PROGRAMMING PARADIGMS

Compiled by

R.D. TENNENT
Queen's University

from works by
Simon Thompson and Ivan Bratko

Taken from:

Haskell: The Craft of Functional Programming, Second Edition
by Simon Thompson

Prolog: Programming for Artificial Intelligence, Third Edition
by Ivan Bratko

PEARSON CUSTOM PUBLISHING
75 Arlington Street, Suite 300, Boston, MA 02116
A Pearson Education Company

PART I

Haskell:
The Craft of Functional Programming

Second Edition

by Simon Thompson

Haskell
The Craft of
Functional
Programming

Second edition

Simon Thompson

Contents

Preface

....

Computer technology changes with frightening speed; the fundamentals, however, remain remarkably static. The architecture of the standard computer is hardly changed from the machines which were built half a century ago, even though their size and power are incomparably different from those of today. In programming, modern ideas like object-orientation have taken decades to move from the research environment into the commercial mainstream. In this light, a functional language like Haskell is a relative youngster, but one with a growing influence to play.

- Functional languages are increasingly being used as **components** of larger systems like Fran (Elliott and Hudak 1997), in which Haskell is used to describe reactive graphical animations, which are ultimately rendered in a lower-level language. This inter-operation is done without sacrificing the semantic elegance which characterizes functional languages.
- Functional languages provide a **framework** in which the crucial ideas of modern programming are presented in the clearest possible way. This accounts for their widespread use in teaching computing science and also for their influence on the design of other languages. A case in point is the design of G-Java, the generics of which are directly modelled on polymorphism in the Haskell mould.

This book provides a tutorial introduction to functional programming in Haskell. The remainder of the preface begins with a brief explanation of functional programming and the reasons for studying it. This is followed by an explanation of the approach taken in the book and an outline of its contents. Perhaps most importantly for readers of the first edition, the changes in approach and content in this second edition are then discussed. A final section explains different possible routes through the material.

What is functional programming?

Functional programming offers a high-level view of programming, giving its users a variety of features which help them to build elegant yet powerful and general libraries of functions. Central to functional programming is the idea of a function, which computes a result that depends on the values of its inputs.

An example of the power and generality of the language is the map function, which is used to transform every element of a list of objects in a specified way. For example, map can be used to double all the numbers in a sequence of numbers or to invert the colours in each picture appearing in a list of pictures.

The elegance of functional programming is a consequence of the way that functions are defined: an equation is used to say what the value of a function is on an arbitrary input. A simple illustration is the function addDouble which adds two integers and doubles their sum. Its definition is

```
addDouble x y = 2*(x+y)
```

where x and y are the inputs and 2*(x+y) is the result.

The model of functional programming is simple and clean: to work out the value of an expression like

```
3 + addDouble 4 5
```

the equations which define the functions involved in the expression are used, so

```
3 + addDouble 4 5
~>    3 + 2*(4+5)
~>    . . .
~>    21
```

This is how a computer would work out the value of the expression, but it is also possible to do exactly the same calculation using pencil and paper, making transparent the implementation mechanism.

It is also possible to discuss how the programs behave in general. In the case of addDouble we can use the fact that x+y and y+x are equal for all numbers x and y to conclude that addDouble x y and addDouble y x are equal for all x and y. This idea of proof is much more tractable than those for traditional imperative and object-oriented (OO) languages.

Haskell and Hugs

This text uses the programming language Haskell, which has freely available compilers and interpreters for most types of computer system. Used here is the Hugs interpreter which provides an ideal platform for the learner, with its fast compile cycle, simple interface and free availability for Windows, Unix and Macintosh systems.

Haskell began life in the late 1980s as an intended standard language for lazy functional programming, and since then it has gone through various changes and modifications. This text is written in Haskell 98, which consolidates work on Haskell thus far, and which is intended to be stable; future extensions will result in Haskell 2 some years down the line, but it is expected that implementations will continue to support Haskell 98 after that point.

While the book covers most aspects of Haskell 98, it is primarily a programming text rather than a language manual. Details of the language and its libraries are contained in the language and library reports available from the Haskell home page,

```
http://www.haskell.org/
```

Why learn functional programming?

A functional programming language gives a simple model of programming: one value, the result, is computed on the basis of others, the inputs.

Because of its simple foundation, a functional language gives the clearest possible view of the central ideas in modern computing, including abstraction (in a function), data abstraction (in an abstract data type), genericity, polymorphism and overloading. This means that a functional language provides not just an ideal introduction to modern programming ideas, but also a useful perspective on more traditional imperative or object-oriented approaches. For example, Haskell gives a direct implementation of data types like trees, whereas in other languages one is forced to describe them by pointer-linked data structures.

Haskell is not just a good 'teaching language'; it is a practical programming language, supported by having extensions such as interfaces to C functions and component-based programming, for example. Haskell has also been used in a number of real-world projects. More information about these extensions and projects can be found in the concluding chapter.

Who should read this book?

This text is intended as an introduction to functional programming for computer science and other students, principally at university level. It can be used by beginners to computer science, or more experienced students who are learning functional programming for the first time; either group will find the material to be new and challenging.

The book can also be used for self-study by programmers, software engineers and others interested in gaining a grounding in functional programming.

The text is intended to be self-contained, but some elementary knowledge of commands, files and so on is needed to use any of the implementations of Haskell. Some logical notation is introduced in the text; this is explained as it appears. In Chapter 19 it would help to have an understanding of the graphs of the $\log$, n^2 and 2^n functions.

The approach taken here

There is a tension in writing about a programming language: one wants to introduce all the aspects of the language as early as possible, yet not to over-burden the reader with too much at once. The first edition of the text introduced ideas 'from the bottom up', which meant that it took more than a hundred pages before any substantial example could be discussed.

The second edition takes a different approach: a case study of 'pictures' introduces a number of crucial ideas informally in the first chapter, revisiting them as the text proceeds. Also, Haskell has a substantial library of built-in functions, particularly over lists, and this edition exploits this, encouraging readers to use these functions before seeing the details of their definitions. This allows readers to progress more quickly, and also accords with practice: most real programs are built using substantial libraries of pre-existing code, and it is therefore valuable experience to work in this way from the start. A section containing details of the other changes in the second edition can be found later in this preface.

Other distinctive features of the approach in the book include the following.

- The text gives a thorough treatment of reasoning about functional programs, beginning with reasoning about list-manipulating functions. These are chosen in preference to functions over the natural numbers for two reasons: the results one can prove for lists seem substantially more realistic, and also the structural induction principle for lists seems to be more acceptable to students.

- The Picture case study is introduced in Chapter 1 and revisited throughout the text; this means that readers see different ways of programming the same function, and so get a chance to reflect on and compare different designs.

- Function design – to be done before starting to code – is also emphasized explicitly in Chapters 4 and 11.

- There is an emphasis on Haskell as a practical programming language, with an early introduction of modules, as well as a thorough examination of the do notation for I/O and other monad-based applications.

- Types play a prominent role in the text. Every function or object defined has its type introduced at the same time as its definition. Not only does this provide a check that the definition has the type that its author intended, but also we view types as the single most important piece of documentation for a definition, since a function's type describes precisely how the function is to be used.

- A number of case studies are introduced in stages through the book: the picture example noted above, an interactive calculator program, a coding and decoding system based on Huffman codes and a small queue simulation package. These are used to introduce various new ideas and also to show how existing techniques work together.

- Support materials on Haskell, including a substantial number of Web links, are included in the concluding chapter. Various appendices contain other backup information including details of the availability of implementations, common Hugs errors and a comparison between functional, imperative and OO programming.

Other support materials appear on the Web site for the book:

`http://www.cs.ukc.ac.uk/people/staff/sjt/craft2e/`

Outline

The introduction in Chapter 1 covers the basic concepts of functional programming: functions and types, expressions and evaluation, definitions and proof. Some of the more advanced ideas, such as higher-order functions and polymorphism, are previewed here from the perspective of the example of pictures built from characters. Chapter 2 looks at the practicalities of the Hugs implementation of Haskell, loading and running scripts written in traditional and 'literate' styles, and the basics of the module system. It also contains a first exercise using the `Picture` type. These two chapters together cover the foundation on which to build a course on functional programming in Haskell.

Information on how to build simple programs over numbers, characters and Booleans is contained in Chapter 3. The basic lessons are backed up with exercises, as is the case for all chapters from here on. With this basis, Chapter 4 steps back and examines the various strategies which can be used to define functions, and particularly emphasizes the importance of using other functions, either from the system or written by the user. It also discusses the idea of 'divide and conquer', as well as introducing recursion over the natural numbers.

Structured data, in the form of tuples and lists, come in Chapter 5. After introducing the idea of lists, programming over lists is performed using two resources: the list comprehension, which effectively gives the power of `map` and `filter`; and the first-order prelude and library functions. Nearly all the list prelude functions are polymorphic, and so polymorphism is brought in here. Chapter 6 contains various extended examples, and only in Chapter 7 is primitive recursion over lists introduced; a text processing case study provides a more substantial example here.

Chapter 8 introduces reasoning about list-manipulating programs, on the basis of a number of introductory sections giving the appropriate logical background. Guiding principles about how to build inductive proofs are presented, together with a more advanced section on building successful proofs from failed attempts.

Higher-order functions are introduced in Chapters 9 and 10. First functional arguments are examined, and it is shown that functional arguments allow the implementation of many of the 'patterns' of computation identified over lists at the start of the chapter. Chapter 10 covers functions as results, defined both as lambda-expressions and as partial applications; these ideas are examined by revisiting the `Picture` example, as well as through an index case study. This is followed by an interlude – Chapter 11 – which discusses the role of the development life cycle in programming.

Type classes allow functions to be overloaded to mean different things at different types; Chapter 12 covers this topic as well as surveying the various classes built into Haskell. The Haskell type system is somewhat complicated because of the presence of classes, and so Chapter 13 explores the way in which types are checked in Haskell. In general, type checking is a matter of resolving the various constraints put upon the possible type of the function by its definition.

In writing larger programs, it is imperative that users can define types for themselves. Haskell supports this in two ways. Algebraic types like trees are the subject of Chapter 14, which covers all aspects of algebraic types from design and proof to their interaction with type classes, as well as introducing numerous examples of algebraic types in practice. These examples are consolidated in Chapter 15, which contains the case study of coding and decoding of information using a Huffman-style code. The foundations of the approach are outlined before the implementation of the case study. Modules are used to break the design into manageable parts, and the more advanced features of the Haskell module system are introduced at this point.

An abstract data type (ADT) provides access to an implementation through a restricted set of functions. Chapter 16 explores the ADT mechanism of Haskell and gives numerous examples of how it is used to implement queues, sets, relations and so forth, as well as giving the basics of a simulation case study.

Chapter 17 introduces lazy evaluation in Haskell which allows programmers a distinctive style incorporating backtracking and infinite data structures. As an example of backtracking there is a parsing case study, and infinite lists are used to give 'process style' programs as well as a random-number generator.

Haskell programs can perform input and output by means of the IO types. Their members – examined in Chapter 18 – represent action-based programs. The programs are most readily written using the do notation, which is introduced at the start of the chapter, and illustrated through a series of examples, culminating in an interactive front-end to the calculator. The foundations of the do notation lie in monads, which can also be used to do action-based programming of a number of different flavours, some of which are examined in the second half of the chapter.

The text continues with an examination in Chapter 19 of program behaviour, by which we mean the time taken for a program to compute its result, and the space used in that calculation. Chapter 20 concludes by surveying various applications and extensions of Haskell as well as looking at further directions for study. These are backed up with Web and other references.

The appendices cover various background topics. The first examines links with functional and OO programing, and the second gives a glossary of commonly used terms in functional programming. The others include a summary of Haskell operators and Hugs errors, together with help on understanding programs and details of the various implementations of Haskell.

The Haskell code for all the examples in the book, as well as other background materials, can be downloaded from the Web site for the book.

What has changed from the first edition?

The second edition of the book incorporates a number of substantial changes, for a variety of reasons.

`Bottom up' or not?

Most importantly, the philosophy of how to introduce material has changed, and this makes most impact on how lists are handled. The first edition was written with a resolutely 'bottom up' approach, first introducing recursive definitions of monomorphic functions, and only later bringing in the built-in functions of the prelude and the libraries. This edition starts by introducing in Chapter 5 the (first-order) polymorphic list-manipulating functions from the prelude as well as list comprehensions, and only introduces recursive definitions over lists in Chapter 7.

The main reason for this change was the author's (and others') experience that once recursion had been introduced early, it was difficult to get students to move on and use other sorts of definitions; in particular it was difficult to get students to use prelude and library functions in their solutions. This is bad in itself, and gives students only a partial view of the language. Moreover, it rests ill with modern ideas about programming, which emphasize the importance of re-use and putting together solutions to utilize a rich programming environment that provides many of the required building blocks.

Introduction

Another consequence of the first-edition approach was that it took some hundred pages before any substantial examples could be introduced; in this edition there is an example of pictures in Chapter 1 which both forms a more substantial case study and is used to preview the ideas of polymorphism, higher-order functions and type abstraction introduced later in the text. The case study is revisited repeatedly as new material is brought in, showing how the same problems can be solved more effectively with new machinery, as well as illustrating the idea of program verification.

The introduction also sets out more clearly some of the basic concepts of functional programming and Haskell, and a separate Chapter 2 is used to discuss the Hugs system, Haskell scripts and modules and so forth.

Haskell 98

The book now has an emphasis on using the full resources of Haskell 98. Hugs now provides an almost complete implementation of Haskell, and so as far as systems are concerned Hugs is the exclusive subject. In most situations Hugs will probably be the implementation of choice for teaching purposes, and if it is not used, it is only the system descriptions which need to be ignored, as none of the language features described are Hugs-specific.

The treatment of abstract data types uses the Haskell mechanism exclusively, rather than the restricted type synonym mechanism of Hugs which was emphasized in the first edition. The material on I/O now starts with the do notation, treating it as a mini language for describing programs with actions. This is followed by a general introduction to monads, giving an example of monadic computation over trees which again uses the do notation.

Finally, functions in the text are given the same names as they have in the prelude or libraries, which was not always the case in the first edition. Type variables are the customary a, b, . . . and list variables are named xs, ys and so on.

Recursion, types and proof

As hinted earlier, recursion is given less emphasis than before.

The material on type checking now takes the approach of looking more explicitly at the constraints put upon types by definitions, and emphasizes this through a sequence of examples. This replaces an approach which stated typing rules but said less about their application in practice.

Students have made the point that proof over lists seems more realistic and indeed easier to understand than proof over the natural numbers. For that reason, proof over lists is introduced in Chapter 8 rather than earlier. This has the advantage that practical examples can be brought in right from the start, and the material on proof is linked with the pictures case study.

Problem solving and patterns of definition

Because of a concern for 'getting students started' in solving problems, there is an attempt to talk more explicitly about strategies for programming, reorganizing and introducing new material in Chapters 4 and 11; this material owes much to Polya's problem-solving approach in mathematics. There is also explicit discussion about various 'patterns of definition' of programs in Section 9.1.

Conclusion and appendices

The new edition contains a concluding chapter which looks to further resources, both printed and on the Web, as well as discussing possible directions for functional programming.

Some material from the appendices has been incorporated into the conclusion, while the appendix that discusses links with other paradigms says rather more about links with OO ideas. The other appendices have been updated, while the one that dealt with 'some useful functions' has been absorbed into the body of the text.

To the reader

This introduction to functional programming in Haskell is designed to be read from start to finish, but some material can be omitted, or read in a different order.

The material is presented in an order that the author finds natural, and while this also reflects some of the logical dependencies between parts of the subject, some material later in the text can be read earlier than it appears. Specifically, the introductions to I/O in the first four sections of Chapter 18 and to algebraic types in the early sections on Chapter 14 can be tackled at any point after reading Chapter 7. Local definitions, given by where and let, are introduced in Chapter 6; they can be covered at any point after Chapter 3.

It is always an option to cover only a subset of the topics, and this can be achieved by stopping before the end; the rest of this section discusses in more detail other ways of trimming the material.

There is a thread on program verification which begins with Chapter 8 and continues in Sections 10.9, 14.7, 16.10 and 17.9; this thread is optional. Similarly, Chapter 19 gives a self-contained treatment of program time and space behaviour which is also optional.

Some material is more technical, and can be omitted on (at least the) first reading. This is signalled explicitly in the text, and is contained in Sections 8.7 and part of Section 13.2.

Finally, it is possible to omit some of the examples and case studies. For example, Sections 6.2 and 6.4 are extended sets of exercises which need not be covered; the text processing (Section 7.6) and indexing (Section 10.8) can also be omitted – their roles are to provide reinforcement and to show the system used on rather larger examples. In the later chapters, the examples in Sections 14.6 and 16.7–16.9 and in Chapter 17 can be skipped, but paring too many examples will run the risk of losing some motivating material.

Chapter 15 introduces modules in the first two sections; the remainder is the Huffman coding case study, which is optional. Finally, distributed through the final chapters are the calculator and simulation case studies. These are again optional, but omission of the calculator case study will remove an important illustration of parsing and algebraic and abstract data types.

Acknowledgements

For feedback on the first edition, I am grateful particularly to Ham Richards, Bjorn von Sydow and Kevin Hammond and indeed to all those who have pointed out errata in that text. In reading drafts of the second edition, thanks to Tim Hopkins and Peter Kenny as well as the anonymous referees.

Emma Mitchell and Michael Strang of Addison-Wesley have supported this second edition from its inception; thanks very much to them.

Particular thanks to Jane for devotion beyond the call of duty in reading and commenting very helpfully on the first two chapters, as well as for her support over the last year while I have been writing this edition. Finally, thanks to Alice and Rory who have more than readily shared our home PC with Haskell.

Simon Thompson
Canterbury, January 1999

Chapter 1

Introducing functional programming

This chapter sets the scene for our exposition of functional programming in Haskell. The chapter has three aims.

- We want to introduce the main ideas underpinning functional programming. We explain what it means to be a function and a type. We examine what it means to find the value of an expression, and how to write an evaluation line-by-line. We look at how to define a function, and also what it means to prove that a function behaves in a particular way.

- We want to illustrate these ideas by means of a realistic example; we use the example of pictures to do this.

Finally, we want to give a preview of some of the more powerful and distinctive ideas in functional programming. This allows us to illustrate how it differs from other approaches like object-oriented programming, and also to show why we consider functional programming to be of central importance to anyone learning computing science. As we proceed with this informal overview we will give pointers to later chapters of the book where we explain these ideas more rigorously and in more detail.

(1.1) Computers and modelling

In the last fifty years computers have moved from being enormous, expensive, scarce, slow and unreliable to being small, cheap, common, fast and (relatively!) dependable. The first computers were 'stand-alone' machines, but now computers can also play different roles, being organized together into networks, or being embedded in domestic machines like cars and washing machines, as well as appearing in personal computers (PCs), organizers and so on.

Despite this, the fundamentals of computers have changed very little in this period: the purpose of a computer is to manipulate symbolic information. This information can represent a simple situation, such as the items bought in a supermarket shopping trip, or more complicated ones, like the weather system above Europe. Given this information, we are required to perform tasks like calculating the total cost of a supermarket trip, or producing a 24-hour weather forecast for southern England.

How are these tasks achieved? We need to write a description of how the information is manipulated. This is called a **program** and it is written in a **programming language**. A programming language is a formal, artificial language used to give instructions to a computer. In other words the language is used to write the **software** which controls the behaviour of the **hardware**. While the structure of computers has remained very similar since their inception, the ways in which they are programmed have developed substantially. Initially programs were written using instructions which controlled the hardware directly, whereas modern programming languages aim to work closer to the level of the problem – a 'high' level – rather than at the 'low' or machine level.

The programming language is made to work on a computer by an **implementation**, which is itself a program and which runs programs written in the higher-level language on the computer in question.

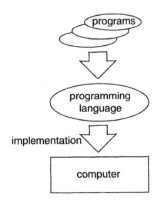

Our task in this text is programming, so we shall be occupied with the upper half of the diagram above, and not the details of implementation (which are discussed in Peyton Jones 1987; Peyton Jones and Lester 1992).

Our subject here is **functional** programming, which is one of a number of different programming styles or **paradigms**; others include object-oriented (OO), structured and logic programming. How can there be different paradigms, and how do they differ? One very fruitful way of looking at programming is that it is the task of **modelling** situations – either real-world or imaginary – within a computer. Each programming paradigm will provide us with different tools for building these models; these different tools allow us – or force us – to think about situations in different ways. A functional programmer will concentrate on the relationships between values, while an OO programmer will concentrate on the objects, say. Before we can say anything more about functional programming we need to examine what it means to be a function.

(1.2) What is a function?

A **function** is something which we can picture as a box with some inputs and an output, thus:

The function gives an **output** value which depends upon the **input** value(s). We will often use the term **result** for the output, and the terms **arguments** or **parameters** for the inputs.

A simple example of a function is addition, +, over numbers. Given input values 12 and 34 the corresponding output will be 46.

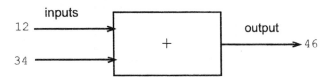

The process of giving particular inputs to a function is called **function application**, and (12 + 34) represents the application of the function + to 12 and 34.

Addition is a mathematical example, but there are also functions in many other situations; examples of these include

- a function giving the distance by road (*output*) between two cities (*inputs*);

- a supermarket check-out program, which calculates the bill (*output*) from a list of bar codes scanned in (*input*); and

- a process controller, which controls valves in a chemical plant. Its inputs are the information from sensors, and its output the signals sent to the valve actuators.

We mentioned earlier that different paradigms are characterized by the different tools which they provide for modelling: in a functional programming language functions will be the central component of our models. We shall see this in our running example of pictures, which we look at now.

(1.3) Pictures and functions

In this chapter, and indeed throughout the book, we will look at an example of two-dimensional pictures, and their representation within a computer system. At this stage we simply want to make the point that many common relationships between pictures are modelled by functions; in the remainder of this section we consider a series of examples of this.

Reflection in a vertical mirror will relate two pictures, and we can model this by a function `flipV`:

where we have illustrated the effect of this reflection on the 'horse' image

In a similar way we have a function `flipH` to represent flipping in a horizontal mirror. Another function models the inversion of the colours in a (monochrome) image

Some functions will take two arguments, among them a function to scale images,

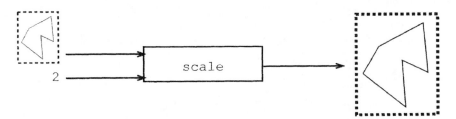

a function describing the superimposition of two images,

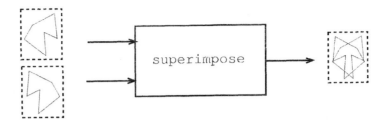

a function to put one picture above another,

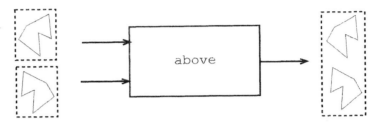

and a function to place two pictures side by side.

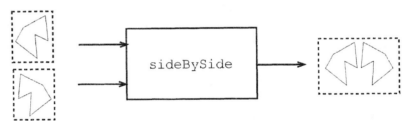

We have now seen what it means to be a function, as well as some examples of functions. Before we explain functional programming, we first have to look at another idea, that of a 'type'.

(1.4) Types

The functions which we use in functional programs will involve all sorts of different kinds of value: the addition function + will combine two numbers to give another number; flipV will transform a picture into a picture; scale will take a picture and a number and return a picture, and so on.

A **type** is a collection of values, such as numbers or pictures, grouped together because although they are different – 2 is not the same as 567 – they are the same *sort* of thing, in that we can apply the same functions to them. It is reasonable to find the larger of two numbers, but not to compare a number and a picture, for instance.

If we look at the addition function, +, it only makes sense to add two numbers but not two pictures, say. This is an example of the fact that the functions we have been talking about themselves have a type, and indeed we can illustrate this diagrammatically, thus:

The diagram indicates that + takes two whole numbers (or Integers) as arguments and gives a whole number as a result. In a similar way, we can label the scale function

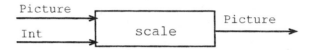

to indicate that its first argument is a Picture and its second is an Int, with its result being a Picture.

We have now explained two of the central ideas in functional programming: a type is a collection of values, like the whole numbers or integers; a function is an operation which takes one or more arguments to produce a result. The two concepts are linked: functions will operate over particular types: a function to scale a picture will take two arguments, one of type Picture and the other of type Int.

In modelling a problem situation, a type can represent a concept like 'picture', while a function will represent one of the ways that such objects can be manipulated, such as placing one picture above another. We shall return to the discussion of types in Section 1.11.

(1.5) The Haskell programming language

Haskell (Peyton Jones and Hughes 1998) is the functional programming language which we use in this text. However, many of the topics we cover are of more general interest and apply to other functional languages (as discussed in Chapter 20), and indeed are lessons for programming in general. Nevertheless, the book is of most value as a text on functional programming in the Haskell language.

Haskell is named after Haskell B. Curry who was one of the pioneers of the λ calculus (lambda calculus), which is a mathematical theory of functions and has been an inspiration to designers of a number of functional languages. Haskell was first specified in the late 1980s, and has since gone through a number of revisions before reaching its current 'standard' state.

There are a variety of implementations of Haskell available; in this text we shall use the **Hugs** (1998) system. We feel that Hugs provides the best environment for the learner, since it is freely available for PC, Unix and Macintosh systems, it is efficient and compact and has a flexible user interface.

Hugs is an interpreter – which means loosely that it evaluates expressions step-by-step as we might on a piece of paper – and so it will be less efficient than a compiler which translates Haskell programs directly into the machine language of a computer. Compiling a language like Haskell allows its programs to run with a speed similar to those written in more conventional languages like C and C++. Details of all the different implementations of Haskell can be found in Appendix E and at the Haskell home page, `http://www.haskell.org/`.

From now on we shall be using the Haskell programming language and the Hugs system as the basis of our exposition of the ideas of functional programming. Details of how to obtain Hugs are in Appendix E. All the programs and examples used in the text can be downloaded from the Web page for this book,

`http://www.cs.ukc.ac.uk/people/staff/sjt/craft2e/`

(1.6) Expressions and evaluation

In our first years at school we learn to **evaluate** an **expression** like (7 - 3) * 2

expression   value

(7−3)*2 ➤━━━━━━━➤ 8

evaluation

to give the **value** 8. This expression is built up from symbols for numbers and for functions over those numbers: subtraction − and multiplication *; the value of the expression is a number. This process of evaluation is automated in an electronic calculator.

In functional programming we do exactly the same: we evaluate expressions to give values, but in those expressions we use functions which model our particular problem. For example, in modelling pictures we will want to evaluate expressions whose values are pictures. If the picture

is called `horse`, then we can form an expression by applying the function `flipV` to the horse. This function application is written by putting the function followed by its argument(s), thus: `flipV horse` and then evaluation will give

expression   value

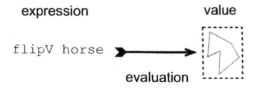

`flipV horse` ➤━━━━━━━➤

evaluation

A more complicated expression is

`invertColour (flipV horse)`

the effect of which is to give a horse reflected in a vertical mirror – `flipV horse` as shown above – and then to invert the colours in the picture to give

To recap, in functional programming, we compute by evaluating expressions which use functions in our area of interest. We can see an implementation of a functional language as something like an electronic calculator: we supply an expression, and the system evaluates the expression to give its value. The task of the programmer is to write the functions which model the problem area.

A **functional program** is made up of a series of **definitions** of functions and other values. We will look at how to write these definitions now.

(1.7) Definitions

A functional program in Haskell consists of a number of **definitions**. A Haskell definition associates a **name** (or **identifier**) with a value of a particular **type**. In the simplest case a definition will have the form

```
name :: type
name = expression
```

as in the example

```
size :: Int
size = 12+13
```

which associates the name on the left-hand side, `size`, with the value of the expression on the right-hand side, 25, a value whose type is `Int`, the type of whole numbers or integers. The symbol '`::`' should be read as 'is of type', so the first line of the last definition reads '`size` is of type `Int`'. Note also that names for functions and other values begin with a small letter, while type names begin with a capital letter.

Suppose that we are supplied with the definitions of `horse` and the various functions over `Picture` mentioned earlier – we will discuss in detail how to download these and use them in a program in Chapter 2 – we can then write definitions which use these operations over pictures. For example, we can say

```
blackHorse :: Picture
blackHorse = invertColour horse
```

so that the `Picture` associated with `blackHorse` is obtained by applying the function `invertColour` to the `horse`, thus giving

Another example is the definition

```
rotateHorse :: Picture
rotateHorse = flipH (flipV horse)
```

and we can picture the evaluation of the right-hand side like this

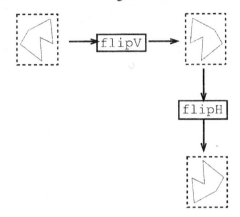

assuming the function `flipH` has the effect of reflecting a `Picture` in a horizontal mirror. The effect of these two reflections is to rotate the picture through 180°.

In Section 1.6 we explained that the Hugs system works rather like a calculator in evaluating expressions. How will it evaluate an expression like

```
size - 17
```

for instance? Using the definition of `size` given earlier, we can replace the left-hand side – `size` – with the corresponding right-hand side – 12+13; this gives us the expression

```
(12+13) - 17
```

and so by doing some arithmetic we can conclude that the value of the expression is 8.

The definitions we have seen so far are simply of constant values; we now turn our attention to how functions are defined.

(1.8) Function definitions

We can also define functions, and we consider some simple examples now. To square an integer we can say

```
square :: Int -> Int
square n = n*n
```

where diagrammatically the definition is represented by

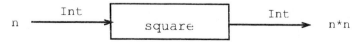

The first line of the Haskell definition of `square` declares the type of the thing being defined: this states that `square` is a function – signified by the arrow `->` – which has a single argument of type `Int` (appearing before the arrow) and which returns a result of type `Int` (coming after the arrow).

The second line gives the definition of the function: the equation states that when `square` is applied to an **unknown** or **variable** n, then the result is n*n. How should we read an equation like this? Because n is an arbitrary, or unknown value, it means that the equation holds *whatever the value of* n, so that it will hold whatever integer expression we put in the place of n, having the consequence that, for instance

```
square 5 = 5*5
```

and

```
square (2+4) = (2+4)*(2+4)
```

This is the way that the equation is used in evaluating an expression which uses `square`. If we are required to evaluate `square` applied to the expression e, we replace the application `square e` with the corresponding right-hand side, e*e.

In general a simple function definition will take the form

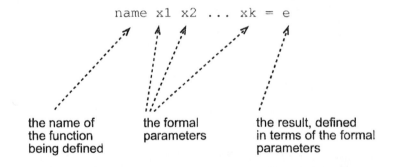

```
name x1 x2 ... xk = e
```

the name of   the formal   the result, defined
the function   parameters   in terms of the formal
being defined   parameters

The variables used on the left-hand side of an equation defining a function are called the **formal parameters** because they stand for arbitrary values of the parameters (or **actual** parameters, as they are sometimes known). We will only use 'formal' and 'actual' in the text when we need to draw a distinction between the two; in most cases it will be obvious which is meant when 'parameter' is used.

Accompanying the definition of the function is a **declaration** of its type. This will take the following form, where we use the function `scale` over pictures for illustration:

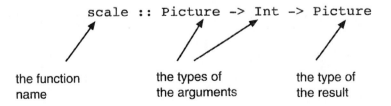

```
scale :: Picture -> Int -> Picture
```

the function   the types of   the type of
name   the arguments   the result

In the general case we have

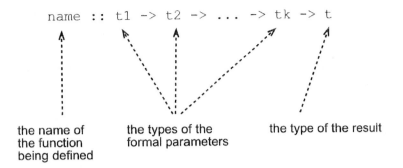

```
name :: t1 -> t2 -> ... -> tk -> t
```

the name of
the function
being defined

the types of the
formal parameters

the type of the result

The definition of rotateHorse in Section 1.7 suggests a general definition of a rotation function. To rotate *any* picture we can perform the two reflections, and so we define

```
rotate :: Picture -> Picture
rotate pic = flipH (flipV pic)
```

We can read the equation thus:

> To rotate a picture pic, we first apply flipV to form (flipV pic); we then reflect this in a horizontal mirror to give flipH (flipV pic).

Given this definition, we can replace the definition of rotateHorse by

```
rotateHorse :: Picture
rotateHorse = rotate horse
```

which states that rotateHorse is the result of applying the function rotate to the picture horse.

The pattern of definition of rotate – 'apply one function, and then apply another to the result' – is so common that Haskell gives a way of combining functions directly in this way. We define

```
rotate :: Picture -> Picture
rotate = flipH . flipV
```

The '.' in the definition signifies **function composition**, in which the output of one function becomes the input of another. In pictures,

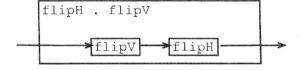

we see the creation of a new function by connecting together the input and output of two given functions: obviously this suggests many other ways of connecting together functions, many of which we will look at in the chapters to come.

The direct combination of functions gives us the first example of the power of functional programming: we are able to combine functions using an operator like '.' just as we can combine numbers using '+'. We use the term '**operator**' here rather than 'function' since '.' is written between its arguments rather than before them; we discuss operators in more detail in Section 3.7.

The direct combination of functions by means of the operator '.' which we have seen here is not possible in other programming paradigms, or at least it would be an 'advanced' aspect of the language, rather than appearing on page 11 of an introductory text.

Type abstraction

Before moving on, we point out another crucial issue which we will explore later in the book. We have just given definitions of

```
blackHorse :: Picture
rotate     :: Picture -> Picture
```

which **use** the type Picture and some functions already defined over it, namely flipH and flipV. We were able to write the definitions of blackHorse and rotate *without knowing anything about* the details of the type Picture or about how the 'flip' functions work over pictures, save for the fact that they behave as we have described.

Treating the type Picture in this way is called **type abstraction**: as users of the type we don't need to concern ourselves with how the type is defined. The advantage of this is that the definitions we give apply *however* pictures are modelled. We might choose to model them in different ways in different situations; whatever the case, the function composition flipH . flipV will rotate a picture through 180°. Chapter 16 discusses this in more detail, and explains the Haskell mechanism to support type abstraction. In the next section we preview other important features of Haskell.

1.9 Looking forward: a model of pictures

We include this section in the first chapter of the book for two reasons. To start with, we want to describe one straightforward way in which Pictures can be modelled in Haskell. Secondly, we want to provide an informal preview of a number of aspects of Haskell which make it a powerful and distinctive programming tool. As we go along we will indicate the parts of the book where we expand on the topics first introduced here.

Our model consists of two-dimensional, monochrome pictures built from **characters**. Characters are the individual letters, digits, spaces and so forth which can be typed at the computer keyboard and which can also be shown on a computer screen. In Haskell the characters are given by the built-in type Char.

This model has the advantage that it is straightforward to view these pictures on a computer terminal window (or if we are using Windows, in the Hugs window). On the other hand, there are other more sophisticated models; details of these can be found at the Web site for the book, mentioned on page 7.

Our version of the horse picture, and the same picture flipped in horizontal and vertical mirrors will be

```
......##...          .....##....          ...##.......
....##..#..          ....#.#....          ..#..##.....
...##.....#.         ....#..#....         .#.....##...
..#.......#.         ...#...#....         .#.......#..
..#...#..#.          ..#...#.....         .#...#...#..
..#...###.#.         .#....#..##.         .#.###...#..
.#....#..##.         ..#...###.#.         .##..#....#.
..#...#.....         ..#...#...#.         .....#...#..
...#...#....         ..#.......#.         ....#...#...
....#..#....         ...##.....#.         ....#..#....
.....#.#....         ....##..#..          ....#.#.....
......##....         .......##...         ....##......
```

horse   flipH horse   flipV horse

where we use dots to show the white parts of the pictures.

How are the pictures built from characters? In our model we think of a picture as being made up of a **list** of lines, that is a collection of lines coming one after another in order. Each line can be seen in a similar way as a list of characters. Because we often deal with collections of things when programming, lists are built into Haskell. More specifically, given any type – like characters or lines – Haskell contains a type of lists of that type, and so in particular we can model pictures as we have already explained, using lists of characters to represent lines, and lists of lines to represent pictures.

With this model of Pictures, we can begin to think about how to model functions over pictures. A first definition comes easily; to reflect a picture in a horizontal mirror each line is unchanged, but the order of the lines is reversed: in other words we reverse the list of lines:

```
flipH = reverse
```

where reverse is a built-in function to reverse the order of items in a list. How do we reflect a picture in a vertical mirror? The ordering of the lines is not affected, but instead *each line is to be reversed*. We can write

```
flipV = map reverse
```

since map is the Haskell function which applies a function to each of the items in a list, individually. In the definitions of flipH and flipV we can begin to see the power and elegance of functional programming in Haskell.

- We have used reverse to reverse a list of lines in flipH and to reverse each line in flipV: this is because the same definition of the function reverse can be used over *every* type of list. This is an example of polymorphism, or generic programming, which is examined in detail in Section 5.7.

- In defining flipV we see the function map applied to its argument reverse, *which is itself a function*. This makes map a very general function, as it can have any desired action on the elements of the list, specified by the function which is its argument. This is the topic of Chapter 9.

Finally, the *result* of applying map to reverse is itself a function. This covered in Chapter 10.

The last two facts show that functions are 'first-class citizens' and can be handled in exactly the same way as any other sort of object like numbers or pictures. The combination of this with polymorphism means that in a functional language we can write very general functions like reverse and map, which can be applied in a multitude of different situations.

The examples we have looked at here are not out of the ordinary. We can see that other functions over pictures have similarly simple definitions. We place one picture above another simply by joining together the two lists of lines to make one list. This is done by the built-in operator ++, which joins together two lists:[1]

```
above = (++)
```

To place two pictures sideBySide we have to join corresponding lines together, thus

```
.......##...    ++    ......##....
.....##..#..    ++    .....#.#....
...##.....#.    ++    ....#..#....
..#.......#.    ++    ...#...#....
..#...#...#.    ++    ..#...#.....
..#...###.#.    ++    .#....#..##.
.#....#..##.    ++    ..#...###.#.
..#...#.....    ++    ..#...#...#.
...#...#....    ++    ..#.......#.
....#..#....    ++    ...##.....#.
.....#.#....    ++    .....##..#..
......##....    ++    ......##...
```

and this is defined using the function zipWith. This function is defined to 'zip together' corresponding elements of two lists using – in this case – the operator ++.

```
sideBySide = zipWith (++)
```

The function superimpose is a rather more complicated application of zipWith, and also we can define invertColour using map. We shall return to these examples in Chapter 10.

1.10 Proof

In this section we explore another characteristic aspect of functional programming: proof. A proof is a logical or mathematical argument to show that something holds *in all circumstances*. For example, given any particular right-angled triangle

---

[1] The operator ++ is surrounded by parentheses (...) in this definition so that it is interpreted as a function; we say more about this in Section 3.7.

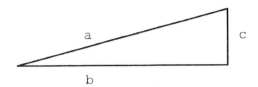

we can check whether or not $a^2=b^2+c^2$ holds. In each case we check, this formula will hold, but this is not in itself enough to show that the formula holds for all a, b and c. A proof, on the other hand, is a general argument which establishes that $a^2=b^2+c^2$ holds whatever right-angled triangle we choose.

How is proof relevant to functional programming? To answer this we will take an example over the `Picture` type to illustrate what can be done. We saw in Section 1.8 that we can define

```
rotate = flipH . flipV
```

but it is interesting to observe that if we reverse the order in which the flip functions are applied then the composition has the same effect, as illustrated here:

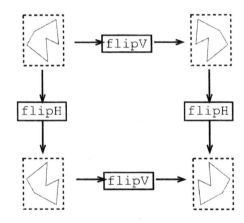

Now, we can express this property as a simple equation between functions:

```
flipH . flipV = flipV . flipH                              (flipProp)
```

Moreover, we can look at our implementations of `flipV` and `flipH` and give a logical **proof** that these functions have the property labelled (`flipProp`) above. The crux of the argument is that the two functions operate independently:

- the function `flipV` affects each line but leaves the lines in the same order while
- the function `flipH` leaves each line unaffected, while reversing the order of the list of lines.

Because the two functions affect different aspects of the list it is immaterial which is applied first, since the overall effect of applying the two in either case is to

- reverse each line and reverse the order of the list of lines.

Proof is possible for most programming languages, but it is substantially easier for functional languages than for any other paradigm. Proof of program properties will be a theme in this text, and we start by exploring proof for list-processing functions in Chapter 8.

What benefit is there in having a proof of a property like (flipProp)? It give us *certainty* that our functions have a particular property. Contrast this with the usual approach in computing where we **test** the value of a function at a selection of places; this only gives us the assurance that the function has the property we seek at the test points, and in principle tells us nothing about the function in other circumstances. There are safety-critical situations in which it is highly desirable to be sure that a program behaves properly, and proof has a role here. We are not, however, advocating that testing is unimportant – merely that testing and proof have complementary roles to play in software development.

More specifically, (flipProp) means that we can be sure that however we apply the functions flipH . flipV and flipV . flipH they will have the same effect. We could therefore **transform** a program using flipH . flipV into one using the functions composed in the reverse order, flipV . flipH, and be certain that the new program will have exactly the same effect as the old. Ideas like this can be used to good effect within implementations of languages, and also in developing programs themselves, as we shall see in Section 10.9.

(1.11) Types and functional programming

What is the role of types in functional programming? Giving a type to a function first of all gives us crucial information about how it is to be used. If we know that

```
scale :: Picture -> Int -> Picture
```

we know two things immediately.

- First, scale has two arguments, the first being a Picture and the second an Int; this means that scale can be applied to horse and 3.
- The result of applying scale to this Picture and Int will be a Picture.

The type thus does two things. First, it expresses a **constraint** on how the function scale is applied: it must be applied to a Picture and an Int. Second, the type tells us what the result is if the function is correctly applied: in this case the result is a Picture.

Giving types to functions and other things not only tells us how they can be used; it is also possible to check automatically that functions are being used in the right way and this process – which is called **type checking** – takes place in Haskell. If we use an expression like

```
scale horse horse
```

we will be told that we have made an error in applying scale to two pictures when a picture and a number are what was expected. Moreover, this can be done without knowing the *values* of scale or horse – all that we need to know to perform the check is the *types* of the things concerned. Thus, **type errors** like these are caught before programs are used or expressions are evaluated.

It is remarkable how many errors, due either to mistyping or to misunderstanding the problem, are made by both novice and experienced programmers. A type system therefore helps the user to write correct programs, and to avoid a large proportion of programming pitfalls, both obvious and subtle.

(1.12) Calculation and evaluation

We have explained that Hugs can be seen as a general calculator, using the functions and other things defined in a functional program. When we evaluate an expression like

```
23 - (double (3+1))                                          (‡)
```

we need to use the definition of the function:

```
double :: Int -> Int
double n = 2*n                                               (dbl)
```

This we do by replacing the unknown n in the definition (dbl) by the expression (3+1), giving

```
double (3+1) = 2*(3+1)
```

Now we can replace double (3+1) by 2*(3+1) in (‡), and evaluation can continue.

One of the distinctive aspects of functional programming is that such a simple 'calculator' model effectively describes computation with a functional program. Because the model is so straightforward, we can perform evaluations in a **step-by-step** manner; in this text we call these step-by-step evaluations **calculations**. As an example, we now show the calculation of the expression with which we began the discussion.

```
    23 - (double (3+1))
⤳   23 - (2*(3+1))                                      using (dbl)
⤳   23 - (2*4)                                          arithmetic
⤳   23 - 8                                              arithmetic
⤳   15                                                  arithmetic
```

where we have used '⤳' to indicate a step of the calculation, and on each line we indicate at the right-hand margin how we have reached that line. For instance, the second line of the calculation:

```
⤳   23 - (2*(3+1))                                      using (dbl)
```

says that we have reached here using the definition of the double function, (dbl).

In writing a calculation it is sometimes useful to underline the part of the expression which gets modified in transition to the next line. This is, as it were, where we need to focus our attention in reading the calculation. The calculation above will have underlining added thus:

```
    23 - (double (3+1))
  ↝   23 - (2*(3+1))                                    using (dbl)
  ↝   23 - (2*4)                                        arithmetic
  ↝   23 - 8                                            arithmetic
  ↝   15                                                arithmetic
```

In what is to come, when we introduce a new feature of Haskell we shall show how it fits into this line-by-line model of evaluation. This has the advantage that we can then explore new ideas by writing down calculations which involve these new concepts.

Summary

As we said at the start, this chapter has three aims. We wanted to introduce some of the fundamental ideas of functional programming; to illustrate them with the example of pictures, and also to give a flavour of what it is that is distinctive about functional programming. To sum up the definitions we have seen,

- a function is something which transforms its inputs to an output;

- a type is a collection of objects of similar sort, such as whole numbers (integers) or pictures;

- every object has a clearly defined type, and we state this type on making a definition;

- functions defined in a program are used in writing expressions to be evaluated by the implementation; and

- the values of expressions can be found by performing calculation by hand, or by using the Hugs interpreter.

In the remainder of the book we will explore different ways of defining new types and functions, as well as following up the topics of polymorphism, functions as arguments and results, data abstraction and proof which we have touched upon in an informal way here.

Getting started with Haskell and Hugs

Chapter 1 introduced the foundations of functional programming in Haskell. We are now ready to use the Hugs system to do some practical programming, and the principal purpose of this chapter is to give an introduction to Hugs.

In beginning to program we will also learn the basics of the Haskell module system, under which programs can be written in multiple, interdependent files, and which can use the `built-in' functions in the prelude and libraries.

Our programming examples will concentrate on using the `Picture` example introduced in Chapter 1 as well as some simple numerical examples. In support of this we will look at how to download the programs and other background materials for the book, as well as how to obtain Hugs.

We conclude by briefly surveying the kinds of error message that can result from typing something incorrect into Hugs.

2.1 A first Haskell program

We begin the chapter by giving a first Haskell program or **script**, which consists of the numerical examples of Chapter 1. As well as definitions, a script will contain comments.

```
{-###########################################################

            FirstScript.hs

            Simon Thompson, June 1998

            The purpose of this script is
                - to illustrate some simple definitions
                  over integers (Int);
                - to give a first example of a script.

############################################################-}


--      The value size is an integer (Int), defined to be
--      the sum of twelve and thirteen.

size :: Int
size = 12+13

--      The function to square an integer.

square :: Int -> Int
square n = n*n

--      The function to double an integer.

double :: Int -> Int
double n = 2*n

--      An example using double, square and size.

example :: Int
example = double (size - square (2+2))
```

Figure 2.1 An example of a traditional script.

A **comment** in a script is a piece of information of value to a human reader rather than to a computer. It might contain an informal explanation about how a function works, how it should or should not be used, and so forth.

There are two different styles of Haskell script, which reflect two different philosophies of programming.

Traditionally, everything in a program file is interpreted as program text, *except* where it is explicitly indicated that something is a comment. This is the style of

```
##########################################################

    FirstLiterate.lhs

    Simon Thompson, June 1998

    The purpose of this script is
      - to illustrate some simple definitions
        over integers (Int);
      - to give a first example of a literate script.

##########################################################
```

The value size is an integer (Int), defined to be the sum of twelve and thirteen.

```
>        size :: Int
>        size = 12+13
```

The function to square an integer.

```
>        square :: Int -> Int
>        square n = n*n
```

The function to double an integer.

```
>        double :: Int -> Int
>        double n = 2*n
```

An example using double, square and size.

```
>        example :: Int
>        example = double (size - square (2+2))
```

Figure 2.2 An example of a literate script.

FirstScript.hs, in Figure 2.1. Scripts of this style are stored in files with an **extension** '.hs'.

Comments are indicated in two ways. The symbol '--' begins a comment which occupies the part of the line to the right of the symbol. Comments can also be enclosed by the symbols '{-' and '-}'. These comments can be of arbitrary length, spanning more than one line, as well as enclosing other comments; they are therefore called **nested comments**.

The alternative, **literate** approach is to make *everything* in the file commentary on the program, and explicitly to signal the program text in some way. A literate version of the script is given in Figure 2.2, where it can be seen that the program text is on lines beginnning with '>', and is separated from the rest of the text in the file by blank lines. Literate scripts are stored in '.lhs' files.

The two approaches emphasize different aspects of programming. The traditional gives primacy to the program, while the literate approach emphasizes that there is more to programming than simply making the right definitions. Design decisions need to be explained, conditions on using functions and so on need to be written down – this is of benefit both for other users of a program and indeed for ourselves if we re-visit a program we have written some time ago, and hope to modify or extend it. We could see this book itself as an extended 'literate script', since commentary here is interspersed by programs which appear in typewriter font on lines of their own. Typewriter font is also used for URLs and proofs in later chapters.

Downloading the programs

All the programs defined in the book, together with other support material and general Haskell and functional programming links, can be found at the Web site for the book,

```
http://www.cs.ukc.ac.uk/people/staff/sjt/craft2e/
```

The scripts we define are given in literate form.

(2.2) Using Hugs

Hugs is a Haskell implementation which runs on both PCs (under Windows 95 and NT) and Unix systems, including Linux. It is freely available via the Haskell home page,

```
http://www.haskell.org/hugs/
```

which is a source of much material on Haskell and its implementations. Further information about downloading and installing Hugs may be found in Appendix E.

In this text we describe the terminal-style interface to Hugs, illustrated in Figure 2.3, because this is common to both Windows and Unix. Experienced PC users should have little difficulty in using the Winhugs system, which gives a Windows-style interface to the Hugs commands, once they have understood how Hugs itself works.

Starting Hugs

To start Hugs on Unix, type hugs to the prompt; to launch Hugs using a particular file, type hugs followed by the name of the file in question, as in

```
hugs FirstLiterate
```

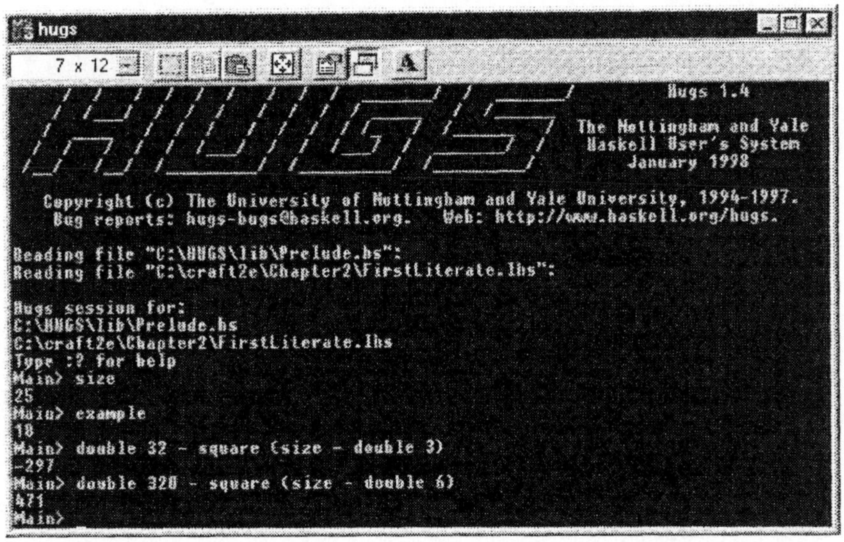

Figure 2.3 A Hugs session on Windows.

On a Windows system, Hugs is launched by choosing it from the appropriate place on the Start menu; to launch Hugs on a particular file, double-click the icon for the file in question.[1]

Haskell scripts carry the extension `.hs` or `.lhs` (for literate scripts); only such files can be loaded, and their extensions can be omitted when they are loaded either when Hugs is launched or by a `:load` command within Hugs.

Evaluating expressions in Hugs

As we said in Section 1.6, the Hugs interpreter will evaluate expressions typed at the prompt. We see in Figure 2.3 the evaluation of `size` to 25, `example` to 18 and two more complex expressions, thus

```
Main> double 32 - square (size - double 3)
-297
Main> double 320 - square (size - double 6)
471
Main>
```

where we have indicated the machine output by using a slanted font; user input appears in unslanted form. The **prompt** here, *Main>*, will be explained in Section 2.4 below.

As can be seen from the examples, we can evaluate expressions which use the definitions in the current script. In this case it is `FirstLiterate.lhs` (or `FirstScript.hs`).

---

[1] This assumes that the appropriate registry entries have been made; we work here with the standard installation of Hugs as discussed in Appendix E.

One of the advantages of the Hugs interface is that it is easy to experiment with functions, trying different evaluations simply by typing the expressions at the keyboard. If we want to evaluate a complex expression, it might be sensible to add it to the program, as in the definition

```
test :: Int
test = double 320 - square (size - double 6)
```

All that we then need to do is to type `test` to the *Main>* prompt.

Hugs commands

Hugs commands begin with a colon, ':'. A summary of the main commands follows.

`:load parrot`	Load the Haskell file `parrot.hs` or `parrot.lhs`. The file extension `.hs` or `.lhs` does not need to be included in the filename.
`:reload`	Repeat the last load command.
`:edit first.lhs`	Edit the file `first.lhs` in the default editor. Note that the file extension `.hs` or `.lhs` is needed in this case. See the following section for more information on editing.
`:type exp`	Give the type of the expression exp. For example, the result of typing `:type size+2` is `Int`.
`:info name`	Give information about the thing named `name`.
`:find name`	Open the editor on the file containing the definition of `name`.
`:quit`	Quit the system.
`:?`	Give a list of the Hugs commands.
`!com`	Escape to perform the Unix or DOS command com.

All the ':' commands can be shortened to their initial letter, giving `:l parrot` and so forth. Details of other commands can be found in the comprehensive on-line Hugs documentation which can be read using a Web browser. On a standard Windows installation it is to be found at

```
C:\hugs\docs\manual-html\manual_contents.html
```

but in general you will need to consult locally to find its location on the system which you are using.

Editing scripts

Hugs can be connected to a 'default' text editor, so that Hugs commands such as `:edit` and `:find` use this editor. This may well be determined by your local set-up. The 'default' default editor on Unix is `vi`; on Windows systems `edit` or `notepad` might be used. Details of how to `:set` values such as the default editor are discussed in Appendix E.

Using the Hugs `:edit` command causes the editor to be invoked on the appropriate file. When the editor is quit, the updated file is loaded automatically. However, it is more convenient to keep the editor running in a separate window and to reload the file by:

● writing the updated file from the editor (without quitting it), and then

● reloading the file in Hugs using `:reload` or `:reload filename`.

In this way the editor is still open on the file should it need further modification.

We now give some introductory exercises for using Hugs on the first example programs.

A first Hugs session

Task 1

Load the file `FirstLiterate.lhs` into Hugs, and evaluate the following expressions

```
square size
square
double (square 2)
$$
square (double 2)
23 - double (3+1)
23 - double 3+1
$$ + 34
13 'div' 5
13 'mod' 5
```

On the basis of this can you work out the purpose of $$?

Task 2

Use the Hugs command `:type` to tell you the type of each of these, apart from $$.

Task 3

What is the effect of typing each of the following?

```
double square
2 double
```

Try to give an explanation of the results that you obtain.

Task 4

Edit the file `FirstLiterate.lhs` to include definitions of functions from integers to integers which behave as follows.

- The function should double its input and square the result of that.
- The function should square its input and double the result of that.

Your solution should include declarations of the types of the functions.

(2.3) The standard prelude and the Haskell libraries

We saw in Chapter 1 that Haskell has various built-in types, such as integers and lists and functions over those types, including the arithmetic functions and the list functions map and ++. Definitions of these are contained in a file, the **standard prelude**, `Prelude.hs`. When Haskell is used, the default is to load the standard prelude, and this can be seen in Figure 2.3 in the line

```
Reading file: "C:\HUGS\lib\Prelude.hs";
```

which precedes the processing of the file `FirstLiterate.lhs` on which Hugs was invoked.

As Haskell has developed over the last decade, the prelude has also grown. In order to make the prelude smaller, and to free up some of the names used in it, many of the definitions have been moved into **standard libraries**, which can be included when they are needed. We shall say more about these libraries as we discuss particular parts of the language.

As well as the standard libraries, the Hugs distribution includes various contributed libraries which support concurrency, functional animations and so forth. Again, we will mention these as we go along. Other Haskell systems also come with contributed libraries, but all systems support the standard libraries.

In order to use the libraries we need to know something about Haskell modules, which we turn to now.

(2.4) Modules

A typical piece of computer software will contain thousands of lines of program text. To make this manageable, we need to split it into smaller components, which we call modules.

A **module** has a name and will contain a collection of Haskell definitions. To introduce a module called `Ant` we begin the program text in the file thus:

```
module Ant where

    . . .
```

A module may also **import** definitions from other modules. The module `Bee` will import the definitions in `Ant` by including an `import` statement, thus:

```
module Bee where
import Ant

    . . .
```

The import statement means that we can use all the definitions in Ant when making definitions in Bee. In dealing with modules in this text we adopt the conventions that

- there is exactly one module per file;
- the file Blah.hs or Blah.lhs contains the module Blah.

The module mechanism supports the libraries we discussed in Section 2.3, but we can also use it to include code written by ourselves or someone else.

The module mechanism allows us to control how definitions are imported and also which definitions are made available or **exported** by a module for use by other modules. We look at this in more depth in Chapter 15, where we also ask how modules are best used to support the design of software systems.

We are now in a position to explain why the Hugs prompt appears as *Main>*. The prompt shows the name of the top-level module currently loaded in Hugs, and in the absence of a name for the module it is called the 'Main' module, discussed in Chapter 15.

In the light of what we have seen so far, we can picture a Hugs session thus:

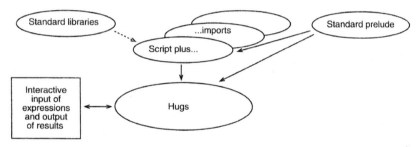

The current script will have access to the standard prelude, and to those modules which it imports; these might include modules from the standard libraries, which are found in the same directory as the standard prelude. The user interacts with Hugs, providing expressions to evaluate and other commands and receiving the results of the evaluations.

The next section revisits the picture example of Chapter 1, which is used to give a practical illustration of modules.

(2.5) A second example: Pictures

The running example in Chapter 1 was of pictures, and in Figure 2.4 we show parts of a script implementing pictures. We have omitted some of the definitions, replacing them with ellipses '...'. The module here is called Pictures, and can be downloaded from the Web page for this text, mentioned on page 22. This module is imported into another module by the statement

```
import Pictures
```

The only new aspect to the example here is the function

```
printPicture :: Picture -> IO ()
```

```
>       module Pictures where

>       type Picture = ....
```

The horse example used in Craft2e, and a completely white picture.

```
>       horse , white :: Picture
>       horse = ....
>       white = ....
```

Getting a picture onto the screen.

```
>       printPicture :: Picture -> IO ()
>       printPicture = ....
```

Reflection in vertical and horizontal mirrors.

```
>       flipV , flipH :: Picture -> Picture
>       flipV = map reverse
>       flipH = reverse
```

One picture above another. To maintain the rectangular property, the pictures need to have the same width.

```
>       above :: Picture -> Picture -> Picture
>       above = (++)
```

One picture next to another. To maintain the rectangular property, the pictures need to have the same height.

```
>       sideBySide :: Picture -> Picture -> Picture
>       sideBySide = zipWith (++)
```

Superimpose two pictures (assumed to be same size).

```
>       superimpose :: Picture -> Picture -> Picture
>       superimpose = ....
```

Invert the black and white in the picture.

```
>       invertColour :: Picture -> Picture
>       invertColour = ....
```

Figure 2.4   A view of the Pictures script.

which is used to display a Picture on the screen. The type IO is a part of the Haskell mechanism for input/output (I/O). We examine this mechanism in detail in Chapter 18; for the present it is enough to know that if horse is the name of the picture used in the earlier examples, then the effect of the function application

```
printPicture horse
```

is the display

```
.......##...
.....##..#..
...##.....#.
..#.......#.
..#...#...#.
..#...###.#.
.#....#..##.
..#...#.....
...#...#....
....#..#....
.....#.#....
......##....
```

first seen in Chapter 1. Any Picture can be printed in a similar way.

In the remainder of this section we present a series of practical exercises designed to use the module Pictures.lhs.

(**Exercises**)───

2.1 Define a module UsePictures which imports Pictures and contains definitions of blackHorse, rotate and rotateHorse which can use the definitions imported from Pictures.

In the remaining questions you are expected to add other definitions to your module UsePictures.

2.2 How would you make a definition of a black rectangle? How could you do this without using white, but assuming that you have a function superimpose defined as discussed on page 5?

2.3 How could you make the picture

Try to find two different ways of getting the result. It may help to work with pieces of white and black paper.

Using your answer to the first part of this question, how would you define a chess (or checkers) board, which is an 8 × 8 board of alternating squares?

2.4 Three variants of the last picture which involve the 'horse' pictures are

 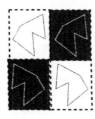 

How would you produce these three?

2.5 Give another variant of the 'horse' pictures in the previous question, and show how it could be created. Note: a nice variant is

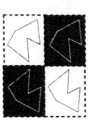

(2.6) Errors and error messages

No system can guarantee that what you type is sensible, and Hugs is no exception. If something is wrong, either in an expression to be evaluated or in a script, you will receive an **error message**. Try typing

```
2+(3+4
```

to the Hugs prompt. The error here is in the **syntax**, and is like a sentence in English which does not have the correct grammatical structure, such as 'Fishcake our camel'.

The expression has too few parentheses: after the '4', a closing parenthesis is expected, to match with the opening parenthesis before '3'. The error message reflects this by saying that what follows '4' is unexpected:

```
ERROR: Syntax error in expression (unexpected end of input)
```

In a similar way typing 2+(3+4)) results in the message

```
ERROR: Syntax error in input (unexpected ')')
```

Now try typing the following expression.

```
double square
```

This gives a **type** error, since double is applied to the function square, rather than an integer:

```
ERROR: Type error in application
*** expression    : double square
*** term          : square
*** type          : Int -> Int
*** does not match : Int
```

The message indicates that something of type Int was expected, but something of type Int -> Int was present instead. Here double expects something of type Int as its argument, but square of type Int -> Int is found in the place of an integer.

When you get an error message like the one above you need to look at how the **term**, in this case square of type Int -> Int, does not match the **context** in which it is used: the context is given in the second line (double square) and the type required by the context, Int, is given in the last line.

Type errors do not always give rise to such well-structured error messages. Typing either 4 double or 4 5 will give rise to a message like

```
ERROR: ... is not an instance of class ...
```

We will explore the technical details behind these messages in a later chapter; for now it is sufficient to read these as 'Type Error!'.

The last kind of error we will see are **program errors**. Try the expression

```
4 'div' (3*2-6)
```

We cannot divide by zero (what would the result be?) and so we get the message

```
Program error: {primDivInt 4 0}
```

indicating that a division of 4 by 0 has occurred. More details about the error messages produced by Hugs can be found in Appendix F.

Summary

The main aim of this chapter is practical, to acquaint the reader with the Hugs implementation of Haskell. We have seen how to write simple Hugs programs, to load them into Hugs and then to evaluate expressions which use the definitions in the module.

Larger Haskell programs are structured into modules, which can be imported into other modules. Modules support the Haskell library mechanism and we illustrate modules in the case study of Pictures introduced in Chapter 1.

We concluded the chapter with an overview of the possible syntax, type and program errors in expressions or scripts submitted to Hugs.

The first two chapters have laid down the theoretical and practical foundations for the rest of the book, which explores the many aspects of functional programming using Haskell and the Hugs interpreter.

Chapter 3

Basic types and definitions

We have now covered the basics of functional programming and have shown how simple programs are written, modified and run in Haskell. This chapter covers Haskell's most important **basic types** and also shows how to write definitions of functions which have multiple **cases** to cover alternative situations. We conclude by looking at some of the details of the **syntax** of Haskell.

Haskell contains a variety of numerical types. We have already seen the `Int` type in use; we shall cover this and also the type `Float` of **floating-point** fractional numbers.

Often in programming we want to make a choice of values, according to whether or not a particular **condition** holds. Such conditions include tests of whether one number is greater than another; whether two values are equal, and so on. The results of these tests – `True` if the condition holds and `False` if it fails – are called the **Boolean** values, after the nineteeth-century logician George Boole, and they form the Haskell type `Bool`. In this chapter we cover the Booleans, and how they are used to give choices in function definitions by means of **guards**.

Finally, we look at the type of characters – individual letters, digits, spaces and so forth – which are given by the Haskell type `Char`.

The chapter provides reference material for the basic types; a reader may skip the treatment of Float and much of the detail about Char, referring back to this chapter when necessary.

Each section here contains examples of functions, and the exercises build on these. Looking ahead, this chapter gives a foundation on top of which we look at a variety of different ways that programs can be designed and written, which is the topic of the next chapter.

3.1 The Booleans: Bool

The Boolean values True and False represent the results of tests, which might, for instance, compare two numbers for equality, or check whether the first is smaller than the second. The Boolean type in Haskell is called Bool. The Boolean operators provided in the language are:

```
&&          and
||          or
not         not
```

Because Bool contains only two values, we can define the meaning of Boolean operators by **truth tables** which show the result of applying the operator to each possible combination of arguments. For instance, the third line of the first table says that the value of False && True is False and that the value of False || True is True.

t_1	t_2	t_1 && t_2	t_1 || t_2		t_1	not t_1
T	T	T	T		T	F
T	F	F	T		F	T
F	T	F	T			
F	F	F	F			

Booleans can be the arguments to or the results of functions. We now look at some examples. 'Exclusive or' is the function which returns True exactly when one but not both of its arguments have the value True; it is like the 'or' of a restaurant menu: you may have vegetarian moussaka or fish as your main course, but not both! The 'built-in or', ||, is 'inclusive' because it returns True if either one or both of its arguments are True.

```
exOr :: Bool -> Bool -> Bool
exOr x y = (x || y) && not (x && y)
```

We can picture the function definition using boxes for functions, and lines for values, as we saw in Chapter 1. Lines coming into a function box represent the arguments, and the line going out the result.

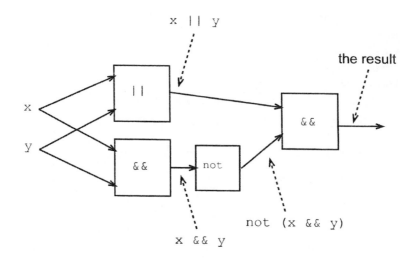

Boolean values can also be compared for equality and inequality using the operators == and /=, which both have the type

```
Bool -> Bool -> Bool
```

Note that /= is the same function as exOr, since both return the result True when exactly one of their arguments is True.

Literals and definitions

Expressions like True and False, and also numbers like 2, are known as **literals**. These are values which are given literally, and which need no evaluation; the result of evaluating a literal is the literal itself.

We can use the literals True and False as arguments, in defining not for ourselves:

```
myNot :: Bool -> Bool
myNot True  = False
myNot False = True
```

We can also use a combination of literals and variables on the left-hand side of equations defining exOr:

```
exOr True  x = not x
exOr False x = x
```

Here we see a definition of a function which uses two equations: the first applies whenever the first argument to exOr is True and the second when that argument is False.

Definitions which use True and False on the left-hand side of equations are often more readable than definitions which only have variables on the left-hand side. This is a simple example of the general **pattern matching** mechanism in Haskell, which we examine in detail in Section 7.1.

Exercises

3.1 Give another version of the definition of 'exclusive or' which works informally thus: 'exclusive or of x and y will be `True` if either x is `True` and y is `False`, or vice versa'.

3.2 Give the 'box and line' diagram corresponding to your answer to the previous question.

3.3 Using literals on the left-hand side we can make the truth table for a function into its Haskell definition. Complete the following definition of `exOr` in this style.

```
exOr True True  = ...
exOr True False = ...
   ...
```

3.4 Give two different definitions of the `nAnd` function

```
nAnd :: Bool -> Bool -> Bool
```

which returns the result `True` except when both its arguments are `True`. Give a diagram illustrating one of your definitions.

3.5 Give line-by-line calculations of

```
nAnd True True
nAnd True False
```

for each of your definitions of `nAnd` in the previous exercise.

3.2 The integers: `Int`

The Haskell type `Int` contains the integers. The integers are the whole numbers, used for counting; they are written thus:

```
0
45
-3452
2147483647
```

The `Int` type represents integers in a fixed amount of space, and so can only represent a finite range of integers. The value `maxBound` gives the greatest value in the type, which happens to be 2147483647. For the majority of integer calculations these fixed size numbers are suitable, but if larger numbers are required we may use the `Integer` type, which can accurately represent whole numbers of any size.[1]

---

[1] We choose to work with `Int` here because various standard Haskell functions which we introduce later in the chapter use the `Int` type.

We do arithmetic on integers using the following operators and functions; the operations we discuss here also apply to the `Integer` type.

+	The sum of two integers.
*	The product of two integers.
^	Raise to the power; 2^3 is 8.
−	The difference of two integers, when infix: a−b; the integer of opposite sign, when prefix: −a.
div	Whole number division; for example div 14 3 is 4. This can also be written 14 `div` 3.
mod	The remainder from whole number division; for example mod 14 3 (or 14 `mod` 3) is 2.
abs	The absolute value of an integer; remove the sign.
negate	The function to change the sign of an integer.

Note that `mod` surrounded by **backquotes** is written between its two arguments, is an **infix** version of the function mod. Any function can be made infix in this way.

Note: Negative literals

A common pitfall occurs with negative literals. For example the number minus twelve is written as −12, but the prefix '−' can often get confused with the infix operator to subtract one number from another and can lead to unforeseen and confusing type error messages. For example, the application

```
negate -34
```

is interpreted as 'negate minus 34' and thus leads to the Hugs error message

```
ERROR: a -> a is not an instance of class "Num"
```

If you are in any doubt about the source of an error and you are dealing with negative numbers you should enclose them in parentheses, thus: negate (−34). See Section 3.7 for more details.

In what follows we will use the term the **natural numbers** for the non-negative integers: 0, 1, 2, ...

Relational operators

There are ordering and (in)equality relations over the integers, as there are over all basic types. These functions take two integers as input and return a `Bool`, that is either `True` or `False`. The relations are

>	greater than (and not equal to)
>=	greater than or equal to
==	equal to
/=	not equal to
<=	less than or equal to
<	less than (and not equal to)

A simple example using these definitions is a function to test whether three `Int`s are equal.

```
threeEqual :: Int -> Int -> Int -> Bool
threeEqual m n p = (m==n) && (n==p)
```

3.6 Explain the effect of the function defined here:

```
mystery :: Int -> Int -> Int -> Bool
mystery m n p = not ((m==n) && (n==p))
```

Hint: if you find it difficult to answer this question directly, try to see what the function does on some example inputs.

3.7 Define a function

```
threeDifferent :: Int -> Int -> Int -> Bool
```

so that the result of `threeDifferent m n p` is True only if all three of the numbers m, n and p are different.

What is your answer for `threeDifferent 3 4 3`? Explain why you get the answer that you do.

3.8 This question is about the function

```
fourEqual :: Int -> Int -> Int -> Int -> Bool
```

which returns the value True only if all four of its arguments are equal.

Give a definition of `fourEqual` modelled on the definition of `threeEqual` above. Now give a definition of `fourEqual` which *uses* the function `threeEqual` in its definition. Compare your two answers.

3.9 Give line-by-line calculations of

```
threeEqual (2+3) 5 (11 'div' 2)
mystery (2+4) 5 (11 'div' 2)
threeDifferent (2+4) 5 (11 'div' 2)
fourEqual (2+3) 5 (11 'div' 2) (21 'mod' 11)
```

3.3 Overloading

Both integers and Booleans can be compared for equality, and the same symbol == is used for both these operations, even though they are different. Indeed, == will be used for equality over any type t for which we are able to define an equality operator. This means that (==) will have the type

```
Int  -> Int  -> Bool
Bool -> Bool -> Bool
```

and indeed `t -> t -> Bool` if the type `t` carries an equality.

Using the same symbol or name for different operations is called **overloading**. A number of symbols in Haskell are overloaded, and we will see in Chapter 12 how overloading is handled in the type system of Haskell, and also how users can define their own overloaded operators or names.

3.4 Guards

Here we explore how conditions or **guards** are used to give alternatives in the definitions of functions. A guard is a Boolean expression, and these expressions are used to express various cases in the definition of a function.

We take as a running example in this section functions which compare integers for size, and start by looking at the example of the function to return the maximum value of two integers. When the two numbers are the same then we call their common value the maximum.

```
max :: Int -> Int -> Int
max x y
  | x >= y      = x
  | otherwise   = y
```

How do we read a definition like this, which appears in the Haskell prelude?

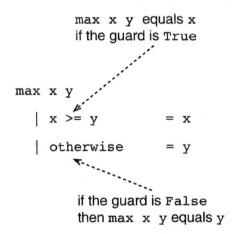

In general, if the first guard (here x>=y) is True then the corresponding value is the result (x in this case). On the other hand, if the first guard is False, then we look at the second, and so on. An otherwise guard will hold whatever the arguments, so that in the case of max the result is x if x>=y and y otherwise, that is in the case that y>x.

An example in which there are multiple guards is a definition of the maximum of three inputs.

```
maxThree :: Int -> Int -> Int -> Int
maxThree x y z
    | x >= y && x >= z    = x
    | y >= z              = y
    | otherwise          = z
```

How does this definition work? The first guard

```
x >= y && x >= z
```

tests whether x is the maximum of the three inputs; if it is True the corresponding result is x. If the guard fails, then x is not the maximum, so there has to be a choice between y and z. The second guard is therefore

```
y >= z
```

If this holds, the result is y; otherwise the result is z. We will go back to the example of maxThree in Section 4.1.

We first gave a general form for simple function definitions in Chapter 1; we can now strengthen this to give a general form for function definitions with guards in Figure 3.1. Note that the otherwise is not compulsory.

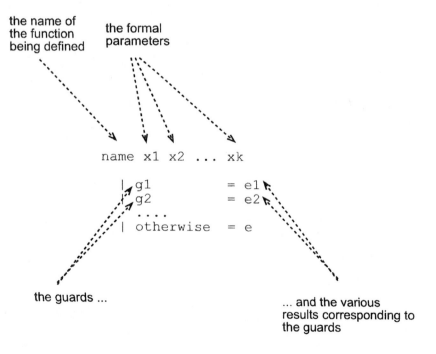

Figure 3.1 The general form for function definitions with guards.

We also saw in Chapter 1 that we can write down line-by-line **calculations** of the values of expressions. How do guards fit into this model? When we apply a function to its arguments we need to know which of the cases applies, and to do this we need to evaluate the guards until we find a guard whose value is True; once we find this, we can evaluate the corresponding result. Taking the example of maxThree, we give two examples in which we perform the evaluation of guards on lines beginning '??'.

```
maxThree 4 3 2
  ?? 4>=3 && 4>=2
  ?? ↝  True && True
  ?? ↝  True
↝  4
```

In this example the first guard we try, 4>=3 && 4>=2, gives True and so the result is the corresponding value, 4. In the second example we have to evaluate more than one guard.

```
maxThree 6 (4+3) 5
  ?? 6>=(4+3) && 6>=5
  ?? ↝  6>=7 && 6>=5
  ?? ↝  False && True
  ?? ↝  False
  ?? 7>=5
  ?? ↝  True
↝  7
```

In this example we first evaluate the first guard, 6>=(4+3) && 6>=5, which results in False; we therefore evaluate the second guard, 7>=5, which gives True, and so the result is 7.

Once we have calculated the value of the second argument, (4+3), we do not re-calculate its value when we look at it again. This is not just a trick on our part; the Hugs system will only evaluate an argument like (4+3) once, keeping its value in case it is needed again, as indeed it is in this calculation. This is one aspect of lazy evaluation, which is the topic of Chapter 17.

Conditional expressions

Guards are conditions which distinguish between different cases in definitions of functions. We can also write general conditional expressions by means of the if... then... else construct of Haskell. The value of

```
if condition then m else n
```

is m if the condition is True and is n if the condition is False, so that the expression if False then 3 else 4 has the value 4, and in general

```
if x >= y then x else y
```

will be the maximum of x and y. This shows that we can write max in a different way thus:

```
max :: Int -> Int -> Int
max x y
  = if x >= y then x else y
```

We tend to use the guard form rather than this, but we will see examples below where the use of `if ... then ... else ...` is more natural.

> **Note: Redefining prelude functions**
>
> The max function is defined in the prelude, `Prelude.hs`, and if a definition
>
> ```
> max :: Int -> Int -> Int
> ```
>
> appears in a script `maxDef.hs` then this definition will conflict with the prelude definition, leading to the Hugs error message
>
> ```
> ERROR "maxDef.hs" (line 3): Definition of variable "max"
> clashes with import
> ```
>
> To redefine the prelude functions `max` and `min`, say, the line
>
> ```
> import Prelude hiding (max,min)
> ```
>
> which overrides the usual import of the prelude should be included at the top of the file `maxDef.hs`, after its `module` statement (if any).
>
> Many of the functions defined in this text are in fact included in the prelude, and so this technique needs to be used whenever you want to redefine one of these.

Exercises

3.10 Give calculations of

```
max (3-2) (3*8)
maxThree (4+5) (2*6) (100 `div` 7)
```

3.11 Give definitions of the functions

```
min      :: Int -> Int -> Int
minThree :: Int -> Int -> Int -> Int
```

which calculate the minimum of two and three integers, respectively.

3.5 The characters: `Char`

People and computers communicate using keyboard input and screen output, which are based on sequences of **characters**, that is letters, digits and 'special' characters like space, tab, newline and end-of-file. Haskell contains a built-in type of characters, called `Char`.

Literal characters are written inside single quotes, thus `'d'` is the Haskell representative of the character d. Similarly `'3'` is the character three. Some special characters are represented as follows

tab	`'\t'`
newline	`'\n'`
backslash (\)	`'\\'`
single quote (')	`'\''`
double quote (")	`'\"'`

There is a standard coding for characters as integers, called the ASCII coding. The capital letters `'A'` to `'Z'` have the sequence of codes from 65 to 90, and the small letters `'a'` to `'z'` the codes 97 to 122. The character with code 34, for example, can be written `'\34'`, and `'9'` and `'\97'` have the same meaning. ASCII has recently been extended to the Unicode standard, which contains characters from fonts other than English.

There are conversion functions between characters and their numerical codes which convert an integer into a character, and vice versa.

```
ord :: Char -> Int
chr :: Int -> Char
```

The coding functions can be used in defining functions over Char. To convert a small letter to a capital an offset needs to be added to its code:

```
offset :: Int
offset = ord 'A' - ord 'a'

toUpper :: Char -> Char
toUpper ch = chr (ord ch + offset)
```

Note that the offset is named, rather than appearing as a part of toUpper, as in

```
toUpper ch = chr (ord ch + (ord 'A' - ord 'a'))
```

This is standard practice, making the program both easier to read and to modify. To change the offset value, we just need to change the definition of offset, rather than having to change the function (or functions) which use it.

Characters can be compared using the ordering given by their codes. So, since the digits 0 to 9 occupy a block of adjacent codes 48 to 57, we can check whether a character is a digit thus:

```
isDigit :: Char -> Bool
isDigit ch = ('0' <= ch) && (ch <= '9')
```

The standard prelude contains a number of conversion functions like toUpper, and discrimination functions like isDigit; details can be found in the file Prelude.hs. Other useful functions over Char are to be found in the library Char.hs.

> **Note: Characters and names**
>
> It is easy to confuse a and 'a'. To summarize the difference, a is a name or a variable, which if defined may have any type whatever, whereas 'a' is a literal character and is therefore of type Char.
>
> In a similar way, it is easy to confuse the number 0 and the character '0'.

Exercises

3.12 Define a function to convert small letters to capitals which returns unchanged characters which are not small letters.

3.13 Define the function

```
charToNum :: Char -> Int
```

which converts a digit like '8' to its value, 8. The value of non-digits should be taken to be 0.

3.6 Floating-point numbers: Float

In Section 3.2 we introduced the Haskell type Int of integers. In calculating we also want to use numbers with fractional parts, which are represented in Haskell by the **floating-point** numbers which make up the type Float. We do not use Float heavily in what follows, and so this section can be omitted on first reading and used as reference material to be consulted when necessary.

Internal to the Haskell system there is a fixed amount of space allocated to representing each Float. This has the effect that not all fractions can be represented by floating-point numbers, and arithmetic over them will not be always be exact. It is possible to use the type of double-precision floating-point numbers, Double for greater precision, or for full-precision fractions built from Integer there is the type Rational. As this is a programming tutorial we restrict our attention to the types Int and Float but we shall survey the numerical types briefly in Chapter 12.

Literal floats in Haskell can be given by decimal numerals, such as

```
0.31426
-23.12
567.347
4523.0
```

The numbers are called floating point because the position of the decimal point is not the same for all Floats; depending upon the particular number, more of the space can be used to store the integer or the fractional part.

Haskell also allows literal floating-point numbers in **scientific notation**. These take the form below, where their values are given in the right-hand column of the table

`+ - *`	`Float -> Float -> Float`	Add, subtract, multiply.
`/`	`Float -> Float -> Float`	Fractional division.
`^`	`Float -> Int -> Float`	Exponentiation $x\char94 n = x^n$ for a natural number n.
`**`	`Float -> Float -> Float`	Exponentiation $x**y = x^y$.
`==,/=,<,>,` `  <=,>=`	`Float -> Float -> Bool`	Equality and ordering operations.
`abs`	`Float -> Float`	Absolute value.
`acos,asin` `  atan`	`Float -> Float`	The inverse of cosine, sine and tangent.

`ceiling`
`  floor`
`  round`
	`Float -> Int`	Convert a fraction to an integer by rounding up, down, or to the closest integer.

`cos,sin` `  tan`	`Float -> Float`	Cosine, sine and tangent.
`exp`	`Float -> Float`	Powers of e.
`fromInt`	`Int -> Float`	Convert an `Int` to a `Float`.
`log`	`Float -> Float`	Logarithm to base e.
`logBase`	`Float -> Float -> Float`	Logarithm to arbitrary base, provided as first argument.
`negate`	`Float -> Float`	Change the sign of a number.
`pi`	`Float`	The constant pi.
`signum`	`Float -> Float`	`1.0`, `0.0` or `-1.0` according to whether the argument is positive, zero or negative.
`sqrt`	`Float -> Float`	(Positive) square root.

Figure 3.2   Floating-point operations and functions.

`231.61e7`	$231.61 \times 10^7\ = 2,316,100,000$
`231.6e-2`	$231.61 \times 10^{-2} = 2.3161$
`-3.412e03`	$-3.412 \times 10^3\ = -3412$

This representation is more convenient than the decimal numerals above for very large and small numbers. Consider the number 2.1^{444}. This will need well over a hundred digits before the decimal point, and this would not be possible in decimal notation of limited size (usually 20 digits at most). In scientific notation, it will be written as `1.162433e+143`.

Haskell provides a range of operators and functions over `Float` in the standard prelude. The table in Figure 3.2 gives their name, type and a brief description of their behaviour. Included are the

- standard mathematical operations: square root, exponential, logarithm and trigonometric functions;

- functions to convert integers to floating-point numbers: `fromInt`, and vice versa: `ceiling`, `floor` and `round`.

Haskell can be used as a numeric calculator. Try typing the expression which follows to the Hugs prompt:

```
sin (pi/4) * sqrt 2
```

Overloaded literals and functions

In Haskell the numbers 4 and 2 belong to both Int and Float; they are overloaded, as discussed in Section 3.3. This is also true of some of the numeric functions; addition, for instance, has both the types

```
Int -> Int -> Int
Float -> Float -> Float
```

and the relational operators == and so forth are available over all basic types. We shall explore this idea of overloading in more detail when we discuss type classes below in Chapter 12.

Note: Converting integers to floating-point numbers

Although literals are overloaded, there is no automatic conversion from Int to Float. In general if we wish to add an integer quantity, like floor 5.6, to a float, like 6.7, we will receive an error message if we type

```
(floor 5.6) + 6.7
```

since we are trying to add quantities of two different types. We have to convert the Int to a Float to perform the addition, thus:

```
fromInt(floor 5.6) + 6.7
```

where fromInt takes an Int to the corresponding Float.

Exercises

_____

3.14 Give a function to return the average of three integers

```
averageThree :: Int -> Int -> Int -> Float
```

Using this function define a function

```
howManyAboveAverage :: Int -> Int -> Int -> Int
```

which returns how many of its inputs are larger than their average value.

The remainder of the questions look at solutions to a quadratic equation

$$a*X^2 + b*X + c = 0.0$$

where a, b and c are real numbers. The equation has

- two real roots, if b^2 > 4.0*a*c;
- one real root, if b^2 == 4.0*a*c; and
- no real roots, if b^2 < 4.0*a*c.

This assumes that a is non-zero — the case which we call **non-degenerate**. In the degenerate case, there are three sub-cases:

- one real root, if b /= 0.0;
- no real roots, if b == 0.0 and c /= 0.0;
- every real number a root, if b == 0.0 and c == 0.0.

3.15 Write a function

```
numberNDroots :: Float -> Float -> Float -> Int
```

that given the coefficients of the quadratic, a, b and c, will return how many roots the equation has. You may assume that the equation is non-degenerate.

3.16 Using your answer to the last question, write a function

```
numberRoots :: Float -> Float -> Float -> Int
```

that given the coefficients of the quadratic, a, b and c, will return how many roots the equation has. In the case that the equation has every number a root you should return the result 3.

3.17 The formula for the roots of a quadratic is

$$\frac{-b \pm \sqrt{b^2 - 4ac}}{2a}$$

Write definitions of the functions

```
smallerRoot, largerRoot :: Float -> Float -> Float -> Float
```

which return the smaller and larger real roots of the quadratic. In the case that the equation has no real roots or has all values as roots you should return zero as the result of each of the functions.

3.7 Syntax

The syntax of a language describes all the properly formed programs. This section looks at various aspects of the syntax of Haskell, and stresses especially those which might seem unusual or unfamiliar at first sight.

Definitions and layout

A script contains a series of definitions, one after another. How is it clear where one definition ends and another begins? In writing English, the end of a sentence is signalled by a full stop, '.'. In Haskell the **layout** of the program is used to state where one definition ends and the next begins.

Formally, a definition is ended by the first piece of text which lies at the same indentation or to the left of the start of the definition.

When we write a definition, its first character opens up a box which will hold the definition, thus

```
mystery x = x*x
```

Whatever is typed in the box forms part of the definition ...

```
mystery x = x*x
       +x
                +2
```

...until something is found which is on the line or to the left of the line. This closes the box, thus

```
mystery x = x*x
       +x
                +2
```

```
next x = ...
```

In writing a sequence of definitions, it is therefore sensible to give them all the same level of indentation. In our scripts we shall always write top-level definitions starting at the left-hand side of the page, and in literate scripts we will indent the start of each definition by a single 'tab'.

This rule for layout is called the **offside rule** because it is reminiscent of the idea of being 'offside' in soccer. The rule also works for conditional equations such as `max` and `maxThree` which consist of more than one clause.

There is, in fact, a mechanism in Haskell for giving an explicit end to part of a definition, just as '.' does in English: the Haskell 'end' symbol is ';'. We can, for instance, use ';' if we wish to write more than one definition on a single line, thus:

```
answer = 42 ;   facSix = 720
```

Note: Layout errors

We see error messages involving ';' even if we have not used it ourselves. If we break the offside rule thus:

```
funny x = x+
1
```

we receive an error message like

```
ERROR .... : Syntax error in expression (unexpected ';')
```

since internally to the system a ';' is placed before the 1 to mark the end of the definition, which does indeed come at an unexpected point.

Recommended layout

The offside rule permits various different styles of layout. In this book for definitions of any size we use the form

```
fun v1 v2 ... vn
  | g1           = e1
  | g2           = e2
  ...
  | otherwise    = er        ( or    | gr        = er)
```

for a **conditional equation** built up from a number of clauses. In this layout, each **clause** starts on a new line, and the guards and results are lined up. Note also that by convention in this text we always specify the type of the function being defined.

If any of the expressions e_i or guards g_i is particularly long, then the guard can appear on a line (or lines) of its own, like this

```
fun v1 v2 ... vn
  | a long guard which may
    go over a number of lines
        = very long expression which goes
          over a number of lines
  | g2        = e2
  ...
```

Names in Haskell

Thus far in the book we have seen a variety of uses of names in definitions and expressions. In a definition like

```
addTwo :: Int -> Int -> Int
addTwo first second = first+second
```

the names or **identifiers** Int, addTwo, first and second are used to name a type, a function and two variables. Identifiers in Haskell must begin with a letter – small or capital – which is followed by an optional sequence of letters, digits, underscores '_' and single quotes.

The names used in definitions of values must begin with a small letter, as must variables and type variables, which are introduced later. On the other hand, capital letters are used to begin type names, such as Int; **constructors**, such as True and False; module names and also the names of type classes, which we shall encounter below.

An attempt to give a function a name which begins with a capital letter, such as

Fun x = x+1

gives the error message 'Undefined constructor function "Fun"'.

There are some restrictions on how identifiers can be chosen. There is a small collection of **reserved words** which cannot be used; these are

```
case class data default deriving do else if import in infix
infixl infixr instance let module newtype of then type where
```

The special identifiers as, qualified, and hiding have special meanings in certain contexts but can be used as ordinary identifiers.

By convention, when we give names built up from more than one word, we capitalize the first letters of the second and subsequent words, as in 'maxThree'.

The same identifier can be used to name both a function and a variable, or both a type and a type constructor; we recommend strongly that this is *not* done, as it can only lead to confusion.

If we want to **redefine** a name that is already defined in the prelude or one of the libraries we have to **hide** that name on import; details of how to do this are given on page 41.

Haskell is built on top of the Unicode character description standard, which allows symbols from fonts other than those in the ASCII standard. These symbols can be used in identifiers and the like, and Unicode characters – which are described by a 16-bit sequence – can be input to Haskell in the form \u*hhhh* where each of the *h* is a hexadecimal (4 bit) digit. In this text we use the ASCII subset of Unicode exclusively.[2]

Operators

The Haskell language contains various operators, like +, ++ and so on. Operators are **infix** functions, so that they are written between their arguments, rather than before them, as is the case for ordinary functions.

In principle it is possible to write all applications of an operator with enclosing parentheses, thus

(((4+8)*3)+2)

but expressions rapidly become difficult to read. Instead two extra properties of operators allow us to write expressions uncluttered by parentheses.

---

[2] Note that at the time of writing, the Hugs system does not support Unicode characters.

Associativity

If we wish to add the three numbers 4, 8 and 99 we can write either 4+(8+99) or (4+8)+99. The result is the same whichever we write, a property we call the **associativity** of addition. Because of this, we can write

4+8+99

for the sum, unambiguously. Not every operator is associative, however; what happens when we write

4-2-1

for instance? The two different ways of inserting parentheses give

(4-2)-1 = 2-1 = 1   left associative
4-(2-1) = 4-1 = 3   right associative

In Haskell each non-associative operator is classified as either left or right associative. If left associative, any double occurrences of the operator will be parenthesized to the left; if right associative, to the right. The choice is arbitrary, but follows custom as much as possible, and in particular '-' is taken to be left associative.

Binding powers

The way in which an operator associates allows us to resolve expressions like

2^3^2

where the same operator occurs twice, but what is done when two different operators occur, as in the following expressions?

2+3*4
3^4*2

For this purpose the **binding power** or **fixity** of the operators need to be compared. * has binding power 7 while + has 6, so that in 2+3*4 the 3 sticks to the 4 rather than the 2, giving

2+3*4 = 2+(3*4)

In a similar way, ^ with binding power 8 binds more tightly than *, so

3^4*2 = (3^4)*2

A full table of the associativities and binding powers of the predefined Haskell operators is given in Appendix C. In the section 'Do-it-yourself operators' below we discuss how operators are defined in scripts and also how their associativity and binding power can be set or changed by declarations.

Note: Function application

 Binding most tightly is function application, which is given by writing the name of the function in front of its argument(s) thus: f v_1 v_2 ... v_n. This binds more tightly than any other operator, so that f n+1 is interpreted as f n plus 1, (f n)+1, rather than f applied to n+1, f (n+1). If in doubt, it is sensible to parenthesize each argument to a function application.

   Similarly, as '−' is both an infix and a prefix operator, there is scope for confusion. f −12 will be interpreted as 12 subtracted from f, rather than f applied to −12; the solution again is to bracket the argument.

Operators and functions

Infix operators can be written *before* their arguments, by enclosing the operator in parentheses. We therefore have, for example,

```
(+) :: Int -> Int -> Int
```

so that

```
(+) 2 3 = 2 + 3
```

This conversion is needed later when we make functions into arguments of other functions. We can also convert functions into operators by enclosing the function name in backquotes, thus `name`. We therefore have, using the maximum function defined earlier,

```
2 `max` 3 = max 2 3
```

This notation can make expressions involving **binary** or two-argument functions substantially easier to read.

   The fixity and associativity of these operators can be controlled; see Appendix C.

Do-it-yourself operators

The Haskell language allows us to define infix operators directly in exactly the same way as functions. Operator names are built from the operator symbols which include the ASCII symbols

```
! # $ % & * + . / < = > ? \ ^ | : - ~
```

together with the Unicode symbols. An operator name may not begin with a colon.

   To define the operator &&& as an integer minimum function, we write

```
(&&&) :: Int -> Int -> Int
x &&& y
   | x > y      = y
   | otherwise  = x
```

The associativity and binding power of the operator can be specified; for details see Appendix C.

3.18 Rewrite your solutions to the earlier exercises to use the recommended layout.

3.19 Given the definitions

```
funny x = x+x
 peculiar y = y
```

explain what happens when you remove the space in front of the `peculiar`.

Summary

This chapter has introduced the base types `Int`, `Float`, `Char` and `Bool` together with various built-in functions over them. We have seen how Boolean expressions – called guards – allow definitions which have various cases, and this was exemplified by the function returning the maximum of two integer arguments. This definition contains two cases, one which applies when the first argument is the larger and the other when the second is the larger.

Finally, we have seen how the layout of a Haskell program is significant – the end of a definition is implicitly given by the first piece of program text 'offside' of the start of the definition; we have also given an overview of operators in Haskell.

This material, together with what we have seen in earlier chapters, gives us a toolkit which we can use to solve programming problems. In the next chapter we will explore various ways of using that toolkit to solve practical problems.

Chapter 4

Designing and writing programs

In this chapter we step back from discussing the details of Haskell and instead look at how to build programs. We present some general strategies for program design; that is we talk about how programs can be planned *before* we start to write the details. The advice we give here is largely independent of Haskell and will be useful whatever programming language we use.

We follow this by discussing recursion. We begin by concentrating on explaining **why** recursion works, and follow this by looking at **how** to find primitive recursive definitions, extending what we have said about design. We conclude with an optional examination of more general forms of recursion.

Once we have written a definition we need to ask whether it does what it is intended to do. We conclude the chapter by exploring the principles of program testing and examining a number of examples.

4.1 *Where do I start?* Designing a program in Haskell

One theme which we want to emphasize in this book is how we can **design** programs to be written in Haskell. Design is used to mean many different things in computing; the way that we want to think of it is like this:

> **Definition**
>
> Design is the stage before we start writing detailed Haskell code.

In this section we will concentrate on looking at examples, and on talking about the different ways we can try to define functions, but we will also try to give some general advice about how to start writing a program. These are set out as questions we can ask ourselves when we are stuck with a programming problem.

Do I understand what I need to do?

Before we can start to solve a programming problem we need to be clear about what we have to do. Often problems are described in an informal way, and this can mean that the problem either is not fully stated or cannot be solved as it is described.

Suppose we are asked to return the middle of three numbers. It is clear that given the numbers 2, 4 and 3 we should return 3, but when presented with 2, 4 and 2 there are two possible responses.

- We could say that 2 is the middle number because when we write the numbers in order: 2 2 4, then 2 is the number that appears in the middle.
- Alternatively we could say that there is no middle number in this case, since 2 is the lower and 4 the higher, and that we therefore cannot return any result.

What can we learn from this illustration?

- First, that even in simple problems there can be things we have to think about before we start programming.
- Secondly, it is important to realize that there is **no right answer** among the two options given just now: it is up to the person wanting the program written and the programmer to work out between them what is wanted.
- Thirdly, a very good way of thinking about whether we understand the problem is to think about how we expect it to work out in various **examples**.
- Finally, it is worth realizing that often difficulties like this come out at the programming stage, when we have already written a whole lot of definitions; the sooner we spot a problem like this, the more wasted effort we can save.

Another example of this came up in the definition of `max` in Section 3.4, where we had to say what the function should return when its two arguments were the same. In that case it was sensible to think of the maximum of, say, 3 and 3 as being 3.

Can I say anything about types at this stage?

One thing we can think about at this stage is the types of the various things we are thinking about. We can write

```
middleNumber :: Int -> Int -> Int -> Int
```

as the name and type of the function returning the middle of three numbers without having any idea about how we are going to define the function itself. Nevertheless, it is progress, and also it gives us something to check our definition against when we have written it: if we manage to write a function `middleNumber` but it does not have the type `Int -> Int -> Int -> Int`, then the function cannot be doing what it should.

What do I already know? How can I use this information?

These are crucial questions for a designer of a program. We need to know what resources are available to us for solving the problem at hand: what definitions have we already written which could be useful, what does the language provide in its prelude and libraries? We will obviously learn more about the latter as we go along, but even when we have written only a small number of programs we should always think about how these might help us solve the problem at hand. For instance, in trying to define the function `maxThree` introduced in Section 3.4, we know that we have already got the `max` function, giving the maximum of two numbers.

As well as knowing our resources we also need to know how we can use them; this we look at now. There are two different ways that a definition we already have can be helpful.

*We can take the definition of a function as a **model** for what we want to do*

In defining `maxThree` we have the resource of already having defined the function `max`. We can think of its definition as a model for how we might define `maxThree`.

In `max` we give the result `x` on condition that it is the maximum of the two, that is

```
x >= y
```

Our definition of `maxThree` does a similar thing, replacing the condition for two values with the condition for three, namely:

```
x >= y && x >= z
```

This way of using `max` is probably the first to spring to mind, but it is not the only way that `max` can help us in defining `maxThree`.

*We can **use** a function we have already defined within the new definition*

We are trying to find the maximum of three numbers, and we are already provided with a function `max` to give us the maximum of two. How could we *use* `max` to give us the result we want? We can take the maximum of the first two, and then the maximum of that and the third. In pictures,

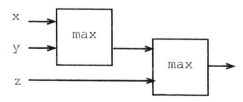

and in Haskell

```
maxThree x y z = max (max x y) z
```

or writing the max in its infix form, 'max',

```
maxThree x y z = (x 'max' y) 'max' z
```

Using max in this way has some advantages.

The definition of maxThree is considerably shorter and easier to read than the original. If at some point we changed the way that max was calculated – perhaps making it a built-in function – then this definition would get the benefit of the 'new' max. This is not such an advantage in a small example like this, but can be of considerable benefit in a larger-scale system where we can expect software to be modified and extended over its lifetime.

Can I break the problem down into simpler parts?

If we cannot solve a problem as it stands, we can think about breaking it down into smaller parts. This principle of 'divide and conquer' is the basis of all larger-scale programming: we solve aspects of the problem separately and then put them together to give an overall solution.

How do we decide how to break a problem down into parts? We can think of solving a simpler problem and then building the full solution on top, or we can ask ourselves the question here.

What if I had any functions I wanted: which could I use in writing the solution?

This *what if . . . ?* is a central question, because it breaks the problem into two parts. First we have to give the solution *assuming* we are given the auxiliary functions we want and thus without worrying about how they are to be defined. Then, we have separately to define these auxiliary functions.

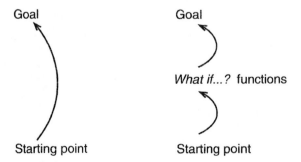

Instead of a single jump from the starting point to the goal, we have two shorter jumps, each of which should be easier to do. This approach is called **top-down** as we start at the top with the overall problem, and work by breaking it down into smaller problems.

This process can be done repeatedly, so that the overall problem is solved in a series of small jumps. We now look at an example; more examples appear in the exercises at the end of the section.

Suppose we are faced with the problem of defining

```
middleNumber :: Int -> Int -> Int -> Int
```

according to the first of the alternatives described on page 54. A model is given by the definition of `maxThree`, in which we give conditions for x to be the solution, y to be the solution and so on. We can therefore sketch out our solution like this

```
middleNumber x y z
  | condition for x to be solution    = x
  | condition for y to be solution    = y
  ....
```

Now, the problem comes in writing down the conditions, but here we say *what if* we had a function to do this. Let us call it `between`. It has three numbers as arguments, and a Boolean result,

```
between :: Int -> Int -> Int -> Bool
```

and is defined so that `between m n p` is True if n is between m and p. We can complete the definition of `middleNumber` now:

```
middleNumber x y z
  | between y x z    = x
  | between x y z    = y
  | otherwise        = z
```

The definition of the function `between` is left as an exercise for the reader.

This section has introduced some of the general ideas which can help us to get started in solving a problem. Obviously, because programming is a creative activity there is not going to be a set of rules which will always lead us mechanically to a solution to a problem. On the other hand, the questions posed here will get us started, and show us some of the alternative strategies we can use to plan how we are going to write a program. We follow up this discussion in Chapter 11.

Exercises

4.1 This question is about the function

```
maxFour :: Int -> Int -> Int -> Int -> Int
```

which returns the maximum of four integers. Give three definitions of this function: the first should be modelled on that of `maxThree`, the second should use the function `max` and the third should use the functions `max` and `maxThree`. For your second and third solutions give diagrams to illustrate your answers. Discuss the relative merits of the three solutions you have given.

4.2 Give a definition of the function

```
between :: Int -> Int -> Int -> Bool
```

discussed in this section. The definition should be consistent with what we said in explaining how `middleNumber` works. You also need to think carefully about the different ways that one number can lie between two others. You might find it useful to define a function

```
weakAscendingOrder :: Int -> Int -> Int -> Bool
```

so that `weakAscendingOrder m n p` is True exactly when m, n and p are in weak ascending order, that is the sequence does not go down at any point. An example of such a sequence is 2 3 3.

4.3 Give a definition of the function

```
howManyEqual :: Int -> Int -> Int -> Int
```

which returns how many of its three arguments are equal, so that

```
howManyEqual 34 25 36 = 0
howManyEqual 34 25 34 = 2
howManyEqual 34 34 34 = 3
```

Think about what functions you have already seen – perhaps in the exercises – which you can use in the solution.

4.4 Give a definition of the function

```
howManyOfFourEqual :: Int -> Int -> Int -> Int -> Int
```

which is the analogue of `howManyEqual` for four numbers. You may need to think *what if ... ?*.

4.2 Recursion

Recursion is an important programming mechanism, in which a definition of a function or other object refers to the object itself. This section concentrates on explaining the idea of recursion, and why it makes sense. In particular we give two complementary explanations of how primitive recursion works in defining the factorial function over the natural numbers. In the section after this we look at how recursion is *used* in practice.

Getting started: a story about factorials

Suppose that someone tells us that the factorial of a natural number is the product of all natural numbers from one up to (and including) that number, so that, for instance

```
fac 6 = 1*2*3*4*5*6
```

Suppose we are also asked to write down a table of factorials, where we take the factorial of zero to be one. We begin thus

```
n        fac n
0         1
1         1
2         1*2 = 2
3         1*2*3 = 6
4         1*2*3*4 = 24
```

but we notice that we are repeating a lot of multiplication in doing this. In working out

```
1*2*3*4
```

we see that we are repeating the multiplication of 1*2*3 before multiplying the result by 4

```
1*2*3 *4
```

and this suggests that we can produce the table in a different way, by saying how to start

```
fac 0 = 1                                              (fac.1)
```

which starts the table thus

```
n       fac n
0         1
```

and then by saying how to go from one line to the next

```
fac n = fac (n-1) * n                                  (fac.2)
```

since this gives us the lines

```
n        fac n
0         1
1         1*1 = 1
2         1*2 = 2
3         2*3 = 6
4         6*4 = 24
```

and so on.

What is the moral of this story? We started off describing the table in one way, but came to see that all we needed was the information in (fac.1) and (fac.2).

- (fac.1) tells us the first line of the table, and

- (fac.2) tells us how to get from one line of the table to the next.

The table is just a written form of the factorial function, so we can see that (fac.1) and (fac.2) actually describe the **function** to calculate the factorial, and putting them together we get

```
fac :: Int -> Int
fac n
  | n==0        = 1
  | n>0         = fac (n-1) * n
```

A definition like this is called **recursive** because we actually use fac in describing fac itself. Put this way it may sound paradoxical: after all, how can we describe something in terms of itself? But, the story we have just told shows that the definition is perfectly sensible, since it gives

- a starting point: the value of fac at 0, and

- a way of going from the value of fac at a particular point, fac (n-1), to the value of fac on the next line, namely fac n.

These recursive rules will give a value to fac n whatever the (positive) value n has – we just have to write out n lines of the table, as it were.

Recursion and calculation

The story in the previous section described how the definition of factorial

```
fac :: Int -> Int
fac n
  | n==0        = 1                          (fac.1)
  | n>0         = fac (n-1) * n              (fac.2)
```

can be seen as generating the table of factorials, starting from fac 0 and working up to fac 1, fac 2 and so forth, up to any value we wish.

We can also read the definition in a calculational way, and see recursion justified in another way. Take the example of fac 4

```
fac 4
↝   fac 3 * 4
```

so that (fac.2) replaces one goal – fac 4 – with a simpler goal – finding fac 3 (and multiplying it by 4). Continuing to use (fac.2), we have

```
fac 4
↝   fac 3 * 4
↝   (fac 2 * 3) * 4
↝   ((fac 1 * 2) * 3) * 4
↝   (((fac 0 * 1) * 2) * 3) * 4
```

Now, we have got down to the simplest case (or **base case**), which is solved by (fac.1).

⤳   (((1 * 1) * 2) * 3) * 4
⤳   ((1 * 2) * 3) * 4
⤳   (2 * 3) * 4
⤳   6 * 4
⤳   24

In the calculation we have worked from the goal back down to the base case, using the **recursion step** (fac.2). We can again see that we get the result we want, because the recursion step takes us from a more complicated case to a simpler one, and we have given a value for the simplest case (zero, here) which we will eventually reach.

We have now seen in the case of fac two explanations for why recursion works.

- The **bottom-up** explanation says that the fac equations can be seen to generate the values of fac one-by-one from the base case at zero.

- A **top-down** view starts with a goal to be evaluated, and shows how the equations simplify this until we hit the base case.

The two views here are related, since we can think of the top-down explanation generating a table too, but in this case the table is generated as it is needed. Starting with the goal of fac 4 we require the lines for 0 to 3 also.

Technically, we call the form of recursion we have seen here **primitive recursion**. We will describe it more formally in the next section, where we examine how to start to find recursive definitions. Before we do that, we discuss another aspect of the fac function as defined here.

Undefined or error values

Our definition of factorial covers zero and the positive integers. What will be the effect of applying fac to a negative number? On evaluating fac (-2) in Hugs we receive the error message

```
Program error: {fac (-2)}
```

because fac is not defined on the negative numbers. We could if we wished extend the definition to zero, on the negative numbers, thus

```
fac n
  | n==0        = 1
  | n>0         = fac (n-1) * n
  | otherwise   = 0
```

or we could include our own error message, as follows

```
fac n
  | n==0        = 1
  | n>0         = fac (n-1) * n
  | otherwise   = error "fac only defined on natural numbers"
```

so that when we evaluate `fac (-2)` we receive the message

```
Program error: fac only defined on natural numbers
```

The error message here is a Haskell string, as discussed in Chapter 5.

Exercises

4.5 Define the function `rangeProduct` which when given natural numbers m and n returns the product

```
m*(m+1)*...*(n-1)*n
```

You should include in your definition the type of the function, and your function should return 0 when n is smaller than m.
Hint: you do not need to use recursion in your definition, but you may if you wish.

4.6 As `fac` is a special case of `rangeProduct`, write a definition of `fac` which *uses* `rangeProduct`.

4.3 Primitive recursion in practice

This section examines how primitive recursion is used in practice by examining a number of examples.

The pattern of primitive recursion says that we can define a function from the natural numbers 0, 1, ... by giving the value at zero, and by explaining how to go from the value at n−1 to the value at n. We can give a **template** for this

```
fun n
  | n==0        = ....                            (prim)
  | n>0         = .... fun (n-1) ....
```

where we have to supply the two right-hand sides.

How can we decide whether a function can be defined in this way? Just as we did earlier in the chapter, we frame a question which summarizes the essential property we need for primitive recursion to apply.

What if *we were given the value* `fun (n-1)`. *How could we define* `fun n` *from it?*

We see how this form of recursion works in practice by looking at some examples.

Examples

---

1. Suppose first that we are asked to define the function to give us powers of two for natural numbers

```
power2 :: Int -> Int
```

so that power2 n is 2^n, that is 2 multiplied by itself n times. The template is

```
power2 n
  | n==0          = ....
  | n>0           = .... power2 (n-1) ....
```

In the zero case the result is 1, and in general 2^n is 2^{n-1} multiplied by 2, so we define

```
power2 n
  | n==0          = 1
  | n>0           = 2 * power2 (n-1)
```

2.   As the next example we take the function

```
sumFacs :: Int -> Int
```

so that

```
sumFacs n = fac 0 + fac 1 + ... + fac (n-1) + fac n
```

If we are told that sumFacs 4 is 34 then we can work out sumFacs 5 in one step: we simply add fac 5, that is 120, giving the result 154. This works in general, and so we can fill in the template like this:

```
sumFacs :: Int -> Int
sumFacs n
  | n==0          = 1
  | n>0           = sumFacs (n-1) + fac n
```

In fact this pattern works for any function f of type Int -> Int in the place of fac, so we can say

```
sumFun :: (Int -> Int) -> Int -> Int
sumFun f n
  | n==0          = f 0
  | n>0           = sumFun f (n-1) + f n
```

where the function whose values are being added is itself an argument of the sumFun function. A sample calculation using sumFun is

```
sumFun fac 3
⤳    sumFun fac 2 + fac 3
⤳    sumFun fac 1 + fac 2 + fac 3
⤳    sumFun fac 0 + fac 1 + fac 2 + fac 3
⤳    fac 0 + fac 1 + fac 2 + fac 3
⤳    ...
⤳    10
```

and we can define sumFacs from sumFun thus:

```
sumFacs n = sumFun fac n
```

We briefly introduced the idea of functions as data in Chapter 1, and we will revisit it in detail in Chapter 9. As we mentioned in Chapter 1, having functions as arguments is powerful and sumFun gives a good example: one definition serves to sum the values of *any* function of type Int -> Int over the range of arguments from 0 to n.

3.   As a last example we look at a geometrical problem. Suppose we want to find out the maximum number of pieces we can get by making a given number of straight-line cuts across a piece of paper. With no cuts we get one piece; what about the general case? Suppose we have n−1 lines already, and that we add one more.

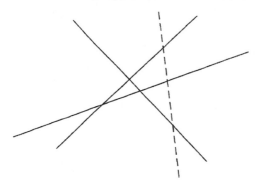

We will get the most new regions if we cross each of these lines; because they are straight lines, we can only cut each one once. This means that the new line crosses exactly n of the regions, and so splits each of these into two. We therefore get n new regions by adding the nth line. Our function definition is given by filling in the template (prim) according to what we have said.

```
regions :: Int -> Int
regions n
  | n==0        = 1
  | n>0         = regions (n-1) + n
```

Exercises

4.7 Using the addition function over the natural numbers, give a recursive definition of multiplication of natural numbers.

4.8 The integer square root of a positive integer n is the largest integer whose square is less than or equal to n. For instance, the integer square roots of 15 and 16 are 3 and 4, respectively. Give a primitive recursive definition of this function.

4.9 Given a function f of type Int -> Int give a recursive definition of a function of type Int -> Int which on input n returns the maximum of the values f 0, f 1,..., f n. You might find the max function defined in Section 3.4 useful.

To test this function, add to your script a definition of some values of f thus:

```
f 0 = 0
f 1 = 44
f 2 = 17
f _ = 0
```

and so on; then test your function at various values.

4.10 Given a function f of type Int -> Int give a recursive definition of a function of type Int -> Bool which on input n returns True if one or more of the values f 0, f 1, ..., f n is zero and False otherwise.

4.11 Can you give a definition of regions which instead of being recursive *uses* the function sumFun?

4.12 [Harder] Find out the maximum number of pieces we can get by making a given number of flat (that is planar) cuts through a solid block. It is *not* the same answer as we calculated for straight-line cuts of a flat piece of paper.

(4.4) General forms of recursion

As we explained in Section 4.2, a recursive definition of a function such as fac would give the value of fac n using the value fac (n-1). We saw there that fac (n-1) is *simpler* in being closer to the base case fac 0. As long as we preserve this property of becoming simpler, different patterns of recursion are possible and we look at some of them in this section. These more general forms of recursion are called **general recursion**. In trying to use recursion to define a function we need to pose the question:

In defining f n which values of f k would help me to work out the answer?

(Examples)────────────────────────────────

1. The sequence of Fibonacci numbers starts with 0 and 1, and subsequent values are given by adding the last two values, so that we get 0+1=1, 1+1=2 and so forth. This can be given a recursive definition as follows

```
fib :: Int -> Int
fib n
  | n==0          = 0
  | n==1          = 1
  | n>1           = fib (n-2) + fib (n-1)
```

where we see in the general case that fib n depends upon not only fib (n-1) but also fib (n-2).

This gives a clear description of the Fibonacci numbers, but unfortunately it gives a very inefficient program for calculating them. We can see that calculating fib n requires us to calculate both fib (n-2) and fib (n-1), and in calculating fib (n-1) we will have to calculate fib (n-2) *again*. We look at ways of overcoming this problem in Section 5.2.

2. Dividing one positive integer by another can be done in many different ways. One of the simplest ways is repeatedly to subtract the divisor from the number being divided, and we give a program doing that here. In fact we will define two functions

```
remainder :: Int -> Int -> Int
divide    :: Int -> Int -> Int
```

which separately give the division's remainder and quotient.

In trying to find a definition it often helps to look at an example. Suppose we want to divide 37 by 10. We expect that

```
remainder 37 10 = 7
divide    37 10 = 3
```

If we subtract the divisor, 10, from the number being divided, 37, how are the values related?

```
remainder 27 10 = 7
divide    27 10 = 2
```

The remainder is the same, and the result of the division is one less. What happens at the base case? An example is

```
remainder 7 10 = 7
divide    7 10 = 0
```

Using these examples as a guide, we have

```
remainder m n
  | m<n        = m
  | otherwise  = remainder (m-n) n

divide m n
  | m<n        = 0
  | otherwise  = 1 + divide (m-n) n
```

These definitions also illustrate another important point: a general recursive function does not always give an answer; instead an evaluation may go on forever. Look at what happens if we evaluate

```
remainder 7 0
↝    remainder (7-0) 0
↝    remainder 7 0
↝    ....
```

This calculation will loop for ever, and indeed we should expect problems if we try to divide by zero! However, the problem also appears if we try to divide by a negative number, for instance

```
divide 4 (-4)
↝    divide (4-(-4)) (-4)
↝    divide 8 (-4)
↝    ...
```

The lesson of this example is that in general there is no guarantee that a function defined by recursion will always **terminate**. We will have termination if we use primitive recursion, and other cases where we are sure that we always go from a more complex case to a simpler one; the problem in the example here is that subtracting a negative number increases the result, giving a more complex application of the function.

Exercises

4.13 Give a recursive definition of a function to find the highest common factor of two positive integers.

4.14 Suppose we have to raise 2 to the power n. If n is even, 2*m say, then

$$2^n = 2^{2*m} = (2^m)^2$$

If n is odd, 2*m+1 say, then

$$2^n = 2^{2*m+1} = (2^m)^2*2$$

Give a recursive function to compute 2^n which uses these insights.

4.5 Program testing

Just because a program is accepted by the Haskell system, it does not mean that it necessarily does what it should. How can we be sure that a program behaves as it is intended to? One option, first aired in Section 1.10, is to prove in some way that it behaves correctly. Proof is, however, an expensive business, and we can get a good deal of assurance that our programs behave correctly by testing the program on selected inputs. The art of testing is then to choose the inputs to be as comprehensive as possible. That is, we want to test data to represent all the different 'kinds' of input that can be presented to the function.

How might we choose test data? There are two possible approaches. We could simply be told the **specification** of the function, and devise test data according to that. This is called **black box** testing, as we cannot see into the box which contains the function. On the other hand, in devising **white box** tests we can use the form of the function definition itself to guide our choice of test data. We will explore these two in turn, by addressing the example of the function which is to return the maximum of three integers,

```
maxThree :: Int -> Int -> Int -> Int
```

Black box testing

How can we make a rational choice of test data for a function, rather than simply picking (supposedly) random numbers out of the air?

What we need to do is try to partition the inputs into different **testing groups** where we expect the function to behave in a similar way for all the values in a given group. In picking the test data we then want to make sure that we choose at least one representative from each group.

We should also pay particular attention to any **special cases**, which will occur on the 'boundaries' of the groups. If we have groups of positive and negative numbers, then we should pay particular attention to the zero case, for instance.

What are the testing groups for the example of maxThree? There is not a single right answer to this, but we can think about what is likely to be relevant to the problem and what is likely to be irrelevant. In the case of maxThree it is reasonable to think that the size or sign of the integers will not be relevant: what will determine the result is their relative ordering. We can make a first subdivision this way

- all three values different;
- all three values the same;
- two items equal, the third different. In fact, this represents two cases
  - two values equal to the maximum, one other;
  - one value equal to the maximum, two others.

We can then pick a set of test data thus

```
6 4 1
6 6 6
2 6 6
2 2 6
```

If we test our definition in Section 3.4 with these data then we see that the program gives the right results. So too does the following program:

```
mysteryMax :: Int -> Int -> Int -> Int
mysteryMax x y z
   | x > y && x > z      = x
   | y > x && y > z      = y
   | otherwise           = z
```

so should we conclude that mysteryMax computes the maximum of the three inputs? If we do, we are wrong, for we have that

```
mysteryMax 6 6 2 ⤳  2
```

This is an important example: it tells us that **testing alone cannot assure us that a function is correct**. How might we have spotted this error in designing our test data? We could have said that not only did we need to consider the groups above, but that we should have looked at all the different possible orderings of the data, giving

- all three values different: six different orderings;
- all three values the same: one ordering;
- two items equal, the third different. In each of the two cases we consider three orderings.

The final case generates the test data 6 6 2 which find the error.

We mentioned special cases earlier: we could see this case of two equal to the maximum in this way. Clearly the author of mysteryMax was thinking about the general case of three different values, so we can see the example as underlining the importance of looking at special cases.

White box testing

In writing white box test data we will be guided by the principles which apply to black box testing, but we can also use the form of the program to help us choose data.

- If we have a function containing guards, we should supply data for each case in the definition. We should also pay attention to 'boundary conditions' by testing the equality case when a guard uses >= or >, for example.
- If a function uses recursion we should test the zero case, the one case and the general case.

In the example of `mysteryMax` we should be guided to the data 6 6 2 since the first two inputs are at the boundaries of the guards

```
x > y && x > z                          y > x && y > z
```

We take up the ideas discussed in this section when we discuss proof in Chapter 8.

Exercises

4.15 Devise test data for a function

```
allEqual :: Int -> Int -> Int -> Bool
```

intended to test whether its three integer inputs are equal.

4.16 Use the test data from the previous question to test the function

```
solution m n p = ((m+n+p)==3*p)
```

Discuss your results.

4.17 The function

```
allDifferent :: Int -> Int -> Int -> Bool
```

should return `True` only if all its inputs are different. Devise black box test data for this function.

4.18 Test the following function

```
attempt m n p = (m/=n) && (n/=p)
```

using the test data written in the previous question. What do you conclude on the basis of your results?

4.19 Devise test data for a function

```
howManyAboveAverage :: Int -> Int -> Int -> Int
```

which returns how many of its three integer inputs are larger than their average value.

4.20 Devise test data for a function to raise two to a positive integer power.

Summary

This chapter has introduced some general principles of program design.

- We should think about how best to use what we already know. If we have already defined a function f we can make use of it in two ways.

  – We can *model* our new definition on the definition of f.

  – We can *use* f in our new definition.

- We should think about how to break the problem into smaller, more easily solved, parts. We should ask *What if I had ...?*.

- We can use recursion to define functions.

We also explained the basics of recursion, and saw how it is used in practice to define a variety of functions. We shall see many more illustrations of this when we look at recursion over lists in Chapter 7.

We concluded by showing that it was possible to think in a principled way about designing test data for function definitions rather than simply choosing the first data that came to mind.

Chapter 5

Data types: tuples and lists

Thus far we have looked at programs which work over the basic types such as `Int`, `Float` and `Bool`, and we have also seen how to approach the design of programs in general. However, in practical problems we will want to represent more complex things, as we saw with our `Picture` example in Chapter 1.

This chapter introduces two ways of building compound data in the Haskell language; these are the **tuple** and the **list**, and together they suffice to let us represent many different kinds of `structured' information. We shall meet other ways of defining data types for ourselves in Chapters 14 and 16.

We concentrate here on explaining the facilities that Haskell provides for defining and manipulating tuples and lists. The repertoire for tuples is small, but for lists the langauge provides many predefined functions and operations. As well as these we can use the `list comprehension' notation to write down descriptions of how lists may be formed from other lists.

In order to describe properly the prelude functions on lists we need to explain **polymorphism**, which is the mechanism by which a Haskell function can act over more than one type: the `length` function on lists can be used over any list type, for instance.

After laying the foundations in this chapter we look at a collection of examples in the chapter to come.

⟨ 5.1 ⟩ Introducing tuples, lists and strings

Both tuples and lists are built up by combining a number of pieces of data into a single object, but they have different properties. In a tuple, we combine a predetermined number of values of predetermined types – which might be different – into a single object. In a list we combine an arbitrary number of values – all of the same type – into a single object.

An example can help to clarify the difference. Suppose we are trying to make a simple model of a supermarket, and as part of that model we want to record the contents of someone's shopping basket. A given item has a name and a price (in pence), and we therefore need somehow to combine these two pieces of information. We do this in a tuple, such as

```
("Salt: 1kg",139)
("Plain crisps",25)
```

where in each tuple a `String` is combined with an `Int`. The literal `String` of characters, written between double quotes, gives the name of the item, and the `Int` gives its price. The `String` is in fact a list of characters, and we discuss that type in Section 5.9.

The values `("Salt: 1kg",139)` and `("Plain crisps",25)` belong to the **tuple type**

```
(String,Int)
```

Every member of this type will have two components – a `String` and an `Int` – as specified in the type `(String,Int)`. If we are given a member of this type we can therefore predict what type its components will have, and this means that we can check that these components are used in an appropriate way: we can check that we deal with the second half as an `Int` and not a `Bool`, for example. We therefore keep the property, first mentioned in Chapter 1, that we can type-check all programs prior to execution, and so any type errors in a program can be found before a program is actually executed.

How are the contents of the basket represented? We know that we have a collection of items, but we do not know in advance how many we have; one basket might contain ten items, another one three. Each item is represented in the same way, as a member of the `(String,Int)` type, and so we represent the contents of the basket by a **list** of these, as in the list

```
[ ("Salt: 1kg",139) , ("Plain crisps",25) , ("Gin: 1lt",1099) ]
```

This is a member of the **list type**

```
[ (String,Int) ]
```

Other members of this list type include the empty list, [], and the basket above with a second packet of crisps replacing the gin:

```
[ ("Salt: 1kg",139) , ("Plain crisps",25) , ("Plain crisps",25) ]
```

Since every member of the list has the same type, we can predict the type of any item chosen from the list. Compare this with a list whose members could have different types: if we choose the first element of such a list we cannot predict its type, and so we lose the ability to type-check programs before they are run. Because we want to keep this important property, Haskell is designed so that lists have to contain elements of the same type, but different lists will contain elements of different types.

We can give names to types in Haskell, so that types are made easier to read. In our example we name the two types

```
type ShopItem = (String,Int)
type Basket   = [ShopItem]
```

where the keyword `type` introduces the fact that this is the definition of a type rather than a value. We can also tell this because the type names `ShopItem` and `Basket` begin with capital letters, as noted in Section 3.7. Built into the system is the definition

```
type String = [Char]
```

so Haskell treats strings as a special case of the list type. Names such as `ShopItem` and `String` are **synonyms** for the types which they name.

We now look at tuple types in more detail, and examine some examples of how tuples are used in practice.

(5.2) Tuple types

The last section introduced the idea of tuple types. In general a tuple type is built up from components of simpler types. The type

$$(t_1, t_2, \ldots, t_n)$$

consists of tuples of values

$$(v_1, v_2, \ldots, v_n)$$

in which $v_1 :: t_1, \ldots, v_n :: t_n$. In other words, each component v_i of the tuple has to have the type t_i given in the corresponding position in the tuple type.

The reason for the name 'tuple' is that these objects are usually called pairs, triples, quadruples, quintuples, sextuples and so on. The general word for them is therefore 'tuple'. In other programming languages, these types are called records or structures; see Appendix A for a more detailed comparison.

We can model a type of supermarket items by the `ShopItem` type defined by

```
type ShopItem = (String,Int)
```

and we saw above that its members include items like ("Gin, 1lt",1099).

A type definition like this is treated as shorthand in Haskell – wherever a name like ShopItem is used, it has exactly the same effect as if (String,Int) had been written. Definitions like this make programs more readable and also lead to more comprehensible type error messages.

How else are tuple types used in programs? We look at a series of examples now.

Examples

1. First, we can use a tuple to return a compound result from a function, as in the example where we are required to return both the minimum and the maximum of two Ints

```
minAndMax :: Int -> Int -> (Int,Int)
minAndMax x y
    | x>=y        = (y,x)
    | otherwise   = (x,y)
```

2. Secondly, suppose we are asked to find a (numerical) solution to a problem when it is uncertain whether a solution actually exists in every case: this might be the question of where a straight line meets the horizontal or x-axis, for instance.

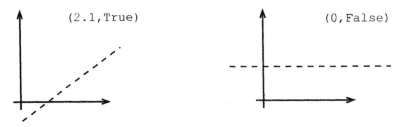

One way of dealing with this is for the function to return a (Float,Bool) pair. If the boolean part is False, this signals that no solution was found; if it is like (2.1,True), it indicates that 2.1 is indeed the solution.

Pattern matching

Next we turn to look at how functions can be defined over tuples. Functions over tuples are usually defined by **pattern matching**. Instead of writing a variable for an argument of type (Int,Int), say, a **pattern**, (x,y) is used.

```
addPair :: (Int,Int) -> Int
addPair (x,y) = x+y
```

On application the components of the pattern are matched by the corresponding components of the argument, so that on applying the function addPair to the argument (5,8) the value 5 is matched to x, and 8 to y, giving the calculation

```
addPair (5,8)
~> 5+8
~> 13
```

Patterns can contain literals and nested patterns, as in the examples

```
addPair (0,y) = y
addPair (x,y) = x+y

shift :: ((Int,Int),Int) -> (Int,(Int,Int))
shift ((x,y),z) = (x,(y,z))
```

Functions which pick out particular parts of a tuple can be defined by pattern matching. For the ShopItem type, the definitions might be

```
name  :: ShopItem -> String
price :: ShopItem -> Int

name  (n,p) = n
price (n,p) = p
```

Haskell has these **selector functions** on pairs built in. They are

```
fst (x,y) = x
snd (x,y) = y
```

Given these selector functions we can avoid pattern matching if we so wish. For instance, we could redefine addPair like this

```
addPair :: (Int,Int) -> Int
addPair p = fst p + snd p
```

but generally a pattern-matching definition is easier to read than one which uses selector functions instead.

Examples

3. We first introduced the Fibonacci numbers

```
0, 1, 1, 2, 3, 5, ... , u, v, (u+v), ...
```

in Section 4.4, where we gave an inefficient recursive definition of the sequence. Using a tuple we can give an efficient solution to the problem. The next value in the sequence is given by adding the previous two, so what we do is to write a function which returns *two consecutive values* as a result. In other words we want to define a function fibPair so that it has the property that

```
fibPair n = (fib n , fib (n+1))
```

then given such a pair, (u,v) we get the next pair as $(v,u+v)$, which is exactly the effect of the fibStep function:

```
fibStep :: (Int,Int) -> (Int,Int)
fibStep (u,v) = (v,u+v)
```

This gives us the definition of the 'Fibonacci pair' function

```
fibPair :: Int -> (Int,Int)
fibPair n
   | n==0        = (0,1)
   | otherwise   = fibStep (fibPair (n-1))
```

and we can define

```
fastFib :: Int -> Int
fastFib = fst . fibPair
```

where recall that '.' composes the two functions, passing the output of `fibPair` to the input of `fst`, which picks out its first component.

Note: One pair or two arguments?

It is important to distinguish between the functions

```
fibStep :: (Int,Int) -> (Int,Int)
fibStep (x,y) = (y,x+y)
```

```
fibTwoStep :: Int -> Int -> (Int,Int)
fibTwoStep x y = (y,x+y)
```

`fibStep` has a single argument which is a pair of numbers, while `fibTwoStep` has two arguments, each of which is a number. We shall see later that the second function can be used in a more flexible way than the first; for the moment it is important to realize that there is a difference, and that type errors will result if we confuse the two and write

```
fibStep 2 3                        fibTwoStep (2,3)
```

We say more about the relationship between these two functions in Section 10.7.

Exercises

5.1 Give a definition of the function

```
maxOccurs :: Int -> Int -> (Int,Int)
```

which returns the maximum of two integers, together with the number of times it occurs. Using this, or otherwise, define the function

```
maxThreeOccurs :: Int -> Int -> Int -> (Int,Int)
```

which does a similar thing for three arguments.

5.2 Give a definition of a function

```
orderTriple :: (Int,Int,Int) -> (Int,Int,Int)
```

which puts the elements of a triple of three integers into ascending order. You might like to use the `maxThree`, `middle` and `minThree` functions defined earlier.

5.3 Define the function which finds where a straight line crosses the x-axis. You will need to think about how to supply the information about the straight line to the function.

5.4 Design test data for the preceding exercises; explain the choices you have made in each case. Give a sample evaluation of each of your functions.

(5.3) Our approach to lists

Lists are a remarkably expressive data type. We can represent a text as a list of lines, each of which is a list of words; we can represent a collection of information, like a supermarket bill, as a list of individual items of data; we can represent a collection of readings from a measuring device as a list of `Floats`, to mention but three potential applications.

At the same time, there are many different things which we can do to lists, some of which first came out in our implementation of `Pictures` by lists in Chapter 1. Given a list we can split it up according to various criteria, we can sort it, select items from it and transform all its members in a particular way. We can combine lists by joining them together or by coalescing corresponding elements. We can combine all the members of a list together – by taking their sum, maximum or conjunction, say – among many other operations. Haskell contains many built-in list functions and operators in the standard prelude `Prelude.hs` and also in the library module `List.hs`.

Because Haskell has so many list functions built in, we can approach our discussion of lists in two very different ways. We could argue that we should start by defining list-manipulating functions for ourselves, and only use library functions after we have understood their definitions.[1] On the other hand, we could adopt a 'toolkit' approach, and simply discuss the library functions and how they can be used. What we aim to do here is to combine the two approaches, often introducing and using functions before they are defined explicitly, but then looking 'under the bonnet' to see how these functions are defined and how we can define other functions for ourselves.

In order fully to appreciate the general operations on lists we have to examine how generic or **polymorphic** functions are handled in Haskell – which we look at in Section 5.7 – as well as the notion of **higher-order functions**, see Section 9.2.

In the remainder of this chapter we introduce the main facilities for list manipulation within Haskell; in the chapters which follow we use these prelude functions, as well as seeing how to define these and other functions for ourselves.

---

[1] This was essentially the approach taken in the first edition of this book.

(5.4) Lists in Haskell

A list in Haskell is a collection of items from a given type. For every type t there is a Haskell type [t] of lists from t.

```
[1,2,3,4,1,4] :: [Int]
[True]        :: [Bool]
```

We read these as '[1,2,3,4,1,4] is a list of Int' and '[True] is a list of Bool'. String is a synonym for [Char] and the two lists which follow are the same.

```
['a','a','b'] :: String
"aab"         :: String
```

We can build lists of items of any particular type, and so we can have lists of functions and lists of lists of numbers, as in

```
[fac,fastFib]     :: [ Int -> Int ]
[[12,2],[2,12],[]] :: [ [Int] ]
```

As can be seen, the list with elements e_1, e_2 to e_n is written by enclosing the elements in square brackets, thus

```
[e1,e2,...,en]
```

As a special case the empty list, [], which contains no items, is an element of every list type.

The order of the items in a list is significant, as is the number of times that an item appears. The three lists of numbers which follow are therefore all different:

```
[1,2,1,2,2]
[2,1,1,2,2]
[2,1,1,2]
```

The first two have length 5, while the third has length 4; the first element of the first list is 1, while the first element of the second is 2. A set is another kind of collection in which the ordering of items and the number of occurrences of a particular item are not relevant; we look at sets in Chapter 16.

There are some other ways of writing down lists of numbers, characters and other enumerated types

● [n .. m] is the list [n,n+1,...,m]; if n exceeds m, the list is empty.

```
[2 .. 7]     = [2,3,4,5,6,7]
[3.1 .. 7.0] = [3.1,4.1,5.1,6.1]
['a' .. 'm'] = "abcdefghijklm"
```

● [n,p .. m] is the list of numbers whose first two elements are n and p and whose last is m, with the numbers ascending in steps of p-n. For example,

```
[7,6 .. 3]        = [7,6,5,4,3]
[0.0,0.3 .. 1.0] = [0.0,0.3,0.6,0.9]
['a','c' .. 'n'] = "acegikm"
```

In both cases it can be seen that if the step size does not allow us to reach m exactly, the last item of the list is the largest/smallest in the sequence which is less/greater than or equal to m. It can also be the case that rounding errors on Float lead to lists being different from what is anticipated; an example is given in the exercises.

In the next section we turn to a powerful method of writing down lists which we can use to define a variety of list-manipulating functions.

Exercises

5.5 What value has the expression [0, 0.1 .. 1]? Check your answer in Hugs and explain any discrepancy there might be between the two.

5.6 How many items does the list [2,3] contain? How many does [[2,3]] contain? What is the type of [[2,3]]?

5.7 What is the result of evaluating [2 .. 2]? What about [2,7 .. 4]? Try evaluating [2,2 .. 2]; to **interrupt evaluation** in Hugs under Windows or Unix you need to type Ctrl-C.

(5.5) List comprehensions

One of the distinct features of a functional language is the list comprehension notation, which has no parallels in other paradigms.

In a list comprehension we write down a description of a list in terms of the elements of another list. From the first list we **generate** elements, which we **test** and **transform** to form elements of the result. We will describe list comprehensions with a single generator in this section; Section 17.3 covers the general case. Nevertheless, the simple case we look at here is very useful in writing a variety of list-processing programs. We introduce the topic by a series of examples.

Examples

1. Suppose that the list ex is [2,4,7], then the list comprehension

[2*n | n<-ex]   (1)

will be

[4,8,14]

as it contains each of the elements n of the list ex, doubled: 2*n. We can read (1) as saying

'Take all 2*n where n comes from ex.'

where the symbol <- is meant to resemble the mathematical symbol for being an element, '∈'. We can write the evaluation of the list comprehension in a table, thus:

```
[ 2*n | n <- [2,4,7] ]
```

```
   n  =   2   4   7
  2*n  =   4   8  14
```

2.   In a similar way,

```
[ isEven n | n<-ex ]  ⤳   [True,True,False]
```

if the function isEven has the definition

```
isEven :: Int -> Bool
isEven n = (n 'mod' 2 == 0)
```

In list comprehensions n<-ex is called a **generator** because it generates the data from which the results are built. On the left-hand side of the '<-' there is a variable, n, while on the right-hand side we put the list, in this case ex, from which the elements are taken.

3.   We can combine a generator with one or more **tests**, which are Boolean expressions, thus:

```
[ 2*n | n <- ex , isEven n , n>3 ]
```
(2)

(2) is paraphrased as

'Take all 2*n where n comes from ex, n is even and greater than 3.'

Again, we can write the evaluation in tabular form.

```
[ 2*n | n <- [2,4,7] , isEven n , n>3 ]
```

```
       n  =   2   4   7
  isEven n  =   T   T   F
      n>3  =   F   T
      2*n  =       8
```

The result of (2) will therefore be the list [8], as 4 is the only even element of [2,4,7] which is greater than 3.

4.   Instead of placing a variable to the left of the arrow '<-', we can put a pattern. For instance,

```
addPairs :: [(Int,Int)] -> [Int]
addPairs pairList = [ m+n | (m,n) <- pairList ]
```

Here we choose all the pairs in the list pairList, and add their components to give a single number in the result list. For example,

```
[ m+n | (m,n) <- [(2,3),(2,1),(7,8)] ]
```

```
    m  =   2   2   7
    n  =   3   1   8
  m+n  =   5   3  15
```

giving the result

```
addPairs  [(2,3),(2,1),(7,8)]  ⤳   [5,3,15]
```

5.   We can add tests in such a situation, too:

```
addOrdPairs :: [(Int,Int)] -> [Int]
addOrdPairs pairList = [ m+n | (m,n) <- pairList , m<n ]
```

so that with the same input example,

```
[ m+n | (m,n) <- [(2,3),(2,1),(7,8)] , m<n ]
```

m	=	2	2	7
n	=	3	1	8
m<n	=	T	F	T
m+n	=	5		15

giving

```
addOrdPairs  [(2,3),(2,1),(7,8)]  ⤳   [5,15]
```

since the second pair in the list, $(2,1)$, fails the test.

6.   Note that we can simply test elements, with the effect that we filter some of the elements of a list, according to a Boolean condition. To find all the digits in a string we can say

```
digits :: String -> String
digits st = [ ch | ch<-st , isDigit ch ]
```

where the prelude function

```
isDigit :: Char -> Bool
```

is True on those characters which are digits: '0', '1' up to '9'.

7.   A list comprehension can form a part of a larger function definition. Suppose that we want to check whether all members of a list of integers are even, or all are odd. We can write

```
allEven xs = (xs == [x | x<-xs, isEven x])
allOdd xs  = ([] == [x | x<-xs, isEven x])
```

We will see list comprehensions in practice in the next section when we examine a simple library database.

5.8 Give a definition of a function

```
doubleAll :: [Int] -> [Int]
```

which doubles all the elements of a list of integers.

5.9 Give a definition of a function

```
capitalize :: String -> String
```

which converts all small letters in a String into capitals, leaving the other characters unchanged. How would you modify this function to give

```
capitalizeLetters :: String -> String
```

which behaves in the same way except that all non-letters are removed from the list? You should check the Char.hs library to see whether it contains any functions useful in solving this problem.

5.10 Define the function

```
divisors :: Int -> [Int]
```

which returns the list of divisors of a positive integer (and the empty list for other inputs). For instance,

```
divisors 12  ⤳  [1,2,3,4,6,12]
```

A prime number n is a number whose only divisors are 1 and n. Using `divisors` or otherwise define a function

```
isPrime :: Int -> Bool
```

which checks whether or not a positive integer is prime (and returns False if its input is not a positive integer).

5.11 Define the function

```
matches :: Int -> [Int] -> [Int]
```

which picks out all occurrences of an integer n in a list. For instance,

```
matches 1 [1,2,1,4,5,1]  ⤳  [1,1,1]
matches 1 [2,3,4,6]      ⤳  []
```

Using `matches` or otherwise, define a function

```
elem :: Int -> [Int] -> Bool
```

which is True if the Int is an element of the list, and False otherwise. For the examples above, we have

```
elem 1 [1,2,1,4,5,1] ⤳  True
elem 1 [2,3,4,6]     ⤳  False
```

Since elem is a prelude function, you need to hide it as described on page 41.

(5.6) A library database

This section presents a simple model of the loan data kept by a library, and illustrates how list comprehensions are used in practice.

A library uses a database to keep a record of the books on loan to borrowers; we first look at which type to use to model the database, and then look at the functions which extract information from a database. This is followed by a discussion of how to model changes to the database, and we conclude by exploring how the database functions can be tested.

Types

In modelling this situation, we first look at the types of the objects involved. People and books are represented by strings

```
type Person = String
type Book   = String
```

The database can be represented in a number of different ways. Three among a number of possibilities are

- We can record each loan as a (Person,Book) pair;
- we could associate with each person the list of books that they have borrowed, using a pair (Person,[Book]), or
- we could record a list of borrowers with each book, thus: ([Person],Book),

Here we choose to make the database a list of (Person,Book) pairs. If the pair ("Alice" , "Asterix") is in the list, it means that "Alice" has borrowed the book called "Asterix". We therefore define

```
type Database = [ (Person , Book) ]
```

We have chosen this representation because it is simple, and also treats people and books in the same way, rather than grouping data in an asymmetrical way.

An example object of this type is

```
exampleBase :: Database
exampleBase
= [ ("Alice" , "Tintin")  , ("Anna" , "Little Women") ,
    ("Alice" , "Asterix"), ("Rory" , "Tintin") ]
```

After defining the types of the objects involved, we consider the functions which work over the database.

- Given a person, we want to find the book(s) that he or she has borrowed, if any.

- Given a book, we want to find the borrower(s) of the book, if any. (It is assumed that there may be more than one copy of any book.)

- Given a book, we want to find out whether it is borrowed.

- Given a person, we may want to find out the number of books that he or she has borrowed.

Each of these **lookup** functions will take a Database, and a Person or Book, and return the result of the query. Their types will be

```
books        :: Database -> Person -> [Book]
borrowers    :: Database -> Book -> [Person]
borrowed     :: Database -> Book -> Bool
numBorrowed  :: Database -> Person -> Int
```

Note that borrowers and books return lists; these can contain zero, one or more items, and so in particular an empty list can signal that a book has no borrowers, or that a person has no books on loan.

Two other functions need to be defined. We need to be able to model a book being loaned to a person and a loaned book being returned. The functions modelling these will take a database, plus the loan information, and return a *different* database, which is the original with the loan added or removed. These **update** functions will have type

```
makeLoan   :: Database -> Person -> Book -> Database
returnLoan :: Database -> Person -> Book -> Database
```

Defining the lookup functions

We concentrate on the definition of the function

```
books :: Database -> Person -> [Book]
```

which forms a model for the other lookup functions. For the exampleBase, we have

```
books exampleBase "Alice" = [ "Tintin" , "Asterix" ]
books exampleBase "Rory"  = [ "Tintin" ]
```

How are these found? In the "Alice" case we need to run through the list exampleBase finding all the pairs whose first component is "Alice"; for each of these we return the second component. As a list comprehension, we have

```
[ book | (person,book) <- exampleBase , person=="Alice" ]
```

person	=	"Alice"	"Anna"	"Alice"	"Rory"
book	=	"Tintin"	"Little Women"	"Asterix"	"Tintin"
(person==	=	T	F	T	F
"Alice")					
book	=	"Tintin"		"Asterix"	

We make this into a general function by saying

```
books        :: Database -> Person -> [Book]            (books.1)
books dBase findPerson
  = [ book | (person,book) <- dBase , person==findPerson ]
```

Note that in this definition Person is a type while person is a variable of type Person.

As we said at the start, books forms a model for the other lookup functions, which we leave as an exercise.

Defining the update functions

The database is modified, or updated, by the functions makeLoan and returnLoan. Making a loan is done by adding a pair to the database, which can be done simply by adding an extra pair to the front of the list of pairs.

```
makeLoan    :: Database -> Person -> Book -> Database
makeLoan dBase pers bk = [ (pers,bk) ] ++ dBase
```

We have used the ++ operator here to join two lists, namely the one element list [(pers,bk)] and the 'old' database dBase.

To return a loan, we need to check through the database, and to remove the pair (pers,bk). We therefore run through all the pairs in the database, and retain those which are not equal to (pers,bk), thus

```
returnLoan    :: Database -> Person -> Book -> Database
returnLoan dBase pers bk
  = [ pair | pair <- dBase , pair /= (pers,bk) ]
```

Note that we have used a simple variable pair rather than a pattern to run over the pairs in the dBase. This is because we do not need to deal with the components separately; all we do is check whether the whole pair is equal to the pair (pers,bk). On the other hand we could use a pattern thus:

```
[ (p,b) | (p,b) <- dBase , (p,b) /= (pers,bk) ]
```

and get exactly the same result.

As we have defined it, the returnLoan function will remove *all* pairs (pers,bk) from the database. We will return to this point in the exercises in Section 9.3.

Testing

A Haskell interpreter acts like a calculator, and this is useful when we wish to test functions like those in the library database. Any function can be tested by typing expressions to the Hugs prompt. For example,

```
makeLoan [] "Alice" "Rotten Romans"
```

To test more substantial examples, it is sensible to put test data into a script, so we might include the definition of exampleBase as well as various tests

```
test1 :: Bool
test1 = borrowed exampleBase "Asterix"

test2 :: Database
test2 = makeLoan exampleBase "Alice" "Rotten Romans"
```

and so on. Adding them to the script means that we can repeatedly evaluate them without having to type them out in full each time. Another device which can help is to use $$, which is short for 'the last expression evaluated'. The following sequence makes a loan, then another, then returns the first.

```
makeLoan exampleBase "Alice" "Rotten Romans"
makeLoan $$ "Rory" "Godzilla"
returnLoan $$ "Alice" "Rotten Romans"
```

Note: Variables in list comprehensions

There is an important pitfall to do with the behaviour of variables in list comprehensions. The definition (books.1) of books above might appear to be over-complicated. We might imagine that we could say

```
books dBase findPerson
 = [ book | (findPerson,book) <- dBase ]              (books.2)
```

The effect of this is to return all the books borrowed by *all* borrowers, not just the particular borrower findPerson.

The reason for this is that the findPerson in (findPerson,book) is a *new* variable, and not the variable on the left-hand side of the definition, so in fact (books.2) has the same effect as

```
books dBase findPerson = [ book | (new,book) <- dBase ]
```

where it is clear that there is no constraint on the value of new to be equal to findPerson.

Exercises

5.12 Go through the calculation of

```
books exampleBase "Charlie"
books exampleBase "Rory"
```

5.13 Define the functions borrowers, borrowed and numBorrowed. To define numBorrowed you will probably need the length function which returns the length of a list.

5.14 Give calculations of

```
returnLoan exampleBase "Alice" "Asterix"
returnLoan exampleBase "Alice" "Little Women"
```

5.15 Discuss how you would implement the database functions had you used the representation [(Person,[Book])] rather than [(Person,Book)] for the database.

(5.7) Generic functions: polymorphism

Before looking in detail at the functions on lists provided in the Haskell prelude and library we need to look at the idea of **polymorphism**, which literally means 'has many shapes'. A function is polymorphic if it 'has many types', and this is the case for many list-manipulating functions. An example is the length function, which returns the length of a list, an Int. This function can be applied to any type of list, so that we can say

```
length :: [Bool] -> Int
length :: [[Char]] -> Int
```

and so forth. How do we write down a type for length which encapsulates this? We say

```
length :: [a] -> Int
```

where a is a **type variable**. Any identifier beginning with a small letter can be used as a type variable; conventionally, letters from the beginning of the alphabet, a, b, c, ... are used. Just as in the definition

```
square x = x*x
```

the variable x stands for an arbitrary value, so a type variable stands for an *arbitrary type*, and so we can see all the types like

```
[Bool] -> Int          [[Char]] -> Int
```

as coming about by replacing the variable a by particular types: here Bool and [Char]. Types like [Bool] -> Int are called **instances** of the type [a] -> Int, and because every type for length is an instance of [a] -> Int we call this type the **most general type** for length.

The type of the function to join together two lists, ++, is

```
[a] -> [a] -> [a]
```

The variable a stands for 'an arbitrary type', but we should be clear that all the a's stand for the same type, just as in

```
square x = x*x
```

the x's all stand for the same (arbitrary) value. Instances of [a]->[a]->[a] will include

```
[Int]->[Int]->[Int]
```

but *not* the type

```
[Int]->[Bool]->[Char]
```

This makes sense: we cannot expect to join a list of numbers and a list of Booleans to give a string!

On the other hand, the functions zip and unzip convert between pairs of lists and lists of pairs, and their types involve two type variables:

```
zip   :: [a] -> [b] -> [(a,b)]
unzip :: [(a,b)] -> ([a],[b])
```

Now, instances of the type of zip include

```
[Int]->[Bool]->[(Int,Bool)]
```

where a and b are replaced by different types (Int and Bool, here). It is, of course, possible to replace both variables by the same type, giving

```
[Int]->[Int]->[(Int,Int)]
```

and the general type [a] -> [a] -> [(a,a)].

Types and definitions

How is a polymorphic function defined? Consider the definition of the identity function,

```
id x = x
```

which returns its argument unchanged. In the definition there is nothing to **constrain** the type of x – all we know about x is that it is returned directly from the function. We know, therefore, that the output type is the same as the input, and so the most general type will be

```
id :: a -> a
```

At work here is the principle that a function's type is as general as possible, consistent with the constraints put upon the types by its definition. In the case of the id function, the only constraint is that the input and output types are the same.

In a similar way, in defining

```
fst (x,y) = x
```

neither x nor y is at all constrained, and so they can come from different types a and b, giving the type

```
fst :: (a,b) -> a
```

A final example is given by

```
mystery (x,y) = if x then 'c' else 'd'
```

Here we see that x is used as a Bool in the if x then ..., whereas y is not used at all, and so is not constrained in the definition, giving mystery the type

```
(Bool,a) -> Char
```

We shall examine the definitions of many of the prelude functions in Chapter 7, and see there that, as outlined above, a function or other object will have as general as possible a type, consistent with the constraints put upon the types by its definition. We look in more depth at the mechanics of type checking in Chapter 13.

Hugs can be used to give the most general type of a function definition, using the :type command. If you have given a type declaration for the function, this can be commented out before asking for the type.

Polymorphism and overloading

Polymorphism and overloading are both mechanisms by which the same function name can be used at different types, but they have an important difference.

A polymorphic function like fst has the same definition, namely

```
fst (x,y) = x
```

at all types, so that it is the **same** function at all its instances.

On the other hand, an overloaded name like == has different definitions over different types, so that the same name is being used to mean **different** but similar functions at different types. For example, == over Int is built in, whereas over pairs it will be defined by

```
(n,m) == (p,q)
  = (n==p) && (m==q)
```

More details about overloading can be found in Chapter 12.

──

Exercises

5.16 Give the most general types for the functions snd and sing defined by

```
snd (x,y) = y
sing x = [x]
```

5.17 Explain why

```
[[a]] -> [[a]]
```

is a type for `id` but why it is not the most general type for this function.

5.18 Earlier in the chapter we saw the example of

```
shift :: ((Int,Int),Int) -> (Int,(Int,Int))
shift ((x,y),z) = (x,(y,z))
```

What is the most general type for `shift`, if the type declaration is omitted?

(5.8) **Haskell list functions in** `Prelude.hs`

Armed with the insight provided by the previous section we can look at the descriptions of the polymorphic list operations from `Prelude.hs` given in Figure 5.1. In this table we give the name of the function or operator, its type, a brief description of its effect and an example, as in the description of `length`

```
length      [a] -> Int              The length of the list.
                                    length "word" ⤳ 4
```

As well as the polymorphic functions in Figure 5.1, the standard prelude provides various operations over specific types; some of these can be seen in Figure 5.2. The types of the functions `sum` and `product`, which are overloaded, will be discussed further in Chapter 12.

The importance of types

The single most useful piece of information about a function is its **type**, and this is particularly true when we look at the polymorphic types of functions in a library like Figure 5.1. Suppose we are looking for a function to make a list from a number of copies of a single element. It must take the item and a count and give a list, so its type will be one of

```
Int -> a -> [a]              a -> Int -> [a]
```

Looking at Figure 5.1 we can quickly locate one function, `replicate`, which does have one of these types and is indeed the function which we seek. If we want a function to reverse a list it will have type `[a] -> [a]` and although there is more than one function with this type, the search is very much narrowed by looking at types.

This insight is not confined to functional languages, but is of particular use when a language supports polymorphic or **generic** functions and operators as we have seen here.

:	`a -> [a] -> [a]`	Add a single element to the front of a list.
		`3:[2,3]` ⇝ `[3,2,3]`
++	`[a] -> [a] -> [a]`	Join two lists together.
		`"Ron"++"aldo"` ⇝ `"Ronaldo"`
!!	`[a] -> Int -> a`	`xs!!n` returns the nth element of `xs`, starting at the beginning and counting from 0.
		`[14,7,3]!!1` ⇝ `7`
concat	`[[a]] -> [a]`	Concatenate a list of lists into a single list.
		`concat [[2,3],[],[4]]` ⇝ `[2,3,4]`
length	`[a] -> Int`	The length of the list.
		`length "word"` ⇝ `4`
head,last	`[a] -> a`	The first/last element of the list.
		`head "word"` ⇝ `'w'`
		`last "word"` ⇝ `'d'`
tail,init	`[a] -> [a]`	All but the first/last element of the list.
		`tail "word"` ⇝ `"ord"`
		`init "word"` ⇝ `"wor"`
replicate	`Int -> a -> [a]`	Make a list of n copies of the item.
		`replicate 3 'c'` ⇝ `"ccc"`
take	`Int -> [a] -> [a]`	Take n elements from the front of a list.
		`take 3 "Peccary"` ⇝ `"Pec"`
drop	`Int -> [a] -> [a]`	Drop n elements from the front of a list.
		`drop 3 "Peccary"` ⇝ `"cary"`
splitAt	`Int -> [a] -> ([a],[a])`	Split a list at a given position.
		`splitAt 3 "Peccary"` ⇝ `("Pec","cary")`
reverse	`[a] -> [a]`	Reverse the order of the elements.
		`reverse [2,1,3]` ⇝ `[3,1,2]`
zip	`[a]->[b]->[(a,b)]`	Take a pair of lists into a list of pairs.
		`zip [1,2] [3,4,5]` ⇝ `[(1,3),(2,4)]`
unzip	`[(a,b)] -> ([a],[b])`	Take a list of pairs into a pair of lists.
		`unzip [(1,5),(3,6)]` ⇝ `([1,3],[5,6])`

Figure 5.1 Some polymorphic list operations from `Prelude.hs`.

and	[Bool] -> Bool	The conjunction of a list of Booleans. and [True,False] ⤳ False
or	[Bool] -> Bool	The disjunction of a list of Booleans. or [True,False] ⤳ True
sum	[Int] -> Int [Float] -> Float	The sum of a numeric list. sum [2,3,4] ⤳ 9
product	[Int] -> Int [Float] -> Float	The product of a numeric list. product [0.1,0.4 .. 1] ⤳ 0.028

Figure 5.2   Some monomorphic list operations from Prelude.hs.

Further functions

We have not described all the functions in the prelude for two different reasons. First, some of the general functions are **higher-order** and we postpone discussion of these until Chapter 9; secondly, some of the functions, such as zip3, are obvious variants of things we have discussed here. Similarly, we have not chosen to enumerate the functions in the library List.hs; readers should consult the library file itself, which contains type information and comments about the effects of the functions.

In the next chapter we explore how to use the prelude functions in making our own definitions of functions; before that we discuss strings, an example of a list type.

(5.9) The String type

The String type is a special case of lists,

```
type String = [Char]
```

and all the polymorphic prelude functions in Figure 5.1 can be used over strings. In Section 3.5 we showed how to write the special characters such as newline and tab using the 'escapes' '\n' and '\t'. These characters can form part of strings, as in the examples

```
"baboon"
""
"\99a\116"
"gorilla\nhippo\nibex"
"1\t23\t456"
```

If we evaluate one of these strings in Hugs, the result is exactly the same as the input. In order to resolve the escape characters and to lose the double quotes we have to perform an output operation. This is done using the primitive Haskell function

```
putStr :: String -> IO ()
```

with the effect of putting the argument string on the screen. Applying putStr to the strings above gives output as follows:

```
baboon

cat
gorilla
hippo
ibex
1       23      456
```

Strings can be joined together using ++, so that "cat"++"\n"++"fish" prints as

```
cat
fish
```

Note: Names, strings and characters

It is easy to confuse a, 'a' and "a". To summarize the difference,

a	is a name or a variable, if defined it may have any type whatever;
'a'	is a character;
"a"	is a string, which just happens to consist of a single character.

Similarly, there is a difference between

emu	a Haskell name or variable;
"emu"	a string.

Other functions over strings can be found in the library String.hs.

Strings and values

Built into Haskell are the overloaded functions show and read, which convert from a value to a String and vice versa; for instance,

```
show (2+3)              ⤳    "5"
show (True || False) ⤳    "True"
```

In the opposite direction, the function read is used to convert a string to the value it represents, so that

```
read "True" ⤳   True
read "3"     ⤳   3
```

In some situations it will not be clear what should be the result type for read – it is then possible to give a type to the application, as in

```
(read "3") :: Int
```

the result of which will be 3 and its type, Int.

A full explanation of the types of read and show can be found in Chapter 12.

5.19 Define a function to convert small letters to capitals which returns unchanged characters which are not small letters.

5.20 Define a function

```
romanDigit :: Char -> String
```

which converts a digit to its representation in Roman numerals, so at '7' it will have the value "VII" and so on.

5.21 Define a function

```
onThreeLines :: String -> String -> String -> String
```

which takes three strings and returns a single string which when printed shows the three strings on separate lines.

5.22 Define a function

```
onSeparateLines :: [String] -> String
```

which takes a list of strings and returns a single string which when printed shows the strings on separate lines.

5.23 Give a function

```
duplicate :: String -> Int -> String
```

which takes a string and an integer, n. The result is n copies of the string joined together. If n is less than or equal to 0, the result should be the empty string, "", and if n is 1, the result will be the string itself.

5.24 Give a function

```
pushRight :: String -> String
```

which takes a string and forms a string of length linelength by putting spaces at the front of the string. If linelength were 12 then pushRight "crocodile" would be "   crocodile". How would you make linelength a parameter of this function?

5.25 Can you criticize the way the previous function is specified? Look for a case in which it is not defined what it should do – it is an exceptional case.

5.26 Define a function

```
fibTable :: Int -> String
```

which produces a table of Fibonacci numbers. For instance, the effect of `putStr` (`fibTable 6`) should be

```
n           fib n
0             0
1             1
2             1
3             2
4             3
5             5
6             8
```

5.27 Define functions to give more readable output from the database operations of Section 5.6.

Summary

This chapter has introduced the structured types of tuples and lists, and explained their differences: in a given tuple type, $(t_1, \ldots t_n)$ the elements all have the same form, namely $(v_1, \ldots v_n)$, with each component v_i being a member of the corresponding type t_i. The list type $[t]$ on the other hand contains elements $[e_1, \ldots, e_n]$ of different lengths but in which all the values e_i have the same type t.

Over tuples we introduced the notion of pattern matching – in which a pattern such as (x,y) could be used to stand for an arbitrary member of a pair type – and saw how this led to more readable definitions.

The bulk of the chapter was an account of the facilities which Haskell provides for working with lists. These include

- various ways of writing lists of elements of base type, including ranges like $[2,4..12]$;
- list comprehensions, in which the members of a list are generated, tested and transformed from the elements of another list, as exemplified by

  `[ toUpper ch | ch <- string , isAlpha ch ]`

  which selects the alphabetic characters from `string`, and converts them to upper case;
- the functions provided by the standard prelude and the `List.hs` library;
- `String` as the list type `[Char]`.

In order to understand the prelude functions it was necessary to discuss polymorphism, by which a function can have 'many types'. Types of functions like this are described by using type variables, as in

`reverse :: [a] -> [a]`

which states that `reverse` can be applied to a list of any type (a is a type variable), returning a member of the same list type.

In the chapters to come we will use the list functions given here in making our own definitions, as well as seeing how the prelude and library functions are themselves defined.

Chapter 7

Defining functions over lists

We have already seen how to define a variety of functions over lists using a combination of list comprehensions and the built-in list processing functions in the Haskell prelude. This chapter looks `under the bonnet' and explains how functions over lists can be defined by means of recursion. This will allow us to define the prelude functions we have already been using, as well as letting us look at a wider class of applications, including sorting and a case study of text processing.

The chapter begins with a summary of the mechanism of pattern matching, and continues with a justification and explanation of recursion echoing the discussion in Chapter 4. We then explore a variety of examples both of functions defined by primitive recursion and of more general recursive functions, and conclude with the case study mentioned earlier.

7.1 Pattern matching revisited

We have seen that function definitions take the form of conditional equations like

```
mystery :: Int -> Int -> Int
```

```
mystery x y
  | x==0       = y
  | otherwise  = x
```

where a choice of two alternatives is made by guards; we can rewrite this into two equations, thus

```
mystery 0 y = y                                              (mystery.1)
mystery x y = x                                              (mystery.2)
```

where we distinguish between the two cases by using a pattern – here the literal 0 – instead of a variable. Just as for guards, the equations are applied **sequentially**, and so (mystery.2) will only be used in cases that (mystery.1) does not apply.

Another aspect of this definition is that y is not used on the right-hand side of (mystery.2). Because of this we do not need to give a name to the second argument in this case, and so we can replace the variable y with the **wildcard** '_' which matches anything, thus

```
mystery 0 y = y
mystery x _ = x
```

We have therefore seen that pattern matching can be used for distinguishing between certain sorts of **cases** in function definitions. We have also seen pattern matching used to **name the components** of tuples, as in

```
joinStrings :: (String,String) -> String
joinStrings (st1,st2) = st1 ++ "\t" ++ st2
```

where the variables st1 and st2 will be matched with the components of any argument.

In working with lists the two aspects of distinguishing cases and extracting components are used together, as we see in the next section.

Summarizing patterns

A pattern can be one of a number of things:

- A **literal value** such as 24, 'f' or True; an argument matches this pattern if it is equal to the value.

- A **variable** such as x or longVariableName; any argument value will match this.

- A **wildcard** '_'; any argument value will match this.

- A **tuple pattern** $(p_1,p_2,\ldots,p_n)$. To match this, an argument must be of the form $(v_1,v_2,\ldots,v_n)$, and each v_k must match p_k.

- A **constructor** applied to a number of patterns; we will examine this case in the next section and in Chapter 14 below.

In a function definition we have a number of conditional equations, each of which will have a left-hand side in which the function is applied to a number of patterns. When the function is applied we try to match the arguments with the patterns in sequence, and we use the first equation which applies; pattern matching in Haskell is thus **sequential**, in a similar way to the conditions expressed by guards.

7.2 Lists and list patterns

Every list is either **empty**, [], or is non-empty. In the latter case – take the example [4,2,3] – then it can be written in the form x:xs, where x is the first item in the list and xs is the remainder of the list; in our example, we have 4:[2,3]. We call 4 the **head** of the list and [2,3] the **tail**.

What is more, every list can be built up from the empty list by repeatedly applying ':', and indeed Haskell lists are represented in that way internally. Our example list can be thought of as being built step-by-step from the right, thus

[]   3:[] = [3]   2:[3] = [2,3]   4:[2,3] = [4,2,3]

and we can write the list using ':' repeatedly thus:

4:2:3:[]

Note that here we use the fact that ':' is **right associative**, so that for any values of x, y and zs,

x:y:zs = x:(y:zs)

It is also not hard to see that 4:2:3:[] is the *only* way that [4,2,3] can be built using ':'. The operator ':', of type

a -> [a] -> [a]

therefore has a special role to play for lists: it is a **constructor** for lists, since every list can be built up in a unique way from [] and ':'. For historical reasons we sometimes call this constructor **cons**. Not all functions are constructors: ++ can be used to build lists, but this construction will not be unique, since, for example

[1] ++ [2,3] = [1,2,3] = [1,2] ++ [3]

Pattern-matching definitions

If we want to make a definition covering all cases of lists we can write

fun xs = ...

but more often than not we will want to distinguish between empty and non-empty cases, as in the prelude functions

```
head              :: [a] -> a
head (x:_)         = x

tail              :: [a] -> [a]
tail (_:xs)        = xs

null              :: [a] -> Bool
null []            = True
null (_:_)         = False
```

where head takes the first item in a non-empty list, tail takes all but the head of a non-empty list and null checks whether or not a list is empty.

In the definition of null the pattern (_:_) will match any non-empty list, but it gives no names for the head and tail; when we need to name one of these, as in tail, then a different pattern, (_:xs), is used.

It has become an informal convention in the Haskell community to write variables over lists in the form xs, ys (pronounced 'exes', 'whyes') and so on, with variables x, y, . . . ranging over their elements. We will – when using short variable names – endeavour to stick to that convention.

We can now explain the final case of pattern matching. A **constructor pattern** over lists will either be [] or will have the form (p:ps) where p and ps are themselves patterns.

- A list matches [] exactly when it is empty.

- A list will match the pattern (p:ps) if it is non-empty, and moreover if its head matches the pattern p and its tail the pattern ps.

In the case of the pattern (x:xs), it is sufficient for the argument to be non-empty to match the pattern; the head of the argument is matched with x and its tail with xs.

A pattern involving a constructor like ':' will always be parenthesized, since function application binds more tightly than any other operation.

The case construction

So far we have seen how to perform a pattern match over the arguments of functions; sometimes we might want to pattern match over other values. This can be done by a case expression, which we introduce by means of an example.

Suppose we are asked to find the first digit in the string st, returning '\0' in case no digit is found. We can use the function digits of Section 5.5 to give us the list of all the digits in the string: digits st. If this is not empty, that is if it matches (x:_), we want to return its first element, x; if it is empty, we return '\0'.

We therefore want to pattern match over the value of (digits st) and for this we use a case expression as follows:

```
firstDigit :: String -> Char

firstDigit st
  = case (digits st) of
      []    -> '\0'
      (x:_) -> x
```

A case expression has the effect of distinguishing between various alternatives – here those of an empty and a non-empty list – and of extracting parts of a value, by associating values with the variables in a pattern. In the case of matching e with (x:_) we associate the head of e with x; as we have used a wild-card pattern in (x:_), the tail of e is not associated with any variable.

In general, a case expression has the form

```
case e of
  p1 -> e1
  p2 -> e2
  ...
  pk -> ek
```

where e is an expression to be matched in turn against the patterns $p_1, p_2, \ldots, p_k$. If p_i is the first pattern which e matches, the result is e_i where the variables in p_i are associated with the corresponding parts of e.

Exercises

7.1 Give a pattern-matching definition of a function which returns the first integer in a list plus one, if there is one, and returns zero otherwise.

7.2 Give a pattern-matching definition of a function which adds together the first two integers in a list, if a list contains at least two elements; returns the head element if the list contains one, and returns zero otherwise.

7.3 Give solutions to the previous two questions *without* using pattern matching.

7.3 Primitive recursion over lists

Suppose we are to find the sum of a list of integers. Just as we described calculating factorial in Section 4.2, we can think of laying out the values of sum in a table thus:

```
        sum [] = 0
....    sum [5] = 5       ....
....    sum [7,5] = 12      ....
....    sum [2,7,5] = 14      ....
....    sum [3,2,7,5] = 17       ....
....
```

and just as in the case of factorial, we can describe the table by describing the first line and how to go from one line to the next, as follows:

```
sum :: [Int] -> Int
sum []     = 0                        (sum.1)
sum (x:xs) = x + sum xs               (sum.2)
```

This gives a definition of sum by **primitive recursion over lists**. In such a definition we give

- a starting point: the value of sum at [], and

- a way of going from the value of sum at a particular point – sum xs – to the value of sum on the next line, namely sum (x:xs).

There is also a calculational explanation for why this form of recursion works; again, this is just like the case put forward in Section 4.2. Consider the calculation of sum [3,2,7,5]. Using the equation (sum.2) repeatedly we have

```
sum [3,2,7,5]
⤳   3 + sum [2,7,5]
⤳   3 + (2 + sum [7,5])
⤳   3 + (2 + (7 + sum [5]))
⤳   3 + (2 + (7 + (5 + sum [])))
```

and now we can use the equation (sum.1) and integer arithmetic to give

```
⤳   3 + (2 + (7 + (5 + 0)))
⤳   17
```

We can see that the recursion used to define sum will give an answer on any finite list since each recursion step takes us closer to the 'base case' where sum is applied to [].

In the next section we look at a collection of examples of definitions by primitive recursion.

Exercises

7.4 Define the function

```
product :: [Int] -> Int
```

which gives the product of a list of integers, and returns 1 for an empty list; why is this particular value chosen as the result for the empty list?

7.5 Define the functions

```
and, or :: [Bool] -> Bool
```

which give the conjunction and disjunction of a list of Booleans. For instance,

```
and [False, True] = False
or  [False, True] = True
```

On an empty list and gives True and or gives False; explain the reason for these choices.

7.4 Finding primitive recursive definitions

We saw in the last section how primitive recursion over lists works, by means of two explanations: tabulating a function and calculating the result of a function. In this section we present a series of examples of primitive recursive definitions over lists. A template for a primitive recursive definition over lists is

```
fun []     = ....
fun (x:xs) = .... x .... xs .... fun xs ....
```

The crucial question to ask in trying to find a primitive recursive definition is:

What if we were given the value `fun xs`. *How could we define* `fun (x:xs)` *from it?*

We explore how definitions are found through a series of examples.

1. By analogy with `sum`, many other functions can be defined by 'folding in' an operator. The prelude functions `product`, `and` and `or` are examples; here we look at how to define the prelude function `concat`,

```
concat :: [[a]] -> [a]
```
(concat.0)

with the effect that

```
concat [e1,e2,...,en] = e1++e2++...++en
```

We can begin our definition

```
concat []     = []
concat (x:xs) = ....
```

How do we find `concat (x:xs)` if we are given `concat xs`? Look at the example where `(x:xs)` is the list $[e_1, e_2, \ldots, e_n]$. The value of `concat xs` is going to be

$$e_2 ++ \ldots ++ e_n$$

and the result we want is $e_1 ++ e_2 ++ \ldots ++ e_n$, and so we simply have to join the list `x` to the front of the joined lists `concat xs`, giving the definition

```
concat []     = []
concat (x:xs) = x ++ concat xs
```
(concat.1)

(concat.2)

Looking at the definition here we can see that `(x:xs)` is a list of lists, since its element is joined to another list in `(concat.2)`; the type of `x` will be the type of the result. Putting these facts together we can conclude that the type of the input is `[[a]]` and the type of the output is `[a]`; this agrees with the type given in `(concat.0)`.

2. How is the function `++` which we used in the previous example itself defined? Can we use primitive recursion? One strategy we can use is to look at examples, so, taking 2 for `x` and `[3,4]` for `xs` we have

```
[2,3,4] ++ [9,8] = [2,3,4,9,8]
  [3,4] ++ [9,8] = [3,4,9,8]
```

so we get `[2,3,4] ++ [9,8]` by putting 2 on the front of `[3,4] ++ [9,8]`. In the case that the first list is empty,

```
    [] ++ [9,8] = [9,8]
```

These examples suggest a definition

```
(++) :: [a] -> [a] -> [a]

[]      ++ ys = ys
(x:xs) ++ ys = x:(xs++ys)
```

Note that the type of ++ allows lists of arbitrary type to be joined, as long as the two lists are of the same type.

3.   A third example is to check whether an Int is an element of an Int list,

```
elem :: Int -> [Int] -> Bool
```

Clearly, no value is an element of [], but under what circumstances is x an element of (y:ys)? If you are not sure about how to answer this question, now is the point to stop and look at an example or two.

Returning to the question, since (y:ys) is built by adding y to the front of ys, x can be an element of y:ys either

- by being equal to y, or

- by being an element of ys.

It is this second case where we use the value elem x ys, and we make the following primitive recursive definition of elem.

```
elem x []      = False                          (elem.1)
elem x (y:ys) = (x==y) || (elem x ys)           (elem.2)
```

Note: Repeated variables in patterns

Another candidate definition of elem is

```
elem x (x:ys) = True                            (elem.3)
elem x (y:ys) = elem x ys
```

in which the equality check is done by repeating the variable x on the left-hand side of (elem.3). Unfortunately, repeated variables like this are not permitted in Haskell patterns.

---

4.   Suppose we wish to double every element of an integer list

```
doubleAll :: [Int] -> [Int]
```

The neatest solution is to use a list comprehension

```
doubleAll xs = [ 2*x | x<-xs ]
```

but we could ask whether this can be done 'by hand', as it were, using primitive recursion. Looking at some examples, we expect that

```
doubleAll [2,3] =   [4,6]
doubleAll [4,2,3] = [8,4,6]
```

so that to double all the elements of (x:xs) we need to double all the elements of xs, and to stick 2*x on the front. Formally, we have

```
doubleAll []     = []                    (doubleAll.1)
doubleAll (x:xs) = 2*x : doubleAll xs     (doubleAll.2)
```

5.   Suppose that we want to select the even elements from an integer list.

```
selectEven :: [Int] -> [Int]
```

Using a list comprehension, we can say

```
selectEven xs = [ x | x<-xs , isEven x ]
```

but can we give a primitive recursive definition of this function? For an empty list, there are no elements to select from,

```
selectEven [] = []                        (selectEven.1)
```

but what happens in the case of a non-empty list? Consider the examples

```
selectEven [2,3,4] = [2,4] = 2 : selectEven [3,4]
selectEven [5,3,4] =   [4] =     selectEven [3,4]
```

It is thus a matter of taking selectEven xs, and adding x to (the front of) this only when x is even. We therefore define

```
selectEven (x:xs)                         (selectEven.2)
  | isEven x    = x : selectEven xs
  | otherwise   =     selectEven xs
```

6.   As a final example, suppose that we want to **sort** a list of numbers into ascending order. One way to sort the list

7	3	9	2

is to sort the tail [3,9,2] to give

2	3	9

It is then a matter of inserting the head, 7, in the right place in this list, to give the result

2	3	7	9

This gives the definition of iSort – the 'i' is for **insertion** sort.

```
iSort :: [Int] -> [Int]

iSort []     = []                         (iSort.1)
iSort (x:xs) = ins x (iSort xs)           (iSort.2)
```

This is a typical example of top-down definition, first discussed in Section 4.1. We have defined iSort assuming we can define ins. The development of the program has been in two separate parts, since we have a definition of the function iSort using a simpler function ins, together with a definition of the function ins itself. Solving each sub-problem is simpler than solving the original problem itself.

Now we have to define the function

```
ins :: Int -> [Int] -> [Int]
```

To get some guidance about how ins should behave, we look at some examples. Inserting 7 into [2,3,9] was given above, while inserting 1 into the same list gives

1	2	3	9

Looking at these two examples we see that

- in the case of 1, if the item to be inserted is no larger than the head of the list, we cons it to the front of the list;

- In the case of 7, if the item is greater than the head, we insert it in the tail of the list, and cons the head to the result, thus:

2 :
3	7	9

The function can now be defined, including the case that the list is empty.

```
ins x []     = [x]                        (ins.1)
ins x (y:ys)
  | x <= y      = x:(y:ys)                 (ins.2)
  | otherwise   = y : ins x ys             (ins.3)
```

We now show the functions in action, in the calculation of iSort [3,9,2]:

```
iSort [3,9,2]
↝   ins 3 (iSort [9,2])                    by (iSort.2)
↝   ins 3 (ins 9 (iSort [2]))              by (iSort.2)
↝   ins 3 (ins 9 (ins 2 (iSort [])))       by (iSort.2)
↝   ins 3 (ins 9 (ins 2 []))               by (iSort.1)
↝   ins 3 (ins 9 [2])                         by (ins.1)
↝   ins 3 (2 : ins 9 [])                      by (ins.3)
↝   ins 3 [2,9]                               by (ins.1)
↝   2 : ins 3 [9]                             by (ins.3)
↝   2 : [3,9]                                 by (ins.2)
↝   [2,3,9]
```

Developing this function has shown the advantage of looking at examples while trying to define a function; the examples can give a guide about how the definition might break into cases, or the pattern of the recursion. We also saw how using top-down design can break a larger problem into smaller problems which are easier to solve.

In the next section we look at definitions by more general forms of recursion.

> (**Exercises**)

7.6 Using primitive recursion over lists, define a function

```
elemNum :: Int -> [Int] -> Int
```

so that `elemNum x xs` returns the number of times that x occurs in the list xs.

Can you define `elemNum` without using primitive recursion, using list comprehensions and built-in functions instead?

7.7 Define a function

```
unique :: [Int] -> [Int]
```

so that `unique xs` returns the list of elements of xs which occur exactly once. For example, `unique [4,2,1,3,2,3]` is `[4,1]`. You might like to think of two solutions to this problem: one using list comprehensions and the other not.

7.8 Give primitive recursive definitions of the prelude functions `reverse` and `unzip`.

7.9 Can you use the `iSort` function to find the minimum and maximum elements of a list of numbers? How would you find these elements without using `iSort`?

7.10 Design test data for the `ins` function. Your data should address different possible points of insertion, and also look at any exceptional cases.

7.11 By modifying the definition of the `ins` function we can change the behaviour of the sort, `iSort`. Redefine `ins` in two different ways so that

- the list is sorted in descending order;
- duplicates are removed from the list. For example,

  ```
  iSort [2,1,4,1,2] = [1,2,4]
  ```

  under this definition.

7.12 Design test data for the duplicate-removing version of `iSort`, explaining your choices.

7.13 By modifying the definition of the `ins` and `iSort` functions, define a function to sort lists of pairs of numbers. The ordering should be **lexicographic** – the dictionary ordering. This ordering first looks at the first halves of the pairs; only if these values are equal are the second halves compared. For instance, `(2,73)` is smaller than `(3,0)`, and this is smaller than `(3,2)`.

(**7.5**) **General recursions over lists**

Just as we argued in Section 4.4, a recursive definition of a function need not always use the value of the function on the tail; any recursive call to a value on a *simpler* list will be legitimate, and so a number of different patterns of recursion are available for finding function definitions over lists. In trying to use recursion over lists to define a function we need to pose the question:

In defining f (x:xs) *which values of* f ys *would help me to work out the answer?*

(**Examples**)———————————————————————————————

1. It is possible to use recursion over two arguments simultaneously, an example being the definition of the prelude function zip. Recall that here we turn two lists into a list of pairs,

```
zip :: [a] -> [b] -> [(a,b)]
```

with the examples

```
zip [1,5] ['c','d']     = [(1,'c'), (5,'d')]
zip [1,5] ['c','d','e'] = [(1,'c'), (5,'d')]
```

If each of the lists is non-empty, we form a pair from their heads, and then zip their tails, giving

```
zip (x:xs) (y:ys) = (x,y) : zip xs ys
```
(zip.1)

but in all other cases – that is when at least one of the lists is empty – the result is empty:

```
zip _ _ = []
```
(zip.2)

Note that we rely on the sequential nature of pattern matching here; we can give the patterns for (zip.2) explicitly if we wish, thus:

```
zip (x:xs) (y:ys) = (x,y) : zip xs ys
zip (x:xs) []     = []
zip []     zs     = []
```

and in the second definition we see the three separate cases given in three separate equations. Using the original definition, an example calculation gives

```
zip [1,5] ['c','d','e']
⤳  (1,'c') : zip [5] ['d','e']              by (zip.1)
⤳  (1,'c') : (5,'d') : zip [] ['e']          by (zip.1)
⤳  (1,'c') : (5,'d') : []                    by (zip.2)
⤳  (1,'c') : [ (5,'d') ]                     by defn of :
⤳  [ (1,'c') , (5,'d') ]                     by defn of :
```

Note that we have used the fact that ':' is right associative in writing this calculation.

2. The function take is used to take a given number of values from a list. For instance,

```
take 5  "Hot Rats" = "Hot R"
take 15 "Hot Rats" = "Hot Rats"
```

In this example we do recursion over an Int and a list

```
take :: Int -> [a] -> [a]
```

There are some special cases, when the Int is zero, or the list is empty

```
take 0 _         = []                                    (take.1)
take _ []        = []                                    (take.2)
```

What about the general case, when the list is non-empty and the Int greater than zero? We take n-1 elements from the tail of the list, and place the head on the front, thus:

```
take n (x:xs)
  | n>0          = x : take (n-1) xs                      (take.3)
```

and in the other cases we give an error

```
take _ _         = error "PreludeList.take: negative argument"
                                                         (take.4)
```

3.   As a final example, we look at another method for sorting lists (of integers). The **quicksort** algorithm works by generating *two* recursive calls to sort. Suppose we are to sort the list

$$[4,2,7,1,4,5,6]$$

we can take off the head, 4, and then split the result $[2,7,1,4,5,6]$ into two parts:

$$[2,1,4] \qquad\qquad [7,5,6]$$

The first contains the elements no larger than 4, the second those exceeding 4. We sort these two, giving

$$[1,2,4] \qquad\qquad [5,6,7]$$

and then we get an ordered version of the original list thus

$$[1,2,4] \ ++ \ [4] \ ++ \ [5,6,7]$$

We can write this now

```
qSort :: [Int] -> [Int]

qSort [] = []                                            (qSort.1)
qSort (x:xs)
  = qSort [ y | y<-xs , y<=x] ++ [x] ++ qSort [ y | y<-xs , y>x]
                                                         (qSort.2)
```

It is striking to see how close this program is to our informal description of the algorithm, and this expressiveness is one of the important advantages of a functional approach.

We can see that this recursion will give an answer for every finite list, since in the recursive calls we apply qSort to two sublists of xs, which are necessarily smaller than (x:xs).

In Chapter 19 we talk about the efficiency of various algorithms, and show that in general quicksort will be more efficient than insertion sort. In the following section we look at a larger example of definitions which use general forms of recursion.

Exercises

7.14 Using the definition of `take` as a guide, define the prelude functions `drop` and `splitAt`.

7.15 What is the value of `take` `(-3)` `[]` according to the definition of `take` given earlier? How would you modify the definition so that there is an error reported whenever the `Int` argument is negative?

7.16 How would you define a function `zip3` which zips together three lists? Try to write a recursive definition and also one which *uses* `zip` instead; what are the advantages and disadvantages of the two different definitions?

7.17 How would you modify qSort to sort a list into descending order? How would you ensure that qSort removed duplicate elements?

7.18 One list is a **sublist** of another if the elements of the first occur in the second, in the same order. For instance, `"ship"` is a sublist of `"Fish & Chips"`, but not of `"hippies"`.

A list is a **subsequence** of another if it occurs as a sequence of elements *next to each other*. For example, `"Chip"` is a subsequence of `"Fish & Chips"`, but not of `"Chin up"`.

Define functions which decide whether one string is a sublist or a subsequence of another string.

(7.6) Example: text processing

In word processing systems it is customary for lines to be filled and broken automatically, to enhance the appearance of the text. This book is no exception. Input of the form

```
The heat bloomed       in December
  as the    carnival  season
              kicked into  gear.
Nearly helpless with sun and glare, I avoided Rio's brilliant
sidewalks
   and glittering beaches,
panting in dark   corners
and waiting out the inverted southern summer.
```

would be transformed by **filling** to

```
The heat bloomed in December as the
carnival season kicked into gear.
Nearly helpless with sun and glare,
I avoided Rio's brilliant sidewalks
and glittering beaches, panting in
dark corners and waiting out the
inverted southern summer.
```

To align the right-hand margin, the text is **justified** by adding extra inter-word spaces on all lines but the last:

```
The heat bloomed in December as the
carnival  season  kicked into gear.
Nearly helpless with sun and glare,
I avoided Rio's brilliant sidewalks
and glittering beaches, panting  in
dark  corners  and  waiting out the
inverted southern summer.
```

An input file in Haskell can be treated as a string of characters, and so string-manipulating operations play an important role here. Also, since strings are lists, this example will exercise general list functions.

Overall strategy

In this section we give an example of bottom-up program development, thinking first about some of the components we will need to solve the problem, rather than decomposing the solution in a top-down way.

The first step in processing text will be to split an input string into **words**, discarding any white space. The words are then rearranged into lines of the required length. These lines can then have spaces added so as to justify the text. We therefore start by looking at how text is split into words.

Extracting words

We first ask, given a string of characters, how should we define a function to take the first word from the front of a string?

A word is any sequence which does not contain the **whitespace** characters space, tab and newline.

```
whitespace = ['\n','\t',' ']
```

In defining getWord we will use the standard function elem, which tests whether an object is an element of a list. For instance, elem 'a' whitespace is False.

To guide the definition, consider two examples.

- getWord " boo" should be "" as the first character is whitespace;

- getWord "cat dog" is "cat". We get this by putting 'c' on the front of "at", which is getWord "at dog".

The definition is therefore given by:

```
getWord :: String -> String
getWord []    = []                              (getWord.1)
getWord (x:xs)
  | elem x whitespace   = []                    (getWord.2)
  | otherwise           = x : getWord xs        (getWord.3)
```

Consider an example

```
getWord "cat dog"
~>    'c' : getWord "at dog"                              by (getWord.3)
~>    'c' : 'a' : getWord "t dog"                         by (getWord.3)
~>    'c' : 'a' : 't' : getWord " dog"                    by (getWord.3)
~>    'c' : 'a' : 't' : []                                by (getWord.2)
~>    "cat"
```

In a similar way, the first word of a string can be dropped.

```
dropWord :: String -> String
dropWord []    = []
dropWord (x:xs)
  | elem x whitespace    = (x:xs)
  | otherwise            = dropWord xs
```

It is easy to check that dropWord "cat dog" = " dog". We aim to use the functions getWord and dropWord to split a string into its constituent words. Note that before we take a word from the string " dog", we should remove the whitespace character(s) from the front. The function dropSpace will do this.

```
dropSpace :: String -> String
dropSpace []    = []
dropSpace (x:xs)
  | elem x whitespace    = dropSpace xs
  | otherwise            = (x:xs)
```

How is a string st to be split into words? Assuming st has no whitespace at the start,

- the first word in the output will be given by applying getWord to st;

- the remainder will be given by splitting what remains after removing the first word and the space following it: dropSpace (dropWord st).

The top-level function splitWords calls split after removing any whitespace at the start of the string.

```
type Word = String

splitWords :: String -> [Word]
splitWords st = split (dropSpace st)

split :: String -> [Word]
split [] = []
split st
  = (getWord st) : split (dropSpace (dropWord st))
```

Consider a short example.

```
splitWords "  dog cat"
⤳   split "dog cat"
⤳   (getWord "dog cat")
          : split (dropSpace (dropWord "dog cat"))
⤳   "dog" : split (dropSpace " cat")
⤳   "dog" : split "cat"
⤳   "dog" : (getWord "cat")
          : split (dropSpace (dropWord "cat"))
⤳   "dog" : "cat" : split (dropSpace [])
⤳   "dog" : "cat" : split []
⤳   "dog" : "cat" : []
⤳   [ "dog" , "cat" ]
```

Splitting into lines

Now we have to consider how to break a list of words into lines. As before, we look to
see how we can take the first line from a list of words.

```
type Line = [Word]
getLine :: Int -> [Word] -> Line
```

getLine takes two parameters. The first is the length of the line to be formed, and the
second the list from which the words are taken. The definition uses length to give the
length of a list. The definition will have three cases

- In the case that no words are available, the line formed is empty.

- If the first word available is w, then this goes on the line if there is room for it: its
  length, length w, has to be no greater than the length of the line, len.
  The remainder of the line is built from the words that remain by taking a line of
  length len-(length w+1).

- If the first word does not fit, the line has to be empty.

```
getLine len []     = []
getLine len (w:ws)
  | length w <= len     = w : restOfLine
  | otherwise           = []
    where
    newlen      = len - (length w + 1)
    restOfLine  = getLine newlen ws
```

Why is the rest of the line of length len-(length w+1)? Space must be allocated
for the word w *and* the inter-word space needed to separate it from the word which
follows. How does the function work in an example?

```
getLine 20 ["Mary","Poppins","looks","like",...
⤳   "Mary" : getLine 15 ["Poppins","looks","like",...
⤳   "Mary" : "Poppins" : getLine 7 ["looks","like",...
```

```
⤳    "Mary" : "Poppins" : "looks" : getLine 1 ["like",...
⤳    "Mary" : "Poppins" : "looks" : []
⤳    [ "Mary" , "Poppins" , "looks" ]
```

A companion function,

```
dropLine :: Int -> [Word] -> Line
```

removes a line from the front of a list of words, just as dropWord is a companion to getWord. The function to split a list of words into lines of length at most (the constant value) lineLen can now be defined:

```
splitLines :: [Word] -> [Line]
splitLines [] = []
splitLines ws
  = getLine lineLen ws
        : splitLines (dropLine lineLen ws)
```

This concludes the definition of the function splitLines, which gives filled lines from a list of words.

Conclusion

To fill a text string into lines, we write

```
fill :: String -> [Line]
fill = splitLines . splitWords
```

To make the result into a single string we need to write a function

```
joinLines :: [Line] -> String
```

This is left as an exercise, as is justification of lines.

Exercises

7.19 Define the function dropLine specified in the text.

7.20 Give a definition of the function

```
joinLine :: Line -> String
```

which turns a line into printable form. For example,

```
joinLine [ "dog" , "cat" ] = "dog cat"
```

7.21 Using the function joinLine, or otherwise, define the function

```
joinLines :: [Line] -> String
```

which joins together the lines, separated by newlines.

7.22 In this case study we have defined separate 'take' and 'drop' functions for words and lines. Redesign the program so that it uses 'split' functions – like the prelude function `splitAt` – instead.

7.23 [Harder] Modify the function `joinLine` so that it justifies the line to length `lineLen` by adding the appropriate number of spaces between the words.

7.24 Design a function

```
wc :: String -> (Int,Int,Int)
```

which when given a text string returns the number of characters, words and lines in the string. The end of a line in the string is signalled by the newline character, '\n'. Define a similar function

```
wcFormat :: String -> (Int,Int,Int)
```

which returns the same statistics for the text *after* it has been filled.

7.25 Define a function

```
isPalin :: String -> Bool
```

which tests whether a string is a palindrome – that is whether it is the same read both backwards and forwards. An example is the string

```
Madam I'm Adam
```

Note that punctuation and white space are ignored in the test, and that no distinction is made between capital and small letters. You might first like to develop a test which simply tests whether the string is exactly the same backwards and forwards, and only afterwards take account of punctuation and capital letters.

7.26 [Harder] Design a function

```
subst :: String -> String -> String -> String
```

so that

```
subst oldSub newSub st
```

is the result of replacing the first occurrence in `st` of the substring `oldSub` by the substring `newSub`. For instance,

```
subst "much  " "tall " "How much  is that?"
  = "How tall is that?"
```

If the substring `oldSub` does not occur in `st`, the result should be `st`.

Summary

This chapter has shown how functions can be defined by recursion over lists, and completes our account of the different ways that list-processing functions can be defined. In the chapter we have looked at examples of the design principles which we first discussed in Chapter 4, including 'divide and conquer' and general pieces of advice about designing recursive programs. The text processing case study provides a broadly bottom-up approach to defining a library of functions.

Generalization: patterns of computation

Chapter 9

Generalization: patterns of computation

Software **reuse** is a major goal of the software industry. One of the great strengths of modern functional programming languages like Haskell is that we can use them to define **general** functions which can be used in many different applications. The Haskell prelude functions over lists, for instance, form a toolkit to which we turn again and again in a host of situations.

We have already seen one aspect of this generality in **polymorphism**, under which the **same** program can be used over many **different** types. The prelude functions over lists introduced in Chapter 5 provide many examples of this including length, ++ and take.

As we said, these functions have the same effect over every argument – length computes the length of a list of any type, for instance. In this chapter we explore a second mechanism, by which we can write functions which embody a **pattern of computation**; two examples of what we mean follow.

 Transform every element of a list in some way. We might turn every alphabetic character into upper case, or double every number.

 Combine the elements of a list using some operator. We could add together the elements of a numeric list in this way, for example.

How can we write general functions which implement patterns like this? We need to make the transformation or operator into a **parameter** of the general function; in other words we need to have functions as arguments of other functions. These **higher-order functions** are the topic of this chapter. Complementing this is the ability to make functions the **results** of functions; we look at that in the next chapter.

We begin the chapter by examining the patterns of computation over lists which we have encountered so far, and in the remaining sections of the chapter we show how these are realized as higher-order Haskell functions. We also re-examine primitive recursive definitions, and see that they generalize the process of combining the elements of a list using an operator.

We conclude with an example of generalization: taking a function over String into a polymorphic, higher-order function. We do this by identifying the parts of the function which make it specific to String and turning those into a parameter of the function. The example serves as a model for how we can generalize functions in any situation thus making them applicable in many more contexts, so that they become suitable candidates for reuse.

(9.1) Patterns of computation over lists

Many of the definitions of list processing functions we have seen so far fall into a small number of different sorts. In this section we look back over the previous chapters and discuss the patterns which emerge. These patterns are realized as Haskell functions later in the chapter.

Applying to all – mapping

Many functions call for all of the elements of a list to be transformed in some way – this we call **mapping**. We have seen examples of this from the first chapter, where we noted that to flip a picture in a vertical mirror – flipV – we needed to reverse each line of the Picture, which is a list of lines.

We also saw mapping in Chapter 5 in our first example of a list comprehension which was to double every element of a list of integers.

```
doubleAll [2,3,71] = [4,6,142]
```

Other examples include

- taking the second element of each pair in a list of pairs, as we do in the library database;
- in the supermarket billing example, converting every item in a list of bar codes to the corresponding (Name,Price) pair;
- formatting each (Name,Price) pair in a list.

Selecting elements – filtering

Selecting all the elements of a list with a given property is also common. Chapter 5 contains the example of the function which selects the digits from a string

```
digits "29 February 2004" = "292004"
```

Among the other cases we have seen are

- select each pair which has a particular person as its first element;
- select each pair which is *not* equal to the loan pair being returned.

Combining the items – folding

The first example of primitive recursion in Chapter 7 was sum, which computes the total of a list of integers. The total of the list is given by **folding** the function + into the list, thus:

```
sum [2,3,71] = 2+3+71
```

In a similar way,

- ++ can be folded into a list of lists to concatenate it, as is done in the definition of concat;
- && can be folded into a list of Booleans to take their conjunction: this is the prelude function and;
- max can be folded into a list of integers to give their maximum.

Breaking up lists

A common pattern in the text processing example of Chapter 7 is to take or drop items from a list while they have some property. A first example is getWord,

```
getWord "cat dog" = "cat"
```

in which we continue to take characters while they are alphabetic. Other examples include dropWord, dropSpace and getLine. In the last of these the property in question depends not only upon the particular list item but also on the part of the list selected so far.

Combinations

These patterns of definition are often used together. In defining books for the library database, which returns all the books on loan to a given person, we filter out all pairs involving the person, and then take all second components of the results. The strength of list comprehensions is that they give this combination of mapping and filtering, which fits some examples – like the library database – particularly well.

Other combinations of functions are also common.

- In the pictures case study the function invertColour inverts the colour of every character in a Picture by inverting every line; inverting a line requires us to invert every character, so here we have two (nested) uses of mapping.
- Formatting the item part of a supermarket bill involves processing each item in some way, then combining the results, using ++.

Primitive recursion and folding

The form of many definitions is primitive recursive. Sorting by insertion is a classic example:

```
iSort []     = []
iSort (x:xs) = ins x (iSort xs)
```

Haskell provides a mechanism to turn a prefix function like ins into an infix version. The name is enclosed by back quotes, 'ins', so

```
iSort (x:xs) = x 'ins' (iSort xs)
```

and, in a given example, we have

```
iSort [4,2,3] = 4 'ins' 2 'ins' 3 'ins' []
```

Looked at this way, the definition looks like 'ins' folded into the list [4,2,3]. We shall look at this again in Section 9.3.

The last 10%

The different kinds of definition discussed so far have all been primitive recursive: we were able to define the result for (x:xs) in terms of the result for xs. It has been said that at least 90% of all definitions of list processing functions are primitive recursive. Some are not, however; in Chapter 7 notable examples are quicksort and the splitLines function,

```
splitLines [] = []
splitLines ws
  = getLine lineLen ws
        : splitLines (dropLine lineLen ws)
```

For a non-empty list of words ws, the result splitLines ws is defined using a recursive call of splitLines not on the tail of ws but on (dropLine lineLen ws). This form of recursion will terminate because (dropLine lineLen ws) will always be shorter than ws itself, at least in sensible cases where no word in the list ws is longer than the line length lineLen.

9.2 Higher-order functions: functions as arguments

A Haskell function is **higher-order** if it takes a function as an argument or returns a function as a result, or both. In this section we show how a variety of functions, including some of the patterns discussed in the last section, can be written using functions as arguments.

Mapping – the `map` function

We can double all the elements in an integer list in two ways, either using a list comprehension,

```
doubleAll :: [Int] -> [Int]
doubleAll xs = [ 2*x | x <- xs ]
```

or using primitive recursion,

```
doubleAll []     = []
doubleAll (x:xs) = 2*x : doubleAll xs
```

In both cases, we can see that the specific operation of multiplying by two is applied to an element of the list in the expression '2*x'.

Suppose that we want to modify every element of a list by another operation – for instance, the function ord that transforms a Char into an Int – we could modify one of the definitions above by replacing the '2*x' by 'ord x' to give a different definition.

Taking this approach would mean that we would write a whole lot of definitions which differ only in the function used to make the transformation. Instead of doing this, we can write a *single* definition in which the function becomes a **parameter** of the definition. Our general definition will be

```
map f xs = [ f x | x <- xs ]                              (map.0)
```

or we can give an explicit primitive recursion

```
map f []     = []                                        (map.1)
map f (x:xs) = f x : map f xs                            (map.2)
```

The function to double all the elements of a list can now be given by applying map to two things: the transformation – double – and the list in question.

```
doubleAll xs = map double xs
```

where double x = 2*x. In a similar way, the function to convert all the characters into their codes will be

```
convertChrs :: [Char] -> [Int]
convertChrs xs = map ord xs
```

In the Picture case study to flip a picture in a vertical mirror we can write

```
flipV :: Picture -> Picture
flipV xs = map reverse xs
```

What is the type of map? It takes two arguments – the first is a function, and the second is a list – and it returns a list.

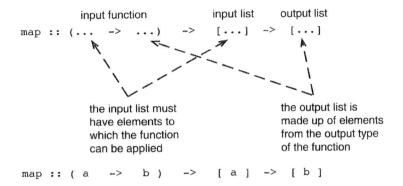

The figure shows how the types of the functions and lists are related, giving map the type

```
map :: (a -> b) -> [a] -> [b]
```

where recall that a and b are type variables, standing for arbitrary types. Instances of the type of map include

```
map :: (Int -> Int) -> [Int] -> [Int]
```

as used in the definition of doubleAll, where map is applied to the function double of type Int -> Int and

```
map :: (Char -> Int) -> [Char] -> [Int]
```

as in the definition of convertChrs.

Modelling properties as functions

Before defining the function to **filter**, or select, those elements of a list having a given property, we need to think about how such properties are to be modelled in Haskell. Take the example of filtering the digits from a string – the function digits mentioned earlier. How is the property of 'being a digit' to be modelled? We have already seen that the prelude contains a function

```
isDigit :: Char -> Bool
```

and we find out whether a particular character like 'd' is a digit or not by applying the function to the character to give a Boolean result, that is True or False.

This is the way that we can model a **property** over any type t. The property is given by a function of type

```
t -> Bool
```

and an element x has the property precisely when f x has the value True. We have already seen the example of isDigit; other examples include

```
isEven :: Int -> Bool
isEven n = (n 'mod' 2 == 0)

isSorted :: [Int] -> Bool
isSorted xs = (xs == iSort xs)
```

where we usually adopt the convention that the names of properties begin with 'is'.

Filtering – the `filter` function

Building on our discussion of properties, we see that the `filter` function will take a property and a list, and return those elements of the list having the property:

```
filter p [] = []                                          (filter.1)
filter p (x:xs)
  | p x         = x : filter p xs                         (filter.2)
  | otherwise   =     filter p xs                         (filter.3)
```

In the case of an empty list, the result is empty. For a non-empty list (`x:xs`) there are two cases. If the guard condition `p x` is true then the element `x` is the first element of the result list; the remainder of the result is given by selecting those elements in `xs` which have the property `p`. If `p x` is `False`, `x` is not included, and the result is given by searching `xs` for elements with property `p`.

A list comprehension also serves to define `filter`,

```
filter p xs = [ x | x <- xs , p x ]                       (filter.0)
```

where again we see that the condition for inclusion of `x` in the list is that it has the property `p`.

Our example `digits` is defined using `filter` as follows

```
digits xs = filter isDigit xs
```

Other applications of `filter` give

```
filter isEven [2,3,4,5]                       ⤳  [2,4]
filter isSorted [[2,3,4,5],[3,2,5],[],[3]] ⤳  [[2,3,4,5],[],[3]]
```

What is the type of `filter`? It takes a property and a list, and returns a list.

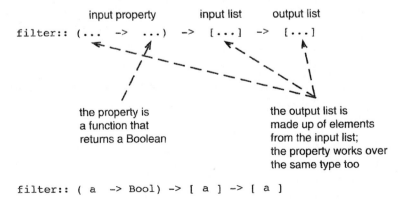

Combining `zip` and `map` – the `zipWith` function

We have already seen the polymorphic function

```
zip :: [a] -> [b] -> [(a,b)]
```

which combines two lists into a list of pairs, where we pair corresponding elements in the two lists. For instance,

```
zip [2,3,4] "Frank" = [(2,'F'),(3,'r'),(4,'a')]
```

What happens if we want to do something to two corresponding elements other than making a pair of them? Recall from Chapter 1 that in our `Picture` case study to define `sideBySide` we wanted to join corresponding lines using (++). To this end we define the `zipWith` function, which combines the effect of zipping and mapping:

```
zipWith f (x:xs) (y:ys) = f x y : zipWith f xs ys
zipWith f _       _     = []
```

In the first case we see that if both lists are non-empty we apply the function f to their heads to give the first element of the result, and zip their tails with f in a similar way. In the second case – when at least one of the inputs is [] – the result is [], just as it was in the definition of `zip`.

Returning to the `Picture` case study, we can then define

```
sideBySide :: Picture -> Picture -> Picture
sideBySide pic1 pic2 = zipWith (++) pic1 pic2
```

What is the type of `zipWith`? The function takes three arguments. The second and third are lists of arbitrary type, [a] and [b] respectively. The result is also a list of arbitrary type, [c]. Now, the first argument is applied to elements of the input lists to give an element of the output list, so it must have type a -> b -> c. Putting this together, we have

```
zipWith :: (a -> b -> c) -> [a] -> [b] -> [c]
```

In the exercises we look further at the examples defined here, as well as introducing other higher-order functions.

Exercises

9.1 Write three line-by-line calculations of `doubleAll [2,1,7]` using the three different definitions of `doubleAll` by means of a list comprehension, primitive recursion and `map`.

9.2 How would you define the `length` function using `map` and `sum`?

9.3 Given the function

```
addUp ns = filter greaterOne (map addOne ns)
```

where

```
greaterOne n = n>1
addOne n     = n+1
```

how would you redefine it using `filter` before map, as in

```
addUp ns = map fun1 (filter fun2 ns)
```

9.4 Describe the effect of

```
map addOne (map addOne ns)
```

Can you conclude anything in general about properties of `map f (map g xs)` where f and g are arbitrary functions?

9.5 What is the effect of

```
filter greaterOne (filter lessTen ns)
```

where `lessTen n = n<10`? What about the general case of

```
filter p (filter q xs)
```

where p and q are arbitrary properties?

9.6 Give definitions of functions to take a list of integers, ns, and

- return the list consisting of the squares of the integers in ns;
- return the sum of squares of items in ns;
- check whether all items of the list are greater than zero.

9.7 Using functions defined already wherever possible, write definitions of functions to

- give the minimum value of a function f on inputs 0 to n;
- test whether the values of f on inputs 0 to n are all equal;
- test if all values of f on inputs 0 to n are greater than zero, and,
- check whether the values f 0, f 1 to f n are in increasing order.

9.8 State the type of and define a function `twice` which takes a function from integers to integers and an input integer, and whose output is the function applied to the input twice. For instance, with the `double` function and 7 as input, the result is 28. What is the most general type of the function you have defined?

9.9 Give the type of and define a function `iter` so that

```
iter n f x = f (f (f ... (f x)...))
```

where f occurs n times on the right-hand side of the equation. For instance, we should have

```
iter 3 f x = f (f (f x))
```

and `iter 0 f x` should return x.

9.10 Using `iter` and `double` define a function which on input n returns 2^n; remember that 2^n means one multiplied by two n times.

(9.3) Folding and primitive recursion

In this section we look at a particular sort of higher-order function which implements the operation of **folding** an operator or function into a list of values. We will see that this operation is more general than we might first think, and that most primitive recursive functions over lists can, in fact, be defined using a fold.

The functions `foldr1` and `foldr`

Here we look at two sorts of folding function. First we look at a function which folds a function into a non-empty list; in the Haskell prelude this is called `foldr1`; we will discuss why it is called this later in the section.

The definition of `foldr1` will have two cases. Folding f into the singleton list [a] gives a. Folding f into a longer list is given by

```
foldr1 f [e1,e2,...,ek]
  = e1 'f' (e2 'f' ( ... 'f' ek)...)
  = e1 'f' (foldr1 f [e2,...,ek])
  = f e1 (foldr1 f [e2,...,ek])
```

The Haskell definition is therefore

```
foldr1 f [x]    = x                      (foldr1.1)
foldr1 f (x:xs) = f x (foldr1 f xs)      (foldr1.2)
```

and the type of `foldr1` will be given by

```
foldr1 :: (a -> a -> a) -> [a] -> a
```

The type shows that `foldr1` has two arguments.

- The first argument is a binary function over the type a; for example, the function (+) over Int.

- The second is a list of elements of type a which are to be combined using the operator; for instance, [3,98,1]

The result is a single value of type a; in the running example we have

```
foldr1 (+) [3,98,1] = 102
```

Other examples which use `foldr1` include

```
foldr1 (||) [False,True,False] = True
foldr1 (++) ["Freak ", "Out" , "", "!"] = "Freak Out!"
foldr1 min [6] = 6
foldr1 (*) [1 .. 6] = 720
```

The function `foldr1` gives an error when applied to an empty list argument.

We can modify the definition to give an extra argument which is the value returned on the empty list, so giving a function defined on all finite lists. This function is called `foldr` and is defined as follows

```
foldr f s []     = s                                    (foldr.1)
foldr f s (x:xs) = f x (foldr f s xs)                   (foldr.2)
```

The 'r' in the definition is for 'fold, bracketing to the **right**'. Using this slightly more general function, whose type we predict is

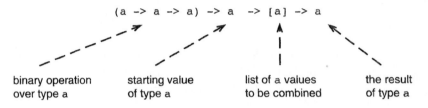

we can now define some of the standard functions of Haskell,

```
concat :: [[a]] -> [a]
concat xs = foldr (++) [] xs
```

```
and :: [Bool] -> Bool
and bs = foldr (&&) True bs
```

Returning to the start of the section, we can now see why `foldr1` is so called: it is fold function, designed to take a list with at least **one** element. We can also define `foldr1` from `foldr`, thus

```
foldr1 f (x:xs) = foldr f x xs                          (foldr1.0)
```

Folding in general – `foldr` again

In fact, the most general type of `foldr` is more general than we predicted. Suppose that the starting value has type b and the elements of the list are of type a, then

```
foldr :: (a -> b -> b) -> b -> [a] -> b
```

We give a full explanation of how this type is derived in Section 13.2.

With this insight about the type of `foldr` we can see that `foldr` can be used to define another whole cohort of list functions. For instance, we can reverse a list thus:

```
rev :: [a] -> [a]
rev xs = foldr snoc [] xs

snoc :: a -> [a] -> [a]
snoc x xs = xs ++ [x]
```

This function is traditionally called `snoc` because it is like 'cons', `:`, in reverse. We can also sort a list in this way

```
iSort :: [Int] -> [Int]
iSort xs = foldr ins [] xs
```

Before we move on, we look for one last time at the definition of `foldr`

```
foldr f s []     = s                    (foldr.1)
foldr f s (x:xs) = f x (foldr f s xs)   (foldr.2)
```

What is the effect of `foldr f s`? We have two cases:

- the value at the empty list is given outright by `s`;
- the value at `(x:xs)` is defined in terms of the value at `xs`, and `x` itself.

This is just like the definition of primitive recursion over lists in Chapter 7.[1] Because of this it is no accident that we can define many of our primitive recursive functions using `foldr`. It is usually mechanical to go from a primitive recursive definition to the corresponding application of `foldr`.

How do the two approaches compare? It is often easier initially to think of a function definition in recursive form and only afterwards to transform it into an application of `foldr`. One of the advantages of making this transformation is that we might then recognize properties of the function by dint of its being a fold. We look at proof for general functions like `map`, `filter` and `foldr` in Section 10.9 and we look at other fold functions in Chapter 19.

⎛ **Exercises** ⎞──

9.11 How would you define the sum of the squares of the natural numbers 1 to n using `map` and `foldr`?

9.12 Define a function to give the sum of squares of the positive integers in a list of integers.

9.13 For the purposes of this exercise you should use `foldr` to give definitions of the prelude functions `unZip`, `last` and `init`, where examples of the latter two are given by

```
last "Greggery Peccary" = 'y'
init "Greggery Peccary" = "Greggery Peccar"
```

───────────────────────────────────

[1] There is an ambiguity in our original characterization. In defining the function g by primitive recursion the value of g (x:xs) is defined in terms of both x and xs as well as the value g xs itself; this makes primitive recursion slightly more general than folding using `foldr`.

9.14 How does the function

```
mystery xs = foldr (++) [] (map sing xs)
```

behave, where `sing x = [x]` for all x?

9.15 The function `formatLines` is intended to format a list of lines using the function

```
formatLine :: Line -> String
```

to format each line in the list. Define a function

```
formatList :: (a -> String) -> [a] -> String
```

which takes as a parameter a function of type

```
a -> String
```

to format each item of the list which is passed as the second parameter. Show how `formatLines` can be defined using `formatList` and `formatLine`.

9.16 Define a function

```
filterFirst :: (a -> Bool) -> [a] -> [a]
```

so that `filterFirst p xs` removes the first element of xs which does not have the property p. Use this to give a version of `returnLoan` which returns only one copy of a book. What does your function do on a list all of whose elements have property p?

9.17 Can you define a function

```
filterLast :: (a -> Bool) -> [a] -> [a]
```

which removes the last occurrence of an element of a list without property p? How could you define it using `filterFirst`?

9.18 How can you simplify some of your earlier definitions in the light of the higher-order functions you have seen here? You could revisit the 'supermarket billing' exercises and try doing those questions again using the functions you have now seen.

(9.4) Generalizing: splitting up lists

As a final example in this chapter we look at how we can generalize the function getWord into a polymorphic, higher-order function. This serves as a model for similar generalizations in many different circumstances.

Many list manipulating programs involve splitting up lists in some way, as a part of their processing. One way of doing this is to select some or all the elements with a particular property – this we have seen with filter. Other ways of processing include taking or dropping elements of the list from the front – this we saw in the text processing example. If we know the number of elements to be dropped, we can use

```
take, drop :: Int -> [a] -> [a]
```

where take n xs and drop n xs are intended to take or drop n elements from the front of the list xs. These functions are defined in Chapter 7.

Also in Chapter 7 we looked at the example of text processing, in which lists were split to yield words and lines. The functions getWord and dropWord defined there were *not* polymorphic, as they were designed to split at whitespace characters.

It is a general principle of functional programming that programs can often be rewritten to use more general polymorphic and/or higher-order functions, and we illustrate that here.

The function getWord was originally defined thus:

```
getWord :: String -> String
getWord []    = []                              (getWord.1)
getWord (x:xs)
  | elem x whitespace    = []                   (getWord.2)
  | otherwise            = x : getWord xs        (getWord.3)
```

What forces this to work over strings is the test in (getWord.2), where x is checked for membership of whitespace. We can generalize the function to have the test – or property – as a parameter.

How is this to be done? Recall that a property over the type a is represented by a function of type (a -> Bool). Making this test a parameter we have

```
getUntil :: (a -> Bool) -> [a] -> [a]
getUntil p []    = []
getUntil p (x:xs)
  | p x         = []
  | otherwise   = x : getUntil p xs
```

in which the test elem x whitespace has been replaced by the test p x, the arbitrary property p applied to x. We can of course recover getWord from this definition:

```
getWord xs
  = getUntil p xs
    where
    p x = elem x whitespace
```

Built into Haskell are the functions takeWhile and dropWhile, which are like getUntil and dropUntil, except that they take or drop elements while the condition is True. For instance,

```
takeWhile :: (a -> Bool) -> [a] -> [a]
takeWhile p []    = []
takeWhile p (x:xs)
  | p x          = x : takeWhile p xs
  | otherwise    = []
```

getUntil can be defined using takeWhile, and vice versa.

Exercises

9.19 Give the type and definition of the generalization dropUntil of the function dropWord.

9.20 How would you define the function dropSpace using dropUntil? How would you define takeWhile using getUntil?

9.21 How would you split a string into lines using getUntil and dropUntil?

9.22 The function getLine of Chapter 7 has a polymorphic type – what is it? How could you generalize the test in this function? If you do this, does the type of the function become more general? Explain your answer.

9.23 Can you give generalizations to polymorphic higher-order functions of the text processing functions getLine, dropLine and splitLines?

Summary

This chapter has shown how the informal patterns of definition over lists can be realized as higher-order, polymorphic functions, such as map, filter and foldr. We saw how these functions arose, and also how their types were derived, as well as reviewing the ways in which they could be used to solve problems.

We concluded with an example of how to generalize a function – the particular example was taken from the text processing case study, but the example serves as a model for how to generalize functions in general.

The chapter has focused on how to write functions which take other functions as arguments; where do these arguments come from? One answer is that they are already defined; another is that they come themselves as the results of Haskell functions – this is the topic of the next chapter.

Chapter 10

Functions as values

As we saw in the previous chapter, functions can be arguments of **higher-order** functions. We shall see in this chapter that functions can also be the **results** of other functions and operators. In this way we create functions as values within our programs, rather than simply being able to create them by defining them in a Haskell script.

This machinery allows us to make the results of some functions into the arguments of other higher-order functions, and lets us exploit these general functions to the full. Using this machinery we see that we are able to give what we call function-level definitions of our functions, which use some of the general functions we have seen earlier. These definitions are both more concise and readable than traditional definitions, as well as being more amenable to proof and program transformation.

In this chapter, after showing a number of ways that we can describe functions in Haskell, we show how functions are returned as results of other functions, especially by means of **partial applications** and **operator sections**. We also re-examine some of our examples to see how the ideas fit into programs we built earlier, and in particular we look again at the `Picture` case study.

A longer example – building an index for a document – is used to show how these new ideas fit into program development. The chapter concludes with some examples of program verification involving higher-order polymorphic objects, where it is shown that the theorems proved about them are reusable in exactly the same way that the functions themselves are reusable.

(10.1) Function-level definitions

One of the reasons that functional programming is called 'functional' is that in such a language we can deal with functions as data, and so treat them much as we might handle integers or lists. Because of this, we will see in this chapter that we can often give a **function-level definition** of a function. What do we mean by this? Rather than explaining how a function operates on one or more parameters, as in the definition

```
rotate :: Picture -> Picture
rotate pic = flipV (flipH pic)                          (rotate.1)
```

a function-level definition gives a direct definition of the function, like

```
rotate = flipV . flipH                                  (rotate.2)
```

In this case we describe `rotate` as the composition of two reflections; of course, the effect of the definitions (rotate.1) and (rotate.2) is exactly the same, but there are two important advantages of the latter approach. First, the second definition is clearer to read and to modify; we see **explicitly** that the definition is a composition of two functions, rather than having to see it as a consequence of the way the right-hand side is defined in (rotate.1).

More importantly, if we state a definition in this form, then we can apply properties of '.' in analysing how `rotate` behaves. This means that in proofs we are able to use properties of composition, as well as being able to see examples of program transformations which will apply because of the form of composition involved. In general these remarks will apply to all higher-order, polymorphic functions, and we see examples of this in Section 10.9 below.

We have already seen other direct definitions, as when we said

```
flipH :: Picture -> Picture
flipH = reverse                                         (flipH.1)
```

We note that this definition has exactly the same effect as saying

```
flipH pic = reverse pic
```

since if we were to use (flipH.1) applied to the picture `horse`, say, the first step of the evaluation would be the step

```
flipH horse
⤳   reverse horse                                       by (flipH.1)
```

in which `flipH` gets replaced by `reverse`.

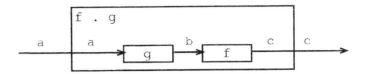

Figure 10.1   Function composition.

10.2) Function composition

We have already used the Haskell function composition operator, '.'; in this section we look at it in more detail, and in particular examine its type.

One of the simplest ways of structuring a program is to do a number of things one after the other – each part can be designed and implemented separately. In a functional program this is achieved by **composing** a number of functions together: the output of one function becomes the input of another, as in Figure 10.1. The annotations of the arrows in the diagram indicate the types of elements involved.

For any functions f and g, the effect of f . g is given by the definition

```
(f . g) x = f (g x)
```
                                                                            (comp.1)

Not all pairs of functions can be composed. The output of g, g x, becomes the input of f, so that the output type of g must equal the input type of f. In the example of rotate from Section 10.1 we see that the output type of flipH and the input type of flipV are both Picture.

In general, the constraint on which functions can be composed is expressed by giving '.' the type

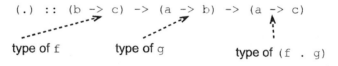

which shows that, if we call the first input f and the second g,

- The input of f and the output of g are of the same type: b.

- The result f . g has the same input type, a, as g and the same output type, c, as f.

Composition is **associative**, that is f . (g . h) is equal to (f . g) . h for all f, g and h. We can therefore write f . g . h unambiguously to mean 'do h, then g, then f'.[1]

Forward composition

The order in f . g is significant, and can be confusing; (f . g) means 'first apply g and then apply f to the result', and so we have to read a composition from right to left in order to appreciate its effect.

---

[1] For technical reasons, the '.' is treated as right associative in the Haskell standard prelude.

The reason we write (f . g) for 'g then f' is that we write arguments to the right of functions. The argument is therefore closer to g than to f, and the order of the functions in (f . g) x is the same as in the nested application, f (g x).

It is simple in Haskell to define an operator for composition which takes its arguments in the opposite order to '.'. This we do thus:

```
infixl 9 >.>
```

```
(>.>) :: (a -> b) -> (b -> c) -> (a -> c)
```

```
g >.> f = f . g                                                (fcomp.1)
```

This definition has the effect that

```
(g >.> f) x = (f . g) x = f (g x)                              (fcomp.2)
```

showing that, as it were, the order of the f and g is swapped before the functions are applied. The rotate example can then be written

```
rotate = flipH >.> flipV
```

which we can read as flipH *then* flipV, with the functions being applied from left to right.

The notation '>.>' contains a '.' to show that it is a form of composition, with the arrows showing the direction in which information is flowing. We will tend to use '>.>' in situations where a number of functions are composed, and it is therefore tiresome to read some lines down the page in order to work out the effect of a function definition.

Pitfalls of composition

There are two pitfalls associated with composition which we need to be aware of:

- There is an error caused by the binding power of function application. It is a common error to write f . g x thinking it means (f . g) applied to x. Because function application binds more tightly than anything else, it is interpreted by the system as f . (g x), which will usually lead to a type error.

  For example, evaluating

  ```
  not . not True
  ```

  gives the type error message

  ```
  ERROR: Type error in application
  *** expression    : not . not True
  *** term          : not True
  *** type          : Bool
  *** does not match : a -> b
  ```

since there is an attempt to treat not True as a function to be composed with not. Such a function needs to have type a->b, whereas it actually has type Bool.

In applying a composition we therefore need to be sure that it is parenthesized, as follows:

```
(not . not) True
```

Function application and composition can get confused. Function composition combines two functions, while application combines a function and an argument (which can be a function, of course).

If, for example, f has type Int -> Bool, then

- f . x means f composed with the *function* x; x therefore needs to be of type s -> Int for some type s.
- f x means f applied to the object x, so x must therefore be an integer.

Exercises

10.1 Redefine the function printBill from the supermarket billing exercise in Section 6.4 so that composition is used. Repeat the exercise using forward composition, >.>.

10.2 If id is the polymorphic identity function, defined by id x = x, explain the behaviour of the expressions

```
(id . f)          (f . id)          id f
```

If f is of type Int -> Bool, at what instance of its most general type a -> a is id used in each case? What type does f have if f id is properly typed?

10.3 Define a function composeList which composes a list of functions into a single function. You should give the type of composeList, and explain why the function has this type. What is the effect of your function on an empty list of functions?

(10.3) Functions as values and results

In this section we begin to look at the ways in which functions can become the results of functions; in the next section we look at the important technique of partial application.

We have already seen that functions can be combined together using the composition operator '.' and the forward composition operator '>.>'; this can be done on the right-hand side of function definitions. The simplest example of this is

```
twice f = (f . f)                                        (twice.1)
```

f is a function, and the result is f composed with itself. For this to work, it needs to have the same input and output type, so we have

```
twice :: (a -> a) -> (a -> a)
```

This states that `twice` takes one argument, a function of type `(a -> a)`, and returns a result of the same type. For instance, if `succ` is the function to add one to an integer,

```
succ :: Int -> Int
succ n = n+1
```

then applying `twice` to it gives the example

```
(twice succ) 12
↝    (succ . succ) 12                                    by (twice.1)
↝    succ (succ 12)                                      by (comp.1)
↝    14
```

We can generalize `twice` so that we pass a parameter giving the number of times the functional argument is to be composed with itself

```
iter :: Int -> (a -> a) -> (a -> a)

iter n f
  | n>0          = f . iter (n-1) f                      (iter.1)
  | otherwise    = id                                    (iter.2)
```

This is a standard primitive recursion over the integer argument; in the positive case we take the composition of `f` with itself `n-1` times and compose once more with `f`. In the zero case we apply `f` no times, so the result is a function which does nothing to its argument, namely `id`. We can give a constructive definition using the standard list functions.

```
iter n f = foldr (.) id (replicate n f)                  (iter.3)
```

In this definition we create the list of n copies of f

```
[f,f,...,f]
```

which is then composed by folding in the composition operator to give

```
f . f . ... . f
```

As an example, we can define 2^n as `iter n double 1`, if `double` doubles its argument.

Expressions defining functions

How else can we write down expressions which describe functions? In writing a function definition we can use a `where` clause to make a definition.

Suppose, for example, that given an integer n we are to return the function (from `Int` to `Int`) which adds n to its argument, we can say

```
addNum :: Int -> (Int -> Int)
addNum n = addN
           where
           addN m = n+m
```

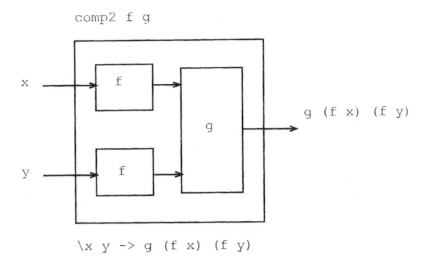

```
comp2 f g
```

```
\x y -> g (f x) (f y)
```

Figure 10.2 Plumbing f and g together.

The result is a function named addN, and addN is itself defined by an equation in the where clause. This method is rather indirect – we say we shall return the function named addN, and then define that function.

Lambda notation

Instead of naming and defining a function that we want to refer to, we can instead write it down directly. In the case of defining addNum we can define the result as

```
\m -> n+m
```

How is this expression to be interpreted?

- Before the arrow are the arguments, in this case the single argument m.
- After the arrow comes the result, here n+m.

That the expression is a function is signalled by its beginning with '\' which is the closest ASCII character to the Greek lambda, λ, which is used in a mathematical theory of functions, called the lambda calculus, for exactly this purpose. The definition of addNum now becomes

```
addNum n = (\m -> n+m)
```

We shall see another way of defining addNum in the next section of this chapter.

Another example which uses the lambda notation is given by the 'plumbing' illustrated in Figure 10.2. The object shown is a function, whose arguments are x and y. The result of the function is

```
g (f x) (f y)
```

so the overall effect is to give a function which applies f to each of its (two) arguments before applying g to the results. The definition states this quite straightforwardly:

```
comp2 :: (a -> b) -> (b -> b -> c) -> (a -> a -> c)
```

```
comp2 f g = (\x y -> g (f x) (f y))
```

To add together the squares of 3 and 4 we can write

```
comp2 sq add 3 4
```

where add and sq have the obvious definitions.

In general, a lambda-defined function is an **anonymous** version of the sort of function we have defined earlier. In other words, the function f defined by

```
f x y z = result
```

and the function

```
\x y z -> result
```

have exactly the same effect.

We shall see in the next section that partial application will make many definitions – including those of the functions here – more straightforward. On the other hand the lambda notation is more general, and thus can be used in situations when a partial application could not.

Exercises

10.4 Give calculations of

```
iter 3 double 1
(comp2 succ (*)) 3 4
comp2 sq add 3 4
```

10.5 What is the type and effect of the function

```
\n -> iter n succ
```

10.6 Given a function f of type a -> b -> c, write down a lambda expression that describes the function of type b -> a -> c which behaves like f but which takes its arguments in the other order. Pictorially,

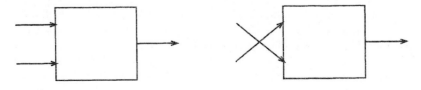

10.7 Using the last exercise, or otherwise, give a definition of the function

$$\texttt{flip :: (a -> b -> c) -> (b -> a -> c)}$$

which reverses the order in which its function argument takes its arguments.

10.8 Using a lambda expression, the Boolean function not and the built-in function elem describe a function of type

```
Char -> Bool
```

which is True only on non-whitespace characters, that is those which are not elements of the list " \t\n".

10.9 Define a function total

```
total :: (Int -> Int) -> (Int -> Int)
```

so that total f is the function which at value n gives the total

```
f 0 + f 1 + ... + f n
```

10.10 [Harder] Define a function

```
slope :: (Float -> Float) -> (Float -> Float)
```

which takes a function f as argument, and returns (an approximation to) its derivative f' as result.

10.11 [Harder] Define a function

```
integrate :: (Float -> Float) -> (Float -> Float -> Float)
```

which takes a function f as argument, and returns (an approximation to) the two argument function which gives the area under its graph between two end points as its result.

⌢10.4⌣ Partial application

The function multiply multiplies together two arguments,

```
multiply :: Int -> Int -> Int
multiply x y = x*y
```

We can view the function as a box, with two input arrows and an output arrow.

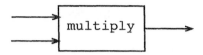

If we apply the function to two arguments, the result is a number; so that, for instance, `multiply` 2 3 equals 6.

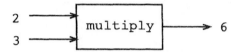

What happens if `multiply` is applied to **one** argument 2? Pictorially, we have

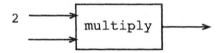

From the picture we can see that this represents a function, as there is still one input arrow to the function awaiting a value. This function will, when given the awaited argument y, return double its value, namely 2*y.

This is an example of a general phenomenon: any function taking two or more arguments can be **partially applied** to one or more arguments. This gives a powerful way of forming functions as results.

To illustrate, we return again to our example in which every element of a list is to be doubled. The function can be defined thus:

```
doubleAll :: [Int] -> [Int]
doubleAll = map (multiply 2)
```

In this definition there are two partial applications:

- `multiply 2` is a function from integers to integers, given by applying `multiply` to one rather than two arguments;

- `map (multiply 2)` is a function from [Int] to [Int], given by partially applying `map`.

Partial application is being put to two different uses here.

- In the first case – `multiply 2` – the partial application is used to form the function which multiplies by two, and which has to be passed to `map` to form the `doubleAll` function;

- the second partial application – of `map` to `multiply 2` – could be avoided by writing the argument to `doubleAll`

```
doubleAll xs = map (multiply 2) xs
```

but, as was argued in Section 10.1, there are advantages to this form of definition.

In Section 10.3 we saw the example of `addNum`,

```
addNum n = (\m -> n+m)
```

which when applied to an integer n was intended to return the function which adds n to its argument. With partial application we have a simpler mechanism, as we can say

```
addNum n m = n+m
```

since when addNum is applied to one argument n it returns the function adding n.

The idea of partial application is important. We have already seen that many functions can be defined as **specializations** of general operations like map, filter and so on. These specializations arise by passing a function to the general operation – this function is often given by a partial application, as in the examples from the pictures case study first seen in Chapter 1:

```
flipV      = map reverse
sideBySide = zipWith (++)
```

We return to look at the Picture case study in greater detail in Section 10.5.

It is not always possible to make a partial application, since the argument to which we want to apply the function may not be its first argument. Consider the function

```
elem :: Char -> [Char] -> Bool
```

We can test whether a character ch is a whitespace character by writing

```
elem ch whitespace
```

where whitespace is the string " \t\n". We would like to write the function to test this by partially applying elem to whitespace, but cannot. We could define a variant of elem which takes its arguments in the other order, as in

```
member xs x = elem x xs
```

and write the function as the partial application

```
member whitespace
```

Alternatively, we can write down this function as a

```
\ch -> elem ch whitespace
```

In a similar vein, to filter all non-whitespace characters from a string, we could write either of the partial applications

```
filter (not . member whitespace)
filter (\ch -> not (elem ch whitespace))
```

The types of partial applications

How is the type of a partial application determined? There is a simple rule which explains it.

Rule of cancellation

If the type of a function f is

$$t_1 \text{->} t_2 \text{->} \ldots \text{->} t_n \text{->} t$$

and it is applied to arguments

$$e_1 \text{::} t_1, e_2 \text{::} t_2, \ldots, e_k \text{::} t_k$$

(where $k \leq n$) then the result type is given by **cancelling** the types t_1 to t_k

$$\cancel{t_1} \text{->} \cancel{t_2} \text{->} \ldots \text{->} \cancel{t_k} \text{->} t_{k+1} \text{->} \ldots \text{->} t_n \text{->} t$$

which gives the type

$$t_{k+1} \text{->} t_{k+2} \text{->} \ldots \text{->} t_n \text{->} t$$

For example, using this rule we can see that we get the following types

```
multiply 2       :: Int -> Int
multiply 2 3     :: Int
doubleAll        :: [Int] -> [Int]
doubleAll [2,3]  :: [Int]
```

The syntax of application and ->

Function application is **left associative** so that

```
f x y = (f x) y
f x y ≠ f (x y)
```

The function space symbol '->' is **right associative**, so that a -> b -> c means

```
a -> (b -> c)
```

and *not*

```
(a -> b) -> c
```

The arrow is not associative. If

```
f :: Int -> Int -> Int
g :: (Int -> Int) -> Int
```

as illustrated

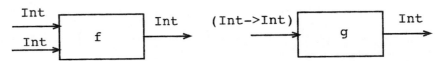

then f will yield a function from Int to Int when given a Int – an example is multiply. On the other hand, when given a function of type Int -> Int, g yields a Int. An example is

```
g :: (Int -> Int) -> Int
g h = (h 0) + (h 1)
```

The function g defined here takes a function h as argument and returns the sum of h's values at 0 and 1, and so g succ will have the value 3.

How many arguments do functions have?

Partial application can appear confusing: in some contexts functions appear to take one argument, and in others more than one. In fact, *every function in Haskell takes exactly one argument*. If this application yields a function, then this function may be applied to a further argument, and so on. Consider the multiplication function again.

```
multiply :: Int -> Int -> Int
```

This is shorthand for

```
multiply :: Int -> (Int -> Int)
```

and so it can therefore be applied to an integer. Doing this gives (for example)

```
multiply 2 :: Int -> Int
```

This can itself be applied to give

```
(multiply 2) 5 :: Int
```

which, since function application is left associative, can be written

```
multiply 2 5 :: Int
```

Our explanations earlier in the book are consistent with this full explanation of the system. We hid the fact that

$$f\ e_1\ e_2\ \ldots\ e_k$$
$$t_1\ \text{->}\ t_2\ \text{->}\ \ldots\ t_n\ \text{->}\ t$$

were shorthand for

$$(\ \ldots((f\ e_1)\ e_2)\ \ldots\ e_k)$$
$$t_1\ \text{->}\ (t_2\ \text{->}\ (\ldots(t_n\ \text{->}\ t)\ldots))$$

but this did no harm to our understanding of how to use the Haskell language. It is to support this shorthand that function application is made left associative and -> is made right associative.

Examples of partial applications will be seen throughout the material to come, and can be used to simplify and clarify many of the preceding examples. Three simple examples are the text processing functions

```
dropSpace = dropWhile (member whitespace)
dropWord  = dropWhile (not . member whitespace)
getWord   = takeWhile (not . member whitespace)
```

where

```
member xs x = elem x xs
```

We look at further examples in the next section, after examining partially applied operators.

Operator sections

The operators of the language can be partially applied, giving what are known as **operator sections**. Examples include

(+2)	The function which adds two to its argument.
(2+)	The function which adds two to its argument.
(>2)	The function which returns whether a number is greater than two.
(3:)	The function which puts the number 3 on the front of a list.
(++"\n")	The function which puts a newline at the end of a string.
("\n"++)	The function which puts a newline at the beginning of a string.

The general rule here is that a section of the operator op will put its argument to the side which completes the application. That is,

```
(op x) y = y op x
(x op) y = x op y
```

When combined with higher-order functions like map, filter and composition, the notation is both powerful and elegant, enabling us to make a whole lot more function-level definitions. For example,

```
filter (>0) . map (+1)
```

is the function which adds one to each member of a list, and then removes those elements which are not positive.

Exercises

10.12 Use partial applications to define the functions comp2 and total given in Section 10.3 and its exercises.

10.13 Find operator sections sec_1 and sec_2 so that

```
map sec₁ . filter sec₂
```

has the same effect as

```
filter (>0) . map (+1)
```

(10.5) Revisiting the `Picture` example

Now that we have been introduced to higher-order functions, and in particular partial application, we can revisit the example of pictures and complete our definitions of the functions over the `Picture` type. The case study was introduced in Chapter 1 and further developed in Sections 2.5 and 6.1.

Recall that a picture is a list of lines, each of which is made up of a list of characters

```
type Picture = [[Char]]
```

We first define reflection in a horizontal mirror, which is given simply by reversing the list of lines,

```
flipH :: Picture -> Picture
flipH = reverse
```

To reflect in a vertical mirror we need to reverse every line – clearly a task for `map`:

```
flipV :: Picture -> Picture
flipV = map reverse
```

To place pictures next to each other we have two functions. To put one picture above the other we join together the two lists of lines

```
above :: Picture -> Picture -> Picture
above = (++)
```

while placing the pictures side-by-side requires corresponding lines to be joined together with ++, using the function `zipWith` first introduced in Section 9.2.

```
sideBySide :: Picture -> Picture -> Picture
sideBySide = zipWith (++)
```

Among the other functions mentioned were

```
invertColour :: Picture -> Picture
superimpose  :: Picture -> Picture -> Picture
printPicture :: Picture -> IO ()
```

and we give their definitions now. To invert the colour in a picture, we need to invert the colour in every line, so

```
invertColour = map ...
```

where ... will be the function to invert the colour in a single line. To invert every character in a line – which is itself a list of characters – we will again use `map`. The function mapped is `invertChar`, first defined in Section 6.1. This gives the definition

```
invertColour :: Picture -> Picture
invertColour = map (map invertChar)
```

which we can read as saying

apply map invertChar to every line in the Picture; that is, apply the function invertChar to every character in the Picture, which is a list of lists of characters.

Suppose we are equipped with a function

```
combineChar :: Char -> Char -> Char
```

which superimposes two characters; how are we to use this in superimposing two pictures? Recall the function

```
zipWith :: (a -> b -> c) -> [a] -> [b] -> [c]
```

where zipWith f xs ys produces a list by applying the function f to corresponding elements chosen from xs and ys, so that, for instance

```
zipWith (*) [2,0] [3,1] = [6,0]
```

To superimpose the pictures, we will need to superimpose corresponding lines, so

```
superimpose = zipWith ...
```

where ... will be required to superimpose two single lines.

In doing this, we have to superimpose corresponding characters, so this is again an application of zipWith. What is used to perform the combination of individual characters? The answer is combineChar, and so we have

```
superimpose :: Picture -> Picture -> Picture
superimpose = zipWith (zipWith combineChar)
```

Our final definition is of printPicture, which outputs a Picture to the screen. We have already seen that to output a String we can use the function

```
putStr :: String -> IO ()
```

so it will be sufficient for us to precede application of this by a function to turn the list of lines making up the Picture into a string, in which the lines are separated by newline characters. This we can write as a composition

```
concat . map (++"\n")
```

since the effect of this is first to add a newline character to every line – the role of map (++"\n") – and then to join this list of strings into a single string – the effect of the concat. We therefore define the printing function thus:

```
printPicture :: Picture -> IO ()
printPicture = putStr . concat . map (++"\n")
```

Exercises

In these exercises we suggest further operations over pictures.

10.14 Define a function

```
chessBoard :: Int -> Picture
```

so that chessBoard n is a picture of an n by n chess board.

10.15 How would you implement invertColour, superimpose and printPicture if Picture was defined to be [[Bool]]?

10.16 Define a function

```
makePicture :: Int -> Int -> [(Int,Int)] -> Picture
```

where the list argument gives the positions of the black points in the picture, and the two integer arguments give the width and height of the picture. For example,

```
makePicture 7 5 [(1,3),(3,2)]
```

will have the form

```
.......
...#...
.......
..#....
.......
```

It is evident from this that positions within lines and lines themselves are counted from zero, with line zero being the top line.

10.17 Define a function

```
pictureToRep :: Picture -> ( Int , Int , [(Int,Int)] )
```

which has the reverse effect of makePicture. For example, if pic is

```
....
.##.
....
```

then pictureToRep pic will be (4 , 3, [(1,1),(1,2)])

10.18 If we make the definition

```
type Rep = ( Int , Int , [(Int,Int)] )
```

discuss how you would define functions over Rep to rotate, reflect and superimpose pictures under this alternative representation. Discuss the advantages and disadvantages of this representation in comparison with the original representation given by the Picture type.

10.19 In the light of the discussion in the last four chapters, redo the exercises of Section 6.2, which deal with positioned pictures.

(10.6) Further examples

This section explores how partial applications and operator sections can be used to simplify and shorten definitions in a number of other examples. Often it is possible to avoid giving an explicit function definition if we can use a partial application to return a function. Revisiting the examples of Chapter 7 we see that to double all the elements in a list we can write

```
doubleAll :: [Int] -> [Int]
doubleAll = map (*2)
```

using an operator section (*2) to replace the double function, and giving the function definition directly by partially applying map.

To filter out the even elements in a numerical list, we have to check whether the remainder on dividing by two is equal to zero. As a function we can write

```
(==0).('mod' 2)
```

This is the composition of two operator sections: first find the remainder on dividing by two, then check if it is equal to zero. (Why can we not write ('mod' 2 == 0)?) The filtering function can then be written

```
getEvens :: [Int] -> [Int]
getEvens = filter ((==0).('mod' 2))
```

Our final example comes from the list splitting study. We defined

```
getWord xs
  = getUntil p xs
    where
    p x = elem x whitespace
```

The local definition is not now needed, as we can define the function p by an operator section:

```
getWord xs = getUntil ('elem' whitespace) xs
```

Note the way that we partially apply a function to its *second* argument, by forming an operator section. This works because

```
('elem' whitespace) x
= x 'elem' whitespace
= elem x whitespace
```

as required.

Finally, the function getWord can itself be given a direct definition, by partial application thus

```
getWord = getUntil ('elem' whitespace)
```

This definition reads like an informal explanation – to get a word, get characters until a whitespace character is found.

10.7 Currying and uncurrying

In Haskell we have a choice of how to model functions of two or more arguments. We usually represent them in what is called a **curried** form, where they take their arguments one at a time. This is called **currying** after Haskell Curry[2] who was one of the pioneers of the λ-calculus and after whom the Haskell language is named. For instance, a function to multiply two integers would normally be defined thus:

```
multiply :: Int -> Int -> Int
multiply x y = x*y
```

while an **uncurried** version can be given by bundling the arguments into a pair, thus:

```
multiplyUC :: (Int,Int) -> Int
multiplyUC (x,y) = x*y
```

Why do we usually opt for the curried form? There are a number of reasons.

- The notation is somewhat neater; we apply a function to a single argument by juxtaposing the two, `f x`, and application to two arguments is done by extending this thus: `g x y`.

- It permits partial application. In the case of multiplication we can write expressions like `multiply 2`, which returns a function, while this is not possible if the two arguments are bundled into a pair, as is the case for `multiplyUC`.

We can in any case move between the curried and uncurried representations with little difficulty, and indeed we can define two higher-order functions which convert between curried and uncurried functions.

Suppose first that we want to write a curried version of a function g, which is itself uncurried and of type `(a,b) -> c`.

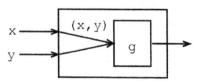

curry g

This function expects its arguments as a pair, but its curried version, `curry g`, will take them separately – we therefore have to form them into a pair before applying g to them:

```
curry :: ((a,b) -> c) -> (a -> b -> c)
curry g x y = g (x,y)
```

`curry multiplyUC` will be exactly the same function as `multiply`.

Suppose now that f is a curried function, of type `a -> b -> c`.

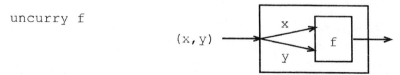

uncurry f

---

[2] In fact the first person to describe the idea was Schönfinkel, but 'Schönfinkeling' does not sound so snappy!

The function `uncurry` `f` will expect its arguments as a pair, and these will have to be separated before `f` can be applied to them:

```
uncurry :: (a -> b -> c) -> ((a,b) -> c)
uncurry f (x,y) = f x y
```

`uncurry multiply` will be exactly the same function as `multiplyUC`. The functions `curry` and `uncurry` are inverse to each other.

Partial application of functions is done on the arguments from left to right, so a function cannot directly be applied to its second argument only. This effect can be achieved indirectly by first transforming the order in which the function takes its arguments and then partially applying it.

```
flip :: (a -> b -> c) -> (b -> a -> c)
flip f x y = f y x
```

`flip map` will takes as its first argument the list and as its second the function to be mapped; it can be applied to its first argument, having the effect of applying `map` to its second only.

Another way of forming the partial application (`'elem'` `whitespace`) is to use the `flip` function. We have

```
flip elem :: [Char] -> Char -> Bool
```

(among other types) and so we can form the partial application thus:

```
flip elem whitespace
```

We now turn to a more substantial example in which we use the ideas of composition, partial application and operator sections in a variety of ways.

(10.8) Example: creating an index

This section explores a different aspect of text processing from those we have looked at already. How can an index for a document be produced automatically? We use the example to illustrate how higher-order functions are used in many parts of the final program. Polymorphism allows their use at different types, and their function parameters mean that they can be used to different effect in different situations.

To make the example texts shorter, a scaled-down version of the indexing problem is investigated. This is only done for ease of presentation, as all the important aspects of the system are explored here.

Specification

We should first specify what the program is to do. The input is a text string, in which lines are separated by the newline character `'\n'`. The index should give every line on which the word in question occurs. Only words of length at least four letters are to be indexed, and an alphabetical listing of the results produced. Within each entry, a line number should not be duplicated. For example, on the input

```
"cathedral doggerel cathedral\nbattery doggerel cathedral\ncathedral"
```

we would expect to get an index

```
battery        2
cathedral      1, 2, 3
doggerel       1, 2
```

Designing the program

We can represent the index as a list, with each entry being an item. What will a single entry be? It has to associate a collection of line numbers with each word in the text; we can therefore represent each entry by a pair consisting of a list of numbers, of type [Int], and a word, of type String. The top-level function will therefore be

```
makeIndex :: Doc -> [ ([Int],Word) ]
```

where we use the type synonyms

```
type Doc  = String
type Line = String
type Word = String
```

to distinguish the different uses of the string type in the design which follows. Note that these are all the same type; we use the names to make our discussion of types carry more information: the definition of 'Line' can be read as saying 'String thought of as representing a line', for example.

How can the program be designed? We focus on the **data structures** which the program will produce, and we can see the program as working by making a series of modifications to the data with which we begin. This **data-directed** design is common in Haskell functional program development.

At the top level, the solution will be a **composition** of functions. These perform the following operations, in turn.

- Split the text, a Doc, into lines, giving an object of type [Line].

- Pair each line with its line number, giving an object of type [(Int,Line)].

- Split the lines into words, associating each word with the number of the line on which it occurs. This gives a list of type [(Int,Word)].

- Sort this list according to the alphabetical ordering of words (Strings), giving a list of the same type.

- Modify the lists so that each word is paired with a list containing a single line number. This gives a result of type [([Int],Word)].

- Amalgamate entries for the same word into a list of numbers, giving a list of type [([Int],Word)].

- Shorten the list by removing all entries for words of less than four letters, giving a list of type [([Int],Word)].

The definition follows; note that we have used comments to give the type of each component function in the forward composition:

```
makeIndex
  = lines        >.>    --  Doc          -> [Line]
    numLines     >.>    --  [Line]        -> [(Int,Line)]
    allNumWords  >.>    --  [(Int,Line)]  -> [(Int,Word)]
    sortLs       >.>    --  [(Int,Word)]  -> [(Int,Word)]
    makeLists    >.>    --  [(Int,Word)]  -> [([Int],Word)]
    amalgamate   >.>    --  [([Int],Word)] -> [([Int],Word)]
    shorten             --  [([Int],Word)] -> [([Int],Word)]
```

Once the type of each of the functions is given, development of each can proceed independently. The only information necessary to use a function is its *type*, and these types are specified in the definition above. Each of the functions can now be given, in turn.

Implementing the component functions

To split a string into a list of lines it must be split at each occurrence of the newline character, '\n'. How is this written as a function? One solution is to write functions analogous to getWord and dropWord, which together were used earlier in splitWords. Alternatively, we can use the functions getUntil and dropUntil from Chapter 7. A third alternative is to look in the standard prelude where we find the function lines already defined; we therefore use that.

```
lines :: Doc -> [Line]
```

The next function should pair each line with its line number. If the list of lines is linels, then the list of line numbers is

```
[1 .. length linels]
```

Stepping back from the problem, it is apparent that the lists of lines and line numbers need to be combined into a **list of pairs**, by zipping the two lists together. The zip function has already been defined to do exactly this, so the required function is

```
numLines :: [Line] -> [ ( Int , Line ) ]
numLines linels
  = zip [1 .. length linels] linels
```

Now the lines have to be split into words, and line numbers attached. We first consider the problem for a single line.

```
numWords :: ( Int , Line ) -> [ ( Int , Word ) ]
```

Splitting into words can be done by the function splitWords of Chapter 7, modified slightly. When we defined splitWords we preserved any punctuation characters, as these were to appear in the output of the text processor. In contrast here we will modify the definition of whitespace to include punctuation, and so remove the punctuation from the resulting words. We define

```
whitespace :: String
whitespace = " \n\t;:.,\'\"!?()-"
```

Each of these words is then to be paired with the (same) line number. Stepping back from the problem, we see that we have to perform an operation on every item of a list, the list of words making up the line. This is a job for map,

```
numWords (number , line)
  = map (\word -> (number,word)) (splitWords line)
```

or a list comprehension

```
numWords (number , line)
  = [ (number , word) | word <- splitWords line ]
```

To apply this to the whole text, the function numWords has to be applied to every line. This is again done by map, and the individual results joined together or **concatenated**. We make a direct definition of the function, by composing its two parts. First we map the function numWords, then we concatenate the results, using concat.

```
allNumWords :: [ ( Int , Line ) ] -> [ ( Int , Word ) ]
allNumWords = concat . map numWords
```

What has been achieved so far? The text has been transformed into a list of line-number/word pairs, from which an index is to be built. For instance, the text

```
"cat dog\nbat dog\ncat"
```

will be converted to

```
[(1,"cat") , (1,"dog") , (2,"bat") , (2,"dog") , (3,"cat")]
```

The list must next be sorted by word order, and lists of lines on which a word appears be built. The ordering relation on pairs of numbers and words is given by

```
orderPair :: ( Int , Word ) -> ( Int , Word ) -> Bool
orderPair ( n1 , w1 ) ( n2 , w2 )
  = w1 < w2 || ( w1 == w2 && n1 < n2 )
```

The words are compared for dictionary order. For pairs containing the same words, ordering is by line number.

Sorting a list is most easily done by a version of the **quicksort** algorithm. The list is split into parts smaller than and larger than a given element; each of these halves can be sorted separately, and then joined together to form the result.

```
sortLs :: [ ( Int , Word ) ] -> [ ( Int , Word ) ]

sortLs []     = []
sortLs (p:ps) = sortLs smaller ++ [p] ++ sortLs larger
```

The lists `smaller` and `larger` are the lists of elements of ps which are smaller (or larger) than the pair p. Note that it is here that duplicate copies are removed – any other occurrence of the pair p in the list ps does not appear in either `smaller` or `larger`.

How are the two lists defined? They are given by selecting those elements of ps with given properties: a job for `filter`, or a list comprehension. Going back to the definition of `sortLs`,

```
sortLs (p:ps)
  = sortLs smaller ++ [p] ++ sortLs larger
    where
    smaller = [ q | q<-ps , orderPair q p ]
    larger  = [ q | q<-ps , orderPair p q ]
```

After sorting the running example will be

```
[(2,"bat") , (1,"cat") , (3,"cat") , (1,"dog") , (2,"dog")]
```

The entries for the same word need to be accumulated together. First each entry is converted to having a *list* of line numbers associated with it, thus

```
makeLists ::  [ (Int,Word) ] -> [ ([Int],Word) ]
makeLists
  = map mklis
    where
    mklis ( n , st ) = ( [n] , st )
```

For our example, this gives

```
[ ([2],"bat") , ([1],"cat") , ([3],"cat") ,
  ([1],"dog") , ([2],"dog") ]
```

After this, the lists associated with the same words are amalgamated.

```
amalgamate :: [ ([Int],Word) ] -> [ ([Int],Word) ]

amalgamate [] = []
amalgamate [p] = [p]
amalgamate ((l1,w1):(l2,w2):rest)
  | w1 /= w2   = (l1,w1) : amalgamate ((l2,w2):rest)   (amalg.1)
  | otherwise  = amalgamate ((l1++l2,w1):rest)         (amalg.2)
```

The first two equations are simple, with the third doing the work.

⬤ If we have two adjacent entries with different words, case (`amalg.1`), then we know that there is nothing to add to the first entry – we therefore have to amalgamate entries in the *tail* only.

⬤ If two adjacent entries have the same word associated, case (`amalg.2`), they are amalgamated and the function is called again on the result. This is because there may be other entries with the same word, also to be amalgamated into the leading entry.

Consider an example

```
amalgamate [ ([2],"bat") , ([1],"cat") , ([3],"cat") ]
 ⤳  ([2],"bat") : amalgamate [([1],"cat"),([3],"cat")] by (amalg.1)
 ⤳  ([2],"bat") : amalgamate [ ([1,3],"cat") ]          by (amalg.2)
 ⤳  ([2],"bat") : [ ([1,3],"cat") ]
 ⤳  [ ([2],"bat") , ([1,3],"cat") ]
```

To meet the requirements, one other operation needs to be performed. 'Small' words of less than four letters are to be removed.

```
shorten
  = filter sizer
    where
    sizer (nl,wd) = length wd > 3
```

Again, the `filter` function proves useful. The index function can now be defined in full:

```
makeIndex :: Doc -> [ ([Int],Word) ]
makeIndex
  = lines >.> numLines >.> allNumWords >.> sortLs >.>
    makeLists >.> amalgamate >.> shorten
```

As was said at the beginning of this section, function composition provides a powerful method for structuring designs: programs are written as a **pipeline** of operations, passing the appropriate data structures between them.

It is easy to see how designs like these can be modified. To take one example, the indexing program above filters out short words only as its final operation. There are a number of earlier points in the chain at which this could have been done, and it is a worthwhile exercise to consider these.

Exercises

10.20 Define the function `lines` using the functions `getUntil` and `dropUntil` from Chapter 9, or the built-in functions `takeWhile` and `dropWhile`. You should be careful that your functions do not give an empty word when there are empty lines in the Doc; this might happen for the examples `"cat\n\ndog"` and `"fish\n"`.

10.21 How would you use lambda expressions to replace the local definitions in `makeLists` and `shorten`? How would you define these functions using list comprehensions?

10.22 In the index for this book, instead of printing an entry like

```
cathedral        3, 5, 6, 7, 9, 10
```

a number of ranges could be given:

```
cathedral        3, 5-7, 9-10
```

How would you redesign your program to do this? Hint: first think about the type of the new index representation and then consider adding another function to the (forward) composition which currently forms the definition of makeIndex.

10.23 How would you re-define sortLs so that duplicate copies of an item are *not* removed? For the index, this means that if a word occurs twice on line 123 say, then 123 occurs twice in the index entry for that word.

10.24 How could the functions getUntil and dropUntil be used in the definition of amalgamate?

10.25 Explain how the function sizer defined locally in shorten can be defined as a composition of built-in functions and operator sections; the role of sizer is to pick the second half of a pair, find its length, and compare the result with 4.

10.26 How is the following definition of the last conditional equation for amalgamate incorrect? Give an example calculation to justify your answer.

```
amalgamate ((l1,w1):(l2,w2):rest)
  | w1 /= w2    = (l1,w1) : amalgamate ((l2,w2):rest)
  | otherwise   = (l1++l2,w1) : amalgamate rest
```

10.27 Give a definition of

```
printIndex :: [ ([Int],Word) ] -> IO ()
```

which gives a neatly laid-out printable version of an index, as shown at the start of the section. You might find it useful to define a function

```
showIndex :: [ ([Int],Word) ] -> String
```

and to use this as a part of your definition of printIndex.

10.28 Modify the program so that words of less than four letters are removed as a part of the definition of allNumWords.

10.29 Modify the makeIndex function so that instead of returning the list of line numbers on which a word occurs, the function returns the total number of times that the word occurs. You will need to make sure that multiple occurrences of a word in a single line are counted. There are two ways of tackling the problem.

- Modify the program as little as is necessary – you could return the length of a list rather than the list itself, for instance.
- Take the program structure as a guide, and write a (simpler) program which calculates the number of occurrences directly.

10.30 Modify the program so that capitalized words like "Dog" are indexed under their uncapitalized equivalents ("dog"). This does not work well for proper names like "Amelia" — what could you do about that?

10.31 The function sortLs is limited to sorting lists of type [(Int,Word)] because it calls the orderPair function. Redefine the function so that it takes the comparison function as a *parameter*. What is its type after this redefinition?

10.32 How would you modify the program if it was to be used to form the index for a Haskell script? Hint: you need to think about what it is sensible to ignore in such an enterprise.

(10.9) Verification and general functions

Verification can take on a different character when we look at higher-order polymorphic functions. We can start to prove equalities between functions, rather than between values of functions, and we shall also see that we are able to prove theorems which resemble their subjects in being general and reusable, and so applicable in many contexts.

Function-level verification

We claimed in Section 10.3 that the function iter is a generalization of twice, since

```
iter 2 f
  = f . iter 1 f                          by (iter.1)
  = f . (f . iter 0 f)                     by (iter.1)
  = f . (f . id)                           by (iter.2)
  = f . f                                  by (compId)
  = twice f                                by (twice.1)
```

In proving this we have used the equality between two functions

```
f . id = f                                      (compId)
```

How is this proved? We examine how each side behaves on an arbitrary argument x

```
(f . id) x
  = f (id x)
  = f x
```

so that for any argument x the two functions have the same behaviour. As black boxes, they are therefore the same. As what interests us here is their behaviour, we say that they are equal. We call this 'black-box' concept of equality **extensional**.

| **Definition** |

Principle of extensionality:

Two functions f and g are equal if they have the same value at every argument.

This is called extensionality in contrast to the idea of **intensionality** in which we say two functions are the same only if they have the same definitions – we no longer think of them as black boxes; we are allowed to look inside them to see how the mechanisms work, as it were. If we are interested in the results of our programs, all that matters are the values given by functions, not how they are arrived at. We therefore use extensionality when we are reasoning about function behaviour in Haskell. If we are interested in **efficiency** or other performance aspects of programs, then the way in which a result is found *will* be significant, however. This is discussed further in Chapter 19.

Exercises

10.33 Using the principle of extensionality, show that function composition is associative: that is, for all f, g and h,

```
f . (g . h) = (f . g) . h
```

10.34 Show that for all f,

```
id . f = f
```

10.35 Show that the function flip defined in Section 10.7 satisfies

```
flip . flip = id
```

Hint: to show this, you might want to prove that for any f,

```
flip (flip f) = f
```

10.36 Two functions f and g are **inverses** if it can be shown that

```
f . g = id            g . f = id
```

Prove that the functions curry and uncurry of Section 10.7 are inverses. Can you think of other pairs of inverse functions?

10.37 Using induction, prove that for all natural numbers n,

```
iter n id = id
```

10.38 A function f is called **idempotent** if

```
f . f = f
```

Show that the functions abs and signum are idempotent. Can you think of any other idempotent functions?

Higher-level proofs

Our verification thus far has concentrated on first-order, monomorphic functions. Just as `map`, `filter` and `fold` generalize patterns of definition, we shall find that proofs about these functions generalize results we have seen already. To give some examples, it is not hard to prove that

```
doubleAll (xs++ys) = doubleAll xs ++ doubleAll ys
```

holds for all finite lists `xs` and `ys`. When `doubleAll` is defined as `map (*2)` it becomes clear that we have an example of a general result,

```
map f (xs++ys) = map f xs ++ map f ys                    (map++)
```

which is valid for *any* function `f`. We also claimed in an earlier exercise that

```
sum (xs++ys) = sum xs + sum ys                           (sum.3)
```

for all finite lists `xs`, `ys`. The function `sum` is given by folding in `(+)`,

```
sum = foldr (+) 0
```

and we have, generally, if `f` is associative, and `st` is an identity for `f`, that is,

```
x 'f' (y 'f' z) = (x 'f' y) 'f' z
x 'f' st = x = st 'f' x
```

for all `x`, `y`, `z` then the equation

```
foldr f st (xs++ys) = f (foldr f st xs) (foldr f st ys)  (foldr.3)
```

holds for all finite `xs` and `ys`. Obviously `(+)` is associative and has 0 as an identity, and so `(sum.3)` is a special case of `(fold.3)`. Now we give three proofs of examples in the same vein.

`map` and composition

A first example concerns `map` and composition. Recall the definitions

```
map f []      = []                                       (map.1)
map f (x:xs) = f x : map f xs                            (map.2)
(f . g) x    = f (g x)                                   (comp.1)
```

It is not hard to see that we should be able to prove that

```
map (f . g) xs = (map f . map g) xs                      (map.3)
```

holds for every finite list `xs`.

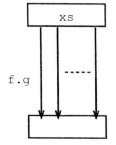 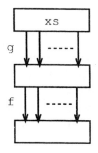

Applying (f . g) to every member of a list should be the same as applying g to every member of the list and then applying f to every member of the result. It is proved just as easily, by structural induction. The (base) case requires the identity to be proved for the empty list.

```
map (f . g) [] = []                                        by (map.1)


(map f . map g) []
  = map f (map g [])                                        by (comp.1)
  = map f []                                                by (map.1)
  = []                                                      by (map.1)
```

Assuming that

```
map (f . g) xs = (map f . map g) xs                            (hyp)
```

is true, it is now necessary to prove that

```
map (f . g) (x:xs) = (map f . map g) (x:xs)                    (ind)
```

Again, it is enough to analyse each side of the equation.

```
map (f . g) (x:xs)
  = (f . g) x : map (f . g) xs                              by (map.2)
  = f (g x) : map (f . g) xs                                by (comp.1)


(map f . map g) (x:xs)
  = map f (map g (x:xs))                                    by (comp.1)
  = map f (g x : map g xs)                                  by (map.2)
  = f (g x) : map f (map g xs)                              by (map.2)
  = f (g x) : (map f . map g) xs                            by (comp.1)
```

The induction hypothesis is exactly what is needed to prove the two sides equal, completing the proof of the induction step and the proof itself.   ■

Each Haskell list type, besides containing finite lists, also contains infinite and partial lists. In Chapter 17 these will be explained and it will be shown that (map.3) is true for *all* lists xs, and therefore that the functional equation

```
map (f . g) = (map f) . (map g)
```

holds in general.

map and filter

The proof above showed how properties of functional programs could be proved from the definitions of the functions in a straightforward way. The properties can state how the program behaves – that a sorting function returns an ordered list, for instance – or can relate one program to another. This latter idea underlies **program transformation** for functional languages. This section introduces an example called **filter promotion** which is one of the most useful of the basic functional transformations.

```
filter p . map f = map f . filter (p . f)
```

The equation says that a map followed by a filter can be replaced by a filter followed by a map. The right-hand side is potentially more efficient than the left, since the map operation will there be applied to a shorter list, consisting of just those elements with the property (p . f). An example is given by the function first defined in Section 10.4.

```
filter (0<) . map (+1)
```

Instead of mapping first, the function can be replaced by

```
map (+1) . filter ((0<) . (+1))
 = map (+1) . filter (0<=)
```

and it is clear that here the transformed version is more efficient, since the test (0<=) is no more costly than (0<). The proof that

```
(filter p . map f) xs = (map f . filter (p . f)) xs
```

for finite lists xs is by structural induction. First we reiterate the definitions of map, filter and composition.

```
map f []        = []                             (map.1)
map f (x:xs)    = f x : map f xs                 (map.2)

filter p []     = []                             (filter.1)
filter p (x:xs)
   | p x        = x : filter p xs                (filter.2)
   | otherwise  =     filter p xs                (filter.3)

(f . g) x       = f (g x)                        (comp.1)
```

The base case consists of a proof of

```
(filter p . map f) [] = (map f . filter (p . f)) []       (base)
```

This is true since

```
(filter p . map f) []
  = filter p (map f [])                          by (comp.1)
  = filter p []                                  by (map.1)
  = []                                           by (filter.1)
```

and

```
(map f . filter (p . f)) []
  = map f (filter (p . f) [])                    by (comp.1)
  = map f []                                      by (filter.1)
  = []                                            by (map.1)
```

In the induction step, a proof of

```
(filter p . map f) (x:xs) = (map f . filter (p . f)) (x:xs)   (ind)
```

is required, using the induction hypothesis

```
(filter p . map f) xs = (map f . filter (p . f)) xs              (hyp)
```

The proof begins with an analysis of the left-hand side of (ind).

```
(filter p . map f) (x:xs)
  = filter p (map f (x:xs))                              by (comp.1)
  = filter p (f x : map f xs)                            by (map.2)
```

There are two[3] cases to consider: whether p (f x) is True or False. Taking the case where p (f x) is True, we continue to examine the left-hand side of (ind), giving

```
  = f x : filter p (map f xs)                            by (filter.2)
  = f x : (filter p . map f) xs                          by (comp.1)
  = f x : (map f . filter (p . f)) xs                    by (hyp)
```

Now we look at the right-hand side of (ind), also assuming that p (f x) is True:

```
(map f . filter (p . f)) (x:xs)
  = map f (filter (p . f) (x:xs))                        by (comp.1)
  = map f (x: (filter (p . f) xs))                       by (filter.2)
  = f x : map f (filter (p . f) xs)                      by (map.2)
  = f x : (map f . filter (p . f)) xs                    by (comp.1)
```

which shows that (ind) holds in the case that p (f x) is True.

A similar chain of reasoning gives the same result in the case where p (f x) is False. This establishes (ind) assuming (hyp), and so together with (base) completes the proof of the filter promotion transformation in the case of finite lists; it holds, in fact, for all lists.   ∎

map, reverse and the Picture case study

When we introduced the Picture case study in Chapter 1 we claimed that we could prove that flipV and flipH can be applied in either order to give the same result. Our implementation defines them thus

```
flipH = reverse
flipV = map reverse
```

and we can see informally that

- reverse affects the order of the elements, while leaving the elements unchanged;
- map reverse affects each of the elements, while keeping their order the same.

The second observation is a consequence of the function being a map, and so we make the more general claim that for all finite lists xs and all functions f,

---

[3] We should also think about what happens when p (f x) is undefined; in this case both sides will be undefined, and so equal.

```
map f (reverse xs) = reverse (map f xs)                    (map/reverse)
```

This has the consequence that

```
flipV (flipH xs) = flipH (flipV xs)
```

if we replace f in (map/reverse) by reverse. We will see in Chapter 17 that we can establish (map/reverse) for all lists xs and so conclude that the functional equations hold:

```
map f . reverse = reverse . map f
flipV . flipH   = flipH . flipV
```

We now prove (map/reverse) by induction over xs.

We have seen the definition of map in the previous examples; reverse is defined thus.

```
reverse []      = []                                       (reverse.1)
reverse (z:zs) = reverse zs ++ [z]                         (reverse.2)
```

Statement   We first have to prove the base case:

```
map f (reverse []) = reverse (map f [])                    (base)
```

and then we need to prove the induction step,

```
map f (reverse (x:xs)) = reverse (map f (x:xs))            (ind)
```

assuming the induction hypothesis:

```
map f (reverse xs) = reverse (map f xs)                    (hyp)
```

Base   Looking at the two sides of the base case in turn, we have

```
map f (reverse [])
  = map f []                                      by (reverse.1)
  = []                                            by (map.1)

reverse (map f [])
  = reverse []                                    by (map.1)
  = []                                            by (reverse.1)
```

and this shows that the two sides of the base case equation have the same value, and so we move on to the induction case.

Induction   We start by examining the left-hand side of (ind):

```
map f (reverse (x:xs))
  = map f (reverse xs ++ [x])                     by (reverse.2)
```

Now, it is not hard to prove that

```
map f (ys++zs) = map f ys ++ map f zs                    (map++)
```

(we leave this proof as an exercise for the reader) and using (map++) we can continue to simplify the left-hand side

```
= map f (reverse xs) ++ map f [x]                    by (map++)
= map f (reverse xs) ++ [f x]            by (map.1),(map.2)
```

Using the induction hypothesis, we can make one more step,

```
= reverse (map f xs) ++ [f x]                        by (hyp)
```

Now looking at the right-hand side,

```
reverse (map f (x:xs))
  = reverse (f x : map f xs)                         by (map.2)
  = reverse (map f xs) ++ [f x]                  by (reverse.2)
```

and now we see that the two sides are equal, which establishes the induction step and so completes the proof. ∎

Libraries of theorems

We have seen in this section that we can prove properties of general functions like map, filter and foldr. This means that when we define a function which uses map, say, we can call on a whole library of properties of map, including, for all finite xs and ys:

```
map (f . g) xs          = (map f . map g) xs
(filter p . map f) xs = (map f . filter (p . f)) xs
map f (reverse xs)      = reverse (map f xs)
map f (ys++zs)          = map f ys ++ map f zs
```

We have seen that using the general functions map, filter and others allowed us to make direct definitions of new functions rather than having to define them 'from scratch' using recursion. In exactly the same way, these general theorems will mean that in many cases we can avoid writing an induction proof about our specific function, and instead simply use one of these theorems.

Exercises

10.39 Prove that for all ys and zs the equation

```
map f (ys++zs) = map f ys ++ map f zs                    (map++)
```

as was used in the proof of the theorem about map and reverse.

10.40 If f is associative, and st is an identity for f – these notions were defined on page 195 – then prove that the equation (foldr.3):

```
foldr f st (xs++ys) = f (foldr f st xs) (foldr f st ys)
```

holds for all finite xs and ys.

10.41 Argue that the result

```
concat (xs ++ ys) = concat xs ++ concat ys
```

is a special case of (foldr.3), using

```
concat = foldr (++) []
```

as the definition of concat.

10.42 Prove that for all finite lists xs, and functions f,

```
concat (map (map f) xs) = map f (concat xs)
```

10.43 Prove that over the type Int

```
(0<) . (+1) = (0<=)
```

as is used in the theorem relating map and filter.

10.44 Prove for all finite lists xs that

```
filter p (filter q xs) = filter (p &&& q) xs
```

where the operator &&& is defined by

```
p &&& q = \x -> (p x && q x)
```

Summary

We have seen in this chapter how we can write functions with functions as results. This means that we can create the functions by applying operations like map, filter and foldr within our programs, and that we can indeed treat functions as 'first-class citizens' of our programming language. A consequence of this has been that we are able to explain the definitions of some of the Picture operations first seen in Chapter 1.

The main mechanisms introduced here have allowed us to create functions by applying functions or operators to fewer arguments than we expected, thus creating partial applications and operator sections. We also saw how the Haskell-type system and syntax were adapted to deal with the curried form of function definitions, by which multi-argument functions take their arguments one at a time.

We concluded by showing that we could prove general properties about general functions like map, and thus build up libraries of results about these functions which can potentially be applied whenever the general function is reused.

Chapter 12

Overloading and type classes

In looking at Haskell so far we have seen two kinds of function which work over more than one type. A **polymorphic** function such as length has a single definition which works over all its types. **Overloaded** functions like equality, + and show can be used at a variety of types, but with different definitions being used at different types.

The chapter starts with a discussion of the benefits of overloading, before looking at **type classes**, which are collections of types; what the members of a class have in common is the fact that certain functions are defined over the type. For instance, the members of the equality type class, Eq, are those types which carry an equality function, ==. Type classes are thus the mechanism by which overloaded functions can be given types in Haskell.

We shall see how to define type classes and types which belong to these classes – so-called **instances** of the class. We will also see that there is a form of inheritance between type classes, which is related to the inheritance of object-oriented programming. We take this up again in Chapter 16 below.

Haskell's prelude and libraries contain a number of classes and instances, particularly for numeric types – we survey these, referring readers to the Haskell report (Peyton Jones and Hughes 1998) for a full exposition.

12.1 **Why overloading?**

This section looks at the reason for including overloading in Haskell; we do this by looking at a scenario.

Suppose that Haskell did not have overloading, and that we wanted to check whether a particular element is a member of a list of type `Bool`. We would define a function like

```
elemBool :: Bool -> [Bool] -> Bool
elemBool x [] = False
elemBool x (y:ys)
  = (x ==Bool y) || elemBool x ys
```

where we have to write $==_{Bool}$ for the equality function over `Bool`.

Suppose now that we want to check whether an integer is a member of an integer list, then we need to define a *new* function

```
elemInt :: Int -> [Int] -> Bool
```

which differs from `elemBool` only in using $==_{Int}$ instead of $==_{Bool}$. Each time we want to check membership of a list of a different type we will have to define yet another – very similar – function.

One way out of this problem is to make the equality function a parameter of a general function

```
elemGen :: (a -> a -> Bool) -> a -> [a] -> Bool
```

but this gives too much generality in a sense, because it can be used with *any* parameter of type `a -> a -> Bool` rather than just an equality check. Also in this case the parameter has to be written down explicitly each time the function `elemGen` is used, as in

```
elemGen (==Bool)
```

making programs less easy to read.

The alternative is to define a function which uses the overloaded equality,

```
elem :: a -> [a] -> Bool
```

where the type `a` has to be restricted to those types which have an equality. The advantages of this approach are

- **Reuse** The definition of `elem` can be used over all types with equality.
- **Readability** It is much easier to read `==` than $==_{Int}$ and so on. This argument holds particularly for numeric operators, where it is more than tiresome to have to write $+_{Int}$, $*_{Float}$ and so on.

What this discussion shows is that a mechanism is needed to give a type to functions like `elem`: that is precisely the purpose of type classes.

(12.2) Introducing classes

The elem function appears to have the type

```
elem :: a -> [a] -> Bool
```

but this type only holds for types a which have an equality function. How is this to be expressed? We need some way of saying whether we have an equality function over a given type. We call the collection of types over which a function is defined a **type class** or simply **class**. For instance, the set of types over which == is defined is the **equality class**, Eq.

Defining the equality class

How do we define a class, such as Eq? We say what is needed for a type a to be in a class. In this case we need a function == defined over a, of type a->a->Bool.

```
class Eq a where
  (==) :: a -> a -> Bool
```

Members of a type class are called its **instances**. Built-in instances of Eq include the base types Int, Float, Bool, Char. Other instances are given by tuples and lists built from types which are themselves instances of Eq; examples include the types (Int,Bool) and [[Char]].

Not all types will necessarily carry an equality; we may choose not to define one, for reasons of information hiding, or there may be no natural way of defining an equality on a particular type. For example, function types like Int -> Int are not instances of Eq, since there is no algorithm which will decide whether two functions over Int have the same behaviour.

It is unfortunate that the term *instance* is used in two quite different ways in Haskell. We talked in Section 5.7 of a type t_1 being an instance of a *type* t_2, when we can substitute for a type variable in t_2 to give t_1. Here we have talked about a type being an instance of a *class*.

Functions which use equality

Many of the functions which we have defined so far use equality over particular types. The function

```
allEqual :: Int -> Int -> Int -> Bool
allEqual m n p = (m==n) && (n==p)
```

decides whether three integers are equal. If we examine the definition itself, it contains nothing which is specific to integers; the only constraint it makes is that m, n and p are compared for equality. Their type can be a for any a *in the type class* Eq. This gives allEqual a most general type thus:

```
allEqual :: Eq a => a -> a -> a -> Bool
allEqual m n p = (m==n) && (n==p)
```

The part before the => is called the **context**. We can read the type as saying that

> if the type a is in the class Eq – that is, if == is defined over the type a – then allEqual has type a -> a -> a -> Bool

This means that allEqual can be used at the following types

```
allEqual :: Char -> Char -> Char -> Bool
allEqual :: (Int,Bool) -> (Int,Bool) -> (Int,Bool) -> Bool
```

since both Char and (Int,Bool) belong to Eq, among many other types. What happens if we break this constraint by trying to compare functions for equality? If we define

```
suc :: Int -> Int
suc = (+1)
```

and try to evaluate

```
allEqual suc suc suc
```

we get the message

```
ERROR: Int -> Int is not an instance of class "Eq"
```

which conveys the fact that (Int -> Int) is not in the Eq class, because it is not an instance of that class.

Further equality examples

The elem example in Section 12.1 will have the type

```
elem :: Eq a => a -> [a] -> Bool
```

and so it will be usable at the types

```
Bool -> [Bool] -> Bool
Int  -> [Int]  -> Bool
```

Many of the functions we have defined already use equality in an overloaded way. We can use the Hugs system to deduce the most general type of a function, such as the books function from the library database of Section 5.6, by commenting out its type declaration in the script, thus

```
-- books :: Database -> Person -> [Book]
```

and then by typing

```
:type books
```

to the prompt. The result we get in that case is

```
books :: Eq a => [ (a,b) ] -> a -> [b]
```

which is perhaps a surprise at first. This is less so if we rewrite the definition with books renamed lookupFirst, because it looks up all the pairs with a particular first part, and returns their corresponding second parts. Here it is with its variables renamed as well

```
lookupFirst :: Eq a => [ (a,b) ] -> a -> [b]

lookupFirst ws x
  = [ z | (y,z) <- ws , y==x ]
```

Clearly from this definition there is nothing specific about books or people and so it is polymorphic, if we can compare objects in the first halves of the pairs for equality. This condition gives rise to the context Eq a. Finally from Section 5.6, as we saw for books,

```
borrowed     :: Eq b => [ (a,b) ] -> b -> Bool
numBorrowed :: Eq a => [ (a,b) ] -> a -> Int
```

Summary

In this section we have introduced the idea of a class, which is a collection of types — its instances — with the property that certain functions are defined over them. One way we can think of a class is **as an adjective**: any particular type is or is not in the class, just as the weather at any particular moment might or might not be sunny.

We saw how equality could be seen as being defined over all the types in the class Eq. This allows many of the functions defined so far to be given polymorphic type, allowing them to be used over any type in the class Eq. In the following sections we explain how classes and instances are defined in general, and explore the consequences of classes for programming in Haskell.

Exercises

12.1 How would you define the 'not equal' operation, /=, from equality, ==? What is the type of /=?

12.2 Define the function numEqual which takes a list of items, xs say, and an item, x say, and returns the number of times x occurs in xs. What is the type of your function? How could you use numEqual to define member?

12.3 Define functions

```
oneLookupFirst  :: Eq a => [ (a,b) ] -> a -> b
oneLookupSecond :: Eq b => [ (a,b) ] -> b -> a
```

oneLookupFirst takes a list of pairs and an item, and returns the second part of the first pair whose first part equals the item. You should explain what your function does if there is no such pair. oneLookupSecond returns the first pair with the roles of first and second reversed.

(12.3) Signatures and instances

In the last section we saw that the operation of equality, ==, is overloaded. This allows == to be used over a variety of types, and also allows for functions using == to be defined over all instances of the class of types Eq. This section explains the mechanics of how classes are introduced, and then how instances of them may be declared. This allows us to program with classes that we define ourselves, rather than simply using the built-in classes of Haskell.

Declaring a class

As we saw earlier, a class is introduced by a declaration like:

```
class Visible a where
  toString :: a -> String
  size     :: a -> Int
```

The declaration introduces the name of the class, Visible, and then follows a **signature**, that is a list of names and their types. Any type a in the Visible class must carry the two functions in the signature:

- the toString function, which converts an object of the type to a String, and,

- the size function, which returns a measure of the size of the argument, as an integer.

Visible things can be viewed, using the toString function, and we can give an estimate of their size: the size of a list might be its length, while a Boolean might have size one.
  The general form of a class definition will be:

```
class Name ty where
  ... signature involving the type variable ty ...
```

Now, how are types made instances of such a class?

Defining the instances of a class

A type is made a member or **instance** of a class by defining the signature functions for the type. For example,

```
instance Eq Bool where
  True  == True  = True
  False == False = True
  _     == _     = False
```

describes how Bool is an instance of the equality class. The declarations that numeric types like Int and Float are in the equality class (and indeed other built-in classes) involve the appropriate primitive equality functions supplied by the implementation.
  Although we have called the class Eq the equality class, there is no requirement that the == function we define has any of the usual properties of equality apart from having

the same type as equality. It is up to the user to ensure that he or she makes sensible definitions, and documents them adequately.

Taking up our other example, we might say

```
instance Visible Char where
  toString ch  = [ch]
  size _       = 1
```

This shows how characters can be turned into strings – by making them into strings of length one – and gives a measure of their size. We can also make Bool an instance, thus:

```
instance Visible Bool where
  toString True  = "True"
  toString False = "False"
  size _         = 1
```

Suppose the type a is visible: this means that we can estimate the size of a value in a, and turn a value into a string. If presented with a list of values of type a, we can use the toString and size on a to define those functions over [a], so we can declare the following instance

```
instance Visible a => Visible [a] where ....
```

in which the **context** Visible a appears, making clear that we are only making visible lists of objects which are themselves visible. We can complete the definition by saying how we print and give the size of a list of a:

```
instance Visible a => Visible [a] where
  toString = concat . map toString
  size     = foldr (+) 1 . map size
```

To turn a list of a into a String, we turn each element of the list into a string (map toString) and then we concatenate the results, using concat. In a similar way we can estimate the size of a list of a: we take the size of each object (map size), and add one to the total of these sizes by foldr (+) 1.

On the right-hand sides of these definitions we use toString and size over the type a; this shows that we need the context which says that a is a Visible type.

There are some limitations to what can be declared as an instance, in other words on what can appear after the => (if any) in an instance declaration. This must either be a base type like Int, or consist of a type former (or constructor) like [...] or (...,...) applied to distinct type variables.

We will *not* be able, for example, to declare (Float,Float) as an instance; nor can we use named types (introduced by a type definition). More details of the mechanism can be found in the Haskell report (Peyton Jones and Hughes 1998). We shall explore more complex examples in the next part of the book, after we have introduced our own type constructors.

Default definitions

To return to our example of equality, the Haskell equality class is in fact defined by

```
class Eq a where
  (==), (/=) :: a -> a -> Bool
  x /= y     = not (x==y)
  x == y     = not (x/=y)
```

To the equality operation is added inequality, /=. As well as this, there are **default** definitions of /= from == and of == from /=. These definitions have two purposes; they give a definition over all equality types, but as defaults they are **overridden** by an instance declaration.

At any instance a definition of at least one of == and /= needs to be supplied for there to be a proper definition of (in)equality, but a definition of either is sufficient to give both, by means of the defaults.

It is also possible to define both of the operations in an instance delaration , so that if we wanted to define a different version of /= over Bool, we could add to our instance declaration for Bool the line

```
  x /= y     = ... our definition ...
```

If we want to *stop* a default being overridden, we should remove the operation from the class, and instead give its definition at the top level and not in the signature. In the case of the operation /= in Eq we would give the top-level definition

```
x /= y      = not (x == y)
```

which has the type

```
(/=) :: Eq a => a -> a -> Bool
```

and will be effective over all types which carry the == operation.

There are some situations when it is better to give default definitions, which can be overridden, rather than top-level definitions, which cannot. Over the numerical types, for instance, an implementation may well supply all the operations as hardware instructions, which will be much more efficient than the default definitions.

Derived classes

Functions and instances can depend upon types being in classes; this is also true of classes. The simplest example in Haskell is the class of ordered types, Ord. To be ordered, a type must carry the operations >, >= and so on, as well as the equality operations. We say

```
class Eq a => Ord a where
  (<), (<=), (>), (>=) :: a -> a -> Bool
  max, min             :: a -> a -> a
  compare              :: a -> a -> Ordering
```

For a type a to be in the class Ord, we must supply over a definitions of the operations of Eq as well as the ones in the signature of Ord. Given a definition of < we can supply default definitions of the remaining operations of Ord. For instance,

```
x <= y    = (x < y || x == y)
x >  y    =  y < x
```

We will explain the type Ordering and the function compare in Section 12.4.

A simple example of a function defined over types in the class Ord is the insertion sort function iSort of Chapter 7. Its most general type is

```
iSort :: Ord a => [a] -> [a]
```

Indeed, any sorting function (which sorts using the ordering given by <=) would be expected to have this type.

From a different point of view, we can see the class Ord as **inheriting** the operations of Eq; inheritance is one of the central ideas of object-oriented programming.

Multiple constraints

In the contexts we have seen so far, we have a single constraint on a type, such as Eq a. There is no reason why we should not have multiple constraints on types. This section introduces the notation we use, and some examples where it is needed.

Suppose we wish to sort a list and then show the results as a string. We can write

```
vSort = toString . iSort
```

To sort the elements, we need the list to consist of elements from an ordered type, as we saw above. To convert the results to a String we need [a] to be Visible; given the instance declaration on page 216, this will hold if a is visible. We therefore have

```
vSort :: (Ord a,Visible a) => [a] -> String
```

showing that a must be in both the classes Ord and Visible. Such types include Bool, [Char] and so on.

In a similar way, suppose we are to use lookupFirst, and then make the results visible. We write

```
vLookupFirst xs x = toString (lookupFirst xs x)
```

We have twin constraints again on our list type [(a,b)]. We need to be able to compare the first halves of the pairs, so Eq a is required. We also want to turn the second halves into strings, so needing Visible b. This gives the type

```
vLookupFirst :: (Eq a,Visible b) => [(a,b)] -> a -> String
```

Multiple constraints can occur in an instance declaration, such as

```
instance (Eq a,Eq b) => Eq (a,b) where
  (x,y) == (z,w)  =  x==z && y==w
```

which shows that a pair of types in Eq again belongs to Eq. Multiple constraints can also occur in the definition of a class,

```
class (Ord a,Visible a) => OrdVis a
```

In such a declaration, the class inherits the operations of both Ord and Visible.

In this particular case, the class declaration contains an empty signature. To be in OrdVis, the type a must simply be in the classes Ord and Visible. We could then modify the type of vSort to say

```
vSort :: OrdVis a => [a] -> String
```

The situation when a class is built on top of two or more classes is called **multiple inheritance**; this has consequences for programming style, explored in Section 14.6.

Summary

This section has explained the basic details of the class mechanism in Haskell. We have seen that a class definition specifies a signature, and that in defining an instance of a class we must provide definitions of each of the operations of the signature. These definitions override any default definitions which are given in the class declaration. Contexts were seen to contain one or more constraints on the type variables which appear in polymorphic types, instance declarations and class declarations.

Exercises

12.4 How would you make Bool, pair types, (a,b), and triple types, (a,b,c), into Visible types?

12.5 Write a function to convert an integer into a String, and hence show how Int can be an instance of Visible.

12.6 What is the type of the function

```
compare x y    = size x <= size y ?
```

12.7 Complete the default definitions for the class Ord.

12.8 Complete the following instance declarations:

```
instance (Ord a, Ord b) => Ord (a,b) where ...
instance Ord b => Ord [b] where ...
```

where pairs and lists should be ordered **lexicographically**, like the words in a dictionary.

(12.4) A tour of the built-in Haskell classes

Haskell contains a number of built-in classes, which we briefly introduce in this section. Many of the classes are numeric, and are built to deal with overloading of the numerical operations over integers, floating-point reals, complex numbers and rationals (that is integer fractions like $\frac{22}{7}$). Rather than give complete details of the numeric types, we give an exposition of their major features.

Equality: Eq

Equality was described above; to recap, we define it by

```
class Eq a where
  (==), (/=) :: a -> a -> Bool
  x /= y   = not (x==y)
  x == y   = not (x/=y)
```

Ordering: Ord

Similarly, we build the ordered class on Eq:

```
class (Eq a) => Ord a where
  compare             :: a -> a -> Ordering
  (<), (<=), (>=), (>) :: a -> a -> Bool
  max, min            :: a -> a -> a
```

The type Ordering contains three values LT, EQ and GT, which represent the three possible outcomes from comparing two elements in the ordering. We shall see how the type Ordering is defined formally in Chapter 14, page 243.

The advantage of using compare is that a single function application decides the exact relationship between two inputs, whereas when using the ordering operators – which return Boolean results – two comparisons might well be necessary. Indeed, we see this in the default definition of compare from == and <=, where two tests are needed to reach the results LT and GT.

```
compare x y
    | x == y     = EQ
    | x <= y     = LT
    | otherwise  = GT
```

The defaults also contain definitions of the ordering operators from compare:

```
x <= y        = compare x y /= GT
x <  y        = compare x y == LT
x >= y        = compare x y /= LT
x >  y        = compare x y == GT
```

There are default definitions for all the operations of Ord, but we need to supply an implementation of either compare or <= in order to give an instance of Ord.

Finally we have default definitions for the maximum and minimum operations,

```
max x y
  | x >= y      = x
  | otherwise   = y
min x y
  | x <= y      = x
  | otherwise   = y
```

Most Haskell types belong to these equality and ordering classes: among the exceptions are function types, and some of the abstract data types we meet below in Chapter 16.

Enumeration: Enum

It is useful to generate lists like [2,4,6,8] using the enumeration expression

```
[2,4 .. 8]
```

but enumerations can be built over other types as well: characters, floating-point numbers, and so on. The class definition is

```
class (Ord a) => Enum a where
  toEnum          :: Int -> a
  fromEnum        :: a -> Int
  enumFrom        :: a -> [a]                -- [n .. ]
  enumFromThen    :: a -> a -> [a]           -- [n,m .. ]
  enumFromTo      :: a -> a -> [a]           -- [n .. m]
  enumFromThenTo  :: a -> a -> a -> [a]      -- [n,n' .. m]
```

where enumFromTo and enumFromThenTo have default definitions, which we leave as exercises for the reader.

The signature of the class also contains operations fromEnum and toEnum which convert between the type and Int. In the case of Char these conversion functions are also known as ord and chr, where these specializations are given by the definitions:

```
ord :: Char -> Int
ord = fromEnum


chr :: Int -> Char
chr = toEnum
```

Confusingly, the Haskell report states that 'these functions [toEnum and fromEnum] are not meaningful for all instances of Enum', and using these operations over floating-point values or full precision integers will result in a run-time error.

Full instances of the class include Int, Char, Bool and other finite types like Ordering. Definable over the class are the successor and predecessor functions,

```
succ, pred :: Enum a => a -> a


succ = toEnum . (+1) . fromEnum
pred = toEnum . (subtract 1) . fromEnum
```

Bounded types: `Bounded`

The `Bounded` class is specified by the declaration

```
class Bounded a where
  minBound, maxBound :: a
```

and the two values give the minimum and maximum values in these types. The types `Int`, `Char`, `Bool`, `Ordering` belong to this class.

Turning values to strings: `Show`

In our introduction to type classes we talked about the class `Visible` as an example of a user-defined class. The standard prelude defines the class `Show`, which contains types whose values can be written as strings.

```
type ShowS = String -> String

class Show a where
  showsPrec :: Int -> a -> ShowS
  show      :: a -> String
  showList  :: [a] -> ShowS
```

The function `showsPrec` supports flexible and efficient conversion of large data values, but in an introductory context, the function

```
show :: a -> String
```

which converts a value into a string is all that is needed. The class contains default definitions of `showsPrec` from `show` and vice versa. Further details about how to exploit the subtleties of `showsPrec` can be found in Hudak, Fasel and Peterson (1997).

Most types belong to the class Show; even if values of the type in question cannot be shown fully, a textutal representation of some sort is given. A function, for example, will be shown as <<`function`>>. For other types, example instance declarations might be

```
instance Show Bool where
  show True  = "True"
  show False = "False"

instance (Show a, Show b) => Show (a,b) where
  show (x,y) = "(" ++ show x ++ "," ++ show y ++ ")"
```

Turning strings to values: `Read`

The class `Read` contains types whose values can be read from strings. To use the class it is enough to know about the function

```
read :: (Read a) => String -> a
```

The result of a `read` may not be properly defined: there needs to be exactly one object of the required type in the input string (which may optionally also contain whitespace or nested comments); in any other case the `read` will fail with an error. More details of how strings are **parsed** in this way can be found in Section 17.5.

It is also important to see that in many cases the type of the result of the `read` has to be specified, since it could potentially be of any type in the class Read. For instance, we can write

```
(read "   1   ")::  Int
```

which indicates that in this case we require the result of the `read` to be an `Int`.

The class Read complements Show, since strings produced by `show` are usually readable by `read`. Many types can be read, but exclusions include function types.

The Haskell numeric types and classes

One of the purposes of the Haskell design was to build a functional programming language which had a strong type system – in which any type errors in definitions and expressions are found before evaluation – yet which contains a rich set of numeric types, as befits a language suitable to substantial 'real world' tasks. Among Haskell's numeric types are

- The fixed precision integers, `Int`, and the full precision integers, `Integer`, which represent *all* integers faithfully.

- The floating-point numbers, `Float`, and the double-precision floating-point numbers, `Double`.

- Rational numbers, that is fractions, represented as ratios of integers; built-in is the type `Rational` of `Integer` fractions.

- Complex numbers, which can be built over other types such as `Float`.

The design also required that the usual operations like + and / and literals such as 23 and 57.4 would be overloaded. For instance, `Int` and `Integer` will carry identical operations[1] and have identical literals, as indeed will `Float` and `Double`; a guide to the operations over integers and floats was given in Sections 3.2 and 3.6. This overloading can lead to situations where the type of an expression is undetermined; in such a case we can give an explicit type to an expression, thus:

```
(2+3)::Int
```

The Haskell report (Peyton Jones and Hughes 1998) discusses a mechanism by which a default type can be given to numeric expressions.

Overloading of numeric functions is achieved by defining a collection of classes. Full details of these can be found in the Haskell report (Peyton Jones and Hughes 1998), and in the standard prelude, `Prelude.hs`; a brief introduction follows here.

The base class to which all numeric types belong is Num, which has the signature

---

[1] Apart from (de)coding of `Char`, `take`, `drop` and so forth.

```
class (Eq a, Show a) => Num a where
  (+), (-), (*)  :: a -> a -> a
  negate         :: a -> a
  abs, signum    :: a -> a
  fromInteger    :: Integer -> a
  fromInt        :: Int -> a

  x - y          = x + negate y
  fromInt        = fromIntegral
```

This signature has the effect that all numeric types carry equality and show functions, together with addition, subtraction, multiplication and related operations. It is also possible to convert an Int or and Integer into a value of any numeric type.

Integer literals are of any numeric type, so that, for example

```
2 :: Num a => a
```

The integer types belong to the class Integral among whose signature functions are

```
quot, rem :: a -> a -> a
div, mod  :: a -> a -> a
```

which give two variants of integer division, 'quot' truncating towards zero, and 'div' truncating below.

Numbers with fractional parts have a substantially richer class structure. Literals of this kind belong to every type in the Fractional class,

```
2.3 :: Fractional a => a
```

which extends Num with fractional division and reciprocal,

```
class (Num a) => Fractional a where
  (/)           :: a -> a -> a
  recip         :: a -> a
  fromRational :: Rational -> a

  recip x       = 1 / x
```

The floating-point numbers in Float and Double belong to the class Floating, which carries the 'mathematical' functions. A part of its signature follows,

```
class (Fractional a) => Floating a where
  pi                 :: a
  exp, log, sqrt     :: a -> a
  (**), logBase      :: a -> a -> a
  sin, cos, tan      :: a -> a
  ....
```

and the full signature is to be found in Prelude.hs. Further details of this and the complex and rational types can be found in the prelude, libraries and the Haskell documentation.

12.9 Investigate the Haskell definition of '<' on the types Bool and $(t_1, t_2, \ldots, t_k)$.

12.10 Define a function

```
showBoolFun :: (Bool -> Bool) -> String
```

which displays a Boolean function as a table. Generalize this to

```
showBoolFunGen :: (a -> String) -> (Bool -> a) -> String
```

whose first argument is a function to show elements of a. This argument is used in giving a table of the results of the function. How would you extend your answer to deal with multiple-argument Boolean functions?

12.11 Using your answer to the previous question, or otherwise, describe how you would make Bool -> Bool an instance of the class Show. (Note, however, that this will *not* be legitimate Haskell, since Bool -> Bool is not of the right form for an instance declaration.)

(12.5) Types and classes

This section discusses the relationship between Haskell type classes and the classes of object-oriented programming; it can be omitted on first reading.

The type system of Haskell can be seen as giving monomorphic types to functions. Polymorphic types like

```
show :: Show a => a -> String
```

which involve type classes can be seen as shorthand for collections of typings, such as

```
show :: Bool -> String
show :: Char -> String
```

for each type Bool, Char, ... belonging to the class.

In Haskell a class is a collection of types. Other languages such as C++ make a type and a class the same thing. Under that approach, introducing the class of visible objects would effectively give us a type[2] ShowType. This class would be characterized by having the function

```
show :: ShowType -> String
```

in its interface. The class ShowType would have Bool and Char among its sub-classes (or sub-types). This would allow us to write values like

---

[2] In C++ teminology this would be an abstract base class, with Bool etc. inheriting and being forced to implement the operations of that class.

```
[True,'N',False] :: [ShowType]
```

Moreover, to convert such a list to a `String` we could write

```
concat . map show :: [ShowType] -> String
```

At different items of the list we use *different* versions of the show function; on the first we use the `Bool` function, on the second the `Char` function and so forth. This so-called **dynamic binding** is a powerful feature of many object-oriented languages, including C++, but it is not a feature of Haskell 98; an extension which would allow dynamic binding is described in Läufer (1996).

Returning to our example, what is the type of `concat . map show` in Haskell? It is not hard to see that it is

```
Show a => [a] -> [Char]
```

so that it can be applied to elements of `[Bool]`, `[Char]` and so on, but not to heterogeneous lists like `[True,'N',False]` which are not legitimately typed in Haskell.

Java allows users to define interfaces, which consist of a signature. A part of a class definition can say which interfaces the class implements. This is very like the way in which Haskell types are made instances of type classes, except that in Haskell it is not necessary to make the instance declaration a part of the type definition itself. This has the effect of allowing *post hoc* extensions to the operations supported by a type, in a way which is not possible for a class in Java.

Summary

This chapter has shown how names such as `read` and `show` and operators like `+` can be overloaded to have different definitions at different types. The mechanism which enables this is the system of Haskell classes. A `class` definition contains a signature which contains the names and types of operations which must be supplied if a type is to be a member of the class. For a particular type, the function definitions are contained in an `instance` declaration.

In giving the type of a function, or introducing a class or an instance, we can supply a context, which constrains the type variables occurring. Examples include

```
member   :: Eq a => [a] -> a -> Bool
instance   Eq a => Eq [a] where ....
class      Eq a => Ord a  where ....
```

In the examples, it can be seen that `member` can only be used over types in the class Eq. Lists of a can be given an equality, provided that a itself can; types in the class Ord must already be in the class Eq.

After giving examples of the various mechanisms, we looked at the classes in the standard preludes of Haskell, and concluded with a discussion of the relationship between the type classes of Haskell and the classes of object-oriented programming. In the final part of the book we shall revisit classes and see how they are used to structure larger-scale systems.

Chapter 13

Checking types

Every value in Haskell has a defined type, which might be monomorphic, polymorphic, or involve one or more type class constraints in a context. For example,

```
'w'   :: Char
flip  :: (a -> b -> c) -> (b -> a -> c)
elem  :: Eq a => a -> [a] -> Bool
```

Strong typing means that we can **check** whether or not expressions we wish to evaluate or definitions we wish to use obey the typing rules of the language without any evaluation taking place. The benefit of this is obvious: we can catch a whole lot of errors before we run a program.

Beyond this, types are a valuable form of program documentation: when we look at a definition, the first relevant piece of information about it is its type, since this explains how it is to be used. In the case of a function, we can read off from its type the types of values to which it has to be applied, and also the type of the result of applying it.

Types are also useful in locating functions in a library. Suppose we want to define a function to remove the duplicate elements from a list, transforming [2,3,2,1,3,4] to [2,3,1,4], for instance. Such a function will have type

```
(Eq a) => [a] -> [a]
```

A search of the standard prelude `Prelude.hs` and the library `List.hs` reveals just one function of this type, namely `nub`, which has exactly the effect we seek. Plainly in practice there might be multiple matches (or missed matches because of the choice of parameter order) but nonetheless the types provide a valuable `handle' on the functions in a library.

In this chapter we give an informal overview of the way in which types are checked. We start by looking at how type checking works in a monomorphic framework, in which every properly typed expression has a single type. Building on this, we then look at the polymorphic case, and see that it can be understood by looking at the **constraints** put on the type of an expression by the way that the expression is constructed. Crucial to this is the notion of **unification**, through which constraints are combined. We conclude the chapter by looking at the **contexts** which contain information about the class membership of type variables, and which thus manage **overloading**.

13.1 Monomorphic type checking

In this section we look at how type checking works in a monomorphic setting, without polymorphism or overloading. The main focus here is type-checking function applications. The simplified picture we see here prepares us for Haskell type checking in general, which is examined in the section after this. When discussing polymorphic operations in this section we will use monomorphic instances, indicated by a type subscript or subscripts. For example, we write

```
+_Int :: Int -> Int -> Int
length_Char :: [Char] -> Int
```

We look first at the way that we type-check expressions, and then look at how definitions are type-checked.

Expressions

In general, an expression is either a literal, a variable or a constant or it is built up by applying a function to some arguments, which are themselves expressions.

The case of function applications includes rather more than we might at first expect. For example, we can see list expressions like [True,False] as the result of applying the constructor function, ':', thus: True:[False]. Also, operators and the if ... then ... else construct act in exactly the same way as functions, albeit with a different syntax.

The rule for type checking a function application is set out in the following diagram, where we see that a function of type s -> t must be applied to an argument of type s. A properly typed application results in an expression of type t.

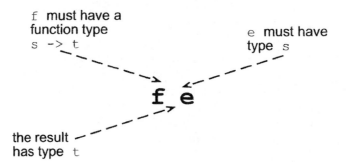

We now look at two examples. First we take ord 'c' $+_{Int}$ 3_{Int}, a correctly typed expression of type Int,

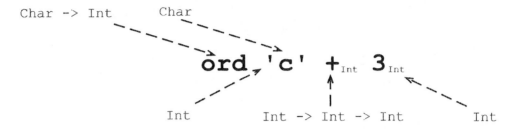

The application of ord to 'c' results in an expression of type Int. The second argument to $+_{Int}$ is also an Int, so the application of $+_{Int}$ is correctly typed, and gives a result of type Int.

If we modify the example to ord 'c' $+_{Int}$ False, we now see a type error, since a Boolean argument, False, is presented to an operator expecting Int arguments, $+_{Int}$.

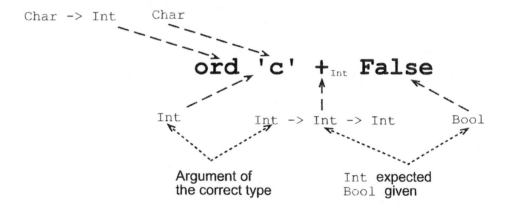

Argument of   Int expected
the correct type   Bool given

Function definitions

In type-checking a monomorphic function definition such as

$$f :: t_1 \rightarrow t_2 \rightarrow \ldots \rightarrow t_k \rightarrow t \qquad \text{(fdef)}$$

```
f p₁ p₂ ··· pₖ
    | g₁      = e₁
    | g₂      = e₂
    ...
    | g₁      = e₁
```

we need to check three things.

- Each of the guards g_i must be of type Bool.
- The value e_i returned in each clause must be of type t.
- The pattern p_j must be consistent with type of that argument, namely t_j.

A pattern is **consistent** with a type if it will match (some) elements of the type. We now look at the various cases. A variable is consistent with any type; a literal is consistent with its type. A pattern (p:q) is consistent with the type [t] if p is consistent with t and q is consistent with [t]. For example, (0:xs) is consistent with the type [Int], and (x:xs) is consistent with any type of lists. The other cases of the definition are similar.

This concludes our discussion of type checking in the monomorphic case; we turn to polymorphism next.

<hr>

Exercise

13.1 Predict the type errors you would obtain by defining the following functions

```
f n      = 37+n
f True   = 34

g 0 = 37
g n = True

h x
   | x>0          = True
   | otherwise    = 37

k x = 34
k 0 = 35
```

Check your answers by typing each definition into a Haskell script, and loading the script into Hugs. Remember that you can use :type to give the type of an expression.

13.2 Polymorphic type checking

In a monomorphic situation, an expression is either well typed, and has a single type, or is not well typed and has none. In a polymorphic language like Haskell, the situation is more complicated, since a polymorphic object is precisely one which has many types.

In this section we first re-examine what is meant by polymorphism, before explaining type checking by means of **constraint satisfaction**. Central to this is the notion of **unification**, by which we find the types simultaneously satisfying two type constraints.

Polymorphism

We are familiar with functions like

```
length :: [a] -> Int
```
(length)

whose types are polymorphic, but how should we understand the type variable a in this type? We can see (length) as shorthand for saying that length has a **set** of types,

```
[Int] -> Int
[(Bool,Char)] -> Int
   . . .
```

in fact containing all the types [t] -> Int where t is a **monotype**, that is a type not containing type variables.

When we apply length we need to determine at which of these types length is being used. For example, when we write

```
length ['c','d']
```

we can see that length is being applied to a list of Char, and so we are using length at type [Char] -> Int.

Constraints

How can we explain what is going on here in general? We can see different parts of an expression as putting different **constraints** on its type. Under this interpretation, type checking becomes a matter of working out whether we can find types which meet the constraints. We have seen some informal examples of this when we discussed the types of map and filter in Section 9.2. We consider some further examples now.

Examples

1. Consider the definition

```
f (x,y) = (x , ['a' .. y])
```

The argument of f is a pair, and we consider separately what constraints there are on the types of x and y. x is completely unconstrained, as it is returned as the first half of a pair. On the other hand, y is used within the expression ['a' .. y], which denotes a range within an enumerated type, starting at the character 'a'. This forces y to have the type Char, and gives the type for f:

```
f :: (a , Char) -> (a , [Char])
```

2. Now we examine the definition

```
g (m,zs) = m + length zs
```

What constraints are placed on the types of m and zs in this definition? We can see that m is added to something, so m must have a numeric type – which one it is remains to be seen. The other argument of the addition is length zs, which tells us two things.

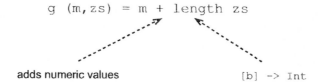

First, we see that `zs` will have to be of type `[b]`, and also that the result is an `Int`. This forces + to be used at `Int`, and so forces `m` to have type `Int`, giving the result

```
g :: (Int , [b]) -> Int
```

3. We now consider the composition of the last two examples,

```
h = g . f
```

In a composition `g . f`, the output of `f` becomes the input of `g`,

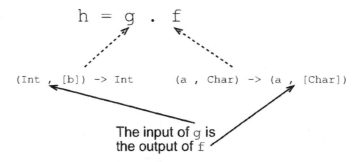

Here we should recall the meaning of types which involve type variables; we can see them as shorthand for sets of types. The output of `f` is described by `(a , [Char])`, and the input of `g` by `(Int , [b])`. We therefore have to look for types which meet both these descriptions. We will now look at this general topic, returning to the example in the course of this dicussion.

Unification

How are we to describe the types which meet the two descriptions `(a , [Char])` and `(Int , [b])`?

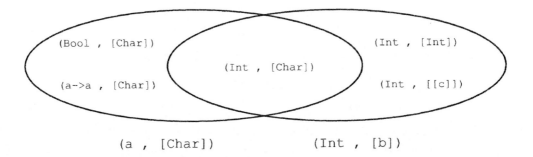

As sets of types, we look for the intersection of the sets given by (a , [Char]) and (Int , [b]). How can we work out a description of this intersection? Before we do this, we revise and introduce some terminology.

Recall that an **instance** of a type is given by replacing a type variable or variables by type expressions. A type expression is a common instance of two type expressions if it is an instance of each expression. The most general common instance of two expressions is a common instance mgci with the property that every other common instance is an instance of mgci.

Now we can describe the intersection of the sets given by two type expressions. It is called the **unification** of the two, which is the **most general common instance** of the two type expressions.

Examples

3 (contd)   In this example, we have

with a single type resulting. This gives the function h the following type

h :: (Int , [Char]) -> Int

and this completes the discussion of example 3.

Unification need not result in a monotype. In the example of unifying the types (a, [a]) and ([b],c),

the result is the type ([b],[[b]]). This is because the expression (a,[a]) constrains the type to have in its second component a list of elements of the first component type, while the expression ([b],c) constrains its first component to be a list. Thus satisfying the two gives the type ([b],[[b]]).

In the last example, note that there are many common instances of the two type expressions, including ([Bool],[[Bool]]) and ([[c]],[[[c]]]), but neither of these examples is the unifier, since ([b],[[b]]) is not an instance of either of them. On the other hand, they are each instances of ([b],[[b]]), as it is the most general common instance, and so the unifier of the two type expressions.

Not every pair of types can be unified: consider the case of [Int] -> [Int] and a -> [a].

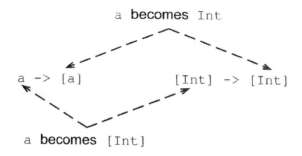

Unifying the argument types requires a to become [Int], while unifying the result types requires a to become Int; clearly these constraints are inconsistent, and so the unification fails.

Type-checking expressions

As we saw in Section 13.1, function application is central to expression formation. This means that type checking also hinges on function applications.

Type-checking polymorphic function application

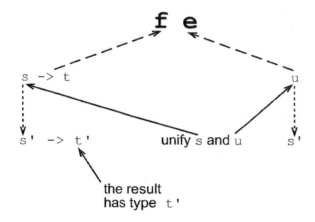

In applying a function f :: s -> t to an argument e :: u we do not require that s and u are equal, but instead that they are unifiable to a type s', say, giving e :: s' and f :: s' -> t'; the result in that case is of type t'. As an example, consider the application map ord where

```
map :: (a -> b) -> [a] -> [b]
ord :: Char -> Int
```

Unifying a -> b and Char -> Int results in a becoming Char and b becoming Int; this gives

```
map :: (Char -> Int) -> [Char] -> [Int]
```

and so

```
map ord :: [Char] -> [Int]
```

As in the monomorphic case, we can use this discussion of typing and function application in explaining type checking all aspects of expressions. We now look at another example, before examining a more technical aspect of type checking.

Example

4. `foldr` again

In Section 9.3 we introduced the `foldr` function

```
foldr f s []     = s                        (foldr.1)
foldr f s (x:xs) = f x (foldr f s xs)       (foldr.2)
```

which could be used to fold an operator into a list, as in

```
foldr (+) 0 [2,3,1] = 2+(3+(1+0))
```

so that it appears as if `foldr` has the type given by

```
foldr :: (a -> a -> a) -> a -> [a] -> a
```

In fact, the most general type of `foldr` is more general than this. Suppose that the starting value has type b and the elements of the list are of type a

```
foldr :: (... -> ... -> ...) -> b -> [a] -> ...
```

Then we can picture the definition thus:

```
                                   b
                                  /
                                 /
                                /
                               ↓
      foldr f s []       = s  / a
                            / /        b
                           ↓ /   ------------------
      foldr f s (x:xs) = f x (foldr f s xs)
                         ------------------------
                                   b
```

s is the result of the first equation, and so the result type of the `foldr` function itself will be b, the type of s

```
foldr :: (... -> ... -> ...) -> b -> [a] -> b
```

In the second equation, f is applied to x as first argument, giving

```
foldr :: (a -> ... -> ...) -> b -> [a] -> b
```

The second argument of f is the result of a `foldr`, and so of type b,

```
foldr :: (a -> b -> ...) -> b -> [a] -> b
```

Finally, the result of the second equation is an application of f; this result must have the same result type as the foldr itself, b.

```
foldr :: (a -> b -> b) -> b -> [a] -> b
```

With this insight about the type of foldr we were able to see that foldr could be used to define another whole cohort of list functions, such as an insertion sort,

```
iSort :: Ord a => [a] -> [a]
iSort = foldr ins []
```

in which ins has the type Ord a => a -> [a] -> [a].

Polymorphic definitions and variables

Here we examine a more technical aspect of how type checking works over polymorphic definitions; it may be omitted on first reading.

Functions and constants can be used at different types in the same expression. A simple instance is

```
expr = length ([]++[True]) + length ([]++[2,3,4])        (expr)
```

The first occurrence of [] is at [Int], whilst the second is at [Bool]. This is completely legitimate, and is one of the advantages of a polymorphic definition. Now suppose that we replace the [] by a variable, and define

```
funny xs = length (xs++[True]) + length (xs++[2,3,4])     (funny)
```

The variable xs is forced to have type [Bool] *and* type [Int]; it is forced to be polymorphic, in other words. This is not allowed in Haskell, as there is no way of expressing the type of funny. It might be thought that

```
funny :: [a] -> Int
```

was a correct type, but this would mean that funny would have all the instance types

```
funny :: [Int] -> Int
funny :: [[Char]] -> Int
    ...
```

which it clearly does not. We conclude that constants and variables are treated differently: constants may very well appear at different incompatible types in the same expression, variables cannot.

What is the significance of disallowing the definition (funny) but allowing the definition (expr)? Taking (expr) first, we have a polymorphic definition of the form [] :: [a] and an expression in which [] occurs twice; the first occurrence is at [Bool], the second at [Int]. To allow these independent uses to occur, we type-check each use of a polymorphic definition with different type variables, so that a constraint on one use does not affect any of the others.

On the other hand, how is the definition of (funny) disallowed? When we type check the use of a variable we will not treat each instance as being of an independent type. Suppose we begin with no constraint on xs, so xs::t, say. The first occurrence of xs forces xs::[Bool], the second requires xs::[Int]; these two constraints cannot be satisfied simultaneously, and thus the definition (funny) fails to type check.

The crucial point to remember from this example is that the definition of a function is not permitted to force any of its arguments to be polymorphic.

Function definitions

In type checking a function definition like (fdef) on page 229 above we have to obey rules similar to the monomorphic case.

- Each of the guards g_i must be of type Bool.
- The value e_i returned in each clause must have a type s_i which is at least as general as t; that is, s_i must have t as an instance.
- The pattern p_j must be **consistent** with type of that argument, namely t_j.

We take up a final aspect of type checking – the impact of type classes – in the next section.

Exercises

13.2 Do the following pairs of types – listed vertically – unify? If so, give a most general unifier for them; if not, explain why they fail to unify.

```
(Int -> b)              (Int,a,a)
(a -> Bool)             (a,a,[Bool])
```

13.3 Show that we can unify (a,[a]) with (b,c) to give (Bool,[Bool]).

13.4 Can the function

```
f :: (a,[a]) -> b
```

be applied to the arguments (2,[3]), (2,[]) and (2,[True]); if so, what are the types of the results? Explain your answers.

13.5 Repeat the previous question for the function

```
f :: (a,[a]) -> a
```

Explain your answers.

13.6 Give the type of f [] [] if f has type

```
f :: [a] -> [b] -> a -> b
```

What is the type of the function h given by the definition

```
h x = f x x ?
```

13.7 How can you use the Haskell system to check whether two type expressions are unifiable, and if so what is their unification? Hint: you can make dummy definitions in Haskell in which the defined value, zircon say, is equated with itself:

```
zircon = zircon
```

Values defined like this can be declared to have any type you wish.

13.8 [Harder] Recalling the definitions of curry and uncurry from Section 10.7, what are the types of

```
curry id
uncurry id
curry (curry id)
uncurry (uncurry id)
uncurry curry
```

Explain why the following expressions do not type-check:

```
curry uncurry
curry curry
```

13.9 [Harder] Give an *algorithm* which decides whether two type expressions are unifiable. If they are, your algorithm should return a most general unifying substitution; if not, it should give some explanation of why the unification fails.

13.3 Type checking and classes

Classes in Haskell restrict the use of some functions, such as ==, to types in the class over which they are defined, in this case Eq. These restrictions are apparent in the **contexts** which appear in some types. For instance, if we define

```
member []     y = False
member (x:xs) y = (x==y) || member xs y
```

its type will be

```
Eq a => [a] -> a -> Bool
```

because x and y of type a are compared for equality in the definition, thus forcing the type a to belong to the equality class Eq.

This section explores the way in which type checking takes place when overloading is involved; the material is presented informally, by means of an example.

Suppose we are to apply the function member to an expression e, whose type is

```
Ord b => [[b]]
```

Informally, e is a list of lists of objects, which belong to a type which carries an ordering. In the absence of the contexts we would unify the type expressions, giving

```
member :: [[b]] -> [b] -> Bool          e :: [[b]]
```

and so giving the application member e the type [b] -> Bool. We do the same here, but we also apply the unification to the contexts, producing the context

```
(Eq [b] , Ord b)                                            (ctx.1)
```

Now, we check and simplify the context.

- The requirements in a context can only apply to type variables, so we need to eliminate requirements like Eq [b]. The only way these can be eliminated is to use the instance declarations. In this case the built-in instance declaration

```
instance Eq a => Eq [a] where ....
```

  allows us to replace the requirement Eq [b] with Eq b in (ctx.1), giving the new context

```
(Eq b , Ord b)                                              (ctx.2)
```

  We repeat this process until no more instances apply.

  If we fail to reduce all the requirements to ones involving a type variable, the application fails, and an error message would be generated. This happens if we apply member to [id];

```
ERROR: a -> a is not an instance of class "Eq"
```

  since id is a function, whose type is not it the class Eq.

- We then simplify the context using the class definitions. In our example we have both Eq b and Ord b, but recall that

```
class Eq a => Ord a where ...
```

  so that any instance of Ord is automatically an instance of Eq; this means that we can simplify (ctx.2) to

```
Ord b
```

This is repeated until no further simplifications result.

For our example, we thus have the type

```
member e :: Ord b => [b] -> Bool
```

This three-stage process of unification, checking (with instances) and simplification is the general pattern for type checking with contexts in Haskell.

Finally, we should explain how contexts are introduced into the types of the language. They originate in types for the functions in class declarations, so that, for instance, we have

```
toString :: Visible a => a -> String
size     :: Visible a => a -> Int
```

The type checking of functions which use these overloaded functions will propagate and combine the contexts as we have seen above.

We have seen informally how the Haskell type system accommodates type checking for the overloaded names which belong to type classes. A more thorough overview of the technical aspects of this, including a discussion of the 'monomorphism restriction' which needs to be placed on certain polymorphic bindings, is to be found in the Haskell 98 report (Peyton Jones and Hughes 1998).

Exercises

13.10 Give the type of each of the individual conditional equations which follow, and discuss the type of the function which together they define.

```
merge (x:xs) (y:ys)
  | x<y          = x : merge xs (y:ys)
  | x==y         = x : merge xs ys
  | otherwise    = y : merge (x:xs) ys
merge (x:xs) []      = (x:xs)
merge []     (y:ys) = (y:ys)
merge []     []      = []
```

13.11 Define a polymorphic sorting function, and show how its type is derived from the type of the ordering relation

```
compare :: Ord a => a -> a -> Ordering
```

13.12 Investigate the types of the following numerical functions; you will find that the types refer to some of the built-in numeric classes.

```
mult x y = x*y
divide x = x 'div' 2
share x  = x / 2.0
```

Recall that these can be given more restrictive types, such as

```
divide :: Int -> Int
```

by explicitly asserting their types as above.

Summary

The chapter explained how type checking of expressions and definitions is performed in Haskell. Initially this was explored in the monomorphic case, and then expanded to deal with polymorphism. In that case we saw type checking as a process of extracting and consolidating constraints, the latter being given by unification of type expressions which contain type variables. We concluded by examining how to manage contexts in types, and thus how overloading is handled in the Haskell type system.

Algebraic types

So far in our discussion of Haskell we have been able to model entities using

- the base types, Int, Float, Bool and Char, and

- composite types: tuple types, $(t_1, t_2, \ldots, t_n)$; list types, $[t_1]$; and function types, $(t_1 \rightarrow t_2)$; where $t_1, \ldots, t_n$ are themselves types.

This gives a wide choice of types and we have seen quite complex structures, like an index for a document, represented by the appropriate combination of types: in the index example, [([Int],[Char])] was used.

However, there are other types which are difficult to model using the constructs we have seen so far. Examples include

- the type of months: January, ..., December;

- the type whose elements are either a number or a string: a house in a street will either have a number or a name, for instance;

- the type of trees, as illustrated in Figure 14.1.

All these types can be modelled by Haskell **algebraic** types, which form the subject of this chapter.

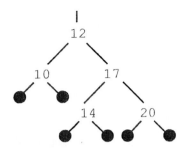

Figure 14.1   An example of a tree of integers.

(14.1) Introducing algebraic types

Algebraic data type definitions are introduced by the keyword data, followed by the name of the type, an equals sign and then the **constructors** of the type being defined. The name of the type and the names of constructors begin with capital letters.

We give a sequence of examples of increasing complexity, before discussing the general form of these type definitions.

Enumerated types

The simplest sort of algebraic type is defined by enumerating the elements of the type. For instance,

```
data Temp   = Cold | Hot
data Season = Spring | Summer | Autumn | Winter
```

introduces two types. The type Temp has two members, Cold and Hot, and Season has four members. More formally, Cold and Hot are called the **constructors** of the type Temp.

To define functions over these types we use pattern matching: we can match against either a literal or a variable. To describe the (British!) weather we might say

```
weather :: Season -> Temp
```

```
weather Summer = Hot
weather _      = Cold
```

Pattern matching is sequential; the first pattern to match an argument will be used. This means that the British weather is only hot in the summer, and it is cold the rest of the year. The built-in Boolean type is defined by

```
data Bool = False | True
```

and the type Ordering, used in the class Ord, by

```
data Ordering = LT | EQ | GT
```

As we have seen, pattern matching is used to define functions over algebraic types. We can use it to define equality over Temp, for instance,

```
Cold == Cold  = True
Hot  == Hot   = True
_    == _     = False
```

to put Temp into the equality class Eq.

It would be tiresome to have to give a definition of equality for every new type which we introduce, and so the Haskell system can be made to generate definitions of ==, ordering, enumeration and text functions automatically. We discuss the details of this at the end of this section, after looking at some more examples.

Product types

Instead of using a tuple we can define a type with a number of components, often called a **product** type, as an algebraic type. An example might be

```
data People = Person Name Age                          (People)
```

where Name is a synonym for String, and Age for Int, written thus:

```
type Name = String
type Age  = Int
```

The definition of People should be read as saying

> To construct an element of type People, you need to supply two values; one, st say, of type Name, and another, n say, of type Age. The element of People formed from them will be Person st n.

Example values of this type include

```
Person "Electric Aunt Jemima" 77
Person "Ronnie" 14
```

As before, functions are defined using pattern matching. A general element of type People has the form Person st n, and we can use this pattern on the left-hand side of a definition,

```
showPerson :: People -> String
showPerson (Person st n) = st ++ " -- " ++ show n
```

(recall that show gives a textual form of an Int, since Int belongs to the Show class). For instance,

```
showPerson (Person "Electric Aunt Jemima" 77)
 = "Electric Aunt Jemima -- 77"
```

In this example, the type has a single constructor, Person, which is **binary** because it takes two elements to form a value of type People. For the enumerated types Temp and Season the constructors are called **nullary** (or *0-ary*) as they take no arguments.

The constructors introduced by algebraic type definitions can be used just like functions, so that `Person st n` is the result of applying the function `Person` to the arguments `st` and `n`; we can interpret the definition (People) as giving the **type of the constructor**, here

```
Person :: Name -> Age -> People
```

An alternative definition of the type of people is given by the type synonym

```
type People = (Name,Age)
```

The advantages of using an algebraic type are threefold.

- Each object of the type carries an explicit **label** of the purpose of the element; in this case that it represents a person.
- It is not possible accidentally to treat an arbitrary pair consisting of a string and a number as a person; a person must be constructed using the `Person` constructor.
- The type will appear in any error messages due to mis-typing; a type synonym might be expanded out and so disappear from any type error messages.

There are also advantages of using a tuple type, with a synonym declaration.

- The elements are more compact, and so definitions will be shorter.
- Using a tuple, especially a pair, allows us to reuse many polymorphic functions such as `fst`, `snd` and `unzip` over tuple types; this will not be the case for the algebraic type.

In each system that we model we will have to choose between these alternatives: our decisions will depend exactly on how we use the products, and on the complexity of the system.

The approach here works equally well with unary constructors, so we might say

```
data Age = Years Int
```

whose elements are `Years 45` and so on. It is clear from a definition like this that 45 is here being used as an age in years, rather than some unrelated numerical quantity. The disadvantage is that we cannot use functions defined over `Int` directly over `Age`.

We can use the same name, for instance `Person`, for both the type and the constructor of a type, as in the definition

```
data Person = Person Name Age
```

We choose not to do this, as using the same name for two related but different objects can easily lead to confusion, but it is an idiom used by a number of Haskell programmers.

The examples of types given here are a special case of what we look at next.

Alternatives

A shape in a simple geometrical program is either a circle or a rectangle. These alternatives are given by the type

```
data Shape = Circle Float |                              (Shape)
             Rectangle Float Float
```

which says that there are two ways of building an element of Shape. One way is to supply the radius of a Circle; the other alternative is to give the sides of a Rectangle. Example objects of this type are

```
Circle 3.0
Rectangle 45.9 87.6
```

Pattern matching allows us to define functions by cases, as in

```
isRound :: Shape -> Bool
isRound (Circle _)      = True
isRound (Rectangle _ _) = False
```

and also lets us use the components of the elements:

```
area :: Shape -> Float
area (Circle r)      = pi*r*r
area (Rectangle h w) = h*w
```

Another way of reading the definition (Shape) is to say that there are two **constructor functions** for the type Shape, whose types are

```
Circle    :: Float -> Shape
Rectangle :: Float -> Float -> Shape
```

These functions are called constructor functions because the elements of the type are constructed by applying these functions.

Extensions of this type, to accommodate the position of an object, are discussed in the exercises at the end of this section.

The general form of algebraic type definitions

The general form of the algebraic type definitions which we have seen so far is

$$
\begin{aligned}
\text{data Typename} & \qquad\qquad\qquad\qquad \text{(Typename)}\\
= \text{Con}_1\ t_{11}\ & \cdots\ t_{1k_1}\ |\\
\text{Con}_2\ t_{21}\ & \cdots\ t_{2k_2}\ |\\
& \cdots\cdots\\
\text{Con}_n\ t_{n1}\ & \cdots\ t_{nk_n}
\end{aligned}
$$

Each Con_i is a constructor, followed by k_i types, where k_i is a non-negative integer which may be zero. We build elements of the type Typename by applying these constructor functions to arguments of the types given in the definition, so that

$$\text{Con}_i\ v_{i1}\ \cdots\ v_{ik_i}$$

will be a member of the type Typename if v_{ij} is in t_{ij} for j ranging from 1 to k_i.

Reading the constructors as functions, the definition (Typename) gives the constructors the following types

```
Con_i :: t_{i1} -> ... -> t_{ik_i} -> Typename
```

In the sections to come, we shall see two extensions of the definitions seen already.

- The types can be **recursive**; we can use the type we are defining, Typename, as (part of) any of the types t_{ij}. This gives us lists, trees and many other data structures.

- The Typename can be followed by one or more type variables which may be used on the right-hand side, making the definition **polymorphic**.

Recursive polymorphic types combine these two ideas, and this powerful mixture provides types which can be reused in many different situations – the built-in type of lists is an example which we have already seen. Other examples are given in the sections which follow.

Before we move on, it is worth contrasting type and data definitions. A synonym given by type is simply a shorthand, and so a synonym type can always be expanded out, and therefore removed from the program. On the other hand, a data definition creates a new type. Because synonyms are simply shorthand, a synonym definition cannot be recursive; data definitions can be and often are recursive, as we shall discover presently.

Deriving instances of classes

As we saw earlier, Haskell has a number of built-in classes including

- Eq, a class giving equality and inequality;

- Ord, built on Eq, giving an ordering over elements of a type;

- Enum, allowing the type to be enumerated, and so giving [n .. m]-style expressions over the type, and

- Show, allowing elements of the type to be turned into textual form, and Read, which allows values of the type to be read from strings.

When we introduce a new algebraic type, such as Temp or Shape, we might well expect to have equality, enumerations and so on. These can be supplied by the system if we ask for them, thus:

```
data Season = Spring | Summer | Autumn | Winter
             deriving (Eq,Ord,Enum,Show,Read)
```

```
data Shape  = Circle Float |
              Rectangle Float Float
              deriving (Eq,Ord,Show,Read)
```

We can thus compare seasons for equality and order, write expressions of the form

```
[Spring .. Autumn]
```

denoting the list

```
[Spring, Summer, Autumn]
```

and show values of the type. The same applies to Shape, except that we cannot enumerate shapes; being in Enum can only be derived for enumerated types such as Season.

We are not forced to use the derived definitions; we can give our own instances, so that, for example, all circles of negative radius are made equal. The definition of showPerson above could also form a model for making People an instance of the type class Show.

Exercises

14.1 Redefine the function weather :: Season -> Temp so that a guard or an if ... is used rather than pattern matching. Which of the definitions is preferable in your opinion?

14.2 Define the type of months as a Haskell algebraic type. Give a function which takes a month to its appropriate season – in doing this you might want to use the ordering on the type, which is derived as explained above.

14.3 What would be the weather function for New Zealand, which is on a similar latitude to Britain, but in the Southern Hemisphere? What would be the definition for Brazil, which is crossed by the Equator?

14.4 Define a function to give the length of the perimeter of a geometrical shape, of type Shape. What is the type of this function?

14.5 Add an extra constructor to Shape for triangles, and extend the functions isRound, area and perimeter to include triangles.

14.6 Define a function which decides whether a Shape is regular: a circle is regular, a square is a regular rectangle and being equilateral makes a triangle regular.

14.7 Investigate the derived definitions for Temp and Shape: what form do the orderings and the show functions take, for example?

14.8 Define == over Shape so that all circles of negative radius are equated. How would you treat rectangles with negative sides?

14.9 The type Shape takes no account of the position or orientation of a shape. After deciding how to represent points, how would you modify the original definition of Shape to contain the **centre** of each object? You can assume that rectangles lie with their sides parallel to the axes, thus:

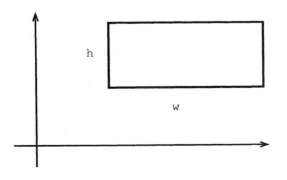

(Rectangle h w ...)

14.10 Calling the new shape type `NewShape`, define a function

```
move :: Float -> Float -> NewShape -> NewShape
```

which moves a shape by the two offsets given:

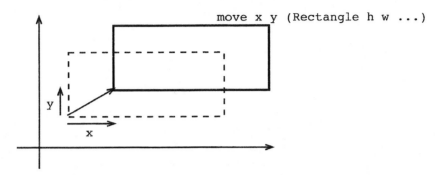

14.11 Define a function to test whether two `NewShapes` overlap.

14.12 Some houses have a number; others have a name. How would you implement the type of 'strings or numbers' used as a part of an address? Write a function which gives the textual form of one of these objects. Give a definition of a type of names and addresses using the type you have defined.

14.13 Reimplement the library database of Section 5.6 to use an algebraic type like `People` rather than a pair. Compare the two approaches to this example.

14.14 The library database of Section 5.6 is to be extended in the following ways.

- CDs and videos as well as books are available for loan.
- A record is kept of the authors of books as well as their titles. Similar information is kept about CDs, but not about videos.
- Each loan has a period: books one month, CDs one week and videos three days.

Explain how you would modify the types used to implement the database, and how the function types might be changed. The system should perform the following operations. For each case, give the types and definitions of the functions involved.

- Find all items on loan to a given person.
- Find all books, CDs or videos on loan to a particular person.
- Find all items in the database due back on or before a particular day, and the same information for any given person.
- Update the database with loans; the constant `today` can be assumed to contain today's date, in a format of your choice.

What other functions would have to be defined to make the system usable? Give their types, but not their definitions.

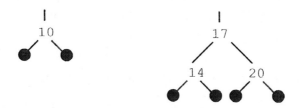

Figure 14.2 Two trees.

14.2 Recursive algebraic types

Types are often naturally described in terms of themselves. For instance, an integer expression is either a **literal** integer, like 347, or is given by combining two expressions using an arithmetic operator such as plus or minus, as in (3–1)+3.

```
data Expr = Lit Int |
            Add Expr Expr |
            Sub Expr Expr
```

Similarly, a tree is either nil or is given by combining a value and two sub-trees. For example, the number 12 and the trees in Figure 14.2 are assembled to give the tree in Figure 14.1. As a Haskell type we say

```
data NTree = NilT |
             Node Int NTree NTree
```

Finally, we have already used the type of lists: a list is either empty ([]) or is built from a head and a tail – another list – using the list constructor ' : '. Lists will provide a good guide to using recursive (and polymorphic) definitions. In particular they suggest how 'general' polymorphic higher-order functions over other algebraic types are defined, and how programs are verified. We now look at some examples in more detail.

Expressions

The type Expr gives a model of the simple numerical expressions discussed above. These might be used in implementing a simple numerical calculator, for instance.

```
data Expr = Lit Int |
            Add Expr Expr |
            Sub Expr Expr
```

Some examples are

```
    2                   Lit 2
    2+3                 Add (Lit 2) (Lit 3)
    (3-1)+3             Add (Sub (Lit 3) (Lit 1)) (Lit 3)
```

where the informal expressions are listed in the left-hand column, and their Expr forms in the right. Given an expression, we might want to evaluate it;

turn it into a string, which can then be printed;

estimate its size – count the operators, say.

Each of these functions will be defined in the same way, using **primitive recursion**. As the type is itself recursive, it is not a surprise that the functions which handle the type are also recursive. Also, the form of the recursive definitions follows the recursion in the type definition. For instance, to evaluate an operator expression we work out the values of the arguments and combine the results using the operator.

```
eval :: Expr -> Int

eval (Lit n)     = n
eval (Add e1 e2) = (eval e1) + (eval e2)
eval (Sub e1 e2) = (eval e1) - (eval e2)
```

Primitive recursive definitions have two parts:

At the non-recursive, *base* cases – (Lit n) here – the value is given outright.

At the recursive cases, the values of the function at the sub-expressions from which the expression is formed – eval e1 and eval e2 here – can be used in calculating the result.

The show function has a similar form

```
show :: Expr -> String

show (Lit n) = show n
show (Add e1 e2)
   = "(" ++ show e1 ++ "+" ++ show e2 ++ ")"
show (Sub e1 e2)
   = "(" ++ show e1 ++ "-" ++ show e2 ++ ")"
```

as does the function to calculate the number of operators in an expression; we leave this as an exercise. Other exercises at the end of the section look at a different representation of expressions for which a separate type is used to represent the different possible operators. Next, we look at another recursive algebraic type, but after that we return to Expr and give an example of a non-primitive-recursive definition of a function to rearrange expressions in a particular way.

Trees of integers

Trees of integers like that in Figure 14.1 can be modelled by the type

```
data NTree = NilT |
              Node Int NTree NTree
```

The null tree is given by NilT, and the trees in Figure 14.2 by

```
Node 10 NilT NilT
Node 17 (Node 14 NilT NilT) (Node 20 NilT NilT)
```

Definitions of many functions are primitive recursive. For instance,

```
sumTree,depth :: NTree -> Int

sumTree NilT            = 0
sumTree (Node n t1 t2) = n + sumTree t1 + sumTree t2

depth NilT              = 0
depth (Node n t1 t2)    = 1 + max (depth t1) (depth t2)
```

with, for example,

```
sumTree (Node 3 (Node 4 NilT NilT) NilT) = 7
depth   (Node 3 (Node 4 NilT NilT) NilT) = 2
```

As another example, take the problem of finding out how many times a number, p say, occurs in a tree. The primitive recursion suggests two cases, depending upon the tree.

- For a null tree, NilT, the answer must be zero.

- For a non-null tree, (Node n t1 t2), we can find out how many times p occurs in the sub-trees t1 and t2 by two recursive calls; we have to make a case split depending on whether p occurs at the particular node, that is depending on whether or not p==n.

The final definition is

```
occurs :: NTree -> Int -> Int

occurs NilT p = 0
occurs (Node n t1 t2) p
  | n==p          = 1 + occurs t1 p + occurs t2 p
  | otherwise     =     occurs t1 p + occurs t2 p
```

The exercises at the end of the section give a number of other examples of functions defined over trees using primitive recursion. We next look at a particular example where a different form of recursion is used.

Rearranging expressions

The next example shows a definition which uses a more general recursion than we have seen so far. After showing why the generality is necessary, we argue that the function we have defined is total: it will give a result on all well-defined expressions.

The operation of addition over the integers is associative, so that the way in which an expression is bracketed is irrelevant to its value. We can, therefore, decide to bracket expressions involving '+' in any way we choose. The aim here is to write a program to turn expressions into right bracketed form, as shown in the following table:

```
(2+3)+4                 2+(3+4)
((2+3)+4)+5             2+(3+(4+5))
((2-((6+7)+8))+4)+5     (2-(6+(7+8)))+(4+5)
```

What is the program to do? The main aim is to spot occurrences of

```
Add (Add e1 e2) e3
```
(AddL)

and to transform them to

```
Add e1 (Add e2 e3)
```
(AddR)

so a first attempt at the program might say

```
try (Add (Add e1 e2) e3)
  = Add (try e1) (Add (try e2) (try e3))
try ...
```

which is primitive recursive: on the right-hand side of their definition the function `try` is only used on sub-expressions of the argument. This function will have the effect of transforming (AddL) to (AddR), but unfortunately (AddExL) will be sent to (AddExR):

```
((2+3)+4)+5                                        (AddExL)
(2+3)+(4+5)                                        (AddExR)
```

The problem is that in transforming (AddL) to (AddR) we may produce another pattern we are looking for at the top level: this is precisely what happens when (AddExL) is transformed to (AddExR). We therefore have to call the function *again* on the result of the rearrangement

```
assoc :: Expr -> Expr

assoc (Add (Add e1 e2) e3)
  = assoc (Add e1 (Add e2 e3))
```
(Add.1)

The other cases in the definition make sure that the *parts* of an expression are rearranged as they should be.

```
assoc (Add e1 e2)
  = Add (assoc e1) (assoc e2)
assoc (Sub e1 e2)
  = Sub (assoc e1) (assoc e2)
assoc (Lit n)
  = Lit n
```
(Add.2)

The equation (Add.2) will only be applied to the cases where (Add.1) does not apply – this is when e1 is either a Sub or a Lit expression. This is always the case in pattern matching; the *first* applicable equation is used.

When we use primitive recursion we can be sure that the recursion will **terminate** to give an answer: the recursive calls are only made on smaller expressions and so, after a finite number of calls to the function, a base case will be reached.

The `assoc` function is more complicated, and we need a more subtle argument to see that the function will always give a result. The equation (Add.1) is the tricky one, but intuitively, we can see that some progress has been made – some of the 'weight' of the tree has moved from left to right. In particular, one addition symbol has swapped sides. None of the other equations moves a plus in the other direction, so that after applying (Add.1) a finite number of times, there will be no more exposed addition symbols at the top level of the left-hand side. This means that the recursion cannot go on indefinitely, and so the function always leads to a result.

Syntax: infix constructors

We have seen that functions can be written in infix form; this also applies to constructors. We can, for example, redefine the function `assoc` thus:

```
assoc ((e1 'Add' e2) 'Add' e3)
  = assoc (e1 'Add' (e2 'Add' e3))
  ...
```

using the infix form of the constructor, given by surrounding it with back-quotes.

When an expression like this is shown, it appears in prefix form, so that the expression (Lit 3) 'Add' (Lit 4) appears as

```
Add (Lit 3) (Lit 4)
```

In a `data` definition we can define Haskell operators which are themselves constructors. These constructors have the same syntax as operator symbols, except that their first character must be a ':', which is reminiscent of ':', itself an infix constructor. For our type of integer expressions, we might define

```
data Expr = Lit Int |
            Expr :+: Expr |
            Expr :-: Expr
```

When an expression involving operator constructors is printed, the constructors appear in the infix position, unlike the quoted constructors above.

It is left as an exercise to complete the redefinition of functions over `Expr` under this redefinition of the `Expr` type.

Mutual recursion

In describing one type, it is often useful to use others; these in turn may refer back to the original type: this gives a pair of **mutually recursive** types. A description of a person might include biographical details, which in turn might refer to other people. For instance:

```
data Person = Adult Name Address Biog |
              Child Name
data Biog   = Parent String [Person] |
              NonParent String
```

In the case of a parent, the biography contains some text, as well as a list of their children, as elements of the type Person.

Suppose that we want to define a function which shows information about a person as a string. Showing this information will require us to show some biographical information, which itself contains further information about people. We thus have two mutually recursive functions:

```
showPerson (Adult nm ad bio)
  = show nm ++ show ad ++ showBiog bio
  ...
showBiog (Parent st perList)
  = st ++ concat (map showPerson perList)
  ...
```

Exercises

14.15 Give calculations of

```
eval (Lit 67)
eval (Add (Sub (Lit 3) (Lit 1)) (Lit 3))
show (Add (Lit 67) (Lit (-34)))
```

14.16 Define the function

```
size :: Expr -> Int
```

which counts the number of operators in an expression.

14.17 Add the operations of multiplication and integer division to the type Expr, and redefine the functions eval, show and size to include these new cases. What does your definition of eval do when asked to perform a division by zero?

14.18 Instead of adding extra constructors to the Expr type, as in the previous question, it is possible to factor the definition thus:

```
data Expr = Lit Int |
            Op Ops Expr Expr

data Ops  = Add | Sub | Mul | Div
```

Show how the functions eval, show and size are defined for this type, and discuss the changes you have to make to your definitions if you add the extra operation Mod for remainder on integer division.

14.19 Give line-by-line calculations of

```
sumTree (Node 3 (Node 4 NilT NilT) NilT)
depth   (Node 3 (Node 4 NilT NilT) NilT)
```

14.20 Complete the redefinition of functions over Expr after it has been defined using the infix constructors :+: and :-:.

14.21 Define functions to return the left- and right-hand sub-trees of an NTree.

14.22 Define a function to decide whether a number is an element of an NTree.

14.23 Define functions to find the maximum and minimum values held in an NTree.

14.24 A tree is reflected by swapping left and right sub-trees, recursively. Define a function to reflect an NTree. What is the result of reflecting twice, reflect . reflect?

14.25 Define functions

```
collapse, sort :: NTree -> [Int]
```

which turn a tree into a list. The function collapse should enumerate the left sub-tree, then the value at the node and finally the right sub-tree; sort should sort the elements in ascending order. For instance,

```
collapse (Node 3 (Node 4 NilT NilT) NilT) = [4,3]
sort     (Node 3 (Node 4 NilT NilT) NilT) = [3,4]
```

14.26 Complete the definitions of showPerson and showBiog which were left incomplete in the text.

14.27 It is possible to extend the type Expr so that it contains *conditional* expressions, If b e1 e2, where e1 and e2 are expressions, and b is a Boolean expression, a member of the type BExp,

```
data Expr = Lit Int |
            Op Ops Expr Expr |
            If BExp Expr Expr
```

The expression

```
If b e1 e2
```

has the value of e1 if b has the value True and otherwise it has the value of e2.

```
data BExp = BoolLit Bool |
            And BExp BExp |
            Not BExp |
            Equal Expr Expr |
            Greater Expr Expr
```

The five clauses here give

      Boolean literals, `BoolLit True` and `BoolLit False`.

      The conjunction of two expressions; it is `True` if both sub-expressions have the value `True`.

      The negation of an expression. `Not be` has value `True` if `be` has the value `False`.

      `Equal e1 e2` is `True` when the two numerical expressions have equal values.

      `Greater e1 e2` is `True` when the numerical expression `e1` has a larger value then `e2`.

Define the functions

```
eval  :: Expr -> Int
bEval :: BExpr -> Bool
```

by mutual recursion, and extend the function `show` to show the redefined type of expressions.

(14.3) Polymorphic algebraic types

Algebraic type definitions can contain the type variables a, b and so on, defining polymorphic types. The definitions are as before, with the type variables used in the definition appearing after the type name on the left-hand side of the definition. A simple example is

```
data Pairs a = Pr a a
```

and example elements of the type are

```
Pr 2 3     :: Pairs Int
Pr [] [3] :: Pairs [Int]
Pr [] []  :: Pairs [a]
```

A function to test the equality of the two halves of a pair is given by

```
equalPair :: Eq a => Pairs a -> Bool
equalPair (Pr x y) = (x==y)
```

The remainder of this section explores a sequence of further examples.

Lists

The built-in type of lists can be given by a definition like

```
data List a = NilList | Cons a (List a)
               deriving (Eq,Ord,Show,Read)
```

where the syntax [a], [] and ':' is used for `List a`, `NilList` and 'Cons'. Because of this, the type of lists forms a useful paradigm for recursive polymorphic types. In particular, we can see the possibility of defining useful families of functions over such types, and the way in which program verification can proceed by induction over the structure of a type.

Binary trees

The trees of Section 14.2 carry numbers at each node; there is nothing special about numbers, and we can equally well say that they have elements of an arbitrary type at the nodes:

```
data Tree a = Nil | Node a (Tree a) (Tree a)
             deriving (Eq,Ord,Show,Read)
```

The definitions of depth and occurs carry over unchanged:

```
depth :: Tree a -> Int
depth Nil           = 0
depth (Node n t1 t2) = 1 + max (depth t1) (depth t2)
```

as do many of the functions defined in the exercises at the end of Section 14.2. One of these is the function collapsing a tree into a list. This is done by visiting the elements of the tree 'inorder', that is visiting first the left sub-tree, then the node itself, then the right sub-tree, thus:

```
collapse :: Tree a -> [a]
collapse Nil = []
collapse (Node x t1 t2)
  = collapse t1 ++ [x] ++ collapse t2
```

For example,

```
collapse (Node 12
               (Node 34 Nil Nil)
               (Node 3 (Node 17 Nil Nil) Nil))
  = [34,12,17,3]
```

Various higher-order functions are definable, also,

```
mapTree :: (a -> b) -> Tree a -> Tree b
mapTree f Nil = Nil
mapTree f (Node x t1 t2)
  = Node (f x) (mapTree f t1) (mapTree f t2)
```

We shall return to trees in Section 16.7, where particular 'search' trees form a case study.

The union type, Either

Type definitions can take more than one parameter. We saw earlier the example of the type whose elements were either a name or a number. In general we can form a type whose elements come either from a or from b:

```
data Either a b = Left a | Right b
                 deriving (Eq,Ord,Read,Show)
```

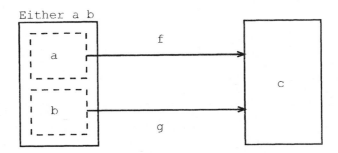

Figure 14.3   Joining together functions.

Members of the 'union' or 'sum' type are (Left x), with x::a, and (Right y) with y::b. The 'name or number' type is given by Either String Int and

```
Left "Duke of Prunes" :: Either String Int
Right 33312           :: Either String Int
```

We can tell whether an element is in the first half of the union by

```
isLeft :: Either a b -> Bool
isLeft (Left _)  = True
isLeft (Right _) = False
```

To define a function from Either a b to Int, say, we have to deal with two cases,

```
fun :: Either a b -> Int
fun (Left x)  = ... x ...
fun (Right y) = ... y ...
```

In the first case, the right-hand side takes x to an Int, so is given by a function from a to Int; in the second case y is taken to an Int, thus being given by a function from b to Int.

Guided by this, we can give a higher-order function which *joins together* two functions defined on a and b to a function on Either a b. The definition follows, and is illustrated in Figure 14.3.

```
either :: (a -> c) -> (b -> c) -> Either a b -> c

either f g (Left x)  = f x
either f g (Right y) = g y
```

If we have a function f::a -> c and we wish to apply it to an element of Either a b, there is a problem: what do we do if the element is in the right-hand side of the Either type? A simple answer is to raise an error

```
applyLeft :: (a -> c) -> Either a b -> c
applyLeft f (Left x)  = f x
applyLeft f (Right _) = error "applyLeft applied to Right"
```

but in the next section we shall explore other ways of handling errors in more detail.

14.28 Investigate which of the functions over trees discussed in the exercises of Section 14.2 can be made polymorphic.

14.29 Define a function `twist` which swaps the order of a union

```
twist :: Either a b -> Either b a
```

What is the effect of (`twist` . `twist`)?

14.30 How would you define `applyLeft` using the function `either`?

14.31 Show that any function of type `a -> b` can be transformed into functions of type

```
a -> Either b c
a -> Either c b
```

14.32 How could you generalize `either` to `join` so that it has type

```
join :: (a -> c) -> (b -> d) -> Either a b -> Either c d
```

You might find the answer to the previous exercise useful here, if you want to define `join` using `either`.

The trees defined in the text are *binary*: each non-nil tree has exactly two sub-trees. We can instead define general trees with an arbitrary list of sub-trees, thus:

```
data GTree a = Leaf a | Gnode [GTree a]
```

The exercises which follow concern these trees.

14.33 Define functions

- to count the number of leaves in a `GTree`;
- to find the depth of a `GTree`;
- to sum a numeric `GTree Int`;
- to find whether an element appears in a `GTree`;
- to map a function over the elements at the leaves of a `GTree`; and
- to flatten a `GTree` to a list.

14.34 How is the completely empty tree represented as a `GTree`?

14.4) Case study: program errors

How should a program deal with a situation which ought not to occur? Examples of such situations include

- attempts to divide by zero, to take the square root of a negative number, and other arithmetical transgressions;

- attempts to take the head of an empty list – this is a special case of a definition over an algebraic type from which one case (here the empty list) is absent.

This section examines the problem, giving three approaches of increasing sophistication. The simplest method is to stop computation and to report the source of the problem. This is indeed what the Haskell system does in the cases listed above, and we can do this in functions we define ourselves using the `error` function,

```
error :: String -> a
```

An attempt to evaluate the expression `error "Circle with negative radius"` results in the message

```
Program error: Circle with negative radius
```

being printed and computation stopping.

The problem with this approach is that all the useful information in the computation is lost; instead of this, the error can be dealt with in some way *without* stopping computation completely. Two approaches suggest themselves, and we look at them in turn now.

Dummy values

The function `tail` is supposed to give the tail of a list, and it gives an error message on an empty list:

```
tail :: [a] -> [a]
tail (_:xs) = xs
tail []     = error "PreludeList.tail: empty list"
```

We could redefine it to say

```
tl :: [a] -> [a]
tl (_:xs) = xs
tl []     = []
```

Now, an attempt to take the tail of *any* list will succeed. In a similar way we could say

```
divide :: Int -> Int -> Int
divide n m
   | (m /= 0)   = n 'div' m
   | otherwise  = 0
```

so that division by zero gives some answer. For `tl` and `divide` there have been obvious choices about what the value in the 'error' case should be; for `head` there is not, and instead we can supply an extra parameter to `head`, which is to be used in the case of the list being empty.

```
hd :: a -> [a] -> a
hd y (x:_) = x
hd y []    = y
```

This approach is completely general; if a function `f` (of one argument, say) usually raises an error when `cond` is `True`, we can define a new function

```
fErr y x
  | cond        = y
  | otherwise   = f x
```

This approach works well in many cases; the only drawback is that we have no way of telling when an error has occurred, since we may get the result `y` from either the error or the 'normal' case. Alternatively we can use an error type to trap and process errors; this we look at now.

Error types

The previous approach works by returning a dummy value when an error has occurred. Why not instead return an error *value* as a result? We define the type

```
data Maybe a = Nothing | Just a
                deriving (Eq,Ord,Read,Show)
```

which is effectively the type a with an extra value `Nothing` added. We can now define a division function `errDiv` thus

```
errDiv :: Int -> Int -> Maybe Int
errDiv n m
  | (m /= 0)    = Just (n 'div' m)
  | otherwise   = Nothing
```

and in the general case, where `f` gives an error when `cond` holds,

```
fErr x
  | cond        = Nothing
  | otherwise   = Just (f x)
```

The results of these functions are now not of the original output type, a say, but of type `Maybe a`. These `Maybe` types allow us to **raise** an error, potentially. We can do two things with a potential error which has been raised

- we can *transmit* the error through a function, the effect of `mapMaybe`;

- we can *trap* an error, the role of `maybe`.

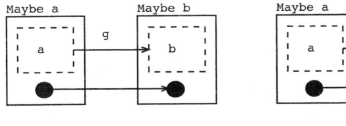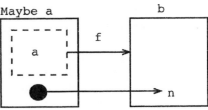

mapMaybe g   maybe n f

Figure 14.4 Error-handling functions.

These two operations are illustrated in Figure 14.4, and we define them now.

The function mapMaybe transmits an error value though the application of the function g. Suppose that g is a function of type a -> b, and that we are to lift it to operate on the type Maybe a. In the case of an argument Just x, g can be applied to the x to give a result, g x, of type b; this is put into Maybe b by applying the constructor function Just. On the other hand, if Nothing is the argument then Nothing is the result.

```
mapMaybe :: (a -> b) -> Maybe a -> Maybe b

mapMaybe g Nothing  = Nothing
mapMaybe g (Just x) = Just (g x)
```

In trapping an error, we aim to return a result of type b, from an input of type Maybe a; we have two cases to deal with

- in the Just case, we apply a function from a to b;
- in the Nothing case, we have to give the value of type b which is to be returned. (This is rather like the value we supplied to hd earlier.)

The higher-order function which achieves this is maybe, whose arguments n and f are used in the Nothing and Just cases respectively.

```
maybe :: b -> (a -> b) -> Maybe a -> b

maybe n f Nothing  = n
maybe n f (Just x) = f x
```

We can see the functions mapMaybe and maybe in action in the examples which follow. In the first, a division by zero leads to a Nothing which passes through the lifting to be trapped – 56 is therefore returned:

```
maybe 56 (1+) (mapMaybe (*3) (errDiv 9 0))
= maybe 56 (1+) (mapMaybe (*3) Nothing)
= maybe 56 (1+) Nothing
= 56
```

In the second, a normal division returns a Just 9. This is multiplied by three, and the maybe at the outer level adds one and removes the Just:

```
maybe 56 (1+) (mapMaybe (*3) (errDiv 9 1))
= maybe 56 (1+) (mapMaybe (*3) (Just 9))
= maybe 56 (1+) (Just 27)
= 1 + 27
= 28
```

The advantage of the approach discussed here is that we can first define the system without error handling, and afterwards add the error handling, using the mapMaybe and maybe functions together with the modified functions to **raise** the error. As we have seen numerous times already, separating a problem into two parts has made the solution of each, and therefore the whole, more accessible.

We revisit the Maybe type in Section 18.8 where we see that it is an example of a more general programming structure, a monad. In particular there we examine the relationship between the function mapMaybe and the map function over lists.

Exercises

14.35 Using the functions mapMaybe and maybe, or otherwise, define a function

```
process :: [Int] -> Int -> Int -> Int
```

so that process xs n m takes the nth and mth items of the list of numbers xs, and returns their sum. Your function should return 0 if either of the numbers is not one of the indices of the list: for a list of length p, the indices are $0, \ldots, p-1$ inclusive.

14.36 Discuss the advantages and disadvantages of the three approaches to error handling presented in this section.

14.37 What are the values of type Maybe (Maybe a)? Define a function

```
squashMaybe :: Maybe (Maybe a) -> Maybe a
```

which will 'squash' Just (Just x) to Just x and all other values to Nothing.

14.38 In a similar way to mapMaybe, define the function

```
composeMaybe :: (a -> Maybe b) ->
                (b -> Maybe c) ->
                (a -> Maybe c)
```

which composes two error-raising functions. How could you use mapMaybe, the function composition operator and the squash function to define composeMaybe?

14.39 The Maybe type could be generalized to allow messages to be carried in the Nothing part, thus:

```
data Err a = OK a | Error String
```

How do the definitions of mapMaybe, maybe and composeMaybe have to be modified to accommodate this new definition?

14.5 Design with algebraic data types

Algebraic data types provide us with a powerful mechanism for modelling types which occur both in problems themselves, and within the programs designed to solve them. In this section we suggest a three-stage method for finding the appropriate algebraic type definitions. We apply it in two examples: finding the 'edit distance' between two words, and a simulation problem.

An important moral of the discussion here is that we can start to design data types *independently* of the program itself. For a system of any size we should do this, as we will be more likely to succeed if we can think about separate parts of the system separately.

We shall have more to say about design of data types in the next two chapters.

Edit distance: problem statement

In discussing the stages of design, we follow the example of finding the **edit distance** between two strings. This is the shortest sequence of simple editing operations which can take us from one string to the other.

The example is a version of a practical problem: in keeping a display (of windows or simple text) up-to-date, the speed with which updates can be done is crucial. It is therefore desirable to be able to make the updates from as few elementary operations as possible; this is what the edit distance program achieves in a different context.

We suppose that there are five basic editing operations on a string. We can change one character into another, copy a character without modifying it, delete or insert a character and delete (kill) to the end of the string. We also assume that each operation has the same cost, except a copy which is free.

To turn the string "fish" into "chips", we could kill the whole string, then insert the characters one-by-one, at a total cost of six. An optimal solution will copy as much of the string as possible, and is given by

- inserting the character 'c',
- changing 'f' to 'h',
- copying 'i',
- inserting 'p',
- copying 's', and finally
- deleting the remainder of the string, "h".

In the remainder of this section we design a type to represent the editing steps, and after looking at another example of data type design, define a function to give an optimal sequence of editing steps from one string to another.

The analysis here can also be used to describe the difference between two lists of arbitrary type. If each item is a line of a file, the behaviour of the function is similar to the Unix `diff` utility, which is used to give the difference between two text files.

Design stages in the edit distance problem

Now we look at the three stages of algebraic type definition in detail.

● First we have to identify the *types* of data involved. In the example, we have to define

```
data Edit = ...
```

which represents the editing operations.

● Next, we have to identify the different sorts of data in each of the types. Each sort of data is given by a **constructor**. In the example, we can change, copy, delete or insert a character and delete (kill) to the end of the string. Our type definition is therefore

```
data Edit = Change ... |
            Copy ... |
            Delete ... |
            Insert ... |
            Kill ...
```

The '...' show that we have not yet said anything about the types of the constructors.

● Finally, for each of the constructors, we need to decide what its **components** or arguments are. Some of the constructors – Copy, Delete and Kill – require no information; the others need to indicate the new character to be inserted, so

```
data Edit = Change Char |
            Copy |
            Delete |
            Insert Char |
            Kill
            deriving (Eq,Show)
```

This completes the definition.

We now illustrate how other type definitions work in a similar way, before returning to give a solution to the 'edit distance' problem.

Simulation

Suppose we want to model, or **simulate**, how the queues in a bank or Post Office behave; perhaps we want to decide how many bank clerks need to be working at particular times of the day. Our system will take as input the arrivals of customers, and give as output their departures. Each of these can be modelled using a type.

- Inmess is the type of input messages. At a given time, there are two possibilities:

  – No-one arrives, represented by the 0-ary constructor No;
  – Someone arrives, represented by the constructor Yes. This will have components giving the arrival time of the customer, and the amount of time that will be needed to serve them.

Hence we have

```
data Inmess = No | Yes Arrival Service

type Arrival = Int
type Service = Int
```

- Similarly, we have Outmess, the type of output messages. Either no-one leaves (None), or a person is discharged (Discharge). The relevant information they carry is the time they have waited, together with when they arrived and their service time. We therefore define

```
data Outmess = None | Discharge Arrival Wait Service

type Wait = Int
```

We return to the simulation example in Chapter 16.

Edit distance: solution

The problem is to find the lowest-cost sequence of edits to take us from one string to another. We can begin the definition thus:

```
transform :: String -> String -> [Edit]

transform [] [] = []
```

To transform the non-empty string st to [], we simply have to Kill it, while to transform [] to st we have to Insert each of the characters in turn:

```
transform xs [] = [Kill]
transform [] ys = map Insert ys
```

In the general case, we have a choice: should we first use Copy, Delete, Insert or Change? If the first characters of the strings are equal we should copy; but if not, there is no obvious choice. We therefore try *all* possibilities and choose the best of them:

```
transform (x:xs) (y:ys)
  | x==y        = Copy : transform xs ys
  | otherwise   = best [ Delete   : transform xs (y:ys) ,
                         Insert y : transform (x:xs) ys ,
                         Change y : transform xs ys ]
```

How do we choose the best sequence? We choose the one with the lowest cost.

```
best :: [[Edit]] -> [Edit]
best [x]    = x
best (x:xs)
  | cost x <= cost b    = x
  | otherwise           = b
    where
    b = best xs
```

The cost is given by charging one for every operation except copy, which is equivalent to 'leave unchanged'.

```
cost :: [Edit] -> Int
cost = length . filter (/=Copy)
```

Exercises

The first four questions are designed to make you think about how data types are designed. These questions are not intended to have a single 'right' answer, rather you should satisfy yourself that you have adequately represented the types which appear in your informal picture of the problem.

14.40 It is decided to keep a record of vehicles which will use a particular car park. Design an algebraic data type to represent them.

14.41 If you knew that the records of vehicles were to be used for comparative tests of fuel efficiency, how would you modify your answer to the last question?

14.42 Discuss the data types you might use in a database of students' marks for classes and the like. Explain the design of any algebraic data types that you use.

14.43 What data types might be used to represent the objects which can be drawn using an interactive drawing program? To give yourself more of a challenge, you might like to think about grouping of objects, multiple copies of objects, and scaling.

14.44 How would you modify the edit distance program to accommodate a Swap operation, which can be used to transform "abxyz" to "baxyz" in a single step?

14.45 Write a definition which when given a list of edits and a string st, returns the sequence of strings given by applying the edits to st in sequence.

14.46 Give a calculation of transform "cat" "am". What do you conclude about the efficiency of the transform function?

⟨14.6⟩ Algebraic types and type classes

We have reached a point where it is possible to explore rather more substantial examples of type classes, first introduced in Chapter 12.

Movable objects

We start by building a class of types whose members are geometrical objects in two dimensions. The operations of the class are those to move the objects in various different ways.

We now work through the definitions, which are illustrated in Figure 14.5. Some moves will be dictated by vectors, so we first define

```
data Vector = Vec Float Float
```

The class definition itself is

```
class Movable a where
  move     :: Vector -> a -> a
  reflectX :: a -> a
  reflectY :: a -> a
  rotate180 :: a -> a
  rotate180 = reflectX . reflectY
```

and it shows the ways in which an object can be moved. First it can be moved by a vector, as in the diagram below.

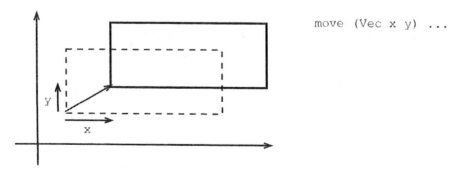

```
move (Vec x y) ...
```

We can also reflect an object in the x-axis (the horizontal axis) or the y-axis (the vertical), or rotate a figure through 180° around the origin (the point where the axes meet). The default definition of rotate180 works by reflecting first in the y-axis and then the x, as we did with the Picture type in Chapter 1.

We can now define a hierarchy of movable objects; first we have the Point,

```
data Vector = Vec Float Float

class Movable a where
  move        :: Vector -> a -> a
  reflectX  :: a -> a
  reflectY  :: a -> a
  rotate180 :: a -> a
  rotate180 = reflectX . reflectY

data Point = Point Float Float
              deriving Show

instance Movable Point where
  move (Vec v1 v2) (Point c1 c2) = Point (c1+v1) (c2+v2)
  reflectX (Point c1 c2)  = Point c1 (-c2)
  reflectY (Point c1 c2)  = Point (-c1) c2
  rotate180 (Point c1 c2) = Point (-c1) (-c2)

data Figure = Line Point Point |
              Circle Point Float
              deriving Show

instance Movable Figure where
  move v (Line p1 p2) = Line (move v p1) (move v p2)
  move v (Circle p r) = Circle (move v p) r

  reflectX (Line p1 p2) = Line (reflectX p1) (reflectX p2)
  reflectX (Circle p r) = Circle (reflectX p) r

  reflectY (Line p1 p2) = Line (reflectY p1) (reflectY p2)
  reflectY (Circle p r) = Circle (reflectY p) r

instance Movable a => Movable [a] where
  move v   = map (move v)
  reflectX = map reflectX
  reflectY = map reflectY
```

Figure 14.5 Movable objects.

```
data Point = Point Float Float
              deriving Show
```

To make Point an instance of Movable we have to give definitions of move, reflectX and reflectY over the Point type.

```
move (Vec v1 v2) (Point c1 c2) = Point (c1+v1) (c2+v2)
```

Here we can see that the move is achieved by adding the components v1 and v2 to the coordinates of the point. Reflection is given by changing the sign of one of the coordinates

```
reflectX (Point c1 c2) = Point c1 (-c2)
reflectY (Point c1 c2) = Point (-c1) c2
```

For this instance we override the default definition of rotate180 by changing the sign of both coordinates. This is a more efficient way of achieving the same transformation than the default definition.

```
rotate180 (Point c1 c2) = Point (-c1) (-c2)
```

Using the type of points we can build figures:

```
data Figure = Line Point Point |
              Circle Point Float
```

and in the instance declaration of Movable for Figure given in Figure 14.5 we use the corresponding operations on Point; for example,

```
move v (Line p1 p2) = Line (move v p1) (move v p2)
move v (Circle p r) = Circle (move v p) r
```

This same approach works again when we consider a list of movable objects:

```
instance Movable a => Movable [a] where
  move v   = map (move v)
  reflectX = map reflectX
```

and so on. Using overloading in this way has a number of advantages.

  The code is much easier to read: at each point we write move, rather than movePoint, and so on.

  We can reuse definitions; the instance declaration for Movable [a] makes lists of any sort of movable object movable themselves. This includes lists of points and lists of figures. Without overloading we would not be able to achieve this.

Named objects

Many forms of data contain some sort of name, a String which identifies the object in question. What do we expect to be able to do with a value of such a type?

  We should be able to identify the name of a value, and

  we ought to be able to give a new name to a value.

These operations are embodied in the Named class:

```
class Named a where
  lookName :: a -> String
  giveName :: String -> a -> a
```

and an example of Named types is given by

```
data Name a = Pair a String
```

the one-constructor type whose two components are of type a and String. The instance declaration for this type is

```
instance Named (Name a) where
  lookName (Pair obj nm) = nm
  giveName nm (Pair obj _) = (Pair obj nm)
```
(1)

Putting together classes

An important aspect of object-oriented software development is the way in which one class can be built upon another, reusing the operations of the original class on the subclass. In this section we explore how to combine the Movable and Named classes, to give objects which are both movable and named. The section is rather more advanced, and can be omitted on first reading.

Suppose we are to add names to our movable objects – how might this be done? We examine one approach in the text, and another in the exercises.

Our approach is to build the type Name a where elements of type a are movable, that is Movable a holds. We then want to establish that the type Name a is in both the classes Movable and Named. We have shown the latter for *any* type a already in (1) above, so we concentrate on the former.

The crucial insight is that the naming is independent of the named type; any operation on the type can be **lifted** to work over named types thus:

```
mapName :: (a -> b) -> Name a -> Name b

mapName f (Pair obj nm) = Pair (f obj) nm
```

We can then argue that all the operations of the Movable class can be lifted.

```
instance Movable a => Movable (Name a) where
  move v   = mapName (move v)
  reflectX = mapName reflectX
  reflectY = mapName reflectY
```
(2)

Now we already know that Named (Name a) by (1) above, so if we define a class combining these attributes

```
class (Movable b, Named b) => NamedMovable b
```
(3)

we can declare the instance

```
instance Movable a => NamedMovable (Name a)
```

This last instance is established by showing that the two constraints of (3) hold when b is replaced by Name a, but this is exactly what (1) and (2) say given the constraint Movable a.

```
data Name a = Pair a String

exam1 = Pair (Point 0.0 0.0) "Dweezil"

instance Named (Name a) where                               (1)
  lookName (Pair obj nm) = nm
  giveName nm (Pair obj _) = (Pair obj nm)

mapName :: (a -> b) -> Name a -> Name b

mapName f (Pair obj nm) = Pair (f obj) nm

instance Movable a => Movable (Name a) where                (2)
  move v   = mapName (move v)
  reflectX = mapName reflectX
  reflectY = mapName reflectY

class (Movable b, Named b) => NamedMovable b               (3)

instance Movable a => NamedMovable (Name a)
```

Figure 14.6 Named movable objects.

This completes the demonstration that NamedMovable (Name a) holds when we know that Movable a. It is worth realising that this demonstration is produced automatically by the Haskell system – we only need to type what is seen in Figure 14.6.

This section has begun to illustrate how classes can be used in the software development process. In particular we have shown how our movable objects can be named in a way which allows reuse of all the code to move the objects.

Exercises

14.47 A different way of combining the classes Named and Movable is to establish the instance

```
instance (Movable b,Named c) => NamedMovable (b,c)
```

This is done by giving the instances

```
instance Movable b => Movable (b,c) where ....
instance Named c   => Named (b,c) where ....
```

Complete these instance declarations.

14.48 Show that the method of the previous question can be used to combine instances of *any* two classes.

14.49 The example in the final part of this section shows how we can combine an arbitrary instance of the Movable class, a, with a *particular* instance of the Named class, String. Show how it can be used to combine an arbitrary instance of one class with a particular instance of another for *any* two classes whatever.

14.50 Extend the collection of operations for moving objects to include scaling and rotation by an arbitrary angle. This can be done by re-defining Movable or by defining a class MovablePlus over the class Movable. Which approach is preferable? Explain your answer.

14.51 Design a collection of classes to model bank accounts. These have different forms: current, deposit and so on, as well as different levels of functionality. Can you reuse the Named class here?

(14.7) Reasoning about algebraic types

Verification for algebraic types follows the example of lists, as first discussed in Chapter 8. The general pattern of structural induction over an algebraic type states that the result has to be proved for each constructor; when a constructor is recursive, we are allowed to use the corresponding induction hypotheses in making the proof. We first give some representative examples in this section, and conclude with a rather more sophisticated proof.

Trees

Structural induction over the type Tree of trees is stated as follows.

Structural induction over trees

To prove the property P(tr) for all finite tr of type Tree t we have to do two things.

Nil **case**	Prove P(Nil).
Node **case**	Prove P(Node x tr1 tr2) for all x of type t
	assuming that P(tr1) and P(tr2) hold already.

The advice of Chapter 8 about finding proofs can easily be carried over to the situation here. Now we give a representative example of a proof. We aim to prove for all finite trees tr that

```
map f (collapse tr) = collapse (mapTree f tr)        (map-collapse)
```

which states that if we map a function over a tree, and then collapse the result we get the same result as collapsing before mapping over the list. The functions we use are defined as follows

```
map f []     = []                                          (map.1)
map f (x:xs) = f x : map f xs                              (map.2)


mapTree f Nil = Nil                                        (mapTree.1)
mapTree f (Node x t1 t2)
  = Node (f x) (mapTree f t1) (mapTree f t2)               (mapTree.2)

collapse Nil = []                                          (collapse.1)
collapse (Node x t1 t2)
  = collapse t1 ++ [x] ++ collapse t2                      (collapse.2)
```

Base   In the `Nil` case, we simplify each side, giving

```
map f (collapse Nil)
  = map f []                                        by (collapse.1)
  = []                                              by (map.1)


collapse (mapTree f Nil)
  = collapse Nil                                    by (mapTree.1)
  = []                                              by (collapse.1)
```

This shows that the base case holds.

Induction   In the Node case, we have to prove:

```
map f (collapse (Node x tr1 tr2))
  = collapse (mapTree f (Node x tr1 tr2))                  (ind)
```

assuming the two induction hypotheses:

```
map f (collapse tr1) = collapse (mapTree f tr1)           (hyp.1)
map f (collapse tr2) = collapse (mapTree f tr2)           (hyp.2)
```

Looking at (ind), we can simplify the left-hand side thus

```
map f (collapse (Node x tr1 tr2))
  = map f (collapse tr1 ++ [x] ++ collapse tr2)     by (collapse.2)
  = map f (collapse tr1) ++ [f x] ++ map f (collapse tr2)
                                                    by (map++)
  = collapse (mapTree f tr1) ++ [f x] ++
    collapse (mapTree f tr2)                        by (hyp1,hyp2)
```

The final step is given by the two induction hypotheses, that the result holds for the two subtrees `tr1` and `tr2`. The result (map++) is the theorem

```
map g (ys++zs) = map g ys ++ map g zs                     (map++)
```

discussed in Chapter 10. Examining the right-hand side now, we have

```
collapse (mapTree f (Node x tr1 tr2))
  = collapse (Node (f x) (mapTree f tr1)
                         (mapTree f tr2))                by (mapTree.2)
  = collapse (mapTree f tr1) ++ [f x] ++
    collapse (mapTree f tr2)                             by (collapse.2)
```

and this finishes the proof in the Node case. As this is the second of the two cases, the proof is complete. ∎

The Maybe type

Structural induction for the type Maybe t becomes proof by cases – because the type is not recursive, in none of the cases is there an appeal to an induction hypothesis. The rule is

Structural induction over the Maybe type

To prove the property P(x) for all defined[1] x of type Maybe t we have to do two things:

Nothing **case**   Prove P(Nothing).

Just **case**   Prove P(Just y) for all defined y of type t.

Our example proof is that, for all defined values x of type Maybe Int,

```
maybe 2 abs x ≥ 0
```

Proof   The proof has two cases. In the first x is replaced by Nothing:

```
maybe 2 abs Nothing
  = 2 ≥ 0
```

In the second, x is replaced by Just y for a defined y.

```
maybe 2 abs (Just y)
  = abs y ≥ 0
```

In both cases the result holds, and so the result is valid in general. ∎

Other forms of proof

We have seen that not all functions are defined by primitive recursion. The example we saw in Section 14.2 was of the function assoc, which is used to rearrange arithmetic expressions represented by the type Expr. Recall that

```
assoc (Add (Add e1 e2) e3)
  = assoc (Add e1 (Add e2 e3))                  (assoc.1)
assoc (Add e1 e2) = Add (assoc e1) (assoc e2)   (assoc.2)
assoc (Sub e1 e2) = Sub (assoc e1) (assoc e2)   (assoc.3)
assoc (Lit n)     = Lit n                       (assoc.4)
```

---

[1] When the type is not recursive, the induction principle gives a proof for all defined objects. An object of this type is defined if it is Nothing, or Just y for a defined y.

with (assoc.1) being the non-primitive recursive case. We would like to prove that the rearrangement does not affect the value of the expression:

eval (assoc ex) = eval ex   (eval-assoc)

for all finite expressions ex. The induction principle for the Expr type has three cases.

Lit **case**	Prove P(Lit n).
Add **case**	Prove P(Add e1 e2), assuming P(e1) and P(e2)
Sub **case**	Prove P(Sub e1 e2), assuming P(e1) and P(e2)

To prove (eval-assoc) for all finite expressions, we have the three cases given above. The Lit and Sub cases are given, respectively, by (assoc.4) and (assoc.3), but the Add case is more subtle. For this we will prove

eval (assoc (Add e1 e2)) = eval (Add e1 e2)   (eval-Add)

by induction on the number of Adds which are left-nested at the top level of the expression e1 – recall that it was by counting these and noting that assoc preserves the total number of Adds overall that we proved the function would always terminate. Now, if there are no Adds at the top-level of e1, the equation (assoc.2) gives (eval-Add). Otherwise we rearrange thus:

eval (assoc (Add (Add f1 f2) e2)))
= eval (assoc (Add f1 (Add f2 e2)))   by (assoc.1)

and since f1 contains fewer Adds at top level,

= eval (Add f1 (Add f2 e2))
= eval (Add (Add f1 f2) e2)   by associativity of +

which gives the induction step, and therefore completes the proof. ∎

This result shows that verification is possible for functions defined in a more general way than primitive recursion.

Exercises

14.52 Prove that the function weather from Section 14.1 has the same behaviour as

```
newWeather = makeHot . isSummer
```

when

```
makeHot True  = Hot
makeHot False = Cold
isSummer = (==Summer)
```

where recall that (==Summer) is an operator section whose effect is to test whether its argument is equal to Summer.

14.53 Is it the case that the area of each Shape from Section 14.1 is non-negative? If so, give a proof; if not, give an example which shows that it is not the case.

14.54 If we define the size of an NTree thus

```
size NilT         = 0
size (Node x t1 t2) = 1 + size t1 + size t2
```

then prove that for all finite nTrees, tr,

```
size tr < 2^(depth tr)
```

14.55 Show for all finite NTrees tr that

```
occurs tr x = length (filter (==x) (collapse tr))
```

The next two exercises refer back to the exercises of Section 14.3.

14.56 Prove that the function twist has the property that

```
twist . twist = id
```

14.57 Explain the principle of structural induction for the type GTree. Formulate and prove the equivalent of the theorem relating map, mapTree and collapse for this type of trees.

Summary

Algebraic types sharpen our ability to model types in our programs: we have seen in this chapter how simple, finite types like Temp can be defined, as well as the more complex Either and recursive types. Many of these recursive types are varieties of tree: we looked at numerical trees; elements of the type Expr can also be thought of as trees representing the underlying structure of arithmetical expressions.

The type of lists gives a guiding example for various aspects of algebraic types.

- The definition of the type is recursive and polymorphic, and many polymorphic higher-order functions can be defined over lists – this carries over to the various types of tree and the error type, Maybe, for example.

- There is a simple principle for reasoning over lists, structural induction, which is the model for structural induction over algebraic types.

The chapter also gives guidelines for defining algebraic types. The definition can be given in three parts: first the type name is identified, then the constructors are named, and finally their component types are specified. As in other aspects of program development, this separation of concerns assists the system developer to produce simple and correct solutions.

Having introduced algebraic data types we are able to give more substantial examples of classes and their instances. We can see that the overloading that classes bring makes code both easier to read and more amenable to reuse; we can see in particular how software can be extended in a way that requires little modification to the code.

In the chapters to come, algebraic types will be an integral part of the systems we develop, and indeed in the next case study we exhibit various aspects of these types. We shall also explore a different approach to types: abstract data types, and see how this approach complements and contrasts with the use of algebraic data types.

Lazy programming

In our calculations so far we have said that the order in which we make evaluation steps will not affect the results produced – it may only affect whether the sequence leads to a result. This chapter describes precisely the **lazy evaluation** strategy which underlies Haskell. Lazy evaluation is well named: a lazy evaluator will only evaluate an argument to a function if that argument's value is **needed** to compute the overall result. Moreover, if an argument is structured (a list or a tuple, for instance), only those parts of the argument which are needed will be examined.

Lazy evaluation has consequences for the style of programs we can write. Since an intermediate list will only be generated **on demand**, using an intermediate list will not necessarily be expensive computationally. We examine this in the context of a series of examples, culminating in a case study of parsing.

To build parsers we construct a **toolkit** of polymorphic, higher-order functions which can be combined in a flexible and extensible way to make language processors of all sorts. One of the distinctive features of a functional language is the collection of facilities it provides for defining such sets of building blocks.

We also take the opportunity to extend the **list comprehension** notation. This does not allow us to write any new programs, but does make a lot of list processing programs

– especially those which work by generating and then testing possible solutions – easier to express and understand.

Another consequence of lazy evaluation is that it is possible for the language to describe **infinite** structures. These would require an infinite amount of time to evaluate fully, but under lazy evaluation, only parts of a data structure need to be examined. Any recursive type will contain infinite objects; we concentrate on lists here, as infinite lists are by far the most widely used infinite structures.

After introducing a variety of examples, such as infinite lists of prime and random numbers, we discuss the importance of infinite lists for **program design**, and see that programs manipulating infinite lists can be thought of as processes consuming and creating `streams' of data. Based on this idea, we explore how to complete the simulation case study.

The chapter concludes with an update on program **verification** in the light of lazy evaluation and the existence of infinite lists; this section can only give a flavour of the area, but contains references to more detailed presentations.

Sections 17.1 and 17.2 are essential reading, but it is possible to follow as much of the remainder as you like: the chapters which follow do not depend upon it.

17.1 Lazy evaluation

Central to evaluation in Haskell is function application. The basic idea behind this is simple; to evaluate the function f applied to arguments a_1, a_2, ..., a_k, we simply **substitute** the expressions a_i for the corresponding variables in the definition of the function. For instance, if

```
f x y = x+y
```

then

```
f (9-3) (f 34 3)
↝   (9-3)+(f 34 3)
```

since we replace x by (9-3) and y by (f 34 3). The expressions (f 34 3) and (9-3) are not evaluated before they are passed to the function.

In this case, for evaluation to continue, we need to evaluate the arguments to '+', giving

```
↝   6+(34+3)
↝   6+37
↝   43
```

In this example, both of the arguments are evaluated eventually, but this is not always the case. If we define

```
g x y = x+12
```

then

```
g (9-3) (g 34 3)
⤳   (9-3)+12
⤳   6+12
⤳   18
```

Here (9-3) is substituted for x, but as y does not appear on the right-hand side of the equation, the argument (g 34 3) will not appear in the result, and so is not evaluated. Here we see the first advantage of lazy evaluation – an argument which is not needed will not be evaluated. This example is rather too simple: why would we write the second argument if its value is never needed? A rather more realistic example is

```
switch :: Int -> a -> a -> a
switch n x y
  | n>0         = x
  | otherwise   = y
```

If the integer n is positive, the result is the value of x; otherwise it is the value of y. Either of the arguments x and y might be used, but in the first case y is not evaluated and in the second x is not evaluated. A third example is

```
h x y = x+x
```

so that

```
h (9-3) (h 34 3)                                    (h-eval)
⤳   (9-3)+(9-3)
```

It appears here that we will have to evaluate the argument (9-3) twice since it is duplicated on substitution. Lazy evaluation ensures that **a duplicated argument is never evaluated more than once**. This can be modelled in a calculation by doing the corresponding steps simultaneously, thus

```
h (9-3) 17
⤳   (9-3)+(9-3)
⤳   6+6
⤳   12
```

In the implementation, there is no duplicated evaluation because calculations are made over **graphs** rather than trees to represent the expressions being evaluated. For instance, instead of duplicating the argument, as in (i) below, the evaluation of (h-eval) will give a graph in which on both sides of the plus there is the *same* expression. This is shown in (ii).

```
i.                              ii.

    ● + ●                           ● + ●


  (9-3)   (9-3)                       (9-3)
```

A final example is given by the pattern matching function,

```
pm (x,y) = x+1
```

applied to the pair $(3+2,4-17)$.

```
pm (3+2,4-17)
⤳   (3+2)+1
⤳   6
```

The argument is examined, and part of it is evaluated. The second half of the pair remains unevaluated, as it is not needed in the calculation. This completes the informal introduction to lazy evaluation, which can be summarized in the three points:

- arguments to functions are evaluated only when this is necessary for evaluation to continue;

- an argument is not necessarily evaluated fully: only the parts that are needed are examined;

- an argument is evaluated at most only once. This is done in the implementation by replacing expressions by graphs and calculating over them.

We now give a more formal account of the calculation rules which embody lazy evaluation.

(17.2) Calculation rules and lazy evaluation

As we first saw in Section 3.7, the definition of a function consists of a number of conditional equations. Each conditional equation can contain multiple clauses and may have a number of local definitions given in a where clause. Each equation will have on its left-hand side the function under definition applied to a number of patterns.

```
f p1 p2 ··· pk
  | g1              = e1
  | g2              = e2
  ···
  | otherwise       = er
    where
      v1   a1,1 ··· = r1
      ····
f q1 q2 ··· qk
  = ···
```

In calculating $f\ a_1\ \dots\ a_k$ there are three aspects.

Calculation – pattern matching

In order to determine which of the equations is used, the arguments are evaluated. The arguments are not evaluated fully, rather they are evaluated sufficiently to see whether they match the corresponding patterns. If they match the patterns p_1 to p_k, then evaluation proceeds using the first equation; if not, they are checked against the second equation, which may require further evaluation. This is repeated until a match is given, or until there are no more equations (which would generate a `Program error`). For instance, given the definition

```
f :: [Int] -> [Int] -> Int
f [] ys          = 0                                        (f.1)
f (x:xs) []      = 0                                        (f.2)
f (x:xs) (y:ys) = x+y                                       (f.3)
```

the evaluation of f [1 .. 3] [1 .. 3] proceeds thus

```
f [1 .. 3] [1 .. 3]                                         (1)
↝   f (1:[2 .. 3]) [1 .. 3]                                 (2)
↝   f (1:[2 .. 3]) (1:[2 .. 3])                             (3)
↝   1+1                                                     (4)
```

At stage (1), there is not enough information about the arguments to determine whether there is a match with (f.1). One step of evaluation gives (2), and shows there is not a match with (f.1).

The first argument of (2) matches the first pattern of (f.2), so we need to check the second. One step of calculation in (3) shows that there is no match with (f.2), but that there is with (f.3); hence we have (4).

Calculation – guards

Suppose that the first conditional equation matches (simply for the sake of explanation). The expressions a_1 to a_k are substituted for the patterns p_1 to p_k throughout the conditional equation. We must next determine which of the clauses on the right-hand side applies. The guards are evaluated in turn, until one is found which gives the value True; the corresponding clause is then used. If we have

```
f :: Int -> Int -> Int -> Int
f m n p
  | m>=n && m>=p        = m
  | n>=m && n>=p        = n
  | otherwise           = p
```

then

```
f (2+3) (4-1) (3+9)
  ??   (2+3)>=(4-1) && (2+3)>=(3+9)
  ??      ↝   5>=3 && 5>=(3+9)
  ??      ↝   True && 5>=(3+9)
  ??      ↝   5>=(3+9)
  ??      ↝   5>=12
  ??      ↝   False
  ??   3>=5 && 3>=12
```

```
   ??    ↝   False && 3>=12
   ??    ↝   False
   ??  otherwise ↝   True
↝   12
```

We leave it as an exercise for the reader to work out which parts of the calculation above are shared.

Calculation – local definitions

Values in where clauses are calculated on demand: only when a value is needed does calculation begin. Given the definitions

```
f :: Int -> Int -> Int

f m n
  | notNil xs    = front xs
  | otherwise    = n
    where
    xs = [m .. n]

front (x:y:zs) = x+y
front [x]      = x

notNil []    = False
notNil (_:_) = True
```

the calculation of f 3 5 will be

```
f 3 5
  ?? notNil xs
  ?? │   where
  ?? │   xs = [3 .. 5]
  ?? │       ↝  3:[4 .. 5]                          (1)
  ?? ↝   notNil (3:[4 .. 5])
  ?? ↝   True
↝   front xs
  │     where
  │     xs = 3:[4 .. 5]
  │         ↝  3:4:[5]                              (2)
↝   3+4                                             (3)
↝   7
```

To evaluate the guard notNil xs, evaluation of xs begins, and after one step, (1) shows that the guard is True. Evaluating front xs requires more information about xs, and so we evaluate by one more step to give (2). A successful pattern match in the definition of front then gives (3), and so the result.

Operators and other expression formers

The three aspects of evaluating a function application are now complete; we should now say something about the built-in operators. If they can be given Haskell definitions, such as

```
True  && x = x
False && x = False
```

then they will follow the rules for Haskell definitions. The left-to-right order means that '&&' will not evaluate its second argument in the case that its first is False, for instance. This is unlike many programming languages, where the 'and' function will evaluate both its arguments.

The other operations, such as the arithmetic operators, vary. Plus needs both its arguments to return a result, but the equality on lists can return False on comparing [] and (x:xs) without evaluating x or xs. In general the language is implemented so that no manifestly unnecessary evaluation takes place.

Recall that if ... then ... else ...; cases; let and lambda expressions can be used in forming expressions. Their evaluation follows the form we have seen for function applications. Specifically, if ... then ... else ... is evaluated like a guard, cases like a pattern match, let like a where clause and a lambda expression like the application of a named function such as f above.

Finally, we turn to the way in which a choice is made between applications.

Evaluation order

What characterizes evaluation in Haskell, apart from the fact that no argument is evaluated twice, is the **order** in which applications are evaluated when there is a choice.

Evaluation is **from the outside in**. In a situation like

$$\underline{f_1\ e_1\ (f_2\ e_2\ 17)}$$

where one application encloses another, as seen in the expression, the outer one, $f_1\ e_1\ (f_2\ e_2\ 17)$, is chosen for evaluation.

Otherwise, evaluation is **from left to right**. In the expression

$$\underline{f_1\ e_1} + \underline{f_2\ e_2}$$

the underlined expressions are both to be evaluated. The left-hand one, $f_1\ e_1$, will be examined first.

These rules are enough to describe the way in which lazy evaluation works. In the sections to come we look at the consequences of a lazy approach for functional programming.

17.3 List comprehensions revisited

The list comprehension notation does not add any new programs to the Haskell language, but it does allow us to (re-)write programs in a new and clearer way. Building on the introduction in Section 5.5, the notation lets us combine multiple maps and filters together in a single expression. Combinations of these functions allow us to write algorithms which generate and test: all the elements of a particular form are generated and combinations of them are tested, before results depending upon them are returned. We begin the section with a re-examination of the syntax of the list comprehension, before giving some simple illustrative examples. After that we give the rules for calculating with list comprehensions, and we finish the section with a series of longer examples.

Syntax

A list comprehension has the form

```
[ e | q₁ , ... , qₖ ]
```

where each **qualifier** q_i has one of two forms.

- It can be a **generator**, p <- lExp, where p is a pattern and lExp is an expression of list type.
- It can be a **test**, bExp, which is a boolean expression.

An expression lExp or bExp appearing in qualifier q_i can refer to the variables used in the patterns of qualifiers q_1 to q_{i-1}.

Simpler examples

Multiple generators allow us to combine elements from two or more lists

```
pairs :: [a] -> [b] -> [(a,b)]
pairs xs ys = [ (x,y) | x<-xs , y<-ys ]
```

This example is important as it shows the way in which the values x and y are chosen.

```
pairs [1,2,3] [4,5]
↝  [(1,4),(1,5),(2,4),(2,5),(3,4),(3,5)]
```

The first element of xs, 1, is given to x, and then *for this fixed value* all possible values of y in ys are chosen. This process is repeated for the remaining values x in xs, namely 2 and 3.

This choice is not accidental, since if we have

```
triangle :: Int -> [(Int,Int)]
triangle n = [ (x,y) | x <- [1 .. n] , y <- [1 .. x] ]
```

the second generator, y <- [1 .. x] depends on the value of x given by the first generator.

```
triangle 3
⤳  [(1,1),(2,1),(2,2),(3,1),(3,2),(3,3)]
```

For the first choice of x, 1, the value of y is chosen from [1 .. 1], for the second choice of x, the value of y is chosen from [1 .. 2], and so on.

Three positive integers form a **Pythagorean triple** if the sum of squares of the first two is equal to the square of the third. The list of all triples with all sides below a particular bound, n, is given by

```
pyTriple n
  = [ (x,y,z) | x <- [2 .. n] , y <- [x+1 .. n] ,
                z <- [y+1 .. n] , x*x + y*y == z*z ]
```

```
pyTriple 100
⤳  [(3,4,5),(5,12,13),(6,8,10),...,(65,72,97)]
```

Here the test combines values from the three generators.

Calculating with list comprehensions

How can we describe the way in which the results of list comprehensions are obtained? One way is to give a translation of the comprehensions into applications of map, filter and concat. We give a different approach here, of calculating *directly* with the expressions.

Before we do this, we introduce one piece of very helpful notation. We write e{f/x} for the expression e in which every occurrence of the variable x has been replaced by the expression f. This is the **substitution** of f for x in e. If p is a pattern, we use e{f/p} for the substitution of the appropriate parts of f for the variables in p. For instance,

```
[ (x,y) | x<-xs ]{[2,3]/xs}    = [ (x,y) | x<-[2,3] ]
```

```
(x + sum xs){(2,[3,4])/(x,xs)} = 2 + sum [3,4]
```

since 2 matches x, and [3,4] matches xs when (2,[3,4]) is matched against (x,xs).

We now explain list comprehensions. The notation looks a bit daunting, but the effect should be clear. The generator v <- [a_1,...,a_n] has the effect of setting v to the values a_1 to a_n in turn. Setting the value appears in the calculation as **substitution** of a value for a variable.

```
[ e | v <- [a1,...,an] , q2 , ... , qk ]
⤳  [ e{a1/v} | q2{a1/v} , ... , qk{a1/v} ]
    ++ ... ++
    [ e{an/v} | q2{an/v} , ... , qk{an/v} ]
```

As a running example for this section we take

```
[ x+y | x <- [1,2] , isEven x , y <- [x .. 2*x] ]
⤳  [ 1+y | isEven 1 , y <- [1 .. 2*1] ] ++
    [ 2+y | isEven 2 , y <- [2 .. 2*2] ]
```

where the values 1 and 2 are substituted for x. The rules for tests are simple,

```
[ e | True  , q2 , ... , qk ]
~>   [ e | q2 , ... , qk ]

[ e | False , q2 , ... , qk ]
~>   []
```

so that our example is

```
~>   [ 1+y | False , y <- [1 .. 2*1] ] ++
     [ 2+y | True  , y <- [2 .. 2*2] ]
~>   [ 2+y | y <- [2,3,4] ]
~>   [ 2+2 | ] ++ [ 2+3 | ] ++ [ 2+4 | ]
```

and when there are no qualifiers,

```
[ e | ] = [ e ]
```

Completing the example, we have

```
[ x+y | x <- [1,2] , isEven x , y <- [x .. 2*x] ]
~>   [4,5,6]
```

Now we consider some more examples.

```
triangle 3
~>   [ (x,y) | x <- [1 .. 3] , y <- [1 .. x] ]
~>   [ (1,y) | y <- [1 .. 1] ] ++
     [ (2,y) | y <- [1 .. 2] ] ++
     [ (3,y) | y <- [1 .. 3] ]
~>   [ (1,1) | ] ++
     [ (2,1) | ] ++ [ (2,2) | ] ++
     [ (3,1) | ] ++ [ (3,2) | ] ++ [ (3,3) | ]
~>   [(1,1),(2,1),(2,2),(3,1),(3,2),(3,3)]
```

as we argued above. Another example contains a test:

```
[ m*m | m <- [1 .. 10] , m*m<50 ]
~>   [ 1*1 | 1*1<50 ] ++ [ 2*2 | 2*2<50 ] ++ ...
     [ 7*7 | 7*7<50 ] ++ [ 8*8 | 8*8<50 ] ++ ...
~>   [ 1  | True ] ++ [ 4  | True ] ++ ...
     [ 49 | True ] ++ [ 64 | False ] ++ ...
~>   [1,4,...49]
```

We now look at two longer examples, the solutions for which are aided by the list comprehension style.

Example

List permutations

A permutation of a list is a list with the same elements in a different order. The perms function returns a list of all permutations of a list.

```
perms :: Eq a => [a] -> [[a]]
```

The empty list has one permutation, itself. If xs is not empty, a permutation is given by picking an element x from xs and putting x at the front of a permutation of the remainder xs\\[x]. (The operation '\\' returns the difference of two lists: xs\\ys is the list xs with each element of ys removed, if it is present.) The definition is therefore

```
perms [] = [[]]
perms xs = [ x:ps | x <- xs , ps <- perms (xs\\[x]) ]
```

Example evaluations give, for a one-element list,

```
perms [2]
⤳   [x:ps| x <- [2] , ps <- perms [] ]
⤳   [x:ps| x <- [2] , ps <- [[]] ]
⤳   [2:ps| ps <- [[]] ]
⤳   [2:[] | ]
⤳   [[2]]
```

for a two-element list,

```
perms [2,3]
⤳   [ x:ps | x <- [2,3] , ps <- perms([2,3]\\[x]) ]
⤳   [ 2:ps | ps <- perms [3] ] ++ [ 3:ps | ps <- perms [2] ]
⤳   [ 2:[3] ] ++ [ 3:[2] ]
⤳   [ [2,3] , [3,2] ]
```

and finally for a three-element list,

```
perms [1,2,3]
⤳   [ x:ps | x <- [1,2,3] , ps <- perms([1,2,3]\\[x]) ]
⤳   [ 1:ps | ps <- perms [2,3]] ++...++ [ 3:ps | ps <- perms [1,2]]
⤳   [ 1:ps | ps<-[[2,3],[3,2]]] ++...++ [ 3:ps | ps<-[[1,2],[2,1]]]
⤳   [[1,2,3],[1,3,2],[2,1,3],[2,3,1],[3,1,2],[3,2,1]]
```

There is another algorithm for permutations: in this, a permutation of a list (x:xs) is given by forming a permutation of xs, and by inserting x into this somewhere. The possible insertion points are given by finding all the possible *splits* of the list into two halves.

```
perm :: [a] -> [[a]]

perm []     = [[]]
perm (x:xs) = [ ps++[x]++qs | rs <- perm xs ,
                              (ps,qs) <- splits rs ]
```

We get the list of all possible `splits` of a list xs after seeing that on splitting (y:ys), we either split at the front of (y:ys), or somewhere inside ys, as given by a split of ys.

```
splits :: [a]->[([a],[a])]
```

```
splits []     = [ ([],[]) ]
splits (y:ys) = ([],y:ys) : [ (y:ps,qs) | (ps,qs) <- splits ys]
```

Before moving on, observe that the type of perms requires that a must be in the class Eq. This is needed for the list difference operator \\ to be defined over the type [a]. There is no such restriction on the type of perm, which uses a different method for calculating the permutations.

Vectors and matrices

In this section we give one model for vectors and matrices of real numbers; others exist, and are suitable for different purposes.

A vector is a sequence of real numbers, [2.1,3.0,4.0], say.

```
type Vector = [Float]
```

The scalar product of two vectors (assumed to be the same length) is given by multiplying together corresponding elements and taking the total of the results.

```
scalarProduct [2.0,3.1] [4.1,5.0]
⤳   2.0*4.1 + 3.1*5.0
⤳   23.7
```

As a first attempt we might write

```
mul xs ys = sum [ x*y | x<-xs , y<-ys ]
```

but this gives

```
mul [2.0,3.1] [4.1,5.0]
⤳   sum [8.2,10.0,12.71,15.5]
⤳   46.41
```

since *all* combinations of pairs from the lists are taken. In order to multiply together corresponding pairs, we first zip the lists together:

```
scalarProduct :: Vector -> Vector -> Float
scalarProduct xs ys = sum [ x*y | (x,y) <- zip xs ys ]
```

and a calculation shows that this gives the required result. (It is also possible to use zipWith to define scalarProduct.) A matrix like

$$\begin{pmatrix} 2.0 & 3.0 & 4.0 \\ 5.0 & 6.0 & -1.0 \end{pmatrix}$$

can be thought of as a list of rows or a list of columns; we choose a list of rows here.

```
type Matrix = [Vector]
```

The example matrix is

```
[[2.0,3.0,4.0],[5.0,6.0,-1.0]]
```

Two matrices M and P are multiplied by taking the scalar products of rows of M with columns of P.

$$\begin{pmatrix} 2.0 & 3.0 & 4.0 \\ 5.0 & 6.0 & -1.0 \end{pmatrix} \times \begin{pmatrix} 1.0 & 0.0 \\ 1.0 & 1.0 \\ 0.0 & -1.0 \end{pmatrix} = \begin{pmatrix} 5.0 & -1.0 \\ 11.0 & 7.0 \end{pmatrix}$$

We therefore define

```
matrixProduct :: Matrix -> Matrix -> Matrix
matrixProduct m p
  = [ [scalarProduct r c | c <- columns p] | r <- m ]
```

where the function `columns` gives the representation of a matrix as a list of columns.

```
columns :: Matrix -> Matrix

columns y = [ [ z!!j | z <- y ] | j <- [0 .. s] ]
            where
            s = length (head y)-1
```

The expression `[ z!!j | z <- y ]` picks the jth element from each row z in y; this is exactly the jth column of y. `length (head y)` is the length of a row in y, and so the indices j will be in the range 0 to `s = length (head y)-1`. Another variant of the `columns` function is `transpose` which is in the library `List.hs`.

Refutable patterns in generators

Some patterns are **refutable**, meaning that an attempt to pattern-match against them may fail. If a refutable pattern is used on the left-hand side of an '<-', its effect is to filter from the list only the elements matching the pattern. For example,

```
[ x | (x:xs) <- [[],[2],[],[4,5]] ]  ⤳  [2,4]
```

The rules for calculation with generators containing a refutable pattern on their left-hand side are similar to those given above, except that before performing the substitution for the pattern, the list is filtered for the elements which match the pattern. The details are left as an exercise.

Exercises

17.1 Give a calculation of the expression

```
[ x+y | x <- [1 .. 4] , y <- [2 .. 4] , x>y ]
```

17.2 Using the list comprehension notation, define the functions

```
subLists,subSequences :: [a] -> [[a]]
```

which return all the sublists and subsequences of a list. A sublist is obtained by omitting some of the elements of a list; a subsequence is a continuous block from a list. For instance, both [2,4] and [3,4] are sublists of [2,3,4], but only [3,4] is a subsequence.

17.3 Give calculations of the expressions

```
perm [2]
perm [2,3]
perm [1,2,3]
```

and of the matrix multiplication

```
matrixProduct [[2.0,3.0,4.0],[5.0,6.0,-1.0]]
              [[1.0,0.0],[1.0,1.0],[0.0,-1.0]]
```

17.4 Give a definition of `scalarProduct` using `zipWith`.

17.5 Define functions to calculate the determinant of a square matrix and, if this is non-zero, to invert the matrix.

17.6 The calculation rules for list comprehensions can be re-stated for the two cases [] and (x:xs), instead of for the arbitrary list $[a_1, \ldots, a_n]$. Give these rules by completing the equations

```
[ e | v <- []      , q2 , ... , qk ] ⤳ ...
[ e | v <- (x:xs) , q2 , ... , qk ] ⤳ ...
```

17.7 Give the precise rules for calculating with a generator containing a refutable pattern, like (x:xs) <- lExp. You might need to define auxiliary functions to do this.

17.8 List comprehensions can be translated into expressions involving `map`, `filter` and `concat` by the following equations.

```
[ x | x<-xs ]              = xs
[ f x | x<-xs ]            = map f xs
[ e | x<-xs , p x , ... ] = [ e | x <- filter p xs , ... ]
[ e | x<-xs , y<-ys , .. ] = concat [ [e|y<-ys, ..] | x<-xs]
```

Translate the expressions

```
[ m*m | m <- [1 .. 10] ]
[ m*m | m <- [1 .. 10] , m*m<50 ]
[ x+y | x <- [1 .. 4] , y <- [2 .. 4] , x>y ]
[ x:p | x <- xs , p <- perms (xs\\[x]) ]
```

using these equations; you will need to define some auxiliary functions as a part of your translation.

(17.4) Data-directed programming

The data structures manipulated by a program will be generated on demand, and indeed may never appear explicitly. This makes possible a style of programming, **data-directed programming**, in which complex data structures are constructed and manipulated. Take the example of finding the sum of fourth powers of numbers from 1 to n. A data-directed solution is to

- build the list of numbers [1 .. n];
- take the power of each number, giving $[1, 16, \ldots, n^4]$, and
- find the sum of this list.

As a program, we have

```
sumFourthPowers n = sum (map (^4) [1 .. n])
```

How does the calculation proceed?

```
sumFourthPowers n
~→   sum (map (^4) [1 .. n])
~→   sum (map (^4) (1:[2 .. n]))
~→   sum ((^4) 1 : map (^4) [2 .. n])
~→   (1^4) + sum (map (^4) [2 .. n])
~→   1 + sum (map (^4) [2 .. n])
~→   ...
~→   1 + (16 + sum (map (^4) [3 .. n]))
~→   ...
~→   1 + (16 + (81 + ... + n^4))
```

As can be seen, none of the intermediate lists is created in this calculation. As soon as the head of the list is created, its fourth power is taken, and it becomes a part of the sum which produces the final result.

Examples

1. List minimum

A more striking example is given by the problem of finding the minimum of a list of numbers. One solution is to sort the list, and take its head! This would be ridiculous if the whole list were sorted in the process, but, in fact we have, using the definition of insertion sort from Chapter 7,

```
iSort [8,6,1,7,5]
~→   ins 8 (ins 6 (ins 1 (ins 7 (ins 5 []))))
~→   ins 8 (ins 6 (ins 1 (ins 7 [5])))
~→   ins 8 (ins 6 (ins 1 (5 : ins 7 [])))
~→   ins 8 (ins 6 (1 : (5 : ins 7 [])))
~→   ins 8 (1 : ins 6 (5 : ins 7 []))
~→   1 : ins 8 (ins 6 (5 : ins 7 []))
```

As can be seen from the underlined parts of the calculation, each application of ins calculates the minimum of a larger part of the list, since the head of the result of ins is given in a single step. The head of the whole list is determined in this case without us working out the value of the tail, and this means that we have a sensible algorithm for minimum given by (head . iSort).

2. Routes through a graph

A graph can be seen as an object of type Relation a, as defined in Section 16.9. How can we find a route from one point in a graph to another? For example, in the graph

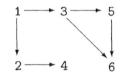

```
graphEx = makeSet [(1,2),(1,3),(2,4),(3,5),(5,6),(3,6)]
```

a route from 1 to 4 is the list [1,2,4].

We solve a slightly different problem: find the list of *all* routes from x to y; our original problem is solved by taking the head of this list. Note that as a list is returned, the algorithm allows for the possibility of there being *no* route from x to y – the empty list of routes is the answer in such a case. This method, which is applicable in many different situations, is often called the **list of successes** technique: instead of returning one result, or an error if there is none, we return a list; the error case is signalled by the empty list. The method also allows for multiple results to be returned, as we shall see.

How do we solve the new problem? For the present we assume that the graph is **acyclic**: there is no circular path from any node back to itself.

- The only route from x to x is [x].

- A route from x to y will start with a step to one of x's neighbours, z say. The remainder will be a path from z to y.

We therefore look for all paths from x to y going through z, for each neighbour z of x.

```
routes :: Ord a => Relation a -> a -> a -> [[a]]
routes rel x y
   | x==y        = [[x]]
   | otherwise   = [ x:r | z <- nbhrs rel x ,
                           r <- routes rel z y ]
```

The nbhrs function is defined by

```
nbhrs :: Ord a => Relation a -> a -> [a]
nbhrs rel x = flatten (image rel x)
```

where flatten turns a set into a list. Now consider the example, where we write routes' for routes graphEx and nbhrs' for nbhrs graphEx, to make the calculation more readable:

```
routes' 1 4
↝    [ 1:r | z <- nbhrs' 1 , r <- routes' z 4 ]
↝    [ 1:r | z <- [2,3] , r <- routes' z 4 ]
↝    [ 1:r | r <- routes' 2 4 ] ++
     [ 1:r | r <- routes' 3 4 ]                                    (†)
↝    [ 1:r | r <- [ 2:s | w <- nbhrs' 2 , s <- routes' w 4 ]]++...
↝    [ 1:r | r <- [ 2:s | w <- [4] , s <- routes' w 4 ] ] ++ ...
↝    [ 1:r | r <- [ 2:s | s <- routes' 4 4 ] ] ++ ...              (‡)
↝    [ 1:r | r <- [ 2:s | s <- [[4]] ] ] ++ ...
↝    [ 1:r | r <- [ [2,4] ] ] ++ ...
↝    [[1,2,4]] ++ ...
```

The head of the list is given by exploring only the first neighbour of 1, namely 2, and its first neighbour, 4. In this case the search for a route leads directly to a result. This is not always so. Take the example of

```
routes' 1 6 = ...
↝    [ 1:r | r <- routes' 2 6 ] ++
     [ 1:r | r <- routes' 3 6 ]                                    (†)
↝    ...
↝    [ 1:r | r <- [ 2:s | s <- routes' 4 6 ] ] ++
     [ 1:r | r <- routes' 3 6 ]                                    (‡)
```

Corresponding points in the calculations are marked by (†) and (‡). The search for routes from 4 to 6 will *fail*, though, as 4 has no neighbours – we therefore have

```
↝    [] ++ [ 1:r | r <- routes' 3 6 ] = ...
↝    [ 1:r | r <- [ 3:s | s <- routes' 5 6 ] ] ++ ...
↝    [[1,3,5,6]] ++ ...
```

The effect of this algorithm is to **backtrack** when a search has failed: there is no route from 1 to 6 via 2, so the other possibility of going through 3 is explored. This is done *only* when the first possibility is exhausted, however, so lazy evaluation ensures that this search through 'all' the paths turns out to be an efficient method of finding a single path.

   We assumed at the start of this development that the graph was acyclic, so that we have no chance of a path looping back on itself, and so of a search going into a loop. We can make a simple addition to the program to make sure that only paths without cycles are explored, and so that the program will work for an arbitrary graph. We add a list argument for the points not to be visited (again), and so have

```
routesC :: Ord a => Relation a -> a -> a -> [a] -> [[a]]
routesC rel x y avoid
  | x==y        = [[x]]
  | otherwise   = [ x:r | z <- nbhrs rel x \\ avoid ,
                          r <- routesC rel z y (x:avoid) ]
```

Two changes are made in the recursive case.

In looking for neighbours of x we look only for those which are not in the list avoid;

in looking for routes from z to y, we exclude visiting both the elements of avoid and the node x itself.

A search for a route from x to y in rel is given by routesC rel x y [].

Exercise

17.9 Defining graphEx2 to be

```
makeSet [(1,2),(2,1),(1,3),(2,4),(3,5),(5,6),(3,6)]
```

try calculating the effect of the original definition on

```
routes graphEx 1 4
```

Repeat the calculation with the revised definition which follows:

```
routes rel x y
  | x==y       = [[x]]
  | otherwise  = [ x:r | z <- nbhrs rel x ,
                         r <- routes rel z y ,
                         not (elem x r) ]
```

and explain why this definition is not suitable for use on cyclic graphs. Finally, give a calculation of

```
routesC graphEx 1 4 []
```

(17.5) Case study: parsing expressions

We have already seen the definition of Expr, the type of arithmetic expressions, in Section 14.2 and in a revised version given on page 255:

```
data Expr = Lit Int | Var Var | Op Ops Expr Expr
data Ops  = Add | Sub | Mul | Div | Mod
```

and showed there how we could calculate the results of these expressions using the function eval. Chapter 16 began with a discussion of how to represent the values held in the variables using the abstract data type Store. Using these components, we can build a calculator for simple arithmetical expressions, but the input is unacceptably crude, as we have to enter members of the Expr type, so that to add 2 and 3, we are forced to type

```
Op Add (Lit 2) (Lit 3)
```
                                                                              (exp)

What we need to make the input reasonable is a function which performs the reverse of show: it will take the text "(2+3)" and return the expression (exp).

Constructing a parser for a type like Expr gives a read function which essentially gives the functionality of the Read class, introduced in Section 12.4 above. Note, however, that the derived definition of read for Expr will parse strings of the form "Op Add (Lit 2) (Lit 3)" rather than the more compact form which we read with our parser.

The type of parsers: Parse

In building a library of parsing functions, we first have to establish the type we shall use to represent parsers. The problem of parsing is to take a list of objects – of type a and characters in our example "(2+3)" – and from it to extract an object of some other type, b, in this case Expr. As a first attempt, we might define the type of parsers thus:

```
type Parse1 a b = [a] -> b
```

Suppose that bracket and number are the parsers of this type which recognize brackets and numbers then we have

```
bracket "(xyz" ⤳    '('
number  "234"  ⤳    2 or 23 or 234?
bracket "234"  ⤳    no result?
```

The problem evident here is that a parser can return more than one result – as in number "234" – or none at all, as seen in the final case. Instead of the original type, we suggest

```
type Parse2 a b = [a] -> [b]
```

where a list of results is returned. In our examples,

```
bracket "(xyz" ⤳    ['(']
number  "234"  ⤳    [2 , 23 , 234]
bracket "234"  ⤳    []
```

In this case an empty list signals failure to find what was sought, while multiple results show that more than one successful parse was possible. We are using the 'list of successes' technique again, in fact.

Another problem presents itself. What if we look for a bracket *followed by* a number, which we have to do in parsing our expressions? We need to know the part of the input which remains after the successful parse. Hence we define

```
type Parse a b = [a] -> [(b,[a])]
```

and our example functions will give

```
bracket "(xyz" ⤳    [('(' , "xyz")]
number  "234"  ⤳    [(2,"34") , (23,"4") , (234,"")]
bracket "234"  ⤳    []
```

Each element in the output list represents a successful parse. In number "234" we see three successful parses, each recognizing a number. In the first, the number 2 is recognized, leaving "34" unexamined, for instance.

The type ReadS b, which appears in the standard prelude and is used in defining the Read class, is a special case of the type Parse a b in which [a] is replaced by String, that is, a is replaced by Char.

Some basic parsers

Now we have established the type we shall use, we can begin to write some parsers. These and the parser-combining functions are illustrated in Figure 17.1; we go through the definitions now.

The first is a parser which always fails, so accepts nothing. There are no entries in its output list.

```
none :: Parse a b
none inp = []
```

On the other hand, we can succeed immediately, without reading any input. The value recognized is a parameter of the function.

```
succeed :: b -> Parse a b
succeed val inp = [(val,inp)]
```

More useful is a parser to recognize a single object or token, t, say. We define

```
token :: Eq a => a -> Parse a a
token t (x:xs)
   | t==x         = [(t,xs)]
   | otherwise    = []
token t []        = []
```

More generally, we can recognize (or spot) objects with a particular property, as represented by a Boolean-valued function.

```
spot :: (a -> Bool) -> Parse a a
spot p (x:xs)
   | p x          = [(x,xs)]
   | otherwise    = []
spot p []         = []
```

These parsers allow us to recognize single characters like a left bracket, or a single digit,

```
bracket = token '('
dig     = spot isDigit
```

and indeed, we can define token from spot:

```
token t = spot (==t)
```

If we are to build parsers for complex structures like expressions we will need to be able to combine these simple parsers into more complicated ones to, for instance, recognize numbers consisting of lists of digits.

```
infixr 5 >*>

type Parse a b = [a] -> [(b,[a])]

none :: Parse a b
none inp = []

succeed :: b -> Parse a b
succeed val inp = [(val,inp)]

token :: Eq a => a -> Parse a a
token t = spot (==t)

spot :: (a -> Bool) -> Parse a a
spot p (x:xs)
   | p x           = [(x,xs)]
   | otherwise     = []
spot p []          = []

alt :: Parse a b -> Parse a b -> Parse a b
alt p1 p2 inp = p1 inp ++ p2 inp

(>*>) :: Parse a b -> Parse a c -> Parse a (b,c)
(>*>) p1 p2 inp
  = [((y,z),rem2) | (y,rem1) <- p1 inp , (z,rem2) <- p2 rem1 ]

build :: Parse a b -> (b -> c) -> Parse a c
build p f inp = [ (f x,rem) | (x,rem) <- p inp ]

list :: Parse a b -> Parse a [b]
list p = (succeed []) 'alt'
         ((p >*> list p) 'build' (uncurry (:)))
```

Figure 17.1   The major parsing functions.

Combining parsers

Here we build a library of higher-order polymorphic functions, which we then use to give our parser for expressions. First we have to think about the ways in which parsers need to be combined.

Looking at the expression example, an expression is *either* a literal, *or* a variable *or* an operator expression. From parsers for the three sorts of expression, we want to build a single parser for expressions. For this we use alt

```
alt :: Parse a b -> Parse a b -> Parse a b
```

```
alt p1 p2 inp = p1 inp ++ p2 inp
```

The parser combines the results of the parses given by parsers p1 and p2 into a single list, so a success in either is a success of the combination. For example,

```
(bracket 'alt' dig) "234"
⤳   [] ++ [(2,"34")]
```

the parse by bracket fails, but that by dig succeeds, so the combined parser succeeds.

For our second function, we look again at the expression example. In recognizing an operator expression we see a bracket *then* a number. How do we put parsers together so that the second is applied to the input that remains after the first has been applied?

We make this function an operator, as we find that it is often used to combine a sequence of parsers, and an infix form with defined associativity is most convenient for this.

```
infixr 5 >*>

(>*>) :: Parse a b -> Parse a c -> Parse a (b,c)

(>*>) p1 p2 inp
  = [((y,z),rem2) | (y,rem1) <- p1 inp , (z,rem2) <- p2 rem1 ]
```

The values (y,rem1) run through the possible results of parsing inp using p1. For each of these, we apply p2 to rem1, which is the input which is unconsumed by p1 in that particular case. The results of the two successful parses, y and z, are returned as a pair.

As an example, assume that number recognizes non-empty sequences of digits, and look at (number >*> bracket) "24(". Applying number to the string "24(" gives two results,

```
number "24(" ⤳   [(2,"4(") , (24,"(")]
```

and so (y,rem1) runs through two cases

```
(number >*> bracket) "24("
⤳   [((y,z),rem2) | (y,rem1) <- [(2,"4(") , (24,"(")] ,
                      (z,rem2)  <- bracket rem1 ]
⤳   [((2,z),rem2)  | (z,rem2)  <- bracket "4(" ] ++
    [((24,z),rem2) | (z,rem2)  <- bracket "(" ]
```

Now, bracket "4(" ⤳ [], so fails, giving

```
⤳   [] ++ [((24,z),rem2) | (z,rem2)  <- bracket "(" ]
```

and

```
bracket "(" ⤳   [('(',"")]
```

which signals success, and finally gives

⤳ [((24,z),rem2) | (z,rem2) <- [(')(',"")]]
⤳ [((24,')(') , "")]

This shows we have one successful parse, in which we have recognized the number 24 followed by the left bracket ')('.

Our final operation is to change the item returned by a parser, or to build something from it. Consider the case of a parser, digList, which returns a list of digits. Can we make it return the number which the list of digits represents? We apply conversion to the results, thus

```
build :: Parse a b -> (b -> c) -> Parse a c
```

```
build p f inp = [ (f x,rem) | (x,rem) <- p inp ]
```

so in an example, we have

```
(digList 'build' digsToNum) "21a3"
⤳  [ (digsToNum x,rem) | (x,rem) <- digList "21a3" ]
⤳  [ (digsToNum x,rem) | (x,rem) <- [("2","1a3"),("21","a3")]]
⤳  [ (digsToNum "2" , "1a3") , (digsToNum "21" , "a3") ]
⤳  [ (2,"1a3") , (21,"a3")]
```

Using the three operations or **combinators** alt, >*> and build together with the primitives of the last section we will be able to define all the parsers we require.

As an example, we show how to define a parser for a **list** of objects, when we are given a parser to recognize a single object. There are two sorts of list:

 A list can be empty, which will be recognized by the parser succeed [].

 Any other list is non-empty, and consists of an object followed by a list of objects. A pair like this is recognized by p >*> list p; we then have to turn this pair (x,xs) into the list (x:xs), for which we use build, applied to the uncurried form of (:), which takes its arguments as a pair, and thus converts (x,xs) to (x:xs).

```
list :: Parse a b -> Parse a [b]
```

```
list p = (succeed []) 'alt'
         ((p >*> list p) 'build' (uncurry (:)))
```

Exercises

17.10 Define the functions

```
neList   :: Parse a b -> Parse a [b]
optional :: Parse a b -> Parse a [b]
```

so that neList p recognizes a non-empty list of the objects which are recognized by p, and optional p recognizes such an object *optionally* – it may recognize an object or succeed immediately.

17.11 Define the function

        nTimes :: Int -> Parse a b -> Parse a [b]

so that nTimes n p recognizes n of the objects recognized by p.

A parser for expressions

Now we can describe our expressions and define the parser for them. Expressions have three forms:

- Literals: 67, ~89, where '~' is used for unary minus.

- Variables: 'a' to 'z'.

- Applications of the binary operations +, *, -, /, %, where % is used for mod, and / gives integer division. Expressions are fully bracketed, if compound, thus: (23+(34-45)), and white space not permitted.

The parser has three parts

```
parser :: Parse Char Expr
parser = litParse 'alt' varParse 'alt' opExpParse
```

corresponding to the three sorts of expression. The simplest to define is

```
varParse :: Parse Char Expr
varParse = spot isVar 'build' Var

isVar :: Char -> Bool
isVar x = ('a' <= x && x <= 'z')
```

(Here the constructor Var is used as a function taking a character to the type Expr.)

An operator expression will consist of two expressions joined by an operator, the whole construct between a matching pair of parentheses:

```
opExpParse
  = (token '(' >*>
     parser     >*>
     spot isOp >*>
     parser     >*>
     token ')')
    'build' makeExpr
```

where the conversion function takes a nested sequence of pairs, like

```
('(',(Lit 23,('+',(Var 'x',')'))))
```

into the expression Op Add (Lit 23) (Var 'x'), thus

```
makeExpr (_,(e1,(bop,(e2,_)))) = Op (charToOp bop) e1 e2
```

Defining the functions isOp and charToOp is left as an exercise.

Finally, we look at the case of literals. A number consists of a non-empty list of digits, with an optional '~' at the front. We therefore use the functions from the exercises of the previous section to say

```
litParse
  = ((optional (token '~')) >*>
     (neList (spot isDigit))
     'build' (charlistToExpr . uncurry (++))
```

Left undefined here is the function charlistToExpr which should convert a list of characters to a literal integer; this is an exercise for the reader.

Exercises

17.12 Define the functions

```
isOp      :: Char -> Bool
charToOp  :: Char -> Ops
```

used in the parsing of expressions.

17.13 Define the function

```
charlistToExpr :: [Char] -> Expr
```

so that

```
charlistToExpr "234" ~> Lit 234
charlistToExpr "~98" ~> Lit (-98)
```

which is used in parsing literal expressions.

17.14 A command to the calculator to assign the value of expr to the variable var is represented thus

```
var:expr
```

Give a parser for these commands.

17.15 How would you change the parser for numbers if decimal fractions are to be allowed in addition to integers?

17.16 How would you change the parser for variables if names longer than a single character are to be allowed?

17.17 Explain how you would modify your parser so that the *whitespace* characters space and tab can be used in expressions, but would be ignored on parsing. (Hint: there is a simple pre-processor which does the trick!)

17.18 (Note: this exercise is for those familiar with Backus-Naur notation for grammars.)

Expressions without bracketing and allowing the multiplicative expressions higher binding power are described by the grammar

```
Expr  ::= Int | Var | (Expr Ops Expr) |
          Lexpr Mop Mexpr | Mexpr Aop Expr
Lexpr ::= Int | Var | (Expr Ops Expr)
Mexpr ::= Int | Var | (Expr Ops Expr) | Lexpr Mop Mexpr
Mop   ::= '*' | '/' | '%'
Aop   ::= '+' | '-'
Ops   ::= Mop | Aop
```

Give a Haskell parser for this grammar. Discuss the associativity of the operator '-' in this grammar.

The top-level parser

The parser defined in the last section, `parser` is of type

```
[Char] -> [ (Expr,[Char]) ]
```

yet what we need is to convert this to a function taking a string to the expression it represents. We therefore define the function

```
topLevel :: Parse a b -> [a] -> b
topLevel p inp
  = case results of
      [] -> error "parse unsuccessful"
      _  -> head results
    where
    results = [ found | (found,[]) <- p inp ]
```

The parse `p inp` is successful if the result contains at least one parse (the second case) in which all the input has been read (the test given by the pattern match to (`found,[]`)). If this happens, the first value `found` is returned; otherwise we are in error.

We can define the type of commands thus

```
data Command = Eval Expr | Assign Var Expr | Null
```

which are intended to cause

- the evaluation of the expression,

- the assignment of the value of the expression to the variable, and

- no effect.

If the assignment command takes the form `var:expr`, then it is not difficult to design a parser for this type,

```
commandParse :: Parse Char Command
```

We will assume this has been built when we revisit the calculator example below.

Conclusions

The type of parsers `Parse a b` with the functions

```
none     :: Parse a b
succeed  :: b -> Parse a b
spot     :: (a -> Bool) -> Parse a a
alt      :: Parse a b -> Parse a b -> Parse a b
>*>      :: Parse a b -> Parse a c -> Parse a (b,c)
build    :: Parse a b -> (b -> c) -> Parse a c
topLevel :: Parse a b -> [a] -> b
```

allow us to construct so-called recursive descent parsers in a straightforward way. It is worth looking at the aspects of the language we have exploited.

- The type `Parse a b` is represented by a function type, so that all the parser combinators are higher order functions.

- Because of polymorphism, we do not need to be specific about either the input or the output type of the parsers we build.

  In our example we have confined ourselves to inputs which are strings of characters, but they could have been *tokens* of any other type, if required: we might take the tokens to be *words* which are then parsed into sentences, for instance.

  More importantly in our example, we can return objects of any type using the same combinators, and in the example we returned lists and pairs as well as simple characters and expressions.

- Lazy evaluation plays a role here also. The possible parses we build are generated *on demand* as the alternatives are tested. The parsers will backtrack through the different options until a successful one is found.

Building general libraries like this parser library is one of the major advantages of using a modern functional programming language with the facilities mentioned above. From a toolkit like this it is possible to build a whole range of parsers and language processors which can form the front ends of systems of all sorts.

We will return to a discussion of parsing in Chapter 18; note also that we could make the type of `Parse a b` into an abstract data type, along the lines discussed in Chapter 16. On the other hand, it would also be useful to leave the implementation open to extension by users, which is the way in which other Haskell libraries are made available.

Exercises

17.19 Define a parser which recognizes strings representing Haskell lists of integers, like `"[2,-3,45]"`.

17.20 Define a parser to recognize simple sentences of English, with a subject, verb and object. You will need to provide some vocabulary, `"cat"`, `"dog"`, and so on, and a parser to recognize a string. You will also need to define a function

```
tokenList :: Eq a => [a] -> Parse a [a]
```

so that, for instance,

```
tokenList "Hello" "Hello Sailor" ⤳ [ ("Hello"," Sailor") ]
```

17.21 Define the function

```
spotWhile :: (a -> Bool) -> Parse a [a]
```

whose parameter is a function which tests elements of the input type, and returns the longest initial part of the input, all of whose elements have the required property. For instance

```
spotWhile digit "234abc"  ⤳  [ ("234","abc") ]
spotWhile digit "abc234"  ⤳  [ ([],"abc234") ]
```

(17.6) **Infinite lists**

One important consequence of lazy evaluation is that it is possible for the language to describe **infinite** structures. These would require an infinite amount of time to evaluate fully, but under lazy evaluation it is possible to compute with only portions of a data structure rather than the whole object. Any recursive type will contain infinite objects; we concentrate on lists here, as these are by far the most widely used infinite structures.

In this section we look at a variety of examples, starting with simple one-line definitions and moving to an examination of random numbers to be used in our simulation case study. The simplest examples of infinite lists are constant lists like

```
ones = 1 : ones
```

Evaluation of this in a Haskell system produces a list of ones, indefinitely. This can be **interrupted** in Hugs by typing Ctrl-C or in the Hugs Windows interface by hitting the 'Stop' button. In either case this produces the result

```
[1, 1, 1, 1, 1, 1, 1^C{Interrupted!}
```

We can sensibly evaluate functions applied to ones. If we define

```
addFirstTwo :: [Int] -> Int
addFirstTwo (x:y:zs) = x+y
```

then applied to ones we have

```
addFirstTwo ones
⤳   addFirstTwo (1:ones)
⤳   addFirstTwo (1:1:ones)
⤳   1+1
⤳   2
```

Built into the system are the lists [n ..], [n,m ..], so that

```
[3 .. ]    = [3,4,5,6,...
[3,5 .. ] = [3,5,7,9,...
```

We can define these ourselves:

```
from :: Int -> [Int]
from n        = n : from (n+1)

fromStep :: Int -> Int -> [Int]
fromStep n m = n : fromStep (n+m) m
```

and an example evaluation gives

```
fromStep 3 2
↝   3 : fromStep 5 2
↝   3 : 5 : fromStep 7 2
↝   ...
```

These functions are also defined over any instance of Enum; details can be found in Prelude.hs.

List comprehensions can also define infinite lists. The list of *all* Pythagorean triples is given by selecting z in [2 ..], and then selecting suitable values of x and y below that.

```
pythagTriples =
   [ (x,y,z) | z <- [2 .. ] , y <- [2 .. z-1] ,
              x <- [2 .. y-1] , x*x + y*y == z*z ]
pythagTriples
= [(3,4,5),(6,8,10),(5,12,13),(9,12,15),(8,15,17),(12,16,20),...
```

The powers of an integer are given by

```
powers :: Int -> [Int]
powers n = [ n^x | x <- [0 .. ] ]
```

and this is a special case of the prelude function iterate, which gives the infinite list

$$[x , f x , .. , f^n x , ..]$$

```
iterate :: (a -> a) -> a -> [a]
iterate f x = x : iterate f (f x)
```

Examples

1. Generating prime numbers

A positive integer greater than one is **prime** if it is divisible only by itself and one. The *Sieve of Eratosthenes* – an algorithm known for over two thousand years – works by

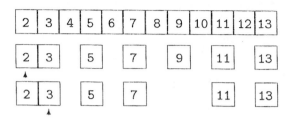

Figure 17.2 The Sieve of Eratosthenes.

cancelling out all the multiples of numbers, once they are established as prime. The primes are the only elements which remain in the list. The process is illustrated in Figure 17.2.

We begin with the list of numbers starting at 2. The head is 2, and we remove all the multiples of 2 from the list. The head of the remainder of the list, 3, is prime, since it was not removed in the sieve by 2. We therefore sieve the remainder of the list of multiples of 3, and repeat the process indefinitely. As a Haskell definition, we write

```
primes :: [Int]

primes        = sieve [2 .. ]
sieve (x:xs) = x : sieve [ y | y <- xs , y 'mod' x > 0]
```

where we test whether x divides y by evaluating y 'mod' x; y is a multiple of x if this value is zero. Beginning the evaluation, we have

```
primes
↝   sieve [2 .. ]
↝   2 : sieve [ y | y <- [3 .. ] , y 'mod' 2 > 0]
↝   2 : sieve (3 : [ y | y <- [4 .. ] , y 'mod' 2 > 0])
↝   2 : 3 : sieve [ z | z <- [ y | y <- [4 .. ] , y 'mod' 2 > 0],
                    z 'mod' 3 > 0]
↝   ...
↝   2 : 3 : sieve [ z | z <- [5,7,9...] , z 'mod' 3 > 0]
↝   ...
↝   2 : 3 : sieve [5,7,11,...]
↝   ...
```

Can we use primes to test for a number being a prime? If we evaluate member primes 7 we get the response True, while member primes 6 gives no answer. This is because an infinite number of elements have to be checked before we conclude that 6 is not in the list. The problem is that member cannot use the fact that primes is ordered. This we do in memberOrd.

```
memberOrd :: Ord a => [a] -> a -> Bool
memberOrd (x:xs) n
```

```
| x<n          = memberOrd xs n
| x==n         = True
| otherwise    = False
```

The difference here is in the final case: if the head of the list (x) is greater than the element we seek (n), the element cannot be a member of the (ordered) list. Evaluating the test again,

```
memberOrd [2,3,5,7,11,...] 6
⤳   memberOrd [3,5,7,11,...] 6
⤳   memberOrd [5,7,11,...] 6
⤳   memberOrd [7,11,...] 6
⤳   False
```

2. Generating random numbers

Many computer systems require us to generate 'random' numbers, one after another. Our queuing simulation is a particular example upon which we focus here, after looking at the basics of the problem.

No Haskell program can produce a truly random sequence; after all, we want to be able to predict the behaviour of our programs, and randomness is inherently unpredictable. What we can do, however, is generate a **pseudo-random** sequence of natural numbers, smaller than modulus. This **linear congruential method** works by starting with a seed, and then by getting the next element of the sequence from the previous value thus

```
nextRand :: Int -> Int
nextRand n = (multiplier*n + increment) 'mod' modulus
```

A (pseudo-)random sequence is given by iterating this function,

```
randomSequence :: Int -> [Int]
randomSequence = iterate nextRand
```

Given the values

```
seed       = 17489
multiplier = 25173
increment  = 13849
modulus    = 65536
```

the sequence produced by randomSequence seed begins

```
[17489,59134,9327,52468,43805,8378,...
```

The numbers in this sequence, which range from 0 to 65535, all occur with the same frequency. What are we to do if instead we want the numbers to come in the (integer) range a to b inclusive? We need to scale the sequence, which is achieved by a map:

```
scaleSequence :: Int -> Int -> [Int] -> [Int]
scaleSequence s t
  = map scale
    where
    scale n = n 'div' denom + s
    range   = t-s+1
    denom   = modulus 'div' range
```

The original range of numbers 0 to modulus-1 is split into range blocks, each of the same length. The number s is assigned to values in the first block, s+1 to values in the next, and so on.

In our simulation example, we want to generate for each arrival the length of service that person will need on being served. For illustration, we suppose that they range from 1 to 6 minutes, but that they are supposed to happen with different probabilities.

Waiting time	1	2	3	4	5	6
Probability	0.2	0.25	0.25	0.15	0.1	0.05

We need a function to turn such a distribution into a transformer of infinite lists. Once we have a function transforming individual values, we can map it along the list.

We can represent a distribution of objects of type a by a list of type [(a,Float)], where we assume that the numeric entries add up to one. Our function transforming individual values will be

```
makeFunction :: [(a,Float)] -> (Float -> a)
```

so that numbers in the range 0 to 65535 are transformed into items of type a. The idea of the function is to give the following ranges to the entries for the list above.

Waiting time	1	2	3	. . .
Range start	0	(m*0.2)+1	(m*0.45)+1	. . .
Range end	m*0.2	m*0.45	m*0.7	. . .

where m is used for modulus. The definition follows:

```
makeFunction dist = makeFun dist 0.0

makeFun ((ob,p):dist) nLast rand
  | nNext >= rand && rand > nLast
        = ob
  | otherwise
      = makeFun dist nNext rand
        where
        nNext = p*fromInt modulus + nLast
```

The makeFun function has an extra argument, which carries the position in the range 0 to modulus-1 reached so far in the search; it is initially zero. The fromInt function used here converts an Int to an equivalent Float.

The transformation of a list of random numbers is given by

```
map (makeFunction dist)
```

and the random distribution of waiting times we require begins thus

```
map (makeFunction dist . fromInt) (randomSequence seed)
= [2,5,1,4,3,1,2,5,4,2,2,2,1,3,2,5,...
```

with 6 first appearing at the 35th position.

Another random number generator is given in the library Random.hs.

> **Note: Infinite list generators**
>
> The list comprehension pythagTriples2, intended to produce the list of all Pythagorean triples, instead produces *no* output to the prompt.
>
> ```
> pythagTriples2 =
>   = [ (x,y,z) | x <- [2 .. ] ,
>                 y <- [x+1 .. ] ,
>                 z <- [y+1 .. ] ,
>                 x*x + y*y == z*z ]
> ```
>
> The problem is in the order of choice of the elements. The first choice for x is 2, and for y is 3; given this, there are an infinite number of values to try for z: 4, 5 and so on, indefinitely. We therefore never try any of the other choices for x or y, among which the triples lie.
>
> Two options present themselves. First we can redefine the solution, as in the original pythagTriples, so that it involves only one infinite list. Alternatively, we can try to write a function which returns all pairs of elements from two infinite lists:
>
> ```
> infiniteProduct :: [a] -> [b] -> [(a,b)]
> ```
>
> This is left as an exercise. Using such a function it is possible to adapt the definition of pythagTriples2 to make it give all the Pythagorean triples.

Exercises

17.22 Define the infinite lists of factorial and Fibonacci numbers,

```
factorial = [1,1,2,6,24,120,720,...]
fibonacci = [0,1,1,2,3,5,8,13,21,...]
```

17.23 Give a definition of the function

```
factors :: Int -> [Int]
```

which returns a list containing the factors of a positive integer. For instance,

```
factors 12 = [1,2,3,4,6,12]
```

Using this function or otherwise, define the list of numbers whose only prime factors are 2, 3 and 5, the so-called **Hamming numbers**:

```
hamming = [1,2,3,4,5,6,8,9,10,12,15,...
```

17.24 Define the function

```
runningSums :: [Int] -> [Int]
```

which calculates the running sums

$$[0, a_0, a_0+a_1, a_0+a_1+a_2, \ldots$$

of a list

$$[a_0, a_1, a_2, \ldots$$

17.25 Define the function `infiniteProduct` specified above, and use it to correct the definition of `pythagTriples2`.

17.7 Why infinite lists?

Haskell supports infinite lists and other infinite structures, and we saw in the last section that we could define a number of quite complicated lists, like the list of prime numbers, and lists of random numbers. The question remains, though, of whether these lists are anything other than a curiosity. There are two arguments which show their importance in functional programming.

First, an infinite version of a program can be more **abstract**, and so simpler to write. Consider the problem of finding the nth prime number, using the Sieve of Eratosthenes. If we work with finite lists, we need to know in advance how large a list is needed to accommodate the first n primes; if we work with an infinite list, this is not necessary: only that part of the list which is needed will be generated as computation proceeds.

In a similar way, the random numbers given by `randomSequence` seed provided an unlimited resource: we can take as many random numbers from the list as we require. There needs to be no decision at the start of programming as to the size of sequence needed. (These arguments are rather like those for **virtual memory** in a computer. It is often the case that predicting the memory use of a program is possible, but tiresome; virtual memory makes this unnecessary, and so frees the programmer to proceed with other tasks.)

The second argument is of wider significance, and can be seen by re-examining the way in which we generated random numbers. We generated an infinite list by means of `iterate`, and we transformed the values using `map`; these operations are pictured

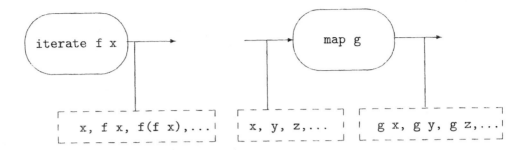

Figure 17.3 A generator and a transformer.

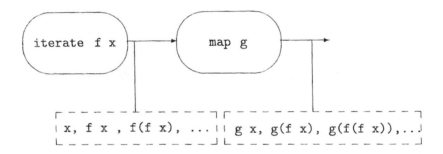

Figure 17.4 Linking processes together.

in Figure 17.3 as a generator of and a transformer of lists of values. These values are shown in the dashed boxes. These components can then be linked together, giving more complex combinations, as in Figure 17.4. This approach **modularizes** the generation of values in a distribution in an interesting way. We have separated the generation of the values from their transformation, and this means we can change each part independently of the other.

Once we have seen the view of infinite lists as the links between processes, other combinations suggest themselves, and in particular we can begin to write process-style programs which involve **recursion**.

Among the exercises in the last section was the problem of finding the running sums

$$[0, a_0, a_0 + a_1, a_0 + a_1 + a_2, \ldots$$

of the list $[a_0, a_1, a_2, \ldots$. Given the sum up to a_k, say, we get the next sum by adding the next value in the input, a_{k+1}. It is as if we *feed the sum back* into the process to have the value a_{k+1} added. This is precisely the effect of the network of processes in Figure 17.5, where the values passing along the links are shown in the dotted boxes.

The first value in the output out is 0, and we get the remaining values by adding the next value in iList to the previous sum, appearing in the list out. This is translated into Haskell as follows. The output of the function on input iList is out. This is

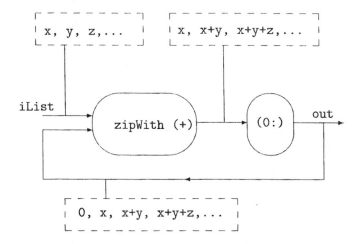

Figure 17.5   A process to compute the running sums of a list.

itself got by adding 0 to the front of the output from the zipWith (+), which itself has inputs iList and out. In other words,

```
listSums :: [Int] -> [Int]

listSums iList = out
                 where
                 out = 0 : zipWith (+) iList out
```

where we recall that zipWith is defined by

```
zipWith f (x:xs) (y:ys) = f x y : zipWith f xs ys
zipWith f _      _       = []
```

and the operator section (0:) puts a zero on the front of a list. We give a calculation of an example now.

```
listSums [1 .. ]
↝   out
↝   0 : zipWith (+) [1 .. ] out
↝   0 : zipWith (+) [1 .. ] (0:...)                              (1)
↝   0 : 1+0 : zipWith (+) [2 .. ] (1+0:...)                      (2)
↝   0 : 1 : 2+1 : zipWith (+) [3 .. ] (2+1:...)   ↝   ...
```

In making this calculation, we replace the occurrence of out in line (1) with the incomplete list (0:...). In a similar way, we replace the tail of out by (1+0:...) in line (2).

The definition of listSums is an example of the general function scanl1', which combines values using the function f, and whose first output is st.

```
scanl1' :: (a -> b -> b) -> b -> [a] -> [b]
scanl1' f st iList
  = out
    where
    out = st : zipWith f iList out
```

The function listSums is given by scanl1' (+) 0, and a function which keeps a running sort of the initial parts of list is sorts = scanl1' ins [], where ins inserts an element in the appropriate place in a sorted list. The list of factorial values, [1,1,2,6,...] is given by scanl1' (*) 1 [1 ..], and taking this as a model, any primitive recursive function can be described in a similar way.

The definition we give here is a minor variant of the prelude function scanl, but we choose to give the definition here because of its close correspondence to the process networks for running sums given in Figure 17.5.

(**Exercises**)───

17.26 Give a definition of the list [2^n | n <- [0 ..]] using a process network based on scanl1'. (Hint: you can take the example of factorial as a guide.)

17.27 How would you select certain elements of an infinite list? For instance, how would you keep running sums of the *positive* numbers in a list of numbers?

17.28 How would you *merge* two infinite lists, assuming that they are sorted? How would you remove duplicates from the list which results? As an example, how would you merge the lists of powers of 2 and 3?

17.29 Give definitions of the lists of Fibonacci numbers [0,1,1,2,3,5,...] and Hamming numbers [1,2,3,4,5,6,8,9,...] (defined on page 370) using networks of processes. For the latter problem, you may find the merge function of the previous question useful.

(17.8) **Case study: simulation**

We are now in a position to put together the ingredients of the queue simulation covered in

- Section 14.5, where we designed the algebraic types Inmess and Outmess,

- Section 16.5, where the abstract types QueueState and ServerState were introduced, and in

- Section 17.6, where we showed how to generate an infinite list of pseudo-random waiting times chosen according to a distribution over the times 1 to 6.

As we said in Section 14.5, our top-level simulation will be a function from a series of input messages to a series of output messages, so

```
doSimulation :: ServerState -> [Inmess] -> [Outmess]
```

where the first parameter is the state of the server at the start of the simulation. In Section 16.5 we presented the function performing one step of the simulation,

```
simulationStep :: ServerState ->
                  Inmess ->
                  (ServerState, [Outmess])
```

which takes the current server state, and the input message arriving at the current minute and returns the state after one minute's processing, paired with the list of the output messages produced by the queues that minute (potentially every queue could release a customer at the same instant, just as no customers might be released.)

The output of the simulation will be given by the output messages generated in the first minute, and after those the results of a new simulation beginning with the updated state:

```
doSimulation servSt (im:messes)
  = outmesses ++ doSimulation servStNext messes
    where
    (servStNext , outmesses) = simulationStep servSt im
```

How do we generate an input sequence? From Section 17.6 we have the sequence of times given by

```
randomTimes
  = map (makeFunction dist . fromInt) (randomSequence seed)
  ↝  [2,5,1,4,3,1,2,5,...
```

We are to have arrivals of one person per minute, so the input messages we generate are

```
simulationInput
  = zipWith Yes [1 .. ] randomTimes
  ↝  [ Yes 1 2 , Yes 2 5 , Yes 3 1 , Yes 4 4 , Yes 5 3 ,...
```

What are the outputs produced when we run the simulation on this input with four queues, by setting the constant numQueues to 4? The output begins

```
doSimulation serverStart simulationInput
  ↝  [Discharge 1 0 2, Discharge 3 0 1, Discharge 6 0 1,
      Discharge 2 0 5, Discharge 5 0 3, Discharge 4 0 4,
      Discharge 7 2 2,...
```

The first six inputs are processed without delay, but the seventh requires a waiting time of 2 before being served.

The infinite number of arrivals represented by simulationInput will obviously generate a corresponding infinite number of output messages. We can make a finite approximation by giving the input

```
simulationInput2 = take 50 simulationInput ++ noes
noes = No : noes
```

where after one arrival in each of the first 50 minutes, no further people arrive. Fifty output messages will be generated, and we define this list of outputs thus:

```
take 50 (doSimulation serverStart simulationInput2)
```

Experimenting

We now have the facilities to begin experimenting with different data, such as the distribution and the number of queues. The total waiting time for a (finite) sequence of Outmess is given by

```
totalWait :: [Outmess] -> Int
totalWait = sum . map waitTime
            where
            waitTime (Discharge _ w _) = w
```

For simulationInput2 the total waiting time is 29, going up to 287 with three queues and down to zero with five. We leave it to the reader to experiment with the **round robin** simulation outlined in the exercises of Section 16.5.

A more substantial project is to model a set-up with a single queue feeding a number of bank clerks – one way to do this is to extend the serverState with an extra queue which feeds into the individual queues: an element leaves the feeder queue when one of the small queues is empty. This should avoid the unnecessary waiting time we face when making the wrong choice of queue, and the simulation shows that waiting times are reduced by this strategy, though by less than we might expect if service times are short.

(17.9) Proof revisited

After summarizing the effect that lazy evaluation has on the types of Haskell, we examine the consequences for reasoning about programs. Taking lists as a representative example, we look at how we can prove properties of infinite lists, and of all lists, rather than simply the set of finite lists, which was the scope of the proofs we looked at in Chapters 8, 10 and 14.

This section cannot give complete coverage of the issues of verification; we conclude with pointers to further reading.

Undefinedness

In nearly every programming language, it is possible to write a program which fails to terminate, and Haskell is no exception. We call the value of such programs the **undefined** value, as it gives no result to a computation.

The simplest expression which gives an undefined result is

```
undef :: a
undef = undef                                                  (undef.1)
```

which gives a non-terminating or undefined value of every type, but of course we can write an undefined program without intending to, as in

```
fak n = (n+1) * fak n
```

where we have confused the use of n and n+1 in attempting to define the factorial function. The value of `fak n` will be the same as `undef`, as they are both non-terminating.

We should remark that we are using the term 'undefined' in two different ways here. The **name** `undef` is given a definition by (undef.1); the **value** that the definition gives it is the undefined value, which represents the result of a calculation or evaluation which fails to terminate (and therefore fails to define a result).

The existence of these undefined values has an effect on the type of lists. What if we define, for example, the list

```
list1 = 2:3:undef
```

The list has a well-defined head, 2, and tail 3:undef. Similarly, the tail has a head, 3, but its tail is undefined. The type [Int] therefore contains **partial** lists like list1, built from the undefined list, undef, parts of which are defined and parts of which are not.

Of course, there are also undefined integers, so we also include in [Int] lists like

```
list2 = undef:[2,3]
list3 = undef:4:undef
```

which contain undefined values, and might also be partial. Note that in list3 the first occurrence of undef is at type Int while the second is at type [Int].

What happens when a function is applied to undef? We use the rules for calculation we have seen already, so that the const function of the standard prelude satisfies

```
const 17 undef  ⤳  17
```

If the function applied to undef has to pattern match, then the result of the function will be undef, since the pattern match has to look at the structure of undef, which will never terminate. For instance, for the functions used in Chapter 8,

```
sum undef        ⤳   undef                                       (sum.u)
doubleAll undef  ⤳   undef                                   (doubleAll.u)
```

In writing proofs earlier in the book we were careful to state that in some cases the results hold only for **defined** values.

An integer is defined if it is not equal to undef; a list is defined if it is a finite list of defined values; using this as a model it is not difficult to give a definition of the defined values of any algebraic type.

A finite list as we have defined it may contain undefined values. Note that in some earlier proofs we stipulated that the results hold only for (finite) lists of defined values, that is for defined lists.

List induction revisited

As we said above, since there is an undefined list, undef, in each list type, lists can be built up from this; there will therefore be two base cases in the induction principle.

Proof by structural induction: fp-lists

To prove the property P(xs) for all finite or partial lists (**fp-lists**) xs we have to do three things:

Base cases	Prove P([]) and P(undef).
Induction step	Prove P(x:xs) assuming that P(xs) holds already.

Among the results we proved by structural induction in Chapter 8 were the equations

```
sum (doubleAll xs) = 2 * sum xs                          (sum-double)
xs ++ (ys ++ zs)   = (xs ++ ys) ++ zs                    (assoc++)
reverse (xs ++ ys) = reverse ys ++ reverse xs            (reverse++)
```

for all **finite** lists xs, ys and zs. For these results to hold for all fp-lists, we need to show that

```
sum (doubleAll undef) = 2 * sum undef              (sum-double.u)
undef ++ (ys ++ zs)   = (undef ++ ys) ++ zs        (assoc++.u)
reverse (undef ++ ys) = reverse ys ++ reverse undef   (reverse++.u)
```

as well as being sure that the induction step is valid for all fp-lists. Now, by (sum.u) and (doubleAll.u) the equation (sum-double.u) holds, and so (sum-double) holds for all fp-lists. In a similar way, we can show (assoc++.u). More interesting is (reverse++.u). Recall the definition of reverse:

```
reverse []     = []
reverse (x:xs) = reverse xs ++ [x]
```

It is clear from this that since there is a pattern match on the parameter, undef as the first parameter will give an undef result, so

```
reverse undef = undef
```

Taking a defined list, like [2,3] for ys in (reverse++.u) gives

```
reverse (undef ++ [2,3])
  = reverse undef
  = undef
```

```
reverse [2,3] ++ reverse undef
  = [3,2] ++ undef
```

This is enough to show that (reverse++.u) does not hold, and that we cannot infer that (reverse++) holds for all fp-lists. Indeed the example above shows exactly that (reverse++) is not valid.

Infinite lists

Beside the fp-lists, there are **infinite** members of the list types. How can we prove properties of infinite lists? A hint is given by our discussion of printing the results of evaluating an infinite list. In practice what happens is that we interrupt evaluation by hitting Ctrl-C after some period of time. We can think of what we see on the screen as an **approximation** to the infinite list.

If what we see are the elements $a_0, a_1, a_2, \ldots, a_n$, we can think of the approximation being the list

a₀:a₁:a₂:...:aₙ:undef

since we have no information about the list beyond the element a_n.

More formally, we say that the partial lists

undef, a₀:undef, a₀:a₁:undef, a₀:a₁:a₂:undef, ...

are approximations to the infinite list $[a_0, a_1, a_2, \ldots, a_n, \ldots]$.

Two lists xs and ys are equal if all their approximants are equal, that is for all natural numbers n, take n xs = take n ys. (The take function gives the defined portion of the nth approximant, and it is enough to compare these parts.) A more usable version of this principle applies to infinite lists only.

Infinite list equality

A list xs is infinite if for all natural numbers n, take n xs $\neq$ take (n+1) xs.
Two infinite lists xs and ys are equal if for all natural numbers n, xs!!n = ys!!n.

Example ───

Two factorial lists

Our example here is inspired by the process-based programs of Section 17.7. If fac is the factorial function

```
fac :: Int -> Int
fac 0 = 1                                              (fac.1)
fac m = m * fac (m-1)                                   (fac.2)
```

one way of defining the infinite list of factorials is

```
facMap = map fac [0 .. ]                               (facMap.1)
```

while a process-based solution is

```
facs = 1 : zipWith (*) [1 .. ] facs                    (facs.1)
```

Assuming these lists are infinite (which they clearly are), we have to prove for all natural numbers n that

```
facMap!!n = facs!!n                                     (facMap.!!)
```

Proof In our proof we will assume for all natural numbers n the results

```
(map f xs)!!n        = f (xs!!n)                    (map.!!)
(zipWith g xs ys)!!n = g (xs!!n) (ys!!n)            (zipWith.!!)
```

which we discuss again later in this section.

(facMap.!!) is proved by mathematical induction, that is we prove the result for 0 outright, and we prove the result for a positive n assuming the result for n−1.

Base We start by proving the result at zero. Examining the left-hand side first,

```
facMap!!0
  = (map fac [0 .. ])!!0                     by (facMap.1)
  = fac ([0 .. ]!!0)                         by (map.!!)
  = fac 0                                    by def of [0 .. ],!!
  = 1                                        by (fac.1)
```

The right-hand side is

```
facs!!0
  = (1 : zipWith (*) [1 .. ] facs)!!0        by (facs.1)
  = 1                                        by def of !!
```

thus establishing the base case.

Induction In the induction case we have to prove (facMap.!!) using the induction hypothesis:

```
facMap!!(n-1) = facs!!(n-1)                              (hyp)
```

The left-hand side of (facMap.!!) is

```
facMap!!n
  = (map fac [0 .. ])!!n                     by (facMap.1)
  = fac ([0 .. ]!!n)                         by (map.!!)
  = fac n                                    by def of [0 .. ],!!
  = n * fac (n-1)                            by (fac.2)
```

It is not hard to see that we have facMap !! (n−1) = fac (n−1) by a similar argument to the first three steps here and so,

```
  ·= n * (facMap!!(n-1))
```

The right-hand side of (facMap.!!) is

```
facs!!n
  = (1 : zipWith (*) [1 .. ] facs)!!n        by (facs.1)
  = (zipWith (*) [1 .. ] facs)!!(n-1)        by def of !!
  = (*) ([1 .. ]!!(n-1)) (facs!!(n-1))       by (zipWith.!!)
  = ([1 .. ]!!(n-1)) * (facs!!(n-1))         by def of (*)
  = n * (facs!!(n-1))                        by def of [1 .. ],!!
  = n * (facMap!!(n-1))                      by (hyp)
```

The final step of this proof is given by the induction hypothesis, and completes the proof of the induction step and the result itself. ∎

Proofs for infinite lists

When are results we prove for all fp-lists valid for all lists? If a result holds for all fp-lists, then it holds for all *approximations* to infinite lists. For some properties it is enough to know the property for all approximations to know that it will be valid for all infinite lists as well. In particular, this is true for all *equations*. This means that, for example, we can assert that for *all* lists xs,

(map f . map g) xs = map (f.g) xs

and therefore by the principle of extensionality for functions,

map f . map g = map (f.g)

Many other of the equations we proved initially for finite lists can be extended to proof for the fp-lists, and therefore to all lists. Some of these are given in the exercises which follow.

Further reading

The techniques we have given here provide a flavour of how to write proofs for infinite lists and infinite data structures in general. We cannot give the breadth or depth of a full presentation, but refer the reader to Paulson (1987) for more details. An alternative approach to proving the factorial list example is given in Thompson (1999), which also gives a survey of proof in functional programming.

Exercises

17.30 Show that for all fp-lists ys and zs,

    undef ++ (ys ++ zs) = (undef ++ ys) ++ zs

to infer that ++ is associative over all lists.

17.31 If rev xs is defined to be shunt xs [], as in Section 8.7, show that

    rev (rev undef) = undef   (rev-rev.1)

In Chapter 8 we proved that

    rev (rev xs) = xs   (rev-rev.2)

for all finite lists xs.

Why can we not infer from (rev-rev.1) and (rev-rev.2) that the equation rev (rev xs) = xs holds for all fp-lists xs?

17.32 Prove for all natural numbers m, n and functions f :: Int -> a that

    (map f [m ..])!!n = f (m+n)

[Hint: you will need to choose the right variable for the induction proof.]

17.33 Prove that the lists

```
facMap = map fac [0 .. ]
facs = 1 : zipWith (*) [1 .. ] facs
```

are infinite.

17.34 If we define indexing thus

```
(x:_)!!0  = x
(_:xs)!!n = xs!!(n-1)
[]!!n     = error "Indexing"
```

show that for all functions f, fp-lists xs and natural numbers n,

```
(map f xs)!!n = f (xs!!n)
```

and therefore infer that the result is valid for all lists xs. State and prove a similar result for zipWith.

17.35 Show that the following equations hold between functions.

```
filter p . map f      = map f . filter (p . f)
filter p . filter q   = filter (q &&& p)
concat . map (map f)  = map f . concat
```

where the operator &&& is defined by

```
(q &&& p) x = q x && p x
```

Summary

Lazy evaluation of Haskell expressions means that we can write programs in a different style. A data structure created within a program execution will only be created on demand, as we saw with the example of finding the sum of fourth powers. In finding routes through a graph we saw that we could explore just that part of the graph which is needed to reveal a path. In these and many more cases the advantage of lazy evaluation is to give programs whose purpose is clear and whose execution is efficient.

We re-examined the list comprehension notation, which makes many list processing programs easier to express; we saw this in the particular examples of route finding and parsing.

A design principle exploited in this chapter involved the use of lazy lists: if a function can return multiple results it is possible to represent this as a list; using lazy evaluation, the multiple results will only be generated one-by-one, as they are required. Also, we are able to represent 'no result' by the empty list, []. This 'list of successes' method is useful in a variety of contexts.

Exploiting this principle as well as higher-order functions, polymorphism and list comprehensions we gave a library of parsing functions, which we saw applied to the type of arithmetical expressions, Expr. This showed one of the strengths of modern functional programming languages, whose constructs are especially well suited to describing general toolkits of this sort.

Rather than being simply a curiosity, this chapter has shown that we can exploit infinite lists for a variety of purposes.

- In giving an *infinite* list of prime or random numbers we provide an unlimited resource: we do not have to know how much of the resource we need while constructing the program; this *abstraction* makes programming simpler and clearer.

- Infinite lists provide a mechanism for process-based programming in a functional setting.

The chapter concluded with a discussion of how proofs could be lifted to the partial and infinite elements of the list type: criteria were given in both cases and we gave examples and counter-examples in illustration.

Conclusion

Chapter 20

Conclusion

This book has covered the basics of functional programming in the lazy language Haskell. It has shown how to craft programs, both by giving extensive examples as each new aspect of the language was introduced, and also by giving general advice on how to design programs, in a distinct phase between giving a precise specification of the problem and writing a solution in Haskell.

The power of functional programming

A functional programmer models the real world at a high level of abstraction, concentrating on what relationships there are between values, embodied in function definitions. This contrasts with a lower-level view in which the details of how items are related predominate. For instance, in Haskell lists are simply values, whereas in C or C++ they become data structures built from pointers, and even in Java it is difficult to present a suitably abstract model of lists. This higher-level approach has a number of consequences, which have come out in the course of the book.

- Higher-order functions and polymorphism combine to support the construction of general-purpose libraries of functions, such as the list functions in the Haskell standard prelude and library. The map function, for instance,

```
map :: (a -> b) -> [a] -> [b]
```

embodies the 'pattern' of applying the same transformation to every element in a list, which will be **reused** in a host of applications of lists.

Also supporting reuse through **overloading** are type classes, used for instance in giving the function

```
elem :: Eq a => a -> [a] -> Bool
```

which tests for membership of a list using the overloaded equality function.

- The definitions of functions are equations which express properties of the functions defined. From the definitions of map and function composition, '.', for example, it is possible to **prove** that for all functions f and g,

```
map (f . g) = map f . map g
```

Proof provides a user with assurance about how a program behaves on all arguments, in contrast to testing which can only give direct information about its behaviour on a – hopefully representative – subset of inputs.

Data structures can be introduced in a directly recursive manner, giving trees, queues and so forth without having to look at their representations. Algorithms are written at the same level as they would be described informally, in contrast with more traditional approaches which make the representation very clear.

A text like this can only provide an introduction to a subject as rich and developed as functional programming; the rest of this concluding chapter discusses other aspects of the subject, as well as giving pointers to other sources on the Web and in books and articles.

Further Haskell

The purpose of this text is to introduce functional programming ideas using the Haskell language. It covers the important aspects of the language, but does not aim to be complete. Among the topics omitted are data types with labelled fields, which resemble records or structures in other languages; strictness annotations, which are used to make data type constructors strict in some or all of their arguments; details of the Read class and the numeric types and classes.

Further information about all these can be found in the Haskell language report (Peyton Jones and Hughes 1998), and the 'Gentle Introduction' of Hudak, Fasel and Peterson (1997) also contains useful information about some of them, as well as providing an overview of the language for an experienced functional programmer. Both of these, as well as many other Haskell resources, can be found at the Haskell home page, `http://www.haskell.org/`

The text has discussed many of the most important functions in the standard prelude but on the whole has avoided discussing the contents of the libraries, which are documented in Peyton Jones and Hughes (1998). These libraries fall into two classes. First there are libraries of utilities, such as `List.hs` which contains a multitude of list-manipulating functions. These are in libraries, which can be included or not by the programmer at will, so as not to clutter up the name space of the language.

Other libraries contain extensions of the language, including a library of arrays, `Array.hs`, as well as facilities for file creation and management, `Directory.hs`, and for system links, `System.hs`. These libraries come with all Haskell implementations; each implementation will also come with particular extensions, usually available in the form of library modules.

Haskell in the future

Haskell was first defined in 1987, and has been modified and extended since then. This text is written in Haskell 98, which is meant to provide a stable base system consisting of tried and tested features. The progress of research in functional programming makes it clear that a language like Haskell will not stand still forever and at the time of writing there is an initiative under way to design Haskell 2, which will extend and modify the language in a number of significant ways. Nevertheless, it is likely that systems will continue to support the features of Haskell 98 as outlined in this text. The Haskell home page can be relied upon to contain up-to-date information on the status of Haskell.

Extending Haskell

As it has been introduced in this text, Haskell is a general-purpose, high-level programming language. Many real-world applications require programs to, for instance, manipulate computer graphics, modify the state of a machine, or operate in parallel, and Haskell as it stands does not provide these facilities directly.

However, there have been extensions to particular Haskell implementations to perform tasks like this. Information about a great number of applications and extensions of Haskell can be found on the home page

```
http://www.haskell.org/libraries.html                    (libraries)
```

or in the documentation for particular implementations, as detailed on the Haskell home page and in Appendix E.

Often languages are not used in isolation, and so links to external libraries and programming languages are important. These interfacing issues are discussed in Finne *et al.* (1998) and Meijer (1998). A variety of graphical user interfaces for Haskell programs have been written; details of these can be found on the (libraries) page.

Other specific extensions include a library to write CGI scripts, which are used to extend the interactive capabilities of Web pages,

```
http://www.cse.ogi.edu/~erik/Personal/cgi.htm
```

to provide a language for describing graphical animations which interact with users (Elliott and Hudak 1997),

```
http://www.research.microsoft.com/~conal/Fran/
```

to give efficient implementations of functional data structures (Okasaki 1998),

```
http://www.cs.columbia.edu/~cdo/edison/
```

to describe musical notation in Haskell (Hudak *et al.* 1996),

```
http://www.haskell.org/haskore/
```

and to support a concurrent version of the language Glasgow Parallel Haskell,

```
http://www.dcs.gla.ac.uk/fp/software/gph/
```

Using a monadic view it is also possible to integrate mutable state into the Haskell model. This is discussed in Peyton Jones and Wadler (1993) and Launchbury and Peyton Jones (1994) and implemented in the Glasgow Haskell Compiler.

Haskell and functional programming on the Web

There are now many resources on Haskell and functional programming to be found on the World Wide Web. This text itself has a home page at

`http://www.cs.ukc.ac.uk/people/staff/sjt/craft2e/`

which lists all the links given here. The Haskell home page is at

`http://www.haskell.org/`

and information about the Haskell mailing list can also be found there.

The Haskell language was named in honour of Haskell Brooks Curry. A short biography and photograph of Curry can be found at

`http://www-groups.dcs.st-and.ac.uk/~history/Mathematicians/Curry.html`

For functional programming in general, the first place to start is the 'FAQ',

`http://www.cs.nott.ac.uk/Department/Staff/gmh/faq.html`

which gives details of all functional programming languages, as well as more general information and indeed answers to frequently asked questions about the basics of functional programming.

Information about a number of real-world applications of functional programming can be found at

`http://www.cs.bell-labs.com/~wadler/realworld/`

Jon Mountjoy has a web page on functional programming,

`http://carol.wins.uva.nl/~jon/func.html`

and Claus Reinke makes available his functional programming bookmarks,

`http://www.cs.nott.ac.uk/~czr/FP.html`

Functional programming languages are used in many universities and other institutions, and resources on functional languages in education are accessible from

`http://www.cs.kun.nl/fple/`

A final resource is the Internet newsgroup

`news:comp.lang.functional`

devoted to discussion of functional programming in general.

Other functional programming languages

Haskell is a lazy, strongly typed functional programming language; another is Miranda (Turner 1986; Thompson 1995). In this text laziness is only examined explicitly in

Chapter 17, and up to that point it looks at aspects of functional programming which are broadly shared with Standard ML (Milner *et al.* 1997; Appel 1993), the best known and most widely used strict and strongly typed functional language, for which Paulson (1996) provides an introduction. It is possible to model lazy evaluation within a strict language, and Haskell provides facilities to make evaluation strict, so the two schools are very close indeed.

A different style of functional programming, eschewing variables as much as possible, was introduced in Backus (1978). Bird and de Moor (1997) is a recent text which emphasizes the benefits of this style in supporting program transformation and also advocates a 'relational' style of programming which extends the functional.

LISP is the oldest established functional lanaguage, but it differs from Haskell and SML in not being strongly typed. An excellent tutorial introduction to programming in the Scheme dialect of LISP is given in Abelson, Sussman and Sussman (1996). An imperative language with similiarities to LISP and used for telephone switching and other real-time applications is Erlang (Armstrong, Virding and Williams 1993).

Two recent surveys of applications of functional programming languages in large-scale projects are Runciman and Wakeling (1995) and Hartel and Plasmeijer (1995b), and there is also information about this on the Web, as cited above.

In the last ten years, powerful techniques of implementation of especially lazy functional languages have been developed. The twin texts (Peyton Jones 1987; Peyton Jones and Lester 1992) describe these in lucid detail.

Where is functional programming going?

The material in this text is an introduction to modern functional programming in a typed, lazy, language. As the field develops, new techniques and approaches are continually being developed; a good place to start in learning about these is the proceedings of two summer schools in Advanced Functional Programming (Jeuring and Meijer 1995; Launchbury, Meijer and Sheard 1996). To see the ways in which functional langauges are being used in education, the proceedings of a meeting on Functional Languages in Education appear in Hartel and Plasmeijer (1995a), and these have been followed up with the creation of the FPLE Web site mentioned above. Research in functional programming is reported in the *Journal of Functional Programming*

```
http://www.dcs.gla.ac.uk/jfp/
```

and at the annual International Conference in Functional Programming (Hudak and Queinnec 1998), as well as at other meetings detailed at the Web sites mentioned above.

It is difficult to predict future directions in a field like computing, but it is clear that one fruitful direction for functional programming is in forming a **component of larger systems**. The Fran system (Elliott and Hudak 1997) uses a functional language to describe animations which are ultimately produced at a lower level using a library written in C++. The opening up of functional systems, so that it is no longer a choice of 'either functional or non-functional, but not both', means that functional languages can take their place in the programmer's toolkit of techniques and prove their worth alongside object-oriented and other languages. This opening up is enabled by systems such as H/Direct (Finne *et al.* 1998) and ActiveHaskell, which links Haskell to COM components; details of this can be found on the (libraries) Web page.

Another direction is in **strengthening type systems** for functional languages, so that only terminating programs can be written. At first sight this seems to exclude too many programs to be practical, but with 'co-data' (Turner 1995), and dependent types – where the type of a result depends upon the value of an argument (Augustsson 1998) – it appears that practical languages can be defined. The advantage of languages like these is that they make reasoning much more straightforward, as well as allowing a programmer to express more of their intuitions about how a program behaves as a part of the program. This text has already shown how a strongly typed language allows for the capture of many errors at compile time, and strengthening the type system can only help this.

A third issue is that of providing **tool support** for developers of functional programs. As was evident in the discussion of lazy evaluation, it is often very difficult indeed to predict the space behaviour of lazy programs; interesting work on this is reported in Runciman and Röjemo (1996).

These are only three of the possible directions for functional languages, and it is clear that they provide a fertile approach to programming which will remain an important element of computing science in years to come.

Functional, imperative and OO programming

In this appendix we compare programming in Haskell to more traditional notions in imperative languages like Pascal and C and object-oriented (OO) languages such as C++ and Java.

Values and states

Consider the example of finding the sum of squares of natural numbers up to a particular number. A functional program describes the values that are to be calculated, directly.

```
sumSquares :: Int -> Int
sumSquares 0 = 0
sumSquares n = n*n + sumSquares (n-1)
```

These equations state what the sum of squares is for a natural number argument. In the first case it is a direct description; in the second it states that the sum to non-zero n is got by finding the sum to n-1 and adding the square of n.

A typical imperative program might solve the problem thus

```
s := 0 ;
i := 0 ;
while i<n do begin
    i := i+1 ;
    s := i*i + s ;
end {while}
```

The sum is the final value of the variable s, which is changed repeatedly during program execution, as is the 'count' variable, i. The effect of the program can only be seen by following the sequence of changes made to these variables by the commands in the program, while the functional program can be read as a series of equations defining the sum of squares. This meaning is **explicit** in the functional program, whereas the imperative program has an overall effect which is not obvious from the program itself.

A more striking algorithm still is one which is completely explicit: 'to find the sum of squares, build the list of numbers 1 to n, square each of them, and sum the result'. This program, which uses neither complex control flow, as does the imperative example, nor recursion as seen in the function sumSquares, can be written in a functional style, thus:

```
newSumSq :: Int -> Int
newSumSq n = sum (map square [1 .. n])
```

where square x = x*x, the operation map applies its first argument to every member of a list, and sum finds the sum of a list of numbers. More examples of this sort of **data-directed** programming can be seen in the body of the text.

Functions and variables

An important difference between the two styles is what is meant by some of the terminology. Both 'function' and 'variable' have different interpretations.

As was explained earlier, a function in a functional program is simply something which returns a value which depends upon some inputs. In imperative and object-oriented languages like Pascal, C, C++ and Java a function is rather different. It will return a value depending upon its arguments, but in general it will also change the values of variables. Rather than being a pure function it is really a procedure which returns a value when it terminates.

In a functional program a variable stands for an **arbitrary** or **unknown** value. Every occurrence of a variable in an equation is interpreted in the same way. They are just like variables in logical formulas, or the mathematical variables familiar from equations like

$$a^2 - b^2 = (a-b)(a+b)$$

In any particular case, the value of all three occurrences of a will be the same. In exactly the same way, in

```
sumSquares n = n*n + sumSquares (n-1)
```

all occurrences of n will be interpreted by the same value. For example

```
sumSquares 7 = 7*7 + sumSquares (7-1)
```

The crucial motto is 'variables in functional programs *do not vary*'.

On the other hand, the value of a variable in an imperative program changes throughout its lifetime. In the sum of squares program above, the variable s will take the values 0,1,5,... successively. Variables in imperative programs *do* vary over time, on the other hand.

Program verification

Probably the most important difference between functional and imperative programs is logical. As well as being a program, a functional definition is a logical equation describing a **property** of the function. Functional programs are **self-describing**, as it were. Using the definitions, other properties of the functions can be deduced.

To take a simple example, for all n>0, it is the case that

```
sumSquares n > 0
```

To start with,

```
sumSquares 1
= 1*1 + sumSquares 0
= 1*1 + 0
= 1
```

which is greater than 0. In general, for n greater than zero,

```
sumSquares n = n*n + sumSquares (n-1)
```

Now, n*n is positive, and if sumSquares (n-1) is positive, their sum, sumSquares n, must be. This proof can be formalized using **mathematical induction**. The body of the text contains numerous examples of proofs by induction over the structure of data structures like lists and trees, as well as over numbers.

Program verification is possible for imperative programs as well, but imperative programs are not self-describing in the way functional ones are. To describe the effect of an imperative program, like the 'sum of squares' program above, we need to add to the program logical formulas or assertions which describe the state of the program at various points in its execution. These methods are both more indirect and more difficult, and verification seems very difficult indeed for 'real' languages like Pascal and C. Another aspect of program verification is **program transformation** in which programs are transformed to other programs which have the same effect but better performance, for example. Again, this is difficult for traditional imperative languages.

Records and tuples

In Chapter 5 the tuple types of Haskell are introduced. In particular we saw the definition

```
type Person = (String,String,Int)
```

This compares with a Pascal declaration of a record

```
type Person = record
  name  : String;
  phone : String;
  age   : Integer
end;
```

which has three fields which have to be named. In Haskell the fields of a tuple can be accessed by pattern matching, but it is possible to define functions called **selectors** which behave in a similar way, if required:

```
name  :: Person -> String
name (n,p,a) = n
```

and so on. If per :: Person then name per :: String, similarly to r.name being a string variable if r is a variable of type Person in Pascal.

Haskell 98 also contains records with named fields, rather more like those of Pascal. For further details, see the Haskell Report (Peyton Jones and Hughes 1998).

Lists and pointers

Haskell contains the type of lists built in, and other recursive types such as trees can be defined directly. We can think of the type of linked lists given by pointers in Pascal as an **implementation** of lists, since in Haskell it is not necessary to think of pointer values, or of storage allocation (new and dispose) as it is in Pascal. Indeed, we can think of Haskell programs as **designs** for Pascal list programs. If we define

```
type list = ^node;
type node = record
   head : value;
   tail : list
end;
```

then we have the following correspondence, where the Haskell head and tail functions give the head and tail of a list.

[]	nil
head ys	ys^.head
tail ys	ys^.tail
(x:xs)	cons(x,xs)

The function cons in Pascal has the definition

```
function cons(y:value;ys:list):list;
  var xs:list;
  begin
    new(xs);
    xs^.head := y;
    xs^.tail := ys;
    cons := xs
  end;
```

Functions such as

```
sumList []      = 0
sumList (x:xs) = x + sumList xs
```

can then be transferred to Pascal in a straightforward way.

```
function sumList(xs:list):integer;
```

```
begin
  if xs=nil
    then sumList := 0
    else sumList := xs^.head + sumList(xs^.tail)
end;
```

A second example is

```
doubleAll []     = []
doubleAll (x:xs) = (2*x) : doubleAll xs
```

where we use cons in the Pascal definition of the function

```
function doubleAll(xs:list):list;
  begin
    if xs=nil
      then doubleAll := nil
      else doubleAll := cons( 2*xs^.head , doubleAll(xs^.tail) )
  end;
```

If we define the functions

```
function head(xs:list):value;      function tail(xs:list):list;
  begin                              begin
    head := xs^.head                   tail := xs^.tail
  end;                               end;
```

then the correspondence is even clearer:

```
function doubleAll(xs:list):list;
  begin
    if xs=nil
      then doubleAll := nil
      else doubleAll := cons( 2*head(xs) , doubleAll( tail(xs) ) )
  end;
```

This is strong evidence that a functional approach can be useful even if we are writing in an imperative language: the functional language can be the high-level *design* language for the imperative implementation. Making this separation can give us substantial help in finding imperative programs – we can think about the design and the lower level implementation *separately*, which makes each problem smaller, simpler and therefore easier to solve.

Higher-order functions

Traditional imperative languages give little scope for higher-order programming; Pascal, Java and C allow functions as arguments, so long as those functions are not themselves higher-order, but has no facility for returning functions as results. In C++ it is possible to return objects which represent functions by overloading the function application operator! This underlies the genericity hailed in the C++ Standard Template Library, which requires advanced features of the language to implement functions like `map` and `filter`.

Control structures like `if-then-else` bear some resemblance to higher-order functions, as they take commands, c_1, c_2 etc. into other commands,

`if b then c₁ else c₂`   `while b do c₁`

just as `map` takes one function to another. Turning the analogy around, we can think of higher-order functions in Haskell as **control structures** which we can define ourselves. This perhaps explains why we form libraries of polymorphic functions: they are the control structures we use in programming particular sorts of system. Examples in the text include libraries for building parsers (Section 17.5) and interactive I/O programs (Chapter 18), as well as the built-in list-processing functions.

Polymorphism

Again, this aspect is poorly represented in many imperative languages; the best we can do in `Pascal`, say, is to use a text editor to copy and modify the list processing code from one type of lists for use with another. Of course, we then run the risk that the different versions of the programs are not modified in step, unless we are very careful to keep track of modifications, and so on.

Polymorphism in Haskell is what is commonly known as **generic** polymorphism: the same 'generic' code works over a whole collection of types. A simple example is the function which reverses the elements in a list.

Haskell classes support what is known as 'ad hoc' polymorphism, or in object-oriented terminology simply 'polymorphism', in which different programs implement the same operation over different types. An example of this is the Eq class of types carrying an equality operation: the way in which equality is checked is completely different at different types. Another way of viewing classes is as **interfaces** which different types can implement in different ways; in this way they resemble the interfaces of object-oriented languages like Java.

As is argued in the text, polymorphism is one of the mechanisms which helps to make programs *reusable* in Haskell; it remains to be seen whether this will also be true of advanced imperative languages.

Defining types and classes

The algebraic type mechanism of Haskell, explained in Chapter 14, subsumes various traditional type definitions. Enumerated types are given by algebraic types all of whose constructors are 0-ary (take no arguments); variant records can be implemented as algebraic types with more then one constructor, and **recursive** types usually implemented by means of pointers become recursive algebraic types.

Just as we explained for lists, Haskell programs over trees and so on can be seen as *designs* for programs in imperative languages manipulating the pointer implementations of the types.

The abstract data types, introduced in Chapter 16, are very like the abstract data types of Modula-2 and so on; the design methods we suggest for use of abstract data types mirror aspects of the **object-based** approach advocated for modern imperative languages such as Ada.

The Haskell class system also has object-oriented aspects, as we saw in Section 14.6. It is important to note that Haskell classes are in some ways quite different from the classes of, for instance, C++. In Haskell classes are made up of types, which themselves have members; in C++ a class is like a type, in that it contains objects. Because of this many of the aspects of object-oriented design in C++ are seen as issues of type design in Haskell.

List comprehensions

List comprehensions provide a convenient notation for **iteration** along lists: the analogue of a for loop, which can be used to run through the indices of an array. For instance, to sum all pairs of elements of xs and ys, we write

```
[ a+b | a <- xs , b <- ys ]
```

The order of the iteration is for a value a from the list xs to be fixed and then for b to run through the possible values from ys; this is then repeated with the next value from xs, until the list is exhausted. Just the same happens for a **nested** for loop

```
for i:=0 to xLen-1 do
  for j:=0 to yLen-1 do                              (twoFor)
    write( x[i]+y[j] )
```

where we fix a value for i while running through all values for j.

In the for loop, we have to run through the indices; a list generator runs through the values directly. The indices of the list xs are given by

```
[0 .. length xs - 1]
```

and so a Haskell analogue of (twoFor) can be written thus:

```
[ xs!!i + ys!!j | i <- [0 .. length xs - 1] ,
                  j <- [0 .. length ys - 1] ]
```

if we so wish.

Lazy evaluation

Lazy evaluation and imperative languages do not mix well. In Pascal, for instance, we can write the function definition

```
function succ(x : integer):integer;
begin
  y    := y+1;
  succ := x+1
end;
```

This function adds one to its argument, but also has the **side-effect** of increasing y by one. If we evaluate $f(y, succ(z))$ we cannot predict the effect it will have.

- If f evaluates its second argument first, y will be increased before being passed to f;
- on the other hand, if f needs its first argument first (and perhaps its second argument not at all), the value passed to f will not be increased, even if it is increased before the function call terminates.

In general, it will not be possible to predict the behaviour of even the simplest programs. Since evaluating an expression can cause a change of the state, the order of expression evaluation determines the overall effect of a program, and so a lazy implementation can behave differently (in unforeseen ways) from the norm.

State, infinite lists and monads

Section 17.6 introduced infinite lists, and one of the first examples given there was an infinite list of random numbers. This list could be supplied to a function requiring a supply of random numbers; because of lazy evaluation, these numbers will only be generated on demand.

If we were to implement this imperatively, we would probably keep in a variable the last random number generated, and at each request for a number we would update this store. We can see the infinite list as supplying *all the values that the variable will take* as a single structure; we therefore do not need to keep the state, and hence have an **abstraction** from the imperative view.

We have seen in Section 18.8 that there has been recent important work on integrating side-effecting programs into a functional system by a monadic approach.

Conclusion

Clearly there are parallels between the functional and the imperative, as well as clear differences. The functional view of a system is often higher-level, and so even if we ultimately aim for an imperative solution, a functional design or **prototype** can be most useful.

We have seen that monads can be used to give an interface to imperative features within a functional framework. Many of the Haskell implementations offer these facilities, and so give a method of uniting the best features of two important programming paradigms without compromising the purity of the language. Other languages, including Standard ML (Milner, Tofte and Harper 1990), combine the functional and the imperative, but these systems tend to lose their pure functional properties in the process.

It is interesting to see the influence of ideas from modern functional programming languages in the design of Java extensions. One of the main drawbacks of Java is that it lacks a generic mechanism; the Pizza language (Odersky and Wadler 1997) adds this, together with Haskell-style pattern matching, and Pizza is a forerunner of the Generic Java extension, GJ, `www.cs.bell-labs.com/who/wadler/pizza/gj/`.

Glossary

We include this glossary to give a quick reference to the most widely used terminology in the book. Words appearing in **bold** in the descriptions have their own entries. Further references and examples are to be found by consulting the index.

Abstract type   An abstract type definition consists of the type name, the **signature** of the type, and the implementation equations for the names in the signature.

Algebraic type   An algebraic type definition states what are the **constructors** of the type. For instance, the declaration

```
data Tree = Leaf Int |
            Node Tree Tree
```

says that the two constructors of the Tree type are Leaf and Node, and that their types are, respectively,

```
Leaf :: Int->Tree
Node :: Tree->Tree->Tree
```

Application   This means giving values to (some of) the arguments of a function. If an n-argument function is given fewer than n arguments, this is called a **partial application**. Application is written using **juxtaposition**.

Argument   A **function** takes one or more arguments into an **output**.

Arguments are also known as **inputs** and **parameters**.

Associativity   The way in which an expression involving two applications of an operator is interpreted. If x#y#z is interpreted as (x#y)#z then # is left associative, if as x#(y#z) it is right associative; if both bracketings give the same result then # is called associative.

Base types   The types of numbers, including Int and Float, **Booleans**, Bool, and **characters**, Char.

Binding power   The 'stickiness' of an operator, expressed as an integer; the higher the number the stickier the operator. For example, 2+3*4 is interpreted as 2+(3*4) as '*' has higher binding power – binds more tightly – than '+'.

Booleans   The type containing the two 'truth values' True and False.

Calculation   A calculation is a line-by-line **evaluation** of a Haskell **expression** on paper. Calculations use the **definitions** which are contained in a **script** as well as the built-in definitions.

Cancellation   The rule for finding the type of a partial application.

Character   A single letter, such as `'s'` or `'\t'`, the tab character. They form the `Char` type.

Class   A collection of types. A class is defined by specifying a **signature**; a type is made an **instance** of the class by supplying an implementation of the definitions of the signature over the type.

Clause   A clause is one of the alternatives making up a **conditional equation**. A clause consists of a **guard** followed by an **expression**. When evaluating a function application, the first clause whose guard evaluates to `True` is chosen.

Combinator   Another name for a **function**.

Comment   Part of a **script** which plays no computational role; it is there for the reader to read and observe. Comments are specified in two ways: the part of the line to the right is made a comment by the symbol `--`; a comment of arbitrary length is enclosed by `{-` and `-}`.

Complexity   A measurement of the time or space behaviour of a function.

Composition   The combination of two functions by passing the **output** of one to the **input** of the other.

Concatenate   To put together a number of lists into a single list.

Conditional equation   A conditional equation consists of a left-hand side followed by a number of **clauses**. Each clause consists of a **guard** followed by an expression which is to be equated with the left-hand side of the **equation** if that particular clause is chosen during evaluation. The clause chosen is the first whose guard evaluates to `True`.

Conformal pattern match   An equation in which a pattern appears on the left-hand side of an equation, as in

`(x,y) = ....`

Constructor   An **algebraic type** is specified by its constructors, which are the functions which build elements of the algebraic type.

In the example in the entry for algebraic types, elements of the type are constructed using `Leaf` and `Node`; the elements are `Leaf n` where `n::Int` and `Node s t` where `s` and `t` are trees.

Context   The hypotheses which appear before `=>` in type and class declarations. A context `M a` means that the type `a` must belong to the class `M` for the function or class definition to apply. For instance, to apply a function of type

`Eq a => [a] -> a -> Bool`

to a list and object, these must come from types over which equality is defined.

Curried function   A function of at least two arguments which takes its arguments one at a time, so having the type

`t1 -> t2 -> ... -> t`

in contrast to the *uncurried* version

`(t1,t2,...) -> t`

The name is in honour of Haskell B. Curry, after whom the Haskell language is also named.

Declaration   A **definition** can be accompanied by a statement of the **type** of the object defined; these are often called type declarations.

Default   A default holds in the absence of any other definition. Used in `class` definitions to give definitions of some of the operations in terms of others; an example is the definition of /= in the Eq class.

Definition   A definition associates a **value** or a **type** with a **name**.

Design   In writing a system, the effort expended *before* implementation is started.

Derived class instance   An instance of a standard class which is derived by the system, rather than put in explicitly by the programmer.

Enumerated type   An **algebraic type** with each constructor having no arguments.

Equation   A **definition** in Haskell consists of a number of equations. On the left-hand side of the equation is a **name** applied to zero or more **patterns**; on the right-hand side is a value. In many cases the equation is **conditional** and has two or more **clauses**. Where the meaning is clear we shall sometimes take 'equation' as shorthand for 'equation or conditional equation'.

Evaluation   Every **expression** in Haskell has a value; evaluation is the process of finding that value. A **calculation** evaluates an expression, as does an interactive Haskell system when that expression is typed to the prompt.

Export   The process of defining which definitions will be visible when a module is **imported** by another.

Expression   An expression is formed by applying a **function** or **operator** to its arguments; these arguments can be **literal** values, or expressions themselves. A simple numerical expression is

(2+8)-10

in which the operator '-' is applied to two arguments.

Extensionality   The principle of proof which says that two functions are equal if they give equal results for every input.

Filter   To pick out those elements of a list which have a particular property, represented by a **Boolean**-valued function.

Floating-point number   A number which is given in decimal (e.g. 456.23) or exponent (e.g. 4.5623e+2) form; these numbers form the type Float.

Fold   To combine the elements of a list using a binary **operation**.

Forward composition   Used for the operator '>.>' with the definition

f >.> g = g . f

f >.> g can be read 'f then g'.

Function   A function is an object which returns a **value**, called the **output** or **result** when it is applied to its **inputs**. The inputs are also known as its **parameters** or **arguments**. Examples include the square root function, whose input and output are numbers, and the function which returns the borrowers (output) of a book (input) in a database (input).

Function types   The type of a **function** is a function type, so that, for instance, the function which checks whether its integer argument is even has type Int->Bool. This is the type of functions with **input** type Int and **output** type Bool.

Generalization   Replacing an object by something of which the original object is an instance.

This might be the replacement of a function by a polymorphic function from which the original is obtained by passing the appropriate parameter, or replacing a logical formula by one which implies the original.

Guard The **Boolean** expression appearing to the right of '|' and to the left of '=' in a **clause** of a **conditional equation** in a Haskell **definition**.

Higher-order function A **function** is higher-order if either one of its **arguments** or its **result**, or both, are functions.

Identifier Another word for **name**.

Implementation The particular **definitions** which make a design concrete; for an **abstract data type**, the definitions of the objects named in the **signature**.

Import The process of including the **exported** definitions of one module in another.

Induction The name for a collection of methods of proof, by which statements of the form 'for all x . . . ' are proved.

Infix An **operation** which appears between its **arguments**. Infix functions are called **operators**.

Inheritance One **class** inherits the operations of another if the first class is in the **context** of the definition of the second. For instance, of the standard classes, Ord inherits (in)equality from Eq.

Input A **function** takes one or more inputs into an **output**. Inputs are also known as **arguments** and **parameters**. The 'square' function takes a single numerical input, for instance.

Instance The term 'instance' is used in two different ways in Haskell.

An instance of a **type** is a type which is given by **substituting** a type expression for a type **variable**. For example,

[(Bool,b)] is an instance of [a], given by substituting the type (Bool,b) for the variable a.

An instance of a **class**, such as Eq (a,b), is given by declaring how the function(s) of the class, in this case ==, are defined over the given type (here (a,b)). Here we would say

```
(x,y) == (z,w)
   = (x==z) && (y==w)
```

Integers The positive and negative whole numbers. In Haskell the type Int represents the integers in a fixed size, while the type Integer represents them exactly, so that evaluating 2 to the power 1000 will give a result consisting of some three hundred digits.

Interactive program A program which reads from and writes to the terminal; reading and writing will be *interleaved*, in general.

Interface The common information which is shared between two program modules.

Juxtaposition Putting one thing next to another; this is the way in which function application is written down in Haskell.

Lambda expression An **expression** which denotes a **function**. After a '\' we list the arguments of the function, then an '->' and then the result. For instance, to add a number to the length of a list we could write

```
\xs n -> length xs + n
```

The term 'lambda' is used since '\' is close to the Greek letter 'λ', or lambda, which is used in a similar way in Church's lambda calculus.

Lazy evaluation The sort of expression **evaluation** in Haskell. In a function application only those arguments whose values are *needed* will be evaluated, and moreover, only the parts of structures which are needed will be examined.

Linear complexity   Order 1, $O(n^1)$, behaviour.

Lists   A list consists of a collection of elements of a particular type, given in some order, potentially containing a particular item more than once. The list [2,1,3,2] is of type [Int], for example.

Literal   Something that is 'literally' a value: it needs no **evaluation**. Examples include 34, [23] and "string".

Local definitions   The definitions appearing in a where clause or a let expression. Their **scope** is the equation or expression to which the clause or let is attached.

Map   To apply an operation to every element of a list.

Mathematical induction   A method of proof for statements of the form 'for all natural numbers n, the statement P(n) holds'.

    The proof is in two parts: the base case, at zero, and the induction step, at which P(n) is proved on the assumption that P(n-1) holds.

Memoization   Keeping the value of a sub-computation (in a list, say) so that it can be reused rather than recomputed, when it is needed.

Module   Another name for a **script**; used particularly when more than one script is used to build a program.

Monad   A monad consists of a type with (at least) two functions, return and >>=. Informally, a monad can be seen as performing some sorts of action before returning an object. The two monad functions respectively return a value

without any action, and sequence two monadic operations.

Monomorphic   A type is **monomorphic** if it is not **polymorphic**.

Most general type   The most general type of an expression is the type t with the property that every other type for the expression is an **instance** of t.

Mutual recursion   Two definitions, each of which depends upon the other.

Name   A **definition** associates a name or **identifier** with a value. Names of **classes**, **constructors** and **types** must begin with capital letters; names of **values**, **variables** and **type variables** begin with small letters. After the first letter, any letter, digit, ' ' ' or '_' can be used.

Natural numbers   The non-negative whole numbers: 0, 1, 2, ...

Offside rule   The way in which the end of a part of a definition is expressed using the *layout* of a **script**, rather than an explicit symbol for the end.

Operation   Another name for **function**.

Operator   A **function** which is written in infix form, between its **arguments**. The function f is made infix thus: 'f'.

Operator section   A partially applied operator.

Output   When a **function** is applied to one or more **inputs**, the resulting value is called the output, or **result**. Applying the 'square' function to (-2) gives the output 4, for example.

Overloading   The use of the same **name** to mean two (or more) different things, at different types. The equality operation, ==, is an example. Overloading is supported in Haskell by the **class** mechanism.

Parameter A **function** takes one or more parameters into an **output**. Parameters are also known as **arguments** and **inputs**, and applying a function to its inputs is sometimes known as 'passing its parameters'.

Parsing Revealing the structure of a sentence in a formal language.

Partial application A **function** of type t_1->t_2->...->t_n->t can be applied to n arguments, or less. In the latter case, the **application** is partial, since the result can itself be passed further parameters.

Pattern A pattern is either a **variable**, a **literal**, a **wild card** or the application of a **constructor** to other patterns.

The term 'pattern' is also used as short for a 'pattern of computation' such as 'applying an operation to every member of a list', a pattern which in Haskell is realised by the map function.

Polymorphism A type is polymorphic if it contains type **variables**; such a type will have many **instances**.

Prefix An **operation** which appears before its **arguments**.

Primitive recursion Over the natural numbers, defining the values of a function outright at zero, and at n greater than zero using the value at n-1. Over an **algebraic type** defining the function by cases over the constructors; recursion is permitted at arguments to a constructor which are of the type in question.

Proof A logical argument which leads us to accept a logical statement as being valid.

Pure programming language A functional programming language is pure if it does not allow **side-effects**.

Quadratic complexity Order two, $O(n^2)$, behaviour.

Recursion Using the name of a value or type in its own **definition**.

Result When a **function** is applied to one or more **inputs**, the resulting value is called the result, or **output**.

Scope The area of a program in which a **definition** or definitions are applicable. In Haskell the scope of top-level definitions is by default the whole **script** in which they appear; it may be extended by importing the module into another. More limited scopes are given by **local definitions**.

Script A script is a file containing **definitions**, **declarations** and module statements.

Set A collection of objects for which the order of elements and the number of occurrences of each element are irrelevant.

Side-effect In a language like Pascal, evaluating an expression can cause other things to happen besides a value being computed. These might be I/O operations, or changes in values stored. In Haskell this does not happen, but a **monad** can be used to give a similar effect, without compromising the simple model of evaluation underlying the language. Examples are IO and State.

Signature A sequence of type **declarations**. These declarations state what are the types of the operations (or functions) over an **abstract type** or a **class** which can be used to manipulate elements of that type.

Stream A stream is a channel upon which items arrive in sequence; in Haskell we can think of **lazy** lists in this way, so it becomes a synonym for lazy list.

String   The type String is a **synonym** for lists of characters, [Char].

Structural induction   A method of proof for statements of the form 'for all finite lists xs, the statement P(xs) holds of xs'. The proof is in two parts: the base case, at [], and the induction step, at which P(y:ys) is proved on the assumption that P(ys) holds.
Also used of the related principle for any algebraic type.

Substitution   The replacement of a **variable** by an **expression**. For example, (9+12) is given by substituting 12 for n in (9+n). Types can also be substituted for type variables; see the entry for **instance**.

Synonym   Naming a type is called a type synonym. The keyword type is used for synonyms.

Syntax   The description of the properly formed programs (or sentences) of a language.

Transformation   Turning one program into another program which computes identical results, but with different behaviour in other respects such as time or space efficiency.

Tuples   A tuple type is built up from a number of component types. Elements of the type consist of tuples of elements of the component types, so that

(2,True,3) :: (Int,Bool,Int)

for instance.

Type   A collection of values. Types can be built from the **base** types using **tuple**, list and **function types**. New types can be defined using the **algebraic** and **abstract** type mechanisms, and types can be named using the type **synonym** mechanism.

Type variable   A **variable** which appears in a **polymorphic type**. An **identifier** beginning with a small letter can be used as a type variable; in this text we use the letters at the start of the alphabet, a, b, c and so on.

Undefinedness   The result of an expression whose evaluation continues forever, rather than giving a *defined* result.

Unification   The process of finding a common **instance** of two (type) expressions containing (type) variables.

Value   A value is a member of some **type**; the value of an **expression** is the result of **evaluating** the expression.

Variable   A variable stands for an *arbitrary* value, or in the case of type variables, an arbitrary type. Variables and type variables have the same syntax as **names**.

Verification   Proving that a function or functions have particular logical properties.

Where clause   Definitions **local** to a (conditional) **equation**.

Wild card   The name for the pattern '_', which is matched by any value of the appropriate type.

Haskell operators

The Haskell operators are listed below in decreasing order of binding power: see Section 3.7 for a discussion of associativity and binding power.

	Left associative	Non-associative	Right associative
9	`!, !!, //`		`.`
8			`**, ^, ^^`
7	`*, /, 'div', 'mod', 'rem', 'quot'`		
6	`+, -`	`:+`	
5		`\\`	`:, ++`
4		`/=, <, <=, ==, >, >=, 'elem', 'notElem'`	
3			`&&`
2			`||`
1	`>>, >>=`	`:=`	
0			`$, 'seq'`

Also defined in this text are the operators

9	`>.>`		
5			`>*>`

The restrictions on names of operators, which are formed using the characters

`! # $ % & * + . / < = > ? \ ^ | : - ~`

are that operators must not start with a colon; this character starts an infix constructor. The operators `-` and `!` can be user-defined, but note that they have a special meaning in certain circumstances – the obvious advice here is not to use them. Finally, certain combinations of symbols are reserved, and cannot be used: `.. :: => = @ \ | ^ <- ->`.

457

To change the associativity or binding power of an operator, &&& say, we make a declaration like

```
infixl 7 &&&
```

which states that &&& has binding power 7, and is a left associative operator. We can also declare operators as non-associative (infix) and right associative (infixr). Omitting the binding power gives a default of 9. These declarations can also be used for back-quoted function names, as in

```
infix 0 'poodle'
```

Understanding programs

This appendix is included to offer help to readers confronted with an unfamiliar function definition. There are various things we can do with the definition, and these are examined in turn here. Given a functional program like

```
mapWhile :: (a -> b) -> (a -> Bool) -> [a] -> [b]

mapWhile f p []     = []                                  (mapWhile.1)
mapWhile f p (x:xs)
  | p x             = f x : mapWhile f p xs               (mapWhile.2)
  | otherwise       = []                                  (mapWhile.3)
```

we can understand what it means in various complementary ways. We can read the program itself, we can write calculations of examples using the program, we can prove properties of the program, and we can estimate its space and time complexity,

Reading the program

Besides any comments which might accompany a program, the program itself is its most important documentation.

The type declaration gives information about the input and output types: for mapWhile, we have to supply three arguments:

- a function, f say, of arbitrary type, a -> b;

- a **property** of objects of type a; that is a function taking an a to a Boolean value; and,

- a list of items of type a.

The output is a list of elements of type b – the output type of f.

The function definition itself is used to give values of mapWhile, but also can be read directly as a description of the program.

- On [], the result is [].

- On a non-empty list, if the head x has property p, then according to (mapWhile.2), we have f x as the first element of the result, with the remainder given by a recursive call on xs.

- If the property p fails of x, the result is terminated, as it were, by returning the empty list [].

In the definition we have a complete description of how the program behaves, but we can animate this by trying specific examples.

Calculating with the program

A more concrete view of what the program does is given by calculating particular examples. For instance,

```
mapWhile (2+) (>7) [8,12,7,13,16]
↝   2+8 : mapWhile (2+) (>7) [12,7,13,16]         by (mapWhile.2)
↝   10 : 2+12 : mapWhile (2+) (>7) [7,13,16]      by (mapWhile.2)
↝   10 : 14 : []                                  by (mapWhile.3)
↝   [10,14]
```

Other examples include

```
mapWhile (2+) (>2) [8,12,7,13,16]  ↝   [10,14,9,15,18]
mapWhile (2+) (>2) []              ↝   []
```

Note that in these examples we use mapWhile at the instance

```
(Int -> Int) -> (Int -> Bool) -> [Int] -> [Int]
```

of its polymorphic type, given by replacing the type variables a and b by the type Int.

Reasoning about the program

We can get a deeper understanding about a program by **proving** properties that the program might have. For mapWhile, we might prove that for all f, p and finite lists xs,

```
mapWhile f p xs            = map f (takeWhile p xs)    (mapWhile.4)
mapWhile f (const True) xs = map f xs                  (mapWhile.5)
mapWhile id p xs           = takeWhile p xs            (mapWhile.6)
```

where we can, in fact, see (mapWhile.5) and (mapWhile.6) as consequences of the characterization of mapWhile given by property (mapWhile.4).

Program behaviour

It is not hard to see that the program will at worst take time linear (that is $O(n^1)$) in the length (n) of the list argument assuming $O(n^0)$ behaviour of f and p, as it runs through the elements of the list once, if at all.

The **space** behaviour is more interesting; because we can output the head of a list once produced, the space required will be constant, as suggested by underlining the parts which can be output in the calculation above.

```
mapWhile (2+) (>7) [8,12,7,13,16]
⤳    2+8 : mapWhile (2+) (>7) [12,7,13,16]
⤳    10 : 2+12 : mapWhile (2+) (>7) [7,13,16]
⤳    10 : 14 : []
⤳    [10,14]
```

Getting started

Each view of the program gives us a different understanding of its behaviour, but when we are presented with an unfamiliar definition we can begin to understand what its effect is by calculating various small examples. If we are given a collection of functions, we can test out the functions from the bottom up, building one calculation on top of another.

The important thing is to realize that rather than being stuck, we can get started by calculating representative examples to show us the way.

Implementations of Haskell

Implementations of Haskell have been built at various sites around the world. This text discusses the Hugs interpreter, which was developed in a joint effort by staff at the Universities of Nottingham in the UK and Yale in the USA. Compilers have been developed at the University of Glasgow, UK, and Chalmers Technical University, Goteborg, Sweden.

Hugs

Hugs is available from

```
http://www.haskell.org/hugs/
```

For the Unix version of Hugs you should follow the installation notes.

Note: Downloading Hugs for Windows

If you want to download the standard installation of Hugs which will set up the appropriate registry entries, you should download one of the

```
selfinstall.exe
selfinstall.zip
```

files which will run an InstallShield script to make the appropriate settings and so on. If you download the **binaries**, you will have to make these settings and so forth for yourself.

You can choose to set the default editor for Hugs. The most straightforward way of doing this under Windows is to run WinHugs and to change the settings there. These changes persist to future invocations of both Hugs and WinHugs. The Programmer's File Editor is a freely available editor for Windows systems:

```
http://www.lancs.ac.uk/people/cpaap/pfe/
```

For the Macintosh, there is a port of Hugs 1.4 to the Power Macintosh OS at

```
ftp://haskell.org/pub/haskell/hugs/mac
    /hugs-June98-MacPPC-binary.sea.bin
```

which has been made by Hans Aberg.

The developers of Hugs recommend it as a Haskell program development system because of its fast compilation cycle, but it cannot offer the speed of execution of the various compilers.

Other Haskell systems

These include the Glasgow Haskell compiler

```
http://www.dcs.gla.ac.uk/fp/software/ghc/
```

developed at the University of Glasgow, the HBC/HBI system

```
http://www.cs.chalmers.se/~augustss/hbc/hbc.html
```

developed at Chalmers Technical University. NHC13

```
http://www.cs.york.ac.uk/fp/nhc13/
```

is a 'lightweight' compiler designed with implementation experimentation in mind.

Further information

Up-to-date information about future developments of these and any other implementations will be available from the Haskell home page,

```
http://www.haskell.org/implementations.html
```

Hugs errors

This appendix examines some of the more common programming errors in Haskell, and shows the error messages to which they give rise in Hugs.

The programs we write all too often contain errors. On encountering an error, the system either halts, and gives an **error message**, or continues, but gives a **warning message** to tell us that something unusual has happened, which might signal that we have made an error. In this appendix, we look at a selection of the messages output by Hugs; we have chosen the messages which are both common and require some explanation; messages like

```
Program error: {head []}
```

are self-explanatory. The messages are classified into roughly distinct areas. Syntax errors show up malformed programs, while type errors show well-formed programs in which objects are used at the wrong types. In fact, an ill-formed expression can often show itself as a type error and not as a syntax error, so the boundaries are not clear.

Syntax errors

A Haskell system attempts to match the input we give to the syntax of the language. Commonly, when something goes wrong, we type something *unexpected*. Typing '2==3)' will provoke the error message

```
ERROR: Syntax error in input (unexpected ')')
```

If a part of a definition is missing, as in

```
fun x
fun 2 = 34
```

we receive the message

```
Syntax error in declaration (unexpected ';')
```

The ';' here is an indication of the end of a definition – the error message therefore tells us that a definition has been ended unexpectedly, as there is no right-hand side corresponding to the fun x.

The inclusion of a type definition in a where clause is signalled by

```
Syntax error in declaration (unexpected keyword "type")
```

The syntax of patterns is more restricted than the full expression syntax, and so we get error messages like

```
Repeated variable "x" in pattern
```

when we use the same variable more than once within a pattern.

In specifying constants, we can make errors: floating-point numbers can be too large, and characters specified by an out-of-range ASCII code:

```
Inf.0
ERROR: Decimal character escape out of range
```

Not every string can be used as a name; some words in Haskell are **keywords** or **reserved identifiers**, and will give an error if used as an identifier. The keywords are

```
case class data default deriving do else if import in infix
infixl infixr instance let module newtype of then type where
```

The special identifiers as, qualified and hiding have special meanings in certain contexts but can be used as ordinary identifiers.

The final restriction on names is that names of constructors and types must begin with a capital letter; nothing else can do so, and hence we get error messages like

```
Undefined constructor function "Montana"
```

if we try to define a function called Montana.

Type errors

As we have seen in the body of the text, the main type error we meet is exemplified by the response to typing 'c' && True to the Hugs prompt:

```
ERROR: Type error in application
*** expression    : 'c' && True
*** term          : 'c'
*** type          : Char
*** does not match : Bool
```

which is provoked by using a Char where an Bool is expected. Other type errors, such as

```
True + 4
```

provoke the error message

```
ERROR: Bool is not an instance of class "Num"
```

This comes from the class mechanism: the system attempts to make `Bool` an instance of the class `Num` of numeric types over which '+' is defined. The error results since there is no such instance declaration making `Bool` belong to the class `Num`.

As we said before, we can get type errors from syntax errors. For example, writing `abs -2` instead of `abs (-2)` gives the error message

```
ERROR: a -> a is not an instance of class "Num"
```

because it is parsed as 2 subtracted from `abs::a->a`, and the operator '-' expects something in the class `Num`, rather than a function of type `a->a`. Other common type errors come from confusing the roles of ' `:` ' and '`++`' as in `2++[2]` and `[2]:[2]`.

We always give type declarations for our definitions; one advantage of this is to spot when our definition does not conform to its declared type. For example,

```
myCheck :: Int -> Bool
myCheck n = ord n == 6
```

gives the error message

```
ERROR "error.hs" (line 8): Type error in function binding
*** term            : myCheck
*** type            : Char -> Bool
*** does not match : Int -> Bool
```

Without the type declaration the definition would be accepted, only to give an error (presumably) when it is used. A final error related to types is given by definitions like

```
type Fred = (Fred,Int)                                          (Fred)
```

a **recursive** type synonym; these are signalled by

```
ERROR "error.hs" (line 11): Recursive type synonym "Fred"
```

The effect of (Fred) can be modelled by the algebraic type definition

```
data Fred = Node Fred Int
```

which introduces the **constructor** `Node` to identify objects of this type.

Program errors

Once we have written a syntactically and type correct script, and asked for the value of an expression which is itself acceptable, other errors can be produced during the **evaluation** of the expression.

The first class of errors comes from missing cases in definitions. If we have written a definition like

```
bat [] = 45
```

and applied it to [34] we get the response

```
Program error: {bat {dict} [Num_Int_fromInt 34]}
```

which shows the point at which evaluation can go no further, since there is no case in the definition of bat to cover a non-empty list. Similar errors come from built-in functions, such as head.

Other errors happen because an **arithmetical constraint** has been broken. These include an out-of-range list index, division by zero, using a fraction where an integer is expected and floating-point calculations which go out of range; the error messages all have the same form:

```
Program error: PreludeList.!!: index too large
Program error: {primDivInt 3 0}
```

If we make a conformal definition, like

```
[a,b] = [1 .. 10]
```

this will fail with a lengthy message

```
Program error: {b_v851_v850_v852 [1, 2, 3] ++ takeWhile (flip (Ord_<= {dict}) 10)
               (_strict (numericEnumFrom {dict}) (Num_Int_+ 3 (Num_Int_fromInt 1)))}
```

which reveals the implementation of this sort of definition.

Evaluation in Haskell is by need, and so a script which uses a name with no corresponding definition for the name will not be in error; only if the value of that name is required, will we get the message

```
ERROR: Undefined variable "cat"
```

Module errors

The module and import statements can provoke a variety of error messages: files may not be present, or may contain errors; names may be included more than once, or an alias on inclusion may cause a name clash. The error messages for these and other errors are self-explanatory.

System messages

In response to some commands and interrupts, the system generates messages, including

```
^C{Interrupted!}
```

signalling the interruption of the current task,

```
ERROR: Garbage collection fails to reclaim sufficient space
```

which shows that the space consumption of the evaluation exceeds that available. One way around this is to increase the size of the heap. To see the current size of the heap and the other settings of the system type

```
:set
```

The message given there shows how the heap size can be changed, as well as how to affect other system parameters.

If the option +s is set, the system prints diagnostic information of the form

```
(2 reductions, 8 cells)
```

The number of `reductions` corresponds to the number of steps in our calculations and the `cells` to the total space usage.

A measure of the space complexity of a function, as described in Chapter 19, is given by the size of the smallest heap in which the evaluation can take place; there is no direct measure of this given by the system.

Bibliography

Abelson, H., G. J. Sussman and J. Sussman (1996). *The Structure and Interpretation of Computer Programs* (2nd edn). MIT Press.

Appel, A. (1993). A critique of Standard ML. *Journal of Functional Programming*, **3**.

Armstrong, J., R. Virding and M. Williams (1993). *Concurrent Programming in ERLANG*. Prentice-Hall.

Augustsson, L. (1998). Cayenne – a language with dependent types. See Hudak and Queinnec (1998).

Backus, J. (1978). Can programming be liberated from the Von Neumann style? *Communications of the ACM*, **21**(8).

Bird, R. and O. de Moor (1997). *Algebra of Programming*. Prentice-Hall.

Cormen, T. H., C. E. Leiserson and R. L. Rivest (1990). *Introduction to Algorithms*. MIT Press.

Elliott, C. and P. Hudak (1997). Functional reactive animation. In *Proceedings of the 1997 ACM SIGPLAN International Conference on Functional Programming (ICFP97)*. ACM Press.

Finne, S., D. Leijen, E. Meijer and S. Peyton Jones (1998). H/direct: A binary foreign language interface for Haskell. See Hudak and Queinnec (1998).

Gordon, A. J. (1994). *Functional Programming and Input/Output*. British Computer Society Distinguished Dissertations in Computer Science. Cambridge University Press.

Peyton Jones, S. and J. Hughes (eds) (1998). *Standard Libraries for the Haskell 98 Programming Language*. http://www.haskell.org/library/.

Hartel, P. and R. Plasmeijer (eds) (1995a). *Functional Programming Languages in Education (FPLE)*. Springer-Verlag, Lecture Notes in Computer Science, 1022.

Hartel, P. and R. Plasmeijer (1995b). Special issue on state-of-the-art applications of pure functional programming languages. *Journal of Functional Programming*, **5**.

Hudak, P., T. Makucevich, S. Gadde and B. Whong (1996). Haskore music notation – An algebra of music. *Journal of Functional Programming*, **6**.

Hudak, P., J. H. Fasel and J. Peterson (1997). A gentle introduction to Haskell. `http://www.haskell.org/tutorial/`

Hudak, P. and C. Queinnec (eds) (1998). *The 1998 International Conference on Functional Programming*. ACM Press.

Hugs (1998). The Hugs System. Available from `http://www.haskell.org/hugs/`

Humphrey, W. S. (1996). *Introduction to the Personal Software Process*. Addison-Wesley.

Jeuring, J. and E. Meijer (eds) (1995). *Advanced Functional Programming*. Springer-Verlag, Lecture Notes in Computer Science, 925.

Läufer, K. (1996). Type classes with existential types. *Journal of Functional Programming*, **6**.

Launchbury, J., E. Meijer and T. Sheard (eds) (1996). *Advanced Functional Programming*. Springer Verlag, Lecture Notes in Computer Science, 1129.

Launchbury, J. and S. Peyton Jones (1994). Lazy functional state threads. In *Programming Languages Development and Implementation*. ACM Press.

Liang, S., P. Hudak and M. Jones (1995). Monad transformers and modular interpreters. In *22nd ACM SIGPLAN-SIGACT Symposium on Principles of Programming Languages (POPL)*. ACM Press.

Meijer, E. (1998). Calling hell from heaven and heaven from hell. See Hudak and Queinnec (1998).

Milner, R., M. Tofte and R. Harper (1990). *The Definition of Standard ML*. MIT Press.

Milner, R., M. Tofte, R. Harper and D. MacQueen (1997). *The Definition of Standard ML* (revised edn). MIT Press.

Odersky, M. and P. Wadler (1997). Pizza into Java: Translating theory into practice. In *24th ACM SIGPLAN-SIGACT Symposium on Principles of Programming Languages*. ACM Press.

Okasaki, C. (1998). *Purely Functional Data Structures*. Cambridge University Press.

Paulson, L. C. (1987). *Logic and Computation — Interactive Proof with Cambridge LCF*. Cambridge University Press.

Paulson, L. C. (1996). *ML for the Working Programmer* (2nd edn). Cambridge University Press.

Peyton Jones, S. (1987). *The Implementation of Functional Programming Languages*. Prentice-Hall.

Peyton Jones, S. and J. Hughes (eds) (1998). *Report on the Programming Language Haskell 98*. `http://www.haskell.org/report/`

Peyton Jones, S. and D. Lester (1992). *Implementing functional languages*. Prentice-Hall.

Peyton Jones, S. and P. Wadler (1993). Imperative functional programming. In *20th ACM SIGPLAN-SIGACT Symposium on Principles of Programming Languages*. ACM Press.

Polya, G. (1988). *How To Solve It* (reissued edn). Princeton University Press.

Runciman, C. and N. Röjemo (1996). New dimensions in heap profiling. *Journal of Functional Programming*, **6**.

Runciman, C. and D. Wakeling (eds) (1995). *Applications of Functional Programming*. UCL Press.

Thompson, S. (1995). *Miranda: The Craft of Functional Programming*. Addison-Wesley.

Thompson, S. (1999). Proof for functional programming. In K. Hammond and G. Michaelson (eds), *Research Directions in Parallel Functional Programming*. Springer Verlag.

Turner, D. (1995). Elementary strong functional programming. In P. Hartel and R. Plasmeijer (eds), *FPLE*, Lecture Notes in Computer Science, Springer Verlag, 1022.

Turner, D. A. (1986). An overview of Miranda. *SIGPLAN Notices*, **21**.

Index

PART II

Prolog:
Programming for
Artificial Intelligence

Third Edition

by Ivan Bratko

Prolog

programming
for artificial
intelligence

Third edition

IVAN BRATKO

Faculty of Computer and Information Science,
Ljubljana University
and
J. Stefan Institute

Contents

From Patrick Winston's Foreword to the Second Edition

I can never forget my excitement when I saw my first Prolog-style program in action. It was part of Terry Winograd's famous Shrdlu system, whose blocks-world problem solver arranged for a simulated robot arm to move blocks around a screen, solving intricate problems in response to human-specified goals.

Winograd's blocks-world problem solver was written in Microplanner, a language which we now recognize as a sort of Prolog. Nevertheless, in spite of the defects of Microplanner, the blocks-world problem solver was organized explicitly around goals, because a Prolog-style language encourages programmers to think in terms of goals. The goal-oriented procedures for grasping, clearing, getting rid of, moving, and ungrasping made it possible for a clear, transparent, concise program to seem amazingly intelligent.

Winograd's blocks-world problem solver permanently changed the way I think about programs. I even rewrote the blocks-world problem solver in Lisp for my Lisp textbook because that program unalterably impressed me with the power of the goal-oriented philosophy of programming and the fun of writing goal-oriented programs.

But learning about goal-oriented programming through Lisp programs is like reading Shakespeare in a language other than English. Some of the beauty comes through, but not as powerfully as in the original. Similarly, the best way to learn about goal-oriented programming is to read and write goal-oriented programs in Prolog, for goal-oriented programming is what Prolog is all about.

In broader terms, the evolution of computer languages is an evolution away from low-level languages, in which the programmer specifies how something is to be done, toward high-level languages, in which the programmer specifies simply *what* is to be done. With the development of Fortran, for example, programmers were no longer forced to speak to the computer in the procrustian low-level language of addresses and registers. Instead, Fortran programmers could speak in their own language, or nearly so, using a notation that made only moderate concessions to the one-dimensional, 80-column world.

Fortran and nearly all other languages are still how-type languages, however. In my view, modern Lisp is the champion of these languages, for Lisp in its Common Lisp form is enormously expressive, but how to do something is still what the Lisp programmer is allowed to be expressive about. Prolog, on the other hand, is a language that clearly breaks away from the how-type languages, encouraging the programmer to describe situations and problems, not the detailed means by which the problems are to be solved.

Consequently, an introduction to Prolog is important for all students of Computer Science, for there is no better way to see what the notion of what-type programming is all about.

In particular, the chapters of this book clearly illustrate the difference between how-type and what-type thinking. In the first chapter, for example, the difference is illustrated through problems dealing with family relations. The Prolog programmer straightforwardly describes the grandfather concept in explicit, natural terms: a grandfather is a father of a parent. Here is the Prolog notation:

```
grandfather( X, Z)  :-  father( X, Y), parent( Y, Z).
```

Once Prolog knows what a grandfather is, it is easy to ask a question: who are Patrick's grandfathers, for example. Here again is the Prolog notation, along with a typical answer:

```
?- grandfather( X, patrick).

X = james;
X = carl
```

It is Prolog's job to figure out how to solve the problem by combing through a database of known father and parent relations. The programmer specifies only what is known and what question is to be solved. The programmer is more concerned with knowledge and less concerned with algorithms that exploit the knowledge.

Given that it is important to learn Prolog, the next question is how. I believe that learning a programming language is like learning a natural language in many ways. For example, a reference manual is helpful in learning a programming language, just as a dictionary is helpful in learning a natural language. But no one learns a natural language with only a dictionary, for the words are only part of what must be learned. The student of a natural language must learn the conventions that govern how the words are put legally together, and later, the student should learn the art of those who put the words together with style.

Similarly, no one learns a programming language from only a reference manual, for a reference manual says little or nothing about the way the primitives of the language are put to use by those who use the language well. For this, a textbook is required, and the best textbooks offer copious examples, for good examples are distilled experience, and it is principally through experience that we learn.

In this book, the first example is on the first page, and the remaining pages constitute an example cornucopia, pouring forth Prolog programs written by a passionate Prolog programmer who is dedicated to the Prolog point of view. By carefully studying these examples, the reader acquires not only the mechanics of the language, but also a personal collection of precedents, ready to be taken apart, adapted, and reassembled together into new programs. With this acquisition of precedent knowledge, the transition from novice to skilled programmer is already under way.

Of course, a beneficial side effect of good programming examples is that they expose a bit of interesting science as well as a lot about programming itself. The science behind the examples in this book is Artificial Intelligence. The reader learns about such problem-solving ideas as problem reduction, forward and backward chaining, 'how' and 'why' questioning, and various search techniques.

In fact, one of the great features of Prolog is that it is simple enough for students in introductory Artificial Intelligence subjects to learn to use immediately. I expect that many instructors will use this book as part of their artificial intelligence subjects so that their students can see abstract ideas immediately reduced to concrete, motivating form.

Among Prolog texts, I expect this book to be particularly popular, not only because of its examples, but also because of a number of other features:

- Careful summaries appear throughout.
- Numerous exercises reinforce all concepts.
- Structure selectors introduce the notion of data abstraction.
- Explicit discussions of programming style and technique occupy an entire chapter.
- There is honest attention to the problems to be faced in Prolog programming, as well as the joys.

Features like this make this a well done, enjoyable, and instructive book.

I keep the first edition of this textbook in my library on the outstanding-textbooks shelf, programming languages section, for as a textbook it exhibited all the strengths that set the outstanding textbooks apart from the others, including clear and direct writing, copious examples, careful summaries, and numerous exercises. And as a programming language textbook, I especially liked its attention to data abstraction, emphasis on programming style, and honest treatment of Prolog's problems as well as Prolog's advantages.

Preface

....

Prolog

Prolog is a programming language centred around a small set of basic mechanisms, including pattern matching, tree-based data structuring and automatic back-tracking. This small set constitutes a surprisingly powerful and flexible programming framework. Prolog is especially well suited for problems that involve objects – in particular, structured objects – and relations between them. For example, it is an easy exercise in Prolog to express spatial relationships between objects, such as the blue sphere is behind the green one. It is also easy to state a more general rule: if object X is closer to the observer than object Y, and Y is closer than Z, then X must be closer than Z. Prolog can now reason about the spatial relationships and their consistency with respect to the general rule. Features like this make Prolog a powerful language for artificial intelligence (AI) and non-numerical programming in general. There are well-known examples of symbolic computation whose implementation in other standard languages took tens of pages of indigestible code. When the same algorithms were implemented in Prolog, the result was a crystal-clear program easily fitting on one page.

Development of Prolog

Prolog stands for *programming in logic* – an idea that emerged in the early 1970s to use logic as a programming language. The early developers of this idea included Robert Kowalski at Edinburgh (on the theoretical side), Maarten van Emden at Edinburgh (experimental demonstration) and Alain Colmerauer at Marseilles (implementation). David D.H. Warren's efficient implementation at Edinburgh in the mid-1970s greatly contributed to the popularity of Prolog. A more recent development is *constraint logic programming* (CLP), usually implemented as part of a Prolog system. CLP extends Prolog with constraint processing, which has proved in practice to be an exceptionally flexible tool for problems like scheduling and logistic planning. In 1996 the official ISO standard for Prolog was published.

Historical controversies about Prolog

There are some controversial views that historically accompanied Prolog. Prolog fast gained popularity in Europe as a practical programming tool. In Japan, Prolog was placed at the centre of the development of the fifth-generation computers. On the other hand, in the United States Prolog was generally accepted with some delay, due to several historical factors. One of these was an early American experience with the Microplanner language, also akin to the idea of logic programming, but inefficiently implemented. Some reservations also came in reaction to the early 'orthodox school' of logic programming, which insisted on the use of pure logic that should not be marred by adding practical facilities not related to logic. This led to some widespread misunderstandings about Prolog in the past. For example, some believed that only backward chaining reasoning can be programmed in Prolog. The truth is that Prolog is a general programming language and any algorithm can be programmed in it. The impractical 'orthodox school's' position was modified by Prolog practitioners who adopted a more pragmatic view, benefiting from combining the new, declarative approach with the traditional, procedural one.

Learning Prolog

Since Prolog has its roots in mathematical logic it is often introduced through logic. However, such a mathematically intensive introduction is not very useful if the aim is to teach Prolog as a practical programming tool. Therefore this book is not concerned with the mathematical aspects, but concentrates on the art of making the few basic mechanisms of Prolog solve interesting problems. Whereas conventional languages are procedurally oriented, Prolog introduces the descriptive, or *declarative*, view. This greatly alters the way of thinking about problems and makes learning to program in Prolog an exciting intellectual challenge. Many believe that every student of computer science should learn something about Prolog at some point because Prolog enforces a different problem-solving paradigm complementary to other programming languages.

Contents of the book

Part I of the book introduces the Prolog language and shows how Prolog programs are developed. Techniques to handle important data structures, such as trees and graphs, are also included because of their general importance. In Part II, Prolog is applied to a number of areas of AI, including problem solving and heuristic search, programming with constraints, knowledge representation and expert systems, planning, machine learning, qualitative reasoning, language processing and game playing. AI techniques are introduced and developed in depth towards their implementation in Prolog, resulting in complete programs. These can be used as building blocks for sophisticated applications. The concluding chapter, on meta-programming, shows how Prolog can be used to implement other languages and programming paradigms, including object-oriented programming, pattern-directed programming and writing interpreters for Prolog in Prolog. Throughout, the emphasis is on the clarity of programs; efficiency tricks that rely on implementation-dependent features are avoided.

Differences between the second and third edition

All the material has been revised and updated. There are new chapters on:

- constraint logic programming (CLP);
- inductive logic programming;
- qualitative reasoning.

Other major changes are:

- addition of belief networks (Bayes networks) in the chapter on knowledge representation and expert systems;
- addition of memory-efficient programs for best-first search (IDA*, RBFS) in the chapter on heuristic search;
- major updates in the chapter on machine learning;
- additional techniques for improving program efficiency in the chapter on programming style and technique.

Throughout, more attention is paid to the differences between Prolog implementations with specific references to the Prolog standard when appropriate (see also Appendix A).

Audience for the book

This book is for students of Prolog and AI. It can be used in a Prolog course or in an AI course in which the principles of AI are brought to life through Prolog. The reader is assumed to have a basic general knowledge of computers, but no knowledge of AI is necessary. No particular programming experience is required; in fact, plentiful experience and devotion to conventional procedural programming – for example in C or Pascal – might even be an impediment to the fresh way of thinking Prolog requires.

The book uses standard syntax

Among several Prolog dialects, the Edinburgh syntax, also known as DEC-10 syntax, is the most widespread, and is the basis of the ISO standard for Prolog. It is also used in this book. For compatibility with the various Prolog implementations, this book only uses a relatively small subset of the built-in features that are shared by many Prologs.

How to read the book

In Part I, the natural reading order corresponds to the order in the book. However, the part of Section 2.4 that describes the procedural meaning of Prolog in a more

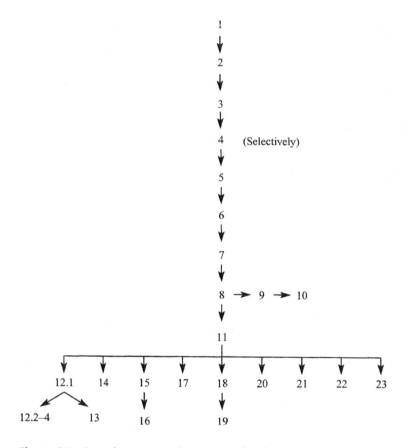

Figure P.1   Precedence constraints among the chapters.

formalized way can be skipped. Chapter 4 presents programming examples that can be read (or skipped) selectively. Chapter 10 on advanced tree representations can be skipped.

Part II allows more flexible reading strategies as most of the chapters are intended to be mutually independent. However, some topics will still naturally be covered before others, such as basic search strategies (Chapter 11). Figure P.1 summarizes the natural precedence constraints among the chapters.

Program code and course materials

Source code for all the programs in the book and relevant course materials are accessible from the companion web site (www.booksites.net/bratko).

Acknowledgements

Donald Michie was responsible for first inducing my interest in Prolog. I am grateful to Lawrence Byrd, Fernando Pereira and David H.D. Warren, once members of the Prolog development team at Edinburgh, for their programming advice and numerous discussions. The book greatly benefited from comments and suggestions to the previous editions by Andrew McGettrick and Patrick H. Winston. Other people who read parts of the manuscript and contributed significant comments include: Damjan Bojadžiev, Rod Bristow, Peter Clark, Frans Coenen, David C. Dodson, Sašo Džeroski, Bogdan Filipič, Wan Fokkink, Matjaž Gams, Peter G. Greenfield, Marko Grobelnik, Chris Hinde, Igor Kononenko, Matevž Kovačič, Eduardo Morales, Igor Mozetič, Timothy B. Niblett, Dušan Peterc, Uroš Pompe, Robert Rodošek, Agata Saje, Claude Sammut, Cem Say, Ashwin Srinivasan, Dorian Šuc, Peter Tancig, Tanja Urbančič, Mark Wallace, William Walley, Simon Weilguny, Blaž Zupan and Darko Zupanič. Special thanks to Cem Say for testing many programs and his gift of finding hidden errors. Several readers helped by pointing out errors in the previous editions, most notably G. Oulsnam and Iztok Tvrdy. I would also like to thank Karen Mosman, Julie Knight and Karen Sutherland of Pearson Education for their work in the process of making this book. Simon Plumtree and Debra Myson-Etherington provided much support in the previous editions. Most of the artwork was done by Darko Simeršek. Finally, this book would not be possible without the stimulating creativity of the international logic programming community.

The publisher wishes to thank Plenum Publishing Corporation for their permission to reproduce material similar to that in Chapter 10 of *Human and Machine Problem Solving* (1989), K. Gilhooly (ed).

Ivan Bratko
January 2000

part 1

The Prolog Language

chapter 1

Introduction to Prolog

This chapter reviews basic mechanisms of Prolog through an example program. Although the treatment is largely informal many important concepts are introduced such as: Prolog clauses, facts, rules and procedures. Prolog's built-in backtracking mechanism and the distinction between declarative and procedural meanings of a program are discussed.

1.1 Defining relations by facts

Prolog is a programming language for symbolic, non-numeric computation. It is specially well suited for solving problems that involve objects and relations between objects. Figure 1.1 shows an example: a family relation. The fact that Tom is a parent of Bob can be written in Prolog as:

```
parent( tom, bob).
```

Here we choose **parent** as the name of a relation; **tom** and **bob** are its arguments. For reasons that will become clear later we write names like **tom** with an initial lower-case letter. The whole family tree of Figure 1.1 is defined by the following Prolog program:

```
parent( pam, bob).
parent( tom, bob).
```

3

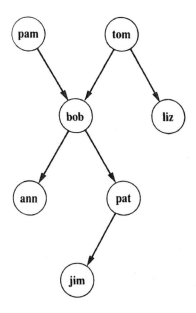

Figure 1.1   A family tree.

> **parent(tom, liz).**
> **parent(bob, ann).**
> **parent(bob, pat).**
> **parent(pat, jim).**

This program consists of six *clauses*. Each of these clauses declares one fact about the **parent** relation. For example, **parent(tom, bob)** is a particular *instance* of the **parent** relation. Such an instance is also called a *relationship*. In general, a relation is defined as the set of all its instances.

When this program has been communicated to the Prolog system, Prolog can be posed some questions about the **parent** relation. For example: Is Bob a parent of Pat? This question can be communicated to the Prolog system by typing into the terminal:

> **?- parent(bob, pat).**

Having found this as an asserted fact in the program, Prolog will answer:

> **yes**

A further query can be:

> **?- parent(liz, pat).**

Prolog answers:

> **no**

because the program does not mention anything about Liz being a parent of Pat. It also answers 'no' to the question:

>   ?- parent(tom, ben).

because the program has not even heard of the name Ben.

More interesting questions can also be asked. For example: Who is Liz's parent?

>   ?- parent(X, liz).

Prolog's answer will not be just 'yes' or 'no' this time. Prolog will tell us what is the value of X such that the above statement is true. So the answer is:

>   X = tom

The question Who are Bob's children? can be communicated to Prolog as:

>   ?- parent(bob, X).

This time there is more than just one possible answer. Prolog first answers with one solution:

>   X = ann

We may now request another solution (by typing a semicolon), and Prolog will find:

>   X = pat

If we request more solutions again, Prolog will answer 'no' because all the solutions have been exhausted.

Our program can be asked an even broader question: Who is a parent of whom? Another formulation of this question is:

>   Find X and Y such that X is a parent of Y.

This is expressed in Prolog by:

>   ?- parent(X, Y).

Prolog now finds all the parent-child pairs one after another. The solutions will be displayed one at a time as long as we tell Prolog we want more solutions, until all the solutions have been found. The answers are output as:

>   X = pam
>   Y = bob;
>
>   X = tom
>   Y = bob;
>
>   X = tom
>   Y = liz;
>
>   ...

We can stop the stream of solutions by typing a return instead of a semicolon.

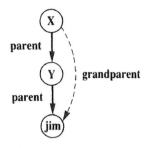

Figure 1.2   The **grandparent** relation expressed as a composition of two **parent** relations.

Our example program can be asked still more complicated questions like: Who is a grandparent of Jim? As our program does not directly know the **grandparent** relation this query has to be broken down into two steps, as illustrated by Figure 1.2.

(1)   Who is a parent of Jim? Assume that this is some Y.

(2)   Who is a parent of Y? Assume that this is some X.

Such a composed query is written in Prolog as a sequence of two simple ones:

    ?- **parent(Y, jim), parent(X, Y).**

The answer will be:

    X = **bob**
    Y = **pat**

Our composed query can be read: Find such X and Y that satisfy the following two requirements:

    parent(Y, jim)   and   **parent(X, Y)**

If we change the order of the two requirements the logical meaning remains the same:

    parent(X, Y)   and   **parent(Y, jim)**

We can indeed do this in our Prolog program, and the query:

    ?- **parent(X, Y), parent(Y, jim).**

will produce the same result.
    In a similar way we can ask: Who are Tom's grandchildren?

    ?- **parent(tom, X), parent(X, Y).**

Prolog's answers are:

    X = **bob**
    Y = **ann;**

X = **bob**
Y = **pat**

Yet another question could be: Do Ann and Pat have a common parent? This can be expressed again in two steps:

(1)   Who is a parent, X, of Ann?

(2)   Is (this same) X a parent of Pat?

The corresponding question to Prolog is then:

?- **parent(X, ann), parent(X, pat).**

The answer is:

X = **bob**

Our example program has helped to illustrate some important points:

- It is easy in Prolog to define a relation, such as the **parent** relation, by stating the n-tuples of objects that satisfy the relation.

- The user can easily query the Prolog system about relations defined in the program.

- A Prolog program consists of *clauses*. Each clause terminates with a full stop.

- The arguments of relations can (among other things) be: concrete objects, or constants (such as **tom** and **ann**), or general objects such as X and Y. Objects of the first kind in our program are called *atoms*. Objects of the second kind are called *variables*.

- Questions to the system consist of one or more *goals*. A sequence of goals, such as:

    parent(X, ann), parent(X, pat)

means the conjunction of the goals:

    X is a parent of Ann, and
    X is a parent of Pat.

The word 'goals' is used because Prolog accepts questions as goals that are to be satisfied.

- An answer to a question can be either positive or negative, depending on whether the corresponding goal can be satisfied or not. In the case of a positive answer we say that the corresponding goal was *satisfiable* and that the goal *succeeded*. Otherwise the goal was *unsatisfiable* and it *failed*.

- If several answers satisfy the question then Prolog will find as many of them as desired by the user.

Exercises

1.1   Assuming the **parent** relation as defined in this section (see Figure 1.1), what will be Prolog's answers to the following questions?

(a)   ?- **parent(jim, X).**

(b)   ?- **parent(X, jim).**

(c)   ?- **parent(pam, X), parent(X, pat).**

(d)   ?- **parent(pam, X), parent(X, Y), parent(Y, jim).**

1.2   Formulate in Prolog the following questions about the **parent** relation:

(a)   Who is Pat's parent?

(b)   Does Liz have a child?

(c)   Who is Pat's grandparent?

1.2   Defining relations by rules

Our example program can be easily extended in many interesting ways. Let us first add the information on the sex of the people that occur in the **parent** relation. This can be done by simply adding the following facts to our program:

```
female( pam).
male( tom).
male( bob).
female( liz).
female( pat).
female( ann).
male( jim).
```

The relations introduced here are **male** and **female**. These relations are unary (or one-place) relations. A binary relation like **parent** defines a relation between *pairs* of objects; on the other hand, unary relations can be used to declare simple yes/no properties of objects. The first unary clause above can be read: Pam is a female. We could convey the same information declared in the two unary relations with one binary relation, sex, instead. An alternative piece of program would then be:

```
sex( pam, feminine).
sex( tom, masculine).
sex( bob, masculine).
...
```

As our next extension to the program let us introduce the **offspring** relation as the inverse of the **parent** relation. We could define **offspring** in a similar way as the

parent relation; that is, by simply providing a list of simple facts about the **offspring** relation, each fact mentioning one pair of people such that one is an offspring of the other. For example:

offspring(liz, tom).

However, the offspring relation can be defined much more elegantly by making use of the fact that it is the inverse of **parent**, and that **parent** has already been defined. This alternative way can be based on the following logical statement:

For all X and Y,
 Y is an offspring of X if
  X is a parent of Y.

This formulation is already close to the formalism of Prolog. The corresponding Prolog clause which has the same meaning is:

offspring(Y, X) :- parent(X, Y).

This clause can also be read as:

For all X and Y,
 if X is a parent of Y then
 Y is an offspring of X.

Prolog clauses such as:

offspring(Y, X) :- parent(X, Y).

are called *rules*. There is an important difference between facts and rules. A fact like:

parent(tom, liz).

is something that is always, unconditionally, true. On the other hand, rules specify things that are true if some condition is satisfied. Therefore we say that rules have:

- a condition part (the right-hand side of the rule) and
- a conclusion part (the left-hand side of the rule).

The conclusion part is also called the *head* of a clause and the condition part the *body* of a clause. For example:

offspring(Y, X) :- parent(X, Y).

          head   body

If the condition **parent(X, Y)** is true then a logical consequence of this is **offspring(Y, X)**.

How rules are actually used by Prolog is illustrated by the following example. Let us ask our program whether Liz is an offspring of Tom:

?- offspring(liz, tom).

There is no fact about offsprings in the program, therefore the only way to consider this question is to apply the rule about offsprings. The rule is general in the sense that it is applicable to any objects X and Y; therefore it can also be applied to such particular objects as liz and tom. To apply the rule to liz and tom, Y has to be substituted with liz, and X with tom. We say that the variables X and Y become instantiated to:

X = tom   and   Y = liz

After the instantiation we have obtained a special case of our general rule. The special case is:

offspring(liz, tom) :- parent(tom, liz).

The condition part has become:

parent(tom, liz)

Now Prolog tries to find out whether the condition part is true. So the initial goal:

offspring(liz, tom)

has been replaced with the subgoal:

parent(tom, liz)

This (new) goal happens to be trivial as it can be found as a fact in our program. This means that the conclusion part of the rule is also true, and Prolog will answer the question with yes.

Let us now add more family relations to our example program. The specification of the **mother** relation can be based on the following logical statement:

For all X and Y,
    X is the mother of Y if
    X is a parent of Y and
    X is a female.

This is translated into Prolog as the following rule:

mother(X, Y) :- parent(X, Y), female(X).

A comma between two conditions indicates the conjunction of the conditions, meaning that *both* conditions have to be true.

Relations such as **parent, offspring** and **mother** can be illustrated by diagrams such as those in Figure 1.3. These diagrams conform to the following conventions. Nodes in the graphs correspond to objects – that is, arguments of relations. Arcs between nodes correspond to binary (or two-place) relations. The arcs are oriented so as to point from the first argument of the relation to the second argument. Unary relations are indicated in the diagrams by simply marking the corresponding objects

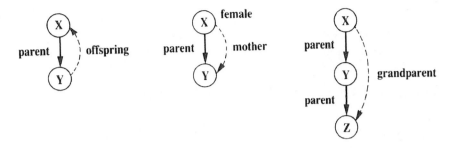

Figure 1.3 Definition graphs for the relations **offspring, mother** and **grandparent** in terms of other relations.

with the name of the relation. The relations that are being defined are represented by dashed arcs. So each diagram should be understood as follows: if the relations shown by solid arcs hold, then the relation shown by a dashed arc also holds. The **grandparent** relation can be, according to Figure 1.3, immediately written in Prolog as:

grandparent(X, Z) :- parent(X, Y), parent(Y, Z).

At this point it will be useful to make a comment on the layout of our programs. Prolog gives us almost full freedom in choosing the layout of the program. So we can insert spaces and new lines as it best suits our taste. In general we want to make our programs look nice and tidy, and, above all, easy to read. To this end we will often choose to write the head of a clause and each goal of the body on a separate line. When doing this, we will indent goals in order to make the difference between the head and the goals more visible. For example, the **grandparent** rule would be, according to this convention, written as follows:

grandparent(X, Z) :-
    parent(X, Y),
    parent(Y, Z).

Figure 1.4 illustrates the **sister** relation:

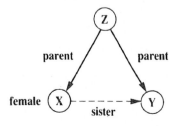

Figure 1.4 Defining the **sister** relation.

For any X and Y,
> X is a sister of Y if
> (1) both X and Y have the same parent, and
> (2) X is a female.

The graph in Figure 1.4 can be translated into Prolog as:

```
sister( X, Y) :-
    parent( Z, X),
    parent( Z, Y),
    female( X).
```

Notice the way in which the requirement 'both X and Y have the same parent' has been expressed. The following logical formulation was used: some Z must be a parent of X, and this *same* Z must be a parent of Y. An alternative, but less elegant way would be to say: Z1 is a parent of X, and Z2 is a parent of Y, and Z1 is equal to Z2.

We can now ask:

```
?- sister( ann, pat).
```

The answer will be 'yes', as expected (see Figure 1.1). Therefore we might conclude that the **sister** relation, as defined, works correctly. There is, however, a rather subtle flaw in our program, which is revealed if we ask the question Who is Pat's sister?:

```
?- sister( X, pat).
```

Prolog will find two answers, one of which may come as a surprise:

```
X = ann;
```

```
X = pat
```

So, Pat is a sister to herself?! This is probably not what we had in mind when defining the **sister** relation. However, according to our rule about sisters Prolog's answer is perfectly logical. Our rule about sisters does not mention that X and Y must not be the same if X is to be a sister of Y. As this is not required Prolog (rightfully) assumes that X and Y can be the same, and will as a consequence find that any female who has a parent is a sister of herself.

To correct our rule about sisters we have to add that X and Y must be different. We will see in later chapters how this can be done in several ways, but for the moment we will assume that a relation **different** is already known to Prolog, and that:

```
different( X, Y)
```

is satisfied if and only if X and Y are not equal. An improved rule for the **sister** relation can then be:

```
sister( X, Y) :-
    parent( Z, X),
    parent( Z, Y),
    female( X),
    different( X, Y).
```

Some important points of this section are:

- Prolog programs can be extended by simply adding new clauses.
- Prolog clauses are of three types: *facts*, *rules* and *questions*.
- *Facts* declare things that are always, unconditionally true.
- *Rules* declare things that are true depending on a given condition.
- By means of *questions* the user can ask the program what things are true.
- Prolog clauses consist of the *head* and the *body*. The body is a list of *goals* separated by commas. Commas are understood as conjunctions.
- Facts are clauses that have a head and the empty body. Questions only have the body. Rules have the head and the (non-empty) body.
- In the course of computation, a variable can be substituted by another object. We say that a variable becomes *instantiated*.
- Variables are assumed to be universally quantified and are read as 'for all'. Alternative readings are, however, possible for variables that appear only in the body. For example:

    hasachild(X) :- parent(X, Y).

can be read in two ways:

(a) *For all* X and Y,
    if X is a parent of Y then
    X has a child.

(b) *For all* X,
    X has a child if
    there is *some* Y such that X is a parent of Y.

Exercises

1.3   Translate the following statements into Prolog rules:

(a) Everybody who has a child is happy (introduce a one-argument relation **happy**).

(b) For all X, if X has a child who has a sister then X has two children (introduce new relation **hastwochildren**).

1.4   Define the relation **grandchild** using the **parent** relation. Hint: It will be similar to the **grandparent** relation (see Figure 1.3).

1.5   Define the relation **aunt(X, Y)** in terms of the relations **parent** and **sister**. As an aid you can first draw a diagram in the style of Figure 1.3 for the **aunt** relation.

1.3   Recursive rules

Let us add one more relation to our family program, the **predecessor** relation. This relation will be defined in terms of the **parent** relation. The whole definition can be expressed with two rules. The first rule will define the direct (immediate) predecessors and the second rule the indirect predecessors. We say that some X is an indirect predecessor of some Z if there is a parentship chain of people between X and Z, as illustrated in Figure 1.5. In our example of Figure 1.1, Tom is a direct predecessor of Liz and an indirect predecessor of Pat.

The first rule is simple and can be formulated as:

> For all X and Z,
> > X is a predecessor of Z if
> > X is a parent of Z.

This is straightforwardly translated into Prolog as:

> **predecessor(X, Z) :-**
> > **parent(X, Z).**

The second rule, on the other hand, is more complicated because the chain of parents may present some problems. One attempt to define indirect predecessors could be as shown in Figure 1.6. According to this, the **predecessor** relation would be defined by a set of clauses as follows:

> **predecessor(X, Z) :-**
> > **parent(X, Z).**
>
> **predecessor(X, Z) :-**
> > **parent(X, Y),**
> > **parent(Y, Z).**

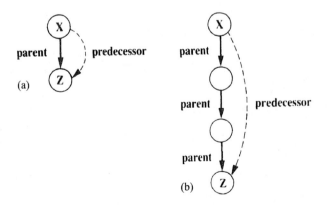

Figure 1.5   Examples of the **predecessor** relation: (a) X is a direct predecessor of Z;
(b) X is an indirect predecessor of Z.

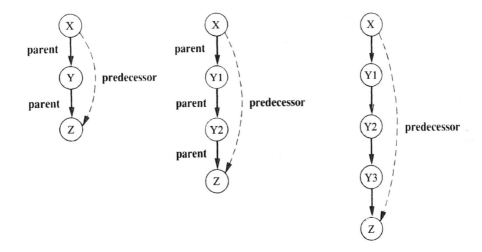

Figure 1.6 Predecessor-successor pairs at various distances.

```
predecessor( X, Z) :-
    parent( X, Y1),
    parent( Y1, Y2),
    parent( Y2, Z).
predecessor( X, Z) :-
    parent( X, Y1),
    parent( Y1, Y2),
    parent( Y2, Y3),
    parent( Y3, Z).
```

...

This program is lengthy and, more importantly, it only works to some extent. It would only discover predecessors to a certain depth in a family tree because the length of the chain of people between the predecessor and the successor would be limited according to the length of our predecessor clauses.

There is, however, an elegant and correct formulation of the **predecessor** relation: it will be correct in the sense that it will work for predecessors at any depth. The key idea is to define the **predecessor** relation in terms of itself. Figure 1.7 illustrates the idea:

For all X and Z,
    X is a predecessor of Z if
    there is a Y such that
    (1) X is a parent of Y and
    (2) Y is a predecessor of Z.

A Prolog clause with the above meaning is:

```
predecessor( X, Z) :-
    parent( X, Y),
    predecessor( Y, Z).
```

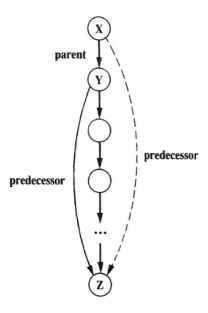

Figure 1.7   Recursive formulation of the **predecessor** relation.

We have thus constructed a complete program for the **predecessor** relation, which consists of two rules: one for direct predecessors and one for indirect predecessors. Both rules are rewritten together here:

predecessor(X, Z) :-
    parent(X, Z).

predecessor(X, Z) :-
    parent(X, Y),
    predecessor(Y, Z).

The key to this formulation was the use of **predecessor** itself in its definition. Such a definition may look surprising in view of the question: When defining something, can we use this same thing that has not yet been completely defined? Such definitions are, in general, called *recursive* definitions. Logically, they are perfectly correct and understandable, which is also intuitively obvious if we look at Figure 1.7. But will the Prolog system be able to use recursive rules? It turns out that Prolog can indeed very easily use recursive definitions. Recursive programming is, in fact, one of the fundamental principles of programming in Prolog. It is not possible to solve tasks of any significant complexity in Prolog without the use of recursion.

Going back to our program, we can ask Prolog: Who are Pam's successors? That is: Who is a person that has Pam as his or her predecessor?

?- predecessor(pam, X).

X = bob;

X = ann;

X = pat;

X = jim

Prolog's answers are, of course, correct and they logically follow from our definition of the **predecessor** and the **parent** relation. There is, however, a rather important question: *How* did Prolog actually use the program to find these answers?

An informal explanation of how Prolog does this is given in the next section. But first let us put together all the pieces of our family program, which was extended gradually by adding new facts and rules. The final form of the program is shown in Figure 1.8. Looking at Figure 1.8, two further points are in order here: the

....

parent(pam, bob).	% Pam is a parent of Bob
parent(tom, bob).	
parent(tom, liz).	
parent(bob, ann).	
parent(bob, pat).	
parent(pat, jim).	
female(pam).	% Pam is female
male(tom).	% Tom is male
male(bob).	
female(liz).	
female(ann).	
female(pat).	
male(jim).	
offspring(Y, X) :-	% Y is an offspring of X if
parent(X, Y).	% X is a parent of Y
mother(X, Y) :-	% X is the mother of Y if
parent(X, Y),	% X is a parent of Y and
female(X).	% X is female
grandparent(X, Z) :-	% X is a grandparent of Z if
parent(X, Y),	% X is a parent of Y and
parent(Y, Z).	% Y is a parent of Z
sister(X, Y) :-	% X is a sister of Y if
parent(Z, X),	
parent(Z, Y),	% X and Y have the same parent and
female(X),	% X is female and
different(X, Y).	% X and Y are different
predecessor(X, Z) :-	% Rule prl: X is a predecessor of Z
parent(X, Z).	
predecessor(X, Z) :-	% Rule pr2: X is a predecessor of Z
parent(X, Y),	
predecessor(Y, Z).	

....

Figure 1.8 The family program.

first will introduce the term 'procedure', the second will be about comments in programs.

The program in Figure 1.8 defines several relations – **parent**, **male**, **female**, **predecessor**, etc. The **predecessor** relation, for example, is defined by two clauses. We say that these two clauses are *about* the **predecessor** relation. Sometimes it is convenient to consider the whole set of clauses about the same relation. Such a set of clauses is called a *procedure*.

In Figure 1.8, the two rules about the **predecessor** relation have been distinguished by the names 'pr1' and 'pr2', added as *comments* to the program. These names will be used later as references to these rules. Comments are, in general, ignored by the Prolog system. They only serve as a further clarification to the person who reads the program. Comments are distinguished in Prolog from the rest of the program by being enclosed in special brackets '/∗' and '∗/'. Thus comments in Prolog look like this:

```
/∗ This is a comment ∗/
```

Another method, more practical for short comments, uses the percent character '%'. Everything between '%' and the end of the line is interpreted as a comment:

```
% This is also a comment
```

Exercise

1.6   Consider the following alternative definition of the **predecessor** relation:

```
predecessor( X, Z) :-
    parent( X, Z).

predecessor( X, Z) :-
    parent( Y, Z),
    predecessor( X, Y).
```

Does this also seem to be a correct definition of predecessors? Can you modify the diagram of Figure 1.7 so that it would correspond to this new definition?

1.4   How Prolog answers questions

This section gives an informal explanation of *how* Prolog answers questions. A question to Prolog is always a sequence of one or more goals. To answer a question, Prolog tries to satisfy all the goals. What does it mean to *satisfy* a goal? To satisfy a goal means to demonstrate that the goal is true, assuming that the relations in the program are true. In other words, to satisfy a goal means to demonstrate that the goal *logically follows* from the facts and rules in the program. If the question contains variables, Prolog also has to find what are the particular objects (in place of variables) for which the goals are satisfied. The particular instantiation of variables to these objects is displayed to the user. If Prolog cannot demonstrate for some instantiation of variables that the goals logically follow from the program, then Prolog's answer to the question will be 'no'.

An appropriate view of the interpretation of a Prolog program in mathematical terms is then as follows: Prolog accepts facts and rules as a set of axioms, and the user's question as a *conjectured theorem*; then it tries to prove this theorem – that is, to demonstrate that it can be logically derived from the axioms.

We will illustrate this view by a classical example. Let the axioms be:

All men are fallible.
Socrates is a man.

A theorem that logically follows from these two axioms is:

Socrates is fallible.

The first axiom above can be rewritten as:

For all X, if X is a man then X is fallible.

Accordingly, the example can be translated into Prolog as follows:

fallible(X) :- man(X).   % All men are fallible

man(socrates).   % Socrates is a man

?- **fallible(socrates).**   % Socrates is fallible?

yes

A more complicated example from the family program of Figure 1.8 is:

?- **predecessor(tom, pat).**

We know that **parent(bob, pat)** is a fact. Using this fact and rule *pr1* we can conclude **predecessor(bob, pat)**. This is a *derived* fact: it cannot be found explicitly in our program, but it can be derived from facts and rules in the program. An inference step, such as this, can be written in a more compact form as:

parent(bob, pat) ==> predecessor(bob, pat)

This can be read: from **parent(bob, pat)** it follows that **predecessor(bob, pat)**, by rule *pr1*. Further, we know that **parent(tom, bob)** is a fact. Using this fact and the derived fact **predecessor(bob, pat)** we can conclude **predecessor(tom, pat)**, by rule *pr2*. We have thus shown that our goal statement **predecessor(tom, pat)** is true. This whole inference process of two steps can be written as:

parent(bob, pat) ==> predecessor(bob, pat)

parent(tom, bob) *and* predecessor(bob, pat) ==> predecessor(tom, pat)

We have thus shown *what* can be a sequence of steps that satisfy a goal – that is, make it clear that the goal is true. Let us call this a proof sequence. We have not, however, shown *how* the Prolog system actually finds such a proof sequence.

Prolog finds the proof sequence in the inverse order to that which we have just used. Instead of starting with simple facts given in the program, Prolog starts with the goals and, using rules, substitutes the current goals with new goals, until new goals happen to be simple facts. Given the question:

?- **predecessor(tom, pat).**

Prolog will try to satisfy this goal. In order to do so it will try to find a clause in the program from which the above goal could immediately follow. Obviously, the only clauses relevant to this end are *pr1* and *pr2*. These are the rules about the **predecessor** relation. We say that the heads of these rules *match* the goal.

The two clauses, *pr1* and *pr2*, represent two alternative ways for Prolog to proceed. Prolog first tries that clause which appears first in the program:

predecessor(X, Z) :- parent(X, Z).

Since the goal is **predecessor(tom, pat)**, the variables in the rule must be instantiated as follows:

X = **tom**, Z = **pat**

The original goal **predecessor(tom, pat)** is then replaced by a new goal:

parent(tom, pat)

This step of using a rule to transform a goal into another goal, as above, is graphically illustrated in Figure 1.9. There is no clause in the program whose head matches the goal **parent(tom, pat)**, therefore this goal fails. Now Prolog *backtracks* to the original goal in order to try an alternative way to derive the top goal **predecessor(tom, pat)**. The rule *pr2* is thus tried:

predecessor(X, Z) :-
　parent(X, Y),
　predecessor(Y, Z).

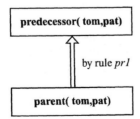

Figure 1.9　The first step of the execution. The top goal is true if the bottom goal is true.

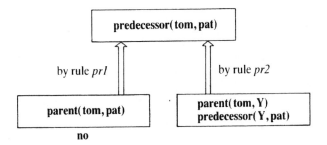

Figure 1.10 Execution trace continued from Figure 1.9.

As before, the variables X and Z become instantiated as:

  X = **tom**, Z = **pat**

But Y is not instantiated yet. The top goal **predecessor(tom, pat)** is replaced by two goals:

  parent(tom, Y),
  predecessor(Y, pat)

This executional step is shown in Figure 1.10, which is an extension to the situation we had in Figure 1.9.

  Being now faced with *two* goals, Prolog tries to satisfy them in the order in which they are written. The first one is easy as it matches one of the facts in the program. The matching forces Y to become instantiated to **bob**. Thus the first goal has been satisfied, and the remaining goal has become:

  predecessor(bob, pat)

To satisfy this goal the rule *pr1* is used again. Note that this (second) application of the same rule has nothing to do with its previous application. Therefore, Prolog uses a new set of variables in the rule each time the rule is applied. To indicate this we shall rename the variables in rule *pr1* for this application as follows:

  predecessor(X', Z') :-
    parent(X', Z').

The head has to match our current goal **predecessor(bob, pat)**. Therefore:

  X' = bob, Z' = pat

The current goal is replaced by:

  parent(bob, pat)

This goal is immediately satisfied because it appears in the program as a fact. This completes the execution trace, which is graphically shown in Figure 1.11.

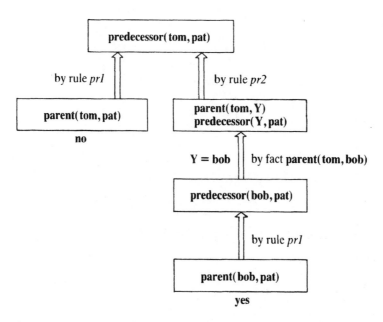

Figure 1.11 The complete execution trace to satisfy the goal **predecessor(tom, pat)**. The right-hand branch proves the goal is satisfiable.

The graphical illustration of the execution trace in Figure 1.11 has the form of a tree. The nodes of the tree correspond to goals, or to lists of goals that are to be satisfied. The arcs between the nodes correspond to the application of (alternative) program clauses that transform the goals at one node into the goals at another node. The top goal is satisfied when a path is found from the root node (top goal) to a leaf node labelled 'yes'. A leaf is labelled 'yes' if it is a simple fact. The execution of Prolog programs is the searching for such paths. During the search Prolog may enter an unsuccessful branch. When Prolog discovers that a branch fails it automatically *backtracks* to the previous node and tries to apply an alternative clause at that node.

Exercise

1.7   Try to understand how Prolog derives answers to the following questions, using the program of Figure 1.8. Try to draw the corresponding derivation diagrams in the style of Figures 1.9 to 1.11. Will any backtracking occur at particular questions?

    (a) ?- **parent(pam, bob).**

    (b) ?- **mother(pam, bob).**

    (c) ?- **grandparent(pam, ann).**

    (d) ?- **grandparent(bob, jim).**

1.5 Declarative and procedural meaning of programs

In our examples so far it has always been possible to understand the results of the program without exactly knowing *how* the system actually found the results. It therefore makes sense to distinguish between two levels of meaning of Prolog programs; namely,

- the *declarative meaning* and

- the *procedural meaning*.

The declarative meaning is concerned only with the *relations* defined by the program. The declarative meaning thus determines *what* will be the output of the program. On the other hand, the procedural meaning also determines *how* this output is obtained; that is, how the relations are actually evaluated by the Prolog system.

The ability of Prolog to work out many procedural details on its own is considered to be one of its specific advantages. It encourages the programmer to consider the declarative meaning of programs relatively independently of their procedural meaning. Since the results of the program are, in principle, determined by its declarative meaning, this should be (in principle) sufficient for writing programs. This is of practical importance because the declarative aspects of programs are usually easier to understand than the procedural details. To take full advantage of this, the programmer should concentrate mainly on the declarative meaning and, whenever possible, avoid being distracted by the executional details. These should be left to the greatest possible extent to the Prolog system itself.

This declarative approach indeed often makes programming in Prolog easier than in typical procedurally oriented programming languages such as C or Pascal. Unfortunately, however, the declarative approach is not always sufficient. It will later become clear that, especially in large programs, the procedural aspects cannot be completely ignored by the programmer for practical reasons of executional efficiency. Nevertheless, the declarative style of thinking about Prolog programs should be encouraged and the procedural aspects ignored to the extent that is permitted by practical constraints.

Summary

- Prolog programming consists of defining relations and querying about relations.

- A program consists of *clauses*. These are of three types: *facts*, *rules* and *questions*.

- A relation can be specified by *facts*, simply stating the n-tuples of objects that satisfy the relation, or by stating *rules* about the relation.

- A *procedure* is a set of clauses about the same relation.

- Querying about relations, by means of *questions*, resembles querying a database. Prolog's answer to a question consists of a set of objects that satisfy the question.

- In Prolog, to establish whether an object satisfies a query is often a complicated process that involves logical inference, exploring among alternatives and possibly *backtracking*. All this is done automatically by the Prolog system and is, in principle, hidden from the user.

- Two types of meaning of Prolog programs are distinguished: declarative and procedural. The declarative view is advantageous from the programming point of view. Nevertheless, the procedural details often have to be considered by the programmer as well.

- The following concepts have been introduced in this chapter:

  clause, fact, rule, question
  the head of a clause, the body of a clause
  recursive rule, recursive definition
  procedure
  atom, variable
  instantiation of a variable
  goal
  goal is satisfiable, goal succeeds
  goal is unsatisfiable, goal fails
  backtracking
  declarative meaning, procedural meaning

References

Various implementations of Prolog use different syntactic conventions. However, most of them follow the tradition of the so-called Edinburgh syntax (also called DEC-10 syntax, established by the historically influential implementation of Prolog for the DEC-10 computer; Pereira *et al.* 1978; Bowen 1981). The Edinburgh syntax also forms the basis of the ISO international standard for Prolog ISO/IEC 13211-1 (Deransart *et al.* 1996). Major Prolog implementations now largely comply with the standard. In this book we use a subset of the standard syntax, with some small and insignificant differences. In rare cases of such differences, there is a note to this effect at an appropriate place.

Bowen, D.L. (1981) *DECsystem-10 Prolog User's Manual*. University of Edinburgh: Department of Artificial Intelligence.

Deransart, P., Ed-Bdali, A. and Ceroni, L. (1996) *Prolog: The Standard*. Berlin: Springer-Verlag.

Pereira, L.M., Pereira, F. and Warren, D.H.D. (1978) *User's Guide to DECsystem-10 Prolog*. University of Edinburgh: Department of Artificial Intelligence.

Syntax and Meaning of Prolog Programs

This chapter gives a systematic treatment of the syntax and semantics of basic concepts of Prolog, and introduces structured data objects. The topics included are:

- simple data objects (atoms, numbers, variables)
- structured objects
- matching as the fundamental operation on objects
- declarative (or non-procedural) meaning of a program
- procedural meaning of a program
- relation between the declarative and procedural meanings of a program
- altering the procedural meaning by reordering clauses and goals.

Most of these topics have already been reviewed in Chapter 1. Here the treatment will become more formal and detailed.

2.1   Data objects

Figure 2.1 shows a classification of data objects in Prolog. The Prolog system recognizes the type of an object in the program by its syntactic form. This is possible because the syntax of Prolog specifies different forms for each type of data object. We have already seen a method for distinguishing between atoms and variables in Chapter 1: variables start with upper-case letters whereas atoms start with lower-case letters. No additional information (such as data-type declaration) has to be communicated to Prolog in order to recognize the type of an object.

2.1.1   Atoms and numbers

In Chapter 1 we have seen some simple examples of atoms and variables. In general, however, they can take more complicated forms – that is, strings of the following characters:

- upper-case letters A, B, ..., Z
- lower-case letters a, b, ..., z
- digits 0, 1, 2, ..., 9
- special characters such as $+ - * / < > = : . \& \_ \sim$

Atoms can be constructed in three ways:

(1)   Strings of letters, digits and the underscore character, '_', starting with a lower-case letter:

        anna
        nil
        x25
        x_25
        x_25AB
        x_
        x___y
        alpha_beta_procedure
        miss_Jones
        sarah_jones

(2)   Strings of special characters:

        <--->
        ======>
        . . .
        . : .
        : : =

When using atoms of this form, some care is necessary because some strings of special characters already have a predefined meaning; an example is ' :- '.

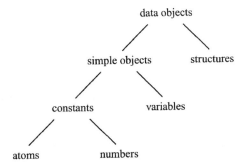

Figure 2.1 Data objects in Prolog.

(3)   Strings of characters enclosed in single quotes. This is useful if we want, for example, to have an atom that starts with a capital letter. By enclosing it in quotes we make it distinguishable from variables:

'Tom'
'South_America'
'Sarah Jones'

Numbers used in Prolog include integer numbers and real numbers. The syntax of integers is simple, as illustrated by the following examples:

1   1313   0   −97

Not all integer numbers can be represented in a computer, therefore the range of integers is limited to an interval between some smallest and some largest number permitted by a particular Prolog implementation.

We will assume the simple syntax of real numbers, as shown by the following examples:

3.14   −0.0035   100.2

Real numbers are not very heavily used in typical Prolog programming. The reason for this is that Prolog is primarily a language for symbolic, non-numeric computation. In symbolic computation, integers are often used, for example, to count the number of items in a list; but there is typically less need for real numbers.

Apart from this lack of necessity to use real numbers in typical Prolog applications, there is another reason for avoiding real numbers. In general, we want to keep the meaning of programs as neat as possible. The introduction of real numbers somewhat impairs this neatness because of numerical errors that arise due to rounding when doing arithmetic. For example, the evaluation of the expression

$10000 + 0.0001 − 10000$

may result in 0 instead of the correct result 0.0001.

2.1.2 Variables

Variables are strings of letters, digits and underscore characters. They start with an upper-case letter or an underscore character:

X
Result
Object2
Participant_list
ShoppingList
_x23
_23

When a variable appears in a clause once only, we do not have to invent a name for it. We can use the so-called 'anonymous' variable, which is written as a single underscore character. For example, let us consider the following rule:

hasachild(X) :- parent(X, Y).

This rule says: for all X, X has a child if X is a parent of some Y. We are defining the property **hasachild** which, as it is meant here, does not depend on the name of the child. Thus, this is a proper place in which to use an anonymous variable. The clause above can thus be rewritten:

hasachild(X) :- parent(X, _).

Each time a single underscore character occurs in a clause it represents a new anonymous variable. For example, we can say that there is somebody who has a child if there are two objects such that one is a parent of the other:

somebody_has_child :- parent(_, _).

This is equivalent to:

somebody_has_child :- parent(X, Y).

But this is, of course, quite different from:

somebody_has_child :- parent(X, X).

If the anonymous variable appears in a question clause then its value is not output when Prolog answers the question. If we are interested in people who have children, but not in the names of the children, then we can simply ask:

?- parent(X, _).

The *lexical scope* of variable names is one clause. This means that, for example, if the name X15 occurs in two clauses, then it signifies two different variables. But each occurrence of X15 within the same clause means the same variable. The situation is different for constants: the same atom always means the same object in any clause – that is, throughout the whole program.

2.1.3 Structures

Structured objects (or simply *structures*) are objects that have several components. The components themselves can, in turn, be structures. For example, the date can be viewed as a structure with three components: day, month, year. Although composed of several components, structures are treated in the program as single objects. In order to combine the components into a single object we have to choose a *functor*. A suitable functor for our example is **date**. Then the date 1 May 2001 can be written as:

date(1, **may**, 2001)

(see Figure 2.2).

All the components in this example are constants (two integers and one atom). Components can also be variables or other structures. Any day in May can be represented by the structure:

date(**Day**, **may**, 2001)

Note that **Day** is a variable and can be instantiated to any object at some later point in the execution.

This method for data structuring is simple and powerful. It is one of the reasons why Prolog is so naturally applied to problems that involve symbolic manipulation.

Syntactically, all data objects in Prolog are *terms*. For example,

may

and

date(1, **may**, 2001)

are terms.

All structured objects can be pictured as trees (see Figure 2.2 for an example). The root of the tree is the functor, and the offsprings of the root are the components. If a component is also a structure then it is a subtree of the tree that corresponds to the whole structured object.

Our next example will show how structures can be used to represent some simple geometric objects (see Figure 2.3). A point in two-dimensional space is defined by its

Figure 2.2 Date is an example of a structured object: (a) as it is represented as a tree; (b) as it is written in Prolog.

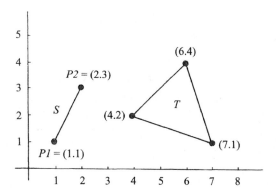

Figure 2.3 Some simple geometric objects.

two coordinates; a line segment is defined by two points; and a triangle can be defined by three points. Let us choose the following functors:

point   for points,
seg   for line segments, and
triangle   for triangles.

Then the objects in Figure 2.3 can be represented as follows:

P1 = **point(1,1)**
P2 = **point(2,3)**
S = **seg(P1, P2)** = **seg(point(1,1), point(2,3))**
T = **triangle(point(4,2), point(6,4), point(7,1))**

The corresponding tree representation of these objects is shown in Figure 2.4. In general, the functor at the root of the tree is called the *principal functor* of the term.

If in the same program we also had points in three-dimensional space then we could use another functor, **point3**, say, for their representation:

point3(X, Y, Z)

We can, however, use the same name, **point**, for points in both two and three dimensions, and write for example:

point(X1, Y1)   and   **point(X, Y, Z)**

If the same name appears in the program in two different roles, as is the case for point above, the Prolog system will recognize the difference by the number of arguments, and will interpret this name as two functors: one of them with two arguments and the other one with three arguments. This is so because each functor is defined by two things:

(1)   the name, whose syntax is that of atoms;

(2)   the *arity* – that is, the number of arguments.

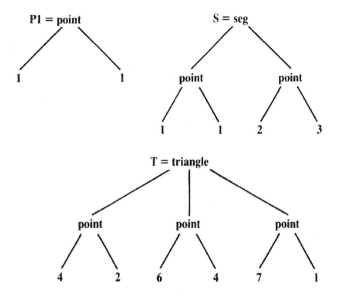

Figure 2.4 Tree representation of the objects in Figure 2.3.

As already explained, all structured objects in Prolog are trees, represented in the program by terms. We will study two more examples to illustrate how naturally complicated data objects can be represented by Prolog terms. Figure 2.5 shows the tree structure that corresponds to the arithmetic expression:

$$(a + b) * (c - 5)$$

According to the syntax of terms introduced so far this can be written, using the symbols '*', '+' and '−' as functors, as follows:

*(+(a, b), −(c, 5))

This is, of course, a legal Prolog term; but this is not the form that we would normally like to have. We would normally prefer the usual, infix notation as used in mathematics. In fact, Prolog also allows us to use the infix notation so that the symbols '*', '+' and '−' are written as infix operators. Details of how the programmer can define his or her own operators will be discussed in Chapter 3.

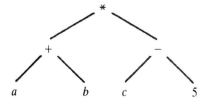

Figure 2.5 A tree structure that corresponds to the arithmetic expression $(a + b) * (c - 5)$.

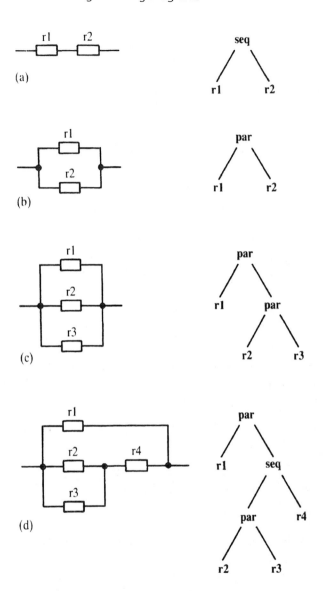

Figure 2.6   Some simple electric circuits and their tree representations: (a) sequential
composition of resistors r1 and r2; (b) parallel composition of two resistors;
(c) parallel composition of three resistors; (d) parallel composition of r1 and
another circuit.

As the last example we consider some simple electric circuits shown in Figure 2.6.
The right-hand side of the figure shows the tree representation of these circuits. The
atoms **r1, r2, r3** and **r4** are the names of the resistors. The functors **par** and **seq** denote
the parallel and the sequential compositions of resistors respectively. The corresponding Prolog terms are:

seq(r1, r2)
par(r1, r2)
par(r1, par(r2, r3))
par(r1, seq(par(r2, r3), r4))

Exercises

2.1   Which of the following are syntactically correct Prolog objects? What kinds of object are they (atom, number, variable, structure)?

(a) **Diana**

(b) **diana**

(c) **'Diana'**

(d) **_diana**

(e) **'Diana goes south'**

(f) **goes(diana, south)**

(g) **45**

(h) **5(X, Y)**

(i)   **+(north, west)**

(j) **three(Black(Cats))**

2.2   Suggest a representation for rectangles, squares and circles as structured Prolog objects. Use an approach similar to that in Figure 2.4. For example, a rectangle can be represented by four points (or maybe three points only). Write some example terms that represent some concrete objects of these types using the suggested representation.

2.2   Matching

In the previous section we have seen how terms can be used to represent complex data objects. The most important operation on terms is *matching*. Matching alone can produce some interesting computation.

Given two terms, we say that they *match* if:

(1)   they are identical, or

(2)   the variables in both terms can be instantiated to objects in such a way that after the substitution of variables by these objects the terms become identical.

For example, the terms **date(D, M, 2001)** and **date(D1, may, Y1)** match. One instantiation that makes both terms identical is:

- D is instantiated to D1
- M is instantiated to **may**
- Y1 is instantiated to **2001**

This instantiation is more compactly written in the familiar form in which Prolog outputs results:

D = D1
M = may
Y1 = 2001

On the other hand, the terms **date(D, M, 2001)** and **date(D1, M1, 1444)** do not match, nor do the terms **date(X, Y, Z)** and **point(X, Y, Z)**.

Matching is a process that takes as input two terms and checks whether they match. If the terms do not match we say that this process *fails*. If they do match then the process *succeeds* and it also instantiates the variables in both terms to such values that the terms become identical.

Let us consider again the matching of the two dates. The request for this operation can be communicated to the Prolog system by the following question, using the operator '=':

?- **date(D, M, 2001) = date(D1, may, Y1)**.

We have already mentioned the instantiation D = D1, M = **may**, Y1 = **2001**, which achieves the match. There are, however, other instantiations that also make both terms identical. Two of them are as follows:

D = 1
D1 = 1
M = may
Y1 = 2001

D = third
D1 = third
M = may
Y1 = 2001

These two instantiations are said to be *less general* than the first one because they constrain the values of the variables D and D1 more strongly than necessary. For making both terms in our example identical, it is only important that D and D1 have the same value, although this value can be anything. Matching in Prolog always results in the *most general* instantiation. This is the instantiation that commits the variables to the least possible extent, thus leaving the greatest possible freedom for further instantiations if further matching is required. As an example consider the following question:

?- **date(D, M, 2001) = date(D1, may, Y1)**,
    date(D, M, 2001) = date(15, M, Y).

To satisfy the first goal, Prolog instantiates the variables as follows:

D = D1
M = may
Y1 = 2001

After having satisfied the second goal, the instantiation becomes more specific as follows:

D = 15
D1 = 15
M = may
Y1 = 2001
Y = 2001

This example also shows that variables, during the execution of consecutive goals, typically become instantiated to increasingly more specific values.

The general rules to decide whether two terms, S and T, match are as follows:

(1)   If S and T are constants then S and T match only if they are the same object.

(2)   If S is a variable and T is anything, then they match, and S is instantiated to T. Conversely, if T is a variable then T is instantiated to S.

(3)   If S and T are structures then they match only if

   (a) S and T have the same principal functor, and

   (b) all their corresponding components match.

   The resulting instantiation is determined by the matching of the components.

The last of these rules can be visualized by considering the tree representation of terms, as in the example of Figure 2.7. The matching process starts at the root (the principal functors). As both functors match, the process proceeds to the arguments where matching of the pairs of corresponding arguments occurs. So the whole matching process can be thought of as consisting of the following sequence of (simpler) matching operations:

triangle = triangle,
point(1,1) = X,
A = point(4,Y),
point(2,3) = point(2,Z).

The whole matching process succeeds because all the matchings in the sequence succeed. The resulting instantiation is:

X = point(1,1)
A = point(4,Y)
Z = 3

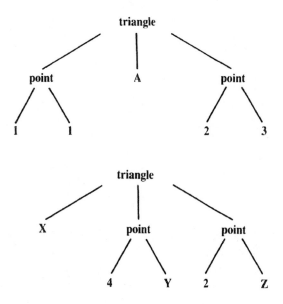

Figure 2.7 Matching **triangle(point(1,1), A, point(2,3)) = triangle(X, point(4,Y), point(2,Z))**.

The following example will illustrate how matching alone can be used for interesting computation. Let us return to the simple geometric objects of Figure 2.4, and define a piece of program for recognizing horizontal and vertical line segments. 'Vertical' is a property of segments, so it can be formalized in Prolog as a unary relation. Figure 2.8 helps to formulate this relation. A segment is vertical if the *x*-coordinates of its end-points are equal, otherwise there is no other restriction on the segment. The property 'horizontal' is similarly formulated, with only *x* and *y* interchanged. The following program, consisting of two facts, does the job:

> **vertical(seg(point(X,Y), point(X,Y1))).**

> **horizontal(seg(point(X,Y), point(X1,Y))).**

The following conversation is possible with this program:

> **?- vertical(seg(point(1,1), point(1,2))).**

> **yes**

> **?- vertical(seg(point(1,1), point(2,Y))).**

> **no**

> **?- horizontal(seg(point(1,1), point(2,Y))).**

> **Y = 1**

The first question was answered 'yes' because the goal in the question matched one of the facts in the program. For the second question no match was possible. In the third question, Y was forced to become 1 by matching the fact about horizontal segments.

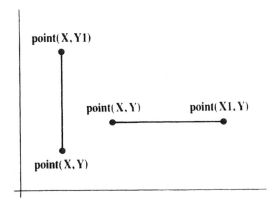

Figure 2.8 Illustration of vertical and horizontal line segments.

A more general question to the program is: Are there any vertical segments that start at the point (2,3)?

?- **vertical(seg(point(2,3), P)).**

P = point(2,Y)

This answer means: Yes, any segment that ends at any point (2,Y), which means anywhere on the vertical line $x = 2$. It should be noted that Prolog's actual answer would probably not look as neat as above, but (depending on the Prolog implementation used) something like this:

P = point(2,_136)

This is, however, only a cosmetic difference. Here _136 is a variable that has not been instantiated. _136 is a legal variable name that the system has constructed during the execution. The system has to generate new names in order to rename the user's variables in the program. This is necessary for two reasons: first, because the same name in different clauses signifies different variables, and second, in successive applications of the same clause, its 'copy' with a new set of variables is used each time.

Another interesting question to our program is: Is there a segment that is both vertical and horizontal?

?- **vertical(S), horizontal(S).**

S = seg(point(X,Y), point(X,Y))

This answer by Prolog says: Yes, any segment that is degenerated to a point has the property of being vertical and horizontal at the same time. The answer was, again, derived simply by matching. As before, some internally generated names may appear in the answer, instead of the variable names X and Y.

Exercises

2.3 Will the following matching operations succeed or fail? If they succeed, what are the resulting instantiations of variables?

(a) **point(A, B) = point(1, 2)**

(b) **point(A, B) = point(X, Y, Z)**

(c) **plus(2, 2) = 4**

(d) **+(2, D) = +(E, 2)**

(e) **triangle(point(−1,0), P2, P3) = triangle(P1, point(1,0), point(0,Y))**

The resulting instantiation defines a family of triangles. How would you describe this family?

2.4 Using the representation for line segments as described in this section, write a term that represents any vertical line segment at $x = 5$.

2.5 Assume that a rectangle is represented by the term **rectangle(P1, P2, P3, P4)** where the P's are the vertices of the rectangle positively ordered. Define the relation:

    regular(R)

which is true if R is a rectangle whose sides are vertical and horizontal.

2.3   Declarative meaning of Prolog programs

We have already seen in Chapter 1 that Prolog programs can be understood in two ways: declaratively and procedurally. In this and the next section we will consider a more formal definition of the declarative and procedural meanings of programs in basic Prolog. But first let us look at the difference between these two meanings again.

Consider a clause:

    P :- Q, R.

where P, Q and R have the syntax of terms. Some alternative declarative readings of this clause are:

    P is true if Q and R are true.
    From Q and R follows P.

Two alternative procedural readings of this clause are:

    To solve problem P, *first* solve the subproblem Q and *then* the subproblem R.
    To satisfy P, *first* satisfy Q and *then* R.

Thus the difference between the declarative readings and the procedural ones is that the latter do not only define the logical relations between the head of the clause and the goals in the body, but also the *order* in which the goals are processed.

Let us now formalize the declarative meaning.

The declarative meaning of programs determines whether a given goal is true, and if so, for what values of variables it is true. To precisely define the declarative meaning we need to introduce the concept of *instance* of a clause. An instance of a clause C is the clause C with each of its variables substituted by some term. A *variant* of a clause C is such an instance of the clause C where each variable is substituted by another variable. For example, consider the clause:

hasachild(X) :- parent(X, Y).

Two variants of this clause are:

hasachild(A) :- parent(A, B).
hasachild(X1) :- parent(X1, X2).

Instances of this clause are:

hasachild(peter) :- parent(peter, Z).
hasachild(barry) :- parent(barry, small(caroline)).

Given a program and a goal G, the declarative meaning says:

A goal G is true (that is, satisfiable, or logically follows from the program) if and only if:

(1)   there is a clause C in the program such that

(2)   there is a clause instance I of C such that

    (a)   the head of I is identical to G, and

    (b)   all the goals in the body of I are true.

This definition extends to Prolog questions as follows. In general, a question to the Prolog system is a *list* of goals separated by commas. A list of goals is true if *all* the goals in the list are true for the *same* instantiation of variables. The values of the variables result from the most general instantiation.

A comma between goals thus denotes the *conjunction* of goals: they *all* have to be true. But Prolog also accepts the *disjunction* of goals: *any one* of the goals in a disjunction has to be true. Disjunction is indicated by a semicolon. For example,

P :- Q ; R.

is read: P is true if Q is true *or* R is true. The meaning of this clause is thus the same as the meaning of the following two clauses together:

P :- Q.
P :- R.

The comma binds stronger than the semicolon. So the clause:

P :- Q, R; S, T, U.

is understood as:

P :- (Q, R); (S, T, U).

and means the same as the clauses:

P :- Q, R.
P :- S, T, U.

Exercises

2.6   Consider the following program:

f(1, one).

f(s(1), two).

f(s(s(1)), three).

f(s(s(s(X))), N) :-
    f(X, N).

How will Prolog answer the following questions? Whenever several answers are possible, give at least two.

(a)   ?- f(s(1), A).

(b)   ?- f(s(s(1)), two).

(c)   ?- f(s(s(s(s(s(s(1)))))), C).

(d)   ?- f(D, three).

2.7   The following program says that two people are relatives if

(a)   one is a predecessor of the other, or

(b)   they have a common predecessor, or

(c)   they have a common successor:

relatives(X, Y) :-
    predecessor(X, Y).

relatives(X, Y) :-
    predecessor(Y, X).

relatives(X, Y) :-   % X and Y have a common predecessor
    predecessor(Z, X),
    predecessor(Z, Y).

relatives(X, Y) :-   % X and Y have a common successor
    predecessor(X, Z),
    predecessor(Y, Z).

Can you shorten this program by using the semicolon notation?

2.8   Rewrite the following program without using the semicolon notation.

```
translate( Number, Word)  :-
    Number = 1, Word = one;
    Number = 2, Word = two;
    Number = 3, Word = three.
```

2.4   Procedural meaning

The procedural meaning specifies *how* Prolog answers questions. To answer a question means to try to satisfy a list of goals. They can be satisfied if the variables that occur in the goals can be instantiated in such a way that the goals logically follow from the program. Thus the procedural meaning of Prolog is a procedure for executing a list of goals with respect to a given program. To 'execute goals' means: try to satisfy them.

Let us call this procedure **execute**. As shown in Figure 2.9, the inputs to and the outputs from this procedure are:

input: a program and a goal list
output: a success/failure indicator and an instantiation of variables

The meaning of the two output results is as follows:

(1)   The success/failure indicator is 'yes' if the goals are satisfiable and 'no' otherwise. We say that 'yes' signals a *successful* termination and 'no' a *failure*.

(2)   An instantiation of variables is only produced in the case of a successful termination; in the case of failure there is no instantiation.

In Chapter 1, we have in effect already discussed informally what procedure **execute** does, under the heading 'How Prolog answers questions'. What follows in the rest of this section is just a more formal and systematic description of this

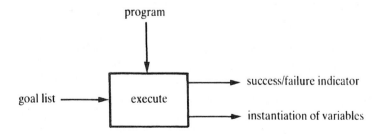

Figure 2.9   Input/output view of the procedure that executes a list of goals.

process, and can be skipped without seriously affecting the understanding of the rest of the book.

Particular operations in the goal execution process are illustrated by the example in Figure 2.10. It may be helpful to study Figure 2.10 before reading the following general description.

To execute a list of goals:

G1, G2, ..., Gm

the procedure **execute** does the following:

- If the goal list is empty then terminate with *success*.
- If the goal list is not empty then continue with (the following) operation called 'SCANNING'.
- *SCANNING*: Scan through the clauses in the program from top to bottom until the first clause, C, is found such that the head of C matches the first goal G1. If there is no such clause then terminate with *failure*.

  If there is such a clause C of the form

    H :- B1, ..., Bn.

  then rename the variables in C to obtain a variant C' of C, such that C' and the list G1, ..., Gm have no common variables. Let C' be

    H' :- B1', ..., Bn'.

  Match G1 and H'; let the resulting instantiation of variables be S.

  In the goal list G1, G2, ..., Gm, replace G1 with the list B1', ..., Bn', obtaining a new goal list

    B1', ..., Bn', G2, ..., Gm

  (Note that if C is a fact then $n = 0$ and the new goal list is shorter than the original one; such shrinking of the goal list may eventually lead to the empty list and thereby a successful termination.)

  Substitute the variables in this new goal list with new values as specified in the instantiation S, obtaining another goal list

    B1", ..., Bn", G2', ..., Gm'

- Execute (recursively with this same procedure) this new goal list. If the execution of this new goal list terminates with success then terminate the execution of the original goal list also with success. If the execution of the new goal list is not successful then abandon this new goal list and go back to SCANNING through the program. Continue the scanning with the clause that immediately follows the clause C (C is the clause that was last used) and try to find a successful termination using some other clause.

PROGRAM

big(bear).	% Clause 1
big(elephant).	% Clause 2
small(cat).	% Clause 3
brown(bear).	% Clause 4
black(cat).	% Clause 5
gray(elephant).	% Clause 6
dark(Z) :- **black(Z).**	% Clause 7: Anything black is dark
dark(Z) :- **brown(Z).**	% Clause 8: Anything brown is dark

QUESTION

?- dark(X), big(X).	% Who is dark and big?

EXECUTION TRACE

(1) Initial goal list: **dark(X), big(X).**

(2) Scan the program from top to bottom looking for a clause whose head matches the first goal **dark(X).** Clause 7 found:

   dark(Z) :- black(Z).

Replace the first goal by the instantiated body of clause 7, giving a new goal list:

   black(X), big(X)

(3) Scan the program to find a match with **black(X).** Clause 5 found: **black(cat).** This clause has no body, so the goal list, properly instantiated, shrinks to:

   big(cat)

(4) Scan the program for the goal **big(cat).** No clause found. Therefore backtrack to step (3) and undo the instantiation X = **cat.** Now the goal list is again:

   black(X), big(X)

Continue scanning the program below clause 5. No clause found. Therefore backtrack to step (2) and continue scanning below clause 7. Clause 8 is found:

   dark(Z) :- brown(Z).

Replace the first goal in the goal list by **brown(X),** giving:

   brown(X), big(X)

(5) Scan the program to match **brown(X),** finding **brown(bear).** This clause has no body, so the goal list shrinks to:

   big(bear)

(6) Scan the program and find clause **big(bear).** It has no body so the goal list shrinks to empty. This indicates successful termination, and the corresponding variable instantiation is:

   X = **bear**

Figure 2.10   An example to illustrate the procedural meaning of Prolog: a sample trace of the procedure **execute.**

This procedure is more compactly written in a Pascal-like notation in Figure 2.11.

Several additional remarks are in order here regarding the procedure **execute** as presented. First, it was not explicitly described how the final resulting instantiation of variables is produced. It is the instantiation S which led to a successful termination, and was possibly further refined by additional instantiations that were done in the nested recursive calls to **execute**.

Whenever a recursive call to **execute** fails, the execution returns to SCANNING, continuing at the program clause C that had been last used before. As the application of the clause C did not lead to a successful termination Prolog has to try an alternative clause to proceed. What effectively happens is that Prolog abandons this whole part of the unsuccessful execution and backtracks to the point (clause C) where this failed branch of the execution was started. When the procedure backtracks to a certain point, all the variable instantiations that were done after that point are undone. This ensures that Prolog systematically examines all the possible alternative paths of execution until one is found that eventually succeeds, or until all of them have been shown to fail.

We have already seen that even after a successful termination the user can force the system to backtrack to search for more solutions. In our description of **execute** this detail was left out.

Of course, in actual implementations of Prolog, several other refinements have to be added to **execute**. One of them is to reduce the amount of scanning through the program clauses to improve efficiency. So a practical Prolog implementation will not scan through all the clauses of the program, but will only consider the clauses about the relation in the current goal.

Exercise

2.9   Consider the program in Figure 2.10 and simulate, in the style of Figure 2.10, Prolog's execution of the question:

   ?- **big(X), dark(X).**

Compare your execution trace with that of Figure 2.10 when the question was essentially the same, but with the goals in the order:

   ?- **dark(X), big(X).**

In which of the two cases does Prolog have to do more work before the answer is found?

procedure *execute* (*Program, GoalList, Success*);

Input arguments:
  Program: list of clauses
  GoalList: list of goals
Output argument:
  Success: truth value; *Success* will become true if *GoalList* is true with respect to *Program*
Local variables:
  Goal: goal
  OtherGoals: list of goals
  Satisfied: truth value
  MatchOK: truth value
  Instant: instantiation of variables
  H, H', B1, B1', ..., Bn, Bn': goals
Auxiliary functions:
  empty(L): returns true if *L* is the empty list
  head(L): returns the first element of list *L*
  tail(L): returns the rest of *L*
  append(L1,L2): appends list *L2* at the end of list *L1*
  match(T1,T2,MatchOK,Instant): tries to match terms *T1* and *T2*; if
      succeeds then *MatchOK* is true and *Instant* is the corresponding instantiation of variables
  substitute(Instant,Goals): substitutes variables in *Goals* according to instantiation *Instant*

begin
  if *empty*(*GoalList*) **then** *Success* := *true*
  else
    begin
      Goal := *head*(*GoalList*);
      OtherGoals := *tail*(*GoalList*);
      Satisfied := *false*;
      while not *Satisfied* **and** *"more clauses in program"* **do**
        begin
          Let next clause in Program be
              H :- B1, ..., Bn.
          Construct a variant of this clause
              H' :- B1', ..., Bn'.
          match(*Goal,H',MatchOK,Instant*);
          if *MatchOK* **then**
            begin
              NewGoals := *append*([*B1',...,Bn'*], *OtherGoals*);
              NewGoals := *substitute*(*Instant,NewGoals*);
              execute(*Program,NewGoals,Satisfied*)
            end
        end;
      Success := *Satisfied*
    end
end;

Figure 2.11   Executing Prolog goals.

2.5   Example: monkey and banana

The monkey and banana problem is used as a simple example of problem solving. Our Prolog program for this problem will show how the mechanisms of matching and backtracking can be used in such exercises. We will develop the program in the non-procedural way, and then study its procedural behaviour in detail. The program will be compact and illustrative.

We will use the following variation of the problem. There is a monkey at the door into a room. In the middle of the room a banana is hanging from the ceiling. The monkey is hungry and wants to get the banana, but he cannot stretch high enough from the floor. At the window of the room there is a box the monkey may use. The monkey can perform the following actions: walk on the floor, climb the box, push the box around (if it is already at the box) and grasp the banana if standing on the box directly under the banana. Can the monkey get the banana?

One important task in programming is that of finding a representation of the problem in terms of the programming language used. In our case we can think of the 'monkey world' as always being in some *state* that can change in time. The current state is determined by the positions of the objects. For example, the initial state of the world is determined by:

(1)   Monkey is at door.

(2)   Monkey is on floor.

(3)   Box is at window.

(4)   Monkey does not have banana.

It is convenient to combine all of these four pieces of information into one structured object. Let us choose the word 'state' as the functor to hold the four components together. Figure 2.12 shows the initial state represented as a structured object.

Our problem can be viewed as a one-person game. Let us now formalize the rules of the game. First, the goal of the game is a situation in which the monkey has the banana; that is, any state in which the last component is 'has':

state(_, _, _, has)

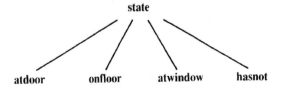

Figure 2.12   The initial state of the monkey world represented as a structured object. The four components are: horizontal position of monkey, vertical position of monkey, position of box, monkey has or has not banana.

Second, what are the allowed moves that change the world from one state to another? There are four types of moves:

(1) grasp banana,

(2) climb box,

(3) push box,

(4) walk around.

Not all moves are possible in every possible state of the world. For example, the move 'grasp' is only possible if the monkey is standing on the box directly under the banana (which is in the middle of the room) and does not have the banana yet. Such rules can be formalized in Prolog as a three-place relation named **move**:

> **move(State1, Move, State2)**

The three arguments of the relation specify a move thus:

> **State1 ⟶ State2**
> **Move**

State1 is the state before the move, **Move** is the move executed and **State2** is the state after the move.

The move 'grasp', with its necessary precondition on the state before the move, can be defined by the clause:

```
move( state( middle, onbox, middle, hasnot),    % Before move
      grasp,                                     % Move
      state( middle, onbox, middle, has) ).      % After move
```

This fact says that after the move the monkey has the banana, and he has remained on the box in the middle of the room.

In a similar way we can express the fact that the monkey on the floor can walk from any horizontal position **Pos1** to any position **Pos2**. The monkey can do this regardless of the position of the box and whether it has the banana or not. All this can be defined by the following Prolog fact:

```
move( state( Pos1, onfloor, Box, Has),
      walk( Pos1, Pos2),                         % Walk from Pos1 to Pos2
      state( Pos2, onfloor, Box, Has) ).
```

Note that this clause says many things, including, for example:

- the move executed was 'walk from some position **Pos1** to some position **Pos2**';

- the monkey is on the floor before and after the move;

- the box is at some point Box which remained the same after the move;

- the 'has banana' status Has remains the same after the move.

The clause actually specifies a whole set of possible moves because it is applicable to any situation that matches the specified state before the move. Such a specification is therefore sometimes also called a move *schema*. Using Prolog variables, such schemas can be easily programmed in Prolog.

The other two types of moves, 'push' and 'climb', can be similarly specified.

The main kind of question that our program will have to answer is: Can the monkey in some initial state State get the banana? This can be formulated as a predicate

canget(State)

where the argument State is a state of the monkey world. The program for canget can be based on two observations:

(1)   For any state in which the monkey already has the banana, the predicate canget must certainly be true; no move is needed in this case. This corresponds to the Prolog fact:

canget(state(_, _, _, has)).

(2)   In other cases one or more moves are necessary. The monkey can get the banana in any state State1 if there is some move Move from State1 to some state State2, such that the monkey can then get the banana in state State2 (in zero or more moves). This principle is illustrated in Figure 2.13. A Prolog clause that corresponds to this rule is:

canget(State1) :-
    move(State1, Move, State2),
    canget(State2).

This completes our program, which is shown in Figure 2.14.

The formulation of canget is recursive and is similar to that of the **predecessor** relation of Chapter 1 (compare Figures 2.13 and 1.7). This principle is used in Prolog again and again.

We have developed our monkey and banana program in the non-procedural way. Let us now study its *procedural* behaviour by considering the following question

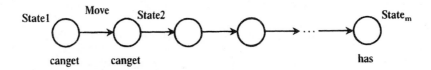

Figure 2.13 Recursive formulation of **canget**.

```
% move( State1, Move, State2): making Move in State1 results in State2;
%    a state is represented by a term:
%      state( MonkeyHorizontal, MonkeyVertical, BoxPosition, HasBanana)

move( state( middle, onbox, middle, hasnot),      % Before move
       grasp,                                      % Grasp banana
       state( middle, onbox, middle, has) ).       % After move

move( state( P, onfloor, P, H),
       climb,                                      % Climb box
       state( P, onbox, P, H) ).

move( state( P1, onfloor, P1, H),
       push( P1, P2),                              % Push box from P1 to P2
       state( P2, onfloor, P2, H) ).

move( state( P1, onfloor, B, H),
       walk( P1, P2),                              % Walk from P1 to P2
       state( P2, onfloor, B, H) ).

% canget( State): monkey can get banana in State

canget( state( _, _, _, has) ).                    % can 1: Monkey already has it

canget( State1) :-                                 % can 2: Do some work to get it
       move( State1, Move, State2),                % Do something
       canget( State2).                            % Get it now
```

Figure 2.14   A program for the monkey and banana problem.

to the program:

   ?- canget(state(atdoor, onfloor, atwindow, hasnot)).

Prolog's answer is 'yes'. The process carried out by Prolog to reach this answer proceeds, according to the procedural semantics of Prolog, through a sequence of goal lists. It involves some search for the right moves among the possible alternative moves. At some point this search will take a wrong move leading to a dead branch. At this stage, backtracking will help it to recover. Figure 2.15 illustrates this search process.

To answer the question Prolog had to backtrack once only. A right sequence of moves was found almost straight away. The reason for this efficiency of the program was the order in which the clauses about the move relation occurred in the program. The order in our case (luckily) turned out to be quite suitable. However, less lucky orderings are possible. According to the rules of the game, the monkey could just as easily try to walk here or there without ever touching the box, or aimlessly push the box around. A more thorough investigation will reveal, as shown in the following section, that the ordering of clauses is, in the case of our program, in fact critical.

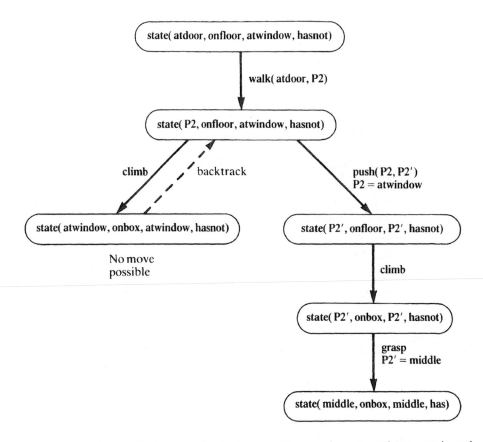

Figure 2.15   The monkey's search for the banana. The search starts at the top node and proceeds downwards, as indicated. Alternative moves are tried in the left-to-right order. Backtracking occurred once only.

2.6   Order of clauses and goals

2.6.1   Danger of indefinite looping

Consider the following clause:

   p :- p.

This says that 'p is true if p is true'. This is declaratively perfectly correct, but procedurally is quite useless. In fact, such a clause can cause problems to Prolog. Consider the question:

   ?- p.

Using the clause above, the goal p is replaced by the same goal p; this will be in turn replaced by p, etc. In such a case Prolog will enter an infinite loop not noticing that no progress is being made.

This example is a simple way of getting Prolog to loop indefinitely. However, similar looping could have occurred in some of our previous example programs if we changed the order of clauses, or the order of goals in the clauses. It will be instructive to consider some examples.

In the monkey and banana program, the clauses about the **move** relation were ordered thus: grasp, climb, push, walk (perhaps 'unclimb' should be added for completeness). These clauses say that grasping is possible, climbing is possible, etc. According to the procedural semantics of Prolog, the order of clauses indicates that the monkey prefers grasping to climbing, climbing to pushing, etc. This order of preferences in fact helps the monkey to solve the problem. But what could happen if the order was different? Let us assume that the 'walk' clause appears first. The execution of our original goal of the previous section

> ?- **canget(state(atdoor, onfloor, atwindow, hasnot)).**

would this time produce the following trace. The first four goal lists (with variables appropriately renamed) are the same as before:

> (1)   **canget(state(atdoor, onfloor, atwindow, hasnot))**

The second clause of **canget** ('can2') is applied, producing:

> (2)   **move(state(atdoor, onfloor, atwindow, hasnot), M', S2'),**
>   **canget(S2')**

By the move **walk(atdoor, P2')** we get:

> (3)   **canget(state(P2', onfloor, atwindow, hasnot))**

Using the clause 'can2' again the goal list becomes:

> (4)   **move(state(P2', onfloor, atwindow, hasnot), M'', S2''),**
>   **canget(S2'')**

Now the difference occurs. The first clause whose head matches the first goal above is now 'walk' (and not 'climb' as before). The instantiation is

> **S2'' = state(P2'', onfloor, atwindow, hasnot)**

Therefore the goal list becomes:

> (5)   **canget(state(P2'', onfloor, atwindow, hasnot))**

Applying the clause 'can2' we obtain:

> (6)   **move(state(P2'', onfloor, atwindow, hasnot), M''', S2'''),**
>   **canget(S2''')**

Again, 'walk' is now tried first, producing:

(7)   **canget(state(P2'''**, **onfloor, atwindow, hasnot))**

Let us now compare the goals (3), (5) and (7). They are the same apart from one variable; this variable is, in turn, P', P'' and P'''. As we know, the success of a goal does not depend on particular names of variables in the goal. This means that from goal list (3) the execution trace shows no progress. We can see, in fact, that the same two clauses, 'can2' and 'walk', are used repetitively. The monkey walks around without ever trying to use the box. As there is no progress made this will (theoretically) go on for ever: Prolog will not realize that there is no point in continuing along this line.

This example shows Prolog trying to solve a problem in such a way that a solution is never reached, although a solution exists. Such situations are not unusual in Prolog programming. Infinite loops are, also, not unusual in other programming languages. What *is* unusual in comparison with other languages is that a Prolog program may be declaratively correct, but at the same time be procedurally incorrect in that it is not able to produce an answer to a question. In such cases Prolog may not be able to satisfy a goal because it tries to reach an answer by choosing a wrong path.

A natural question to ask at this point is: Can we not make some more substantial change to our program so as to drastically prevent any danger of looping? Or shall we always have to rely just on a suitable ordering of clauses and goals? As it turns out programs, especially large ones, would be too fragile if they just had to rely on some suitable ordering. There are several other methods that preclude infinite loops, and these are much more general and robust than the ordering method itself. These techniques will be used regularly later in the book, especially in those chapters that deal with path finding, problem solving and search.

2.6.2   Program variations through reordering of clauses and goals

Already in the example programs of Chapter 1 there was a latent danger of producing a cycling behaviour. Our program to specify the **predecessor** relation in Chapter 1 was:

```
predecessor( Parent, Child) :-
    parent( Parent, Child).

predecessor( Predecessor, Successor) :-
    parent( Predecessor, Child),
    predecessor( Child, Successor).
```

Let us analyze some variations of this program. All the variations will clearly have the same declarative meaning, but not the same procedural meaning. According to the declarative semantics of Prolog we can, without affecting the declarative meaning, change:

(1)   the order of clauses in the program, and

(2)   the order of goals in the bodies of clauses.

The **predecessor** procedure consists of two clauses, and one of them has two goals in the body. There are, therefore, four variations of this program, all with the same declarative meaning. The four variations are obtained by:

(1)   swapping both clauses, and

(2)   swapping the goals for each order of clauses.

The corresponding four procedures, called **pred1**, **pred2**, **pred3** and **pred4**, are shown in Figure 2.16.

....

```
% Four versions of the predecessor program

% The original version

pred1( X, Z) :-
  parent( X, Z).

pred1( X, Z) :-
  parent( X, Y),
  pred1( Y, Z).

% Variation a: swap clauses of the original version

pred2( X, Z) :-
  parent( X, Y),
  pred2( Y, Z).

pred2( X, Z) :-
  parent( X, Z).

% Variation b: swap goals in second clause of the original version

pred3( X, Z) :-
  parent( X, Z).

pred3( X, Z) :-
  pred3( X, Y),
  parent( Y, Z).

% Variation c: swap goals and clauses of the original version

pred4( X, Z) :-
  pred4( X, Y),
  parent( Y, Z).

pred4( X, Z) :-
  parent( X, Z).
```

....

Figure 2.16 Four versions of the **predecessor** program.

There are important differences in the behaviour of these four declaratively equivalent procedures. To demonstrate these, consider the parent relation as shown in Figure 1.1 of Chapter 1. Now, what happens if we ask whether Tom is a predecessor of Pat using the four variations of the **predecessor** relation:

?- **pred1**(tom, pat).

yes

?- **pred2**(tom, pat).

yes

?- **pred3**(tom, pat).

yes

?- **pred4**(tom, pat).

In the last case Prolog cannot find the answer. This is manifested on the terminal by a Prolog message such as 'More core needed' or 'Stack overflow'.

Figure 1.11 in Chapter 1 showed the trace of **pred1** (in Chapter 1 called **predecessor**) produced for the above question. Figure 2.17 shows the corresponding traces for **pred2**, **pred3** and **pred4**. Figure 2.17(c) clearly shows that **pred4** is hopeless, and Figure 2.17(a) indicates that **pred2** is rather inefficient compared to **pred1**: **pred2** does much more searching and backtracking in the family tree.

This comparison should remind us of a general practical heuristic in problem solving: it is usually best to try the simplest idea first. In our case, all the versions of the **predecessor** relation are based on two ideas:

(1)   the simpler idea is to check whether the two arguments of the **predecessor** relation satisfy the **parent** relation;

(2)   the more complicated idea is to find somebody 'between' both people (somebody who is related to them by the **parent** and **predecessor** relations).

Of the four variations of the **predecessor** relation, **pred1** does simplest things first. On the contrary, **pred4** always tries complicated things first. **pred2** and **pred3** are in between the two extremes. Even without a detailed study of the execution traces, **pred1** should be preferred merely on the grounds of the rule 'try simple things first'. This rule will be in general a useful guide in programming.

Our four variations of the **predecessor** procedure can be further compared by considering the question: What types of questions can particular variations answer, and what types can they not answer? It turns out that **pred1** and **pred2** are both able to reach an answer for any type of question about predecessors; **pred4** can never reach an answer; and **pred3** sometimes can and sometimes cannot. One example in which **pred3** fails is:

?- **pred3**(liz, jim).

This question again brings the system into an infinite sequence of recursive calls. Thus **pred3** also cannot be considered procedurally correct.

2.6.3   Combining declarative and procedural views

The foregoing section has shown that the order of goals and clauses does matter. Furthermore, there are programs that are declaratively correct, but do not work in practice. Such discrepancies between the declarative and procedural meaning may

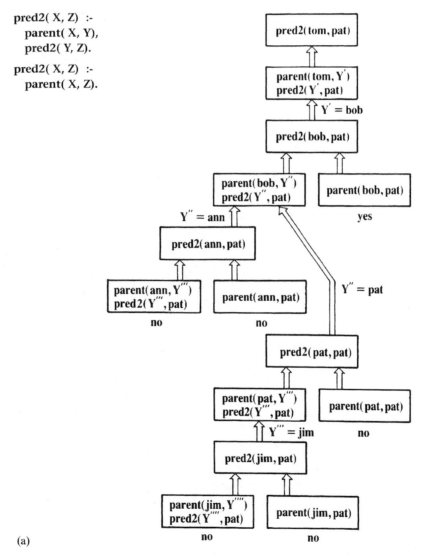

pred2(X, Z) :-
  parent(X, Y),
  pred2(Y, Z).

pred2(X, Z) :-
  parent(X, Z).

(a)

Figure 2.17   The behaviour of three formulations of the **predecessor** relation on the question: Is Tom a predecessor of Pat?

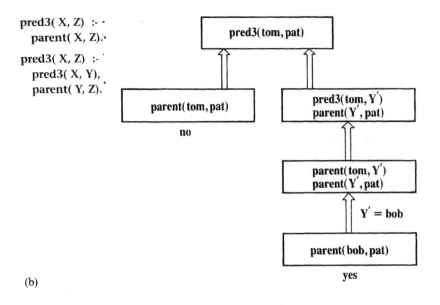

pred3(X, Z) :-
    parent(X, Z).

pred3(X, Z) :-
    pred3(X, Y),
    parent(Y, Z).

(b)

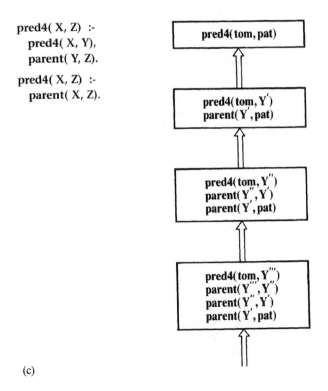

pred4(X, Z) :-
    pred4(X, Y),
    parent(Y, Z).

pred4(X, Z) :-
    parent(X, Z).

(c)

Figure 2.17   *contd*

appear annoying. One may argue: Why not simply forget about the declarative meaning? This argument can be brought to an extreme with a clause such as:

predecessor(X, Z) :- predecessor(X, Z).

which is declaratively correct, but is completely useless as a working program.

The reason why we should not forget about the declarative meaning is that progress in programming technology is achieved by moving away from procedural details toward declarative aspects, which are normally easier to formulate and understand. The system itself, not the programmer, should carry the burden of filling in the procedural details. Prolog does help toward this end, although, as we have seen in this section, it only helps partially: sometimes it does work out the procedural details itself properly, and sometimes it does not. The philosophy adopted by many is that it is better to have at least *some* declarative meaning rather than *none* ('none' is the case in most other programming languages). The practical aspect of this view is that it is often rather easy to get a working program once we have a program that is declaratively correct. Consequently, a useful practical approach that often works is to concentrate on the declarative aspects of the problem, then test the resulting program, and if it fails procedurally try to rearrange the clauses and goals into a suitable order.

2.7   The relation between Prolog and logic

Prolog is related to mathematical logic, so its syntax and meaning can be specified most concisely with references to logic. Prolog is indeed often defined that way. However, such an introduction to Prolog assumes that the reader is familiar with certain concepts of mathematical logic. These concepts are, on the other hand, certainly not necessary for understanding and using Prolog as a programming tool, which is the aim of this book. For the reader who is especially interested in the relation between Prolog and logic, the following are some basic links to mathematical logic, together with some appropriate references.

Prolog's syntax is that of the *first-order predicate logic* formulas written in the so-called *clause form* (a conjunctive normal form in which quantifiers are not explicitly written), and further restricted to Horn clauses only (clauses that have at most one positive literal). Clocksin and Mellish (1987) give a Prolog program that transforms a first-order predicate calculus formula into the clause form. The procedural meaning of Prolog is based on the *resolution principle* for mechanical theorem proving introduced by Robinson in his classic paper (1965). Prolog uses a special strategy for resolution theorem proving called SLD. An introduction to the first-order predicate calculus and resolution-based theorem proving can be found in several general books on artificial intelligence (Genesereth and Nilsson 1987; Ginsberg 1993; Poole *et al.* 1998; Russell and Norvig 1995; see also Flach 1994). Mathematical questions regarding the properties of Prolog's procedural meaning with respect to logic are analyzed by Lloyd (1991).

Matching in Prolog corresponds to what is called *unification* in logic. However, we avoid the word unification because matching, for efficiency reasons in most Prolog systems, is implemented in a way that does not exactly correspond to unification (see Exercise 2.10). But from the practical point of view this approximation to unification is quite adequate. Proper unification requires the so-called *occurs check*: does a given variable occur in a given term? The occurs check would make matching inefficient.

Exercise

2.10   What happens if we ask Prolog:

?-   X = f(X).

Should this request for matching succeed or fail? According to the definition of unification in logic this should fail, but what happens according to our definition of matching in Section 2.2? Try to explain why many Prolog implementations answer the question above with:

X = f(f(f(f(f(f(f(f(f(f(f(f(f(f(...

Summary

So far we have covered a kind of basic Prolog, also called 'pure Prolog'. It is 'pure' because it corresponds closely to formal logic. Extensions whose aim is to tailor the language toward some practical needs will be covered later in the book (Chapters 3, 5, 6, 7). Important points of this chapter are:

- Simple objects in Prolog are *atoms*, *variables* and *numbers*. Structured objects, or *structures*, are used to represent objects that have several components.

- Structures are constructed by means of *functors*. Each functor is defined by its name and arity.

- The type of object is recognized entirely by its syntactic form.

- The *lexical* scope of variables is one clause. Thus the same variable name in two clauses means two different variables.

- Structures can be naturally pictured as trees. Prolog can be viewed as a language for processing trees.

- The *matching* operation takes two terms and tries to make them identical by instantiating the variables in both terms.

- Matching, if it succeeds, results in the *most general* instantiation of variables.

- The *declarative semantics* of Prolog defines whether a goal is true with respect to a given program, and if it is true, for what instantiation of variables it is true.

- A comma between goals means the conjunction of goals. A semicolon between goals means the disjunction of goals.

- The *procedural semantics* of Prolog is a procedure for satisfying a list of goals in the context of a given program. The procedure outputs the truth or falsity of the goal list and the corresponding instantiations of variables. The procedure automatically backtracks to examine alternatives.

- The declarative meaning of programs in 'pure Prolog' does not depend on the order of clauses and the order of goals in clauses.

- The procedural meaning does depend on the order of goals and clauses. Thus the order can affect the efficiency of the program; an unsuitable order may even lead to infinite recursive calls.

- Given a declaratively correct program, changing the order of clauses and goals can improve the program's efficiency while retaining its declarative correctness. Reordering is one method of preventing indefinite looping.

- There are other more general techniques, apart from reordering, to prevent indefinite looping and thereby make programs procedurally robust.

- Concepts discussed in this chapter are:

      data objects: atom, number, variable, structure
      term
      functor, arity of a functor
      principal functor of a term
      matching of terms
      most general instantiation
      declarative semantics
      instance of a clause, variant of a clause
      procedural semantics
      executing goals

References

Clocksin, W.F. and Mellish, C.S. (1987) *Programming in Prolog*, second edition. Berlin: Springer-Verlag.

Flach, P. (1994) *Simply Logical: Intelligent Reasoning by Example*. Chichester, UK: Wiley.

Genesereth, M.R. and Nilsson, N.J. (1987) *Logical Foundation of Artificial Intelligence*. Palo Alto, CA: Morgan Kaufmann.

Ginsberg, M. (1993) *Essentials of Artificial Intelligence*. San Francisco, CA: Morgan Kaufmann.

Lloyd, J.W. (1991) *Foundations of Logic Programming*, second edition. Berlin: Springer-Verlag.

Robinson, A.J. (1965) A machine-oriented logic based on the resolution principle. *JACM* **12**: 23–41.

Poole, D., Mackworth, A. and Gaebel, R. (1998) *Computational Intelligence: A Logical Approach.* Oxford University Press.

Russell, S. and Norvig, P. (1995) *Artificial Intelligence: A Modern Approach.* Englewood Cliffs, NJ: Prentice Hall.

chapter 3

Lists, Operators, Arithmetic

In this chapter we will study a special notation for lists, one of the simplest and most useful structures, and some programs for typical operations on lists. We will also look at simple arithmetic and the operator notation, which often improves the readability of programs. Basic Prolog of Chapter 2, extended with these three additions, becomes a convenient framework for writing interesting programs.

3.1   Representation of lists

The *list* is a simple data structure widely used in non-numeric programming. A list is a sequence of any number of items, such as **ann, tennis, tom, skiing**. Such a list can be written in Prolog as:

[ann, tennis, tom, skiing]

This is, however, only the external appearance of lists. As we have already seen in Chapter 2, all structured objects in Prolog are trees. Lists are no exception to this.

How can a list be represented as a standard Prolog object? We have to consider two cases: the list is either empty or non-empty. In the first case, the list is simply written as a Prolog atom, [ ]. In the second case, the list can be viewed as consisting of two things:

(1)   the first item, called the *head* of the list;

(2)   the remaining part of the list, called the *tail*.

61

For our example list,

[ann, tennis, tom, skiing]

the head is **ann** and the tail is the list:

[tennis, tom, skiing]

In general, the head can be anything (any Prolog object, for example, a tree or a variable); the tail has to be a list. The head and the tail are then combined into a structure by a special functor,

.(Head, Tail)

Since **Tail** is in turn a list, it is either empty or it has its own head and tail. Therefore, to represent lists of any length no additional principle is needed. Our example list is then represented as the term:

.(ann, .(tennis, .(tom, .(skiing, []))))

Figure 3.1 shows the corresponding tree structure. Note that the empty list appears in our term. This is because the one but last tail is a single item list:

[skiing]

This list has the empty list as its tail:

[skiing] = .(skiing, [])

This example shows how the general principle for structuring data objects in Prolog also applies to lists of any length. As our example also shows, the straight-forward notation with dots and possibly deep nesting of subterms in the tail part can produce rather confusing expressions. This is the reason why Prolog provides the neater notation for lists, so that they can be written as sequences of items enclosed in square brackets. A programmer can use both notations, but the square bracket notation is, of course, normally preferred. We will be aware, however, that this is

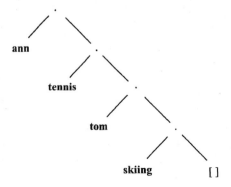

Figure 3.1 Tree representation of the list [**ann, tennis, tom, skiing**].

only a cosmetic improvement and that our lists will be internally represented as binary trees. When such terms are output they will be automatically converted into their neater form. Thus the following conversation with Prolog is possible:

```
?- List1 = [a,b,c],
   List2 = .( a, .( b, .( c, [ ] ) ) ).

List1 = [a,b,c]
List2 = [a,b,c]

?- Hobbies1 = .( tennis, .( music, [ ] ) ),
   Hobbies2 = [ skiing, food],
   L = [ ann, Hobbies1, tom, Hobbies2].

Hobbies1 = [ tennis, music]
Hobbies2 = [ skiing, food]
L = [ ann, [tennis,music], tom, [skiing,food] ]
```

This example also reminds us that the elements of a list can be objects of any kind; in particular they can also be lists.

It is often practical to treat the whole tail as a single object. For example, let:

L = [a,b,c]

Then we could write:

Tail = [b,c]   and   L = .(a, Tail)

To express this in the square bracket notation for lists, Prolog provides another notational extension, the vertical bar, which separates the head and the tail:

L = [a | Tail]

The vertical bar notation is in fact more general: we can list any number of elements followed by '|' and the list of remaining items. Thus alternative ways of writing the above list are:

[a,b,c] = [a | [b,c]] = [a,b | [c]] = [a,b,c | [ ]]

To summarize:

- A list is a data structure that is either empty or consists of two parts: a *head* and a *tail*. The tail itself has to be a list.

- Lists are handled in Prolog as a special case of binary trees. For improved readability Prolog provides a special notation for lists, thus accepting lists written as:

    [Item1, Item2, . . .]

  or

    [Head | Tail]

  or

    [Item1, Item2, . . . | Others]

3.2   Some operations on lists

Lists can be used to represent sets, although there is a difference: the order of elements in a set does not matter while the order of items in a list does; also, the same object can occur repeatedly in a list. Still, the most common operations on lists are similar to those on sets. Among them are:

- checking whether some object is an element of a list, which corresponds to checking for the set membership;
- concatenation of two lists, obtaining a third list, which may correspond to the union of sets;
- adding a new object to a list, or deleting some object from it.

In the remainder of this section we give programs for these and some other operations on lists.

3.2.1   Membership

Let us implement the membership relation as:

member(X, L)

where X is an object and L is a list. The goal **member(X, L)** is true if X occurs in L. For example,

member(b, [a,b,c])

is true,

member(b, [a,[b,c]])

is not true, but

member([b,c], [a,[b,c]])

is true. The program for the membership relation can be based on the following observation:

X is a member of L if either:
(1) X is the head of L, or
(2) X is a member of the tail of L.

This can be written in two clauses; the first is a simple fact and the second is a rule:

member(X, [X | Tail]).

member(X, [Head | Tail]) :-
   member(X, Tail).

3.2.2 Concatenation

For concatenating lists we will define the relation:

> **conc(L1, L2, L3)**

Here L1 and L2 are two lists, and L3 is their concatenation. For example,

> **conc([a,b], [c,d], [a,b,c,d])**

is true, but

> **conc([a,b], [c,d], [a,b,a,c,d])**

is false. In the definition of **conc** we will have again two cases, depending on the first argument, L1:

(1)   If the first argument is the empty list then the second and the third arguments must be the same list (call it L); this is expressed by the following Prolog fact:

> **conc([ ], L, L).**

(2)   If the first argument of **conc** is a non-empty list then it has a head and a tail and must look like this:

> **[X | L1]**

Figure 3.2 illustrates the concatenation of [X | L1] and some list L2. The result of the concatenation is the list [X | L3] where L3 is the concatenation of L1 and L2. In Prolog this is written as:

> **conc([X | L1], L2, [X | L3]) :-**
> **conc(L1, L2, L3).**

This program can now be used for concatenating given lists, for example:

> **?- conc([a,b,c], [1,2,3], L).**

> **L = [a,b,c,1,2,3]**

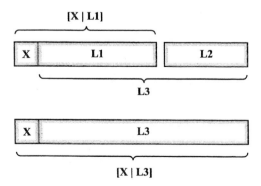

Figure 3.2 Concatenation of lists.

```
?- conc( [a,[b,c],d], [a,[ ],b], L).

L = [a, [b,c], d, a, [ ], b]
```

Although the conc program looks rather simple it can be used flexibly in many other ways. For example, we can use conc in the inverse direction for *decomposing* a given list into two lists, as follows:

```
?- conc( L1, L2, [a,b,c] ).

L1 = [ ]
L2 = [a,b,c];

L1 = [a]
L2 = [b,c];

L1 = [a,b]
L2 = [c];

L1 = [a,b,c]
L2 = [ ];

no
```

It is possible to decompose the list [a,b,c] in four ways, all of which were found by our program through backtracking.

We can also use our program to look for a certain pattern in a list. For example, we can find the months that precede and the months that follow a given month, as in the following goal:

```
?- conc( Before, [may | After],
           [jan,feb,mar,apr,may,jun,jul,aug,sep,oct,nov,dec] ).

Before = [jan,feb,mar,apr]
After = [jun,jul,aug,sep,oct,nov,dec].
```

Further we can find the immediate predecessor and the immediate successor of May by asking:

```
?- conc( _ , [Month1,may,Month2 | _],
           [jan,feb,mar,apr,may,jun,jul,aug,sep,oct,nov,dec] ).

Month1 = apr
Month2 = jun
```

Further still, we can, for example, delete from some list, L1, everything that follows three successive occurrences of z in L1 together with the three z's. For example:

```
?- L1 = [a,b,z,z,c,z,z,z,d,e],
conc( L2, [z,z,z | _], L1).

L1 = [a,b,z,z,c,z,z,z,d,e]
L2 = [a,b,z,z,c]
```

We have already programmed the membership relation. Using conc, however, the membership relation could be elegantly programmed by the clause:

```
member1( X, L) :-
    conc( L1, [X | L2], L).
```

This clause says: X is a member of list L if L can be decomposed into two lists so that the second one has X as its head. Of course, **member1** defines the same relation as **member**. We have just used a different name to distinguish between the two implementations. Note that the above clause can be written using anonymous variables as:

```
member1( X, L) :-
    conc( _, [X | _], L).
```

It is interesting to compare both implementations of the membership relation, **member** and **member1**. **member** has a rather straightforward procedural meaning, which is as follows:

To check whether some X is a member of some list L:
(1) first check whether the head of L is equal to X, and then
(2) check whether X is a member of the tail of L.

On the other hand, the declarative reading of **member1** is straightforward, but its procedural meaning is not so obvious. An interesting exercise is to find how **member1** actually computes something. An example execution trace will give some idea: let us consider the question:

```
?- member1( b, [a,b,c] ).
```

Figure 3.3 shows the execution trace. From the trace we can infer that **member1** behaves similarly to **member**. It scans the list, element by element, until the item in question is found or the list is exhausted.

Exercises

3.1   (a) Write a goal, using **conc**, to delete the last three elements from a list L producing another list L1. Hint: L is the concatenation of L1 and a three-element list.

(b) Write a goal to delete the first three elements and the last three elements from a list L producing list L2.

3.2   Define the relation

      last(Item, List)

so that **Item** is the last element of a list **List**. Write two versions: (a) using the **conc** relation, (b) without **conc**.

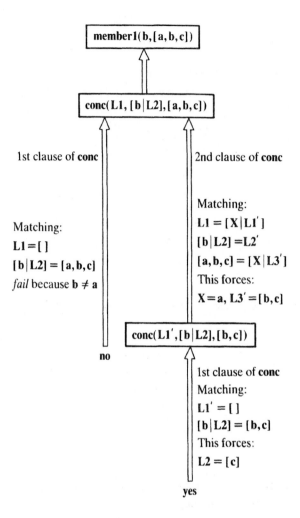

Figure 3.3 Procedure **member1** finds an item in a given list by sequentially searching the list.

3.2.3 Adding an item

To add an item to a list, it is easiest to put the new item in front of the list so that it becomes the new head. If X is the new item and the list to which X is added is L then the resulting list is simply:

[X | L]

So we actually need no procedure for adding a new element in front of the list. Nevertheless, if we want to define such a procedure explicitly, it can be written as the fact:

add(X, L, [X | L]).

3.2.4 Deleting an item

Deleting an item, X, from a list, L, can be programmed as a relation

del(X, L, L1)

where L1 is equal to the list L with the item X removed. The **del** relation can be defined similarly to the membership relation. We have, again, two cases:

(1)   If X is the head of the list then the result after the deletion is the tail of the list.

(2)   If X is in the tail then it is deleted from there.

> **del(X, [X | Tail], Tail).**
>
> **del(X, [Y | Tail], [Y | Tail1]) :-**
> **del(X, Tail, Tail1).**

Like **member**, **del** is also non-deterministic. If there are several occurrences of X in the list then **del** will be able to delete any one of them by backtracking. Of course, each alternative execution will only delete one occurrence of X, leaving the others untouched. For example:

> ?- **del(a, [a,b,a,a], L).**
>
> L = [b,a,a];
>
> L = [a,b,a];
>
> L = [a,b,a];
>
> **no**

del will fail if the list does not contain the item to be deleted.

   del can also be used in the inverse direction, to add an item to a list by inserting the new item anywhere in the list. For example, if we want to insert **a** at any place in the list [1,2,3] then we can do this by asking the question: What is L such that after deleting **a** from L we obtain [1,2,3]?

> ?- **del(a, L, [1,2,3]).**
>
> L = [a,1,2,3];
>
> L = [1,a,2,3];
>
> L = [1,2,a,3];
>
> L = [1,2,3,a];
>
> **no**

In general, the operation of inserting X at any place in some list **List** giving **BiggerList** can be defined by the clause:

> **insert(X, List, BiggerList) :-**
> **del(X, BiggerList, List).**

In **member1** we elegantly implemented the membership relation by using **conc**. We can also use **del** to test for membership. The idea is simple: some X is a member of List if X can be deleted from List:

member2(X, List) :-
    del(X, List, _).

3.2.5   Sublist

Let us now consider the sublist relation. This relation has two arguments, a list L and a list S such that S occurs within L as its sublist. So,

sublist([c,d,e], [a,b,c,d,e,f])

is true, but

sublist([c,e], [a,b,c,d,e,f])

is not. The Prolog program for **sublist** can be based on the same idea as **member1**, only this time the relation is more general (see Figure 3.4). Accordingly, the relation can be formulated as:

S is a sublist of L if:
(1) L can be decomposed into two lists, L1 and L2, and
(2) L2 can be decomposed into two lists, S and some L3.

As we have seen before, the **conc** relation can be used for decomposing lists. So the above formulation can be expressed in Prolog as:

sublist(S, L) :-
    conc(L1, L2, L),
    conc(S, L3, L2).

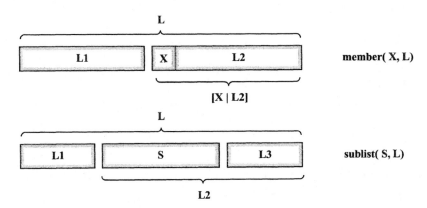

Figure 3.4 The **member** and **sublist** relations.

Of course, the **sublist** procedure can be used flexibly in several ways. Although it was designed to check if some list occurs as a sublist within another list it can also be used, for example, to find all sublists of a given list:

?- sublist(S, [a,b,c]).

S = [ ];

S = [a];

S = [a,b];

S = [a,b,c];

S = [ ];

S = [b];

. . .

3.2.6 Permutations

Sometimes it is useful to generate permutations of a given list. To this end, we will define the **permutation** relation with two arguments. The arguments are two lists such that one is a permutation of the other. The intention is to generate permutations of a list through backtracking using the **permutation** procedure, as in the following example:

?- permutation([a,b,c], P).

P = [a,b,c];

P = [a,c,b];

P = [b,a,c];

. . .

The program for **permutation** can be, again, based on the consideration of two cases, depending on the first list:

(1)   If the first list is empty then the second list must also be empty.

(2)   If the first list is not empty then it has the form [X | L], and a permutation of such a list can be constructed as shown in Figure 3.5: first permute L obtaining L1 and then insert X at any position into L1.

Two Prolog clauses that correspond to these two cases are:

```
permutation( [ ], [ ] ).

permutation( [X | L], P)  :-
   permutation( L, L1),
   insert( X, L1, P).
```

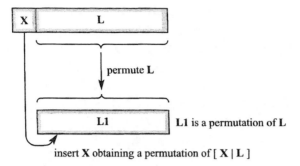

insert **X** obtaining a permutation of [**X | L**]

Figure 3.5 One way of constructing a permutation of the list **[X | L]**.

One alternative to this program would be to delete an element, X, from the first list, permute the rest of it obtaining a list P, and then add X in front of P. The corresponding program is:

permutation2([], []).

permutation2(L, [X | P]) :-
  del(X, L, L1),
  permutation2(L1, P).

It is instructive to do some experiments with our permutation programs. Its normal use would be something like this:

?- permutation([red,blue,green], P).

This would result in all six permutations, as intended:

P = [red, blue, green];

P = [red, green, blue];

P = [blue, red, green];

P = [blue, green, red];

P = [green, red, blue];

P = [green, blue, red];

no

Another attempt to use **permutation** is:

?- permutation(L, [a,b,c]).

Our first version, **permutation**, will now instantiate L successfully to all six permutations. If the user then requests more solutions, the program would never answer 'no' because it would get into an infinite loop trying to find another permutation when there is none. Our second version, **permutation2**, will in this case find only the first (identical) permutation and then immediately get into an infinite loop. Thus, some care is necessary when using these permutation programs.

Exercises

3.3 Define two predicates

evenlength(List) and **oddlength(List)**

so that they are true if their argument is a list of even or odd length respectively. For example, the list [a,b,c,d] is 'evenlength' and [a,b,c] is 'oddlength'.

3.4 Define the relation

reverse(List, ReversedList)

that reverses lists. For example, **reverse([a,b,c,d], [d,c,b,a])**.

3.5 Define the predicate **palindrome(List)**. A list is a palindrome if it reads the same in the forward and in the backward direction. For example, [m,a,d,a,m].

3.6 Define the relation

shift(List1, List2)

so that List2 is List1 'shifted rotationally' by one element to the left. For example,

    ?- shift([1,2,3,4,5], L1),
       shift(L1, L2).

produces:

    L1 = [2,3,4,5,1]
    L2 = [3,4,5,1,2]

3.7 Define the relation

translate(List1, List2)

to translate a list of numbers between 0 and 9 to a list of the corresponding words. For example:

translate([3,5,1,3], [three,five,one,three])

Use the following as an auxiliary relation:

means(0, zero).   means(1, one).   means(2, two).   ...

3.8 Define the relation

subset(Set, Subset)

where **Set** and **Subset** are two lists representing two sets. We would like to be able to use this relation not only to check for the subset relation, but also to generate all possible subsets of a given set. For example:

```
?- subset( [a,b,c], S).
S = [a,b,c];
S = [a,b];
S = [a,c];
S = [a];
S = [b,c];
S = [b];
...
```

3.9 Define the relation

dividelist(List, List1, List2)

so that the elements of **List** are partitioned between **List1** and **List2**, and **List1** and **List2** are of approximately the same length. For example, **dividelist([a,b,c,d,e], [a,c,e], [b,d])**.

3.10 Rewrite the monkey and banana program of Chapter 2 as the relation

canget(State, Actions)

to answer not just 'yes' or 'no', but to produce a sequence of monkey's actions represented as a list of moves. For example:

Actions = [walk(door,window), push(window,middle), climb, grasp]

3.11 Define the relation

flatten(List, FlatList)

where **List** can be a list of lists, and **FlatList** is **List** 'flattened' so that the elements of **List's** sublists (or sub-sublists) are reorganized as one plain list. For example:

```
?- flatten( [a,b,[c,d],[ ],[[[e]]],f], L).
L = [a,b,c,d,e,f]
```

3.3 Operator notation

In mathematics we are used to writing expressions like

$2*a + b*c$

where $+$ and $*$ are operators, and 2, a, b, are arguments. In particular, $+$ and $*$ are said to be *infix* operators because they appear *between* the two arguments. Such expressions can be represented as trees, as in Figure 3.6, and can be written as Prolog terms with $+$ and $*$ as functors:

+(*(2,a), *(b,c))

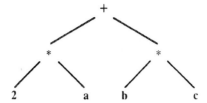

Figure 3.6 Tree representation of the expression **2∗a + b∗c**.

Since we would normally prefer to have such expressions written in the usual, infix style with operators, Prolog caters for this notational convenience. Prolog will therefore accept our expression written simply as:

    2∗a + b∗c

This will be, however, only the external representation of this object, which will be automatically converted into the usual form of Prolog terms. Such a term will be output for the user, again, in its external, infix form.

Thus operators in Prolog are merely a notational extension. If we write **a + b**, Prolog will handle it exactly as if it had been written **+(a,b)**. In order that Prolog properly understands expressions such as **a + b∗c**, Prolog has to know that ∗ binds stronger than +. We say that + has higher precedence than ∗. So the precedence of operators decides what is the correct interpretation of expressions. For example, the expression **a + b∗c** can be, in principle, understood either as

    +(a, ∗(b,c))

or as

    ∗(+(a,b), c)

The general rule is that the operator with the highest precedence is the principal functor of the term. If expressions containing + and ∗ are to be understood according to our normal conventions, then + has to have a higher precedence than ∗. Then the expression **a + b∗c** means the same as **a + (b∗c)**. If another interpretation is intended, then it has to be explicitly indicated by parentheses – for example, **(a + b)∗c**.

A programmer can define his or her own operators. So, for example, we can define the atoms **has** and **supports** as infix operators and then write in the program facts like:

    peter has information.
    floor supports table.

These facts are exactly equivalent to:

    has(peter, information).
    supports(floor, table).

A programmer can define new operators by inserting into the program special kinds of clauses, sometimes called *directives*, which act as operator definitions. An operator definition must appear in the program before any expression containing that operator. For our example, the operator **has** can be properly defined by the directive:

:- **op(600, xfx, has).**

This tells Prolog that we want to use 'has' as an operator, whose precedence is 600 and its type is 'xfx', which is a kind of infix operator. The form of the specifier 'xfx' suggests that the operator, denoted by 'f', is between the two arguments denoted by 'x'.

Notice that operator definitions do not specify any operation or action. In principle, *no operation on data is associated with an operator* (except in very special cases). Operators are normally used, as functors, only to combine objects into structures and not to invoke actions on data, although the word 'operator' appears to suggest an action.

Operator names are atoms. An operator's precedence must be in some range which depends on the implementation. We will assume that the range is between 1 and 1200.

There are three groups of operator types which are indicated by type specifiers such as xfx. The three groups are:

(1)   infix operators of three types:

   xfx   xfy   yfx

(2)   prefix operators of two types:

   fx   fy

(3)   postfix operators of two types:

   xf   yf

The specifiers are chosen so as to reflect the structure of the expression where 'f' represents the operator and 'x' and 'y' represent arguments. An 'f' appearing between the arguments indicates that the operator is infix. The prefix and postfix specifiers have only one argument, which follows or precedes the operator respectively.

There is a difference between 'x' and 'y'. To explain this we need to introduce the notion of the *precedence of argument*. If an argument is enclosed in parentheses or it is an unstructured object then its precedence is 0; if an argument is a structure then its precedence is equal to the precedence of its principal functor. 'x' represents an argument whose precedence must be strictly lower than that of the operator. 'y' represents an argument whose precedence is lower or equal to that of the operator.

These rules help to disambiguate expressions with several operators of the same precedence. For example, the expression

   a − b − c

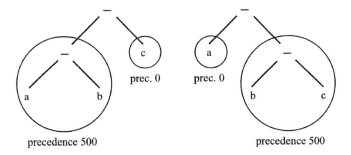

Figure 3.7 Two interpretations of the expression **a** − **b** − **c** assuming that '−' has precedence 500. If '−' is of type **yfx**, then interpretation 2 is invalid because the precedence of **b** − **c** is not less than the precedence of '−'.

is normally understood as (**a** − **b**) − **c**, and not as **a** − (**b** − **c**). To achieve the normal interpretation the operator '−' has to be defined as yfx. Figure 3.7 shows why the second interpretation is then ruled out.

As another example consider the prefix operator **not**. If not is defined as **fy** then the expression

not not p

is legal; but if **not** is defined as **fx** then this expression is illegal because the argument to the first **not** is **not p**, which has the same precedence as **not** itself. In this case the expression has to be written with parentheses:

not(not p)

For convenience, some operators are predefined in the Prolog system so that they can be readily used, and no definition is needed for them. What these operators are and what their precedences are depends on the implementation of Prolog. We will assume that this set of 'standard' operators is as if defined by the clauses in Figure 3.8. The operators in this figure are a subset of those defined in the Prolog standard, plus the operator **not**. As Figure 3.8 also shows, several operators can be declared by one clause if they all have the same precedence and if they are all of the same type. In this case the operators' names are written as a list.

The use of operators can greatly improve the readability of programs. As an example let us assume that we are writing a program for manipulating Boolean expressions. In such a program we may want to state, for example, one of de Morgan's equivalence theorems, which can in mathematics be written as:

$\sim$(A & B)   <$\Longrightarrow$> $\sim$A v $\sim$B

One way to state this in Prolog is by the clause:

equivalence(not(and(A, B)), or(not(A), not(B))).

```
:- op( 1200, xfx, [ :-, -->] ).
:- op( 1200, fx [ :-, ?-] ).
:- op( 1100, xfy, ';' ).
:- op( 1050, xfy, -> ).
:- op( 1000, xfy, ',' ).
:- op( 900, fy, [ not, '\+'] ).
:- op( 700, xfx, [ =, \=, ==, \==, =.. ] ).
:- op( 700, xfx, [ is, =:=, =\=, <, =<, >, >=, @<, @=<, @>, @>=] ).
:- op( 500, yfx, [ +, -] ).
:- op( 400, yfx, [ *, /, //, mod] ).
:- op( 200, xfx, **).
:- op( 200, xfy, ^).
:- op( 200, fy, - ).
```

Figure 3.8 A set of predefined operators.

However, it is in general a good programming practice to try to retain as much resemblance as possible between the original problem notation and the notation used in the program. In our example, this can be achieved almost completely by using operators. A suitable set of operators for our purpose can be defined as:

```
:- op( 800, xfx, <===>).
:- op( 700, xfy, v).
:- op( 600, xfy, &).
:- op( 500, fy, ~).
```

Now the de Morgan's theorem can be written as the fact:

~(A & B) <===> ~A v ~B.

According to our specification of operators above, this term is understood as shown in Figure 3.9.

To summarize:

- The readability of programs can be often improved by using the operator notation. Operators can be infix, prefix or postfix.

- In principle, no operation on data is associated with an operator except in special cases. Operator definitions do not define any action, they only introduce new notation. Operators, as functors, only hold together components of structures.

- A programmer can define his or her own operators. Each operator is defined by its name, precedence and type.

- The precedence is an integer within some range, usually between 1 and 1200. The operator with the highest precedence in the expression is the principal functor of the expression. Operators with lowest precedence bind strongest.

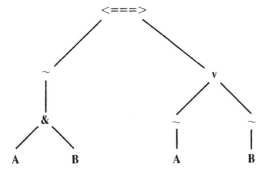

Figure 3.9 Interpretation of the term ~(A & B) <===> ~A v ~B.

- The type of an operator depends on two things: (1) the position of the operator with respect to the arguments, and (2) the precedence of the arguments compared to the precedence of the operator itself. In a specifier like **xfy**, **x** indicates an argument whose precedence is strictly lower than that of the operator; **y** indicates an argument whose precedence is less than or equal to that of the operator.

Exercises

3.12   Assuming the operator definitions

> :- **op(300, xfx, plays).**
> :- **op(200, xfy, and).**

then the following two terms are syntactically legal objects:

> **Term1 = jimmy plays football and squash**
> **Term2 = susan plays tennis and basketball and volleyball**

How are these terms understood by Prolog? What are their principal functors and what is their structure?

3.13   Suggest an appropriate definition of operators ('was', 'of', 'the') to be able to write clauses like

> **diana was the secretary of the department.**

and then ask Prolog:

> **?- Who was the secretary of the department.**
>
> **Who = diana**
>
> **?- diana was What.**
>
> **What = the secretary of the department**

3.14   Consider the program:

t(0+1, 1+0).

t(X+0+1, X+1+0).

t(X+1+1, Z) :-
    t(X+1, X1),
    t(X1+1, Z).

How will this program answer the following questions if '+' is an infix operator of type yfx (as usual):

(a)   ?- t(0+1, A).

(b)   ?- t(0+1+1, B).

(c)   ?- t(1+0+1+1+1, C).

(d)   ?- t(D, 1+1+1+0).

3.15   In the previous section, relations involving lists were written as:

member(Element, List),
conc(List1, List2, List3),
del(Element, List, NewList), ...

Suppose that we would prefer to write these relations as:

Element in List,
concatenating List1 and List2 gives List3,
deleting Element from List gives NewList, ...

Define 'in', 'concatenating', 'and', etc. as operators to make this possible. Also, redefine the corresponding procedures.

3.4   Arithmetic

Some of the predefined operators can be used for basic arithmetic operations. These are:

+	addition
−	subtraction
*	multiplication
/	division
**	power
//	integer division
mod	modulo, the remainder of integer division

Notice that this is an exceptional case in which an operator may in fact invoke an operation. But even in such cases an additional indication to perform arithmetic will be necessary. The following question is a naive attempt to request arithmetic computation:

?- X = 1 + 2.

Prolog will 'quietly' answer

X = 1 + 2

and not X = 3 as we might possibly expect. The reason is simple: the expression 1 + 2 merely denotes a Prolog term where + is the functor and 1 and 2 are its arguments. There is nothing in the above goal to force Prolog to actually activate the addition operation. A special predefined operator, **is**, is provided to circumvent this problem. The **is** operator will force evaluation. So the right way to invoke arithmetic is:

?- X **is** 1 + 2.

Now the answer will be:

X = 3

The addition here was carried out by a special procedure that is associated with the operator **is**. We call such procedures *built-in procedures*.

Different implementations of Prolog may use somewhat different notations for arithmetics. For example, the '/' operator may denote integer division or real division. In this book, '/' denotes real division, the operator // denotes integer division, and **mod** denotes the remainder. Accordingly, the question:

?- X **is** 5/2,
    Y **is** 5//2,
    Z **is** 5 **mod** 2.

is answered by:

X = 2.5
Y = 2
Z = 1

The left argument of the **is** operator is a simple object. The right argument is an arithmetic expression composed of arithmetic operators, numbers and variables. Since the **is** operator will force the evaluation, all the variables in the expression must already be instantiated to numbers at the time of execution of this goal. The precedence of the predefined arithmetic operators (see Figure 3.8) is such that the associativity of arguments with operators is the same as normally in mathematics. Parentheses can be used to indicate different associations. Note that +, −, *, / and **div** are defined as yfx, which means that evaluation is carried out from left to right. For example,

X **is** 5 − 2 − 1

is interpreted as:

X is (5 – 2) – 1

Prolog implementations usually also provide standard functions such as sin(X), cos(X), atan(X), log(X), exp(X), etc. These functions can appear to the right of operator **is**.

Arithmetic is also involved when *comparing* numerical values. We can, for example, test whether the product of 277 and 37 is greater than 10000 by the goal:

?- 277 * 37 > 10000.

yes

Note that, similarly to **is**, the '>' operator also forces the evaluation.

Suppose that we have in the program a relation **born** that relates the names of people with their birth years. Then we can retrieve the names of people born between 1980 and 1990 inclusive with the following question:

?- **born(Name, Year),**
   Year >= 1980,
   Year =< 1990.

The comparison operators are as follows:

X > Y	X is greater than Y
X < Y	X is less than Y
X >= Y	X is greater than or equal to Y
X =< Y	X is less than or equal to Y
X =:= Y	the values of X and Y are equal
X =\= Y	the values of X and Y are not equal

Notice the difference between the matching operator '=' and '=:='; for example, in the goals X = Y and X =:= Y. The first goal will cause the matching of the objects X and Y, and will, if X and Y match, possibly instantiate some variables in X and Y. There will be no evaluation. On the other hand, X =:= Y causes the arithmetic evaluation and cannot cause any instantiation of variables. These differences are illustrated by the following examples:

?- 1 + 2 =:= 2 + 1.

yes

?- 1 + 2 = 2 + 1.

no

?- 1 + A = B + 2.

A = 2
B = 1

Let us further illustrate the use of arithmetic operations by two simple examples. The first is computing the greatest common divisor; the second, counting the items in a list.

Given two positive integers, X and Y, their greatest common divisor, D, can be found according to three cases:

(1)   If X and Y are equal then D is equal to X.

(2)   If X < Y then D is equal to the greatest common divisor of X and the difference Y − X.

(3)   If Y < X then do the same as in case (2) with X and Y interchanged.

It can be easily shown by an example that these three rules actually work. Choosing, for example, X = 20 and Y = 25, the above rules would give D = 5 after a sequence of subtractions.

These rules can be formulated into a Prolog program by defining a three-argument relation, say:

gcd(X, Y, D)

The three rules are then expressed as three clauses, as follows:

gcd(X, X, X).

gcd(X, Y, D) :-
    X < Y,
    Y1 is Y − X,
    gcd(X, Y1, D).

gcd(X, Y, D) :-
    Y < X,
    gcd(Y, X, D).

Of course, the last goal in the third clause could be equivalently replaced by the two goals:

X1 is X − Y,
gcd(X1, Y, D)

Our next example involves counting, which usually requires some arithmetic. An example of such a task is to establish the length of a list; that is, we have to count the items in the list. Let us define the procedure:

length(List, N)

which will count the elements in a list **List** and instantiate N to their number. As was the case with our previous relations involving lists, it is useful to consider two cases:

(1)   If the list is empty then its length is 0.

(2)   If the list is not empty then **List** = [**Head** | **Tail**]; then its length is equal to 1 plus the length of the tail **Tail**.

These two cases correspond to the following program:

```
length( [ ], 0).

length( [_ | Tail], N) :-
    length( Tail, N1),
    N is 1 + N1.
```

An application of **length** can be:

```
?- length( [a,b,[c,d],e], N).

N = 4
```

Note that in the second clause of **length**, the two goals of the body cannot be swapped. The reason for this is that N1 has to be instantiated before the goal:

```
N is 1 + N1
```

can be processed. With the built-in procedure **is**, a relation has been introduced that is sensitive to the order of processing and therefore the procedural considerations have become vital.

It is interesting to see what happens if we try to program the **length** relation without the use of **is**. Such an attempt can be:

```
length1( [ ], 0).

length1( [_ | Tail], N) :-
    length1( Tail, N1),
    N = 1 + N1.
```

Now the goal

```
?- length1( [a,b,[c,d],e], N).
```

will produce the answer:

```
N = 1+(1+(1+(1+0))).
```

The addition was never explicitly forced and was therefore not carried out at all. But in **length1** we can, unlike in **length**, swap the goals in the second clause:

```
length1( [_ | Tail], N) :-
    N = 1 + N1,
    length1( Tail, N1).
```

This version of **length1** will produce the same result as the original version. It can also be written shorter, as follows,

```
length1( [_ | Tail], 1 + N) :-
    length1( Tail, N).
```

still producing the same result. We can, however, use **length1** to find the number of elements in a list as follows:

?- length1([a,b,c], N), Length is N.

N = 1+(1+(1+0))
Length = 3

Finally we note that the predicate **length** is often provided as a built-in predicate. To summarize:

- Built-in procedures can be used for doing arithmetic.

- Arithmetic operations have to be explicitly requested by the built-in procedure **is**. There are built-in procedures associated with the predefined operators +, −, *, /, **div** and **mod**.

- At the time that evaluation is carried out, all arguments must be already instantiated to numbers.

- The values of arithmetic expressions can be compared by operators such as <, =<, etc. These operators force the evaluation of their arguments.

Exercises

3.16   Define the relation

    max(X, Y, Max)

so that **Max** is the greater of two numbers X and Y.

3.17   Define the predicate

    maxlist(List, Max)

so that **Max** is the greatest number in the list of numbers **List**.

3.18   Define the predicate

    sumlist(List, Sum)

so that **Sum** is the sum of a given list of numbers **List**.

3.19   Define the predicate

    ordered(List)

which is true if **List** is an ordered list of numbers. For example,

    ordered([1,5,6,6,9,12]).

3.20   Define the predicate

    subsum(Set, Sum, SubSet)

so that **Set** is a list of numbers, **SubSet** is a subset of these numbers, and the sum of the numbers in **SubSet** is **Sum**. For example:

```
?- subsum( [1,2,5,3,2], 5, Sub).
Sub = [1,2,2];
Sub = [2,3];
Sub = [5];
...
```

3.21 Define the procedure

between(N1, N2, X)

which, for two given integers N1 and N2, generates through backtracking all the integers X that satisfy the constraint N1 ≤ X ≤ N2.

3.22 Define the operators 'if', 'then', 'else' and ':=' so that the following becomes a legal term:

if X > Y then Z := X else Z := Y

Choose the precedences so that 'if' will be the principal functor. Then define the relation 'if' as a small interpreter for a kind of 'if-then-else' statement of the form

if Val1 > Val2 then Var := Val3 else Var := Val4

where **Val1**, **Val2**, **Val3** and **Val4** are numbers (or variables instantiated to numbers) and **Var** is a variable. The meaning of the 'if' relation should be: if the value of **Val1** is greater than the value of **Val2** then **Var** is instantiated to Val3, otherwise to Val4. Here is an example of the use of this interpreter:

```
?- X = 2, Y = 3,
   Val2 is 2*X,
   Val4 is 4*X,
   if Y > Val2 then Z := Y else Z := Val4,
   if Z > 5 then W := 1 else W := 0.

X = 2
Y = 3
Z = 8
W = 1
Val2 = 4
Val4 = 8
```

Summary

- The list is a frequently used structure. It is either empty or consists of a *head* and a *tail* which is a list as well. Prolog provides a special notation for lists.

- Common operations on lists, programmed in this chapter, are: list membership, concatenation, adding an item, deleting an item, sublist.

- The *operator notation* allows the programmer to tailor the syntax of programs toward particular needs. Using operators the readability of programs can be greatly improved.

- New operators are defined by the directive **op**, stating the name of an operator, its type and precedence.

- In principle, there is no operation associated with an operator; operators are merely a syntactic device providing an alternative syntax for terms.

- Arithmetic is done by built-in procedures. Evaluation of an arithmetic expression is forced by the procedure **is** and by the comparison predicates <, =<, etc.

- Concepts introduced in this chapter are:

  list, head of list, tail of list
  list notation
  operators, operator notation
  infix, prefix and suffix operators
  precedence of an operator
  arithmetic built-in procedures

chapter 4

Using Structures: Example Programs

Data structures, with matching, backtracking and arithmetic, are a powerful programming tool. In this chapter we will develop the skill of using this tool through programming examples: retrieving structured information from a database, simulating a non-deterministic automaton, travel planning, and eight queens on the chessboard. We will also see how the principle of data abstraction can be carried out in Prolog. The programming examples in this chapter can be read selectively.

4.1   Retrieving structured information from a database

This exercise develops techniques of representing and manipulating structured data objects. It also illustrates Prolog as a natural database query language.

A database can be naturally represented in Prolog as a set of facts. For example, a database about families can be represented so that each family is described by one clause. Figure 4.1 shows how the information about each family can be structured. Each family has three components: husband, wife and children. As the number of children varies from family to family the children are represented by a list that is capable of accommodating any number of items. Each person is, in turn, represented by a structure of four components: name, surname, date of birth, job. The job information is 'unemployed', or it specifies the working organization and salary. The family of Figure 4.1 can be stored in the database by the clause:

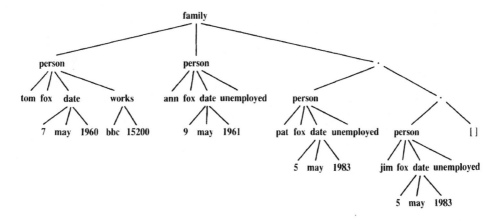

Figure 4.1 Structuring information about the family.

```
family(
    person( tom, fox, date(7,may,1960), works(bbc,15200) ),
    person( ann, fox, date(9,may,1961), unemployed),
    [ person( pat, fox, date(5,may,1983), unemployed),
      person( jim, fox, date(5,may,1983), unemployed) ] ).
```

Our database would then be comprised of a sequence of facts like this describing all families that are of interest to our program.

Prolog is, in fact, a very suitable language for retrieving the desired information from such a database. One nice thing about Prolog is that we can refer to objects without actually specifying all the components of these objects. We can merely indicate the *structure* of objects that we are interested in, and leave the particular components in the structures unspecified or only partially specified. Figure 4.2 shows some examples. So we can refer to all Armstrong families by:

family(person(_ , armstrong, _ , _), _ , _)

The underscore characters denote different anonymous variables; we do not care about their values. Further, we can refer to all families with three children by the term:

family(_ , _ , [_ , _ , _])

To find all married women that have at least three children we can pose the question:

?- family(_ , person(Name, Surname, _ , _), [_ , _ , _ | _]).

The point of these examples is that we can specify objects of interest not by their content, but by their structure. We only indicate their structure and leave their arguments as unspecified slots.

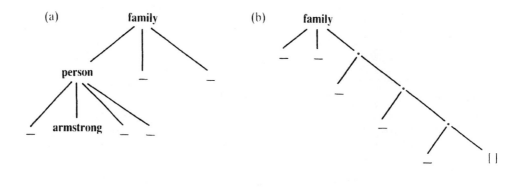

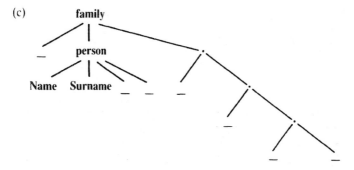

Figure 4.2 Specifying objects by their structural properties: (a) any Armstrong family; (b) any family with exactly three children; (c) any family with at least three children. Structure (c) makes provision for retrieving the wife's name through the instantiation of the variables **Name** and **Surname**.

We can provide a set of procedures that can serve as a utility to make the interaction with the database more comfortable. Such utility procedures could be part of the user interface. Some useful utility procedures for our database are:

```
husband( X) :-                        % X is a husband
   family( X, _, _).

wife( X) :-                           % X is a wife
   family( _, X, _).

child( X) :-                          % X is a child
   family( _, _, Children),
   member( X, Children).              % X in list Children

exists( Person) :-                    % Any person in the database
   husband( Person)
   ;
   wife( Person)
   ;
   child( Person).
```

dateofbirth(person(_, _, Date, _), Date).

salary(person(_, _, _, works(_, S)), S).   % Salary of working person

salary(person(_, _, _, unemployed), 0).   % Salary of unemployed

We can use these utilities, for example, in the following queries to the database:

- Find the names of all the people in the database:

    ?- exists(person(Name, Surname, _, _)).

- Find all children born in 2000:

    ?- child(X),
       dateofbirth(X, date(_, _, 2000)).

- Find all employed wives:

    ?- wife(person(Name, Surname, _, works(_, _))).

- Find the names of unemployed people who were born before 1973:

    ?- exists(person(Name, Surname, date(_, _, Year), unemployed)),
       Year < 1973.

- Find people born before 1960 whose salary is less than 8000:

    ?- exists(Person),
       dateofbirth(Person, date(_, _, Year)),
       Year < 1960,
       salary(Person, Salary),
       Salary < 8000.

- Find the names of families with at least three children:

    ?- family(person(_, Name, _, _), _, [_, _, _ | _]).

To calculate the total income of a family it is useful to define the sum of salaries of a list of people as a two-argument relation:

total(List_of_people, Sum_of_their_salaries)

This relation can be programmed as:

total([], 0).   % Empty list of people

total([Person | List], Sum) :-
    salary(Person, S),   % S: salary of first person
    total(List, Rest),   % Rest: sum of salaries of others
    Sum is S + Rest.

The total income of families can then be found by the question:

    ?- family(Husband, Wife, Children),
       total([Husband, Wife | Children], Income).

Let the **length** relation count the number of elements of a list, as defined in Section 3.4. Then we can specify all families that have an income per family member of less than 2000 by:

```
?- family( Husband, Wife, Children),
   total( [Husband, Wife | Children], Income),
   length( [Husband, Wife | Children], N),        % N: size of family
   Income/N < 2000.
```

Exercises

4.1   Write queries to find the following from the family database:

(a) names of families without children;

(b) all employed children;

(c) names of families with employed wives and unemployed husbands;

(d) all the children whose parents differ in age by at least 15 years.

4.2   Define the relation

twins(Child1, Child2)

to find twins in the family database.

4.2   Doing data abstraction

Data abstraction can be viewed as a process of organizing various pieces of information into natural units (possibly hierarchically), thus structuring the information into some conceptually meaningful form. Each such unit of information should be easily accessible in the program. Ideally, all the details of implementing such a structure should be invisible to the user of the structure – the programmer can then just concentrate on objects and relations between them. The point of the process is to make the use of information possible without the programmer having to think about the details of how the information is actually represented.

Let us discuss one way of carrying out this principle in Prolog. Consider our family example of the previous section again. Each family is a collection of pieces of information. These pieces are all clustered into natural units such as a person or a family, so they can be treated as single objects. Assume again that the family information is structured as in Figure 4.1. In the previous section, each family was represented by a Prolog clause. Here, a family will be represented as a structured object, for example:

FoxFamily = family(person(tom, fox, _ , _), _ , _)

Let us now define some relations through which the user can access particular components of a family without knowing the details of Figure 4.1. Such relations can be called *selectors* as they select particular components. The name of such a selector relation will be the name of the component to be selected. The relation will have two arguments: first, the object that contains the component, and second, the component itself:

> selector_relation(Object, Component_selected)

Here are some selectors for the family structure:

> husband(family(Husband, _ , _), Husband).
>
> wife(family(_ , Wife, _), Wife).
>
> children(family(_ , _ , ChildList), ChildList).

We can also define selectors for particular children:

> firstchild(Family, First) :-
>   children(Family, [First | _]).
>
> secondchild(Family, Second) :-
>   children(Family, [_ , Second | _]).
>
> ...

We can generalize this to selecting the Nth child:

> nthchild(N, Family, Child) :-
>   children(Family, ChildList),
>   nth_member(N, ChildList, Child).   % Nth element of a list

Another interesting object is a person. Some related selectors according to Figure 4.1 are:

> firstname(person(Name, _ , _ , _), Name).
>
> surname(person(_ , Surname, _ , _), Surname).
>
> born(person(_ , _ , Date, _), Date).

How can we benefit from selector relations? Having defined them, we can now forget about the particular way that structured information is represented. To create and manipulate this information, we just have to know the names of the selector relations and use these in the rest of the program. In the case of complicated representations, this is easier than always referring to the representation explicitly. In our family example in particular, the user does not have to know that the children are represented as a list. For example, assume that we want to say that Tom Fox and Jim Fox belong to the same family and that Jim is the second child of Tom. Using the selector relations above, we can define two persons, call them **Person1** and **Person2**, and the family. The following list of goals does this:

> firstname(Person1, tom), surname(Person1, fox),   % Person1 is Tom Fox
> firstname(Person2, jim), surname(Person2, fox),   % Person2 is Jim Fox
> husband(Family, Person1),
> secondchild(Family, Person2)

As a result, the variables **Person1**, **Person2** and **Family** are instantiated as:

> **Person1** = **person(tom, fox, _, _)**

> **Person2** = **person(jim, fox, _, _)**

> **Family** = **family(person(tom, fox, _, _), _, [_, person(jim, fox) | _])**

The use of selector relations also makes programs easier to modify. Imagine that we would like to improve the efficiency of a program by changing the representation of data. All we have to do is to change the definitions of the selector relations, and the rest of the program will work unchanged with the new representation.

Exercise

4.3   Complete the definition of **nthchild** by defining the relation

> **nth_member(N, List, X)**

which is true if X is the Nth member of **List**.

4.3   Simulating a non-deterministic automaton

This exercise shows how an abstract mathematical construct can be translated into Prolog. In addition, our resulting program will turn out to be much more flexible than initially intended.

A *non-deterministic finite automaton* is an abstract machine that reads as input a string of symbols and decides whether to *accept* or to *reject* the input string. An automaton has a number of *states* and it is always in one of the states. It can change its state by moving from the current state to another state. The internal structure of the automaton can be represented by a transition graph such as that in Figure 4.3. In this example, s_1, s_2, s_3 and s_4 are the *states* of the automaton. Starting from the initial state (s_1 in our example), the automaton moves from state to state while reading the input string. Transitions depend on the current input symbol, as indicated by the arc labels in the transition graph.

A transition occurs each time an input symbol is read. Note that transitions can be non-deterministic. In Figure 4.3, if the automaton is in state s_1 and the current input symbol is *a* then it can transit into s_1 or s_2. Some arcs are labelled *null* denoting the 'null symbol'. These arcs correspond to 'silent moves' of the automaton. Such a

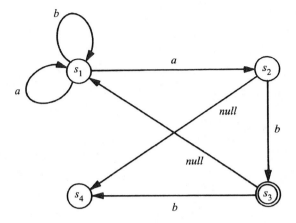

Figure 4.3   An example of a non-deterministic finite automaton.

move is said to be *silent* because it occurs without any reading of input, and the observer, viewing the automaton as a black box, will not be able to notice that any transition has occurred.

The state s_3 is double circled, which indicates that it is a *final state*. The automaton is said to *accept* the input string if there is a transition path in the graph such that

(1)   it starts with the initial state,

(2)   it ends with a final state, and

(3)   the arc labels along the path correspond to the complete input string.

It is entirely up to the automaton to decide which of the possible moves to execute at any time. In particular, the automaton may choose to make or not to make a silent move, if it is available in the current state. But abstract non-deterministic machines of this kind have a magic property: if there is a choice then they always choose a 'right' move; that is, a move that leads to the acceptance of the input string, if such a move exists. The automaton in Figure 4.3 will, for example, accept the strings *ab* and *aabaab*, but it will reject the strings *abb* and *abba*. It is easy to see that this automaton accepts any string that terminates with *ab*, and rejects all others.

In Prolog, an automaton can be specified by three relations:

(1)   a unary relation **final** which defines the final states of the automaton;

(2)   a three-argument relation **trans** which defines the state transitions so that

   trans(S1, X, S2)

   means that a transition from a state S1 to S2 is possible when the current input symbol X is read;

(3)   a binary relation

silent(S1, S2)

meaning that a silent move is possible from S1 to S2.

For the automaton in Figure 4.3 these three relations are:

final(s3).

trans(s1, a, s1).
trans(s1, a, s2).
trans(s1, b, s1).
trans(s2, b, s3).
trans(s3, b, s4).

silent(s2, s4).
silent(s3, s1).

We will represent input strings as Prolog lists. So the string *aab* will be represented by [a,a,b]. Given the description of the automaton, the simulator will process a given input string and decide whether the string is accepted or rejected. By definition, the non-deterministic automaton accepts a given string if (starting from an initial state), after having read the whole input string, the automaton can (possibly) be in its final state. The simulator is programmed as a binary relation, **accepts**, which defines the acceptance of a string from a given state. So

accepts(State, String)

is true if the automaton, starting from the state **State** as initial state, accepts the string **String**. The **accepts** relation can be defined by three clauses. They correspond to the following three cases:

(1)   The empty string, [], is accepted from a state **State** if **State** is a final state.

(2)   A non-empty string is accepted from **State** if reading the first symbol in the string can bring the automaton into some state **State1**, and the rest of the string is accepted from **State1**. Figure 4.4(a) illustrates.

(3)   A string is accepted from **State** if the automaton can make a silent move from **State** to **State1** and then accept the (whole) input string from **State1**. Figure 4.4(b) illustrates.

These rules can be translated into Prolog as:

```
accepts( State, [ ] ) :-              % Accept empty string
    final( State).

accepts( State, [X | Rest] ) :-       % Accept by reading first symbol
    trans( State, X, State1),
    accepts( State1, Rest).

accepts( State, String) :-            % Accept by making silent move
    silent( State, State1),
    accepts( State1, String).
```

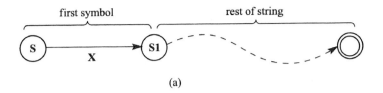

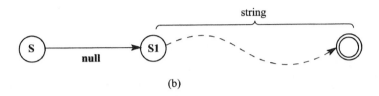

Figure 4.4   Accepting a string: (a) by reading its first symbol X; (b) by making a silent move.

The program can be asked, for example, about the acceptance of the string *aaab* by:

?- **accepts(s1, [a,a,a,b]).**

yes

As we have already seen, Prolog programs are often able to solve more general problems than problems for which they were originally developed. In our case, we can also ask the simulator which state our automaton can be in initially so that it will accept the string *ab*:

?- **accepts(S, [a,b]).**

S = s1;

S = s3

Amusingly, we can also ask: What are all the strings of length 3 that are accepted from state s_1?

?- **accepts(s1, [X1,X2,X3]).**

X1 = a
X2 = a
X3 = b;

X1 = b
X2 = a
X3 = b;

no

If we prefer the acceptable input strings to be typed out as lists then we can formulate the question as:

?- String = [_, _, _], accepts(s1, String).

String = [a,a,b];

String = [b,a,b];

no

We can make further experiments asking even more general questions, such as: From what states will the automaton accept input strings of length 7?

Further experimentation could involve modifications in the structure of the automaton by changing the relations **final**, **trans** and **silent**. The automaton in Figure 4.3 does not contain any cyclic 'silent path' (a path that consists only of silent moves). If in Figure 4.3 a new transition

silent(s1, s3)

is added then a 'silent cycle' is created. But our simulator may now get into trouble. For example, the question

?- accepts(s1, [a]).

would induce the simulator to cycle in state s_1 indefinitely, all the time hoping to find some way to the final state.

Exercises

4.4   Why could cycling not occur in the simulation of the original automaton in Figure 4.3, when there was no 'silent cycle' in the transition graph?

4.5   Cycling in the execution of **accepts** can be prevented, for example, by counting the number of moves made so far. The simulator would then be requested to search only for paths of some limited length. Modify the **accepts** relation this way. Hint: Add a third argument: the maximum number of moves allowed:

accepts(State, String, MaxMoves)

4.4   Travel agent

In this section we will construct a program that gives advice on planning air travel. The program will be a rather simple advisor, yet it will be able to answer some useful questions, such as:

- What days of the week is there a direct evening flight from Ljubljana to London?

- How can I get from Ljubljana to Edinburgh on Thursday?

●   I have to visit Milan, Ljubljana and Zurich, starting from London on Tuesday and returning to London on Friday. In what sequence should I visit these cities so that I have no more than one flight each day of the tour?

The program will be centred around a database holding the flight information. This will be represented as a three-argument relation:

timetable(Place1, Place2, ListOfFlights)

where **ListOfFlights** is a list of structured items of the form:

DepartureTime / ArrivalTime / FlightNumber / ListOfDays

Here the operator '/' only holds together the components of the structure, and of course does not mean arithmetic division. **ListOfDays** is either a list of weekdays or the atom **alldays**. One clause of the **timetable** relation can be, for example:

timetable(london, edinburgh,
            [9:40 / 10:50 / ba4733 / alldays,
            19:40 / 20:50 / ba4833 / [mo,tu,we,th,fr,su]]).

The times are represented as structured objects with two components, hours and minutes, combined by the operator ':'.

The main problem is to find exact routes between two given cities on a given day of the week. This will be programmed as a four-argument relation:

route(Place1, Place2, Day, Route)

Here **Route** is a sequence of flights that satisfies the following criteria:

(1)   the start point of the route is **Place1**;

(2)   the end point is **Place2**;

(3)   all the flights are on the same day of the week, **Day**;

(4)   all the flights in **Route** are in the **timetable** relation;

(5)   there is enough time for transfer between flights.

The route is represented as a list of structured objects of the form:

From / To / FlightNumber / Departure_time

We will also use the following auxiliary predicates:

(1)   **flight(Place1, Place2, Day, FlightNum, DepTime, ArrTime)**

       This says that there is a flight, **FlightNum**, between **Place1** and **Place2** on the day of the week **Day** with the specified departure and arrival times.

(2)   **deptime(Route, Time)**

       Departure time of **Route** is **Time**.

(3)   **transfer(Time1, Time2)**

There is at least 40 minutes between **Time1** and **Time2**, which should be sufficient for transfer between two flights.

The problem of finding a route is reminiscent of the simulation of the non-deterministic automaton of the previous section. The similarities of both problems are as follows:

- The states of the automaton correspond to the cities.

- A transition between two states corresponds to a flight between two cities.

- The **transition** relation of the automaton corresponds to the **timetable** relation.

- The automaton simulator finds a path in the transition graph between the initial state and a final state; the travel planner finds a route between the start city and the end city of the tour.

Not surprisingly, therefore, the **route** relation can be defined similarly to the **accepts** relation, with the exception that here we have no 'silent moves'. We have two cases:

(1)   Direct flight connection: if there is a direct flight between places **Place1** and **Place2** then the route consists of this flight only:

```
route( Place1, Place2, Day, [ Place1 / Place2 / Fnum / Dep ] ) :-
    flight( Place1, Place2, Day, Fnum, Dep, Arr).
```

(2)   Indirect flight connection: the route between places P1 and P2 consists of the first flight, from P1 to some intermediate place P3, followed by a route between P3 to P2. In addition, there must be enough time between the arrival of the first flight and the departure of the second flight for transfer.

```
route( P1, P2, Day, [P1 / P3 / Fnum1 / Dep1 | RestRoute] ) :-
    route( P3, P2, Day, RestRoute),
    flight( P1, P3, Day, Fnum1, Dep1, Arr1),
    deptime( RestRoute, Dep2),
    transfer( Arr1, Dep2).
```

The auxiliary relations **flight**, **transfer** and **deptime** are easily programmed and are included in the complete travel planning program in Figure 4.5. Also included is an example timetable database.

Our route planner is extremely simple and may examine paths that obviously lead nowhere. Yet it will suffice if the flight database is not large. A really large database would require more intelligent planning to cope with the large number of potential candidate paths.

Some example questions to the program are as follows:

% A FLIGHT ROUTE PLANNER

:- **op(50, xfy, :).**

% route(Place1, Place2, Day, Route):
%   Route is a sequence of flights on Day, starting at Place1, ending at Place2

route(P1, P2, Day, [P1 / P2 / Fnum / Deptime]) :-   % Direct flight
  flight(P1, P2, Day, Fnum, Deptime, _).

route(P1, P2, Day, [(P1/P3/Fnum1/Dep1) | RestRoute]) :-   % Indirect connection
  route(P3, P2, Day, RestRoute),
  flight(P1, P3, Day, Fnum1, Dep1, Arr1),
  deptime(RestRoute, Dep2),   % Departure time of Route
  transfer(Arr1, Dep2).   % Enough time for transfer

flight(Place1, Place2, Day, Fnum, Deptime, Arrtime) :-
  timetable(Place1, Place2, Flightlist),
  member(Deptime / Arrtime / Fnum / Daylist , Flightlist),
  flyday(Day, Daylist).

flyday(Day, Daylist) :-
  member(Day, Daylist).

flyday(Day, alldays) :-
  member(Day, [mo,tu,we,th,fr,sa,su]).

deptime([P1 / P2 / Fnum / Dep | _], Dep).

transfer(Hours1:Mins1, Hours2:Mins2) :-
  60 ∗ (Hours2 − Hours1) + Mins2 − Mins1 >= 40.

member(X, [X | L]).

member(X, [Y | L]) :-
  member(X, L).

% A FLIGHT DATABASE

timetable(edinburgh, london,
        [9:40 / 10:50 / ba4733 / alldays,
         13:40 / 14:50 / ba4773 / alldays,
         19:40 / 20:50 / ba4833 / [mo,tu,we,th,fr,su]]).

timetable(london, edinburgh,
        [9:40 / 10:50 / ba4732 / alldays,
         11:40 / 12:50 / ba4752 / alldays,
         18:40 / 19:50 / ba4822 / [mo,tu,we,th,fr]]).

timetable(london, ljubljana,
        [13:20 / 16:20 / jp212 / [mo,tu,we,fr,su],
         16:30 / 19:30 / ba473 / [mo,we,th,sa]]).

timetable(london, zurich,
        [9:10 / 11:45 / ba614 / alldays,
         14:45 / 17:20 / sr805 / alldays]).

Figure 4.5   A flight route planner and an imaginary flight timetable.

Figure 4.5 *contd*

```
timetable( london, milan,
            [  8:30 / 11:20 / ba510 / alldays,
              11:00 / 13:50 / az459 / alldays ] ).
timetable( ljubljana, zurich,
            [ 11:30 / 12:40 / jp322 / [tu,th] ] ).
timetable( ljubljana, london,
            [ 11:10 / 12:20 / jp211 / [mo,tu,we,fr,su],
              20:30 / 21:30 / ba472 / [mo,we,th,sa] ] ).
timetable( milan, london,
            [  9:10 / 10:00 / az458 / alldays,
              12:20 / 13:10 / ba511 / alldays ] ).
timetable( milan, zurich,
            [  9:25 / 10:15 / sr621 / alldays,
              12:45 / 13:35 / sr623 / alldays ] ).
timetable( zurich, ljubljana,
            [ 13:30 / 14:40 / jp323 / [tu,th] ] ).
timetable( zurich, london,
            [  9:00 /  9:40 / ba613 / [mo,tu,we,th,fr,sa],
              16:10 / 16:55 / sr806 / [mo,tu,we,th,fr,su] ] ).
timetable( zurich, milan,
            [  7:55 /  8:45 / sr620 / alldays ] ).
```

- What days of the week is there a direct evening flight from Ljubljana to London?

  ?- flight(ljubljana, london, Day, _, DeptHour: _, _), DeptHour >= 18.

  Day = mo;
  Day = we;
  ...

- How can I get from Ljubljana to Edinburgh on Thursday?

  ?- route(ljubljana, edinburgh, th, R).

  R = [ljubljana / zurich / jp322 / 11:30, zurich / london / sr806 / 16:10,
  **   london / edinburgh / ba4822 / 18:40]**

- How can I visit Milan, Ljubljana and Zurich, starting from London on Tuesday and returning to London on Friday, with no more than one flight each day of the tour? This question is somewhat trickier. It can be formulated by using the **permutation** relation, programmed in Chapter 3. We are asking for a permutation of the cities Milan, Ljubljana and Zurich such that the corresponding flights are possible on successive days:

?- permutation([milan, ljubljana, zurich], [City1, City2, City3]),
flight(london, City1, tu, FN1, _ , _),
flight(City1, City2, we, FN2, _ , _),
flight(City2, City3, th, FN3, _ , _),
flight(City3, london, fr, FN4, _ , _).

City1 = milan
City2 = zurich
City3 = ljubljana
FN1 = ba510
FN2 = sr621
FN3 = jp323
FN4 = jp211

Finally let us note that this program is susceptible to indefinite loops, which happens for example if we ask it to find a route not in the timetable:

?- route (moscow, edinburgh, mo, R).

It is better therefore to keep questions safe by limiting the length of the route. We can use the usual trick with **conc**:

?- conc(R, _ , [_ ,_ ,_ ,_]), route(moscow, edinburgh, mo, R).

no

The **conc** goal limits the list **R** to length 4 and also forces the search to consider shortest routes first.

4.5   The eight queens problem

The problem here is to place eight queens on the empty chessboard in such a way that no queen attacks any other queen. The solution will be programmed as a unary predicate

solution(Pos)

which is true if and only if **Pos** represents a position with eight queens that do not attack each other. It will be interesting to compare various ideas for programming this problem. Therefore we will present three programs based on somewhat different representations of the problem.

4.5.1   Program 1

First we have to choose a representation of the board position. One natural choice is to represent the position by a list of eight items, each of them corresponding to one queen. Each item in the list will specify a square of the board on which the

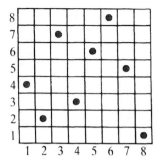

Figure 4.6 A solution to the eight queens problem. This position can be specified by the list
[1/4, 2/2, 3/7, 4/3, 5/6, 6/8, 7/5, 8/1].

corresponding queen is sitting. Further, each square can be specified by a pair of coordinates (X and Y) on the board, where each coordinate is an integer between 1 and 8. In the program we can write such a pair as:

X/Y

where, of course, the '/' operator is not meant to indicate division, but simply combines both coordinates together into a square. Figure 4.6 shows one solution of the eight queens problem and its list representation.

Having chosen this representation, the problem is to find such a list of the form:

[X1/Y1, X2/Y2, X3/Y3, ..., X8/Y8]

which satisfies the no-attack requirement. Our procedure **solution** will have to search for a proper instantiation of the variables X1, Y1, X2, Y2, ..., X8, Y8. As we know that all the queens will have to be in different columns to prevent vertical attacks, we can immediately constrain the choice and so make the search task easier. We can thus fix the X-coordinates so that the solution list will fit the following, more specific template:

[1/Y1, 2/Y2, 3/Y3, ..., 8/Y8]

We are interested in the solution on a board of size 8 by 8. However, in programming, the key to the solution is often in considering a more general problem. Paradoxically, it is often the case that the solution for the more general problem is easier to formulate than that for the more specific, original problem. The original problem is then simply solved as a special case of the more general problem.

The creative part of the problem is to find the correct generalization of the original problem. In our case, a good idea is to generalize the number of queens (the number of columns in the list) from 8 to any number, including zero. The **solution** relation can then be formulated by considering two cases:

Case 1   The list of queens is empty: the empty list is certainly a solution because there is no attack.

Case 2   The list of queens is non-empty: then it looks like this:

[X/Y | Others]

In case 2, the first queen is at some square X/Y and the other queens are at squares specified by the list **Others**. If this is to be a solution then the following conditions must hold:

(1)   There must be no attack between the queens in the list **Others**; that is, **Others** itself must also be a solution.

(2)   X and Y must be integers between 1 and 8.

(3)   A queen at square X/Y must not attack any of the queens in the list **Others**.

To program the first condition we can simply use the **solution** relation itself. The second condition can be specified as follows: Y will have to be a member of the list of integers between 1 and 8 – that is, [1,2,3,4,5,6,7,8]. On the other hand, we do not have to worry about X since the solution list will have to match the template in which the X-coordinates are already specified. So X will be guaranteed to have a proper value between 1 and 8. We can implement the third condition as another relation, **noattack**. All this can then be written in Prolog as follows:

```
solution( [X/Y | Others] )  :-
  solution( Others),
  member( Y, [1,2,3,4,5,6,7,8] ),
  noattack( X/Y, Others).
```

It now remains to define the **noattack** relation:

noattack(Q, Qlist)

Again, this can be broken down into two cases:

(1)   If the list **Qlist** is empty then the relation is certainly true because there is no queen to be attacked.

(2)   If **Qlist** is not empty then it has the form [**Q1** | **Qlist1**] and two conditions must be satisfied:

(a)   the queen at Q must not attack the queen at Q1, and

(b)   the queen at Q must not attack any of the queens in **Qlist1**.

To specify that a queen at some square does not attack another square is easy: the two squares must not be in the same row, the same column or the same diagonal. Our solution template guarantees that all the queens are in different columns, so it only remains to specify explicitly that:

• the Y-coordinates of the queens are different, and

• they are not in the same diagonal, either upward or downward; that is, the distance between the squares in the X-direction must not be equal to that in the Y-direction.

....

% solution(BoardPosition) if BoardPosition is a list of non-attacking queens

solution([ ]).

solution([X/Y | Others]) :-   % First queen at X/Y, other queens at Others
  solution(Others),
  member(Y, [1,2,3,4,5,6,7,8]),
  noattack(X/Y, Others).   % First queen does not attack others

noattack(_, [ ]).   % Nothing to attack

noattack(X/Y, [X1/Y1 | Others]) :-
  Y = \ = Y1,   % Different Y-coordinates
  Y1 – Y = \ = X1 – X,   % Different diagonals
  Y1 – Y = \ = X – X1,
  noattack(X/Y, Others).

member(Item, [Item | Rest]).

member(Item, [First | Rest]) :-
  member(Item, Rest).

% A solution template

template([1/Y1,2/Y2,3/Y3,4/Y4,5/Y5,6/Y6,7/Y7,8/Y8]).

....

Figure 4.7   Program 1 for the eight queens problem.

Figure 4.7 shows the complete program. To alleviate its use a template list has been added. This list can be retrieved in a question for generating solutions. So we can now ask:

  ?- template(S), solution(S).

and the program will generate solutions as follows:

  S = [1/4, 2/2, 3/7, 4/3, 5/6, 6/8, 7/5, 8/1];

  S = [1/5, 2/2, 3/4, 4/7, 5/3, 6/8, 7/6, 8/1];

  S = [1/3, 2/5, 3/2, 4/8, 5/6, 6/4, 7/7, 8/1];

  . . .

Exercise
....

4.6   When searching for a solution, the program of Figure 4.7 explores alternative values for the Y-coordinates of the queens. At which place in the program is the order of alternatives defined? How can we easily modify the program to change the order? Experiment with different orders with the view of studying the time efficiency of the program.

4.5.2 Program 2

In the board representation of program 1, each solution had the form

    [1/Y1, 2/Y2, 3/Y3, ..., 8/Y8]

because the queens were simply placed in consecutive columns. No information is lost if the X-coordinates were omitted. So a more economical representation of the board position can be used, retaining only the Y-coordinates of the queens:

    [Y1, Y2, Y3, ..., Y8]

To prevent the horizontal attacks, no two queens can be in the same row. This imposes a constraint on the Y-coordinates. The queens have to occupy all the rows 1, 2, ..., 8. The choice that remains is the *order* of these eight numbers. Each solution is therefore represented by a permutation of the list

    [1,2,3,4,5,6,7,8]

Such a permutation, S, is a solution if all the queens are safe. So we can write:

    solution(S) :-
        permutation([1,2,3,4,5,6,7,8], S),
        safe(S).

We have already programmed the **permutation** relation in Chapter 3, but the **safe** relation remains to be specified. We can split its definition into two cases:

(1)   S is the empty list: this is certainly safe as there is nothing to be attacked.

(2)   S is a non-empty list of the form [**Queen** | **Others**]. This is safe if the list **Others** is safe, and **Queen** does not attack any queen in the list **Others**.

In Prolog, this is:

    safe([ ]).

    safe([Queen | Others]) :-
        safe(Others),
        noattack(Queen, Others).

The **noattack** relation here is slightly trickier. The difficulty is that the queens' positions are only defined by their Y-coordinates, and the X-coordinates are not explicitly present. This problem can be circumvented by a small generalization of the **noattack** relation, as illustrated in Figure 4.8. The goal

    noattack(Queen,Others)

is meant to ensure that **Queen** does not attack **Others** when the X-distance between **Queen** and **Others** is equal to 1. What is needed is the generalization of the X-distance between **Queen** and **Others**. So we add this distance as the third argument of the **noattack** relation:

    noattack(Queen, Others, Xdist)

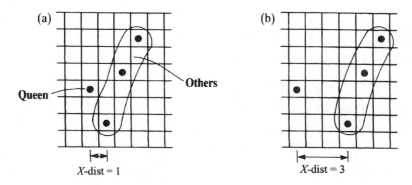

Figure 4.8   (a) X-distance between **Queen** and **Others** is 1. (b) X-distance between **Queen** and **Others** is 3.

Accordingly, the **noattack** goal in the **safe** relation has to be modified to

noattack(Queen, Others, 1)

The **noattack** relation can now be formulated according to two cases, depending on the list **Others**: if **Others** is empty then there is no target and certainly no attack; if **Others** is non-empty then **Queen** must not attack the first queen in **Others** (which is **Xdist** columns from **Queen**) and also the tail of **Others** at **Xdist** + 1. This leads to the program shown in Figure 4.9.

4.5.3   Program 3

Our third program for the eight queens problem will be based on the following reasoning. Each queen has to be placed on some square; that is, into some column, some row, some upward diagonal and some downward diagonal. To make sure that all the queens are safe, each queen must be placed in a different column, a different row, a different upward and a different downward diagonal. It is thus natural to consider a richer representation with four coordinates:

x columns
y rows
u upward diagonals
v downward diagonals

The coordinates are not independent: given x and y, u and v are determined (Figure 4.10 illustrates). For example, as:

$$u = x - y$$
$$v = x + y$$

% solution(Queens) if Queens is a list of Y-coordinates of eight non-attacking queens

```
solution( Queens) :-
  permutation( [1,2,3,4,5,6,7,8], Queens),
  safe( Queens).

permutation( [], [] ).

permutation( [Head | Tail], PermList) :-
  permutation( Tail, PermTail),
  del( Head, PermList, PermTail).                    % Insert Head in permuted Tail
```

% del(Item, List, NewList): deleting Item from List gives NewList

```
del( Item, [Item | List], List).

del( Item, [First | List], [First | List1] ) :-
  del( Item, List, List1).
```

% safe(Queens) if Queens is a list of Y-coordinates of non-attacking queens

```
safe( [] ).

safe( [Queen | Others] ) :-
  safe( Others),
  noattack( Queen, Others, 1).

noattack( _, [], _).

noattack( Y, [Y1 | Ylist], Xdist) :-
  Y1 – Y =\= Xdist,
  Y – Y1 =\= Xdist,
  Dist1 is Xdist + 1,
  noattack( Y, Ylist, Dist1).
```

Figure 4.9   Program 2 for the eight queens problem.

The domains for all four dimensions are:

$$Dx = [1,2,3,4,5,6,7,8]$$

$$Dy = [1,2,3,4,5,6,7,8]$$

$$Du = [-7,-6,-5,-4,-3,-2,-1,0,1,2,3,4,5,6,7]$$

$$Dv = [2,3,4,5,6,7,8,9,10,11,12,13,14,15,16]$$

The eight queens problem can now be stated as follows: select eight 4-tuples (X,Y,U,V) from the domains (X from Dx, Y from Dy, etc.), never using the same element twice from any of the domains. Of course, once X and Y are chosen, U and V are determined. The solution can then be, roughly speaking, as follows: given all four domains, select the position of the first queen, delete the corresponding items from the four domains, and then use the rest of the domains for placing the rest of the queens. A program based on this idea is shown in Figure 4.11. The board

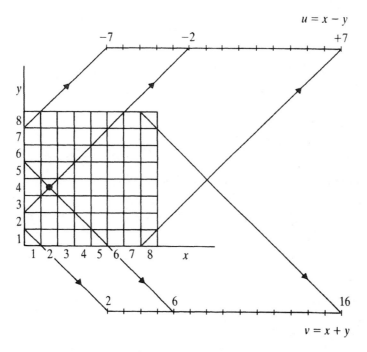

Figure 4.10   The relation between columns, rows, upward and downward diagonals. The
indicated square has coordinates: $x = 2$, $y = 4$, $u = 2 - 4 = -2$, $v = 2 + 4 = 6$.

% solution(Ylist) if Ylist is a list of Y-coordinates of eight non-attacking queens

```
solution( Ylist) :-
    sol( Ylist,                              % Y-coordinates of queens
        [1,2,3,4,5,6,7,8],                   % Domain for X-coordinates
        [1,2,3,4,5,6,7,8],                   % Domain for Y-coordinates
        [-7,-6,-5,-4,-3,-2,-1,0,1,2,3,4,5,6,7],   % Upward diagonals
        [2,3,4,5,6,7,8,9,10,11,12,13,14,15,16] ).  % Downward diagonals

sol( [], [], Dy, Du, Dv).

sol( [Y | Ylist], [X | Dx1], Dy, Du, Dv)  :-
    del( Y, Dy, Dy1),                        % Choose a Y-coordinate
    U is X-Y,                                % Corresponding upward diagonal
    del( U, Du, Du1),                        % Remove it
    V is X+Y,                                % Corresponding downward diagonal
    del( V, Dv, Dv1),                        % Remove it
    sol( Ylist, Dx1, Dy1, Du1, Dv1).         % Use remaining values

del( Item, [Item | List], List).

del( Item, [First | List], [First | List1] )  :-
    del( Item, List, List1).
```

Figure 4.11   Program 3 for the eight queens problem.

position is, again, represented by a list of Y-coordinates. The key relation in this program is

sol(Ylist, Dx, Dy, Du, Dv)

which instantiates the Y-coordinates (in **Ylist**) of the queens, assuming that they are placed in consecutive columns taken from Dx. All Y-coordinates and the corresponding U and V-coordinates are taken from the lists Dy, Du and Dv. The top procedure, **solution**, can be invoked by the question:

?- solution(S).

This will cause the invocation of **sol** with the complete domains that correspond to the problem space of eight queens.

The **sol** procedure is general in the sense that it can be used for solving the N-queens problem (on a chessboard of size N by N). It is only necessary to properly set up the domains Dx, Dy, etc.

It is practical to mechanize the generation of the domains. For that we need a procedure

gen(N1, N2, List)

which will, for two given integers N1 and N2, produce the list:

List = [N1, N1 + 1, N1 + 2, ..., N2 − 1, N2]

Such a procedure is:

```
gen( N, N, [N] ).

gen( N1, N2, [N1 | List] ) :-
    N1 < N2,
    M is N1 + 1,
    gen( M, N2, List).
```

The top level relation, **solution**, has to be accordingly generalized to

solution(N, S)

where N is the size of the board and S is a solution represented as a list of Y-coordinates of N queens. The generalized **solution** relation is:

```
solution( N, S) :-
    gen( 1, N, Dxy),                    % Dxy – domain for X and Y
    Nu1 is 1 − N, Nu2 is N − 1,
    gen( Nu1, Nu2, Du),
    Nv2 is N + N,
    gen( 2, Nv2, Dv),
    sol( S, Dxy, Dxy, Du, Dv).
```

For example, a solution to the 12-queens problem would be generated by:

?- solution(12, S).

S = [1,3,5,8,10,12,6,11,2,7,9,4]

4.5.4   Concluding remarks

The three solutions to the eight queens problem show how the same problem can be approached in different ways. We also varied the representation of data. Sometimes the representation was more economical, sometimes it was more explicit and partially redundant. The drawback of the more economical representation is that some information always has to be recomputed when it is required.

At several points, the key step toward the solution was to generalize the problem. Paradoxically, by considering a more general problem, the solution became easier to formulate. This generalization principle is a kind of standard technique that can often be applied.

Of the three programs, the third one illustrates best how to approach general problems of constructing under constraints a structure from a given set of elements.

A natural question is: Which of the three programs is most efficient? In this respect, program 2 is far inferior while the other two programs are similar. The reason is that permutation-based program 2 constructs complete permutations while the other two programs are able to recognize and reject unsafe permutations when they are only partially constructed. Program 3 avoids some of the arithmetic computation that is essentially captured in the redundant board representation this program uses.

Exercise

4.7   Let the squares of the chessboard be represented by pairs of their coordinates of the form X/Y, where both X and Y are between 1 and 8.

(a) Define the relation **jump(Square1, Square2)** according to the knight jump on the chessboard. Assume that **Square1** is always instantiated to a square while **Square2** can be uninstantiated. For example:

        ?- jump(1/1, S).

        S = 3/2;

        S = 2/3;

        no

(b) Define the relation **knightpath(Path)** where **Path** is a list of squares that represent a legal path of a knight on the empty chessboard.

(c) Using this **knightpath** relation, write a question to find any knight's path of length 4 moves from square 2/1 to the opposite edge of the board (Y = 8) that goes through square 5/4 after the second move.

Summary

The examples of this chapter illustrate some strong points and characteristic features of Prolog programming:

- A database can be naturally represented as a set of Prolog facts.

- Prolog's mechanisms of querying and matching can be flexibly used for retrieving structured information from a database. In addition, utility procedures can be easily defined to further alleviate the interaction with a particular database.

- *Data abstraction* can be viewed as a programming technique that makes the use of complex data structures easier, and contributes to the clarity of programs. It is easy in Prolog to carry out the essential principles of data abstraction.

- Abstract mathematical constructs, such as automata, can often be readily translated into executable Prolog definitions.

- As in the case of eight queens, the same problem can be approached in different ways by varying the representation of the problem. Often, introducing redundancy into the representation saves computation. This entails trading space for time.

- Often, the key step toward a solution is to generalize the problem. Paradoxically, by considering a more general problem the solution may become easier to formulate.

chapter 5

Controlling Backtracking

We have already seen that a programmer can control the execution of a program through the ordering of clauses and goals. In this chapter we will look at another control facility, called 'cut', for preventing backtracking. The cut also extends the expressive power of Prolog and enables the definition of a kind of negation, called 'negation as failure' and associated with the 'closed world assumption'.

5.1 Preventing backtracking

Prolog will automatically backtrack if this is necessary for satisfying a goal. Automatic backtracking is a useful programming concept because it relieves the programmer of the burden of programming backtracking explicitly. On the other hand, uncontrolled backtracking may cause inefficiency in a program. Therefore we sometimes want to control, or to prevent, backtracking. We can do this in Prolog by using the 'cut' facility.

Let us first study the behaviour of a simple example program whose execution involves some unnecessary backtracking. We will identify those points at which the backtracking is useless and leads to inefficiency.

Consider the double-step function shown in Figure 5.1. The relation between X and Y can be specified by three rules:

Rule 1: if X < 3 then Y = 0

Rule 2: if 3 ≤ X and X < 6 then Y = 2

Rule 3: if 6 ≤ X then Y = 4

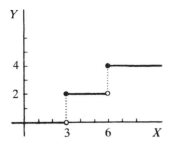

Figure 5.1 A double-step function.

This can be written in Prolog as a binary relation:

f(X, Y)

as follows:

f(X, 0) :- X < 3.	% Rule 1
f(X, 2) :- 3 =< X, X < 6.	% Rule 2
f(X, 4) :- 6 =< X.	% Rule 3

This program, of course, assumes that before f(X, Y) is executed X is already instantiated to a number, as this is required by the comparison operators.

We will make two experiments with this program. Each experiment will reveal some source of inefficiency in the program, and we will remove each source in turn by using the cut mechanism.

5.1.1 Experiment 1

Let us analyze what happens when the following question is posed:

?- f(1, Y),   2 < Y.

When executing the first goal, **f(1, Y)**, Y becomes instantiated to 0. So the second goal becomes

2 < 0

which fails, and so does the whole goal list. This is straightforward, but before admitting that the goal list is not satisfiable, Prolog tries, through backtracking, two useless alternatives. The detailed trace is shown in Figure 5.2.

The three rules about the f relation are mutually exclusive so that one of them at most will succeed. Therefore we, not Prolog, know that as soon as one rule succeeds there is no point in trying to use the others, as they are bound to fail. In the example of Figure 5.2, rule 1 has become known to succeed at the point indicated by 'CUT'. In order to prevent futile backtracking at this point we have to tell Prolog explicitly

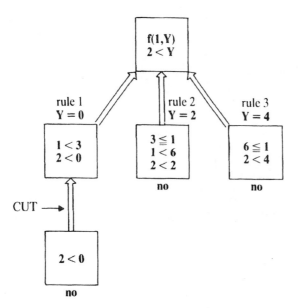

Figure 5.2   At the point marked 'CUT' we already know that the rules 2 and 3 are bound to fail.

not to backtrack. We can do this by using the cut mechanism. The 'cut' is written as ! and is inserted between goals as a kind of pseudo-goal. Our program, rewritten with cuts, is:

```
f( X, 0)  :-  X < 3, !.

f( X, 2)  :-  3 =< X, X < 6, !.

f( X, 4)  :-  6 =< X.
```

The ! symbol will now prevent backtracking at the points at which it appears in the program. If we now ask:

```
?-  f( 1, Y), 2 < Y.
```

Prolog will produce the same left-hand branch as in Figure 5.2. This branch will fail at the goal 2 < 0. Now Prolog will try to backtrack, but not beyond the point marked ! in the program. The alternative branches that correspond to 'rule 2' and 'rule 3' will not be generated.

The new program, equipped with cuts, is in general more efficient than the original version without cuts. When the execution fails, the new program will in general recognize this sooner than the original program.

To conclude, we have improved the efficiency by adding cuts. If the cuts are now removed in this example, the program will still produce the same result; it will perhaps only spend more time. In our case, by introducing the cut we only changed the procedural meaning of the program; that is, the results of the program were not affected. We will see later that using a cut may affect the results as well.

5.1.2   Experiment 2

Let us now perform a second experiment with the second version of our program. Suppose we ask:

    ?- f(7, Y).

    Y = 4

Let us analyze what has happened. All three rules were tried before the answer was obtained. This produced the following sequence of goals:

Try rule 1:   7 < 3 fails, backtrack and try rule 2 (cut was not reached)

Try rule 2:   3 ≦ 7 succeeds, but then 7 < 6 fails, backtrack and try rule 3 (cut was not reached)

Try rule 3:   6 ≦ 7 succeeds

This trace reveals another source of inefficiency. First it is established that X < 3 is not true (7 < 3 fails). The next goal is 3 =< X (3 =< 7 succeeds). But we know that once the first test has failed the second test is bound to succeed as it is the negation of the first. Therefore the second test is redundant and the corresponding goal can be omitted. The same is true about the goal 6 =< X in rule 3. This leads to the following, more economical formulation of the three rules:

    if X < 3 then Y = 0,
    otherwise if X < 6 then Y = 2,
    otherwise Y = 4.

We can now omit the conditions in the program that are guaranteed to be true whenever they are executed. This leads to the third version of the program:

    f(X, 0) :- X < 3, !.
    f(X, 2) :- X < 6, !.
    f(X, 4).

This program produces the same results as our original version, but is more efficient than both previous versions. But what happens if we *now* remove the cuts? The program becomes:

    f(X, 0) :- X < 3.
    f(X, 2) :- X < 6.
    f(X, 4).

This may produce multiple solutions, some of which are not correct. For example:

    ?- f(1, Y).

    Y = 0;

Y = 2;

Y = 4;

no

It is important to notice that, in contrast to the second version of the program, this time the cuts do not only affect the procedural behaviour, but also change the results of the program.

A more precise meaning of the cut mechanism is as follows:

Let us call the 'parent goal' the goal that matched the head of the clause containing the cut. When the cut is encountered as a goal it succeeds immediately, but it commits the system to all choices made between the time the 'parent goal' was invoked and the time the cut was encountered. All the remaining alternatives between the parent goal and the cut are discarded.

To clarify this definition consider a clause of the form:

H :- B1, B2, ..., Bm, !, ..., Bn.

Let us assume that this clause was invoked by a goal G that matched H. Then G is the parent goal. At the moment that the cut is encountered, the system has already found some solution of the goals **B1, ..., Bm**. When the cut is executed, this (current) solution of **B1, ..., Bm** becomes frozen and all possible remaining alternatives are discarded. Also, the goal G now becomes committed to this clause: any attempt to match G with the head of some other clause is precluded.

Let us apply these rules to the following example:

C :- P, Q, R, !, S, T, U.

C :- V.

A :- B, C, D.

?- A.

Here A, B, C, D, P, etc. have the syntax of terms. The cut will affect the execution of the goal C as illustrated by Figure 5.3. Backtracking will be possible within the goal list P, Q, R; however, as soon as the cut is reached, all alternative solutions of the goal list P, Q, R are suppressed. The alternative clause about C,

C :- V.

will also be discarded. However, backtracking will still be possible within the goal list S, T, U. The 'parent goal' of the clause containing the cut is the goal C in the clause:

A :- B, C, D.

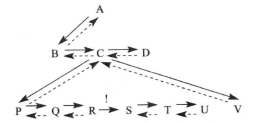

Figure 5.3 The effect of the cut on the execution. Starting with **A**, the solid arrows indicate the sequence of calls; the dashed arrows indicate backtracking. There is 'one way traffic' between **R** and **S**.

Therefore the cut will only affect the execution of the goal C. On the other hand, it will be 'invisible' from goal A. So automatic backtracking within the goal list B, C, D will remain active regardless of the cut within the clause used for satisfying C.

5.2 Examples using cut

5.2.1 Computing maximum

The procedure for finding the larger of two numbers can be programmed as a relation

    max(X, Y, Max)

where Max = X if X is greater than or equal to Y, and Max is Y if X is less than Y. This corresponds to the following two clauses:

    max(X, Y, X) :- X >= Y.

    max(X, Y, Y) :- X < Y.

These two rules are mutually exclusive. If the first one succeeds then the second one will fail. If the first one fails then the second must succeed. Therefore a more economical formulation, with 'otherwise', is possible:

    If X ≥ Y then Max = X,
    otherwise Max = Y.

This is written in Prolog using a cut as:

    max(X, Y, X) :- X >= Y, !.

    max(X, Y, Y).

It should be noted that the use of this procedure requires care. It is safe if in the goal **max(X,Y,Max)** the argument Max is not instantiated. The following example of incorrect use illustrates the problem:

```
?- max( 3, 1, 1).

yes
```

The following reformulation of **max** overcomes this limitation:

```
max( X, Y, Max) :-
    X >= Y, !, Max = X
    ;
    Max = Y.
```

5.2.2   Single-solution membership

We have been using the relation

```
member( X, L)
```

for establishing whether X is in list L. The program was:

```
member( X, [X | L] ).
member( X, [Y | L] ) :- member( X, L).
```

This is non-deterministic: if X occurs several times then any occurrence can be found. Let us now change **member** into a deterministic procedure which will find only the first occurrence. The change is simple: we only have to prevent back-tracking as soon as X is found, which happens when the first clause succeeds. The modified program is:

```
member( X, [X | L] ) :- !.
member( X, [Y | L] ) :- member( X, L).
```

This program will generate just one solution. For example:

```
?- member( X, [a,b,c] ).

X = a;

no
```

5.2.3   Adding an element to a list without duplication

Often we want to add an item X to a list L so that X is added only if X is not yet in L. If X is already in L then L remains the same because we do not want to have redundant duplicates in L. The **add** relation has three arguments:

```
add( X, L, L1)
```

where X is the item to be added, L is the list to which X is to be added and L1 is the resulting new list. Our rule for adding can be formulated as:

If X is a member of list L then L1 = L,
otherwise L1 is equal to L with X inserted.

It is easiest to insert X in front of L so that X becomes the head of L1. This is then programmed as follows:

add(X, L, L) :- member(X, L), !.

add(X, L, [X | L]).

The behaviour of this procedure is illustrated by the following example:

?- **add(a, [b,c], L).**

L = [a,b,c]

?- **add(X, [b,c], L).**

L = [b,c]
X = b

?- **add(a, [b,c,X], L).**

L = [b,c,a]
X = a

Similar to the foregoing example with **max**, **add(X, L1, L2)** is intended to be called with L2 uninstantiated. Otherwise the result may be unexpected: for example **add(a, [a], [a,a])** succeeds.

This example is instructive because we cannot easily program the 'non-duplicate add' without the use of cut or another construct derived from the cut. If we omit the cut in the foregoing program then the **add** relation will also add duplicate items. For example:

?- **add(a, [a,b,c], L).**

L = [a,b,c];

L = [a,a,b,c]

So the cut is necessary here to specify the intended relation, and not only to improve efficiency. The next example also illustrates this point.

5.2.4 Classification into categories

Assume we have a database of results of tennis games played by members of a club. The pairings were not arranged in any systematic way, so each player just played some other players. The results are in the program represented as facts like:

```
beat( tom, jim).
beat( ann, tom).
beat( pat, jim).
```

We want to define a relation

class(Player, Category)

that ranks the players into categories. We have just three categories:

winner: every player who won all his or her games is a winner
fighter: any player that won some games and lost some
sportsman: any player who lost all his or her games

For example, if all the results available are just those above then Ann and Pat are winners, Tom is a fighter and Jim is a sportsman.

It is easy to specify the rule for a fighter:

X is a fighter if
    there is some Y such that X beat Y and
    there is some Z such that Z beat X.

Now a rule for a winner:

X is a winner if
    X beat some Y and
    X was not beaten by anybody.

This formulation contains 'not' which cannot be directly expressed with our present Prolog facilities. So the formulation of **winner** appears trickier. The same problem occurs with **sportsman**. The problem can be circumvented by combining the definition of **winner** with that of **fighter**, and using the 'otherwise' connective. Such a formulation is:

If X beat somebody and X was beaten by somebody
    then X is a fighter,
    otherwise if X beat somebody
        then X is a winner,
        otherwise if X got beaten by somebody
            then X is a sportsman.

This formulation can be readily translated into Prolog. The mutual exclusion of the three alternative categories is indicated by the cuts:

```
class( X, fighter) :-
  beat( X, _),
  beat( _, X), !.
class( X, winner) :-
  beat( X, _), !.
```

```
class( X, sportsman) :-
    beat( _, X).
```

Notice that the cut in the clause for **winner** is not necessary. Care is needed when using such procedures containing cuts. Here is what can happen:

```
?- class( tom, C).

C = fighter;                        % As intended

no

?- class( tom, sportsman).

yes                                 % Not as intended
```

The call of **class** is safe if the second argument is not instantiated. Otherwise we may get an unintended result.

Exercises

5.1   Let a program be:

```
p( 1).
p( 2) :- !.
p( 3).
```

Write all Prolog's answers to the following questions:

(a) ?- p(X).

(b) ?- p(X), p(Y).

(c) ?- p(X), !, p(Y).

5.2   The following relation classifies numbers into three classes: positive, zero and negative:

```
class( Number, positive)  :-  Number > 0.
class( 0, zero).
class( Number, negative)  :-  Number < 0.
```

Define this procedure in a more efficient way using cuts.

5.3   Define the procedure

```
split( Numbers, Positives, Negatives)
```

which splits a list of numbers into two lists: positive ones (including zero) and negative ones. For example:

```
split( [3,−1,0,5,−2], [3,0,5], [−1,−2] )
```

Propose two versions: one with a cut and one without.

5.3   Negation as failure

'Mary likes all animals but snakes'. How can we say this in Prolog? It is easy to express one part of this statement: Mary likes any X if X is an animal. This is in Prolog:

    likes(mary, X) :- animal(X).

But we have to exclude snakes. This can be done by using a different formulation:

    If X is a snake then 'Mary likes X' is not true,
    otherwise if X is an animal then Mary likes X.

That something is not true can be said in Prolog by using a special goal, **fail**, which always fails, thus forcing the parent goal to fail. The above formulation is translated into Prolog, using **fail**, as follows:

    likes(mary, X) :-
       snake(X), !, fail.
    likes(mary, X) :-
       animal(X).

The first rule here will take care of snakes: if X is a snake then the cut will prevent backtracking (thus excluding the second rule) and **fail** will cause the failure. These two clauses can be written more compactly as one clause:

    likes(mary, X) :-
       snake(X), !, fail
       ;
       animal(X).

We can use the same idea to define the relation

    different(X, Y)

which is true if X and Y are different. We have to be more precise, however, because 'different' can be understood in several ways:

- X and Y are not literally the same;
- X and Y do not match;
- the values of arithmetic expressions X and Y are not equal.

Let us choose here that X and Y are different if they do not match. The key to saying this in Prolog is:

    If X and Y match then **different**(X, Y) fails,
    otherwise **different**(X, Y) succeeds.

We again use the cut and **fail** combination:

different(X, X) :- !, **fail**.

different(X, Y).

This can also be written as one clause:

different(X, Y) :-
    X = Y, !, **fail**
    ;
    true.

true is a goal that always succeeds.

These examples indicate that it would be useful to have a unary predicate 'not' such that

not(Goal)

is true if **Goal** is not true. We will now define the **not** relation as follows:

If **Goal** succeeds then **not**(Goal) fails,
otherwise **not**(Goal) succeeds.

This definition can be written in Prolog as:

not(P) :-
    P, !, **fail**
    ;
    true.

Henceforth, we will assume that **not** is a built-in Prolog procedure that behaves as defined here. We will also assume that **not** is defined as a prefix operator, so that we can also write the goal

not(snake(X))

as:

not snake(X)

Some Prolog implementations, in fact, support this notation. If not, then we can always define **not** ourselves. Alternatively, **not Goal** is written as \+ **Goal**. This more mysterious notation is also recommended in the Prolog standard for the following reason. **not** defined as failure, as here, does not exactly correspond to negation in mathematical logic. This difference can cause unexpected behaviour if **not** is used without care. This will be discussed later in the chapter.

Nevertheless, **not** is a useful facility and can often be used advantageously in place of cut. Our two examples can be rewritten with **not** as:

likes(mary, X) :-
    animal(X),
    not snake(X).

```
solution( [ ] ).

solution( [X/Y | Others] ) :-
   solution( Others),
   member( Y, [1,2,3,4,5,6,7,8] ),              % Usual member predicate
   not attacks( X/Y, Others).

attacks( X/Y, Others) :-
   member( X1/Y1, Others),
   ( Y1 = Y;
     Y1 is Y + X1 – X;
     Y1 is Y – X1 + X ).
```

Figure 5.4 Another eight queens program.

```
different( X, Y) :-
   not( X = Y).
```

This certainly looks better than our original formulations. It is more natural and is easier to read.

Our tennis classification program of the previous section can also be rewritten, using **not**, in a way that is closer to the initial definition of the three categories:

```
class( X, fighter) :-
   beat( X, _),
   beat( _, X).

class( X, winner) :-
   beat( X, _),
   not beat( _, X).

class( X, sportsman) :-
   beat( _, X),
   not beat( X, _).
```

As another example of the use of **not** let us reconsider program 1 for the eight queens problem of the previous chapter (Figure 4.7). We specified the **no_attack** relation between a queen and other queens. This relation can be formulated also as the negation of the **attack** relation. Figure 5.4 shows a program modified accordingly.

Exercises

5.4   Given two lists, **Candidates** and **RuledOut**, write a sequence of goals (using **member** and **not**) that will through backtracking find all the items in **Candidates** that are not in **RuledOut**.

5.5 Define the set subtraction relation

> **set_difference(Set1, Set2, SetDifference)**

where all the three sets are represented as lists. For example:

> **set_difference([a,b,c,d], [b,d,e,f], [a,c])**

5.6 Define the predicate

> **unifiable(List1, Term, List2)**

where **List2** is the list of all the members of **List1** that match **Term**, but are not instantiated by this matching. For example:

> **?- unifiable([X, b, t(Y)], t(a), List).**
>
> **List = [X, t(Y)]**

Note that X and Y have to remain uninstantiated although the matching with **t(a)** does cause their instantiation. Hint: Use **not(Term1 = Term2)**. If **Term1 = Term2** succeeds then **not(Term1 = Term2)** fails and the resulting instantiation is undone!

5.4   Problems with cut and negation

Using the cut facility we get something, but not for nothing. The advantages and disadvantages of using cut were illustrated by examples in the previous sections. Let us summarize, first the advantages:

(1) With cut we can often improve the efficiency of the program. The idea is to explicitly tell Prolog: do not try other alternatives because they are bound to fail.

(2) Using cut we can specify mutually exclusive rules; so we can express rules of the form:

> *if* condition P *then* conclusion Q,
> *otherwise* conclusion R

In this way, cut enhances the expressive power of the language.

The reservations against the use of cut stem from the fact that we can lose the valuable correspondence between the declarative and procedural meaning of programs. If there is no cut in the program we can change the order of clauses and goals, and this will only affect the efficiency or termination of the program, not the declarative meaning. On the other hand, in programs with cuts, a change in the order of clauses may affect the declarative meaning. This means that we can get different results. The following example illustrates:

```
p :- a, b.

p :- c.
```

The declarative meaning of this program is: p is true if and only if a and b are both true or c is true. This can be written as a logic formula:

p   <==>   (a & b) ∨ c

We can change the order of the two clauses and the declarative meaning remains the same. Let us now insert a cut:

```
p :- a, !, b.

p :- c.
```

The declarative meaning is now:

p   <==>   (a & b) ∨ (∼a & c)

If we swap the clauses,

```
p :- c.

p :- a, !, b.
```

then the meaning becomes:

p   <==>   c ∨ (a & b)

The important point is that when we use the cut facility we have to pay more attention to the procedural aspects. Unfortunately, this additional difficulty increases the probability of a programming error.

In our examples in the previous sections we have seen that sometimes the removal of a cut from the program can change the declarative meaning of the program. But there were also cases in which the cut had no effect on the declarative meaning. The use of cuts of the latter type is less delicate, and therefore cuts of this kind are sometimes called 'green cuts'. From the point of view of readability of programs, green cuts are 'innocent' and their use is quite acceptable. When reading a program, green cuts can simply be ignored.

On the contrary, cuts that do affect the declarative meaning are called 'red cuts'. Red cuts are the ones that make programs hard to understand, and they should be used with special care.

Cut is often used in combination with a special goal, **fail**. In particular, we defined the negation of a goal (**not**) as the failure of the goal. The negation, so defined, is just a special, more restricted way of using cut. For reasons of clarity we will prefer to use **not** instead of the *cut–fail* combination (whenever possible), because the negation is intuitively clearer than the *cut–fail* combination.

It should be noted that **not** may also cause problems, and so should also be used with care. The problem is that **not**, as defined here, does not correspond exactly to negation in mathematics. If we ask Prolog:

?- **not human(mary).**

Prolog will probably answer 'yes'. But this should not be understood as Prolog saying 'Mary is not human'. What Prolog really means to say is: 'There is not enough information in the program to prove that Mary is human'. This arises because when processing a **not** goal, Prolog does not try to prove this goal directly. Instead, it tries to prove the opposite, and if the opposite cannot be proved then Prolog assumes that the **not** goal succeeds.

Such reasoning is based on the so-called *closed world assumption*. According to this assumption *the world is closed* in the sense that everything that exists is stated in the program or can be derived from the program. Accordingly then, if something is not in the program (or cannot be derived from it) then it is not true and consequently its negation is true. This deserves special care because we do not normally assume that 'the world is closed'. When we do not explicitly enter the clause

human(mary).

into our program, we do not mean to imply that Mary is not human.

To further study the special care that **not** requires, consider the following example about restaurants:

good_standard(jeanluis).

expensive(jeanluis).

good_standard(francesco).

reasonable(Restaurant) :-
   not expensive(Restaurant).

If we ask:

?- **good_standard(X), reasonable(X).**

Prolog will answer:

X = **francesco**

If we ask apparently the same question

?- **reasonable(X), good_standard(X).**

then Prolog will answer:

no

The reader is invited to trace the program to understand why we get different answers. The key difference between both questions is that the variable X is, in the first case, already instantiated when **reasonable(X)** is executed, whereas X is not yet instantiated in the second case. The general hint is: **not Goal** works safely if the variables in **Goal** are instantiated at the time **not Goal** is called. Otherwise we may get unexpected results due to reasons explained in the sequel.

The problem with uninstantiated negated goals arises from unfortunate change of the quantification of variables in negation as failure. In the usual interpretation in Prolog, the question:

?- expensive(X).

means: Does there *exist* X such that **expensive(X)** is true? If yes, what is X? So X is *existentially* quantified. Accordingly Prolog answers X = **jeanluis**. But the question:

?- not expensive(X).

is not interpreted as: Does there exist X such that **not expensive(X)**? The expected answer would be X = **francesco**. But Prolog answers 'no' because negation as failure changes the quantification to universal. The question **not expensive(X)** is interpreted as:

not(exists X such that expensive(X))

This is equivalent to:

For *all* X: not expensive(X)

We have discussed problems with cut, which also indirectly occur in **not**, in detail. The intention has been to warn users about the necessary care, not to definitely discourage the use of cut. Cut is useful and often necessary. And after all, the kind of complications that are incurred by cut in Prolog commonly occur when programming in other languages as well.

Summary

- The cut facility prevents backtracking. It is used both to improve the efficiency of programs and to enhance the expressive power of the language.

- Efficiency is improved by explicitly telling Prolog (with cut) not to explore alternatives that we know are bound to fail.

- Cut makes it possible to formulate mutually exclusive conclusions through rules of the form:

    if Condition *then* Conclusion1 *otherwise* Conclusion2

- Cut makes it possible to introduce *negation as failure*: **not Goal** is defined through the failure of **Goal**.

- Two special goals are sometimes useful: **true** always succeeds, **fail** always fails.

- There are also some reservations against cut: inserting a cut may destroy the correspondence between the declarative and procedural meaning of a program. Therefore, it is part of good programming style to use cut with care and not to use it without reason.

- **not** defined through failure does not exactly correspond to negation in mathematical logic. Therefore, the use of **not** also requires special care.

References

The distinction between 'green cuts' and 'red cuts' was proposed by van Emden (1982). Le (1993) proposes a different negation for Prolog which is mathematically advantageous, but computationally more expensive.

Le, T.V. (1993) *Techniques of Prolog Programming*. John Wiley & Sons.
van Emden, M. (1982) Red and green cuts. *Logic Programming Newsletter*: **2**.

chapter 6

Input and Output

In this chapter we will investigate some built-in facilities for reading data from computer files and for outputting data to files. These procedures can also be used for formatting data objects in the program to achieve a desired output representation of these objects. We will also look at facilities for reading programs and for constructing and decomposing atoms.

6.1 Communication with files

The method of communication between the user and the program that we have been using up to now consists of user questions to the program and program answers in terms of instantiations of variables. This method of communication is simple and suffices to get the information in and out. However, it is often not quite sufficient because it is too rigid. Extensions to this basic communication method are needed in the following areas:

- input of data in forms other than questions – for example, in the form of English sentences,
- output of information in any format desired, and
- input from and output to any computer file or device and not just the user terminal.

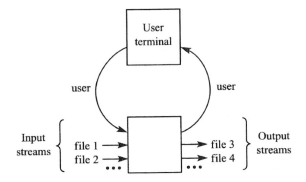

Figure 6.1 Communication between a Prolog program and several files.

Built-in predicates aimed at these extensions depend on the implementation of Prolog. We will study here a simple and handy repertoire of such predicates, which is part of many Prolog implementations. However, the implementation manual should be consulted for details and specificities. Many Prolog implementations provide various additional facilities not covered here. Such extra facilities handle windows, provide graphics primitives for drawing on the screen, input information from the mouse, and so on.

We will first consider the question of directing input and output to files, and then how data can be input and output in different forms.

Figure 6.1 shows a general situation in which a Prolog program communicates with several files. The program can, in principle, read data from several input files, also called *input streams*, and output data to several output files, also called *output streams*. Data coming from the user's terminal is treated as just another input stream. Data output to the terminal is, analogously, treated as another output stream. Both of these 'pseudo-files' are referred to by the name **user**. The names of other files can be chosen by the programmer according to the rules for naming files in the computer system used.

At any time during the execution of a Prolog program, only two files are 'active': one for input and one for output. These two files are called the *current input stream* and the *current output stream* respectively. At the beginning of execution these two streams correspond to the user's terminal. The current input stream can be changed to another file, **Filename**, by the goal:

    see(Filename)

Such a goal succeeds (unless there is something wrong with **Filename**) and causes, as a side effect, that input is switched from the previous input stream to **Filename**. So a typical example of using the **see** predicate is the following sequence of goals, which reads something from **file1** and then switches back to the terminal:

```
...
see( file1),
read_from_file( Information),
see( user),
...
```

The current output stream can be changed by a goal of the form:

tell(Filename)

A sequence of goals to output some information to file3, and then redirect succeeding output back to the terminal, is:

```
...
tell( file3),
write_on_file( Information),
tell( user),
...
```

The goal

seen

closes the current input file. The goal

told

closes the current output file.

We will assume here that files can only be processed sequentially although many Prolog implementations also handle files with random access. Sequential files behave in the same way as the terminal. Each request to read something from an input file will cause reading at the current position in the current input stream. After the reading, the current position will be, of course, moved to the next unread item. So the next request for reading will start reading at this new current position. If a request for reading is made at the end of a file, then the information returned by such a request is the atom **end_of_file**.

Writing is similar; each request to output information will append this information at the end of the current output stream. It is not possible to move backward and to overwrite part of the file.

We will here only consider 'text-files' – that is, files of characters. Characters are letters, digits and special characters. Some of them are said to be non-printable because when they are output on the terminal they do not appear on the screen. They may, however, have other effects, such as spacing between columns and lines.

There are two main ways in which files can be viewed in Prolog, depending on the form of information. One way is to consider the character as the basic element of the file. Accordingly, one input or output request will cause a single character to be read or written. We assume the built-in predicates for this are **get**, **get0** and **put**.

The other way of viewing a file is to consider bigger units of information as basic building blocks of the file. Such a natural bigger unit is the Prolog term. So each input/output request of this type would transfer a whole term from the current input stream or to the current output stream respectively. Predicates for transfer of terms are **read** and **write**. Of course, in this case, the information in the file has to be in a form that is consistent with the syntax of terms.

What kind of file organization is chosen will, of course, depend on the problem. Whenever the problem specification will allow the information to be naturally squeezed into the syntax of terms, we will prefer to use a file of terms. It will then be possible to transfer a whole meaningful piece of information with a single request. On the other hand, there are problems whose nature dictates some other organization of files. An example is the processing of natural language sentences, say, to generate a dialogue in English between the system and the user. In such cases, files will have to be viewed as sequences of characters that cannot be parsed into terms.

6.2   Processing files of terms

6.2.1   *read* and *write*

The built-in predicate **read** is used for reading terms from the current input stream. The goal

read(X)

will cause the next term, T, to be read, and this term will be matched with X. If X is a variable then, as a result, X will become instantiated to T. If matching does not succeed then the goal **read(X)** fails. The predicate **read** is deterministic, so in the case of failure there will be no backtracking to input another term. Each term in the input file must be followed by a full stop and a space or carriage-return.

If **read(X)** is executed when the end of the current input file has been reached then X will become instantiated to the atom **end_of_file**.

The built-in predicate **write** outputs a term. So the goal

write(X)

will output the term X on the current output file. X will be output in the same standard syntactic form in which Prolog normally displays values of variables. A useful feature of Prolog is that the **write** procedure 'knows' to display any term no matter how complicated it may be.

Typically, there are additional built-in predicates for formatting the output. They insert spaces and new lines into the output stream. The goal

tab(N)

causes N spaces to be output. The predicate **nl** (which has no arguments) causes the start of a new line at output.

The following examples will illustrate the use of these procedures.

Let us assume that we have a procedure that computes the cube of a number:

```
cube( N, C)  :-
    C is N * N * N.
```

Suppose we want to use this for calculating the cubes of a sequence of numbers. We could do this by a sequence of questions:

```
?- cube( 2, X).
```

X = 8

```
?- cube( 5, Y).
```

Y = 125

```
?- cube( 12, Z).
```

Z = 1728

For each number, we had to type in the corresponding goal. Let us now modify this program so that the **cube** procedure will read the data itself. Now the program will keep reading data and outputting their cubes until the atom **stop** is read:

```
cube  :-
    read( X),
    process( X).

process( stop)  :-  !.

process( N)  :-
    C is N * N * N,
    write( C),
    cube.
```

This is an example of a program whose declarative meaning is awkward to formulate. However, its procedural meaning is straightforward: to execute **cube**, first read X and then process it; if X = **stop** then everything has been done, otherwise write the cube of X and recursively call the **cube** procedure to process further data. A table of the cubes of numbers can be produced using this new procedure as follows:

```
?- cube.
2.
8
5.
125
12.
1728
stop.
yes
```

The numbers 2, 5 and 12 were typed in by the user on the terminal; the other numbers were output by the program. Note that each number entered by the user had to be followed by a full stop, which signals the end of a term.

It may appear that the above **cube** procedure could be simplified. However, the following attempt to simplify is not correct:

```
cube :-
   read( stop), !.

cube :-
   read( N),
   C is N * N * N,
   write( C),
   cube.
```

The reason why this is wrong can be seen easily if we trace the program with input data 5, say. The goal **read(stop)** will fail when the number is read, and this number will be lost for ever. The next **read** goal will input the next term. On the other hand, it could happen that the **stop** signal is read by the goal **read(N)**, which would then cause a request to multiply non-numeric data.

The **cube** procedure conducts interaction between the user and the program. In such cases it is usually desirable that the program, before reading new data from the terminal, signals to the user that it is ready to accept the information, and perhaps also says what kind of information it is expecting. This is usually done by sending a 'prompt' signal to the user before reading. Our **cube** procedure would be accordingly modified, for example, as follows:

```
cube :-
   write( 'Next item, please: '),
   read( X),
   process( X).

process( stop) :- !.

process( N) :-
   C is N * N * N,
   write( 'Cube of '), write( N), write( ' is '),
   write( C), nl,
   cube.
```

A conversation with this new version of **cube** would then be, for example, as follows:

```
?- cube.
Next item, please: 5.
Cube of 5 is 125
Next item, please: 12.
Cube of 12 is 1728
Next item, please: stop.
yes
```

Depending on the implementation, an extra request (like **ttyflush**, say) after writing the prompt might be necessary in order to force the prompt to actually appear on the screen before reading.

In the following sections we will look at some typical examples of operations that involve reading and writing.

6.2.2   Displaying lists

Besides the standard Prolog format for lists, there are several other natural forms for displaying lists which have advantages in some situations. The following procedure

```
writelist( L)
```

outputs a list L so that each element of L is written on a separate line:

```
writelist( [ ] ).

writelist( [X | L] ) :-
   write( X), nl,
   writelist( L).
```

If we have a list of lists, one natural output form is to write the elements of each list in one line. To this end, we will define the procedure **writelist2**. An example of its use is:

```
?- writelist2( [ [a,b,c], [d,e,f], [g,h,i] ] ).

a b c
d e f
g h i
```

A procedure that accomplishes this is:

```
writelist2( [ ] ).

writelist2( [L | LL] ) :-
   doline( L), nl,
   writelist2( LL).

doline( [ ] ).

doline( [X | L] ) :-
   write( X), tab( 1),
   doline( L).
```

A list of integer numbers can be sometimes conveniently shown as a bar graph. The following procedure, **bars**, will display a list in this form, assuming that the numbers in the list are sufficiently small. An example of using **bars** is:

```
?- bars( [3,4,6,5] ).
***
****
******
*****
```

The **bars** procedure can be defined as follows:

```
bars( [ ] ).

bars( [N | L] ) :-
   stars( N), nl,
   bars( L).

stars( N) :-
   N > 0,
   write( *),
   N1 is N − 1,
   stars( N1).

stars( N) :-
   N =< 0.
```

6.2.3 Processing a file of terms

A typical sequence of goals to process a whole file, F, would look something like this:

> ..., see(F), processfile, see(user), ...

Here **processfile** is a procedure to read and process each term in F, one after another, until the end of the file is encountered. A typical schema for **processfile** is:

```
processfile :-
   read( Term),              % Assuming Term not a variable
   process( Term).

process( end_of_file) :- !.  % All done

process( Term) :-
   treat( Term),             % Process current item
   processfile.              % Process rest of file
```

Here **treat(Term)** represents whatever is to be done with each term. An example would be a procedure to display on the terminal each term together with its consecutive number. Let us call this procedure **showfile**. It has to have an additional argument to count the terms read:

```
showfile( N) :-
   read( Term),
   show( Term, N).

show( end_of_file, _) :- !.

show( Term, N) :-
   write( N), tab( 2), write( Term), nl,
   N1 is N + 1,
   showfile( N1).
```

Exercises

6.1   Let **f** be a file of terms. Define a procedure

findterm(Term)

that displays on the terminal the first term in **f** that matches **Term**.

6.2   Let **f** be a file of terms. Write a procedure

findallterms(Term)

that displays on the terminal all the terms in **f** that match **Term**. Make sure that **Term** is not instantiated in the process (which could prevent its match with terms that occur later in the file).

6.3   Manipulating characters

A character is written on the current output stream with the goal

put(C)

where C is the ASCII code (a number between 0 and 127) of the character to be output. For example, the question

?- put(65), put(66), put(67).

would cause the following output:

ABC

65 is the ASCII code of 'A', 66 of 'B', 67 of 'C'.
      A single character can be read from the current input stream by the goal

get0(C)

This causes the current character to be read from the input stream, and the variable C becomes instantiated to the ASCII code of this character. A variation of the predicate get0 is **get**, which is used for reading non-blank characters. So the goal

get(C)

will cause the skipping over of all non-printable characters (blanks in particular) from the current input position in the input stream up to the first printable character. This character is then also read and C is instantiated to its ASCII code.
      As an example of using predicates that transfer single characters let us define a procedure, **squeeze**, to do the following: read a sentence from the current input stream, and output the same sentence reformatted so that multiple blanks between words are replaced by single blanks. For simplicity we will assume that any input

sentence processed by **squeeze** ends with a full stop and that words are separated simply by one or more blanks, but no other character. An acceptable input is then:

The   robot tried   to pour wine out   of the   bottle.

The goal **squeeze** would output this in the form:

The robot tried to pour wine out of the bottle.

The **squeeze** procedure will have a similar structure to the procedures for processing files in the previous section. First it will read the first character, output this character, and then complete the processing depending on this character. There are three alternatives that correspond to the following cases: the character is either a full stop, a blank or a letter. The mutual exclusion of the three alternatives is achieved in the program by cuts:

```
squeeze :-
   get0( C),
   put( C),
   dorest( C).

dorest( 46) :- !.                    % 46 is ASCII for full stop, all done

dorest( 32) :- !,                    % 32 is ASCII for blank
   get( C),                          % Skip other blanks
   put( C),
   dorest( C).

dorest( Letter) :-
   squeeze.
```

Exercise

6.3   Generalize the **squeeze** procedure to handle commas as well. All blanks immediately preceding a comma are to be removed, and we want to have one blank after each comma.

6.4   Constructing and decomposing atoms

It is often desirable to have information, read as a sequence of characters, represented in the program as an atom. There is a built-in predicate, **name**, which can be used to this end. **name** relates atoms and their ASCII encodings. Thus,

name(A, L)

is true if L is the list of ASCII codes of the characters in A. For example, name(zx232, [122,120,50,51,50])

is true. There are two typical uses of **name**:

(1)   given an atom, break it down into single characters;

(2)   given a list of characters, combine them into an atom.

An example of the first kind of application would be a program that deals with orders, taxis and drivers. These would be, in the program, represented by atoms such as:

order1, order2, driver1, driver2, taxia1, taxilux

The following predicate:

taxi(X)

tests whether an atom X represents a taxi:

```
taxi( X) :-
    name( X, Xlist),
    name( taxi, Tlist),
    conc( Tlist, _, Xlist).          % Is word 'taxi' prefix of X?
```

Predicates **order** and **driver** can be defined analogously.

The next example illustrates the use of combining characters into atoms. We will define a predicate:

getsentence(Wordlist)

that reads a free-form natural language sentence and instantiates **Wordlist** to some internal representation of the sentence. A natural choice for the internal representation, which would enable further processing of the sentence, is this: each word of the input sentence is represented as a Prolog atom; the whole sentence is represented as a list of atoms. For example, if the current input stream is:

Mary was pleased to see the robot fail.

then the goal **getsentence(Sentence)** will cause the instantiation:

Sentence = ['Mary', was, pleased, to, see, the, robot, fail]

For simplicity, we will assume that each sentence terminates with a full stop and that there are no punctuation symbols within the sentence.

The program is shown in Figure 6.2. The procedure **getsentence** first reads the current input character, **Char**, and then supplies this character to the procedure **getrest** to complete the job. **getrest** has to react properly according to three cases:

(1)   **Char** is the full stop: then everything has been read.

(2)   **Char** is the blank: ignore it, **getsentence** from rest of input.

```
/*
    Procedure getsentence reads in a sentence and combines the words into a list of atoms.
    For example

        getsentence( Wordlist)

    produces

        Wordlist = [ 'Mary', was, pleased, to, see, the, robot, fail]

    if the input sentence is:

        Mary was pleased to see the robot fail.

*/

getsentence( Wordlist) :-
    get0( Char),
    getrest( Char, Wordlist).

getrest( 46, [ ] ) :- !.                              % End of sentence: 46 = ASCII for '.'

getrest( 32, Wordlist) :- !,                          % 32 = ASCII for blank
    getsentence( Wordlist).                           % Skip the blank

getrest( Letter, [Word | Wordlist] ) :-
    getletters( Letter, Letters, Nextchar),           % Read letters of current word
    name( Word, Letters),
    getrest( Nextchar, Wordlist).

getletters( 46, [], 46) :- !.                         % End of word: 46 = full stop

getletters( 32, [], 32) :- !.                         % End of word: 32 = blank

getletters( Let, [Let | Letters], Nextchar) :-
    get0( Char),
    getletters( Char, Letters, Nextchar).
```

Figure 6.2   A procedure to transform a sentence into a list of atoms.

(3)   Char is a letter: first read the word, **Word**, which begins with Char, and then use **getsentence** to read the rest of the sentence, producing **Wordlist**. The cumulative result is the list [**Word | Wordlist**].

The procedure that reads the characters of one word is:

    getletters(Letter, Letters, Nextchar)

The three arguments are:

(1)   **Letter** is the current letter (already read) of the word being read.

(2)   **Letters** is the list of letters (starting with **Letter**) up to the end of the word.

(3)   **Nextchar** is the input character that immediately follows the word read. **Nextchar** must be a non-letter character.

We conclude this example with a comment on the possible use of the **getsentence** procedure. It can be used in a program to process text in natural language. Sentences represented as lists of words are in a form that is suitable for further processing in Prolog. A simple example is to look for certain keywords in input sentences. A much more difficult task would be to understand the sentence; that is, to extract from the sentence its meaning, represented in some chosen formalism. This is an important research area of Artificial Intelligence, and is introduced in Chapter 21.

Exercises

6.4   Define the relation

    starts(Atom, Character)

to check whether **Atom** starts with **Character**.

6.5   Define the procedure **plural** that will convert nouns into their plural form. For example:

    ?- plural(table, X).

    X = tables

6.6   Write the procedure

    search(KeyWord, Sentence)

that will, each time it is called, find a sentence in the current input file that contains the given **KeyWord**. **Sentence** should be in its original form, represented as a sequence of characters or as an atom (procedure **getsentence** of this section can be accordingly modified).

6.5   Reading programs

We can communicate our programs to the Prolog system by means of built-in predicates that *consult* or *compile* files with programs. The details of 'consulting' and compiling files depend on the implementation of Prolog. Here we look at some basic facilities that are available in many Prologs.

We tell Prolog to read a program from a file F with a goal of the form **consult(F)**, for example:

    ?- consult(program3).

Depending on the implementation, the file name **program3** will possibly have to have an extension indicating that it is a Prolog program file. The effect of this goal will be that all the clauses in file **program3** are read and loaded into the memory. So they will be used by Prolog when answering further questions from the user. Another file may be 'consulted' at some later time during the same session. Basically, the effect is again that the clauses from this new file are added into the memory. However, details depend on the implementation and other circumstances. If the new file contains clauses about a procedure defined in the previously consulted file, then the new clauses may be simply added at the end of the current set of clauses, or the previous definition of this procedure may be entirely replaced by the new one.

Several files may be consulted by the same **consult** goal, for example:

> ?- consult([program3, program4, queens]).

Such a question can also be written more simply as:

> ?- [program3, program4, queens].

Consulted programs are used by a Prolog *interpreter*. If a Prolog implementation also features a *compiler*, then programs can be loaded in a compiled form. This enables more efficient execution with a typical speed-up factor of 5 or 10 between the interpreted and compiled code. Programs are loaded into memory in the compiled form by the built-in predicate **compile**, for example:

> ?- compile(program3).

or

> ?- compile([program4, queens, program6]).

Compiled programs are more efficiently executed, but interpreted programs are easier to debug because they can be inspected and traced by Prolog's debugging facilities. Therefore an interpreter is typically used in the program development phase, and a compiler is used with the final program.

It should be noted, again, that the details of consulting and compiling files depend on the implementation of Prolog. Usually a Prolog implementation also allows the user to enter and edit the program interactively.

Summary

- Input and output (other than that associated with querying the program) is done using built-in procedures. This chapter introduced a simple and practical repertoire of such procedures that can be found in many Prolog implementations.

- This repertoire assumes that files are sequential. There is the *current input stream* and the *current output stream*. The user terminal is treated as a file called **user**.

- Switching between streams is done by:

see(File)	**File becomes the current input stream**
tell(File)	**File becomes the current output stream**
seen	close the current input stream
told	close the current output stream

- Files are read and written in two ways:

  as sequences of characters
  as sequences of terms

  Built-in procedures for reading and writing characters and terms are:

read(Term)	input next term
write(Term)	output **Term**
put(CharCode)	output character with the given ASCII code
get0(CharCode)	input next character
get(CharCode)	input next 'printable' character

- Two procedures help formatting:

nl	output new line
tab(N)	output N blanks

- The procedure **name(Atom, CodeList)** decomposes and constructs atoms. **CodeList** is the list of ASCII codes of the characters in **Atom.**

- Many Prolog implementations provide additional facilities to handle non-sequential files, windows, provide graphics primitives, input information from the mouse, etc.

Reference to Prolog standard

For some of the predicates mentioned in this chapter, ISO standard for Prolog (Deransart *et al.* 1996) recommends different names from those used in most Prolog implementations. However, the predicates are conceptually the same, so compatibility is only a matter of renaming. The concerned predicates in this chapter are: **see(Filename)**, **tell(Filename)**, **get(Code)**, **put(Code)**, **name(Atom,CodeList)**. The corresponding predicate names in the standard are: **set_input(Filename)**, **set_output(Filename)**, **get_code(Code)**, **put_code(Code)**, **atom_codes(Atom,CodeList)**.

Deransart, P., Ed-Bdali, A. and Ceroni, L. (1996) *Prolog: The Standard.* Berlin: Springer-Verlag.

chapter 7

More Built-in Predicates

In this chapter we will examine some more built-in predicates for advanced Prolog programming. These features enable the programming of operations that are not possible using only the features introduced so far. One set of such predicates manipulate terms: testing whether some variable has been instantiated to an integer, taking terms apart, constructing new terms, etc. Another useful set of procedures manipulates the 'database': they add new clauses to the program or remove existing ones.

The built-in predicates largely depend on the implementation of Prolog. However, the predicates discussed in this chapter are provided by many Prolog implementations. Various implementations may provide additional features.

7.1   Testing the type of terms

7.1.1   Predicates *var, nonvar, atom, integer, float, number, atomic, compound*

Terms may be of different types: variable, integer, atom, etc. If a term is a variable then it can be, at some point during the execution of the program, instantiated or uninstantiated. Further, if it is instantiated, its value can be an atom, a structure, etc. It is sometimes useful to know what the type of this value is. For example, we may want to add the values of two variables, X and Y, by:

Z is X + Y

Before this goal is executed, X and Y have to be instantiated to numbers. If we are not sure that X and Y will indeed be instantiated to numbers at this point then we should check this in the program before arithmetic is done.

To this end we can use the built-in predicate **number**. number(X) is true if X is a number or if it is a variable whose value is a number. We say that X must 'currently stand for' a number. The goal of adding X and Y can then be protected by the following test on X and Y:

..., **number(X), number(Y), Z is X + Y, ...**

If X and Y are not both numbers then no arithmetic will be attempted. So the **number** goals 'guard' the goal Z is X + Y before meaningless execution.

Built-in predicates of this sort are: **var, nonvar, atom, integer, float, number, atomic, compound**. Their meaning is as follows:

var(X)	succeeds if X is currently an uninstantiated variable
nonvar(X)	succeeds if X is not a variable, or X is an already instantiated variable
atom(X)	is true if X currently stands for an atom
integer(X)	is true if X currently stands for an integer
float(X)	is true if X currently stands for a real number
number(X)	is true if X currently stands for a number
atomic(X)	is true if X currently stands for a number or an atom
compound(X)	is true if X currently stands for a compound term (a structure)

The following example questions to Prolog illustrate the use of these built-in predicates:

?- **var(Z), Z = 2.**

Z = 2

?- **Z = 2, var(Z).**

no

?- **integer(Z), Z = 2.**

no

?- **Z = 2, integer(Z), nonvar(Z).**

Z = 2

?- **atom(3.14).**

no

```
?-  atomic( 3.14).

yes

?-  atom( ==> ).

yes

?-  atom( p(1) ).

no

?-  compound ( 2 + X)

yes
```

We will illustrate the need for **atom** by an example. We would like to count how many times a given atom occurs in a given list of objects. To this purpose we will define a procedure:

```
count( A, L, N)
```

where A is the atom, L is the list and N is the number of occurrences. The first attempt to define **count** could be:

```
count( _, [], 0).
count( A, [A | L], N)  :-  !,
   count( A, L, N1),                  % N1 = number of occurrences in tail
   N is N1 + 1.
count( A, [_ | L], N)  :-
   count( A, L, N).
```

Now let us try to use this procedure on some examples:

```
?-  count( a, [a,b,a,a], N).

N = 3

?-  count( a, [a,b,X,Y], Na).

Na = 3

...

?-  count( b, [a,b,X,Y], Nb).

Nb = 3

...

?-  L = [a, b, X, Y], count( a, L, Na), count( b, L, Nb).

Na = 3
Nb = 1
X = a
Y = a

...
```

In the last example, X and Y both became instantiated to a and therefore we only got Nb = 1; but this is not what we had in mind. We are interested in the number of real occurrences of the given *atom*, and not in the number of terms that *match* this atom. According to this more precise definition of the count relation we have to check whether the head of the list is an atom. The modified program is as follows:

```
count( _, [], 0).

count( A, [B | L], N) :-
    atom( B), A = B, !,        % B is atom A?
    count( A, L, N1),          % Count in tail
    N is N1 + 1
    ;
    count( A, L, N).           % Otherwise just count the tail
```

The following, more complex programming exercise in solving cryptarithmetic puzzles makes use of the **nonvar** predicate.

7.1.2   A cryptarithmetic puzzle using *nonvar*

A popular example of a cryptarithmetic puzzle is

```
  D O N A L D
+ G E R A L D
  ───────────
  R O B E R T
```

The problem here is to assign decimal digits to the letters D, O, N, etc., so that the above sum is valid. All letters have to be assigned different digits, otherwise trivial solutions are possible – for example, all letters equal zero.

We will define a relation

sum(N1, N2, N)

where N1, N2 and N represent the three numbers of a given cryptarithmetic puzzle. The goal **sum(N1, N2, N)** is true if there is an assignment of digits to letters such that N1 + N2 = N.

The first step toward a solution is to decide how to represent the numbers N1, N2 and N in the program. One way of doing this is to represent each number as a list of decimal digits. For example, the number 225 would be represented by the list [2,2,5]. As these digits are not known in advance, an uninstantiated variable will stand for each digit. Using this representation, the problem can be depicted as:

```
  [D, O, N, A, L, D]
+ [G, E, R, A, L, D]
= [R, O, B, E, R, T]
```

Number1 $= [D_{11}, D_{12}, \ldots, D_{1i}, \ldots]$
Number2 $= [D_{21}, D_{22}, \ldots, D_{2i}, \ldots]$
Number3 $= [D_{31}, D_{32}, \ldots, D_{3i}, \ldots]$

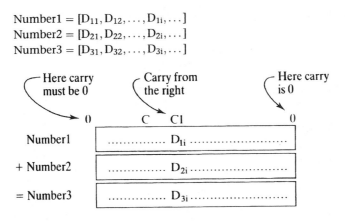

Figure 7.1 Digit by digit summation. The relations at the indicated ith digit position are:
$D_{3i} = (C1 + D_{1i} + D_{2i}) \bmod 10;\ C = (C1 + D_{1i} + D_{2i}) \text{ div } 10.$

The task is to find such an instantiation of the variables D, O, N, etc., for which the sum is valid. When the **sum** relation has been programmed, the puzzle can be stated to Prolog by the question:

?- **sum([D,O,N,A,L,D], [G,E,R,A,L,D], [R,O,B,E,R,T]).**

To define the **sum** relation on lists of digits, we have to implement the actual rules for doing summation in the decimal number system. The summation is done digit by digit, starting with the right-most digits, continuing toward the left, always taking into account the carry digit from the right. It is also necessary to maintain a set of available digits; that is, digits that have not yet been used for instantiating variables already encountered. So, in general, besides the three numbers N1, N2 and N, some additional information is involved, as illustrated in Figure 7.1:

- carry digit before the summation of the numbers;
- carry digit after the summation;
- set of digits available before the summation;
- remaining digits, not used in the summation.

To formulate the **sum** relation we will use, once again, the principle of generalization of the problem: we will introduce an auxiliary, more general relation, **sum1. sum1** has some extra arguments, which correspond to the foregoing additional information:

sum1(N1, N2, N, C1, C, Digits1, Digits)

N1, N2 and N are our three numbers, as in the **sum** relation, C1 is carry from the right (before summation of N1 and N2), and C is carry to the left (after the summation). The following example illustrates:

?- sum1([H,E], [6,E], [U,S], 1, 1, [1,3,4,7,8,9], Digits).

H = 8
E = 3
S = 7
U = 4
Digits = [1,9]

This corresponds to the following summation:

$$1 \leftarrow \quad \leftarrow 1$$

$$
\begin{array}{cc}
8 & 3 \\
6 & 3 \\
\hline
4 & 7
\end{array}
$$

As Figure 7.1 shows, C1 and C have to be 0 if N1, N2 and N are to satisfy the **sum** relation. **Digits1** is the list of available digits for instantiating the variables in N1, N2 and N; **Digits** is the list of digits that were not used in the instantiation of these variables. Since we allow the use of any decimal digit in satisfying the **sum** relation, the definition of **sum** in terms of **sum1** is as follows:

sum(N1, N2, N) :-
    sum1(N1, N2, N, 0, 0, [0,1,2,3,4,5,6,7,8,9], _).

The burden of the problem has now shifted to the **sum1** relation. This relation is, however, general enough that it can be defined recursively. We will assume, without loss of generality, that the three lists representing the three numbers are of equal length. Our example problem, of course, satisfies this constraint; if not, a 'shorter' number can be prefixed by zeros.

The definition of **sum1** can be divided into two cases:

(1)   The three numbers are represented by empty lists. Then:

   sum1([ ], [ ], [ ], C, C, Digs, Digs).

(2)   All three numbers have some left-most digit and the remaining digits on their right. So they are of the form:

   [D1 | N1],   [D2 | N2],   [D | N]

In this case two conditions must be satisfied:

(a)   The three numbers N1, N2 and N have to satisfy the **sum1** relation, giving some carry digit, C2, to the left, and leaving some unused subset of decimal digits, **Digs2**.

(b)   The left-most digits D1, D2 and D, and the carry digit C2 have to satisfy the relation indicated in Figure 7.1: C2, D1 and D2 are added giving D and a carry to the left. This condition will be formulated in our program as a relation **digitsum**.

Translating this case into Prolog we have:

```
sum1( [D1 | N1], [D2 | N2], [D | N], C1, C, Digs1, Digs) :-
    sum1( N1, N2, N, C1, C2, Digs1, Digs2),
    digitsum( D1, D2, C2, D, C, Digs2, Digs).
```

It only remains to define the **digitsum** relation in Prolog. There is one subtle detail that involves the use of the metalogical predicate **nonvar**. D1, D2 and D have to be decimal digits. If any of them is not yet instantiated then it has to become instantiated to one of the digits in the list **Digs2**. This digit has to be deleted from the set of available digits. If D1, D2 or D is already instantiated then, of course, none

---

```
% Solving cryptarithmetic puzzles

sum( N1, N2, N) :-                              % Numbers represented as lists of digits
    sum1( N1, N2, N,
          0, 0,                                % Carries from right and to left both 0
          [0,1,2,3,4,5,6,7,8,9], _).           % All digits available

sum1( [ ], [ ], [ ], C, C, Digits, Digits).

sum1( [D1 | N1], [D2 | N2], [D | N], C1, C, Digs1, Digs) :-
    sum1( N1, N2, N, C1, C2, Digs1, Digs2),
    digitsum( D1, D2, C2, D, C, Digs2, Digs).

digitsum( D1, D2, C1, D, C, Digs1, Digs) :-
    del_var( D1, Digs1, Digs2),                % Select an available digit for D1
    del_var( D2, Digs2, Digs3),                % Select an available digit for D2
    del_var( D, Digs3, Digs),                  % Select an available digit for D
    S is D1 + D2 + C1,
    D is S mod 10,                             % Remainder
    C is S // 10.                              % Integer division

del_var( A, L, L) :-
    nonvar( A), !.                             % A already instantiated

del_var( A, [A | L], L).                       % Delete the head

del_var( A, [B | L], [B | L1] ) :-
    del_var( A, L, L1).                        % Delete from tail

% Some puzzles

puzzle1( [D,O,N,A,L,D],
         [G,E,R,A,L,D],
         [R,O,B,E,R,T] ).

puzzle2( [0,S,E,N,D],
         [0,M,O,R,E],
         [M,O,N,E,Y] ).
```

Figure 7.2 A program for cryptarithmetic puzzles.

of the available digits will be spent. This is realized in the program as a non-deterministic deletion of an item from a list. If this item is non-variable then nothing is deleted (no instantiation occurs). This is programmed as:

```
del_var( Item, List, List) :-
    nonvar( Item), !.                          % Item already instantiated

del_var( Item, [Item | List], List).          % Delete the head

del_var( Item, [A | List], [A | List1] ) :-
    del_var( Item, List, List1).               % Delete Item from tail
```

A complete program for cryptarithmetic puzzles is shown in Figure 7.2. The program also includes the definition of two puzzles. The question to Prolog about DONALD, GERALD and ROBERT, using this program, would be:

```
?- puzzle1( N1, N2, N), sum( N1, N2, N).
```

Sometimes this puzzle is made easier by providing part of the solution as an additional constraint that D be equal 5. The puzzle in this form could be communicated to Prolog using sum1:

```
?- sum1( [5,O,N,A,L,5],
         [G,E,R,A,L,5],
         [R,O,B,E,R,T],
         0, 0, [0,1,2,3,4,6,7,8,9], _).
```

It is interesting that in both cases there is only one solution. That is, there is only one way of assigning digits to letters.

Exercises

7.1   Write a procedure **simplify** to symbolically simplify summation expressions with numbers and symbols (lower-case letters). Let the procedure rearrange the expressions so that all the symbols precede numbers. These are examples of its use:

```
?- simplify( 1 + 1 + a, E).
```
$E = a + 2$

```
?- simplify( 1 + a + 4 + 2 + b + c, E).
```
$E = a + b + c + 7$

```
?- simplify( 3 + x + x, E).
```
$E = 2*x + 3$

7.2   Define the procedure:

add_to_tail(Item, List)

to store a new element into a list. Assume that all of the elements that can be stored are non-variables. List contains all the stored elements followed by a tail that is not instantiated and can thus accommodate new elements. For example, let the existing elements stored be **a**, **b** and **c**. Then

> **List = [a, b, c | Tail]**

where **Tail** is a variable. The goal

> **add_to_tail(d, List)**

will cause the instantiation

> **Tail = [d | NewTail]**   and   **List = [a, b, c, d | NewTail]**

Thus the structure can, in effect, grow by accepting new items. Define also the corresponding membership relation.

7.2   Constructing and decomposing terms: =.., *functor, arg, name*

There are three built-in predicates for decomposing terms and constructing new terms: **functor**, **arg** and '=..'. We will first look at =.., which is written as an infix operator and reads as 'univ'. The goal

> **Term =.. L**

is true if L is a list that contains the principal functor of **Term**, followed by its arguments. The following examples illustrate:

> **?- f(a, b) =.. L.**
>
> **L = [f, a, b]**
>
> **?- T =.. [rectangle, 3, 5].**
>
> **T = rectangle(3, 5)**
>
> **?- Z =.. [p, X, f(X,Y)].**
>
> **Z = p(X, f(X,Y))**

Why would we want to decompose a term into its components – its functor and its arguments? Why construct a new term from a given functor and arguments? The following example illustrates the need for this.

Let us consider a program that manipulates geometric figures. Figures are squares, rectangles, triangles, circles, etc. They can, in the program, be represented as terms such that the functor indicates the type of figure, and the arguments specify the size of the figure, as follows:

> **square(Side)**
> **triangle(Side1, Side2, Side3)**
> **circle(R)**

One operation on such figures can be enlargement. We can implement this as a three-argument relation

    enlarge(Fig, Factor, Fig1)

where Fig and Fig1 are geometric figures of the same type (same functor), and the parameters of Fig1 are those of Fig multiplicatively enlarged by Factor. For simplicity, we will assume that all the parameters of Fig are already known; that is, instantiated to numbers, and so is Factor. One way of programming the **enlarge** relation is:

    enlarge(square(A), F, square(A1)) :-
        A1 is F*A.

    enlarge(circle(R), F, circle(R1)) :-
        R1 is F*R1.

    enlarge(rectangle(A,B), F, rectangle(A1,B1)) :-
        A1 is F*A, B1 is F*B.

    ...

This works, but it is awkward when there are many different figure types. We have to foresee all types that may possibly occur. Thus, we need an extra clause for each type although each clause says essentially the same thing: take the parameters of the original figure, multiply all the parameters by the factor, and make a figure of the same type with new parameters.

One (unsuccessful) attempt to handle, at least, all one-parameter figures with one clause could be:

    enlarge(Type(Par), F, Type(Par1)) :-
        Par1 is F*Par.

However, this is normally not allowed in Prolog because the functor has to be an atom; so the variable Type would not be accepted syntactically as a functor. The correct method is to use the predicate '=..'. Then the **enlarge** procedure can be stated completely generally, for any type of object, as follows:

    enlarge(Fig, F, Fig1) :-
        Fig =.. [Type | Parameters],
        multiplylist(Parameters, F, Parameters1),
        Fig1 =.. [Type | Parameters1].

    multiplylist([], _, []).

    multiplylist([X | L], F, [X1 | L1]) :-
        X1 is F*X, multiplylist(L, F, L1).

Our next example of using the '=..' predicate comes from symbolic manipulation of formulas where a frequent operation is to substitute some subexpression by another expression. We will define the relation

    substitute(Subterm, Term, Subterm1, Term1)

as follows: if all occurrences of **Subterm** in **Term** are substituted by **Subterm1** then we get **Term1**. For example:

?- **substitute(sin(x), 2*sin(x)*f(sin(x)), t, F).**

F = 2*t*f(t)

By 'occurrence' of **Subterm** in **Term** we will mean something in **Term** that *matches* Subterm. We will look for occurrences from top to bottom. So the goal

?- **substitute(a+b, f(a, A+B), v, F).**

will produce

F = f(a, v)		**F = f(a, v+v)**
A = a	and not	**A = a+b**
B = b		**B = a+b**

In defining the **substitute** relation we have to consider the following decisions depending on the case:

If **Subterm = Term** then **Term1 = Subterm1**;
otherwise if **Term** is 'atomic' (not a structure)
  then **Term1 = Term** (nothing to be substituted),
  otherwise the substitution is to be carried out on the arguments of **Term**.

These rules can be converted into a Prolog program, shown in Figure 7.3.

....

```
% substitute( Subterm, Term, Subterm1, Term1):
%    if all occurrences of Subterm in Term are substituted with Subterm1 then we get Term1.

% Case 1: Substitute whole term

substitute( Term, Term, Term1, Term1)  :-  !.

% Case 2: Nothing to substitute if Term atomic

substitute( _, Term, _, Term) :-
   atomic( Term), !.

% Case 3: Do substitution on arguments

substitute( Sub, Term, Sub1, Term1) :-
   Term =.. [F | Args],                          % Get arguments
   substlist( Sub, Args, Sub1, Args1),           % Perform substitution on them
   Term1 =.. [F | Args1].

substlist( _, [], _, [] ).

substlist( Sub, [Term | Terms], Sub1, [Term1 | Terms1] ) :-
   substitute( Sub, Term, Sub1, Term1),
   substlist( Sub, Terms, Sub1, Terms1).
```

....

Figure 7.3 A procedure for substituting a subterm of a term by another subterm.

Terms that are constructed by the '=..' predicate can, of course, be also used as goals. The advantage of this is that the program itself can, during execution, generate and execute goals of forms that were not necessarily foreseen at the time of writing the program. A sequence of goals illustrating this effect would be something like the following:

obtain(Functor),
compute(Arglist),
Goal =.. [Functor | Arglist],
Goal

Here, **obtain** and **compute** are some user-defined procedures for getting the components of the goal to be constructed. The goal is then constructed by '=..', and invoked for execution by simply stating its name, **Goal**.

Some implementations of Prolog may require that all the goals, as they appear in the program, are *syntactically* either atoms or structures with an atom as the principal functor. Thus a variable, regardless of its eventual instantiation, in such a case may not be syntactically acceptable as a goal. This problem is circumvented by another built-in predicate, **call**, whose argument is the goal to be executed. Accordingly, the above example would be rewritten as:

    . . .
Goal =.. [Functor | Arglist],
call(Goal)

Sometimes we may want to extract from a term just its principal functor or one of its arguments. We can, of course, use the '=..' relation. But it can be neater, and also more efficient, to use one of the other two built-in procedures for manipulating terms: **functor** and **arg**. Their meaning is as follows: a goal

functor(Term, F, N)

is true if F is the principal functor of **Term** and N is the arity of F. A goal

arg(N, Term, A)

is true if A is the Nth argument in **Term**, assuming that arguments are numbered from left to right starting with 1. The following examples illustrate:

?- functor(t(f(X), X, t), Fun, Arity).

Fun = t
Arity = 3

?- arg(2, f(X, t(a), t(b)), Y).

Y = t(a)

?- functor(D, date, 3),
**   arg(1, D, 29),**
**   arg(2, D, june),**
**   arg(3, D, 1982).**

D = date(29, june, 1982)

The last example shows a special application of the **functor** predicate. The goal **functor(D, date, 3)** generates a 'general' term whose principal functor is **date** with three arguments. The term is general in that the three arguments are uninstantiated variables whose names are generated by Prolog. For example:

> **D = date(_5, _6, _7)**

These three variables are then instantiated in the example above by the three **arg** goals.

Related to this set of built-in predicates is the predicate **name** for constructing/decomposing atoms, introduced in Chapter 6. We will repeat its meaning here for completeness.

> **name(A, L)**

is true if L is the list of ASCII codes of the characters in atom A.

Exercises

7.3   Define the predicate **ground(Term)** so that it is true if **Term** does not contain any uninstantiated variables.

7.4   The **substitute** procedure of this section only produces the 'outer-most' substitution when there are alternatives. Modify the procedure so that all possible alternative substitutions are produced through backtracking. For example:

> **?- substitute(a+b, f(A+B), new, NewTerm).**
>
> **A = a**
> **B = b**
> **NewTerm = f(new);**
>
> **A = a+b**
> **B = a+b**
> **NewTerm = f(new+new)**

Our original version only finds the first answer.

7.5   Define the relation

> **subsumes(Term1, Term2)**

so that **Term1** is more general than **Term2**. For example:

> **?- subsumes(X, c).**
>
> **yes**
>
> **?- subsumes(g(X), g(t(Y))).**
>
> **yes**
>
> **?- subsumes(f(X,X), f(a,b)).**
>
> **no**

7.3   Various kinds of equality and comparison

When do we consider two terms to be equal? Until now we have introduced three kinds of equality in Prolog. The first was based on matching, written as:

X = Y

This is true if X and Y match. Another type of equality was written as:

X is E

This is true if X matches the value of the arithmetic expression E. We also had:

E1 =:= E2

This is true if the values of the arithmetic expressions E1 and E2 are equal. In contrast, when the values of two arithmetic expressions are not equal, we write:

E1 =\= E2

Sometimes we are interested in a stricter kind of equality: the *literal equality* of two terms. This kind of equality is implemented as another built-in predicate written as an infix operator '==':

T1 == T2

This is true if terms T1 and T2 are identical; that is, they have exactly the same structure and all the corresponding components are the same. In particular, the names of the variables also have to be the same. The complementary relation is 'not identical', written as:

T1 \== T2

Here are some examples:

?- **f(a, b) == f(a, b).**

yes

?- **f(a, b) == f(a, X).**

no

?- **f(a, X) == f(a, Y).**

no

?- **X \== Y.**

yes

?- **t(X, f(a,Y)) == t(X, f(a,Y)).**

yes

As an example, let us redefine the relation

count(Term, List, N)

from Section 7.1. This time let N be the number of literal occurrences of the term **Term** in a list **List**:

```
count( _, [ ], 0).

count( Term, [Head | L ], N)  :-
  Term == Head, !,
  count( Term, L, N1),
  N is N1 + 1
  ;
  count( Term, L, N).
```

We have already seen predicates that compare terms arithmetically, for example X+2 < 5. Another set of built-in predicates compare terms alphabetically and thus define an ordering relation on terms. For example, the goal

```
X @< Y
```

is read: term X precedes term Y. The precedence between simple terms is determined by alphabetical or numerical ordering. The precedence between structures is determined by the precedence of their principal functors. If the principal functors are equal, then the precedence between the top-most, left-most functors in the subterms in X and Y decides. Examples are:

```
?- paul @< peter.

yes

?- f(2) @< f(3).

yes

?- g(2) @< f(3).

no

?- g(2) @>= f(3).

yes

?- f( a, g(b), c) @< f( a, h(a), a).

yes
```

All the built-in predicates in this family are @<, @=<, @>, @>= with their obvious meanings.

7.4   Database manipulation

According to the relational model of databases, a database is a specification of a set of relations. A Prolog program can be viewed as such a database: the specification of relations is partly explicit (facts) and partly implicit (rules). Some built-in predicates make it possible to update this database during the execution of the program. This is done by adding (during execution) new clauses to the program or by deleting existing clauses. Predicates that serve these purposes are **assert**, **asserta**, **assertz** and **retract**.

A goal

assert(C)

always succeeds and, as its side effect, causes a clause C to be 'asserted' – that is, added to the database. A goal

retract(C)

does the opposite: it deletes a clause that matches C. The following conversation with Prolog illustrates:

?- crisis.

no

?- assert(crisis).

yes

?- crisis.

yes

?- retract(crisis).

yes

?- crisis.

no

Clauses thus asserted act exactly as part of the 'original' program. The following example shows the use of **assert** and **retract** as one method of handling changing situations. Let us assume that we have the following program about weather:

nice :-
   sunshine, not raining.

funny :-
   sunshine, raining.

disgusting :-
   raining, fog.

raining.

fog.

The following conversation with this program will gradually update the database:

?- nice.

no

```
?-  disgusting.

yes

?-  retract( fog).

yes

?-  disgusting.

no

?-  assert( sunshine).

yes

?-  funny.

yes

?-  retract( raining).

yes

?-  nice.

yes
```

Clauses of any form can be asserted or retracted. However, depending on the implementation of Prolog, it may be required that predicates manipulated through assert/retract be declared as *dynamic*, using the directive **dynamic(PredicateIndicator)**. Predicates that are only brought in by assert, and not by consult, are automatically assumed as dynamic.

The next example illustrates that **retract** is also non-deterministic: a whole set of clauses can, through backtracking, be removed by a single **retract** goal. Let us assume that we have the following facts in the 'consulted' program:

```
fast( ann).
slow( tom).
slow( pat).
```

We can add a rule to this program, as follows:

```
?-  assert(
         ( faster(X,Y)  :-
              fast(X), slow(Y) ) ).

yes

?-  faster( A, B).

A = ann
B = tom

?-  retract( slow(X) ).

X = tom;
X = pat;
no
```

```
?- faster( ann, _).

no
```

Notice that when a rule is asserted, the syntax requires that the rule (as an argument to **assert**) be enclosed in parentheses.

When asserting a clause, we may want to specify the position at which the new clause is inserted to the database. The predicates **asserta** and **assertz** enable us to control the position of insertion. The goal

```
asserta( C)
```

adds C at the beginning of the database. The goal

```
assertz( C)
```

adds C at the end of the database. We will assume that **assert** is equivalent to **assertz**, as usual in Prolog implementations. The following example illustrates these effects:

```
?- assert( p(b) ), assertz( p(c) ), assert( p(d) ), asserta( p(a) ).

yes

?- p( X).

X = a;
X = b;
X = c;
X = d
```

There is a relation between **consult** and **assertz**. Consulting a file can be defined in terms of **assertz** as follows: to consult a file, read each term (clause) in the file and assert it at the end of the database.

One useful application of **asserta** is to store already computed answers to questions. For example, let there be a predicate

```
solve( Problem, Solution)
```

defined in the program. We may now ask some question and request that the answer be remembered for future questions.

```
?- solve( problem1, Solution),
     asserta( solve( problem1, Solution) ).
```

If the first goal above succeeds then the answer (**Solution**) is stored and used, as any other clause, in answering further questions. The advantage of such a 'memoization' of answers is that a further question that matches the asserted fact will normally be answered much quicker than the first one. The result now will be simply retrieved as a fact, and not computed through a possibly time-consuming process. This technique of storing derived solutions is also called 'caching'.

An extension of this idea is to use asserting for generating all solutions in the form of a table of facts. For example, we can generate a table of products of all pairs of integers between 0 and 9 as follows: generate a pair of integers X and Y, compute Z is X*Y, assert the three numbers as one line of the product table, and then force the failure. The failure will cause, through backtracking, another pair of integers to be found and so another line tabulated, etc. The following procedure **maketable** implements this idea:

```
maketable :-
    L = [0,1,2,3,4,5,6,7,8,9],
    member( X, L),                    % Choose first factor
    member( Y, L),                    % Choose second factor
    Z is X*Y,
    assert( product(X,Y,Z) ),
    fail.
```

The question

```
?- maketable.
```

will, of course, not succeed, but it will, as a side effect, add the whole product table to the database. After that we can ask, for example, what pairs give the product 8:

```
?- product( A, B, 8).
```

A = 1
B = 8;

A = 2
B = 4;

...

A remark on the style of programming should be made at this stage. The foregoing examples illustrate some obviously useful applications of **assert** and **retract**. However, their use requires special care. Excessive and careless use of these facilities cannot be recommended as good programming style. By asserting and retracting we, in fact, modify the program. Therefore relations that hold at some point will not be true at some other time. At different times the same questions receive different answers. A lot of asserting and retracting may thus obscure the meaning of the program. The resulting behaviour of the program may become difficult to understand, difficult to explain and to trust.

Exercises

7.6   (a) Write a Prolog question to remove the whole **product** table from the database.

       (b) Modify the question so that it only removes those entries where the product is 0.

7.7   Define the relation

```
copy_term( Term, Copy)
```

which will produce a copy of **Term** so that **Copy** is **Term** with all its variables renamed. This can be easily programmed by using **asserta** and **retract**. In some Prologs **copy_term** is provided as a built-in predicate.

7.5   Control facilities

So far we have covered most of the extra control facilities except **repeat**. For completeness the complete set is presented here.

- *cut*, written as '!', prevents backtracking. It was introduced in Chapter 5. A useful predicate is **once(P)** defined in terms of cut as:

  once(P) :- P, !.

  once(P) produces one solution only. The cut, nested in **once**, does not prevent backtracking in other goals.

- **fail** is a goal that always fails.

- **true** is a goal that always succeeds.

- **not(P)** is negation as failure that behaves exactly as if defined as:

  not(P) :- P, !, fail; true.

  Some problems with cut and **not** were discussed in detail in Chapter 5.

- **call(P)** invokes a goal P. It succeeds if P succeeds.

- **repeat** is a goal that always succeeds. Its special property is that it is non-deterministic; therefore, each time it is reached by backtracking it generates another alternative execution branch. **repeat** behaves as if defined by:

  repeat.
  repeat :- repeat.

  A typical way of using **repeat** is illustrated by the following procedure **dosquares** which reads a sequence of numbers and outputs their squares. The sequence is concluded with the atom **stop**, which serves as a signal for the procedure to terminate.

  dosquares :-
    repeat,
    read(X),
    (X = stop, !
    ;
    Y is X∗X, write(Y),
    fail
).

7.6   *bagof, setof* and *findall*

We can generate, by backtracking, all the objects, one by one, that satisfy some goal. Each time a new solution is generated, the previous one disappears and is not accessible any more. However, sometimes we would prefer to have all the generated objects available together – for example, collected into a list. The built-in predicates **bagof, setof** and **findall** serve this purpose.

The goal

   bagof(X, P, L)

will produce the list L of all the objects X such that a goal P is satisfied. Of course, this usually makes sense only if X and P have some common variables. For example, let us have these facts in the program:

   age(peter, 7).
   age(ann, 5).
   age(pat, 8).
   age(tom, 5).

Then we can obtain the list of all the children of age 5 by the goal:

   ?- bagof(Child, age(Child, 5), List).

   List = [ann, tom]

If, in the above goal, we leave the age unspecified, then we get, through back-tracking, three lists of children, corresponding to the three age values:

   ?- bagof(Child, age(Child, Age), List).

   Age = 7
   List = [peter];

   Age = 5
   List = [ann, tom];

   Age = 8
   List = [pat];

   no

We may prefer to have all of the children in one list regardless of their age. This can be achieved by explicitly stating in the call of **bagof** that we do not care about the value of Age as long as such a value exists. This is stated as:

   ?- bagof(Child, Age ^ age(Child, Age), List).

   List = [peter, ann, pat, tom]

Syntactically, '^' is a predefined infix operator of type **xfy**.

If there is no solution for P in the goal **bagof**(X, P, L), then the **bagof** goal simply fails. If the same object X is found repeatedly, then all of its occurrences will appear in L, which leads to duplicate items in L.

The predicate **setof** is similar to **bagof**. The goal

> **setof**(X, P, L)

will again produce a list L of objects X that satisfy P. Only this time the list L will be ordered, and duplicate items, if there are any, will be eliminated. The ordering of the objects is according to built-in predicate @<, which defines the precedence among terms. For example:

> ?- **setof**(Child, Age ^ age(Child, Age), ChildList),
>   **setof**(Age, Child ^ age(Child, Age), AgeList).
>
> ChildList = [ann, pat, peter, tom]
> AgeList = [5, 7, 8]

There is no restriction on the kind of objects that are collected. So we can, for example, construct the list of children ordered by their age, by collecting pairs of the form Age/Child:

> ?- **setof**(Age/Child, age(Child, Age), List).
>
> List = [5/ann, 5/tom, 7/peter, 8/pat]

Another predicate of this family, similar to **bagof**, is **findall**.

> **findall**(X, P, L)

produces, again, a list of objects that satisfy P. The difference with respect to **bagof** is that *all* of the objects X are collected regardless of (possibly) different solutions for variables in P that are not shared with X. This difference is shown in the following example:

> ?- **findall**(Child, age(Child, Age), List).
>
> List = [peter, ann, pat, tom]

If there is no object X that satisfies P then **findall** will succeed with L = [].

If **findall** is not available as a built-in predicate in the implementation used then it can be easily programmed as follows. All solutions for P are generated by forced backtracking. Each solution is, when generated, immediately asserted into the database so that it is not lost when the next solution is found. After all the solutions have been generated and asserted, they have to be collected into a list and retracted from the database. This whole process can be imagined as all the solutions generated forming a queue. Each newly generated solution is, by assertion, added to the end of this queue. When the solutions are collected the queue dissolves. Note, in addition, that the end of this queue has to be marked, for example, by the atom 'bottom' (which, of course, should be different from any solution that is possibly expected). An implementation of **findall** along these lines is shown as Figure 7.4.

```
findall( X, Goal, Xlist) :-
    call( Goal),                          % Find a solution
    assertz( queue(X) ),                  % Assert it
    fail;                                 % Try to find more solutions
    assertz( queue(bottom) ),             % Mark end of solutions
    collect( Xlist).                      % Collect the solutions

collect( L) :-
    retract( queue(X) ), !,               % Retract next solution
    ( X == bottom, !, L = [ ]             % End of solutions?
    ;
      L = [X | Rest], collect( Rest) ).   % Otherwise collect the rest
```

Figure 7.4 An implementation of the **findall** relation.

Exercises

7.8   Use **bagof** to define the relation **powerset(Set, Subsets)** to compute the set of all subsets of a given set (all sets represented as lists).

7.9   Use **bagof** to define the relation

      copy_term(Term, Copy)

such that **Copy** is **Term** with all its variables renamed.

Summary

- A Prolog implementation normally provides a set of built-in procedures to accomplish several useful operations that are not possible in pure Prolog. In this chapter, such a set of predicates available in many Prolog implementations was introduced.

- The type of a term can be tested by the following predicates:

var(X)	X is a (non-instantiated) variable
nonvar(X)	X is not a variable
atom(X)	X is an atom
integer(X)	X is an integer
float(X)	X is a real number
atomic(X)	X is either an atom or a number
compound(X)	X is a structure

- Terms can be constructed or decomposed:

  Term =.. [Functor | ArgumentList]
  functor(Term, Functor, Arity)
  arg(N, Term, Argument)
  name(Atom, CharacterCodes)

- Terms can be compared:

X = Y	X and Y match
X == Y	X and Y are identical
X \== Y	X and Y are not identical
X =:= Y	X and Y are arithmetically equal
X =\= Y	X and Y are not arithmetically equal
X < Y	arithmetic value of X is less than Y (related: =<, >, >=)
X @< Y	term X precedes term Y (related: @=<, @>, @>=)

- A Prolog program can be viewed as a relational database that can be updated by the following procedures:

assert(Clause)	add **Clause** to the program
asserta(Clause)	add at the beginning
assertz(Clause)	add at the end
retract(Clause)	remove a clause that matches **Clause**

- All the objects that satisfy a given condition can be collected into a list by the predicates:

bagof(X, P, L)	L is the list of all X that satisfy condition P
setof(X, P, L)	L is the sorted list of all X that satisfy condition P
findall(X, P, L)	similar to **bagof**

- **repeat** is a control facility that generates an unlimited number of alternatives for backtracking.

chapter 8

Programming Style and Technique

In this chapter we will review some general principles of good programming and discuss the following questions in particular: How to think about Prolog programs? What are elements of good programming style in Prolog? How to debug Prolog programs? How to make Prolog programs more efficient?

8.1 General principles of good programming

What is a good program? Answering this question is not trivial as there are several criteria for judging how good a program is. Generally accepted criteria include the following:

- *Correctness* Above all, a good program should be correct. That is, it should do what it is supposed to do. This may seem a trivial, self-explanatory requirement. However, in the case of complex programs, correctness is often not attained. A common mistake when writing programs is to neglect this obvious criterion and pay more attention to other criteria, such as efficiency or external glamour of the program.

- *User-friendliness* A good program should be easy to use and interact with.

- *Efficiency* A good program should not needlessly waste computer time and memory space.

- *Readability*   A good program should be easy to read and easy to understand. It should not be more complicated than necessary. Clever programming tricks that obscure the meaning of the program should be avoided. The general organization of the program and its layout help its readability.

- *Modifiability*   A good program should be easy to modify and to extend. Transparency and modular organization of the program help modifiability.

- *Robustness*   A good program should be robust. It should not crash immediately when the user enters some incorrect or unexpected data. The program should, in the case of such errors, stay 'alive' and behave reasonably (should report errors).

- *Documentation*   A good program should be properly documented. The minimal documentation is the program's listing including sufficient program comments.

The importance of particular criteria depends on the problem and on the circumstances in which the program is written, and on the environment in which it is used. There is no doubt that correctness has the highest priority. The issues of readability, user-friendliness, modifiability, robustness and documentation are usually given, at least, as much priority as the issue of efficiency.

There are some general guidelines for practically achieving the above criteria. One important rule is to first *think* about the problem to be solved, and only then to start writing the actual code in the programming language used. Once we have developed a good understanding of the problem and the solution is well thought through, the actual coding will be fast and easy, and there is a good chance that we will soon get a correct program.

A common mistake is to start writing the code even before the full definition of the problem has been understood. A fundamental reason why early coding is bad practice is that the thinking about the problem and the ideas for a solution should be done in terms that are most relevant to the problem. These terms are usually far from the syntax of the programming language used, and they may include natural language statements and pictorial representation of ideas.

Such a formulation of the solution will have to be transformed into the programming language, but this transformation process may not be easy. A good approach is to use the principle of *stepwise refinement*. The initial formulation of the solution is referred to as the 'top-level solution', and the final program as the 'bottom-level solution'.

According to the principle of stepwise refinement, the final program is developed through a sequence of transformations, or 'refinements', of the solution. We start with the first, top-level solution and then proceed through a sequence of solutions; these are all equivalent, but each solution in the sequence is expressed in more detail. In each refinement step, concepts used in previous formulations are elaborated to greater detail and their representation gets closer to the programming language. It should be realized that refinement applies both to procedure definitions and to data structures. In the initial stages we normally work with more abstract, bulky units of information whose structure is refined later.

Such a strategy of top-down stepwise refinement has the following advantages:

- it allows for formulation of rough solutions in terms that are most relevant to the problem;

- in terms of such powerful concepts, the solution should be succinct and simple, and therefore likely to be correct;

- each refinement step should be small enough so that it is intellectually manage-able; if so, the transformation of a solution into a new, more detailed representation is likely to be correct, and so is the resulting solution at the next level of detail.

In the case of Prolog we may talk about the stepwise refinement of *relations*. If the problem suggests thinking in algorithmic terms, then we can also talk about refinement of *algorithms*, adopting the procedural point of view in Prolog.

In order to properly refine a solution at some level of detail, and to introduce useful concepts at the next lower level, we need ideas. Therefore programming is creative, especially so for beginners. With experience, programming gradually becomes less of an art and more of a craft. But, nevertheless, a major question is: How do we get ideas? Most ideas come from experience, from similar problems whose solutions we know. If we do not know a direct programming solution, another similar problem could be helpful. Another source of ideas is everyday life. For example, if the problem is to write a program to sort a list of items we may get an idea from considering the question: How would I myself sort a set of exam papers according to the alphabetical order of students?

General principles of good programming outlined in this section basically apply to Prolog as well. We will discuss some details with particular reference to Prolog in the following sections.

8.2   How to think about Prolog programs

One characteristic feature of Prolog is that it allows for both the procedural and declarative way of thinking about programs. The two approaches have been discussed in detail in Chapter 2, and illustrated by examples throughout the text. Which approach will be more efficient and practical depends on the problem. Declarative solutions are usually easier to develop, but may lead to an inefficient program.

During the process of developing a solution we have to find ideas for reducing problems to one or more easier subproblems. An important question is: How do we find proper subproblems? There are several general principles that often work in Prolog programming. These will be discussed in the following sections.

8.2.1   Use of recursion

The principle here is to split the problem into cases belonging to two groups:

(1)   trivial, or 'boundary' cases;

(2)   'general' cases where the solution is constructed from solutions of (simpler) versions of the original problem itself.

In Prolog we use this technique all the time. Let us look at one more example: processing a list of items so that each item is transformed by the same transformation rule. Let this procedure be

   maplist(List, F, NewList)

where **List** is an original list, F is a transformation rule (a binary relation) and **NewList** is the list of all transformed items. The problem of transforming **List** can be split into two cases:

(1)   Boundary case: **List** = [ ]

   if **List** = [ ] then **NewList** = [ ], regardless of F

(2)   General case: **List** = [X | **Tail**]

   To transform a list of the form [X | **Tail**], do:
      transform the item X by rule F obtaining **NewX**, and
      transform the list **Tail** obtaining **NewTail**;
      the whole transformed list is [NewX | NewTail].

In Prolog:

   maplist([ ], _, [ ]).

   maplist([X | Tail], F, [NewX | NewTail]) :-
   G =.. [F, X, NewX],
   call(G),
   maplist(Tail, F, NewTail).

Suppose we have a list of numbers and want to compute the list of their squares. **maplist** can be used for this as follows:

   square(X, Y) :-
   Y is X∗X.

   ?- maplist([2, 6, 5], square, Squares).
   Squares = [4, 36, 25]

One reason why recursion so naturally applies to defining relations in Prolog is that data objects themselves often have recursive structure. Lists and trees are such objects. A list is either empty (boundary case) or has a head and a tail that is itself a list (general case). A binary tree is either empty (boundary case) or it has a root and two subtrees that are themselves binary trees (general case). Therefore, to process a whole non-empty tree, we must do something with the root, and process the subtrees.

8.2.2 Generalization

It is often a good idea to generalize the original problem, so that the solution to the generalized problem can be formulated recursively. The original problem is then solved as a special case of its more general version. Generalization of a relation typically involves the introduction of one or more extra arguments. A major problem, which may require deeper insight into the problem, is how to find the right generalization.

As an example let us revisit the eight queens problem. The original problem was to place eight queens on the chessboard so that they do not attack each other. Let us call the corresponding relation:

eightqueens(Pos)

This is true if **Pos** is a position with eight non-attacking queens. A good idea in this case is to generalize the number of queens from eight to N. The number of queens now becomes the additional argument:

nqueens(Pos, N)

The advantage of this generalization is that there is an immediate recursive formulation of the **nqueens** relation:

(1) Boundary case: N = 0

   To safely place zero queens is trivial.

(2) General case: N > 0

   To safely place N queens on the board, satisfy the following:

   - achieve a safe configuration of (N − 1) queens; and

   - add the remaining queen so that she does not attack any other queen.

Once the generalized problem has been solved, the original problem is easy:

eightqueens(Pos) :- nqueens(Pos, 8).

8.2.3 Using pictures

When searching for ideas about a problem, it is often useful to introduce some graphical representation of the problem. A picture may help us to perceive some essential relations in the problem. Then we just have to describe what we *see* in the picture in the programming language.

The use of pictorial representations is often useful in problem solving in general; it seems, however, that it works with Prolog particularly well. The following arguments explain why:

(1) Prolog is particularly suitable for problems that involve objects and relations between objects. Often, such problems can be naturally illustrated by graphs in which nodes correspond to objects and arcs correspond to relations.

(2) Structured data objects in Prolog are naturally pictured as trees.

(3) The declarative meaning of Prolog facilitates the translation of pictorial representations into Prolog because, in principle, the order in which the picture is described does not matter. We just put what we see into the program in any order. (For practical reasons of the program's efficiency this order will possibly have to be polished later.)

8.3   Programming style

The purpose of conforming to some stylistic conventions is:

• to reduce the danger of programming errors; and

• to produce programs that are readable and easy to understand, easy to debug and to modify.

We will review here some ingredients of good programming style in Prolog: some general rules of good style, tabular organization of long procedures and commenting.

8.3.1 Some rules of good style

• Program clauses should be short. Their body should typically contain no more than a few goals.

• Procedures should be short because long procedures are hard to understand. However, long procedures are acceptable if they have some uniform structure (this will be discussed later in this section).

• Mnemonic names for procedures and variables should be used. Names should indicate the meaning of relations and the role of data objects.

- The layout of programs is important. Spacing, blank lines and indentation should be consistently used for the sake of readability. Clauses about the same procedure should be clustered together; there should be blank lines between clauses (unless, perhaps, there are numerous facts about the same relation); each goal can be placed on a separate line. Prolog programs sometimes resemble poems for the aesthetic appeal of ideas and form.

- Stylistic conventions of this kind may vary from program to program as they depend on the problem and personal taste. It is important, however, that the same conventions are used consistently throughout the whole program.

- The cut operator should be used with care. Cut should not be used if it can be easily avoided. It is better to use, where possible, 'green cuts' rather than 'red cuts'. As discussed in Chapter 5, a cut is called 'green' if it can be removed without altering the declarative meaning of the clause. The use of 'red cuts' should be restricted to clearly defined constructs such as **not** or the selection between alternatives. An example of the latter construct is:

  if **Condition** *then* **Goal1** *else* **Goal2**

  This translates into Prolog, using cut, as:

Condition, !,	% Condition true?
Goal1	% If yes then Goal1
;	
Goal2	% Otherwise Goal2

- The **not** procedure can also lead to surprising behaviour, as it is related to cut. We have to be well aware of how **not** is defined in Prolog. However, if there is a dilemma between **not** and cut, the former is perhaps better than some obscure construct with cut.

- Program modification by **assert** and **retract** can grossly degrade the transparency of the program's behaviour. In particular, the same program will answer the same question differently at different times. In such cases, if we want to reproduce the same behaviour we have to make sure that the whole previous state, which was modified by assertions and retractions, is completely restored.

- The use of a semicolon may obscure the meaning of a clause. The readability can sometimes be improved by splitting the clause containing the semicolon into more clauses; but this will, possibly, be at the expense of the length of the program and its efficiency.

  To illustrate some points of this section consider the relation

  merge(List1, List2, List3)

where **List1** and **List2** are ordered lists that merge into **List3**. For example:

  merge([2,4,7], [1,3,4,8], [1,2,3,4,4,7,8])

The following is an implementation of **merge** in bad style:

```
merge( List1, List2, List3)  :-
    List1 = [], !, List3 = List2;          % First list empty
    List2 = [], !, List3 = List1;          % Second list empty
    List1 = [X | Rest1],
    List2 = [Y | Rest2],
    ( X < Y, !,
      Z = X,                               % Z is head of List3
      merge( Rest1, List2, Rest3);
      Z = Y,
      merge( List1, Rest2, Rest3) ),
    List3 = [Z | Rest3].
```

Here is a better version which avoids semicolons:

```
merge( [], List, List)  :-
    !.                                      % Prevent redundant solutions

merge( List, [], List).

merge( [X | Rest1], [Y | Rest2], [X | Rest3] )  :-
    X < Y, !,
    merge( Rest1, [Y | Rest2], Rest3).

merge( List1, [Y | Rest2], [Y | Rest3] )  :-
    merge( List1, Rest2, Rest3).
```

8.3.2 Tabular organization of long procedures

Long procedures are acceptable if they have some uniform structure. Typically, such a form is a set of facts when a relation is effectively defined in the tabular form. Advantages of such an organization of a long procedure are:

- Its structure is easily understood.

- Incrementability: it can be refined by simply adding new facts.

- It is easy to check and correct or modify (by simply replacing some fact independently of other facts).

8.3.3 Commenting

Program comments should explain in the first place what the program is about and how to use it, and only then the details of the solution method used and other programming details. The main purpose of comments is to enable the user to use the program, to understand it and to possibly modify it. Comments should describe, in the shortest form possible, everything that is essential to these ends.

Undercommenting is a usual fault, but a program can also be overcommented. Explanation of details that are obvious from the program code itself is only a needless burden to the program.

Long passages of comments should precede the code they refer to, while short comments should be interspersed with the code itself. Information that should, in general, be included in comments comprises the following:

- What the program does, how it is used (for example, what goal is to be invoked and what are the expected results), examples of using the program.

- What are top-level predicates?

- How are main concepts (objects) represented?

- Execution time and memory requirements of the program.

- What are the program's limitations?

- Are there any special system-dependent features used?

- What is the meaning of the predicates in the program? What are their arguments? Which arguments are 'input' and which are 'output', if known? (Input arguments have fully specified values, without uninstantiated variables, when the predicate is called.)

- Algorithmic and implementation details.

- The following conventions are often used when describing predicates. References to a predicate are made by stating the predicate's name and its arity, written as:

    PredicateName / Arity

    For example, **merge(List1, List2, List3)** would be referred to as **merge/3**. The input/output modes of the arguments are indicated by prefixing arguments' names by '+' (input) or '-' (output). For example, **merge(+List1, +List2, -List3)** indicates that the first two arguments of **merge** are input, and the third one is output.

8.4   Debugging

When a program does not do what it is expected to do the main problem is to locate the error(s). It is easier to locate an error in a part of the program (or a module) than in the program as a whole. Therefore, a good principle of debugging is to start by testing smaller units of the program, and when these can be trusted, to test bigger modules or the whole program.

Debugging in Prolog is facilitated by two things: first, Prolog is an interactive language so any part of the program can be directly invoked by a proper question to the Prolog system; second, Prolog implementations usually provide special debugging aids. As a result of these two features, debugging of Prolog programs can, in general, be done more efficiently than in most other programming languages.

The basis for debugging aids is *tracing*. 'Tracing a goal' means that the information regarding the goal's satisfaction is displayed during execution. This information includes:

- Entry information: the predicate name and the values of arguments when the goal is invoked.

- Exit information: in the case of success, the values of arguments that satisfy the goal; otherwise an indication of failure.

- Re-entry information: invocation of the same goal caused by backtracking.

Between entry and exit, the trace information for all the subgoals of this goal can be obtained. So we can trace the execution of our question all the way down to the lowest level goals until facts are encountered. Such detailed tracing may turn out to be impractical due to the excessive amount of tracing information; therefore, the user can specify selective tracing. There are two selection mechanisms: first, suppress tracing information beyond a certain level; second, trace only some specified subset of predicates, and not all of them.

Such debugging aids are activated by system-dependent built-in predicates. A typical subset of such predicates is as follows:

trace

triggers exhaustive tracing of goals that follow.

notrace

stops further tracing.

spy(P)

specifies that a predicate P be traced. This is used when we are particularly interested in the named predicate and want to avoid tracing information from other goals (either above or below the level of a call of P). Several predicates can be simultaneously active for 'spying'.

nospy(P)

stops 'spying' P.

Tracing beyond a certain depth can be suppressed by special commands during execution. There may be several other debugging commands available, such as returning to a previous point of execution. After such a return we can, for example, repeat the execution at a greater detail of tracing.

8.5   Improving efficiency

There are several aspects of efficiency, including the most common ones, execution time and space requirements of a program. Another aspect is the time needed by the programmer to develop the program.

The traditional computer architecture is not particularly suitable for the Prolog style of program execution – that is, satisfying a list of goals. Therefore, the limitations of time and space may be experienced earlier in Prolog than in many other programming languages. Whether this will cause difficulties in a practical application depends on the problem. The issue of time efficiency is practically meaningless if a Prolog program that is run a few times per day takes 1 second of CPU time and a corresponding program in some other language, say Fortran, takes 0.1 seconds. The difference in efficiency will perhaps matter if the two programs take 50 minutes and 5 minutes respectively.

On the other hand, in many areas of application Prolog will greatly reduce the program development time. Prolog programs will, in general, be easier to write, to understand and to debug than in traditional languages. Problems that gravitate toward the 'Prolog domain' involve symbolic, non-numeric processing, structured data objects and relations between them. In particular, Prolog has been successfully applied in areas such as symbolic solving of equations, planning, databases, general problem solving, prototyping, implementation of programming languages, discrete and qualitative simulation, architectural design, machine learning, natural language understanding, expert systems, and other areas of artificial intelligence. On the other hand, numerical mathematics is an area for which Prolog is not a natural candidate.

With respect to the execution efficiency, executing a *compiled* program is generally more efficient than *interpreting* the program. Therefore, if the Prolog system contains both an interpreter and a compiler, then the compiler should be used if efficiency is critical.

If a program suffers from inefficiency then it can often be radically improved by improving the algorithm itself. However, to do this, the procedural aspects of the program have to be studied. A simple way of improving the executional efficiency is to find a better ordering of clauses of procedures, and of goals in the bodies of procedures. Another relatively simple method is to provide guidance to the Prolog system by means of cuts.

Ideas for improving the efficiency of a program usually come from a deeper understanding of the problem. A more efficient algorithm can, in general, result from improvements of two kinds:

- Improving search efficiency by avoiding unnecessary backtracking and stopping the execution of useless alternatives as soon as possible.

- Using more suitable data structures to represent objects in the program, so that operations on objects can be implemented more efficiently.

We will study both kinds of improvements by looking at examples. Yet another technique of improving efficiency will be illustrated by an example. This technique, called caching, is based on asserting into the database intermediate results that are likely to be needed again in the future computation. Instead of repeating the computation, such results are simply retrieved as already known facts.

8.5.1   Improving the efficiency of an eight queens program

As a simple example of improving the search efficiency let us revisit the eight queens problem (see Figure 4.7). In this program, the Y-coordinates of the queens are found by successively trying, for each queen, the integers between 1 and 8. This was programmed as the goal:

> **member(Y, [1,2,3,4,5,6,7,8])**

The way that **member** works is that $Y = 1$ is tried first, and then $Y = 2$, $Y = 3$, etc. As the queens are placed one after another in adjacent columns on the board, it is obvious that this order of trials is not the most appropriate. The reason for this is that the queens in adjacent columns will attack each other if they are not placed at least two squares apart in the vertical direction. According to this observation, a simple attempt to improve the efficiency is to rearrange the candidate coordinate values. For example:

> **member(Y, [1,5,2,6,3,7,4,8])**

This minor change will reduce the time needed to find the first solution by a factor of 3 or 4.

In the next example, a similarly simple idea of reordering will convert a practically unacceptable time complexity into a trivial one.

8.5.2   Improving the efficiency in a map colouring program

The map colouring problem is to assign each country in a given map one of four given colours in such a way that no two neighbouring countries are painted with the same colour. There is a theorem which guarantees that this is always possible.

Let us assume that a map is specified by the neighbour relation

> **ngb(Country, Neighbours)**

where **Neighbours** is the list of countries bordering on **Country**. So the map of Europe, with 30 countries, would be specified (in alphabetical order) as:

> **ngb(albania, [greece, macedonia, yugoslavia]).**
> **ngb(andorra, [france, spain]).**

ngb(austria, [czech_republic, germany, hungary, italy, liechtenstein,
                 slovakia, slovenia, switzerland]).

. . .

Let a solution be represented as a list of pairs of the form

Country/Colour

which specifies a colour for each country in a given map. For the given map, the names of countries are fixed in advance, and the problem is to find the values for the colours. Thus, for Europe, the problem is to find a proper instantiation of variables C1, C2, C3, etc. in the list:

[albania/C1, andorra/C2, austria/C3, . . .]

Now let us define the predicate

colours(Country_colour_list)

which is true if the Country_colour_list satisfies the map colouring constraint with respect to a given ngb relation. Let the four colours be yellow, blue, red and green. The condition that no two neighbouring countries are of the same colour can be formulated in Prolog as follows:

```
colours( [ ] ).

colours( [Country/Colour | Rest] ) :-
  colours( Rest),
  member( Colour, [yellow, blue, red, green] ),
  not( member( Country1/Colour, Rest), neighbour( Country, Country1) ).

neighbour( Country, Country1) :-
  ngb( Country, Neighbours),
  member( Country1, Neighbours).
```

Here, member(X,L) is, as usual, the list membership relation. This will work well for simple maps, with a small number of countries. Europe might be problematic, however. Assuming that the built-in predicate setof is available, one attempt to colour Europe could be as follows. First, let us define an auxiliary relation:

```
country( C) :- ngb( C, _).
```

Then the question for colouring Europe can be formulated as:

```
?- setof( Cntry/Colour, country( Cntry), CountryColourList),
   colours( CountryColourList).
```

The setof goal will construct a template country/colour list for Europe in which uninstantiated variables stand for colours. Then the colours goal is supposed to instantiate the colours. However, this attempt will probably fail because of inefficiency.

A detailed study of the way Prolog tries to satisfy the **colours** goal reveals the source of inefficiency. Countries in the country/colour list are arranged in alphabetical order, and this has nothing to do with their geographical arrangement. The order in which the countries are assigned colours corresponds to the order in the list (starting at the end), which is in our case independent of the **ngb** relation. So the colouring process starts at some end of the map, continues at some other end, etc., moving around more or less randomly. This may easily lead to a situation in which a country that is to be coloured is surrounded by many other countries, already painted with all four available colours. Then backtracking is necessary, which leads to inefficiency.

It is clear, then, that the efficiency depends on the order in which the countries are coloured. Intuition suggests a simple colouring strategy that should be better than random: start with some country that has many neighbours, and then proceed to the neighbours, then to the neighbours of neighbours, etc. For Europe, then, Germany (having most neighbours) is a good candidate to start with. Of course, when the template country/colour list is constructed, Germany has to be put at the end of the list and other countries have to be added at the front of the list. In this way the colouring algorithm, which starts at the rear end, will commence with Germany and proceed from there from neighbour to neighbour.

Such a country/colour template dramatically improves the efficiency with respect to the original, alphabetical order, and possible colourings for the map of Europe will be now produced without difficulty.

We can construct a properly ordered list of countries manually, but we do not have to. The following procedure, **makelist**, does it. It starts the construction with some specified country (Germany in our case) and collects the countries into a list called **Closed**. Each country is first put into another list, called **Open**, before it is transferred to **Closed**. Each time that a country is transferred from **Open** to **Closed**, its neighbours are added to **Open**.

```
makelist( List) :-
    collect( [germany], [ ], List).

collect( [ ], Closed, Closed).                      % No more candidates for Closed

collect( [X | Open], Closed, List) :-
    member( X, Closed), !,                          % X has already been collected?
    collect( Open, Closed, List).                   % Discard X

collect( [X | Open], Closed, List) :-
    ngb( X, Ngbs),                                  % Find X's neighbours
    conc( Ngbs, Open, Open1),                       % Put them to Open1
    collect( Open1, [X | Closed], List).            % Collect the Rest
```

The **conc** relation is, as usual, the list concatenation relation.

8.5.3   Improving efficiency of list concatenation by difference lists

In our programs so far, the concatenation of lists has been programmed as:

conc([ ], L, L).

conc([X | L1], L2, [X | L3]) :-
    conc(L1, L2, L3).

This is inefficient when the first list is long. The following example explains why:

?- conc([a,b,c], [d,e], L).

This produces the following sequence of goals:

conc([a,b,c], [d,e], L)
    conc([b,c], [d,e], L')   where L = [a | L']
        conc([c], [d,e], L'')   where L' = [b | L'']
            conc([ ], [d,e], L''')   where L'' = [c | L''']
                true   where L''' = [d,e]

From this it is clear that the program in effect scans all of the first list, until the empty list is encountered.

But could we not simply skip the whole of the first list in a single step and append the second list, instead of gradually working down the first list? To do this, we need to know where the end of a list is; that is, we need another representation of lists. One solution is the data structure called *difference lists*. So a list is represented by a pair of lists. For example, the list

[a,b,c]

can be represented by the two lists:

L1 = [a,b,c,d,e]
L2 = [d,e]

Such a pair of lists, which we will for brevity choose to write as L1-L2, represents the 'difference' between L1 and L2. This of course only works under the condition that L2 is a suffix of L1. Note that the same list can be represented by several 'difference pairs'. So the list [a,b,c] can be represented, for example, by

[a,b,c] - [ ]

or

[a,b,c,d,e] - [d,e]

or

[a,b,c,d,e | T] - [d,e | T]

or

[a,b,c | T] - T

where T is any list. The empty list is represented by any pair of the form L-L.

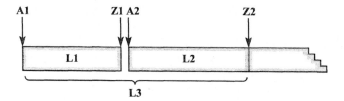

Figure 8.1 Concatenation of lists represented by difference pairs. **L1** is represented by **A1-Z1**, **L2** by **A2-Z2**, and the result **L3** by **A1-Z2** when **Z1** = **A2** must be true.

As the second member of the pair indicates the end of the list, the end is directly accessible. This can be used for an efficient implementation of concatenation. The method is illustrated in Figure 8.1. The corresponding concatenation relation translates into Prolog as the fact:

concat(A1 - Z1, Z1 - Z2, A1 - Z2).

Let us use **concat** to concatenate the lists **[a,b,c]**, represented by the pair **[a,b,c | T1]**-**T1**, and the list **[d,e]**, represented by **[d,e | T2]**-**T2**:

?- concat([a,b,c | T1] - T1, [d,e | T2] - T2, L).

The concatenation is done just by matching this goal with the clause about **concat**, giving:

T1 = [d,e | T2]
L = [a,b,c,d,e | T2] - T2

Due to its efficiency, this *difference lists* technique for list concatenation is very popular, although it cannot be used as flexibly as our usual **conc** procedure.

8.5.4 Last call optimization and accumulators

Recursive calls normally take up memory space, which is only freed after the return from the call. A large number of nested recursive calls may lead to shortage of memory. In special cases, however, it is possible to execute nested recursive calls without requiring extra memory. In such a case a recursive procedure has a special form, called *tail recursion*. A tail-recursive procedure only has one recursive call, and this call appears as the *last goal* of the *last clause* in the procedure. In addition, the goals preceding the recursive call must be deterministic, so that no backtracking occurs after this last call. We can force this determinism by placing a cut just before the recursive call. Typically a tail-recursive procedure looks like this:

p(...) :- ....   % No recursive call in the body of this clause
p(...) :- ....   % No recursive call in the body of this clause
...

```
p( ... ) :-
    ..., !,                    % The cut ensures no backtracking
    p( ... ).                  % Tail-recursive call
```

In the cases of such tail-recursive procedures, no information is needed upon the return from a call. Therefore such recursion can be carried out simply as iteration in which a next cycle in the loop does *not* require additional memory. A Prolog system will typically notice such an opportunity of saving memory and realize tail recursion as iteration. This is called *tail recursion optimization*, or *last call optimization*.

When memory efficiency is critical, tail-recursive formulations of procedures help. Often it is indeed possible to re-formulate a recursive procedure into a tail-recursive one. Let us consider the predicate for computing the sum of a list of numbers:

```
sumlist( List, Sum)
```

Here is a simple first definition:

```
sumlist( [ ], 0).

sumlist( [ First | Rest], Sum) :-
    sumlist( Rest, Sum0),
    Sum is X + Sum0.
```

This is not tail recursive, so the summation over a very long list will require many recursive calls and therefore a lot of memory. However, we know that in a typical procedural language such summation can be carried out as a simple iterative loop. How can we make **sumlist** tail recursive and enable Prolog too to carry it out as iteration? Unfortunately we cannot simply swap the goals in the body of the second clause, because the is goal can only be executed *after* Sum0 has been computed. But the following is a common trick that does it:

```
sumlist( List, Sum) :-
    sumlist( List, 0, Sum).              % Call auxiliary predicate

% sumlist( List, PartialSum, TotalSum):
%    TotalSum = PartialSum + sum over List

sumlist( [ ], Sum, Sum).                 % Total sum = partial sum

sumlist( [ First | Rest ], PartialSum, TotalSum) :-
    NewPartialSum is PartialSum + First,
    sumlist( Rest, NewPartialSum, TotalSum).
```

This is now tail recursive and Prolog can benefit from last call optimization.

The technique of making our **sumlist** procedure tail recursive as above is frequently used. To define our target predicate **sumlist/2**, we introduced an auxiliary predicate **sumlist/3**. The additional argument, **PartialSum**, enabled a tail-recursive formulation. Such extra arguments are common and they are called *accumulators*. The final result is gradually accumulated in such an accumulator during successive recursion calls.

Here is another famous example of tail-recursion formulation through introducing an accumulator argument:

reverse(List, ReversedList)

ReversedList has the same elements as **List**, but in the reverse order. The following is a first, straightforward attempt:

reverse([ ], [ ]).

reverse([X | Rest], Reversed) :-
    reverse(Rest, RevRest),
    conc(RevRest, [X], Reversed).   % Append X at end

This is not tail recursive. Apart from that, it is also very inefficient because of the goal **conc(RevRest, [X], Reversed)**, which requires time proportional to the length of **RevRest**. Therefore, to reverse a list of length n, the procedure above will require time proportional to n^2. But, of course, a list can be reversed in linear time. Therefore, due to its inefficiency, the procedure above is also known as 'naive reverse'. A much more efficient version below introduces an accumulator:

reverse(List, Reversed) :-
    reverse(List, [ ], Reversed).

% reverse(List, PartReversed, Reversed):
%   Reversed is obtained by adding the elements of List in reverse order
%   to PartReversed

reverse([ ], Reversed, Reversed).

reverse([X | Rest], PartReversed, TotalReversed) :-
    reverse(Rest, [X | PartReversed], TotalReversed).   % Add X to accumulator

This is efficient (time is linear in the length of list) and tail recursive.

8.5.5 Simulating arrays with *arg*

The list structure is the easiest representation for sets in Prolog. However, accessing an item in a list is done by scanning the list. This takes time proportional to the length of the list. For long lists this is very inefficient. Tree structures, discussed in Chapters 9 and 10, offer much more efficient access. However, often it is possible to access an element of a structure through the element's *index*. In such cases, *array* structures, provided in other programming languages, are the most effective because they enable direct access to a required element.

There is no array facility in Prolog, but arrays can be simulated to some extent by using the built-in predicates **arg** and **functor**. Here is an example. The goal:

functor(A, f, 100)

makes a structure with 100 elements:

A = **f**(_, _, _, ...)

In other languages, a typical example statement that involves direct access to an element of an array is:

A[60] := 1

This initializes the value of the 60th element of array A to 1. We can achieve analogous effect in Prolog by the goal:

arg(60, A, 1)

This directly accesses the 60th component of the compound term A, which as the result gets instantiated to:

A = f(_, ..., _, 1, _, ..., _)   % 60th component equal 1

The point is that time needed to access the Nth component of a structure does not depend on N. Another typical example statement from other programming languages is:

X := A[60]

This translates into our simulated array in Prolog as:

arg(60, A, X)

This is much more efficient than having a list of 100 elements and accessing the 60th element by nested recursion down the list. However, the updating of the value of an element in a simulated array is awkward. Once the values in an array have been initialized, they can be changed, for example:

A[60] := A[60] + 1

A straightforward way to simulate such update of a *single* value in an array in Prolog would be as follows: build a *whole* new structure with 100 components using **functor**, insert the new value at the appropriate place in the structure, and fill all the other components by the corresponding components of the previous structure. All this is awkward and very inefficient. One idea to improve this is to provide uninstantiated 'holes' in the components of the structure, so that future values of array elements can be accommodated in these holes. So we can, for example, store successive update values in a list in which the rest of the list is an uninstantiated variable – a 'hole' for future values. As an example consider the following updates of the value of variable X in a procedural language:

X := 1;   X := 2;   X := 3

These updates can be simulated in Prolog with the 'holes' technique as follows:

X = [1 | Rest1]   % Corresponds to X := 1, Rest1 is hole for future values
Rest1 = [2 | Rest2]   % Corresponds to X := 2, Rest 2 is hole for future values
Rest2 = [3 | Rest3]   % Corresponds to X := 3

At this point X =[1, 2, 3 | **Rest3**]. Obviously the whole history of the values of X is maintained, and the current value is the one just preceding the 'hole'. If there are many successive updates, the 'current' value gets nested deep, and the technique becomes inefficient again. A further idea, to overcome this source of inefficiency, is to throw away the previous values at the moment when a list gets too long, and start again with a list consisting of just a head and an uninstantiated tail.

In spite of these potential complications, in many cases the simulation of arrays with **arg** is simple and works well. One such example is our solution 3 for the eight queens problem in Chapter 4 (Figure 4.11). This program places a next queen into a currently free column (X-coordinate), row (Y-coordinate), upward diagonal (U-coordinate) and downward diagonal (V-coordinate). The sets of currently free coordinates are maintained, and when a new queen is placed the corresponding occupied coordinates are deleted from these sets. The deletion of U and V coordinates in Figure 4.11 involves scanning the corresponding lists, which is inefficent. Efficiency can easily be improved by simulated arrays. So the set of all 15 upward diagonals can be represented by the following term with 15 components:

Du = **u**(_, _, _, _, _, _, _, _, _, _, _, _, _, _, _)

Consider placing a queen at the square (X,Y) = (1,1). This square lies on the 8th upward diagonal. The fact that this diagonal is now occupied can be marked by instantiating the 8th component of **Du** to 1 (that is, the corresponding X-coordinate):

arg(8, **Du**, 1)

Now **Du** becomes:

Du = **u**(_, _, _, _, _, _, _, 1, _, _, _, _, _, _, _)

If later a queen is attempted to be placed at (X,Y) = (3,3), also lying on the 8th diagonal, this would require:

arg(8, **Du**, 3)   % Here X = 3

This will fail because the 8th component of **Du** is already 1. So the program will not allow another queen to be placed on the same diagonal. This implementation of the sets of upward and downward diagonals leads to a considerably more efficient program than the one in Figure 4.11.

8.5.6   Improving efficiency by asserting derived facts

Sometimes during computation the same goal has to be satisfied again and again. As Prolog has no special mechanism to discover such situations whole computation sequences are repeated.

As an example consider a program to compute the Nth Fibonacci number for a given N. The Fibonacci sequence is:

1, 1, 2, 3, 5, 8, 13, . . .

Each number in the sequence, except for the first two, is the sum of the previous two numbers. We will define a predicate

fib(N, F)

to compute, for a given N, the Nth Fibonacci number, F. We count the numbers in the sequence starting with N = 1. The following **fib** program deals first with the first two Fibonacci numbers as two special cases, and then specifies the general rule about the Fibonacci sequence:

```
fib( 1, 1).                    % 1st Fibonacci number

fib( 2, 1).                    % 2nd Fibonacci number

fib( N, F)  :-                 % Nth Fib. number, N > 2
  N > 2,
  N1 is N - 1, fib( N1, F1),
  N2 is N - 2, fib( N2, F2),
  F is F1 + F2.                % Nth number is the sum of its two predecessors
```

This program tends to redo parts of the computation. This is easily seen if we trace the execution of the following goal:

?- fib(6, F).

Figure 8.2 illustrates the essence of this computational process. For example, the third Fibonacci number, $f(3)$, is needed in three places and the same computation is repeated each time.

This can be easily avoided by remembering each newly computed Fibonacci number. The idea is to use the built-in procedure **asserta** and to add these (intermediate) results as facts to the database. These facts have to precede other clauses about **fib** to prevent the use of the general rule in cases where the result is already known. The modified procedure, **fib2**, differs from **fib** only in this assertion:

```
fib2( 1, 1).                   % 1st Fibonacci number

fib2( 2, 1).                   % 2nd Fibonacci number

fib2( N, F)  :-                % Nth Fib. number, N > 2
  N > 2,
  N1 is N - 1, fib2( N1, F1),
  N2 is N - 2, fib2( N2, F2),
  F is F1 + F2,
  asserta( fib2( N, F) ).      % Remember Nth number
```

This program will try to answer any **fib2** goal by first looking at stored facts about this relation, and only then resort to the general rule. As a result, when a goal **fib2**(N, F) is executed all Fibonacci numbers, up to the Nth number, will get

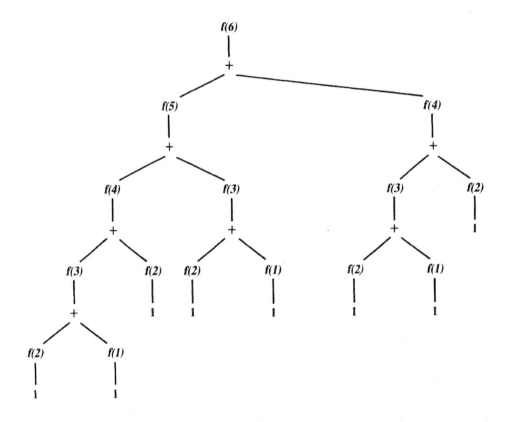

Figure 8.2 Computation of the 6th Fibonacci number by procedure **fib**.

tabulated. Figure 8.3 illustrates the computation of the 6th Fibonacci number by fib2. A comparison with Figure 8.2 shows the saving in the computational complexity. For greater N, the savings would be much more substantial.

Asserting intermediate results, also called *caching*, is a standard technique for avoiding repeated computations. It should be noted, however, that in the case of Fibonacci numbers we can preferably avoid repeated computation by using another algorithm, rather than by asserting intermediate results. This other algorithm will lead to a program that is more difficult to understand, but more efficient to execute. The idea this time is not to define the Nth Fibonacci number simply as the sum of its two predecessors and leave the recursive calls to unfold the whole computation 'downwards' to the two initial Fibonacci numbers. Instead, we can work 'upwards', starting with the initial two numbers, and compute the numbers in the sequence one by one in the forward direction. We have to stop when we have computed the Nth number. Most of the work in such a program is done by the procedure:

forwardfib(M, N, F1, F2, F)

Here, F1 and F2 are the (M − 1)st and Mth Fibonacci numbers, and F is the Nth Fibonacci number. Figure 8.4 helps to understand the **forwardfib** relation. According

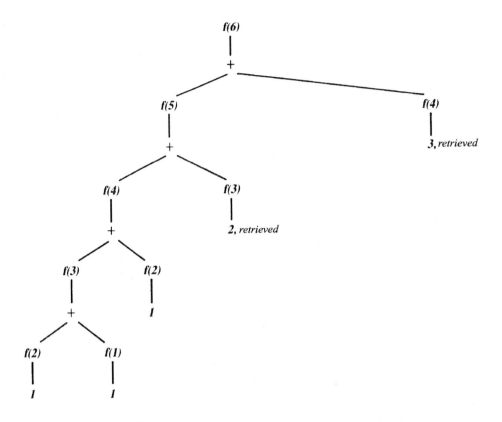

Figure 8.3 Computation of the 6th Fibonacci number by procedure **fib2**, which remembers previous results. This saves some computation in comparison with **fib**, see Figure 8.2.

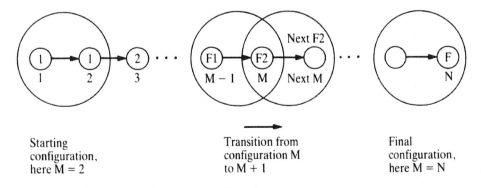

Figure 8.4 Relations in the Fibonacci sequence. A 'configuration', depicted by a large circle, is defined by three things: an index M and two consecutive Fibonacci numbers $f(M - 1)$ and $f(M)$.

to this figure, **forwardfib** finds a sequence of transformations to reach a final configuration (when M = N) from a given starting configuration. When **forwardfib** is invoked, all the arguments except F have to be instantiated, and M has to be less than or equal to N. The program is:

```
fib3( N, F)  :-
    forwardfib( 2, N, 1, 1, F).                 % The first two Fib. numbers are 1

forwardfib( M, N, F1, F2, F2) :-
    M >= N.                                     % Nth Fibonacci number reached

forwardfib( M, N, F1, F2, F)  :-
    M < N,                                      % Nth number not yet reached
    NextM is M + 1,
    NextF2 is F1 + F2,
    forwardfib( NextM, N, F2, NextF2, F).
```

Notice that **forwardfib** is tail recursive, and M, F1 and F2 are accumulator arguments.

Exercises

8.1   Procedures **sub1**, **sub2** and **sub3**, shown below, all implement the sublist relation. **sub1** is a more procedural definition whereas **sub2** and **sub3** are written in a more declarative style. Study the behaviour, with reference to efficiency, of these three procedures on some sample lists. Two of them behave nearly equivalently and have similar efficiency. Which two? Why is the remaining one less efficient?

```
sub1( List, Sublist)  :-
    prefix( List, Sublist).

sub1( [ _ | Tail], Sublist)  :-
    sub1( Tail, Sublist).                       % Sublist is sublist of Tail

prefix( _, [ ] ).

prefix( [X | List1], [X | List2] )  :-
    prefix( List1, List2).

sub2( List, Sublist)  :-
    conc( List1, List2, List),
    conc( List3, Sublist, List1).

sub3( List, Sublist)  :-
    conc( List1, List2, List),
    conc( Sublist, _, List2).
```

8.2   Define the relation

```
add_at_end( List, Item, NewList)
```

to add **Item** at the end of **List** producing **NewList**. Let both lists be represented by difference pairs.

8.3   Define the relation

   reverse(List, ReversedList)

where both lists are represented by difference pairs.

8.4   Rewrite the **collect** procedure of Section 8.5.2 using difference pair representation for lists so that the concatenation can be done more efficiently.

8.5   The following procedure computes the maximum value in a list of numbers:

```
max( [X], X).

max( [X | Rest], Max) :-
  max( Rest, MaxRest),
  ( MaxRest >= X, !, Max = MaxRest
  ;
    Max = X ).
```

Transform this into a tail-recursive procedure. Hint: Introduce accumulator argument **MaxSoFar**.

8.6   Rewrite program 3 for eight queens (Figure 4.11) using simulated array with **arg** to represent the sets of free diagonals, as discussed in Section 8.5.5. Measure the improvement in efficiency.

8.7   Implement the updating of the value of an element of an array simulated by **functor** and **arg**, using 'holes' for future values along the lines discussed in Section 5.5.5.

Summary

- There are several criteria for evaluating programs:

   correctness
   user-friendliness
   efficiency
   readability
   modifiability
   robustness
   documentation

- The principle of *stepwise refinement* is a good way of organizing the program development process. Stepwise refinement applies to relations, algorithms and data structures.

- In Prolog, the following techniques often help to find ideas for refinements:

   Using recursion: identify boundary and general cases of a recursive definition.

   Generalization: consider a more general problem that may be easier to solve than the original one.

Using pictures: graphical representation may help to identify important relations.

- It is useful to conform to some stylistic conventions to reduce the danger of programming errors, make programs easier to read, debug and modify.

- Prolog systems usually provide program debugging aids. Trace facilities are most useful.

- There are many ways of improving the efficiency of a program. Simple techniques include:

  reordering of goals and clauses

  controlling backtracking by inserting cuts

  remembering (by **asserta**) solutions that would otherwise be computed again

- More sophisticated techniques aim at better algorithms (improving search efficiency in particular) and better data structures. Frequently used programming techniques of this kind are:

  difference lists

  tail recursion, last call optimization

  accumulator arguments

  simulating arrays with **functor** and **arg**

References

Ross (1989) and O'Keefe (1990) explore in depth the efficiency issues, program design and programming style in Prolog. Sterling (1990) edited a collection of papers describing the design of large Prolog programs for a number of practical applications.

O'Keefe, R.A. (1990) *The Craft of Prolog*. Cambridge, MA: MIT Press.

Ross, P. (1989) *Advanced Prolog: Techniques and Examples*. Harlow: Addison-Wesley.

Sterling, L. (1990) *The Practice of Prolog*. Cambridge, MA: MIT Press.

chapter 9

Operations on Data Structures

One fundamental question in programming is how to represent complex data objects, such as sets, and efficiently implement operations on such objects. The theme of this chapter is some frequently used data structures that belong to three big families: lists, trees and graphs. We will examine ways of representing these structures in Prolog, and develop programs for some operations on these structures, such as sorting a list, representing data sets by tree structures, storing data in trees and retrieving data from trees, path finding in graphs, etc. We will study several examples because these operations are extremely instructive for programming in Prolog.

9.1 Sorting lists

A list can be sorted if there is an ordering relation between the items in the list. We will for the purpose of this discussion assume that there is an ordering relation

gt(X, Y)

meaning that X is *greater than* Y, whatever 'greater than' means. If our items are numbers then the gt relation will perhaps be defined as:

gt(X, Y) :- X > Y.

If the items are atoms then the gt relation can correspond to the alphabetical order, for example defined by:

gt(X, Y) :- X @> Y.

Remember that this relation also orders compound terms.

Let

sort(List, Sorted)

denote a relation where **List** is a list of items and **Sorted** is a list of the same items sorted in the ascending order according to the gt relation. We will develop three definitions of this relation in Prolog, based on different ideas for sorting a list. The first idea is as follows:

To sort a list, **List**:

- Find two adjacent elements, X and Y, in **List** such that gt(X, Y) and swap X and Y in **List**, obtaining **List1**; then sort **List1**.

- If there is no pair of adjacent elements, X and Y, in **List** such that gt(X, Y), then **List** is already sorted.

The purpose of swapping two elements, X and Y, that occur out of order, is that after the swapping the new list is closer to a sorted list. After a sufficient amount of swapping we should end up with all the elements in order. This principle of sorting is known as *bubble sort*. The corresponding Prolog procedure will be therefore called **bubblesort**:

```
bubblesort( List, Sorted) :-
    swap( List, List1), !,           % A useful swap in List?
    bubblesort( List1, Sorted).

bubblesort( Sorted, Sorted).         % Otherwise list is already sorted

swap( [X, Y | Rest], [Y, X | Rest] ) :-   % Swap first two elements
    gt( X, Y).

swap( [Z | Rest], [Z | Rest1] ) :-   % Swap elements in tail
    swap( Rest, Rest1).
```

Another simple sorting algorithm is *insertion sort*, which is based on the following idea:

To sort a non-empty list, L = [X | T]:

(1) Sort the tail T of L.

(2) Insert the head, X, of L into the sorted tail at such a position that the resulting list is sorted. The result is the whole sorted list.

This translates into Prolog as the following **insertsort** procedure:

```
insertsort( [], [] ).

insertsort( [X | Tail], Sorted)  :-
    insertsort( Tail, SortedTail),        % Sort the tail
    insert( X, SortedTail, Sorted).       % Insert X at proper place

insert( X, [Y | Sorted], [Y | Sorted1] )  :-
    gt( X, Y), !,
    insert( X, Sorted, Sorted1).

insert( X, Sorted, [X | Sorted] ).
```

The sorting procedures **bubblesort** and **insertsort** are simple, but inefficient. Of the two procedures, insertion sort is the more efficient one. However, the average time that **insertsort** requires for sorting a list of length n grows proportionally to n^2. For long lists, therefore, a much better sorting algorithm is *quicksort*. This is based on the following idea, which is illustrated in Figure 9.1.

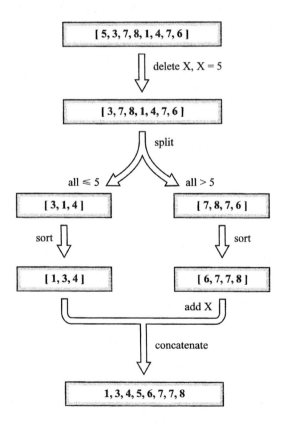

Figure 9.1 Sorting a list by *quicksort.*

To sort a non-empty list, L:

(1) Delete some element X from L and split the rest of L into two lists, called **Small** and **Big**, as follows: all elements in L that are greater than X belong to **Big**, and all others to **Small**.

(2) Sort **Small** obtaining **SortedSmall**.

(3) Sort **Big** obtaining **SortedBig**.

(4) The whole sorted list is the concatenation of **SortedSmall** and [X | **SortedBig**].

If the list to be sorted is empty then the result of sorting is also the empty list. A Prolog implementation of quicksort is shown in Figure 9.2. A particular detail of this implementation is that the element, X, that is deleted from L is always simply the head of L. The splitting is programmed as a four-argument relation:

split(X, L, Small, Big)

The time complexity of this algorithm depends on how lucky we are when splitting the list to be sorted. If the list is split into two lists of approximately equal lengths then the time complexity of this sorting procedure is of the order $n \log n$ where n is the length of the list to be sorted. If, on the contrary, splitting always results in one list far bigger than the other, then the complexity is in the order of n^2. Analysis would show that the average performance of quicksort is, fortunately, closer to the best case than to the worst case.

The program in Figure 9.2 can be further improved by a better implementation of the concatenation operation. Using the difference-pair representation of lists, introduced in Chapter 8, concatenation is reduced to triviality. To use this idea in

....

```
% quicksort( List, SortedList): sort List by the quicksort algorithm

quicksort( [], [] ).

quicksort( [X | Tail], Sorted) :-
    split( X, Tail, Small, Big),
    quicksort( Small, SortedSmall),
    quicksort( Big, SortedBig),
    conc( SortedSmall, [X | SortedBig], Sorted).

split( X, [], [], [] ).

split( X, [Y | Tail], [Y | Small], Big) :-
    gt( X, Y), !,
    split( X, Tail, Small, Big).

split( X, [Y | Tail], Small, [Y | Big] ) :-
    split( X, Tail, Small, Big).
```

....

Figure 9.2 Quicksort.

% quicksort(List, SortedList): sort List with the quicksort algorithm

```
quicksort( List, Sorted)  :-
  quicksort2( List, Sorted - [] ).
```

% quicksort2(List, SortedDiffList): sort List, result is represented as difference list

```
quicksort2( [], Z - Z).

quicksort2( [X | Tail], A1 - Z2)  :-
  split( X, Tail, Small, Big),
  quicksort2( Small, A1 - [X | A2] ),
  quicksort2( Big, A2 - Z2).
```

Figure 9.3 A more efficient implementation of **quicksort** using difference-pair representation for lists. Relation **split(X, List, Small, Big)** is as defined in Figure 9.2.

our sorting procedure, the lists in the program of Figure 9.2 can be represented by pairs of lists of the form A-Z as follows:

SortedSmall	is represented by	**A1 - Z1**
SortedBig	is represented by	**A2 - Z2**

Then the concatenation of the lists **SortedSmall** and [X | **SortedBig**] corresponds to the concatenation of pairs:

A1 - Z1   and   [X | A2] - Z2

The resulting concatenated list is represented by:

A1 - Z2   where   Z1 = [X | A2]

The empty list is represented by any pair Z-Z. Introducing these changes systematically into the program of Figure 9.2 we get a more efficient implementation of quicksort, programmed as **quicksort2** in Figure 9.3. The procedure **quicksort** still uses the usual representation of lists, but the actual sorting is done by the more efficient **quicksort2**, which uses the difference-pair representation. The relation between the two procedures is:

```
quicksort( L, S)  :-
  quicksort2( L, S - [] ).
```

Exercises

9.1   Write a procedure to merge two sorted lists producing a third list. For example:

?- **merge**([2,5,6,6,8], [1,3,5,9], L).

L = [1,2,3,5,5,6,6,8,9]

9.2   The difference between the sorting programs of Figures 9.2 and 9.3 is in the representation of lists – the latter uses difference-lists. Transformation between plain lists and difference-lists is straightforward and could be mechanized. Carry out the corresponding changes systematically in the program of Figure 9.2 to transform it into the program of Figure 9.3.

9.3   Our **quicksort** program performs badly when the list to be sorted is already sorted or almost sorted. Analyze why.

9.4   Another good idea for sorting a list that avoids the weakness of **quicksort** is based on dividing the list, then sorting smaller lists, and then merging these sorted smaller lists. Accordingly, to sort a list L:

- divide L into two lists, L1 and L2, of approximately equal length;
- sort L1 and L2 giving S1 and S2;
- merge S1 and S2 giving L sorted.

This is known as the merge-sort algorithm. Implement merge-sort and compare its efficiency with the **quicksort** program.

9.2   Representing sets by binary trees

One usual application of lists is to represent sets of objects. A disadvantage of using a list for representing a set is that the set membership testing is relatively inefficient. The predicate **member(X, L)** to test whether X is a member of a list L is usually programmed as:

member(X, [X | L]).

member(X, [Y | L]) :-
   member(X, L).

To find X in a list L, this procedure scans the list element by element until X is found or the end of the list is encountered. This is very inefficient in the case of long lists.
   For representing sets, there are various tree structures that facilitate more efficient implementation of the set membership relation. We will here consider binary trees.
   A binary tree is either empty or it consists of three things:

- a root;
- a left subtree;
- a right subtree.

The root can be anything, but the subtrees have to be binary trees again. Figure 9.4 shows an example. This tree represents the set {a, b, c, d}. The elements of the set are

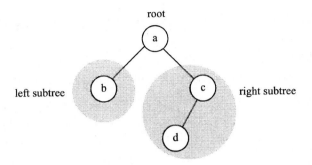

Figure 9.4 A binary tree.

stored as nodes of the tree. In Figure 9.4, the empty subtrees are not pictured; for example, the node b has two subtrees that are both empty.

There are many ways to represent a binary tree by a Prolog term. One simple possibility is to make the root of a binary tree the principal functor of the term, and the subtrees its arguments. Accordingly, the example tree of Figure 9.4 would be represented by:

> **a(b, c(d))**

Among other disadvantages, this representation requires another functor for each node of the tree. This can lead to troubles if nodes themselves are structured objects.

A better and more usual way to represent binary trees is as follows: we need a special symbol to represent the empty tree, and we need a functor to construct a non-empty tree from its three components (the root and the two subtrees). We will make the following choice regarding the functor and the special symbol:

- Let the atom **nil** represent the empty tree.

- Let the functor be t so the tree that has a root X, a left subtree L and a right subtree R is represented by the term t(L, X, R) (see Figure 9.5).

In this representation, the example tree of Figure 9.4 is represented by the term:

> **t(t(nil, b, nil), a, t(t(nil, d, nil), c, nil))**

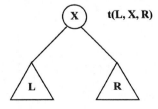

Figure 9.5 A representation of binary trees.

Let us now consider the set membership relation, here named in. A goal

in(X, T)

is true if X is a node in a tree T. The **in** relation can be defined by the following rules:

X is in a tree T if:

- the root of T is X, or
- X is in the left subtree of T, or
- X is in the right subtree of T.

These rules directly translate into Prolog:

in(X, t(_ , X, _)).

in(X, t(L, _ , _)) :-
   in(X, L).

in(X, t(_ , _ , R)) :-
   in(X, R).

Obviously, the goal

in(X, nil)

will fail for any X.

Let us investigate the behaviour of this procedure. In the following examples, T is the tree of Figure 9.4. The goal

in(X, T)

will, through backtracking, find all the data in the set in the following order:

X = a;   **X = b;**   **X = c;**   **X = d**

Now let us consider efficiency. The goal

in(a, T)

succeeds immediately by the first clause of the procedure **in**. On the other hand, the goal

in(d, T)

will cause several recursive calls of **in** before d is eventually found. Similarly, the goal

in(e, T)

will fail only after the whole tree has been searched by recursive calls of **in** on all the subtrees of T.

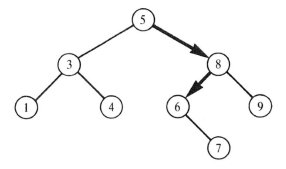

Figure 9.6   A binary dictionary. Item 6 is reached by following the indicated path 5 → 8 → 6.

This is, then, as inefficient as simply representing a set by a list. A major improvement can, however, be achieved if there is an ordering relation between the data in the set. Then the data in the tree can be ordered from left to right according to this relation. We say that a non-empty tree t(**Left**, **X**, **Right**) is ordered from left to right if:

(1)   all the nodes in the left subtree, **Left**, are less than X; and

(2)   all the nodes in the right subtree, **Right**, are greater than X; and

(3)   both subtrees are also ordered.

Such a binary tree will be called a *binary dictionary*. Figure 9.6 shows an example.

The advantage of ordering is that, to search for an object in a binary dictionary, it is always sufficient to search at most one subtree. The key to this economization when searching for X is that we can by comparing X and the root immediately discard at least one of the subtrees. For example, let us search for the item 6 in the tree of Figure 9.6. We start at the root, 5, compare 6 and 5, and establish 6 > 5. As all the data in the left subtree must be less than 5, the only remaining possibility to find 6 is the right subtree. So we continue the search in the right subtree, moving to node 8, etc.

The general method for searching in the binary dictionary is:

To find an item X in a dictionary D:

* if X is the root of D then X has been found, otherwise
* if X is less than the root of D then search for
  X in the left subtree of D, otherwise
* search for X in the right subtree of D;
* if D is empty the search fails.

% in(X, Tree): X in binary dictionary Tree

in(X, t(_ , X, _)).

in(X, t(Left, Root, Right)) :-
  gt(Root, X),   % Root greater than X
  in(X, Left).   % Search left subtree

in(X, t(Left, Root, Right)) :-
  gt(X, Root),   % X greater than Root
  in(X, Right).   % Search right subtree

Figure 9.7 Finding an item X in a binary dictionary.

These rules are programmed as the procedure **in** in Figure 9.7. The relation **gt(X, Y)** means: X is greater than Y. If the items stored in the tree are numbers then this relation is simply X > Y.

In a way, the **in** procedure itself can be also used for *constructing* a binary dictionary. For example, the following sequence of goals will construct a dictionary D that contains the elements 5, 3, 8:

?- **in(5, D), in(3, D), in(8, D).**

D = t(t(D1, 3, D2), 5, t(D3, 8, D4)).

The variables D1, D2, D3 and D4 are four unspecified subtrees. They can be anything and D will still contain the given items 3, 5 and 8. The dictionary that is constructed depends on the order of the goals in the question (Figure 9.8).

A comment is in order here on the search efficiency in dictionaries. Generally speaking, the search for an item in a dictionary is more efficient than searching in a

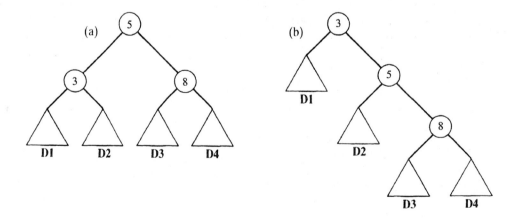

Figure 9.8 (a) Tree **D** that results from the sequence of goals: **in(5, D), in(3, D), in(8, D)**. (b) Tree resulting from: **in(3, D), in(5, D), in(8, D)**.

list. What is the improvement? Let n be the number of items in our data set. If the set is represented by a list then the expected search time will be proportional to its length n. On average, we have to scan the list up to something like half-way through it. If the set is represented by a binary dictionary, the search time will be roughly proportional to the height of the tree. The height of a tree is the length of a longest path between the root and a leaf in the tree. The height, however, depends on the shape of the tree.

We say that a tree is (approximately) *balanced* if, for each node in the tree, its two subtrees accommodate an approximately equal number of items. If a dictionary with n nodes is nicely balanced then its height is proportional to $\log n$. We say that a balanced tree has *logarithmic complexity*. The difference between n and $\log n$ is the improvement of a balanced dictionary over a list. This holds, unfortunately, only when a tree is approximately balanced. If the tree gets out of balance its performance will degrade. In extreme cases of totally unbalanced trees, a tree is in effect reduced to a list. In such a case the tree's height is n, and the tree's performance is equally poor as that of a list. Therefore we are always interested in balanced dictionaries. Methods of achieving this objective will be discussed in Chapter 10.

Exercises

9.5   Define the predicates

(a) **binarytree(Object)**

(b) **dictionary(Object)**

to recognize whether **Object** is a binary tree or a binary dictionary respectively, written in the notation of this section.

9.6   Define the procedure

height(BinaryTree, Height)

to compute the height of a binary tree. Assume that the height of the empty tree is 0, and that of a one-element tree is 1.

9.7   Define the relation

linearize(Tree, List)

to collect all the nodes in **Tree** into a list.

9.8   Define the relation

maxelement(D, Item)

so that **Item** is the largest element stored in the binary dictionary D.

9.9   Modify the procedure

      in(Item, BinaryDictionary)

by adding the third argument, **Path**, so that **Path** is the path between the root of the dictionary and **Item**.

9.3   Insertion and deletion in a binary dictionary

When maintaining a dynamic set of data we may want to insert new items into the set and also delete some old items from the set. So one common repertoire of operations on a set of data, S, is:

in(X, S)	X is a member of S
add(S, X, S1)	Add X to S giving S1
del(S, X, S1)	Delete X from S giving S1

Let us now define the *add* relation. It is easiest to insert new data at the bottom level of the tree, so that a new item becomes a leaf of the tree at such a position that the ordering of the tree is preserved. Figure 9.9 shows changes in a tree during a sequence of insertions. Let us call this kind of insertion **addleaf(D, X, D1)**.

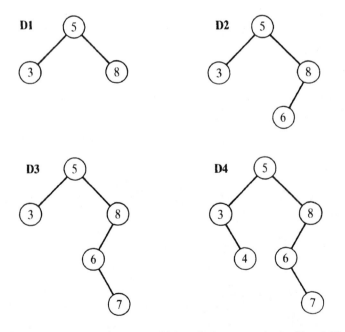

Figure 9.9   Insertion into a binary dictionary at the leaf level. The trees correspond to the following sequence of insertions: **add(D1, 6, D2), add(D2, 7, D3), add(D3, 4, D4).**

```
% addleaf( Tree, X, NewTree):
%    inserting X as a leaf into binary dictionary Tree gives NewTree

addleaf( nil, X, t( nil, X, nil) ).

addleaf( t( Left, X, Right), X, t( Left, X, Right) ).

addleaf( t( Left, Root, Right), X, t( Left1, Root, Right) ) :-
   gt( Root, X),
   addleaf( Left, X, Left1).

addleaf( t( Left, Root, Right), X, t( Left, Root, Right1) ) :-
   gt( X, Root),
   addleaf( Right, X, Right1).
```

Figure 9.10 Inserting an item as a leaf into the binary dictionary.

Rules for adding at the leaf level are:

- The result of adding X to the empty tree is the tree t(nil, X, nil).

- If X is the root of D then D1 = D (no duplicate item gets inserted).

- If the root of D is greater than X then insert X into the left subtree of D; if the root of D is less than X then insert X into the right subtree.

Figure 9.10 shows a corresponding program.

Let us now consider the *delete* operation. It is easy to delete a leaf, but deleting an internal node is more complicated. The deletion of a leaf can be in fact defined as the inverse operation of inserting at the leaf level:

```
delleaf( D1, X, D2) :-
   addleaf( D2, X, D1).
```

Unfortunately, if X is an internal node then this does not work because of the problem illustrated in Figure 9.11. X has two subtrees, **Left** and **Right**. After X is

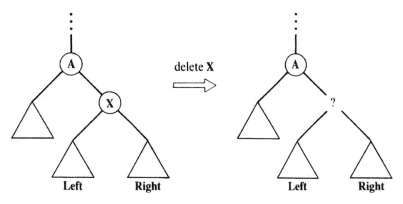

Figure 9.11 Deleting X from a binary dictionary. The problem is how to patch up the tree after X is removed.

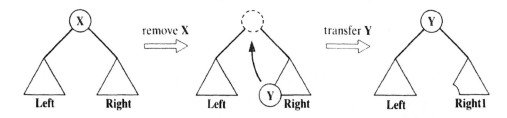

Figure 9.12   Filling the gap after removal of X.

removed, we have a hole in the tree and **Left** and **Right** are no longer connected to the rest of the tree. They cannot both be directly connected to the father of X, A, because A can accommodate only one of them.

If one of the subtrees **Left** and **Right** is empty then the solution is simple: the non-empty subtree is connected to A. If they are both non-empty then one idea is as shown in Figure 9.12. The left-most node of **Right**, Y, is transferred from its current position upwards to fill the gap after X. After this transfer, the tree remains ordered. Of course, the same idea works symmetrically, with the transfer of the right-most node of **Left**.

According to these considerations, the operation to delete an item from the binary dictionary is programmed in Figure 9.13. The transfer of the left-most node of the right subtree is accomplished by the relation

    delmin(Tree, Y, Tree1)

where Y is the minimal (that is, the left-most) node of **Tree**, and **Tree1** is **Tree** with Y deleted.

There is another elegant solution to *add* and *delete*. The *add* relation can be defined non-deterministically so that a new item is inserted at any level of the tree, not just at the leaf level. The rules are:

To add X to a binary dictionary D either:

- add X at the root of D (so that X becomes the new root), or
- if the root of D is greater than X then insert X into the left subtree of D, otherwise insert X into the right subtree of D.

The difficult part of this is the insertion at the root of D. Let us formulate this operation as a relation

    addroot(D, X, D1)

where X is the item to be inserted at the root of D and D1 is the resulting dictionary with X as its root. Figure 9.14 illustrates the relations between X, D and D1. The

% del(Tree, X, NewTree):
%   deleting X from binary dictionary Tree gives NewTree

del(t(nil, X, Right), X, Right).

del(t(Left, X, nil), X, Left).

del(t(Left, X, Right), X, t(Left, Y, Right1)) :-
  delmin(Right, Y, Right1).

del(t(Left, Root, Right), X, t(Left1, Root, Right)) :-
  gt(Root, X),
  del(Left, X, Left1).

del(t(Left, Root, Right), X, t(Left, Root, Right1)) :-
  gt(X, Root),
  del(Right, X, Right1).

% delmin(Tree, Y, NewTree):
%   delete minimal item Y in binary dictionary Tree producing NewTree

delmin(t(nil, Y, Right), Y, Right).

delmin(t(Left, Root, Right), Y, t(Left1, Root, Right)) :-
  delmin(Left, Y, Left1).

Figure 9.13 Deleting from the binary dictionary.

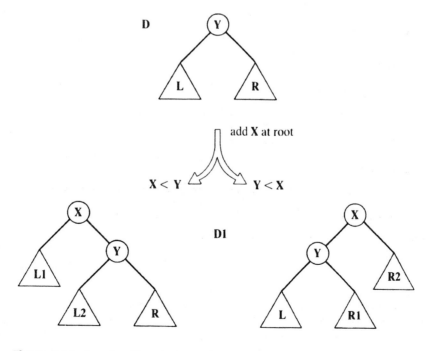

Figure 9.14 Inserting X at the root of a binary dictionary.

remaining question is now: What are the subtrees L1 and L2 in Figure 9.14 (or R1 and R2 alternatively)? The answer can be derived from the following constraints:

- L1 and L2 must be binary dictionaries;
- the set of nodes in L1 and L2 is equal to the set of nodes in L;
- all the nodes in L1 are less than X, and all the nodes in L2 are greater than X.

The relation that imposes all these constraints is just our **addroot** relation. Namely, if X were added as the root into L, then the subtrees of the resulting tree would be just L1 and L2. In Prolog, L1 and L2 must satisfy the goal:

   addroot(L, X, t(L1, X, L2))

The same constraints apply to R1 and R2:

   addroot(R, X, t(R1, X, R2))

Figure 9.15 shows a complete program for the 'non-deterministic' insertion into the binary dictionary.

The nice thing about this insertion procedure is that there is no restriction on the level of insertion. Therefore *add* can be used in the inverse direction in order to delete an item from the dictionary. For example, the following goal list constructs

```
% add( Tree, X, NewTree):
%    inserting X at any level of binary dictionary Tree gives NewTree

add( Tree, X, NewTree) :-
   addroot( Tree, X, NewTree).              % Add X as new root

add( t( L, Y, R), X, t( L1, Y, R) ) :-      % Insert X into left subtree
   gt( Y, X),
   add( L, X, L1).

add( t( L, Y, R), X, t( L, Y, R1) ) :-      % Insert X into right subtree
   gt( X, Y),
   add( R, X, R1).

% addroot( Tree, X, NewTree): inserting X as the root into Tree gives NewTree

addroot( nil, X, t( nil, X, nil) ).         % Insert into empty tree

addroot( t( L, Y, R), X, t( L1, X, t( L2, Y, R) ) ) :-
   gt( Y, X),
   addroot( L, X, t( L1, X, L2) ).

addroot( t( L, Y, R), X, t( t( L, Y, R1), X, R2) ) :-
   gt( X, Y),
   addroot( R, X, t( R1, X, R2) ).
```

Figure 9.15 Insertion into the binary dictionary at any level of the tree.

a dictionary D containing the items 3, 5, 1, 6, and then deletes 5 yielding a dictionary DD:

> **add(nil, 3, D1), add(D1, 5, D2), add(D2, 1, D3),**
> **add(D3, 6, D), add(DD, 5, D)**

9.4 Displaying trees

Like all data objects in Prolog, a binary tree, T, can be directly output by the built-in procedure **write**. However, the goal

> **write(T)**

will only output all the information, but will not graphically indicate the actual tree structure. It can be rather tiring to imagine the actual tree structure from a Prolog term that represents that tree. Therefore it is often desirable to have a tree typed out in a way that graphically indicates its structure.

There is a relatively simple method for displaying trees in such a form. The trick is to display a tree growing from left to right, and not from top to bottom as trees are usually pictured. The tree is rotated to the left so that the root becomes the left-most element, and the leaves are moved to the right. Figure 9.16 illustrates.

Let us define a procedure

> **show(T)**

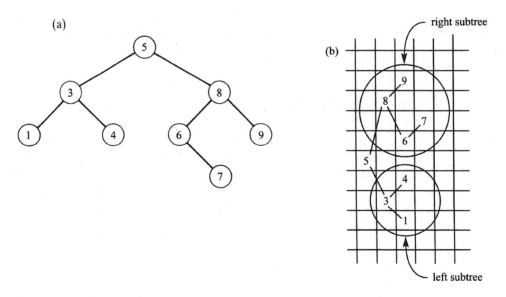

Figure 9.16 (a) A tree as normally pictured. (b) The same tree as typed out by the procedure **show** (arcs are added for clarity).

```
% show( Tree): display binary tree

show( Tree) :-
    show2( Tree, 0).

% show2( Tree, Indent): display Tree indented by Indent

show2( nil, _).
show2( t( Left, X, Right), Indent) :-
    Ind2 is Indent + 2,                    % Indentation of subtrees
    show2( Right, Ind2),                    % Display right subtree
    tab( Indent), write( X), nl,            % Write root
    show2( Left, Ind2).                     % Display left subtree
```

Figure 9.17 Displaying a binary tree.

to display a tree T in the form indicated in Figure 9.16. The principle is:

To show a non-empty tree, T:

(1)   show the right subtree of T, indented by some distance, H, to the right;

(2)   write the root of T;

(3)   show the left subtree of T indented by distance H to the right.

The indentation distance H, which can be appropriately chosen, is an additional parameter for displaying trees. Introducing H we have the procedure

    show2(T, H)

to display T indented H spaces from the left margin. The relation between the procedures **show** and **show2** is:

    show(T) :- show2(T, 0).

The complete program, which indents by 2, is shown in Figure 9.17. The principle of achieving such an output format can be easily adopted for displaying other types of trees.

Exercise

9.10   Our procedure for displaying trees shows a tree in an unusual orientation, so that the root is on the left and the leaves of the tree are on the right. Write a (more difficult) procedure to display a tree in the usual orientation with the root at the top and the leaves at the bottom.

9.5   Graphs

9.5.1   Representing graphs

Graph structures are used in many applications, such as representing relations, situations or problems. A graph is defined by a set of *nodes* and a set of *edges*, where each edge is a pair of nodes. When the edges are directed they are also called *arcs*. Arcs are represented by *ordered* pairs. Such a graph is a *directed* graph. The edges can be attached costs, names, or any kind of labels, depending on the application. Figure 9.18 shows examples.

Graphs can be represented in Prolog in several ways. One method is to represent each edge or arc separately as one clause. The graphs in Figure 9.18 can be thus represented by sets of clauses, for example:

connected(a, b).
connected(b, c).
...

arc(s, t, 3).
arc(t, v, 1).
arc(u, t, 2).
...

Another method is to represent a whole graph as one data object. A graph can be thus represented as a pair of two sets: nodes and edges. Each set can be represented as a list; each edge is a pair of nodes. Let us choose the functor **graph** to combine both sets into a pair, and the functor **e** for edges. Then one way to represent the (undirected) graph in Figure 9.18 is:

G1 = graph([a,b,c,d], [e(a,b), e(b,d), e(b,c), e(c,d)])

To represent a directed graph we can choose the functors **digraph** and **a** (for arcs). The directed graph of Figure 9.18 is then:

G2 = digraph([s,t,u,v], [a(s,t,3), a(t,v,1), a(t,u,5), a(u,t,2), a(v,u,2)])

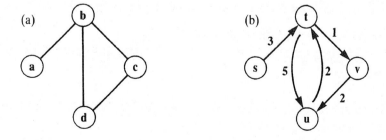

Figure 9.18   (a) A graph. (b) A directed graph with costs attached to the arcs.

If each node is connected to at least one other node then we can omit the list of nodes from the representation as the set of nodes is then implicitly specified by the list of edges.

Yet another method is to associate with each node a list of nodes that are adjacent to that node. Then a graph is a list of pairs consisting of a node plus its adjacency list. Our example graphs can then, for example, be represented by:

G1 = [**a** -> [**b**], **b** -> [**a,c,d**], **c** -> [**b,d**], **d** -> [**b,c**]]

G2 = [**s** -> [**t/3**], **t** -> [**u/5, v/1**], **u** -> [**t/2**], **v** -> [**u/2**]]

The symbols '->' and '/' above are, of course, infix operators.

What will be the most suitable representation will depend on the application and on operations to be performed on graphs. Two typical operations are:

- find a path between two given nodes;
- find a subgraph, with some specified properties, of a graph.

Finding a spanning tree of a graph is an example of the latter operation. In the following sections we will look at some simple programs for finding a path and for finding a spanning tree.

9.5.2   Finding a path

Let G be a graph, and A and Z two nodes in G. Let us define the relation

path(A, Z, G, P)

where P is an acyclic path between A and Z in G. P is represented as a list of nodes on the path. If G is the graph in the left-hand side of Figure 9.18 then:

path(a, d, G, [a,b,d])

path(a, d, G, [a,b,c,d])

Since a path must not contain any cycle, a node can appear in the path at most once. One method to find a path is:

To find an acyclic path, P, between A and Z in a graph, G:

If A = Z then P = [A], otherwise
find an acyclic path, P1, from some node Y to Z, and find a path from A to Y avoiding the nodes in P1.

This formulation implies another relation: find a path under the restriction of avoiding some subset of nodes (P1 above). We will, accordingly, define another procedure:

path1(A, Path1, G, Path)

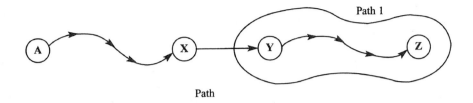

Figure 9.19 The **path1** relation: **Path** is a path between A and Z; the last part of **Path** overlaps with **Path1**.

As illustrated in Figure 9.19, the arguments are:

- A is a node,
- G is a graph,
- **Path1** is a path in G,
- **Path** is an acyclic path in G that goes from A to the beginning of **Path1** and continues along **Path1** up to its end.

The relation between **path** and **path1** is:

  path(A, Z, G, Path) :- path1(A, [Z], G, Path).

Figure 9.19 suggests a recursive definition of **path1**. The boundary case arises when the start node of **Path1** (Y in Figure 9.19) coincides with the start node of **Path**, A. If the start nodes do not coincide then there must be a node, X, such that:

(1)   Y is adjacent to X, and

(2)   X is not in **Path1**, and

(3)   **Path** must satisfy the relation **path1(A, [X | Path1], G, Path).**

A complete program is shown in Figure 9.20. In this program, **member** is the list membership relation. The relation

  adjacent(X, Y, G)

....

% path(A, Z, Graph, Path): Path is an acyclic path from A to Z in Graph

path(A, Z, Graph, Path) :-
  path1(A, [Z], Graph, Path).

path1(A, [A | Path1], _, [A | Path1]).

path1(A, [Y | Path1], Graph, Path) :-
  adjacent(X, Y, Graph),
  not member(X, Path1),   % No-cycle condition
  path1(A, [X, Y | Path1], Graph, Path).

....

Figure 9.20 Finding an acyclic path, **Path**, from A to Z in **Graph**.

means that there is an arc from X to Y in graph G. The definition of this relation depends on the representation of graphs. If G is represented as a pair of sets (nodes and edges),

G = graph(Nodes, Edges)

then:

adjacent(X, Y, graph(Nodes, Edges)) :-
  member(e(X,Y), Edges)
  ;
  member(e(Y,X), Edges).

A classical problem on graphs is to find a Hamiltonian path; that is, an acyclic path comprising all the nodes in the graph. Using **path** this can be done as follows:

hamiltonian(Graph, Path) :-
  path(_, _, Graph, Path),
  covers(Path, Graph).

covers(Path, Graph) :-
  not (node(N, Graph), not member(N, Path)).

Here, node(N, Graph) means: N is a node in **Graph**.

We can attach costs to paths. The cost of a path is the sum of the costs of the arcs in the path. If there are no costs attached to the arcs then we can talk about the length instead, counting 1 for each arc in the path. Our **path** and **path1** relations can be modified to handle costs by introducing an additional argument, the cost, for each path:

path(A, Z, G, P, C)

path1(A, P1, C1, G, P, C)

Here, C is the cost of P and C1 is the cost of P1. The relation **adjacent** now also has an extra argument, the cost of an arc. Figure 9.21 shows a path-finding program that computes a path and its cost.

This procedure can be used for finding a minimum cost path. We can find such a path between two nodes, **node1** and **node2**, in some graph **Graph** by the goals:

path(node1, node2, Graph, MinPath, MinCost),
not (path(node1, node2, Graph, _, Cost), Cost < MinCost)

We can also find a maximum cost path between any pair of nodes in a graph **Graph** by the goals:

path(_, _, Graph, MaxPath, MaxCost),
not (path(_, _, Graph, _, Cost), Cost > MaxCost)

It should be noted that this is a very inefficient way for finding minimal or maximal paths. This method unselectively investigates possible paths and is completely unsuitable for large graphs because of its high time complexity. The path-finding

```
% path( A, Z, Graph, Path, Cost):
%    Path is an acyclic path with cost Cost from A to Z in Graph

path( A, Z, Graph, Path, Cost)  :-
   path1( A, [Z], 0, Graph, Path, Cost).

path1( A, [A | Path1], Cost1, Graph, [A | Path1], Cost1).

path1( A, [Y | Path1], Cost1, Graph, Path, Cost)  :-
   adjacent( X, Y, CostXY, Graph),
   not member( X, Path1),
   Cost2 is Cost1 + CostXY,
   path1( A, [X, Y | Path1], Cost2, Graph, Path, Cost).
```

Figure 9.21 Path-finding in a graph: **Path** is an acyclic path with cost **Cost** from A to Z in **Graph**.

problem frequently arises in Artificial Intelligence. We will study more sophisticated methods for finding optimal paths in Chapters 11 and 12.

9.5.3 Finding a spanning tree of a graph

A graph is said to be *connected* if there is a path from any node to any other node. Let G = (V, E) be a connected graph with the set of nodes V and the set of edges E. A *spanning tree* of G is a connected graph T = (V, E′) where E′ is a subset of E such that:

(1)   T is connected, and

(2)   there is no cycle in T.

These two conditions guarantee that T is a tree. For the left-hand side graph of Figure 9.18, there are three spanning trees, which correspond to three lists of edges:

Tree1 = [a-b, b-c, c-d]

Tree2 = [a-b, b-d, d-c]

Tree3 = [a-b, b-d, b-c]

Here each term of the form X-Y denotes an edge between nodes X and Y. We can pick any node in such a list as the root of a tree. Spanning trees are of interest, for example, in communication problems because they provide, with the minimum number of communication lines, a path between any pair of nodes.

We will define a procedure

stree(G, T)

where T is a spanning tree of G. We will assume that G is connected. We can imagine constructing a spanning tree algorithmically as follows: Start with the empty set of edges and gradually add new edges from G, taking care that a cycle is never created, until no more edge can be added because it would create a cycle. The resulting set of edges defines a spanning tree. The no-cycle condition can be maintained by a simple rule: an edge can be added only if one of its nodes is already in the growing tree, and the other node is not yet in the tree. A program that implements this idea is shown in Figure 9.22. The key relation in this program is:

spread(Tree1, Tree, G)

All the three arguments are sets of edges. G is a connected graph; **Tree1** and **Tree** are subsets of G such that they both represent trees. **Tree** is a spanning tree of G obtained by adding zero or more edges of G to **Tree1**. We can say that 'Tree1 gets spread to **Tree**'.

It is interesting that we can also develop a working program for constructing a spanning tree in another, completely declarative way, by simply stating

....

```
% Finding a spanning tree of a graph
%
% Trees and graphs are represented by lists of their edges.
% For example: Graph = [a-b, b-c, b-d, c-d]

% stree( Graph, Tree): Tree is a spanning tree of Graph

stree( Graph, Tree)  :-
    member( Edge, Graph),
    spread( [Edge], Tree, Graph).

% spread( Tree1, Tree, Graph): Tree1 'spreads to' spanning tree Tree of Graph

spread( Tree1, Tree, Graph)  :-
    addedge( Tree1, Tree2, Graph),
    spread( Tree2, Tree, Graph).

spread( Tree, Tree, Graph)  :-
    not addedge( Tree, _, Graph).          % No edge can be added without creating a cycle

% addedge( Tree, NewTree, Graph):
%    add an edge from Graph to Tree without creating a cycle

addedge( Tree, [A-B | Tree], Graph)  :-
    adjacent( A, B, Graph),                % Nodes A and B adjacent in Graph
    node( A, Tree),                        % A in Tree
    not node( B, Tree).                    % A-B doesn't create a cycle in Tree

adjacent( Node1, Node2, Graph)  :-
    member( Node1-Node2, Graph)
    ;
    member( Node2-Node1, Graph).

node( Node, Graph)  :-                     % Node is a node in Graph if
    adjacent( Node, _, Graph).             % Node is adjacent to anything in Graph
```

....

Figure 9.22 Finding a spanning tree of a graph: an 'algorithmic' program. The program assumes that the graph is connected.

mathematical definitions. We will assume that both graphs and trees are represented by lists of their edges, as in the program of Figure 9.22. The definitions we need are:

(1)   T is a spanning tree of G if:

   • T is a subset of G, and

   • T is a tree, and

   • T 'covers' G; that is, each node of G is also in T.

(2)   A set of edges T is a tree if:

   • T is connected, and

   • T has no cycle.

```
% Finding a spanning tree
% Graphs and trees are represented as lists of edges.

% stree( Graph, Tree): Tree is a spanning tree of Graph

stree( Graph, Tree)  :-
   subset( Graph, Tree),
   tree( Tree),
   covers( Tree, Graph).

tree( Tree)  :-
   connected( Tree),
   not hasacycle( Tree).

% connected( Graph): there is a path between any two nodes in Graph

connected( Graph)  :-
   not ( node( A, Graph), node( B, Graph), not path( A, B, Graph, _) ).

hasacycle( Graph)  :-
   adjacent( Node1, Node2, Graph),
   path( Node1, Node2, Graph, [Node1, X, Y | _] ).          % Path of length > 1

% covers( Tree, Graph): every node of Graph is in Tree

covers( Tree, Graph)  :-
   not ( node( Node, Graph), not node( Node, Tree) ).

% subset( List1, List2): List2 represents a subset of List1

subset( [], [] ).

subset( [X | Set], Subset)  :-                              % X not in subset
   subset( Set, Subset).

subset( [X | Set], [X | Subset])  :-                        % X included in subset
   subset( Set, Subset).
```

Figure 9.23   Finding a spanning tree of a graph: a 'declarative' program. Relations **node** and **adjacent** are as in Figure 9.22.

Using our **path** program of the previous section, these definitions can be stated in Prolog as shown in Figure 9.23. It should be noted, however, that this program is, in this form, of little practical interest because of its inefficiency.

Exercises

9.11   Consider spanning trees of graphs that have costs attached to edges. Let the *cost* of a spanning tree be defined as the sum of the costs of all the edges in the tree. Write a program to find a minimum-cost spanning tree of a given graph.

9.12   Experiment with the spanning tree programs in Figures 9.22 and 9.23, and measure their execution times. Identify the sources of inefficiency in the second program.

Summary

In this chapter we studied Prolog implementations of some frequently used data structures and associated operations on them. These include:

- Lists:

    sorting lists:
        bubble sort
        insertion sort
        quicksort
    efficiency of these procedures

- Representing sets as binary trees and binary dictionaries:

    searching for an item in a tree
    adding an item
    deleting an item
    adding as a leaf, adding as the root
    the balance of trees, how balance affects the efficiency of these operations
    displaying trees

- Graphs:

    representing graphs
    finding a path in a graph
    finding a spanning tree of a graph

References

In this chapter we have tackled in Prolog classical topics of sorting and of maintaining data structures for representing sets. These topics are covered in general books on algorithms and data structures, for example, Aho, Hopcroft and Ullman (1974, 1983), Cormen, Leiserson and

Rivest (1990), Gonnet and Baeza-Yates (1991) and Kingston (1998). The Prolog program for insertion at any level of the binary tree (Section 9.3) was first shown to the author by M. van Emden (personal communication).

Aho, A.V., Hopcroft, J.E. and Ullman, J.D. (1974) *The Design and Analysis of Computer Algorithms*. Addison-Wesley.

Aho, A.V., Hopcroft, J.E. and Ullman, J.D. (1983) *Data Structures and Algorithms*. Addison-Wesley.

Cormen, T.H., Leiserson, C.E. and Rivest, R.L. (1990) *Introduction to Algorithms* (second edition 2000). MIT Press.

Gonnet, G.H. and Baeza-Yates, R. (1991) *Handbook of Algorithms and Data Structures in Pascal and C* (second edition). Addison-Wesley.

Kingston, J.H. (1998) *Algorithms and Data Structures* (second edition). Addison-Wesley.

chapter 10

Advanced Tree Representations

In this chapter we look at advanced techniques for representing data sets by trees. The key idea is to keep the tree balanced, or approximately balanced, in order to prevent the tree from degenerating toward a list. Such tree-balancing schemes guarantee relatively fast, logarithmic-time data-access even in the worst case. Two such schemes are presented in this chapter: 2-3 trees and AVL-trees. (The knowledge of this chapter is not a prerequisite to any other chapter.)

10.1   The 2-3 dictionary

A binary tree is said to be well balanced if both its subtrees are of approximately equal height (or size) and they are also balanced. The height of a balanced tree is approximately $\log n$ where n is the number of nodes in the tree. The time needed to evaluate the relations **in**, **add** and **delete** on binary dictionaries grows proportionally with the height of the tree. On balanced dictionaries, then, all these operations can be done in time that is in the order of $\log n$. The logarithmic growth of the complexity of the set membership testing is a definite improvement over the list representation of sets, where the complexity grows linearly with the size of the data set. However, poor balance of a tree will degrade the performance of the dictionary. In extreme cases, the binary dictionary degenerates into a list, as shown in Figure 10.1. The form of the dictionary depends on the sequence in which the data is inserted. In the best case we get a good balance with performance in the order $\log n$, and in the worst case the performance is in the order n. Analysis shows that on average, assuming that any sequence of data is equally likely, the complexity of **in**, **add** and **delete** is still in the order $\log n$. So the average performance is, fortunately, closer to the best case than to the worst case. There are, however, several rather

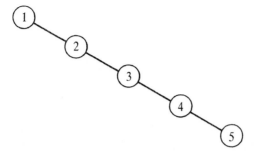

Figure 10.1 A totally unbalanced binary dictionary. Its performance is reduced to that of a list.

simple schemes for keeping good balance of the tree regardless of the data sequence. Such schemes guarantee the *worst case* performance of **in, add** and **delete** in the order $\log n$. One of them is the 2-3 tree; another scheme is the AVL-tree.

The *2-3* tree is defined as follows: it is either empty, or it consists of a single node, or it is a tree that satisfies the following conditions:

- each internal node has two or three children, and
- all the leaves are at the same level.

A 2-3 dictionary is a 2-3 tree in which the data items are stored in the leaves, ordered from left to right. Figure 10.2 shows an example. The internal nodes contain labels that specify the minimal elements of the subtrees as follows:

- if an internal node has two subtrees, this internal node contains the minimal element of the second subtree;
- if an internal node has three subtrees then this node contains the minimal elements of the second and of the third subtree.

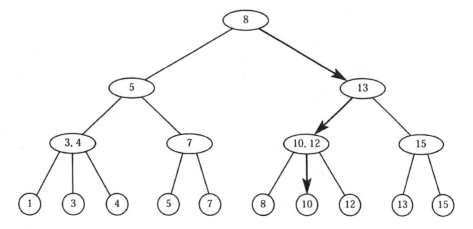

Figure 10.2 A 2-3 dictionary. The indicated path corresponds to searching for the item 10.

To search for an item, X, in a 2-3 dictionary we start at the root and move toward the bottom level according to the labels in the internal nodes. Let the root contain the labels M1 and M2. Then:

- if X < M1 then continue the search in the left subtree, otherwise
- if X < M2 then continue the search in the middle subtree, otherwise
- continue the search in the right subtree.

If the root only contains one label, M, then proceed to the left subtree if X < M, and to the right subtree otherwise. This is repeated until the leaf level is reached, and at this point X is either successfully found or the search fails.

As all the leaves are at the same level, the 2-3 tree is perfectly balanced with respect to the heights of the subtrees. All search paths from the root to a leaf are of the same length which is of the order $\log n$, where n is the number of items stored in the tree.

When inserting new data, the 2-3 tree can also grow in breadth, not only in depth. Each internal node that has two children can accommodate an additional child, which results in the breadth-wise growth. If, on the other hand, a node with three children accepts another child then this node is split into two nodes, each of them taking over two of the total of four children. The so-generated new internal node gets incorporated further up in the tree. If this happens at the top level then the tree is forced to grow upwards. Figure 10.3 illustrates these principles.

Insertion into the 2-3 dictionary will be programmed as the relation

add23(Tree, X, NewTree)

where **NewTree** is obtained by inserting X into **Tree**. The main burden of insertion will be transferred to two auxiliary relations, both called **ins**. The first one has three arguments:

ins(Tree, X, NewTree)

where **NewTree** is the result of inserting X into **Tree**. **Tree** and **NewTree** have the *same height*. But, of course, it is not always possible to preserve the same height after

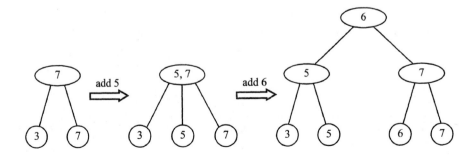

Figure 10.3   Inserting into a 2-3 dictionary. The tree first grows in breadth and then upwards.

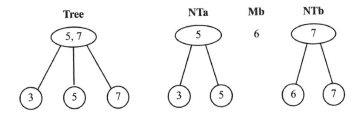

Figure 10.4 The objects in the figure satisfy the relation **ins(Tree, 6, NTa, Mb, NTb)**.

insertion. Therefore we have another **ins** relation, with five arguments, to cater for this case:

  ins(Tree, X, NTa, Mb, NTb)

Here, when inserting X into **Tree**, **Tree** is split into two trees: **NTa** and **NTb**. Both **NTa** and **NTb** have the same height as **Tree**. **Mb** is the minimal element of **NTb**. Figure 10.4 shows an example.

  In the program, a 2-3 tree will be represented, depending on its form, as follows:

- **nil** represents the empty tree.

- l(X) represents a single node tree, a leaf with item X.

- n2(T1, M, T2) represents a tree with two subtrees, T1 and T2; M is the minimal element of T2.

- n3(T1, M2, T2, M3, T3) represents a tree with three subtrees, T1, T2 and T3; M2 is the minimal element of T2, and M3 is the minimal element of T3.

T1, T2 and T3 are all 2-3 trees.

  The relation between **add23** and **ins** is: if after insertion the tree does not grow upwards then simply:

  add23(Tree, X, NewTree) :-
  ins(Tree, X, NewTree).

If, however, the height after insertion increases, then **ins** determines the two subtrees, T1 and T2, which are then combined into a bigger tree:

  add23(Tree, X, n2(T1, M, T2)) :-
  ins(Tree, X, T1, M, T2).

The **ins** relation is more complicated because it has to deal with many cases: inserting into the empty tree, a single node tree, a tree of type n2 or n3. Additional subcases arise from insertion into the first, second or third subtree. Accordingly, **ins** will be defined by a set of rules so that each clause about **ins** will deal with one of the cases. Figure 10.5 illustrates some of these cases. The cases in this figure translate into Prolog as follows:

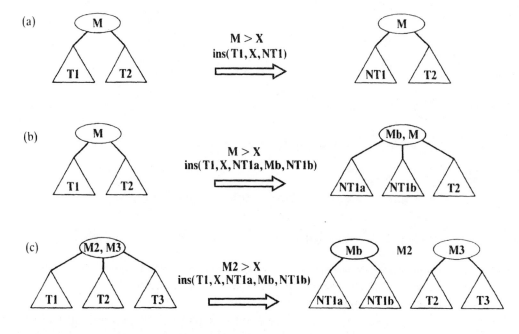

Figure 10.5 Some cases of the **ins** relation.
(a) **ins(n2(T1, M, T2), X, n2(NT1, M, T2));**
(b) **ins(n2(T1, M, T2), X, n3(NT1a, Mb, NT1b, M, T2));**
(c) **ins(n3(T1, M2, T2, M3, T3), X, n2(NT1a, Mb, NT1b),
            M2, n2(T2, M3, T3))**

Case a

    ins(n2(T1, M, T2), X, n2(NT1, M, T2)) :-
       gt(M, X),   % M greater than X
       ins(T1, X, NT1).

Case b

    ins(n2(T1, M, T2), X, n3(NT1a, Mb, NT1b, M, T2)) :-
       gt(M, X),
       ins(T1, X, NT1a, Mb, NT1b).

Case c

    ins(n3(T1, M2, T2, M3, T3), X, n2(NT1a, Mb, NT1b), M2, n2(T2, M3, T3)) :-
       gt(M2, X),
       ins(T1, X, NT1a, Mb, NT1b).

Figure 10.6 shows the complete program for inserting into the 2-3 dictionary.
Figure 10.7 shows a program for displaying 2-3 trees.

Our program occasionally does some unnecessary backtracking. If the three-
argument **ins** fails then the five-argument **ins** is called, which redoes part of the

% Insertion in the 2-3 dictionary

add23(Tree, X, Tree1) :-   % Add X to Tree giving Tree1
  ins(Tree, X, Tree1).   % Tree grows in breadth

add23(Tree, X, n2(T1, M2, T2)) :-   % Tree grows upwards
  ins(Tree, X, T1, M2, T2).

add23(nil, X, l(X)).

ins(l(A), X, l(A), X, l(X)) :-
  gt(X, A).

ins(l(A), X, l(X), A, l(A)) :-
  gt(A, X).

ins(n2(T1, M, T2), X, n2(NT1, M, T2)) :-
  gt(M, X),
  ins(T1, X, NT1).

ins(n2(T1, M, T2), X, n3(NT1a, Mb, NT1b, M, T2)) :-
  gt(M, X),
  ins(T1, X, NT1a, Mb, NT1b).

ins(n2(T1, M, T2), X, n2(T1, M, NT2)) :-
  gt(X, M),
  ins(T2, X, NT2).

ins(n2(T1, M, T2), X, n3(T1, M, NT2a, Mb, NT2b)) :-
  gt(X, M),
  ins(T2, X, NT2a, Mb, NT2b).

ins(n3(T1, M2, T2, M3, T3), X, n3(NT1, M2, T2, M3, T3)) :-
  gt(M2, X),
  ins(T1, X, NT1).

ins(n3(T1, M2, T2, M3, T3), X, n2(NT1a, Mb, NT1b), M2, n2(T2, M3, T3)) :-
  gt(M2, X),
  ins(T1, X, NT1a, Mb, NT1b).

ins(n3(T1, M2, T2, M3, T3), X, n3(T1, M2, NT2, M3, T3)) :-
  gt(X, M2), gt(M3, X),
  ins(T2, X, NT2).

ins(n3(T1, M2, T2, M3, T3), X, n2(T1, M2, NT2a), Mb, n2(NT2b, M3, T3)) :-
  gt(X, M2), gt(M3, X),
  ins(T2, X, NT2a, Mb, NT2b).

ins(n3(T1, M2, T2, M3, T3), X, n3(T1, M2, T2, M3, NT3)) :-
  gt(X, M3),
  ins(T3, X, NT3).

ins(n3(T1, M2, T2, M3, T3), X, n2(T1, M2, T2), M3, n2(NT3a, Mb, NT3b)) :-
  gt(X, M3),
  ins(T3, X, NT3a, Mb, NT3b).

Figure 10.6 Inserting in the 2-3 dictionary. In this program, an attempt to insert a duplicate
item will fail.

....

```
% Displaying 2-3 dictionary

show( T) :-
  show( T, 0).

show( nil, _ ).

show( l(A), H) :-
  tab( H), write( A), nl.

show( n2( T1, M, T2), H) :-
  H1 is H + 5,
  show( T2, H1),
  tab( H), write( --), nl,
  tab( H), write( M), nl,
  tab( H), write( --), nl,
  show( T1, H1).

show( n3( T1, M2, T2, M3, T3), H) :-
  H1 is H + 5,
  show( T3, H1),
  tab( H), write( --), nl,
  tab( H), write( M3), nl,
  show( T2, H1),
  tab( H), write( M2), nl,
  tab( H), write( --), nl,
  show( T1, H1).
```

```
                                    15
                               --
                               15
                               --
                               13
                          --
                          13
                          --
                                    12
                               --
                               12
                                    10
                               10
                               --
                                    8
                     --
                     8
                     --
                                    7
                               --
                               7
                               --
                                    5
                          --
                          5
                          --
                                    4
                               --
                               4
                                    3
                               3
                               --
                                    1
```

Figure 10.7   Left: a program to display a 2-3 dictionary. Right: the dictionary of Figure 10.2 as displayed by this program.

....

work. This source of inefficiency can easily be eliminated by, for example, redefining ins as:

    ins2(Tree, X, NewTrees)

NewTrees is a list of length 1 or 3, as follows:

    NewTrees = [NewTree]   if   ins(Tree, X, NewTree)

    NewTrees = [NTa, Mb, NTb]   if   ins(Tree, X, NTa, Mb, NTb)

The **add23** relation would be, accordingly, redefined as:

add23(T, X, T1) :-
    ins2(T, X, Trees),
    combine(Trees, T1).

The **combine** relation has to produce a single tree, T1, from the list **Trees**.

Exercises

10.1   Define the relation

in(Item, Tree)

to search for **Item** in a 2-3 dictionary **Tree**.

10.2   Modify the program of Figure 10.6 to avoid backtracking (define relations **ins2** and **combine**).

10.2   AVL-tree: an approximately balanced tree

AVL-tree is a binary tree that has the following properties:

(1)   Its left subtree and right subtree differ in height by 1 at the most.

(2)   Both subtrees themselves are also AVL-trees.

This definition allows for trees that are slightly out of balance. It can be shown that the height of an AVL-tree is always, even in the worst case, roughly proportional to $\log n$ where n is the number of nodes in the tree. This guarantees the logarithmic performance for the operations **in, add** and **del**.

Operations on the AVL-dictionary are essentially the same as on binary dictionaries, with some additions to maintain approximate balance of the tree. If the tree gets out of approximate balance after an insertion or deletion then some additional mechanism will get it back into the required degree of balance. To implement this mechanism efficiently, we have to maintain some additional information about the balance of the tree. Essentially we only need the difference between the heights of its subtrees, which is either -1, 0 or $+1$. For the sake of simplicity of the operations involved we will, however, prefer to maintain the complete heights of trees and not only the differences.

We will define the insertion relation as:

addavl(Tree, X, NewTree)

where both **Tree** and **NewTree** are AVL-dictionaries such that **NewTree** is **Tree** with X inserted. AVL-trees will be represented by terms of the form:

t(Left, A, Right) / Height

where A is the root, **Left** and **Right** are the subtrees, and **Height** is the height of the tree. The empty tree is represented by **nil/0**. Now let us consider the insertion of X into a non-empty AVL-dictionary:

Tree = t(L, A, R)/H

We will start our discussion by only considering the case where X is greater than A. Then X is to be inserted into R and we have the following relation:

addavl(R, X, t(R1, B, R2)/Hb)

Figure 10.8 illustrates the following ingredients from which **NewTree** is to be constructed:

L, A, R1, B, R2

What can be the heights of L, R, R1 and R2? L and R can only differ in height by 1 at the most. Figure 10.8 shows what the heights of R1 and R2 can be. As only one item, X, has been inserted into R, at most one of the subtrees R1 and R2 can have the height $h + 1$.

In the case that X is less than A then the situation is analogous with left and right subtrees interchanged. Therefore, in any case, we have to construct **NewTree** from three trees (let us call them **Tree1**, **Tree2** and **Tree3**), and two single items, A and B. Let us now consider the question: How can we combine these five ingredients to make

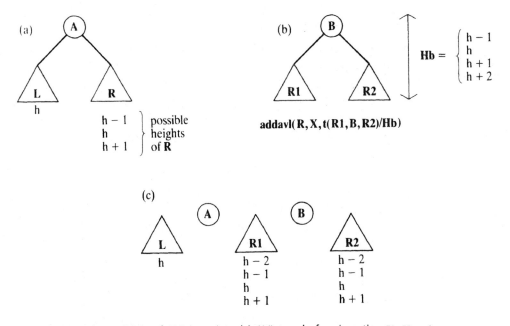

Figure 10.8   The problem of AVL insertion: (a) AVL-tree before inserting **X**, **X** > **A**; (b) AVL-tree after inserting **X** into **R**; (c) ingredients from which the new tree is to be constructed.

NewTree so that NewTree is an AVL-dictionary? The order from left to right in NewTree has to be:

Tree1, A, Tree2, B, Tree3

We have to consider three cases:

(1)   The middle tree, **Tree2**, is taller than both other trees.

(2)   **Tree1** is at least as tall as **Tree2** and **Tree3**.

(3)   **Tree3** is at least as tall as **Tree2** and **Tree1**.

Figure 10.9 shows how **NewTree** can be constructed in each of these cases. In case 1, the middle tree **Tree2** has to be decomposed and its parts incorporated into NewTree. The three rules of Figure 10.9 are easily translated into Prolog as a relation:

combine(Tree1, A, Tree2, B, Tree3, NewTree)

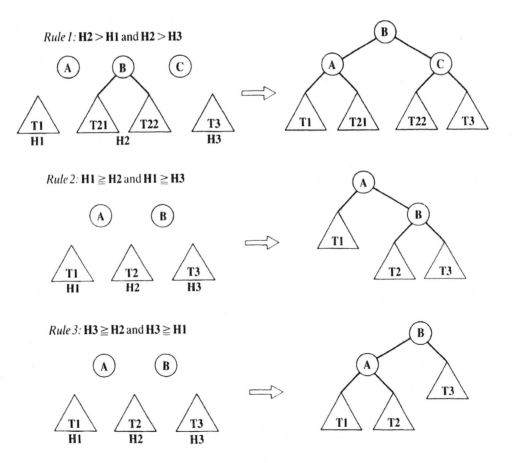

Figure 10.9   Three combination rules for AVL-trees.

The last argument, NewTree, is an AVL-tree constructed from five ingredients, the first five arguments. Rule 1, for example, becomes:

```
combine(
    T1/H1, A, t(T21,B,T22) / H2, C, T3/H3,                          % Five ingredients
    t( t(T1/H1,A,T21)/Ha, B, t(T22,C,T3/H3)/Hc)/Hb) :-             % Their combination

    H2 > H1, H2 > H3,                                               % Middle tree is tallest
    Ha is H1 + 1,                                                   % Height of left subtree
    Hc is H3 + 1,                                                   % Height of right subtree
    Hb is Ha + 1.                                                   % Height of the whole tree
```

....

```
% addavl( Tree, X, NewTree): insertion into AVL-dictionary
%    Tree = t( Left, Root, Right)/HeightOfTree
%    Empty tree = nil/0

addavl( nil/0, X, t( nil/0, X, nil/0)/1).                          % Add X to empty tree
addavl( t( L, Y, R)/Hy, X, NewTree) :-                            % Add X to non-empty tree
    gt( Y, X),
    addavl( L, X, t( L1, Z, L2)/_ ),                              % Add into left subtree
    combine( L1, Z, L2, Y, R, NewTree).                          % Combine ingredients of NewTree
addavl( t( L, Y, R)/Hy, X, NewTree) :-
    gt( X, Y),
    addavl( R, X, t( R1, Z, R2)/_ ),                             % Add into right subtree
    combine( L, Y, R1, Z, R2, NewTree).

% combine( Tree1, A, Tree2, B, Tree3, NewTree):
%    combine Tree1, Tree2, Tree3 and nodes A and B into an AVL-tree

combine( T1/H1, A, t( T21, B, T22)/H2, C, T3/H3,
        t( t(T1/H1,A,T21)/Ha, B, t(T22,C,T3/H3)/Hc)/Hb) :-
    H2 > H1, H2 > H3,                                            % Middle subtree tallest
    Ha is H1 + 1,
    Hc is H3 + 1,
    Hb is Ha + 1.
combine( T1/H1, A, T2/H2, C, T3/H3, t( T1/H1, A, t(T2/H2,C,T3/H3)/Hc)/Ha) :-
    H1 >= H2, H1 >= H3,                                          % Tall left subtree
    max1( H2, H3, Hc),
    max1( H1, Hc, Ha).
combine( T1/H1, A, T2/H2, C, T3/H3, t( t(T1/H1,A,T2/H2)/Ha, C, T3/H3)/Hc) :-
    H3 >= H2, H3 >= H1,                                          % Tall right subtree
    max1( H1, H2, Ha),
    max1( Ha, H3, Hc).
max1( U, V, M) :-                                                % M is 1 + max. of U and V
    U > V, !, M is U + 1
    ;
    M is V + 1.
```

....

Figure 10.10   AVL-dictionary insertion. In this program, an attempt to insert a duplicate will fail. See Figure 10.9 for **combine**.

A complete **addavl** program, which also computes the heights of the tree and the subtrees, is shown as Figure 10.10.

Our program works with the heights of trees. A more economical representation is, as said earlier, possible. In fact, we only need the balance, which can only be -1, 0 or $+1$. The disadvantage of such economization would be, however, somewhat more complicated combination rules.

Exercises

10.3   Define the relation

    avl(Tree)

to test whether a binary tree **Tree** is an AVL-tree; that is, all the sibling subtrees may differ in their heights by 1 at the most. Let binary trees be represented by terms of the form **t(Left, Root, Right)** or **nil**.

10.4   Trace the execution of the AVL insertion algorithm, starting with the empty tree and successively inserting 5, 8, 9, 3, 1, 6, 7. How is the root item changing during this process?

Summary

- 2-3 trees and AVL-trees, implemented in this chapter, are types of balanced trees.

- Balanced, or approximately balanced, trees guarantee efficient execution of the three basic operations on trees: looking for an item, adding or deleting an item. All these operations can be done in time proportional to $\log n$, where n is the number of nodes in the tree.

References

2-3 trees are described in detail by, for example, Aho, Hopcroft and Ullman (1974, 1983). In their 1983 book an implementation in Pascal is also given. Wirth (1976) gives a Pascal program to handle AVL-trees. 2-3 trees are a special case of more general B-trees. This and several other variations or data structures related to 2-3 trees and AVL-trees are covered, among others, by Gonnet and Baeza-Yates (1991) together with various results on the behaviour of these structures. A program for AVL-tree insertion that only uses tree-bias information (that is, the difference between the heights of the subtrees -1, 0 or $+1$, and not the complete height) was published by van Emden (1981).

Aho, A.V., Hopcroft, J.E. and Ullman, J.D. (1974) *The Design and Analysis of Computer Algorithms*. Addison-Wesley.

Aho, A.V., Hopcroft, J.E. and Ullman, J.D. (1983) *Data Structures and Algorithms*. Addison-Wesley.

Gonnet, G.H. and Baeza-Yates, R. (1991) *Handbook of Algorithms and Data Structures in Pascal and C*. Addison-Wesley.

van Emden, M. (1981) *Logic Programming Newsletter* 2.

Wirth, N. (1976) *Algorithms + Data Structures = Programs*. Englewood Cliffs, NJ: Prentice Hall.

Some Differences Between Prolog Implementations

The syntax for Prolog in this book follows the tradition of the Edinburgh Prolog, which has been adopted by the majority of Prolog implementations and also the ISO standard for Prolog. Typically implementations of Prolog offer many additional features. Generally, the programs in the book use a subset of what is provided in a typical implementation, and is included in the ISO standard. However, there are still some differences between various Prologs that may require small changes when executing the programs in the book with a particular Prolog. This appendix draws attention to some of such more likely differences.

Dynamic and static predicates

The ISO standard and some Prolog implementations distinguish between *static* and *dynamic* predicates. Static predicates may be compiled into a more efficient code than dynamic ones. Only dynamic predicates can be manipulated by **assert(a/z)** and **retract**, and can be retrieved by **clause(Head, Body)**. A predicate is assumed static, unless announced in the program by a declaration of the form:

>:- **dynamic PredicateName(PredicateArity).**

e.g. :- **dynamic member(2).**

Predicates introduced through **assert(a/z)** only, are automatically assumed as dynamic.

Assert and retract

The standard only includes the predicates **asserta** and **assertz**, but not **assert**. Virtually all the implementations also provide **assert**. If **assert** is not available, **assertz** can simply be used instead. To remove all the clauses about a predicate, built-in predicates **retractall(Clause)** or **abolish(PredicateName/Arity)** may be provided.

Undefined predicates

In some Prologs, a call to a predicate not defined in the program at all, simply fails. Other Prologs in such cases complain with an error message. In such Prologs, undefined predicates can be made to fail (without error messages) by a built-in predicate like: **unknown(_, fail)**.

Negation as failure: *not* and '\+'

In this book we use **not Goal** for negation as failure. Many Prologs (and the standard) use the (somewhat less pretty) notation:

    \+ **Goal**

to emphasize that this is not the proper logical negation, but negation defined through failure. For compatibility with these Prologs, 'not' should be replaced by '\+', or (with less work), **not** introduced as a user-defined predicate (see Appendix B).

Predicate *name(Atom, CodeList)*

This predicate is provided by most implementations, but not included in the standard (instead: **atom_codes/2**). There are small differences between Prologs in the behaviour of **name** in special cases, e.g. when the first argument is a number.

Loading programs with *consult* and *reconsult*

Loading programs with **consult** and **reconsult** varies between implementations. Differences occur when programs are loaded from multiple files and the same predicate is defined in more than one file (the new clauses about the same predicate may simply be added to the old clauses; alternatively, just the clauses in the most recent file are loaded, abandoning the previous clauses about the same predicate).

Modules

In some Prologs, the program can be divided into *modules* so that predicate names are local to a module unless they are specifically made visible from other modules. This is useful when writing large programs, when predicates with the same name and arity may mean different things in different modules.

Some Frequently Used Predicates

Some basic predicates such as **member/2** and **conc/3** are used in many programs throughout the book. To avoid repetition, the definition of such predicates is usually not included in the program's listing. To run a program, these frequently used predicates also have to be loaded into Prolog. This is done most easily by consulting (or compiling) a file, such as one given in this appendix, that defines these predicates. The listing below includes some predicates that may already be included among the built-in predicates, depending on the implementation of Prolog. For example, negation as failure written as **not Goal** is also included below for compatibility with Prologs that use the notation \+ **Goal** instead. When loading into Prolog the definition of a predicate that is already built-in, Prolog will typically just issue a warning message and ignore the new definition.

```
% File frequent.pl: Library of frequently used predicates

% Negation as failure
%    This is normally available as a built-in predicate,
%    often written with the prefix operator '\+', e.g. \+ likes(mary,snakes)
%    The definition below is only given for compatibility among Prolog implementations

:- op( 900, fy, not).

not Goal  :-
   Goal, !, fail
   ;
   true.

% once( Goal): produce one solution of Goal only (the first solution only)
%    This may already be provided as a built-in predicate

once( Goal)  :-
   Goal, !.

% member( X, List): X is a member of List

member( X, [ X | _]).                    % X is head of list

member( X, [ _ | Rest])  :-
   member( X, Rest).                     % X is in body of list
```

% conc(L1, L2, L3): list L3 is the concatenation of lists L1 and L2

```
conc( [ ], L, L).

conc( [X | L1], L2, [X | L3]) :-
    conc( L1, L2, L3).
```

% del(X, L0, L): List L is equal to list L0 with X deleted
%   Note: Only one occurrence of X is deleted
%   Fail if X is not in L0

```
del( X, [X | Rest], Rest).              % Delete the head

del( X, [Y | Rest0], [Y | Rest]) :-
    del( X, Rest0, Rest).               % Delete from tail
```

% subset(Set, Subset): list Set contains all the elements of list Subset
%   Note: The elements of Subset appear in Set in the same order as in Subset

```
subset( [ ], [ ]).

subset( [First | Rest], [First | Sub]) :-    % Retain First in subset
    subset( Rest, Sub).

subset( [First | Rest], Sub) :-              % Remove First
    subset( Rest, Sub).
```

% set_difference(Set1, Set2, Set3): Set3 is the list representing
%   the difference of the sets represented by lists Set1 and Set2
%   Normal use: Set1 and Set2 are input arguments, Set3 is output

```
set_difference( [], _, []).

set_difference( [X | S1], S2, S3) :-
    member( X, S2), !,                  % X in set S2
    set_difference( S1, S2, S3).

set_difference( [X | S1], S2, [X | S3]) :-  % X not in S2
    set_difference( S1, S2, S3).
```

% length(List, Length): Length is the length of List
%   Note: length/2 may already be included among built-in predicates
%   The definition below is tail-recursive
%   It can also be used to generate efficiently list of given length

```
length( L, N) :-
    length( L, 0, N).

length( [ ], N, N).

length( [_ | L], N0, N) :-
    N1 is N0 + 1,
    length( L, N1, N).
```

% max(X, Y, Max): Max = max(X,Y)

```
max( X, Y, Max)  :-
  X > = Y, !, Max = X
  ;
  Max = Y.
```

% min(X, Y, Min): Min = min(X,Y)

```
min( X, Y, Min)  :-
  X = < Y, !, Min = X
  ;
  Min = Y.
```

% copy_term(T1, T2): term T2 is equal to T1 with variables renamed
%   This may already be available as a built-in predicate
%   Procedure below assumes that copy_term is called so that T2 matches T1

```
copy_term( Term, Copy)  :-
  asserta( term_to_copy( Term)),
  retract( term_to_copy( Copy)), !.
```

Solutions to Selected Exercises

Chapter 1

1.1   (a) **no**

       (b) X = **pat**

       (c) X = **bob**

       (d) X = **bob**, Y = **pat**

1.2   (a) **?- parent(X, pat).**

       (b) **?- parent(liz, X).**

       (c) **?- parent(Y, pat), parent(X, Y).**

1.3   (a) **happy(X) :-**
           parent(X, Y).

       (b) **hastwochildren(X) :-**
           parent(X, Y),
           sister(Z, Y).

1.4   **grandchild(X, Z) :-**
       parent(Y, X),
       parent(Z, Y).

1.5   **aunt(X, Y) :-**
       parent(Z, Y),
       sister(X, Z).

1.6   Yes it is.

1.7   (a) no backtracking

       (b) no backtracking

       (c) no backtracking

       (d) backtracking

Chapter 2

2.1   (a) variable

       (b) atom

       (c) atom

       (d) variable

(e) atom

(f) structure

(g) number

(h) syntactically incorrect

(i) structure

(j) syntactically incorrect

2.3   (a) A = 1, B = 2

(b) no

(c) no

(d) D = 2, E = 2

(e) P1 = point(−1,0)
P2 = point(1,0)
P3 = point(0,Y)

This can represent the family of triangles with two vertices on the *x*-axis at 1 and −1 respectively, and the third vertex anywhere on the *y*-axis.

2.4   seg(point(5,Y1), point(5,Y2))

2.5   regular(rectangle(point(X1,Y1), point(X2,Y1), point(X2,Y3),
point(X1,Y3))).

% This assumes that the first point is the left bottom vertex.

2.6   (a) A = **two**

(b) **no**

(c) C = **one**

(d) D = s(s(1));
D = s(s(s(s(s(1)))))

2.7   relatives(X, Y) :-
predecessor(X, Y)
;
predecessor(Y, X)
;
predecessor(Z, X),
predecessor(Z, Y)
;
predecessor(X, Z),
predecessor(Y, Z).

2.8   translate(1, one).
translate(2, two).
translate(3, three).

2.9   In the case of Figure 2.10 Prolog does slightly more work.

2.10   According to the definition of matching of Section 2.2, this succeeds. X becomes a sort of circular structure in which X itself occurs as one of the arguments.

Chapter 3

3.1   (a) conc(L1, [_, _, _], L)

   (b) conc([_, _, _ | L2], [_, _, _], L)

3.2   (a) last(Item, List) :-
           conc(_, [Item], List).

   (b) last(Item, [Item]).

   last(Item, [First | Rest]) :-
      last(Item, Rest).

3.3   evenlength([ ]).

   evenlength([First | Rest]) :-
      oddlength(Rest).

   oddlength([First | Rest]) :-
      evenlength(Rest).

3.4   reverse([ ], [ ]).

   reverse([First | Rest], Reversed) :-
      reverse(Rest, ReversedRest),
      conc(ReversedRest, [First], Reversed).

3.5   % This is easy using reverse

   palindrome(List) :-
      reverse(List, List).

   % Alternative solution, not using reverse

   palindrome1([ ]).

   palindrome1([_]).

   palindrome1(List) :-
      conc([First | Middle], [First], List),
      palindrome1(Middle).

3.6   shift([First | Rest], Shifted) :-
      conc(Rest, [First], Shifted).

3.7   translate([ ], [ ]).

   translate([Head | Tail], [Head1 | Tail1]) :-
      means(Head, Head1),
      translate(Tail, Tail1).

3.8   % The following assumes the order of elements in Subset as in Set

   subset([ ], [ ]).

   subset([First | Rest], [First | Sub]) :-   % Retain First in subset
      subset(Rest, Sub).

   subset([First | Rest], Sub) :-   % Remove First
      subset(Rest, Sub).

3.9   dividelist([ ], [ ], [ ]).   % Nothing to divide

dividelist([X], [X], [ ]).   % Divide one-element list

dividelist([X, Y | List], [X | List1], [Y | List2]) :-
    dividelist(List, List1, List2).

3.10   canget(state(_ , _ , _ , has), [ ]).   % Nothing to do

canget(State, [Action | Actions]) :-
    move(State, Action, NewState),   % First action
    canget(NewState, Actions).   % Remaining actions

3.11   flatten([Head | Tail], FlatList) :-   % Flatten non-empty list
    flatten(Head, FlatHead),
    flatten(Tail, FlatTail),
    conc(FlatHead, FlatTail, FlatList).

flatten([ ], [ ]).   % Flatten empty list

flatten(X, [X]).   % Flatten a non-list

% Note: On backtracking this program produces rubbish

3.12   Term1 = plays(jimmy, and(football, squash))
Term2 = plays(susan, and(tennis, and(basketball, volleyball)))

3.13   :- op(300, xfx, was).
:- op(200, xfx, of).
:- op(100, fx, the).

3.14   (a) A = 1 + 0

(b) B = 1 + 1 + 0

(c) C = 1 + 1 + 1 + 1 + 0

(d) D = 1 + 1 + 0 + 1;
    D = 1 + 0 + 1 + 1;
    D = 0 + 1 + 1 + 1   % Further backtracking causes indefinite cycling

3.15   :- op(100, xfx, in).
:- op(300, fx, concatenating).
:- op(200, xfx, gives).
:- op(100, xfx, and).
:- op(300, fx, deleting).
:- op(100, xfx, from).

% List membership

Item in [Item | List].

Item in [First | Rest] :-
    Item in Rest.

% List concatenation

concatenating [ ] and List gives List.

concatenating [X | L1] and L2 gives [X | L3] :-
    concatenating L1 and L2 gives L3.

% Deleting from a list

deleting Item from [Item | Rest] gives Rest.

deleting Item from [First | Rest] gives [First | NewRest] :-
    deleting Item from Rest gives NewRest.

3.16   **max(X, Y, X) :-**
        X >= Y.

        max(X, Y, Y) :-
        X < Y.

3.17   **maxlist([X], X).**   % Maximum of single-element list

        maxlist([X, Y | Rest], Max) :-   % At least two elements in list
            maxlist([Y | Rest], MaxRest),
            max(X, MaxRest, Max).   % Max is the greater of X and MaxRest

3.18   **sumlist([ ], 0).**

        sumlist([First | Rest], Sum) :-
            sumlist(Rest, SumRest),
            Sum is First + SumRest.

3.19   **ordered([X]).**   % Single-element list is ordered

        ordered([X, Y | Rest]) :-
            X = < Y,
            ordered([Y | Rest]).

3.20   **subsum([ ], 0, [ ]).**

        subsum([N | List], Sum, [N | Sub]) :-   % N is in subset
            Sum1 is Sum - N,
            subsum(List, Sum1, Sub).

        subsum([N | List], Sum, Sub) :-   % N is not in subset
            subsum(List, Sum, Sub).

3.21   **between(N1, N2, N1) :-**
            N1 = < N2

        between(N1, N2, X) :-
            N1 < N2,
            NewN1 is N1 + 1,
            between(NewN1, N2, X).

3.22   **:- op(900, fx, if).**
        :- op(800, xfx, then).
        :- op(700, xfx, else).
        :- op(600, xfx, :=).

        if Val1 > Val2 then Var := Val3 else Anything :-
            Val1 > Val2,
            Var = Val3.

        if Val1 > Val2 then Anything else Var := Val4 :-
            Val1 = < Val2,
            Var = Val4.

Chapter 4

4.1 (a) ?- **family(person(_ , Name, _ , _), _ , [ ]).**

(b) ?- **child(person(Name, SecondName, _ , works(_ , _))).**

(c) ?- **family(person(_ , Name, _ , unemployed),**
person(_ , _ , _ , works(_ , _)), _).

(d) ?- **family(Husband, Wife, Children),**
dateofbirth(Husband, date(_ , _ , Year1)),
dateofbirth(Wife, date(_ , _ , Year2)),
(Year1 - Year2 > = 15
;
Year2 - Year1 > = 15
),
member(Child, Children).

4.2 **twins(Child1, Child2) :-**
family(_ , _ , Children),
del(Child1, Children, OtherChildren), % Delete Child1
member(Child2, OtherChildren),
dateofbirth(Child1, Date),
dateofbirth(Child2, Date).

4.3 **nth_member(1, [X | L], X).**   % X is first element of list [X | L]

nth_member(N, [Y | L], X) :-   % X is nth element of [Y | L]
N1 is N - 1,
nth_member(N1, L, X).

4.4 The input string shrinks on each non-silent cycle, and it cannot shrink indefinitely.

4.5 **accepts(State, [ ], _) :-**
final(State).

accepts(State, [X | Rest], MaxMoves) :-
MaxMoves > 0,
trans(State, X, State1),
NewMax is MaxMoves - 1,
accepts(State1, Rest, NewMax).

accepts(State, String, MaxMoves) :-
MaxMoves > 0,
silent(State, State1),
NewMax is MaxMoves - 1,
accepts(State1, String, NewMax).

4.6 The order is defined in the goal **member(Y, [1,2,3,4,5,6,7,8]).**

4.7 (a) **jump(X/Y, X1/Y1) :-**   % Knight jump from X/Y to X1/Y1
(
dxy(Dx, Dy)   % Knight distances in x and y directions
;
dxy(Dy, Dx),   % or the other way round
),

```
        X1 is X + Dx,
        inboard( X1),                    % X1 is within chessboard
        Y1 is Y + Dy,
        inboard( Y1).                    % Y1 is within chessboard

     dxy( 2, 1).                         % 2 squares to right, 1 forward
     dxy( 2, -1).                        % 2 squares to right, 1 backward
     dxy( -2, 1).                        % 2 to left, 1 forward
     dxy( -2, -1).                       % 2 to left, 1 backward

     inboard( Coord) :-                  % Coordinate within chessboard
        0 < Coord,
        Coord < 9.
```

(b)   `knightpath( [Square] ).`   % Knight sitting on Square

```
   knightpath( [S1, S2 | Rest] ) :-
      jump( S1, S2),
      knightpath( [S2 | Rest] ).
```

(c)   `?- knightpath( [ 2/1,R,5/4,S,X/8] ).`

Chapter 5

5.1   (a)   X = 1;
                X = 2;

        (b)   X = 1
                Y = 1;

                X = 1
                Y = 2;

                X = 2
                Y = 1;

                X = 2
                Y = 2;

        (c)   X = 1
                Y = 1;

                X = 1
                Y = 2;

5.2   Assume that procedure **class** is called with second argument uninstantiated.

```
class( Number, positive) :-
   Number > 0, !.

class( 0, zero) :- !.

class( Number, negative).
```

5.3   `split( [ ], [ ], [ ] ).`

```
split( [X | L], [X | L1], L2) :-
   X >= 0, !,
   split( L, L1, L2).
```

```
split( [X | L], L1, [X | L2] ) :-
   split( L, L1, L2).
```

5.4   member(Item, Candidates), not member(Item, RuledOut)

5.5   set_difference([], _, []).

```
set_difference( [X | L1], L2, L) :-
   member( X, L2), !,
   set_difference( L1, L2, L).

set_difference( [X | L1], L2, [X | L] ) :-
   set_difference( L1, L2, L).
```

5.6   unifiable([], _, []).

```
unifiable( [First | Rest], Term, List) :-
   not( First = Term), !,
   unifiable( Rest, Term, List).

unifiable( [First | Rest], Term, [First | List] ) :-
   unifiable( Rest, Term, List).
```

Chapter 6

6.1
```
findterm( Term) :-                    % Assuming current input stream is file f
   read( Term), !,                    % Current term in F matches Term?
   write( Term)                       % If yes, display it
   ;
   findterm( Term).                   % Otherwise process the rest of file
```

6.2
```
findallterms( Term) :-
   read( CurrentTerm),                % Assuming CurrentTerm not a variable
   process( CurrentTerm, Term).

process( end_of_file, _) :- !.

process( CurrentTerm, Term) :-
   ( not( CurrentTerm = Term), !      % Terms do not match
   ;
     write( CurrentTerm), nl          % Otherwise output current term
   ),
   findallterms( Term).               % Do the rest of file
```

6.4
```
starts( Atom, Character) :-
   name( Character, [Code] ),
   name( Atom, [Code | _] ).
```

6.5
```
plural( Noun, Nouns) :-
   name( Noun, CodeList),
   name( s, CodeS),
   conc( CodeList, CodeS, NewCodeList),
   name( Nouns, NewCodeList).
```

Chapter 7

7.2   **add_to_tail(Item, List) :-**
       var(List), !,   % List represents empty list
       List = [Item | Tail].

   add_to_tail(Item, [_ | Tail]) :-
   add_to_tail(Item, Tail).

   member(X, List) :-
       var(List), !,   % List represents empty list
       fail.   % so X cannot be a member

   member(X, [X | Tail]).

   member(X, [_ | Tail]) :-
   member(X, Tail).

7.5   % subsumes(Term1, Term2):
       %   Term1 subsumes Term2, e.g. subsumes(t(X,a,f(Y)), t(A,a,f(g(B))))
       % Assume Term1 and Term2 do not contain the same variable
       % In the following procedure, subsuming variables get instantiated
       % to terms of the form literally(SubsumedTerm)

   subsumes(Atom1, Atom2) :-
       atomic(Atom1), !,
       Atom1 == Atom2.

   subsumes(Var, Term) :-
       var(Var), !,   % Variable subsumes anything
       Var = literally(Term).   % To handle other occurrences of Var

   subsumes(literally(Term1), Term2) :- !, % Another occurrence of Term2
       Term1 == Term2.

   subsumes(Term1, Term2) :-   % Term1 not a variable
       nonvar(Term2),
       Term1 =.. [Fun | Args1],
       Term2 =.. [Fun | Args2],
       subsumes_list(Args1, Args2).

   subsumes_list([ ], [ ]).

   subsumes_list([First1 | Rest1], [First2 | Rest2]) :-
       subsumes(First1, First2),
       subsumes_list(Rest1, Rest2).

7.6   (a) **?- retract(product(X, Y, Z)), fail.**

       (b) **?- retract(product(X, Y, 0)), fail.**

7.7   **copy_term(Term, Copy) :-**
       asserta(term_to_copy(Term)),
       retract(term_to_copy(Copy)).

7.9   **copy_term(Term, Copy) :-**
       bagof(X, X = Term, [Copy]).

Chapter 8

8.2   **add_at_end(L1 - [Item | Z2], Item, L1 - Z2).**

8.3   **reverse(A - Z, L - L) :-**   % Result is empty list if
          A == Z, !.   % A - Z represents empty list

   reverse([X | L] - Z, RL - RZ) :-   % Non-empty list
          reverse(L - Z, RL - [X | RZ]).

8.6   % Eight queens program

   sol(Ylist) :-
          functor(Du, u, 15),   % Set of upward diagonals
          functor(Dv, v, 15),   % Set of downward diagonals
          sol(Ylist,
                [1,2,3,4,5,6,7,8],   % Set of X-coordinates
                [1,2,3,4,5,6,7,8],   % Set of Y-coordinates
                Du, Dv).

   sol([ ], [ ], [ ], _ , _).

   sol([Y | Ys], [X | XL], YL0, Du, Dv) :-
          del(Y, YL0, YL),   % Choose a Y coordinate
          U is X+Y-1,
          arg(U, Du, X),   % Upward diagonal free
          V is X-Y+8,
          arg(V, Dv, X),   % Downward diagonal free
          sol(Ys, XL, YL, Du, Dv).

   del(X, [X | L], L).

   del(X, [Y | L0], [Y | L]) :-
          del(X, L0, L).

Chapter 9

9.4   %mergesort(List, SortedList): use the merge-sort algorithm

   mergesort([ ], [ ]).

   mergesort([X], [X]).

   mergesort(List, SortedList) :-
          divide(List, List1, List2),   % Divide into approx. equal lists
          mergesort(List1, Sorted1),
          mergesort(List2, Sorted2),
          merge(Sorted1, Sorted2, SortedList). % Merge sorted lists

   divide([ ], [ ], [ ]).

   divide([X], [X], [ ]).

   divide([X, Y | L], [X | L1], [Y | L2]) :-   % Put X, Y into separate lists
          divide(L, L1, L2).

   % merge(List1, List2, List3): See Section 8.3.1

9.5   (a) **binarytree(nil).**

       binarytree(t(Left, Root, Right)) :-
          binarytree(Left),
          binarytree(Right).

9.6   **height(nil, 0).**

    height(t(Left, Root, Right), H) :-
      height(Left, LH),
      height(Right, RH),
      max(LH, RH, MH),
      H is 1 + MH.

    max(A, B, A) :-
      A > = B, !.

    max(A, B, B).

9.7   **linearize(nil, [ ]).**

    linearize(t(Left, Root, Right), List) :-
      linearize(Left, List1),
      linearize(Right, List2),
      conc(List1, [Root | List2], List).

9.8   **maxelement(t(_, Root, nil), Root) :- !.**   % Root is right-most element

    maxelement(t(_, _, Right), Max) :-   % Right subtree non-empty
      maxelement(Right, Max).

9.9   **in(Item, t(_, Item, _), [Item]).**

    in(Item, t(Left, Root, _), [Root | Path]) :-
      gt(Root, Item),
      in(Item, Left, Path).

    in(Item, t(_, Root, Right), [Root | Path]) :-
      gt(Item, Root),
      in(Item, Right, Path).

9.10   % Display a binary tree from top to bottom
    % This program assumes that each node is just one character

    show(Tree) :-
      dolevels(Tree, 0, more).   % Do all levels from top

    dolevels(Tree, Level, alldone) :- !.   % No more nodes beyond Level

    dolevels(Tree, Level, more) :-   % Do all levels from Level
      traverse(Tree, Level, 0, Continue), nl,   % Output nodes at Level
      NextLevel is Level + 1,
      dolevels(Tree, NextLevel, Continue).   % Do lower levels

    traverse(nil, _, _, _).

    traverse(t(Left, X, Right), Level, Xdepth, Continue) :-
      NextDepth is Xdepth + 1,
      traverse(Left, Level, NextDepth, Continue),   % Traverse left subtree

```
    ( Level = Xdepth, !,                          % Node X at Level?
      write( X), Continue = more                   % Output node, more to do
      ;
      write(' ')                                    % Otherwise leave space
    ),
    traverse( Right, Level, NextDepth, Continue).  % Traverse right subtree
```

Chapter 10

10.1   `in( Item, l( Item) ).`   % Item found in leaf

```
in( Item, n2( T1, M, T2) ) :-                    % Node has two subtrees
    gt( M, Item), !,                              % Item not in second subtree
    in( Item, T1)                                 % Search first subtree
    ;
    in( Item, T2).                                % Otherwise search the second
in( Item, n3( T1, M2, T2, M3, T3) ) :-           % Node has three subtrees
    gt( M2, Item), !,                             % Item not in second or third
    in( Item, T1)                                 % Search first subtree
    ;
    gt( M3, Item), !,                             % Item not in third subtree
    in( Item, T2)                                 % Search second subtree
    ;
    in( Item, T3).                                % Search third subtree
```

10.3
```
avl( Tree) :-
    avl( Tree, Height).                          % Tree is AVL-tree with height Height

avl( nil, 0).                                     % Empty tree is AVL and has height 0

avl( t( Left, Root, Right), H) :-
    avl( Left, HL),
    avl( Right, HR),
    ( HL is HR; HL is HR + 1; HL is HR - 1),     % Subtrees heights almost equal
    max1( HL, HR, H).

max1( U, V, M) :-                                 % M is 1 + max of U and V
    U > V, !, M is U + 1
    ;
    M is V + 1.
```

10.4   The item at the root is initially 5, then 8, and finally 5 again.

Index